Comanche Dictionary and Grammar
Second Edition

SIL International®
Publications in Linguistics
92

This Comanche dictionary is based on research drawn from the files of the late Elliot Canonge which he initiated in the early 1940s under the auspices of the Summer Institute of Linguistics. Dr. Robinson has rescued and enhanced this important body of data which spans traditional and contemporary varieties of Comanche speech styles and four geographically identifiable dialects. The Comanche-English section of the work, as complete as current sources permit, constitutes the central portion of the dictionary, but an English-Comanche section indexes Comanche entries to aid in locating Comanche forms from the point of view of their English equivalents. In turn, Dr. Armagost's provision of an introductory exploration of Comanche morphology and syntax further enhances this volume as an important contribution to our knowledge of this branch of the Uto-Aztecan family of languages.

Series Editors

Virgil Poulter
University of Texas at Arlington

William R. Merrifield
SIL International®

Volume Editors

Alan C. Wares
Mickey Brussow

Iris M. Wares

Consulting Editors

Doris A. Bartholomew
Pamela M. Bendor-Samuel
Desmond C. Derbyshire
Robert A. Dooley
Jerold A. Edmondson

Austin Hale
Robert E. Longacre
Eugene E. Loos
Kenneth L. Pike
Viola G. Waterhouse

Production Staff

Bonnie Brown, Managing Editor
Judy Benjamin, Compositor
Patrick Gourley, Cover design
Wekeah Bradley and Ron Burgess, Drawings

Comanche Dictionary and Grammar
Second Edition

Lila Wistrand-Robinson
and
James Armagost

SIL International®
Dallas, Texas

Copies of this and other publications of SIL International® may be obtained from:

SIL International Publications
7500 W. Camp Wisdom Road
Dallas, TX 75236-5629

Voice: 972-708-7404
Fax: 972-708-7363
publications_intl@sil.org
www.ethnologue.com/bookstore.asp

Contents

Elliott Donton Canonge

1921 - 1971
Friend of the Comanches

Mary Redbird

Artist Wekeah Bradley
with daughter Hawana

Eva Tooahnipah

Mary Wahkinney
and May Wanqua

Ron Burgess, artist

Rev. & Mrs. Ned Timbo

Eva Watchetaker

Daisy Waters

George Smith
Watchetaker

Acknowledgments

This Comanche-English dictionary and grammar is an outgrowth of the work of the late Elliott Canonge, whose field work was done between 1945 and 1963 under the auspices of the Summer Institute of Linguistics. Various SIL scholars influenced him in the analysis of the Comanche vowel system described in his 1957 article Voiceless vowels in Comanche. His Comanche Texts, first published in 1958, includes in the appendix a list of words retrieved from the text materials by computer. Since his dictionary file of approximately 3500 words was not available to the public, his widow gave permission for it to be edited and published.

Through Kansas State University, a grant was received for this purpose from the National Endowment for the Humanities (Project 1366) for a fourteen-month period during 1978 and 1979, eight months covering only half-time work. The grant period included nine weeks of fieldwork in Oklahoma, consulting with fluent speakers of Comanche and checking both Canonge's list and words encountered in previous bibliographic research. The language associates were Felix Kowena, Mary Redbird, Daisy Waters, Ned Timbo, Mary Wahkinney, Eva Tooahnipah, Watchetaker, and Maude Blevins. Consulting sessions were recorded on audio tape and archived at Kansas State University.

The dictionary portion of this study and recent fieldwork associated with it are primarily the work of Lila Wistrand-Robinson, but SIL editor Iris Wares needs also to be mentioned and thanked for her indefatigable work in preparing this part of the volume for publication. James Armagost, of Kansas State University, became associated with the project in connection with the NEH grant and is primarily responsible for the grammar portion of the study.

Sketches are the work of talented Comanche artists Weckeah Bradley and Ron Burgess.

Finally, we wish to acknowledge the work of the editorial staff of SIL's Academic Publications Department (currently called Global Publishing Services) and its computer operators in preparing this volume for publication.

Lila Wistrand-Robinson
James Armagost
June, 1990

Preface

The Comanche people are at present located around Walters, Cache, and Lawton, in the State of Oklahoma. They seem to have originated in the Southwest, although at one time they lived and ranged from the Northwest Coast, down the Pacific Coast, and across to what is now Oklahoma, Texas, and Mexico. They moved back and forth in the latter area until the coming of white colonists in the eighteenth and nineteenth centuries. This dark and painful period was marked by the needless slaughter of the Comanche people, who fought relentlessly for their land and their rights; but they were unable to gain the victory. Land was bought and fenced off, and buffalo were slaughtered until the days of the massive hunts came to a close, bringing to an end the traditional, nomadic Comanche way of life.

Sent to English-language schools, where they were punished for speaking their own language, many Comanche students lost proficiency in their native tongue. With the coming of compulsory education, English gradually became the first language of recent generations of Comanche children. Cultural changes took place in Indian schools where children in dormitories away from home were required to wear clothing and eat food of the white men. In spite of this, present-day Comanches have preserved many aspects of their native culture, some of which have been recorded in this dictionary.

The Comanche language is a member of the Uto-Aztecan language family, Numic branch, and Shoshone group. Other Uto-Aztecan groups are Piman and Nahuatlan. Shoshone is the nearest sister language, so closely related that a Comanche speaker immediately recognizes the similarity when he hears it spoken. Other members of the Shoshonean group are Hopi, Northern and Southern Paiute, Snake, and Ute. Also related are Papago, Mono, and Tubatulabal in the Southwest. Finally, in Mexico are Yaqui-Mayo, Huichol, Cora, Tarahumara, and the various dialects of Nahuatl or Aztec, completing the Uto-Aztecan language family.

This volume is designed not only to record and preserve Comanche speech but also to help younger generations of Comanches learn about their history and culture. For this reason, names of outstanding Comanche tribal members have been included, as well as historical dates, fauna and flora of the area, and facts about cultural artifacts and their use or construction.

Comanche words are listed in the Comanche-English dictionary (Part I) along with dialectal variants, grammatical categories, simple etymologies, and illustrative sentences. The reader may use the dictionary to find linguistic, historical, or cultural information, or to look for particular Comanche words with their accompanying information.

Following Part I there are five appendixes listing fauna (animals, birds, reptiles, fish, and insects), flora, body parts, months of the year, and personal names. Appendix E has been included here by request as a reference for finding names for Comanche children. Trees and plants listed in Appendix B are a key to the ecological setting of the Comanches and to many of the medicinal plants used in Comanche culture. Some items in this list include scientific names for more specific identification.

The English-Comanche lexicon (Part II), is a reference to Comanche terms for speakers of English. Each English word is followed by corresponding Comanche words or phrases. To find a particular Comanche entry, one may use the lexicon first and then go to the dictionary to find a more complete explanation of a Comanche word.

By use of the dictionary and the grammar (Part III) in conjunction with the narratives in Comanche Texts, a student should be able to gain a rudimentary knowledge of the language.

A brief bibliography lists books and articles on the history, culture, language, and linguistic studies of Comanche.

Abbreviations

A	accusative	DA	daughter
ABS	absolutive	DAT	dative
ABSTR	abstract	DECL	declarative
AFF	affirmative	DEF	definite
AG	agentive	DEM	demonstrative
AJ	adjective	DERIV	derivational
ALL	allative	DIR	direction
AN	animate	DO	definite object
ARCH	archaic	DS	different subject
AUG	augmentative	DUR	durative
AUX	subordinate verb	DV	ditransitive verb
AV	adverb	EMPH	emphasis
BEN	benefactive	ENGL	English
BR	brother	EVID	evidential
C	Comanche	EXCL	exclamation
C&J	Carlson and Jones	FA	father
CAUS	causative	G	genitive
cf.	compare	HU	husband
CMPL	completive	HUM	human
CO	coreferential	!	imperative
COG	cognate	I	inclusive
CONT	continuative	IMM	immediate
CTR	contrast	INAN	inanimate
D	dual	INCEP	inceptive
D1	immediate proximal	INDEF	indefinite
D2	removed proximal	INFER	inference
D3	immediate distal	INSTR	instrument
D4	removed distal	INTENS	intensifier
D5	scattered	INTERJ	interjection

IO	indirect object	QUES	interrogative
IRREG	irregular	QUOT	quotative
IV	intransitive verb	RDP	reduplication
K	Kwahere (dialect)	REAL	realized
L	locative	RECIP	reciprocal
M	manner	REF	reference (to)
MEAS	measure	REFL	reflexive
MO	mother	REL	relative clause
MV	main verb		marker
N	nominative	REP	repetitive
N	Nookoni (dialect)	S	singular
NEC	necessity	SB	sibling
NEG	negative	SEP	separate
NOM	nominal	SH	Shoshone
NONHUM	nonhuman	SO	son
NP	noun phrase	SP	Spanish
NTOP	nontopic	sp.	species
NUM	numeral	SS	same subject
O	Ohnono (dialect)	ST	stative
OBJ	object	SUBJ	subject
OBL	obligation	T	time
P	Pehnanɨɨ (dialect)	TMP	temporary
P	plural	TOP0	topic
PART	partitive	TV	transitive verb
PERS	person/personal	UNR	unrealized
PFX	prefix	UNSP	unspecified referent
PN	pronoun	VB	verbalizer
PO	possessor	VOC	vocative
PPL	participle	VP	verb phrase
PREP	preposition	W	Wia?nɨɨ (dialect)
PROG	progressive	WI	wife
PST	narrative past	Y	Yapai?nɨɨ (dialect)
PUA	Proto-Uto-Aztecan	X	exclusive
Q	quantifier	?	analysis unknown

Part I

Comanche-English Dictionary

Introduction

1. Entries. Comanche entry words are printed in boldface type at the left-hand margin of each column. For easy reference, the first word on each page also appears at the left-hand margin at the top of the page, and the last word on the page appears on the same line at the right-hand margin. Instead of pronunciation being indicated in each entry, a guide to pronunciation is presented immediately following this preface. Unless otherwise marked, all entries are singular; verbs are cited with the progressive suffix *-tʉ* or *-rʉ*.

Many Comanche nouns have a long form, such as *aawo* 'cup, vessel, container', and a shortened form, such as *awo*, which combines with other lexical roots to form compounds, such as *awo noʔo* 'armadillo' and *awo tahwi* 'cupboard'. Such long and short forms are often listed separately in the dictionary in their normal alphabetical order, but are cross-referenced to each other. The reader should beware that separately-listed combining forms are sometimes labeled as prefixes to indicate their dependent character, even though they are more properly lexical rather than inflectional from a strictly linguistic point of view.

Alphabetic order is the same as in English except that voiceless (underlined) vowels are ordered immediately after their voiced counterparts, the sixth vowel ʉ, and glottal stop *(ʔ)* is placed at the end of the alphabet, following *y*.

As is customary in other dictionaries, word space takes precedence over consonants or vowels so that the open compound precedes the closed sequence in alphabetic order. Once again, the reader needs to beware that more work needs to be done to define the rules of word formation for Comanche, especially in respect to compounding of lexical material. It is not at all clear how open and closed compounds should be treated and we are aware that this matter is not handled with complete consistency in these pages. Some compounds are left open, with word space, others are closed, without word space. Earlier versions of this manuscript employed hyphen for some compounds but these were edited out for lack of firm guidelines regarding their use.

2. Variants. Variations in pronunciation or meaning, as spoken by different Comanche clans, are indicated by abbreviations of clan names. These variants are not otherwise listed in the dictionary. Most of the entries originally collected by Canonge came from the *Wia?nʉʉ* (W) 'worn-away people' of the Walters area (also called *Mahnenʉʉ*). Wistrand-Robinson's word checking took place chiefly with members of the *Kwahare* (K) 'antelope' clan in the Cache and Lawton areas of Oklahoma. She did brief checking, also, with four other groups. The *Yapai?nʉʉ* (Y) 'root-eaters' (reportedly named because they ate roots in the winter months when nothing else was available) roamed the Arkansas River valley in earlier times. The *Pehnanʉʉ* (P) were so named because a deer reportedly went through their camp at one time and the people shouted so much that the deer died of fright. They are located ten miles west of Duncan, Oklahoma, which is also called Comanche City. Brief checks also took place with the *Noyʉhkanʉʉ* or *Nookoni* (N) 'wanderers', located between the Red River and the Peace River, and with the *Ohnono* (O) clan in the Lawton area, yielding a few variants from each of these groups.

3. Case and number. Following a main entry with or without dialectal variants, there may be special accusative or plural forms listed for a noun or verb. Singular (sg) or plural (pl) marking follows forms to which they apply. Examples of separate forms for singular and plural subjects are:

ʉhpʉitʉ (v) *pl* **ʉhkooitʉ**   sleep.
okweetʉ (v) *pl* **o?okwetʉ**   flow.

Examples of verbs with separate forms for singular and plural objects are:

pa?wʉhtiarʉ *(v, sg obj)*, *pl obj* **pawʉ?weniitʉ**   baptize.
tʉkʉhpehkarʉ *(v, sg obj)*, *pl obj* **tʉkʉwasʉrʉ**   kill for food.

4. Grammatical Classification. Only a very broad grammatical classification of Comanche words is attempted in the dictionary. Consult the grammar for more details.

5. Definitions. Definitions include basic meanings in concise form, and may include scientific names for specificity of fauna and flora. The denotata of kinship terms are abbreviated as in the list of abbreviations that accompanies the grammar.

Some archaic definitions, marked arch, are included where these have been identified, in order to document this information; e.g.,

namuwoo, (n, arch) husband.

6. Etymologies. For some dictionary entries, simple morphological analyses are given in terms of the literal meaning of separate morphemes comprising a total entry. These analyses take two forms, as follows:

awo nohi? (n) dice game (*lit* playing container; refers to bowl or containerused in playing dice).
keto?kapaa (n) kerosene [**ke** not + *to?ka* dark + **paa** liquid].

7. Examples. Example sentences of two types are presented—those given by Comanche language associates, and sentences taken from Canonge's *Comanche Texts*. Numbers in parentheses after an illustrative sentence refer to page number and sentence number in *Comanche Texts*; e.g. 115:3 refers to page 115, sentence 3 in *texts*.

8. Cross Reference. As an additional aid in locating dialectal variants or related words, many entries are cross-referenced.

Guide to Pronunciation

The Comanche alphabet, consisting of six vowels and twelve consonants, is as follows, with vowels having both voiced and voiceless realizations. These occur in the following order:

$$a \; \underline{a} \; b \; e \; \underline{e} \; h \; i \; \underline{i} \; k \; m \; n \; o \; \underline{o} \; p \; r \; s \; t \; u \; \underline{u} \; ʉ \; \underline{ʉ} \; w \; y \; ʔ$$

Single vowels are pronounced as follows:		Examples:	
a	as in *a* of *father*	*ma*	'my, his'
e	as in *ei* of *eight*	*ke*	'no'
i	as in *ee* of *see*	*hini*	'what?'
o	as in *o* of *go*	*ahó*	'hello, thank you
u	as in *oo* of *boot*	*hubiyaʔ*	'song, hymn'
ʉ	as *u* with the lips spread; not found in English.	*sʉmʉʔ*	'one'

Long vowels are written as a sequence of two like vowels, as in *aa* or *ee*. They are pronounced like simple vowels, but are longer in duration. Examples:

haa	'yes'
ma eeko	'his tongue'
marii	'them'
noobi	'hill'
pimorooʔ	'cow'
yuupʉ	'fat (person)'
ʉnʉʉʔ	'insect, bug'

Voiceless (or whispered) vowels in Comanche are underlined. Examples:

7

a̠	*kasa̠*	'wing'	o	*aawo̠*	'cup, vessel'
e̠	*taabe̠*	'sun'	u̠	*yuhu̠*	'fat, grease'
i̠	*noo'bi̠*	'hill, knoll'	ʉ̠	*nakwʉsiʔ*	'pumpkin'

Stress is marked (´) when it does not fall on the first syllable and yet is primary stress, and marked (`) when it is secondary stress. Examples:

aakáaʔ	'devil's horn'	amawóoʔa-paa	'apple juice
atakwásʉʔ	'corn soup'	naʔbukuwàaʔa-nábaa	'gasoline'
pasawíʔooʔ	'frog'	pòhotʉ-naʔsʉkía	'heavy shawl'

In shorter words, the stress on the first syllable usually becomes secondary to the marked primary stress, as a rule of thumb. On compounds, the relationship between the two words may cause the stress to fall on either the first or on the second word of the compound.

Consonants:

b	made with air blown lightly through slightly parted lips,		
	or like English *v* in 'a van'	*tabe*	'sun'
h	as in *h* of *hot*	*husi̠*	'cactus'
k	as in *k* of *ski* (unaspirated)	*kakuʔ*	'grandmother'
m	as in *m* of *move*	*moowiʔ*	'lariat'
n	as in *n* of *no*	*ma namiʔ*	'his sister'
p	as in *p* of *spin* (unaspirated)	*ma puukʉ̠*	'his horse'
r	as in *tt* of *batter*	*nʉ araʔ*	'my uncle'
s	as in *s* of *sun*	*ma soʔo*	'his cheek'
t	as in *t* of *stop* (unaspirated)	*tabe*	'sun'
w	as in *w* of *wish*	*wahi*	'cedar'
y	as in *y* of *you*	*yuyu*	'grease'
ʔ	as in *ohʔoh*, where air is cut off in the throat		
	between syllables (glottal stop)	*poʔaʔ*	'skin, bark'

Combinations of the above consonants which should be noted are:

| kw | as in *qu* of *quick* | *ma kwahi* | 'his back' |
| ts | as in *ts* of *beets* | *tseenaʔ* | 'wolf' |

In the Kwahare band and a few other bands, word-medial gw occurs, as follows:

| gw | as in *gu* of *guano* | *nigwaitʉ* | 'ask for' |

Preaspiration and preglottalization of certain consonants occur word-medially, as follows:

hn	aworahna	'cupboard'	ʔn	sʉsʉmʉʔnʉʉ	'some'
hk	eka-huhkupʉ	'cardinal'	ʔb	hunuʔbiʔ	'creek'
hp	ekasahpanaʔ	'soldier'	ʔw	taʔwoʔiʔ	'gun'
ht	ahotabenihtʉ	'thanksgiving'	ʔr	ekaʔeʔree	'swamp rabbit'

Comanche-English Dictionary

A

aa (n) animal horn. **ekakuura?aa**
young buffalo's horn. *See* **na?aa.**

aahe, ahe (interj) I claim it! (said
when claiming coup in time past).

aakaa?, ahkaa? (n) banana
(domestic fruit introduced; so
named because it appeared similar
to native plant, devil's horn).

aakáa?, ahkáa? (n) devil's horn,
devil's claw (native weed: grows
in barnyard or where cattle are
fed; has edible black seeds).

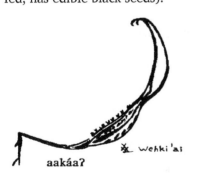

aakáa?

aakwusitu (v), *pl* **aakwusina** sneeze.

aamuyake? (n) horn (wind
instrument). *See* **woinu.**

aanatsihtuye? (n) animal horn
comb, horn brush.

aatakíi?, ahtakíi? (n) grasshopper
(small species).

aatamúu?, ahtamúu? (n)
grasshopper (large, no wings).

aawo (n) cup, vessel, container;
arch basket. **Nu pia? tsa? aawo
makotsetu.** My mother is washing
dishes. *See* **awo-.**

aawuì utama?, aakwuhtama? (n)
yarn (*lit* tie horn; *arch* used for
braiding men's hair).

aawusipu, aakwusipu (n) braid.

aawusitu, aakwusi?aru (v) braid.

ahna (n) underarm, armpit, side of
chest. *See* **ana-,** anatukate.

ahó (adv) thank you, hello. *See* **ura.**

ahotabenihtu (n) thanksgiving,
prayer of thanks.

Ahotabenihtu mua (n) November
(Thanksgiving month).

ahpu? (n), *acc* **ahpu?a** father.

ahra (n) jaw.

ahweniitu (v) root around (as a
hog). *See* **muwainitu.**

ahwepu (n) tuber (any food dug
up from soil). *See* **totohtu,**

11

to?roponii?, ta?wahkóo?,
payaape̞, tutupi̞tu̞.

ai (interj) Expression of disgust.

aibuniitu̞, ahi?bu̞niitu̞ P (v)
destroy, waste, torment.

aihinahanitu̞, aikuhaniitu̞
(v) sin (do evil, do wrong).
Aihinahaniitu̞. He did something
bad.

aikurekwatu̞ (v) curse (use profane
language).

aimi?aru̞ (v), *pl* **wahkami?aru̞** lope,
trot, move in slow motion. **Aru̞ka
tsa? aimi?aru̞.** The deer is loping.
See **pohyami?aru̞.**

aitu̞ (adj) bad, wicked, evil. **Uru̞
tsa? aitu̞.** That (over there) is no
good. *See* **tu̞tsu̞, kesuatu̞.**

ai?bihinu̞u̞sukatu̞ (adj)
discouraged, downhearted. *See*
narahtokwetu̞.

akwaru̞tu̞ (v), *pl* **akwaru̞?ru̞kina**
belch, burp.

akwaru̞? (n) belch, burp.

ama- (pfx) underarm to waist, side
of chest. *See* **ahna, ana-.**

amawóo (n) apple (*lit* wormy
chest[?]). *Pyrus malus* L.

amawóo?a pàa (n) sweet cider,
apple juice.

amawosa (n) pocket (*lit* underarm
bag).

amawo?a? po?a? (n) apple skin.

amawu̞nu̞tu̞ (v) suffer chest pain
(have pneumonia in side of chest).
See **tu̞?inawu̞nu̞ru̞.**

aná, anáa (interj) ouch!
(exclamation when suffering
physical pain other than burn).

ana-, ahna (n) underarm, armpit.

anáabi, anabi (n) one hill. *See*
ku?ebi, nookaru̞ru̞.

anahabiniitu̞ (v) seek (vision quest;
seek power or blessing by fasting
on a mountain).

anakwanare? (n) gourd (wild taxon;
lit underarm odor). *Cucurbita
foetida* (wild gourd having strong
odor similar to garlic).

anapu̞hu̞, anapu̞, ahnapu̞ (n)
underarm hair (*lit* underarm fuzz).

anatukate, ahnatukate (n) armpit.
See **ahma.**

ania, ani̞a (n) mane. **tu̞hu̞ya ania**
horse mane.

anikwita mi?aru̞ (v) roll along (as a
ball); tumble, summersault (turn a
flip). *See* **nakkuminooru̞.**

anitu̞ (v, hum subj), *pl* **aanearu̞** give
up exhausted, die in accident;
nonhum subj fall over (as a plant).

ani̞kuura? (n) ant.

ani̞mui̞ (n) housefly.

ani̞mui̞ wasu̞ (n) fly spray (*lit* fly
kill).

ani̞mui̞ wu̞htokwe?a? (n) flyswatter
(*lit* thing with which to hit and
kill flies).

arai, ahrai W, P, ahra?i (n) bridle
(*lit* for the jaw).

arakwu̞?u̞tu̞ (n) marriage of uncle
and niece.

arapu̞, ahrapu̞ W, P (n) jaw.

aratsi? (n) wheel game (the wheel is
a willow rim with rawhide spokes
radiating from a rawhide circle
a half-inch in diameter in the
middle; a special throwing arrow
is used).

aratuhku, ahraruhku (n) jowl meat
(meat of jaw).

ara? (n) uncle (mother's brother,
father's brother), niece, nephew
(man's sister's child).

Aruka páa? (name) Deer-water (a Comanche chief).

aruka tuhku K, O, P (n) deer meat.

arukáa kuhma (n) buck (single male deer).

arukáa ruhkapu, W arukáa tuhkapu Y (n) deer meat, deer food **K, O.**

aruka? (n), *acc* **aruka?a** deer.

aruka? nukuhma (n) buck (male deer leading herd of does).

ata-, atah-, atu- (adj) different, other, another. **Atuma.** It is a different one.

atabaro?itu (v) rise, swell (tend to flood; as water in a creek or river). *See* **paro?ikitu.**

atabitsi W (n) foreigner (other than of Comanche origin).

atabitsunoi (n) button snakeroot. *Liatris punetata* Hook (roots chewed for juice; also used as remedy).

atahunubi, atuhunu?bi P (n) tributary, branch of a creek, fork of a stream. *See* **nabatai.**

Atakuni, Ata kahni (name) Lone-tipi (person).

atakwá?su? (n) quick-cook corn soup (made of fresh, roasted, dried corn with meat, bones added).

atakwa?su?aipu (n) quick-dried corn, roasted corn.

atakwa?su?aitu (v) roast corn (quick-dry corn over fire). **Atakwa?su?aitu ma.** He is making quick-dried corn.

atana?i (n) foreigner, *adj* **atanaitu** foreign.

atapu, atahpu K, atapuku Y (adv man) doing differently, doing another way. **Atapuku ma nahaniitu.** He is fixing it another way.

ata?okwetu (v) overflow (flowing over banks, as a creek), *adj* **ata?okwetu** overflow.

Atsabi? (name) Creator, Holy Spirit (name of deity).

aturu (adj) different, wrong one. **Aturu ma.** It is the wrong one.

aturuu (n) others.

atusokoobi, atuhusokoobi (n) foreign country.

aweru, ahwetu (v) dig up (as roots). **Paapasi ahwetu.** He is digging potatoes.

awi-, ahwi- (v) miss aim. **Puhimataka ma tsa? u ahwinu.** He just barely missed it. *See* **tsimi?akuru.**

awo- (pfx) cup, vessel, container. *See* **aawo.**

awomakotse (n) dishwasher (person who washes dishes).

awomakotseru (v) wash dishes.

awonohi? (n) dice game (*lit* playing container; refers to bowl or container used in playing Indian dice).

awono?o? (n) armadillo (*lit* carries its own container).

awotsawuni?itu, awotsawuni-tsiitu (v) set the table.

awomatsuma? (n) teatowel, dishtowel, towel.

aworahna (n), *pl* **aworahni?i** cupboard (*lit* shelf or box for dishes).

E

ebi- (pfx) blue.

ebihuutsuu? (n) bluejay, bluebird.

ebikahni, ebikuni (n) plaster (*lit* blue house).

ebikuyuutsi? (n) roadrunner, chaparral cock (*lit* blue quail). *Geococcyx californianus* (of the cuckoo family).

ebimuura ya?ke? (n) bullfrog. *Rana catesbiana* (*lit* gray mule that cries). *See* **pasawí?oo?.**

ebimuutaroo?, ebimuhtaroo? K (n) mountain boomer (type of lizard).

ebipaboko?ai? P (n) mountain boomer (type of lizard).

ebipitu̱, ebipi̱tu̱ (adj) blue-gray, light blue.

ebitotsiya? (n) Texas thistle. *Cirsium texanum.*

ebi̱ wu̱mi̱na? (n) influenza, flu (*lit* blue illness).

ebu (dem pro) different, various directions.

eebi, ehbi (adj) blue.

eetu̱, etu̱- (n) bow for shooting arrows, bois d'arc wood for archery bows.

ehka, eeka (dem adj, acc sg scattered) those.

eka-, eku̱- (pfx) red color.

ekaamawoo?, ekaamagwoo? (n) crab apple (*lit* red apple). *Malus* spp. *See* **tu̱e amawóo?.**

ekae?ree W (n) swamp rabbit. *Lagomorpha* (species with red color on forehead). *See* **ta?wokina?e?reeka.**

Ekahohtu̱pahi hunu?bi (n) Red River (*lit* red bank river).

ekahuukupu̱, ekahuhkupu̱ (n) red soil (with iron content). *See* **eka sokoobi.**

ekakuhtabearu̱ (v) shine red (give forth a red light as from fire or sun).

Eka kura (name) Red-buffalo (person).

ekakúura? (n) buffalo calf (*lit* red buffalo).

ekakuyáa? (n) jack (in card game; *lit* redhead).

ekaku̱ma? (n) bay horse (reddish brown male).

ekakwitse?e (n), *pl* **ekakwitsi-bai?etu̱** lightning flash.

ekakwitse?eru̱ (v), *pl* **ekakwitsimi?aru̱** discharge a flash of lightning.

ekamitsáa?, ekamitsonaa? (n) cactus (*lit* red hackberry).

Ekamurawa (name) Red-crooked-nose (person).

ekamurora?i huupi (n) redbud (*lit* red-bursting tree). *Cercis canadensis.* L.

ekanaru̱mu̱u̱? (n) red store, trading post (type of store for Indians in earlier years).

ekanatsu̱, eka naropa? (n) eriogonum root (*lit* red medicine). *Eriogonum longifolium* Nutt. (used for treating stomach trouble).

ekapaa, ekahpaa (n) wine (*lit* red juice).

ekapia?, ekahpia? (n) sorrel mare (*lit* red female).

ekaohapitu̱ (adj) orange (*lit* red-yellow). *See* **ohaekapitu̱.**

ekapokopi, ekapokòo? (n) yaupon holly (*lit* red berries). *Ilex omitoria* sp? (leaves used for making a type of tea).

ekapokopi (n) strawberry. *Fragaria vesca* L.

ekapuhihwi (n) gold, money, coins. *See* **puhihwi.**

ekapu̱si?a̱, ekapusi? (n) flea (*lit* red louse).

ekasahpana? (n) soldier (*lit* red chested; early Spanish uniforms had red sashes). *See* **taibo ekɥsahpana?.**

ekasokoobi (n) red soil. *See* **eka huukupɥ.**

ekasonipɥ (n) grass, little bluestem (*lit* red stem). *Andropogon scoparius* Michx. (grass makes good pastures; stems used as switches in sweat lodge; ashes from stems used for treating syphilitic sores [C & J]).

ekatasia, ekatɥsi?a, tasia (n) measles (*lit* red bumps).

ekatotsạ (n) bank of stream, river bank (*lit* red gully).

ekatseena? (n) red fox. *Vulpes* sp. *See* **kɥ?kwɥria?, tseena?.**

ekatsiira?, ekahtsiira? (n) red pepper. *Piper Cayenne.*

ekatɥɥpi (n) red brick, red rock.

ekaɥnɥɥ (n) red ant (*lit* red insect).

ekaɥnɥɥ?a tɥhka?eetɥ (n) anteater.

ekawaapị, ekawaapɥ (n) juniper, red cedar. **Juniperus virginiana** (fruits eaten; smoke from leaves used in purifying).

ekawehaarɥ (v) burn red, turn red hot.

Ekawokani (name) Red-young- man (person).

ekawoni (n) smartweed. *Polygonum* (digs into flesh and burns; saliva causes it to release hold for removal).

ekawɥkwiapɥ (n) blister (*lit* red raw place). **Nɥ nape tsa? eka wɥkwiapɥ.** My foot is blistered.

ekawɥpisị K, ekạwipɥsa? P (n) rouge (made from a type of red sandstone; can be mixed with tallow or tree sap as a salve).

ekabapị (n) redheaded buzzard (*lit* redhead). *Buteo* sp.

ekahkoni (n) Indian breadroot. *Psoralea hypogeae* Nutt. [?] (roots used for food; eaten raw).

ekahwi (adj) gold color, shiny. *See* **puhihwi.**

ekapị, ekapitɥ (adj) red.

ekapisa? (n) rouge (*lit* red powder; made from a type of red sandstone).

ekapo?, ekapoho (n) mescal bean. *Sophora secundiflora* (bake beans in oven, drill holes for stringing as ornaments; used for decoration or ceremonies).

ekayɥ?yɥ?ka? (n) jelly (*lit* quivering red [substance]).

eka?otɥ, ekapisiapɥ (n, adj) pink.

ekạhuutsu?, ekahuhkupɥ (n) cardinal, redbird.

ekạsahpana? paraiboo? (n) army officer (*lit* soldier chief).

eko-, eeko, eekọ (n) tongue.

ekotɥwɥni? (n) glottis.

ekotɥyaipɥ (n) tongue-tied person.

ekwakɥɥpi?, egwakɥɥpi? (n) ground squirrel.

ekwi (n) fish.

ekwipisạ? (n) red rock.

ekwɥsibeniitɥ (v) lick (with tongue).

emɥahkatɥ (v, adj) to deceive, deceptive.

emɥahkatɥ, emɥaro?ịkatɥ (adj) mischievous, deceitful, lunatic (beyond reason or advising).

Esahibi (name) Wolf-drinking (historical personage; a brave warrior and leader).

Esatai (name) Little-wolf (person).

esi- (pfx) gray.

esiebipi̱tʉ (adj) lavender (*lit* gray-blue).

esiekapi̱tʉ (adj) pale pink (*lit* gray-red).

Esihabiitʉ (name) Gray-streak, Gray-flat-lying-object (former Comanche chief).

esi inapʉ (n) dried meat, jerky (very dry). *See* **inapʉ.**

esikakwoʔa, eshi kawoʔa, (n) gray face (used in making fun of someone or in name calling).

Esikono (name) Gray-box (war chief of Antelope Eaters around 1836–1916; moved to live west of Old Post Oak Mission in Oklahoma before the time of the roads).

esikooitʉ (v, pl) faint repeatedly, convulse. *See* **esi tʉyaitʉ.**

esiku̱hma? (n) horse (gray male).

esimuura? (n) mule (*lit* gray mule).

esinabuniitʉ (adj) appear gray. *See* **esitsʉnʉʔiitʉ.**

esinʉʉhparabi (n) loco weed. *Astragalus* sp.

esipia? (n) gray mare.

esipipi̱kuurʉ (v) murmur, mumble (*lit* make strange or unclear sounds).

esipohoobi, esipohobi (n) sage (white, lobed cudweed). *Artemisia ludoviciana* Nutt. (multipurpose medicine to cure mental trouble, cold, backache, liver disorders, kidney problems).

Esitami? (name) Asetammy (*lit* gray brother; person).

Esitohi? (n) Milky Way (name of distant stars).

esitoyaabi̱ (n) gray mountain.

Esitoyanʉʉ (n) Mexicans captured by the Comanches (named for the Esitoya mountains).

Esitoya? (n), *pl* **esitoyapitʉ** mountains east of El Paso, Texas.

esitsʉnʉʔiitʉ (v) gray appearance. *See* **esi nabuniitʉ.**

esitʉyaitʉ (v) faint, convulse (*lit* death gray). *See* **esi kooitʉ.**

esiʉnʉʉ? (n) elephant (*lit* gray animal).

esiwanaʔʉhʉ, esikwahaʔhʉ (n) blanket (cotton bed blanket).

esipi̱tʉ (adj) gray, slate color.

Esʉnapʉ (name) Asenap (*lit* gray foot).

etʉhuupi (n) osage orange, hedge apple, bois d'arc wood. **Maclura pomifera** [Raf.] Schn.

etʉsikawoʔarʉ W (v) accuse someone of being gray-faced.

etʉʉ (dem adj, nom pl scattered) those.

etʉsipʉ (n) ashes.

ewa kʉʉpi? (n) ground squirrel (*lit* striped squirrel).

eʔbootsiarʉ (v) mildew, decay, rot.

eʔbootsia? (n) mildew, decay, rot.

eʔmʉarʉ (v) go crazy, act without self-dignity (ref. to women).

eʔrée (n) forehead.

H

haa (interj) yes.

haahpi (adj) prone position, lying down.

haahpitʉ (v, inan subj), *pl* **haniòkatʉìsituated**, lying somewhere; *pl, anim subj* **kwabi** lie down, stretch out. **Habiitʉ nʉ.**

I am lying down. **Kima habiki.** Come lie down (48:20).

haakaru (v), *pl* **hakaakaru** find room for someone or something.

haapane, hahpane, hahpaniitu O (n) level valley.

habiitu (v) sleep, lie down.

habikuni, habikahni (n) bedroom, sleeping quarters (*lit* night dwelling), night cradleboard (baby's cradleboard is of simple construction of hide laced up, sometimes with padding, for baby to sleep by mother's side).

habikuno? (n) day cradleboard (used to transport baby on mother's back). *See* **waakohno.**

habikuno?

꙰ wehki'ai

habikwasuu, habikwasu?u W (n) nightgown, pajamas (*lit* night dress).

hagwoitu W (adj) loose.

hahka (dem pro, acc sg) whom.

haipia? (n) opposite-sex sibling-in-law (BrWi, WiSs, BrWiSs, SsHu, HuBr, SsHuBr), opposite-sex cross cousin (parallel or cross).

haitsíi (n voc) dear friend.

haitsi (n) same-sex friend, same-sex cousin (parallel or cross).

haitsi ihtaipu (n) former friend (*lit* thrown away; one who is no longer a friend).

haitsi wihtaitu (v) disown a friend (give up a friendship).

hakaapu, hakahpu (adv interrog) which way? where to? **Hakaaputu suru mi?ai?** Which way is that one going?

hakai (adv interrog, state of being) how? **Hakai unu nuusuka?** How do you feel?

hakani (adv interrog, manner) how?. **Hakani unu nahanu?** What happened to you? (*lit* what way did you become?).

hakaniiku, hakanihku (adv interrog) what way? how? **Hakanihku unu ma poomia?** How are you writing this?

hakani?yu, hakani?yutu (adv interrog) why? **Hakani?yutu unu sinihku tai hanituni?** Why are you telling us to do it this way?

hakaru (pro interrog, nom) who? which? *pl* **hakaruu. Hakaru narumukahtu mi?ai?** Who is going to town?

hakuse? (adv interrog, loc) where?

haku, hakuru (adv interrog) where? what place?

hani- (pfx) maize, corn, ear of corn.

haníibi (n) corn, maize, ear of corn (sweet or field corn). *See* **numu hani.**

hanikotsapu (n) cornmeal mush.

hanikwasukuru (v) toast corn, roast corn. *See* **atakwa?su?aitu.**

haninookopu, haninohkopu (n) corn bread.

hanitusupu (n) ground corn, cornmeal.

haniwo?ora K, hanibitawo?oraa W, O (n) corncob.

hani buhipu (n) corn shucks, corn leaves.

hanipu (n) prepared food.

hanisahoba, hanisahuupa (n) corn soup (not quick-cook type).

Hanitaibo (n) Corn People (Comanche band).

hanitu (v), *pl* **hanikatu** do, fix, repair.

hanituniru (v) order, command (*lit* tell to do, give orders).

hapiana?, hapinna (n) suspenders.

haya kwasiku (adv) at last. *See* **kwasiku.**

hayarokwetu (num) four.

ha?íi (interj) Oh, my! (used by women only). *See* **ubia.**

ha?nii (n) beaver.

ha?wo?itu, ha?wokahtu (adj) hollow, loose (not tight).

hehékitu (v, anim subj) pant, breathe heavily. **Oru sarii tsa? hehékuka.** The dog is panting.

hehekubuniitu (v) pant with tongue hanging down, pant heavily.

hekwi?, hehkwi? (n) spleen.

hibiawo (n) drinking cup.

hibikahti (n) cup.

hibikutu (v) water an animal. **Sarii?a ma hibikutui.** He will give water to the dog.

hibikutu (v) drink alcoholic beverage (be made drunk).

hibipu, hibitu (n) drunk person, intoxicated person.

hibipu, hibitu, hibihkatu O (adj) drunk, intoxicated. *See* **kwinumapu.**

hibitu (v) drink. **Paa nu? hibitu.** I am drinking water.

hihini (n) thing.

hiitoo? K, N (n) meadowlark, field lark. *See* **ohanunapu.**

Hiitoo? K, N (name) Meadowlark, Field-lark (personal name).

himaku (pro interrog, acc) with what? on what? **Himaku nahaniitu?** On what (am I) going to attach (it)?

himataaka, himataku W (adv man) barely. **Oru tsa? naboko?a himataka mi?aru.** That car is just barely going.

hima?aru (v, pl), *sg* **yaaru** pick up several objects, take several objects. **mahimamiaru** keep on taking objects.

hima?ikaru (v), *pl* **himawekwiitu** carry in.

himiitu, himikatu (v, pl) give several objects. *See* **utukatu.**

hina (interrog pro, acc) what? **Hina munu hanibui ni??** What are you all doing so much? (5:3). *See* **hini.**

hinanahimitu (v, pl obj) exchange gifts. *See* **na?uhturu.**

hinanahimitu waipu (n) gift-exchanging partner (woman).

hini, hiini (pro interrog, nom) what? **Osu hini ohto huhkúwunukina?** What is that coming stirring up dust along there? (7:38). *See* **hina.**

hipa?a (adv interrog) on what?

hipe? (adv interrog) when? **Hipe tanu piarukaru?** When are we having thanksgiving (prayer)?

hipeka?i (num interrog) how many? how much?

hipetᵾ (num interrog) how many? how much? **Hipetᵾ itᵾ nawe hᵾpai?** How much does this cost?

hipᵾ (adj) possessed, owned, belonging to. **Oko ma hipᵾ.** It belongs to that person (over there).

hipᵾkatᵾ (v) own, possess. **Sariia hipᵾkatᵾ nᵾ.** I own the dog. See **mahípᵾrᵾmᵾtᵾ.**

hi?oo- (pfx) ref. to sunflowers.

hi?ookwana? (n) sunflower salve (cold remedy for nose and throat; contains eucalyptol and mint; *lit* sunflower odor).

hi?oosanahkòo (n) weed wax (plant from whose sap chewing gum was made).

hi?oopi, hi?ohpi (n) sunflower stalk or plant.

hi?oopitaohayaa, hi?opitatotsiyaa (n) sunflower head.

homo-, homobi (n) powder, flour.

homobi saapi, homobi sahpi (n) face powder (*lit* powder-paint).

homopisarᵾ (v) powder the body, flour, powder something (powder the body with talcum powder).

homoketᵾma? (n) powdery (fine and dry).

homonabisakatᵾ (v) apply powder to oneself.

homonutsaitᵾ (v) crumble (like dust). See **mahomonutsarᵾ, tahhomonutsarᵾ.**

homopᵾ (n) powder, flour. See **pisahpi.**

homorohtía? (n) packaged flour (*lit* bread flour; packaged wheat flour).

homoroso?yoki? (n) talcum powder.

hooki (n), *pl* **po?ropᵾnᵾᵾ, po?ro?nᵾᵾhog.** See **mubipo?roo?.**

hooki tᵾᵾhtᵾmapᵾ (n) hog-pen fence. See **po?ro tᵾhtᵾmapᵾ.**

hoora (n) hole dug in soil.

horarᵾ (v) dig a hole. See **tᵾhorarᵾ.**

ho?aitᵾ, hoekwarᵾ (v) hunt (look for prey). **Wasape?a u hoekwai.** He went hunting for a bear.

ho?aniitᵾ (v) sneak around, spy on, look for. **Ohkanᵾ usukwaitᵾ u ho?aniitᵾ.** I have found what I have been looking for. See **kuhiyarᵾ.**

ho?yopitᵾ (v) ill (feel malaise). See **keho?yopitᵾ.**

ho?yopi (adj) sickly, ill.

ho?yopipᵾ (adj) uneven, inexact.

hu- (pfx) ref. to tree, wood, stick. See **huu-.**

huaawo, huakwo, huagwo (n) mortar. See **huuaawo.**

huba (n) coffee.

huba aawo? (n) coffeepot.

huba aikᵾtᵾ (v) brew coffee (boil coffee). **Tai huba aikᵾtᵾ mᵾ.** I am boiling some coffee for us.

huba aitᵾ (v) make coffee.

hubebitᵾ (v) drink coffee.

hubinitᵾ (v) groan, cry out.

hubiyaarᵾ (v) cry, yell noisily.

hubiya piayakeetᵾ (n) death wail.

hubiyaa piayakeetᵾ, hubiha piayaketᵾ (v) cry loudly, wail.

hubiyairᵾ (v) make noise yelling.

hubiya? (n) song, hymn (*lit* sounds mournful, like crying).

hubᵾhka? (n) illness (the type a child contracts).

huhku-, huuku- (pfx) ref. to dust.

huhkukwᵾnᵾrᵾ (v) blow dust, dust storm. See **huukunatsirᵾ, huuku kwᵾmᵾrᵾ.**

huhkupᵾ (n) dust.

humasuapu (n) domestic tree.

hunaku (post) outside, before, in front of.

hunaku, hunakwu, huuku, hu?nakwu (post) outside. hunakuhu toward the outside. hunakwuhi from outside.

hunu?bi (n) creek, stream. *See* okwèetu.

hupimi?aru (v) back up, go backwards.

husi (n) cactus. *Cactaceae* sp. (edible and used as medicine), peyote (hallucinogenic drug for ceremonies).

huu-, huupi, huuhpi, huh- (n) tree, wood. *See* hu-, tuhhuu?.

huu aawo (n) mortar, barrel, wooden vessel (*arch* sandrock in natural bowl shape used with a pestle). *See* huaawo.

huuba? (n) coffee (*lit* tree water).

huuhimaru (v, pl obj), *sg* huuyaaru possess sticks.

Huuhunu?bi (n) Timber Creek.

Huuhwiya, Huwiya (name) Refuse-to-come (a medicine man who refused to attend the council at Fort Sill).

Huuh?inuu (n) Timber People (Comanche band, Southern Comanches).

huukabatu, huhkabatu (n) woods, clump of trees. *See* soohuuhpi.

huukisaakitu (v) hear or make noise in timber.

huukono?itu (n) natural windbreak.

huuku, huhku (n) collarbone. *See* sihkupu.

huukukatu, huhkukatu (adj) dusty (be dusty).

huukukwumuru (v) blow dust. *See* huhkukwunuru.

huukumatsumaru, huhkumatsumaru (v) dust off by hand.

huukunatsiru, huhkunatsiru (v) blow dust. *See* huhkukwunuru.

huukunatsiru, huhkunatsiru (v) dust off.

huukuna? (n) match (to strike for fire).

huukunuetu, huhkunuetu (v) blow dust.

huukupu, huhkupu (n) dust.

huukumuyake?, huhku muyake? (n) whistle (made of collarbone or substitute; used by medicine men).

huukuhunuru, huhkuwunuru (v) dust storm, raise dust, stir up dust.

huumara?, huhmara? (n) falcon. *Falco* sp.

huunakaru? (n) wooden bench.

huunaro?i? (n) ladder, stairs.

huunarumuu? (n) lumberyard (*lit* wood store).

huunatsihtu?ye?, huu natsihtu?ye? (n) wooden comb.

huuna? (n) groundhog, woodchuck.

huupi kasamawu (adj), *pl* huupi-takobi?i battered tree (as by winds).

huupi po?a? (n) tree bark.

huupiso?na?aitu (v) make a bird nest. *See* pisona?aitu.

huupita homoketu (n) sawdust (*lit* tree powder). *See* huupita pisoni, huutusupu.

huupita kwiita, huupi kwiita (n) tree stump. *See* huupita turahna.

huupita mooka (n) tree limb.

huupita pisoni (n) sawdust. *See* huupita homoketu.

huupita poʔa (n) tree bark.

huupita tʉrahna (n) tree root, stump. *See* **huupita kwiita.**

huupitan pihnàa, hupitan sanahpi (n) rosin (*lit* juice of a tree).

huupihnàa (n) syrup, molasses, sugar cane.

huusibeʔ (n) drawknife, wood plane, peeling tool (cobbler's tool, modern carpenter's tool; *arch* artifact used by early Comanches to peel bark off trees).

huutsi piahpʉ? (n) daughter-in-law (SoWi, SbSoWi).

huutsihkaaʔ, huutsihkaʔa (n) two-man handsaw. *See* **moʔo huutsihkaʔaʔ.**

huutsikaʔarʉ (v) saw something with a saw.

huutsiyaaʔ (n) teepee pole (holds flap on top of teepee; *lit* pole-that-holds-up).

huutsi, huhtsi (n) paternal grandmother, woman's agnatic grandchild.

huutsi piahpʉ, hutsi piahpʉ (n) daughter-in-law (of man or woman).

huutsúu, huhtsúaʔ (n) bird (general term).

huutsúʔa kàhni (n) bird nest, birdhouse, sensitive pea (*lit* bird house). *Cassia nictitana.*

huutsúʔa pisooʔni (n) bird nest (so named for strings, rags, etc. used in building it).

huutsúʔa tʉahkapʉ (n) sumac. *Rhus* sp. (*lit* bird food).

huutubuʔitʉ W (adj) slender (*lit* like a tree).

huutunaakatʉ K (adj) slender (*lit* like a tree is straight).

huutusupʉ W (n) sawdust (*lit* wood ground up). *See* **huupita homoketʉ, huupita pisoni.**

huutʉrohpakoʔiʔi (n) wooden mallet.

Huuwʉhtʉkwaʔ (name) Take-a-stick-and-hit-someone (person).

huuyaarʉ (v), *pl* **huuhimarʉ** possess, carry a stick.

huuyʉkkwiʔ (n), *pl* **huu yʉkkwʉʔnʉʉ** lumberman, white man (from homesteaders' practice of making log cabins).

huwaboʔkóoʔ (n) wild currant, mulberry, huckleberry. *Ribes odoratum* Wendl.

huyubaʔatʉ, huyubatʉ (adj) oblong, long and flat. *See* **piahuyubatʉ.**

huyuni (adj) oval.

hʉa- (pfx) ref. to fish or fishing.

hʉahuupi, hʉaana huupʉ (n) fishing pole.

hʉarʉ (v) to trap, to fish.

Hʉarʉ u. He is fishing.

hʉarʉʔ (n) trap (general term for all traps).

hʉato (n) fish (unknown species).

hʉawapi, tahʉawapi (n), *pl* **hʉaʔetʉ** fisherman, trapper.

hʉaʔ W, **hʉaʔeetʉ** K (n) fish hook.

hʉbi, hʉʉbi, hʉbi waipʉ (n) middle-aged woman (grown, possibly heavy-set).

hʉbi tsiitsiʔ, hʉʉbi tsihtsiʔ (n) elderly woman (little old lady).

hʉhkiapʉ (n) shadow.

hʉhkʉnarʉ, nʉhkʉnarʉ (v) cover something. **Sonipʉ tsaʔ nʉhkʉnarʉ.** The hay is covered. *See* **wʉhkʉnarʉ.**

hʉhtsawʉkatʉ (v) feel cool.

huitsi, huihtutsi (num) a few, a
little bit. *See* tutaatu.

Hukiyani (name) Carrying-her-
sunshade (person).

hukiai (n) umbrella.

hukikʉ (n) shade. *See* huuki.

hukitu (adj) shaded.

hunu- (pfx) ref. to thinness.

hunupoʔaʔ (n) human skin. *See*
mapóʔaʔ.

hunubi pokaaʔ (n) bat (*lit* thin
cockleburr).

hunuketʉ, huʔnuketʉ (adj) thin
(as thin paper or onion skin). *See*
tapituhtsi.

huu (num interrog) how many? Unu
huu tomopʉ? How old are you?

huu, huutu (num) a few; n huutʉtsi
just a few. Huutʉtsi maʔ. There
are just a few.

huukatu, hukatu, hukai (v, inan
subj) cool off (as food).

huukiaʔ, hukiapʉ (n) shadow. Ma
huukiaʔ tsaʔ mamaʔaitu usúni.
His shadow is always with him.

huukina huupi (n) poles for
constructing brush arbor.

huukiʔaitu (n) brush arbor (usually
made of horseweed, blackjack
oak, or willow branches). *See*
sonihuuki.

huukiʔaiʔ (n) umbrella.

huuki (n) shade. huukikʉ in the
shade. *See* hukikʉ.

huunuʔ (n) porcupine (*lit* thin, for
thin quills). *See* yuhnu.

huusu (num) a few times. Nah
huusu uruu maʔaipisikwanuuʔii
ma. He slid with them just a few
times.

huutsaʔwetu, huutsaʔwuru (v,
hum subj) cool off.

huutsaʔwʉ miʔaru (v) go on
vacation (*lit* go to cool off).

huutsipʉ, huhtsipʉ (n) saliva. *See*
kupisiʔ.

Huwuni (name) Dawn (person).

huwuni (n time) dawn. *See* kuhu
wunʉkatʉ, tosa huwunikatʉmaʔ.

huʔniipʉʔ (n) hiccough.

huʔniitu, huuʔnitu (v), *pl*
hʉʔnipʉbu hiccough.

Huʔnipitʉ (name) Hiccough-
daughter (person).

I

ibu (adv dem, prox) this direction.
Ibu nu miaruʔi. I will go this
direction.

ibuʔikʉru (v) fill (cause to be full).
See pawʉsaʔnaitu.

ibuʔitu (v) filled to the brim. *See*
paa maʔibuʔikutu.

ibuniitu, ipuniitu (v) come this way.

Idahi (n) Snakes (Athapascan name
for the Comanches—their enemies).

ihka (pro dem, prox acc sg) this.
Ihka masukaa. Feel this (60:22).
Ihka puni tuihú. Look at this,
friend (41:7).

Ihtataʔo (n) Burned Meat (small
Comanche band that became
extinct).

ikaru (v), *pl* wekwiitu,
wekwimiʔaru enter. Itu tsaʔ
ikaruʔi. This person is going
to enter. Tenahpuʔ tsaʔ
ikahkii. The man came in. *See*
sutenaʔikuru.

iki (adv dem, prox) here. Iki tanu
yukwi. Let's sit here (60:16).
ikʉhu to here.

inaarʉ, inasʉ (adj compar) younger than, smaller than. **Ma tamiʔa inasʉ ma.** He is younger than his brother.

inakwata, inagwata, inawaata, inawata, inawàata (n) meat-drying A-frame (poles for preparing jerky).

inakwʉ (adv dem, prox) this direction. **Inakwʉhi nʉ? puniwatuʔi.** I will go to look in this direction (104:11).

inapʉ (n), *acc* inapa jerky, jerked meat. *See* **esiinapʉ.**

inarʉ (n) meat jerky, jerked meat.

inaʔetʉ (v) jerk meat, hang meat up to dry (one step in the process of making jerky). **Sitʉ waʔihpʉ? ma inaʔetʉ.** This woman prepares jerky.

Isananakaʔ, Isʉnanika (n) Howling-coyote, Echo-of-the-wolf-howl (star name; former chief and one of the signers of the Medicine Lodge Treaty).

isananarʉmuʔipʉ? (n) gossip.

isanaramuʔitʉ? (n) one who gossips.

isapʉ, ishapʉ? (n) lie, liar. *See* **nayaʔisaʔaitʉ, kaawosą.**

Isatekwa (name) Liar, Lie-talk (person).

isawasʉ? (n) pesticide, poison.

isawasʉ wanakotse? (n) lye (*lit* soap poison).

Isawʉra (name) Crazy-bear (person).

isaʔaitʉ (v) lie (tell an untruth).

Ishatai (name) Coyote-droppings (Comanche messiah who predicted Coggia's Comet to last for five days and to be followed by drought; he instituted Sun Dance in 1874).

isʉ (pro dem, prox acc sg) this. **Isʉ hakʉku ʉ yaaʔį?** Where was this you took? (82:22).

itsa, itsee (n) snake root, church root. *Liatris* sp. (from Mexico; good for curing asthma or emphysema; rub on legs to repel rattlesnakes). *See* **timʉihʉ?.**

itsaraitʉ ʉnʉa kahni (n) den, animal hole.

itsiną, itsini (n, acc) agent, Indian agent (fr Engl *agency*).

itʉ (pro dem, prox nom sg), *pl* **itʉʉ** this. **Paakʉhu tsa? itʉ nʉhi tsayumaʔi.** This one made us fall in the water.

itʉkwʉ (pro dem, prox nom du) these two. **Itʉkwʉ tsa? nikwanarʉkwʉ.** These two have been talking.

iyaaʔitʉ (v) watch for (be a guard). **Surʉ tsa? tabeni ma naharuʔiha iyaaʔitʉ.** That one watches for when it will be noon.

iʔa (adv loc, prox) somewhere (near). **Iʔa tsa? miibeʔtu haniitʉ.** There is a meeting someplace close by.

K

kaabehkarʉ, kaabehkatʉ (v) trick, fool, deceive, cheat, play dead. **Ke nʉ bʉmi kaabehka- waʔitʉ.** I can't be cheated myself (11:30).

kaahaniitʉ (v) fool, deceive, cheat.

Kaaiwanʉʉ (n) Kiowa people.

kaakwakurʉ, kaakaku (v) defeat by cheating, win in a contest by cheating. **Nʉmasʉ ʉ kaakwakui.** I beat you by cheating.

kahni

kaanatsaka?uhtupʉ (n) one who betrays.

kaanatsaka?uhturʉ (v) betray someone.

kaasuarʉ (v), *pl* **kaayʉkwiitʉ** intend to deceive or cheat, pretend (even if not successful), kid around. *See* **nohitekwarʉ.**

Kaatʉ, Katinʉ (n) God.

kaawosa̱ (n) fox, jackal; liar, dishonest person, shyster. *See* **isapʉ?.**

kaayʉkwi̱tʉ (adj) cheater.

kabitsi̱ (n) cabbage.

kabʉrʉʉ? (n) sheep.

kabʉrʉʉ?a tua (n) lamb (*lit* sheep child).

kabʉrʉʉ?a pʉhʉ (n) sheep wool.

kabʉrʉ?a tahkoni wapi̱ (n) shepherd (hired sheep lord).

kabʉrʉʉ tʉhkapʉ (n) mutton (*lit* sheep meat).

kah- (pfx) house, teepee, room, home.

kahku?e (n) smoke hole (in teepees), upper story, upstairs (in any house or building). *See* **kahniku?e.**

kahni, -kʉni (n) house, teepee, room, home. **Sitʉkwʉ pʉhʉ kahni betu mi?arʉ.** These two are going toward their house.

kahni (n) house. *See* **puku kahni.**

kahni ku?e (n) housetop, smoke hole. *See* **ku?e, kahku?e.**

kahni mi?a (v) visit, go visiting (*lit* house go).

kahni nasiyuuki? K (n) shingle.

kahni tai (n) room, cave. *See* **taina.**

kahni tʉbanaa (n) wall (of house). *See* **tʉbanaa?.**

kahni tʉbitsika? K (n) trailer house. [**kahni** house + **tʉ** (unspec) + **bitsika?** pulled]. *See* **tʉbiyaakʉ?.**

kahni busi?a (n) house bug of any kind, bedbug (*lit* house louse).

kahni nahʉʉki (n) porch (*lit* house shade).

kahnitaikʉ (n) tunnel, burrow. **Tʉ?rikuu tsa? pʉ kahnitaikʉ ikanʉ.** The prairie dog went into his burrow.

kahnitʉeka (n) Indian paintbrush. *Scrophulariaceae Castilleja indivisa.*

kahni?aitʉ (v) build a house, construct a house or other building. **Kahni?aitʉ ma.** He is building a house.

kahni̱ ebi̱ (n) W plaster; K house paint.

kahni̱ tʉboopʉ, kahni̱ tʉbana rʉboopʉ (n) wallpaper.

kahpe (n) bed.

Kahpewai (name) No-bed (person).

kahpinakwʉ (adv) west (*lit* bed-behind; since teepees faced east).

kahtʉiʔ (n) neighbor (*lit* house friend). **Nʉ kahʔtʉiʔ tsaʔ nʉ makai.** My neighbor has given me some food.

kahtʉ (v) sit, live. **Tʉtaatʉ kuyuutsiʔ tsaʔ suʔna sonikku kahtʉ.** A little quail is sitting somewhere there in the grass.

Kahúu nihku pipikurẹ (name) Squeaky-like-a-mouse (person). *See* **Pipikuʔ.**

kahúu pipikuniitʉ, kahúu pipikurʉ (v) squeak (as a mouse).

kahúu pʉmata hʉarʉʔ (n) mousetrap, rattrap.

kahúuʔ, kahhúuʔ (n) house mouse.

kakuʔ (n) maternal grandmother, maternal great aunt, woman's uterine grandchild.

kamakʉna W, **kamakʉnʉa** K (n) loved one, beloved.

kamakʉrʉ (v) love (want someone to remain present). **Ʉnʉ nʉ kamakʉnʉ?** Do you love me?

kamatʉ (v) taste. **Tsaa maʔ kamatʉ.** It tastes good. **Moha maʔ kamatʉ.** It tastes sour, bitter, acid. **Otʉ maʔ kamatʉ.** It tastes neither sweet nor sour.

kamúutaʔ (n) sweet potato.

kanabaʔaitʉ (adj) stand tall, tall and slender. **Tenahpʉʔ orʉ kanabawʉnʉ.** That man is tall and slender. *See* **huutubuʔitʉ.**

kanabʉʉtsiʔ, kanabʉhtsiʔ (n) thin person.

karʉkatʉ (v, adj), *pl* **yʉkwi miʔarʉ** sit down, stay; *adj* **yʉkwiitʉ** seated.

karʉkʉrʉ, karʉʉkʉkatʉ (v), *pl* **yʉkwikʉkatʉset** up (as a teepee);

cook, boil food. **Pihuura nʉ karʉʉkʉkatʉ.** I am cooking beans.

karʉʉrʉ (adj) stationary (remaining in place).

kasabipikurʉ, kasapiipikurʉ (v) flap wings, whir (make wing noises while flying).

kasamaarʉ (n) club (of playing cards).

kasamawʉrʉ (v, adj) batter; battered (as by wind). **Huuhpi kasaʔmawʉrʉ.** The tree is battered (by the wind).

kasaráibooʔ (n) angel (*lit* winged stranger).

kasa (n) wing.

kasakatʉ (adj) winged. **Sitʉ kwasinabooʔ kasakatʉ mawakatu yʉtsʉhkina.** This snake having wings came flying towards him (27:6).

katakakitʉ W, **katatakitʉ** K, **O** (v) woman's whoop (cry of excitement).

katsonakwʉ (n) rear, rump.

kawonokatʉ (n) street (*lit* wolf separate camp).

kawohwitʉ (v) ring (as a bell). **Kawohwitʉ.** It is ringing (*lit* it is belling). *See* **tuʔtsayaketʉ.**

kawohwiʔ (n) bell. **Kawohwiʔ tsaʔ yakeetʉ.** The bell is ringing (*lit* bell is crying).

kaʔamoorʉ (v) lap with the tongue (as a dog laps water).

kaʔi (n) forehead.

kaʔibʉhʉ, kaʔibʉʉ (n) eyebrow (*lit* forehead fuzz). *See* **pʉhʉ.**

Kaʔmʉtʉhiʔ W, Kamʉrʉʔiʔ K (name) Looking-from-side-to-side (person).

ka?ra?áa?, ka?ara?áa? (n) tick.

ka?wekitʉ (adj compar) greater than. I ka?wekitʉ. This is greater.

ka?witsetʉ K, kawʉtʉ?itʉ W (v) shake head in disagreement.

ka?witʉ (v, hum subj) hold council, gather together. Ka?witʉ urʉ. They are gathering (to hold council).

ke-, kee (pfx) no, negative.

Ketokwe hina haniitʉ (name) Satan, devil (lit not exact whatever do). See Tuhkwasi taiboo?.

Kebakowe? (name) Coyote (lit does-not-go-in-water; nickname for Coyote).

kebayʉmʉkitʉ (adj) quiet (not moving), still (unmoving). Paa tsa? kebayʉmʉkikatʉ. The water is (very) still.

kebisa?makarʉ, kepisa?makarʉ (v) encourage, strengthen.

Kehaitsipaapi (name) Bald (lit without hair).

kehe, kehena (num) nothing.

kehewa?itʉ (v) be missing, exhaust supply, run short. Urʉʉ kahninʉʉ kehewa?i. Their teepees were gone (37:8).

keho?yopitʉ, keóyo?bahtʉ (adj) healthy, whole. See kenama?ʉbʉ?itʉ.

kekʉnabeniitʉ (v) leave person alone, stop quarreling (lit stop biting; used when person is aggravated).

kemabana?itʉ (v) reject, dislike, lack knowledge of. Kema mabana?itʉ. He doesn't like anything. Ke hina mabana?itʉ. He doesn't know how to do anything.

kemahpʉ?arʉ, kemahpʉ?a (v, adj) fail to do something, unable to do something (even though one has the desire to comply). See tsuhitʉ.

kemakʉmapʉ, kemakʉmahpʉ (adj) dulled edge, dulled. See kʉmakwa?i.

kemarʉkwisʉ (adv time) soon. See miitʉtsi.

kemenikwitʉ W, keme?oniikwitʉ K (v, adj) reject someone, rejected.

kemi?arʉtatsino (n) north star (lit not-moving star).

kenama?ʉbʉ?itʉ (adj) healthy, well (not sickly). See nama?abʉ.

kenanawatsitʉ, kenanakwatsitʉ (adj) clear, plain, understood. See nanawatsikarʉ.

kenaninabenitʉ (adj) distraught, continue uncontrollably (unable to stop when one should, as talking or crying).

kenatsʉwitʉ (adj) weak.

kenawʉnʉrʉ, kenagwʉnʉrʉ (adj) be in deep water (lit cannot stand up; as in water over one's head).

keno, kenu (n) hillside, hill.

kesósoorʉ (adj nonhum) tame, gentle.

kesósoorʉ (adj, human) humble, calm, relaxed.

kesuatʉ (adj) mean, rough. See aitʉ, tʉtsʉ-.

Kesʉ (adv) never.

keta? (neg) Don't! (used in commands). Keta? tekwaarʉ. Don't talk!

ketekwa (adj) dumb (unable to speak).

ketokwetʉ (adj) deficient, not good enough.

keto?kapaa (n) kerosene [**ke** not + **to?ka** dark + **paa** liquid]. *See* **tuka?anabaa.**

Ketse na?bo (name) Painted- feather (*lit* striped wing).

ketsihanabenitu (adj) starving (extremely hungry; without food).

ketunabunitu (adj) dark, darken (be dark, get dark).

ketunakatu (adj) deaf, disobedient. *See* **tunakatu.**

kewáhabahku (adv) doubtless, surely.

kewesikatu, kewesiketu (adj) straight (not curly).

kewesiketu (adv) be straight (not curled, unable to curl). **Kewesiketu u.** It won't curl.

keyu K (adv time) late, tardy (after the appointed time). **Keyu u? pitui.** He arrived late.

keyu?u, keyuu W (adv time) late.

kia (adv) maybe, perhaps (expresses wonder, doubt, inquisitiveness). **Nah kia u? po?ayaahkwa?i.** Guess it just blew away (49:29). *See* **suukutsa?noo.**

kiahbitu (v, pl), *sg* **to?ibitu** come out at a particular place.

kibo?aru (v) peel off skin, skin something. *See* **kwuru?aru.**

kihtsi? (adv time) now (right now), immediately. **Ukihtsi nu? mi?aru.** I am going right now. *See* **meeku.**

kii (n) corner.

kiinaboo (n) diamond (in playing cards, *lit* striped or spotted corner).

kiipu (n) elbow.

kimaru (v), *pl* **sumunokima** come. **Situkuse? tutaatu tuinuhpu?**

mawakatu kimaru. This little boy is coming toward her (82:16).

Kiyu (name) Horseback (person).

ki?aru (v) cut something.

ko- (pfx) ref. to cut.

kobe-, koobe (n) face. **Uruu pia? tsa? u kobekuhu wihii.** Their mother threw it in his face (17:24).

kobe kiihtu?eka? W, **kobe wihtu?eka?** K (n) face cream.

kobe matsuma? (n) towel, face towel (*lit* face-wiping cloth).

kobe nabo? K (n) camera (*lit* face marking). *See* **numiboo?etu.**

kobe tsa?nika? (n) mask, false face (*lit* face loincloth).

Kohi (name) Narrow-gut (person).

kohikamutu (v) suffer abdominal pain.

kohikamukatu (n) stomach ache, intestinal flu.

kohinehkitu (v) wear something around the waist (men's apparel only).

kohinehki?, kohineeki? (n) belt, G-string. *See* **tsa?nika?.**

Kohitu se?tanuku (name) Sitting-bear (Comanche chief about 1821–1871).

kohi, kohhi? (n) small intestine, waist area, abdomen.

koho?aaitu (v) harvest. **U koho?aiitu?i u.** He will harvest corn (cut ears).

kohpapu (n), *pl* **kohbiapu** broken object.

kohparu (v), *pl* **kohbi?aitu, wuhkobi?** break up. **Huupita kohbiaru.** (It) is breaking up trees.

kohpooru (v) brand (mark with heat). *See* **tsihpooru.**

kohtoo rʉnahpʉ (n) fireman (one who puts out fires).

kohtoo wapi (n) fire-builder (one who builds fires).

kohtoopʉ (n) fire, heat of fire.

kohtóorʉ (v) build a fire. **Surʉʉ tsaʔ wihnu pia kohtóoi.** Then they made a big fire.

kohtsáarʉ (v) stew, cook (as apples or corn mush).

kohtsáaʔ, kohtsapʉ, kohtsaarʉ (n) cooked cereal, stewed food. *See* **tʉkarʉkʉpʉ.**

kokáaʔ (n), du **kokáaʔnʉkwʉ,** *pl* **kokáanʉ** guinea fowl. *Numido meleagris.*

kokoráʔa (n) chicken.

kokoráʔa kahni (n) chicken coop.

kokoráʔa kuhma W, **kokoráʔa nʉʉahpʉ** K (n) rooster.

kokoráʔa nooyo (n, arch) chicken egg.

kokoráʔa aràhimaʔetʉ, kokoraʔa ʔatahimaʔetʉ (n) chicken hawk.

kokoráʔa arʉhtʉmaʔ, kokoraʔa arʉhtʉmapʉ (n) chicken wire (*lit* chicken's fence).

kokoráʔa atùapʉ (n, modern) chicken egg (*lit* chicken child).

kokoráʔa pokopi (n) egg (*lit* chicken fruit).

kokoráʔa tasiʔa (n) chicken pox (*lit* chicken rash).

kokoráʔa yaketʉ K (v) cluck (as a hen), crow (as a rooster).

Komanche, Comanche (n) Those-who-are-always-against.

kono-, konóopʉ (n) firewood (load of, stacked in place).

kono honiitʉ (v), *pl* **kono hoyʉkatʉ** bring back firewood.

kono miʔarʉ (v) fetch firewood.

kono honiitʉ

konóorʉ (v) bring in firewood.

koobetʉ (adj) be hard and brittle (as leather curls in fire).

kooipʉ (n), *pl* **kooi- pʉnʉʉ** dead person.

kooitʉ (v, pl) to die. *See* **tʉyaaitʉ.**

koonitʉ (v) turn around. **Ibʉ niitʉ kooni.** Turn this way.

kooniʔetʉ (v) turn around.

koono, kohno, -kʉno (n) cradle, box, container, resting place.

kooʔ (n) mush, cornmeal mush.

kooʔitʉ (v) cut up something, slice, chop.

korohko (n) necktie. *See* **yuʔakorohko.**

korohkorʉ (v) wear something around the neck.

koropitʉ, korʉpitʉ (adj) brown, khaki, tan, dust-colored, beige.

kotsana (n) flank of living animal, hindquarter. *See* **tohoobe.**

koʔabitsipʉ (n) cheese (*lit* cut milk).

koʔitʉ (v), *pl* **koyama-** return, come back.

Kuhiyai (name) Peeping-from-behind-tree (person).

kuhiyarʉ (v) peep at, spy on someone. *See* **hoʔaniitʉ.**

kuhkerʉ (v) chop firewood.

kuhkuparʉ (v), *pl* kuhtokwe kill with heat, cremate, burn to death accidentally.

kuhkwarʉkitʉ (v, adj) take a steam bath, bathed.

kuhma (n) male, man.

kuhmaru (v) marry (of a woman).

kuhmito?ai? (n) popcorn (*lit* heated turns inside out).

kuhnu?itʉ W (v, adj) boil, boiled.

kuhparʉ (adj) melted.

kuhpawikʉ?itʉ (v) melt something (as in rendering lard). *See* **yuhukarʉ, ku?okwerʉ.**

kuhpitsʉni?arʉ W, **kuhpitsoonitʉ** K (v) render lard, fry out fat. *See* **yuhukarʉ.**

kuhporákitʉ (v) crackle, make popping noise. *See* **kukʉbihkutʉ.**

kuhpuru?airʉ (v) pop on someone, splatter. *See* **puruarʉ.**

kuhpuru?aitʉ (adj) splattered.

kuhtabearʉ (v) flash (as a light).

kuhtakwitsoo?nitʉ W, **kuhtso?okitʉ, kuhtsookitʉ** K (v) wrinkle, wither, shrivel up from heat.

kuhtsahwirʉ (v) throw into the fire, burn something up.

kuhtsiyarʉ (v, sg obj), *pl obj* **kuhtsihimaarʉ** roast on a stick (make a shish kebob) [**kuhtsu** cow + **hima?arʉ** pick up (pl)].

kuhtsu pokàa? (n) cocklebur, burr (*lit* cow berry).

kuhtsu taibo napʉ (n) cowboy boots.

kuhtsu taibo nohhiitʉ W (n) rodeo (*lit* cowboy play). *See* **tukumakwʉyetʉ?.**

kuhtsu taibo? (n) cowboy, cattleman.

kuhtsu tʉbini? (n) horned toad.

Kuhtsu tʉhka (n) Buffalo Eaters (middle Comanche band in western Oklahoma along the Canadian River and north of it; said to have left the northwest for Colorado, Kansas, New Mexico, Oklahoma, and Texas about 900 A.D.).

Kuhtsu kwi?ta (name) Cow-dung (person).

Kuhtsuna kwahipʉ (name) Buffalo-hump (Comanche chief of earlier years).

Kuhtsunu kwahipʉ (name) One-who-rides-buffalo (Comanche chief of early years).

kuhtsu? W (n) cow. *See* **kuutsu?.**

kuhtsu?marʉ (v) burn down (*lit* finished by fire).

kuhtsʉnikʉrʉ (v) heat something.

kuhtsʉni? (n) fever (*lit* going through heat).

kuhtsʉnitʉ (adj) be feverish (have a fever).

Kuhtu (name) Coals-in-a-wood-fire.

kuhtu tʉkʉmanirʉ K (v) cook over charcoal, barbecue.

kuhtuubi K (n) charcoal.

kuhtʉyarʉ (v) burn oneself to death, self-immolate.

kuitsi (n) throat.

kuitsɨkwaitʉ K (v) gag oneself (by putting something in the throat).

kuitsɨmarʉkitʉ (adj) strangled.

kuitsɨmarʉkʉtʉ (v) strangle someone.

kuitsɨsʉatʉ, kuitsʉatʉ (v) have a sore throat.

kuitsɨtsɨwoirʉ W (v) gag (put a finger down the throat to induce vomiting).

kuitsitukwuni, kuitsituwunuʔ (n) adam's apple. *See* **pia kuitsiʔ.**

Kukapu (name) Cooks-dried-meat (person).

kukubihkutu (v) crackle, pop, sizzle. *See* **kuhporákitu.**

kukumepu (n) parched corn, toasted maize.

kukumeru (v) parch corn.

kukumeʔawe (n) skillet (used for parching corn). **Nu kukumeʔawetuku nu? nasuwatsiʔ.** I lost my skillet (122:20).

kumahpuʔ, kuhmapuʔ (n) husband. **U kumahpuʔ tsaʔ hunuʔbetu aainukwa.** Her husband loped off toward the creek.

kumaʔomeru, kutsaniru (v) stir up fire.

kumiitsanatsu (n) milkweed. *Asclepiadaceae.*

kuna-, kuuna (n) firewood.

kunapisoʔni (n) wood shavings, chips (*lit* firewood nest).

kunawaikina puʔe (n) railroad tracks (*lit* firewood wagon road).

kunawaikinu, kunawaikina (n) train, railroad car (*lit* firewood wagon).

kunawobipuuku (n) train, railroad car.

kunakuaru K (v), *pl* **kunakuuʔetaruappear,** bob up, protrude. *See* **kuroʔitu.**

kunanatsu (n) prickly ash, toothache tree. *Zanthoxylum americanum* Mill (has yellow roots; grows in sandy soil; grind bark with prehistoric bones as medicine for arthritis, fever, sore throat, and toothache). *See* **tupinatsu.**

kuna naʔmahpeeʔ (n) lightning bug (*lit* firewood ball).

Kunaʔituʔ (n) Onion Creek, Texas (*lit* firewood rock; named for volcanic plug located on south bank of creek).

kuparu (v) cut something or someone down.

kupisaru (v) dry by heating (as on a stove) [**kuh-** fire + **pisa-** dry].

kupisi, kubisi (n) brain.

kupisinamaya, kupisimawa (n) croton weed (leaves mixed with animal brains for use in tanning hides). *Croton monanthogynus* Michx.

kupisiʔaru (v) rub with brains (one of last steps in tanning a hide).

kupitaru (v) light a lamp or fire, throw a light on something.

kupitaʔ (n) light, lamp, flashlight. *See* **tukaʔ.**

kuputsaru (v) explode from heat, burst from overheating.

kuroʔitu W (v), *pl* **kunakuuʔitu** appear, bob up, protrude. *See* **kunakuaru.**

Kurupitsoni (name) Looks-brown (person).

kuruupe (n) opening in clothing.

kusi- (pfx) ref. to gray color of ashes. *See* **kusipu.**

kusiebipitu (adj) K light blue; W lavender.

kusikwaʔaaʔ (n) crane (*lit* gray thing that flaps wings). *See* **paʔatoyokatu huutsuuʔ.**

kusikwiʔiiʔ (n) Mexican blanket (gray-blue, previously issued by government to Native Americans); W blue-gray bird (sp. unknown).

kusimuura (n) donkey (*lit* gray mule).

kusinʉʉhparabi (n) gray-colored plant (sp. unknown).

Kusiokwe (n) Pecos River (*lit* gray stream).

kusisaiʔ (n) small gray bird (generally found around cattle; sp. unkown).

kusisʉkʉi, kusi sʉkʉ (n) fall plum. Prunussp. (fruits either eaten fresh or dried and stored for later use; *lit* gray plum). *See* **yusʉkʉ**.

kusipi̱ W, **kusipi̱tʉ** K (adj) gray, light blue.

kusipʉ (n) ashes.

kusitekwarʉ, kusihtakwarʉ (v) whistle.

kusiwʉhpima W (v) roast in ashes (formerly made bread or cooked meat by placing in coals, covering with ashes). **Surii kusiwʉhpimanu ma.** He roasted them in the ashes.

kusiwʉʉnʉ (n) shrub (similar to sage tree; grows by river; used as medicine; sp. unknown).

kusiyunaʔ (n) shovel (for ashes). *See* **tʉtsiyunaʔ**.

kusuatʉ (v) warm (feel warm from weather).

kusʉwetʉ, kusʉkwetʉ (v) radiate heat, blow heat toward one.

kutsani, kutsuhpi̱ (n) fire poker.

kutsihpʉʔ (n) donkey (*lit* fire end).

Kutsiokwe (n) Peace River (*lit* clear water).

kutsiyaapʉ (n) shish kebob.

kutsiʔomo (n) shin or shin bone.

kutsiʔwobiʔ (n) donkey (*lit* fire-end-board or hoof).

kutsi̱tonarʉ (v), *pl obj* kutsi̱towa-karʉ set on fire, burn.

kutʉhorapʉ W, **kutóorapʉ** K (n) fireplace, hearth, fire hole.

kutʉhorarʉ, kutoorarʉ (v) dig a fire hole. **Nʉ piaʔ tsaʔ wihnu nʉmi kutʉhórakʉʔeeyʉ.** My mother then would dig a fire hole for us (109:6).

kutʉhubihtaa ohweetʉ (n) coal mine.

kutʉhuubi̱ W, **kutuubʉ** K (n) coal.

kutʉhuyunaʔ W, **kutʉʉyunaʔ** K (n) coal shovel.

kuuma, kuhma (n) male animal.

kuumabaitʉ, kuhmabai (v) be married, have a husband.

kuumarurʉ, kuhmarukatʉ (v) marry a man.

kuupʉ (n) cache (food stored by animals or birds).

kuura (n) pack rat.

kuurʉ (v) cache (storage of food by animals or birds).

kuutsuʔ K (n), *pl* kuutsuhnanʉʉ cow, cattle. *See* **kuhtsuʔ**.

kuwaaitʉ (v) dry up.

kuwikʉsii (n) pony tail.

kuwoʔnepʉ (n) hollow, burned out tree trunk.

kuwʉhoraʔ, kuhworaʔ (n) hoe, mattock.

kuyaarʉ, kuyaami̱ʔarʉ (v) carry on the head.

kuyaʔakatʉ (adj) afraid, scared, frightened. **Sitʉ tʉseʔ waʔihpʉʔ tʉbitsi kuyaʔanʉ.** This woman was really scared (52:19). *See* **wʉʔyʉrʉhkikatʉ**.

kuyaʔarʉ (v) frighten.

kuyúusiʔ, kuyúutsiʔ (n) quail. *See* **tʉebasuuʔ**.

kuyuʔnii, kuyunii̱ʔ (n), *pl* kuyu-nii̱ʔnʉʉ, *acc pl* kuyunii̱ʔa turkey.

Kuyuníi?nʉʉ pisikwanuu?i.
The turkeys were sliding (5:1).
tosa kuynii? white turkey,
eka kuyunii? red turkey, **tuu
kuyunii?** black turkey.
ku?e (n) top, summit, on top of.
ku?ebi, ku?ekarʉ (n) hill, peak
(standing alone). *See* **anáabi.**
Ku?e kwʉsih taibo? (n) Chinese (*lit*
spinner-braided foreigners).
ku?e kwʉsi? (n) spinner (hair style;
braid from top or back of head;
style worn by early Comanches and
other Native American peoples).
**ku?e naba wʉhtia, ku?e nabaa
kwʉhtia** (v) baptize by sprinkling
(*lit* to pour out water on top).
ku?e tsasimapʉ (n) scalp (war
trophy).
ku?e tsasimarʉ (v) scalp someone.
ku?e wóo? (n) dove, pigeon (*lit* top
moaning, moaning on top). *See*
pasahòo, taibo huutsuu?.
ku?e wʉnʉrʉ, ku?e kwʉnʉ (v)
buck off, pitch off (as does a
horse).
ku?hiboo?, ku?hiboorʉ (n) nurse
cape (dress with a large round
collar).
ku?inapʉ (n), *acc* **ku?inapʉha**
roasted meat (possibly jerked).
**Suhka pʉ ku?inapʉha u?
tsayumi?ii.** He took off his
roasted meat (7:39). *See*
tʉkwʉsʉkʉpʉ?.
ku?inarʉ (v) roast meat over fire or
dry it for jerky, barbecue.
ku?inawaata̱, ku?inakwaata̱ (n)
grill, barbecue grate.
ku?miitsa̱ (n) wart.
ku?nikakʉrʉ (v), **pl obj kuwekwa
kʉrʉ** rope someone or something

while moving. **Tʉnahpʉ tsa?
pimoroo?a tua?a ku?nikakʉi.**
The man roped the calf.
ku?nikarʉ, kuwekwarʉ (v) slip a
rope around something.
ku?nika? (n) mourning cape (worn by
mother or grandmother of deceased;
so named because of tightness on
the neck of the wearer).
ku?nuitʉ (v) to swallow.
ku?okwerʉ W (v) render lard (*lit*
with heat liquify). *See* **yuhukarʉ,
kuhpitsʉni?arʉ.**
ku?tsiyaarʉ (v), *pl obj* **ku?tsihi-
marʉ** roast on sticks. **Pʉʉ
kohtoopʉba?a urʉʉ u ku?tsi-
yaa?eeyʉ.** They roasted it over
their fire on sticks (73:10).
kʉarʉ (v), *pl* **to?itʉ** escape, come
out, climb out.
kʉayʉka?etʉ W (v) ride horseback.
See **tʉhʉyakarʉ.**

kʉayʉka?etʉ   wehki'al

kʉbʉráata̱ (adj) tall and slender.
kʉhkarʉ?itʉ (v) bite together.
kʉhkarʉkatʉ (v) bite into and not
turn loose.
kʉhka?arʉ (v) bite off. **Nʉmatitʉ
sʉmʉsʉ piakʉhka?a.** Take a big
bite from me once (22:14).
kʉhkihtserʉ (v) W spit out; K mash
in the mouth.

kʉhkobarʉ (v), *pl obj* **kʉhtokwe** bite to death, break or sever with the teeth. **Itʉ tsaʔ ihka kʉhkobaʔi.** He broke this with his teeth. *See* **kʉnutsanʉ.**

kʉhkwatuubirʉ K, kʉhtsobokikatʉ W (v) roll in the mouth.

kʉhkwibikitʉ (v) quiver (lips), chatter (teeth). *See* **sʉhkwibitʉ, kuuhtarakii.**

kʉhkwitsitʉ (v), *pl* **kʉhtoroki, kʉhtoromi** grit the teeth, clack the teeth (once, or many times as does a hog).

kʉhpararʉ (v) straighten something (holding in mouth, as an arrow shaft).

kʉhparoʔaitʉ K, kʉhparuuburʉ W (v) moisten in the mouth.

kʉhpitsoonitʉ (v) grind (with teeth), extract juice (by mouth).

kʉhpohtorʉ (v) burst with the mouth, pop with the mouth (as chewing gum).

kʉhpomarʉ (v) trim, prune (to shape a tree). **Huupihta mooke kʉhpomai.** (He) trimmed the branches of the tree. *See* **wʉhʉwʉʔniitʉ, wʉʔyʉkwitʉ, kʉmakoorʉ.**

kʉhpomiʔitʉ (v) W chew up fine; K bite off.

kʉhporokitʉ (v) grit the teeth, grind the teeth.

kʉhpunitʉ (v) taste, try out. *See* **kʉʔkwiyarʉ.**

kʉhtáa mubitaiʔ (n) hickory (*lit* hard shelled; named for the nut).

kʉhtáa nuʔyaʔa W, kʉhtaa nuhye K (n) racer snake.

kʉhtáaku (adv) tightly. **Mʉʉ kahni nʉʉʔka kʉhtáaku tsahtʉmiʔinʉ.** All of you shut your house tightly (3:7).

kʉhtáatʉ (adj) strong, tight, hard.

kʉhtabai (n) pecan.

kʉhtáanʉetʉ (v) storm, blow hard. **Sukʉhu sitʉ urii kʉhtáanʉenʉ.** This (wind) blew hard on them there (53:26).

kʉhtoponarʉ W, kʉhtoponirʉ K (v) make round with the mouth.

kʉhtoʔyarʉ K (v) unwrap something with the mouth.

kʉhtsakarʉ (v) catch something with the mouth. **Kʉhtsakaʔaitʉ ma.** He is catching something with his mouth.

kʉhtsayaʔyaʔkeʔ (n, arch) coyote (*lit* yowling animal). *See* **kʉʔkwʉriaʔ.**

kʉhtsiarʉ (v), *pl* **kʉsoʔi** bite (mainly used in speaking of dogs or babies who bite). **Sitʉ kwasi- nabooʔ ubinai u kʉhtsianuʉ.** This snake bit him from behind (27:9).

kʉhtsuukarʉ (v) close the mouth.

kʉhtsuʔmarʉ (v) eat up, finish off by eating. **Pihuura tsaʔ kʉhtsu-ʔmai nʉ.** I ate up all the beans.

kʉhtsutsʉʉʔniʔ (n) poisonous wild onion (**lit** cause teeth to clench). *Allium* sp.? (similar to large wild onion). *See* **kuʉkạ.**

kʉhtʉkʉtoʔipʉ, kʉhtoʔipʉ (n) leftover food (something from mouth). **Pʉʉ kʉhtoʔipʉha urʉʉ sitii tʉrʉeʔtii makamaʔeeyʉ.** They fed their leftovers to these children (74:14).

kʉhʉwʉnʉkatʉ (n) dawn (before sunup). *See* **hʉwʉni.**

kʉhyaarʉ (v), *pl obj* **kʉhhimarʉ** take something in the mouth.

kʉkʉbʉraakwaʔsiʔ (n) scissortail,
fork-tailed flycatcher. *Muscivora
fortificata.*

kʉmakoorʉ (v) trim, prune (as to
shape a tree). **U kʉmakooʔi u.** He
trimmed it. *See* **kʉhpomarʉ.**

kʉmakwaʔi, kʉmakwai, kʉmawa-
htʉ (adj) dull **nahu kʉmakwaʔi**
dull knife. *See* **kemakʉmapʉ.**

kʉmapʉ (n) sharpened edge, knife
edge, can opener.

kʉmaʔ (adv loc) beside, along the
edge of.

kʉmaʔkʉ (post) beside.

kʉmaʔrʉ (post) alongside.

kʉminarʉ (v) break something,
break a bone (using instrument).

kʉmiʔakʉrʉ (v) send (make go by
talking; talk someone into going,
persuade someone to go).

kʉnabenitʉ (v) bite (as an insect).

kʉnorʉ (v) graze (eat grass, as cattle
do).

kʉnuaitʉ (v) move something with
the mouth.

kʉnutsarʉ (v) break up with the
teeth. *See* **kʉhkobarʉ.**

kʉnuʔ (n) paternal grandfather,
paternal great uncle; man's
agnatic grandchild, man's agnatic
grandnephew.

kʉpisoʔaitʉ K, kʉpʉhisoʔaitʉ W
(v) anger someone, annoy. *See*
mahrubʉhkaitʉ.

kʉpisiʔ, kʉpʉsiʔ (n) saliva. *See*
hʉʉtsipʉ, tusi-.

kʉpʉtsarʉ (v) break open with the
teeth.

kʉrahúuʔ K, kʉʔraʔhúuʔ W (n)
hackberry. *Celtis occidentalis
var. canina.* Raf. (used to cure
diarrhea).

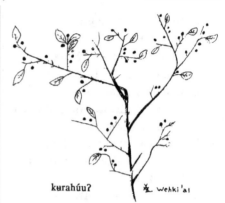

kʉrahúuʔ   ᴿ wehki'ai

kʉriata (n) yellow pond lily.
Nymphaea advena Ait.? (roots
boiled and eaten).

kʉrʉʔatsi̱ (n) yellow lotus. *Nelum-
bo luteo* [Willd.] Pers.? (roots
boiled or eaten raw; nutritious).

kʉsarʉ (v) open the mouth.

kʉsiʔkwarʉ (v) tear with the teeth.

kʉsukarʉ (v) taste. **Pokopi̱hta u
kʉsukai.** He tasted the fruit.

kʉtáatʉ, kʉhtaatʉ (adj) tight,
strong, hard.

kʉtsuʔtsuʔkitʉ, kʉtsʉbarʉ (v)
squeak, creak (make squeak as a
floor or shoes).

Kʉtsʉkwipʉ (name) Chew-up
(person).

kʉtsʉbakitʉ (v) bite together.

kʉtsʉkwetʉ (v) chew. *See*
kʉyuʔnetʉ.

kʉtsʉweʔ (n) chewing gum.

kʉtu (adv) yesterday.

kʉtubarʉ W, kʉtʉrʉkwaitʉ K (v)
click, snap (make snapping sound
as a trigger).

kʉtʉbarʉ (v) crack with the teeth.

kʉʉhtarakiitʉ (v) chatter the teeth.
See **kʉhkwibikitʉ.**

kʉʉkanarʉhkaʔ (n) wild onion
(roots roasted in coals and eaten).

kuuka̱, kuka (n), *acc pl* **kuukewild** onion. *Allium* sp. (edible root). *See* **kuhtsutsuuhni?.**

kuukume?, kuhkume? (n) stranger. (archany nonkinsman).

kuutsi̱ (n) wisdom tooth.

kuwokaru, kuhpiwokaru (v) drag something (by mouth). **Sarii tsa? u kuhpiwokaru.** The dog is dragging it (by its mouth).

kuyu?netu (v) chew. *See* **kutsukwetu.**

ku?kwiyaru (v) nibble, taste (eat a small amount). *See* **kuhpunitu.**

ku?kwuriaru (v) dribble, spill (from the mouth). *See* **ku?okwetu.**

ku?kwuria? (n) fox, coyote. *See* **kaawosa̱, oha ahnakatu̱, kuhtsaya?ya?ke?.**

ku?okwetu (v) slobber, dribble from the mouth. *See* **ku?kwuriaru.**

ku?tseena (n), *pl* **kutseenanuu** fox, wolf, coyote (long form). *See* **tseena?, kuhtsaya?ya?ke?.**

ku?uru (v) have hope. **Nu ku?uru suni.** I hope it is like that. **Ku?uru hai.** I do hope so.

ku?wikeetu (v) shake something (holding it in the mouth). **Sarii tsa? tabukina?a ku?wikeetu.** The dog is shaking the rabbit (with his mouth).

ku?wonuhubai (n, arch) handcar.

ku?wunubaa?i̱, ku?wunuhubai (n) railroad handcar. *See* **pi?yupu káa?i̱.**

kwaabih kahni (n) rooming house.

kwabaru, kwabatu (v) hug, squeeze, carry in the arms. *See* **toyokwabaru.**

kwabitu (v, pl), *sg* **habiitu** lie down.

Kwahari tuhka, Kwaharunuu (n) Antelope Eaters (Comanche band now located in Cache and Lawton, OK; said to have originated in 1100 A.D. from the Tejas (tuhka) group, Deer Hunters).

kwahi (n) back (of person or animal).

kwahi kupisi̱ (n) spinal cord (excluding any bones).

kwahi nooru (v) carry on the back, backpack.

kwahinupu (n) spine, backbone.

kwahiporopu, kwahiwo?oraa (n) spinal column, backbone.

Kwahira (name) Robe-on-his-back (person).

kwahisiapu (n) covetous person.

kwahisi?a (v) covet, envy another person. *See* **nasuyaketu.**

kwahitsuhni̱ (n) vertebra (one bone of the backbone).

kwahituki? (n) saddle blanket.

kwahtsu W (n), *acc* **kwahtsuna** rib.

kwakuru K (v) defeat, win over someone. *See* **tahni?aru.**

Kwana (name) Quanah Parker (Comanche chief, eldest son of Narua and Nokona; born in 1847, was the last war chief of the Comanches; died in 1911).

Kwana kuhtsu paa? (n) Rio Grande (*lit* stinking buffalo river; named in Comanche for dead buffalo killed by the Comanches because they crossed the river and could not be driven back).

Kwana pekwasu (n) Rio Frio (*lit* stinking fish river; named in Comanche for dead fish in dried water holes).

kwanaru (v) have odor, have bad odor, *modern* smell good. **Totsiyaa tsaʔ tsaa kwanaru.** The flower smells good (has pleasant odor).

kwanuʔitu K, **kwaʔnuʔitu** W (v) throw body on the ground, squat. *See* **wunuhkaruru.**

Kwaru (n) Comanche band (*lit* loud-speaking people; located in Cache-Lawton area).

kwasi- (pfx) ref. to animal tail.

kwasi nuruuʔwuʔ (n) snapping turtle. *Chelydra serpentina. See* **paʔkwakume.**

kwasi taibooʔ (n) monkey (*lit* tailed foreigner).

kwasi taibooʔa naʔkuhtabai (n) coconut (*lit* monkey pecan).

kwasi taibooʔa tuhkapu (n) coconut (*lit* monkey food).

kwasi tonaʔ (n) scorpion (*lit* stinging tail, or tail that stings).

Kwasia (name) Eagle-tail-feather (person).

kwasiku (adv time) last, next time. *See* **hayakwasiku.**

kwasinaboo pekwi (n) eel (*lit* snake fish).

kwasinaboo wuhkitsuʔtsuʔikatu (n) rattlesnake. *See* **wuhtsabeyakatu.**

kwasinabooʔ (n) snake (general term). **Situ kwasinabooʔ ubinai u kuhtsianu.** The snake bit him from behind (27:9).

kwasinabooʔa tuahkapu (n) tomato, *arch* goat rue (*lit* snake food). *Leguminosae Tephrosia virginiana.*

kwasi (n) animal tail.

kwasuʔu sakweni, kwasuʔu tohtsanaʔ (n) clothes hanger.

kwasuʔukatu K, **kwasuʔu tuaru** W (v) own an article of clothing.

Kwasuʔukatu nu. I have a dress.

kwasuʔu (n) dress, shirt, coat. *See* **tenahpuʔa kwasuʔu.**

kwasuʔu tumuuru (v) buy an article of clothing.

kwasukupu (n) cooked food.

kwasukuru (v) roast food, fry meat or vegetables.

kwasupu (adj) ripe.

kwasutu (v) cook. **Suru u kwasuhka, pu turueʔtii nimainu.** When it was cooked, he called his children.

kwetusapu, kwetsapu N (adj) unfriendly. *See* **nakahanupu.**

kwetusuakuru W, **kwetusaʔitu** K (v) ignore, reject. **U kwetusua-kutu nu.** I am ignoring him.

kweʔyaru (v, nonhum subj) shed (as a tree sheds leaves).

kweʔyuku sohóobi (n) silver maple (*lit* shedding cottonwood).

kweʔyukatu (v, hum subj) tire out. **Oha ahnakatu tsaʔ kweʔ- yukatu.** Coyote is tired out (10:23).

kwibihpikitu W, **kwibibikitu** K (v) tremble. *See* **suhkwibitu.**

kwibukitu (v) lash (as hard rain or hail), switch, whip. **Nu tuaʔa nu kwibukii.** I switched my boy. *See* **tukwibukiitu.**

kwihitu (v) throw overhand.

kwihnai (n) eagle (considered sacred). *See* **piakwihnai.**

kwihne kahpinakwu (n) northwest.

kwihne muhyunakwu (n) northeast.

Kwihne tosabitu (name) White-eagle (person).

kwihnenakwu (n) north (*lit* cold direction).

kwihnai

kwihneru (v) be cold, turn cold (weather).

kwihne? (n) wintertime.

kwiipusiaru (v) tan a hide (by smoke).

kwiisuatu W (adj) foggy. See pakunaikatu.

kwiita (n) buttocks.

kwiita, kwitaku P (n, nonhum sub) bottom.

kwiitsuba?itu (v) dart, flash, flicker (as a snake's tongue).

kwinumakatu (adj) dizzy.

kwinumapu (n) drunk, intoxicated person. See hibipu.

kwinumaru (v) make dizzy.

kwinumasuaru (v) feel faint. See sua watsikatu.

kwinu?yaru (v) spin around, turn around. See natsahkwinu?itu.

kwipunaru (v) twist. See makwipunaru.

kwipu, kwiipu (n) smoke.

kwipusiapu (n) palomino horse (smoked-tan color).

kwisihka (adj) tangled. See sakwusikutu.

kwisihkaru (v) make, cause to tangle.

kwisikatu K (v) tangle, braid. Wanaramu tsa? kwisikatu. The thread is tangled. See kwusipu.

kwita maropona (n) doodlebug, sowbug (lit excrement roller).

kwitapu (n) feces, excrement.

kwitatsi (n) large intestine.

kwitso?aitu (v) recover (get well, improve in health).

kwitso?aru (v) save, rescue (as from a tragedy). See makwitso- ?aru, wuhkwitso?aru.

kwitsunairu (v) twist the body. See nuukwitsunaru.

Kwi?ena mua (n) September.

kwuhti? (n) wounded person (from gunshot).

kwuhuniwaitu, kwuhunikwaitu (v) propose marriage (ask a girl for her hand; ask parents for hand of their daughter).

kwuhupu, kwuupu (n) captive (must have possessor). nu kwuhupu my captive.

kwuhuru (v) arrest, capture, catch.

kwuhu? (n) wife.

kwuru?aru (v) peel off (as skin, fruit peeling, furniture finish). See kiabo?aru.

kwusiberu W (v) brush off. See wusiberu.

kwusipu W (adj) tangled, braided. See kwisiru.

kwuuhtikuru, kwutikuru (v), pl kwutikukuru shoot something.

kwuuhturu (v) marry (take a wife). U kwuuhturu?i nu. I will marry her.

kwuuhtukatu W, K, kwuukatu P (adj) married (of a man). See kumahpu?.

M

ma (pro, 3rd prox acc sg) him, her, it. **Ma marʉkʉtsi, nʉ ma tʉhkaruʔi̱.** After finishing it, I will eat it.

maa (adv dem, prox) with or on someone or something [**ma** (dem) + **ma** on, with]. **Sitʉʉ maa yʉkwihkatʉ.** These ones are sitting on it (120:14).

maaitʉ (adv dem, prox) at or to someone or something [**ma** (dem) + **metʉ** at, to]. **Wakareʔeeʔ maaitʉ yahnéeyʉ.** The turtle is laughing at him (10:26).

maatu (adv dem, prox) up to or onto someone or something [**ma** (dem) + **matu** up to, onto]. **Sitʉʉ kwasinabooʔ maatu tunehtsʉnʉ.** This snake ran up to him (35:10).

mabáakuʔneetʉ (adj) baptized (*lit* hands put under water).

mabáaʔaitʉ (adj) watered, moistened.

mabararʉ (v) massage, press down, rub medicine on body. *See* **narʉʔekarʉ.**

mabarʉ W (v) knead, mix. *See* **tʉmabarʉ.**

mabasahtʉkitʉ K (v) sit in sun to dry. *See* **pasahtahtʉkitʉ.**

mabaʔisokitʉ (adj) dampened, sponged. *See* **paʔi̱soketʉ.**

mabekakʉrʉ W (v) pay medicine man. *See* **tʉmabekarʉ.**

mabeʔakatʉ W (adj) parted (hair).

mabihtʉʔuyarʉ (v) exchange one item for another (*lit* with hands give back).

mabisoʔàitʉ (adj) angry, angered.

mabisukiitʉ (adj) crushed into small pieces.

mabitsiarʉ (v) respect, honor, care for (*lit* take hand). *See* **maritsiakatʉ.**

mabitsoorʉ (v) press down with hands to expel water.

mabohto, mabohtoʔitʉ (v) snap fingers.

maboʔayarʉ (v) take off, be carried away by wind, blew away. **Yʉtsʉnohiʔa maboʔoyanʉ.** The kite flew.

mabunihkarʉ (v) tempt or test someone (*lit* see hand).

mabʉarʉ (v) release from hands.

mahbotsetʉ, mahpotse (v) push away (jerk hand away from body).

mahikoʔitʉ (v) return from warpath. **Hayarokwetʉʉ tuibihtsiʔanʉʉ mahíkoʔi̱ka̱.** Four young men were returning from the warpath (93:1).

mahimiʔarʉ (v) go on warpath.

mahípʉrʉmʉrʉ (v) buy for oneself, possess (hold in hand).

mahípʉrʉmʉtʉ (v) possess (hold in hand). *See* **hipʉkatʉ.**

mahiyaitʉ (v) reach out, offer hand. **U hina mahiyai nʉ.** I am reaching for it. *See* **makwʉbʉtsʉrʉ.**

mahiyarʉ (v) swear, take oath (ref. to holding up hand). **Mahi- yarʉ nʉ.** I am taking an oath.

mahka (pro, 3rd prox acc sg) him, her, it.

mahkarʉ W (v) hitch up (as horse and buggy). *See* **nomohkarʉ.**

mahkʉkitʉ K (v) drive in animals (*lit* cause to come in).

mahkʉrʉ W (v) drive up animals.

mahkᵾsuwaitᵾ (v) drive along or away.

mahkwᵾmarᵾ (v) loosen with hands, unwrap.

mahoinitᵾ (v) go in circles, encircle.

mahomonutsarᵾ (v) crumble to powder (with hands), mash into small particles. *See* **manutsaʔarᵾ, tahhomonutsarᵾ, homonuhtsaitᵾ.**

mahooikatᵾ (adj) stalked, ambushed.

mahorarᵾ (v) scoop up, dig (with hands). *See* **tsahhorarᵾ.**

mahri (pro, 3rd prox acc du) two of them.

mahrubᵾhkaitᵾ (v) anger someone. *See* **kᵾpisoʔaitᵾ.**

mahrᵾ (pro, 3rd prox nom du) of two of them. **Sitᵾkᵾseʔ wihnu mahrᵾmaʔai.** This one then went with them (two).

mahtokooʔ (n) thumb (*lit* hand grandfather).

mahtokwᵾnaitᵾ K, **mahtokwᵾnᵾ-ʔitᵾ** W (v) lean on something, rest on something (as a broom against or on a wall). **Huunaro-ʔiʔ mahtu namahtokwᵾnᵾka.** A ladder was leaning along it (92:10).

mahtsokaitᵾ (v) close the hand. **Nᵾ moʔe nᵾ matsokai.** I closed my hand. *See* **moʔo-.**

mahtsukitᵾ (v) close someone's hand.

mahtuaʔ (n) little finger.

mahtᵾpináaʔ K (n) middle finger. *See* **masᵾwᵾhkiʔ.**

mahuihkatᵾ, mahwikatᵾ (adj) pushed over, knocked over.

mahuinoorᵾ (v) come slowly (*lit* come walking being pushed).

mahuyubakatᵾ (adj) oblong (formed by rolling between the hands).

mahuʔnetᵾ (v) crawl on hands and knees (pulling forward with the hands). *See* **wᵾhuʔnerᵾ, tahuʔnerᵾ.**

mahᵾrᵾhwakatᵾ (adj) opened [**mahu-** push + **tᵾhwaʔ** open].

mahyarᵾ (v) defile, break a taboo, law, treaty. **Marii mahyaʔi marᵾ.** They broke the treaty against them.

maihtᵾkᵾ (adv man) openly, plainly.

makaarᵾ (v) feed. **Nᵾ maaka!** Feed me!

makahtᵾnikatᵾ (v) tell to feed [**maka-** feed + **tᵾni-** tell].

makamaitᵾ (v) wait for someone.

makamᵾkarᵾ (v) ambush. *See* **tᵾkamᵾrᵾ.**

makaʔmukitᵾ (v) prepare for (as a room for a guest). **Marᵾᵾ nanawaʔihpᵾʔanᵾᵾ sihka tᵾha tsaaku makaʔmukiᵾ.** Their womenfolk prepared this meat good (69:9).

makitsarᵾ (v) mash, squash, hand grind.

makitsetᵾ (adj) squashed, mashed.

makoobikatᵾ (adj) broken up.

makoʔitᵾ (v) regain possession (get something back).

makuhpᵾkatᵾ (adj) strangled, choked.

Makutabai (name) dog hero (notorious in tales).

makuyaʔaitᵾ (adj) frightened. *See* **wᵾʔyᵾrᵾhkikatᵾ.**

makɨetɨ W (v) refuse, prohibit.

makɨma?aitɨ (adj) sharpened.

makɨnaitɨ (v) hold down with hand (as in catching animal).

makɨ (adv dem, prox) right here. **Sitɨwɨ tsa? makɨ pitɨnɨ.** These two arrived here (115:3).

makɨtserɨ, makiitsetɨ (v) mash. **Nɨ mo?o ma makɨtsenɨ.** I mashed it with my hands. *See* **mapitserɨ.**

makwatubiitɨ (adj) folded, rolled up.

makwarɨ (v) feel around (with hands). *See* **mawa-.**

makwe (n) back of the hand.

makwihtserɨ (v) persecute, afflict.

makwineetɨ, makwineerɨ (v) wipe off with the hand.

makwipunarɨ K, makwɨpetɨ W (v) twist, crease with the hands (as a rope). *See* **takwɨperɨ, kwipunarɨ.**

makwitso?aitɨ (v) save someone, rescue, prevent someone's death. **Nɨmatu to?itsi ɨnɨ, nɨ makwitso?ainɨ.** Coming out onto me, you saved me (105:28). *See* **kwitso?arɨ.**

makwiyetɨ, makwɨyeerɨ (v, adj) chase someone, chased.

makwi?numaitɨ (v) be made dizzy, made drunk, intoxicated. **Po?saba tsa? ma makwi?numai.** The whiskey made him drunk.

makwiteerɨ (v) strip off (as seeds from a plant).

makwɨbɨtsɨrɨ W (v) reach for (with hand). *See* **mahiyaitɨ, maruru?arɨ.**

makwɨmutsiarɨ (v) sharpen an edge [**ma-** (dem) + **kwɨ-** edge + **mutsia** sharpen].

makwɨri?aikatɨ (adj) spilled accidentally.

makwɨrɨ?eka? W (n) hand lotion (*lit* something spilled on the hand). *See* **mo?okwitɨ?eka?.**

makwɨ?netɨ (v) rub lightly, touch lightly with the hand.

makwɨ?nikɨtɨ K (v) smooth (with hand).

makwɨ?nikɨ W (n) tire, wheel. *See* **na?bukuwà?a narahpaanạ.**

makwɨsaitɨ (v) open the hand.

makwɨsà? (n) sleeve.

makwɨsetɨ (adj) sprained.

makwɨsikɨkatɨ (adj) tangled by hand.

mamámutsiakatɨ (adj) formed to a point (by hand, as in greenware).

mamamɨekatɨ (adj) delayed, detained.

mamárɨmarɨ (v) close up, cover (as with a lid).

mami?akɨtɨ (v) operate manually. *See* **nɨɨmi?akɨrɨ.**

mamutsiakatɨ (adj) sharpened to a point.

mamutsiarɨ (v) make pointed. **Ma mamutsiarɨ ma?.** He is sharpening it to a point. *See* **manutsiarɨ.**

mamɨsuakatɨ K (adj) prohibited, taboo.

manáawɨnɨ?etɨ (v) incite to rear up.

manahkerɨ (v) measure. **U manahkeki u.** He came to measure it. *See* **tɨmanahketɨ.**

manakɨarɨ (v, sg obj), *pl obj* **manakɨɨ?irɨ** cause to protrude). **Sitɨ wakare?ee? u kwasitaka etɨsipɨka manakɨɨ?ikɨnɨ.** This turtle made just their tails stick out of (*lit* at) the fire (10:22).

manakwʉ K, manaanakwʉ W
(adv loc) far away (long distance,
on the other side). **Surʉʉkʉse?
manakwʉhi tuu?eeyʉ.** Those
(people) carried water far (81:2).

mananaa?waihkarʉ (v) wait
on, care for, entertain, extend
hospitality to a guest.

manawʉnʉkatʉ (adj) reared up,
standing on hind feet (as a horse
or bear).

mana?koroomitʉ (v) K cover the
head (as with a cloth); W cover
something over.

manekihtʉ? (num) full house in
card game, arch five.

manímʉarʉ (v) blame, criticize,
find fault.

manitʉ (v) cross over (as a river or
bridge). **Manitu?i ma.** He will
cross over.

manookatʉ (adj) carried on back.

manoorʉ (v) carry, haul in a vehicle
(give someone a lift).

manuarʉ W (v) rake together. *See*
marʉ?okitʉ.

manutsa?arʉ W (v) break up,
crumble (with the hands). *See*
homonuhtsaitʉ, tahnutsa?erʉ.

manutsiarʉ W (v) form into a point
(as greenware). *See* **mamutsiarʉ.**

manʉkikʉrʉ, manʉkikʉrʉ (v,
sg obj), *pl* **objmanurakʉ-** shoo
away (make something run). *See*
tanʉkikʉtʉ.

manʉʉsukaarʉ (v) excite, give
sensation (cause good or bad
feeling in body or spirit).

manʉʉtsikwa? W (n) pain, ache.

manʉʉ?maitʉ (v) tire of
something. *See* **wʉ?tsikwarʉ,
nakʉnʉʉ?maitʉ.**

manʉarʉ (v) raise someone, rear a
child.

manʉkʉtʉ (adj) pressed down,
packed in tightly.

manʉsutarʉ (v) surrender (give up
to a victor).

manʉsuta?aitʉ (v) surrender
someone.

manʉsu?narʉ W (v) tame a wild
thing.

mapaana? (n) palm reader,
fortuneteller. *See* **nipʉkaa?eetʉ.**

mapaana (n) palm of hand.

mapitserʉ (v) mash up something.
See **makʉtserʉ.**

mapó?a? (n) human skin. *See* **hʉnʉ
po?a?.**

mapʉhʉ, mapʉhʉ (n) hair on lower
arm or hand (*lit* arm fuzz).

mapʉnukeerʉ (v) polish by hand.
See **tapʉnukeerʉ.**

mapʉtsarʉ (v) burst open, break
open (with hand).

marahpunihkatʉ (adj) tried on, tested.

marátʉbaitʉ (v), *pl* **maráhtata?i-**
crack something (with hand). *See*
marʉbarʉ.

marebunitʉ (v) cure partially
through touch. **Ma marebuni nʉ.**
I made him better.

marii (pro, 3rd prox acc pl) them.
Marii punihtsi ma ikahkị. Looking at them, he came in. **Marii
ʉkʉniwʉnʉka, marʉʉkʉhu
kʉahkị.** As they just spoke,
something bright came out in
sight (86:15).

maritsiakatʉ (adj) honored,
respected. *See* **mabitsiarʉ.**

marohtʉmarʉ (v) close up with
hand (put on lid) [**ma-** hand +
tohtʉma- close up].

maropoʔnarʉ (v), *pl obj*
maropoʔniʔitʉ roll around, coil
(by hand). **U sʉmʉrayuʔnẹtsi**
urʉʉ, u maroponiʔinụ.
Completely pounding it, they
made balls of it (116:17).

maropoʔniʔipụ (n) round object
(formed by hand). *See* **tohto-**
ponitụ.

marukarʉ (v) quench by hand, snuff
out.

maruruʔarʉ (v) reach for, stretch
out arm. **Waʔihpʉʔ maruruʔah-**
tsi huabokooʔa pomanụ.
The woman, stretching out her
arm, picked a huckleberry. *See*
mahiyaitʉ, makwʉbʉtsʉrʉ.

marʉa (n) herd.

Marʉhke (n) Eating-tribe (Shoshoni
band; Snake People).

marʉkarʉ (v) finish (by hand).
Soone nʉ marʉkai. I finished
(making) the quilt.

marʉkitʉ (v) touch (with hand).
Nʉma ma marʉkị. He touched me.

marʉkiʔnetʉ (v) flatten something
(with hand, as a tortilla; *lit* cause
to be flat).

marʉmabunipụ (n) tested item,
tried item.

marʉmarʉ (v) close, cover (with lid,
as a box).

marʉị mʉrʉ (v) buy something.

marʉpịsuʔarʉ W (v) unfold (by hand)
[**ma-** hand + **tupụisuʔa** unfold].

marʉrooniitʉ K (adj) braced,
supported. *See* **tohtʉrooniitụ.**

marʉroonitʉ (v) brace (by hand)
[**ma-** hand + **tụrooni-** brace].

marʉʉ (pro, 3rd prox gen pl) their
marʉʉ paraibooʔ their chief
(70:11).

marʉʉʔnitʉ (v) beg.

marʉʔokitʉ K (v) rake together. *See*
manuarʉ.

marʉbarʉ (v) crack something with
hands. *See* **marátụbaitʉ.**

marʉhnikatʉ (v) respect someone.

masiito (n) fingernail.

masitotsarʉ W (v) pinch (*lit* take
hold with the fingernail).

masiʔwarʉ (v) tear (by hand), *adj*
masikwaitʉ torn (by hand).

masuabetaitʉ (v) learn by
experience, know by experience.
See **suabetai.**

masukaarʉ (v) feel, touch (with the
hand) [**ma-** hand + **suka-** touch].

masutsarʉ (v) offer someone help.

masuyakerʉ (v) be tempted, suffer
temptation (by something one is
handling).

masuyuʔikarʉ K (v) tame an
animal, break a horse. **Tenahpʉʔ**
tsaʔ pʉ puukị masuyui. The man
tamed his horse.

masuʔnaitʉ K (v) rub the wrong
way (as of fur). *See* **masʉroonitʉ.**

masuʔnerʉ (v) rub applying
pressure with the hands.

masuʔwaʔnekitʉ (v) dog paddle,
paddle water, waddle or move
clumsily. **Sarii masuʔwaʔnekitʉ.**
The dog is swimming (dog
paddling). *See* **paruhparʉ.**

masʉapụ W (n) home-grown garden
product.

masʉarʉ W (v) raise garden
product.

masʉroonitʉ W (v) rub the wrong
way (as of fur). *See* **masuʔnaitʉ.**

masʉsʉʔnitʉ (v) numb the hand
[**ma-** hand + **sʉsụʔni** numb]. *See*
tsasʉsʉʔnikatʉ.

masɨwɨhki? (n) fingers (including thumb).

masɨwɨhki? W (n) middle finger. *See* **mahtɨpináa?**.

matsaaihkakurɨ (v) lead along (as horse or blind person). *See* **tsakami?arɨ**.

matsáapikaarɨ (v) pull to make noise (as a bell rope).

matsáhtsurɨ (v) squeeze hand.

matsákwɨnɨkɨrɨ (v) help up from sitting to standing position (by the hand).

matsarɨ W (v) grasp (with hand).

matsáyɨtsurɨ (v) help up (from lying to sitting position (by the hand).

matsíhtuyeetɨ P (v) comb someone's hair.

matsi?okwɨkatɨ (adj) hand gathered (as with a needle).

matsobokɨkatɨ (adj) rolled (by hand).

matsokatɨ (adj) held (in hand).

matsumarɨ (v) wipe.

matsuma? (n) cloth (piece of fabric).

matsurɨ (v) nudge, pinch.

matsɨkikatɨ (adj) tight (on the hand) [**ma-** hand + **tsɨki-** tight].

matsɨbakikatɨ (adj) glued, pasted, sealed.

matuwetɨ (v) limp (human, or front leg of animal). *See* **pituwetɨ**.

matɨhwarɨ (v) open something (as a door).

matɨsohpe? (n) wildcat.

mawa- (pfx) feel around with hand. *See* **makwarɨ**.

mawaatsa (n) rib.

mawakatu (adv dem, prox) toward someone or something.

mawo?a?aiyu (n) cement.

mawɨmerɨ (v) hurt someone (make suffer).

mayaketɨ (v) play instrument (with hands) [**ma-** hand + **yake-** cry].

mayake? (n) piano.

mayɨ?yɨrɨ (v) hand jerk, hand twitch.

ma? (pro, 3rd prox nom sg) he, she, it. **Nɨ tohtɨkwai ma?.** He hit me.

ma?aikɨrɨ (v) row (as a boat), push something that rolls. *See* **wɨ?aikɨrɨ, tsi?aikɨrɨ**.

ma?itsa?bɨkatɨ (adj) cramped hand, paralyzed hand. *See* **sɨkwe tɨyai**.

ma?kwe?yarɨ (v) lose something from hand or wrist.

ma?nika? (n, arch) finger ring. *See* **mo?otsi?nika?**.

ma?nɨ sarii? (n) dachshund (*lit* short-legged dog).

ma?ohta?aitɨ (v) hill up (put soil around base of plant). *See* **wɨno?karɨrɨ**.

ma?okwerɨ (v) milk something, squeeze to a head (*lit* cause to flow, as a boil). *See* **tɨma?okwetɨ**.

ma?omerɨ (v) stir up fire.

ma?urarɨ (v) find something with the hand [**ma-** hand + **ura** find]. *See* **urarɨ**.

ma?wiitsa (n) wrist.

ma?wikarɨ, ma?wikerɨ (v) push, shove. *See* **wɨtsɨkitɨ**.

ma?witsohko (n) bracelet [**ma?-wiitsa** wrist + **tsoohko** bead].

ma?wɨminarɨ (v) reach out and touch. *See* **wɨminarɨ**.

ma?wɨtsa ro?ponitɨ (v) have cramp in hand).

ma?yʉkwiitʉ (v) fix up, set up, doll up someone. *See* nama?yʉkwitʉ.

ma?yʉneetʉ (v) entertain (make smile or laugh). **Ohna?a ma?yʉneetʉ u.** He made the baby laugh.

me, meh (quotative particle, indicates something spoken). **Surʉkʉse? oha?ahnakatʉ, 'Mʉi nahubiyaaru?i̱ nʉ? me urii niikwiiyu̱.'** 'I'll sing for you,' said the coyote. (3:6).

meeku (adv time) right now. **Meeku takwʉ nararʉʉna̱.** Now let us two run a race (9:8). *See* kihtsi?.

miakʉrʉ (v) run after, chase.

miakʉtʉ K (v) chase. **U miakʉi, tʉhʉyabai.** He chased him on horseback.

miarʉ, mi?arʉ (v) go. **Ma pia? pʉhi muhnehtsi mi?anu̱.** His mother went leading them (81:9).

miibe?tu̱, miihbe?tu̱ (adv loc) farther along, adv time temporarily.

miihtsi̱ (n) ankle.

miitu̱tsi, miihtsi? (adv loc) near, adv time soon, shortly. *See* kemarʉkwi̱su̱.

mitsokokʉkatʉ (adj) sleepy.

mitsonaa? (n) southern hackberry. *Celtis laevigata* [Willd.]

mitʉko?o (n) roof of mouth.

moha-, moha (adj) sour, bitter, acidic.

mohakamarʉ (v) taste sour, bitter, acid.

mohatsi̱ (adv intens) very. **Mohatsi̱kuna sʉsuatʉ nʉ.** I am very cold *See* nohi.

mohatsʉkuekapi̱tʉ (adj) bright red.

mohto?a (n) K pimple; mohto?a W rash (red bumps on skin).

momʉsaka (n) fire-tender in a peyote meeting.

monahpʉ? (n), *pl* nonanʉʉ son-in-law (DaHu, SbDaHu).

monʉ ohni (n) tuberculosis.

mooka (n), *acc* mooke branch (of plant). **huupita mooka** tree branch.

mookʉsʉaitʉ (v) branch out.

moonʉ?ʉakatʉ (adj) cancerous, chronic.

mootekwo?pʉ (n) sign language (*lit* hand talk).

moowi? (n) lariat (*lit* hand rope; made of plaited rawhide for roping).

Moo?wetʉ (name) No-hand (person).

Mopai (name) Owl (person).

Mota, Tatseni (name) Lee Motah (b. Nov. 12, 1911).

motso sarii? (n) poodle (*lit* bearded dog).

motso taiboo? (n) bearded white man.

motso̱, motso- (n) beard.

moya?itʉ (v) slander (speak against someone).

mo?o (n), *acc* mo?e hand. **Nʉ mo?e nʉ matsukai.** I closed my hand.

mo?o huutsihka?a? (n) handsaw, ripsaw. *See* huutsihkaa?.

mo?o kwitʉ?eka? K (n) hand lotion (*lit* hand ointment). *See* makwʉrʉ?eka?.

mo?o narʉso (n) glove (*lit* hand sack).

mo?o rʉboo? (n) typewriter (*lit* hand writer).

mo?o tsaaitʉ (v) hold hands.

moʔo tsiʔnikaʔ (n, modern) finger ring. *See* **maʔnikaʔ**.

moʔo wɨhtamarɨ (v) hobble an animal, handcuff a person.

moʔo wɨhtamaʔ (n) a hobble (tied on animal).

moʔobeʔ (num) five. **Surɨ kɨseʔ moʔobeʔkaa u miʔaʔi̱ tomonu̱.** That one went for five years (85:3).

Moʔpi tsokopɨ (name) Old-owl (former Comanche chief).

mu-, mubi̱ (n) nose. *See* **muhbi**.

mubitai, muʔbitai, muʔbitai huuhpi (n) walnut. *Juglans regia* L. (nuts eaten, leaves used to treat ringworm).

mubi̱ poʔroo rɨhkapɨ W (n) pork (*lit* pig meat). *See* **poʔro rɨhkapɨ**.

mubi̱ poʔroo rɨhtɨmaʔ W (n) hog fence.

mubi̱ poʔrooʔ (n) pig, hog.

mubi̱ poʔroʔa poʔaa W (n) pork rind.

mubi̱ sariiʔ (n) greyhound (*lit* nose dog).

mubi̱situ (v) blow the nose. **Ketaʔka mubi̱situu.** Don't blow your noses (127:7). *See* **wɨmupɨsitɨ**.

mubi̱ tsooʔnitɨ (v) suck (as on candy; *lit* draw up the nose).

mubi̱ tsooʔniʔ (n) candy sucker. *See* **mukwiteʔ**.

mubohtohkipɨ (n) bubble, balloon.

mubohtohkirɨ (v) inflate (as a balloon). *See* **pohtokɨrɨ**.

mubohtohkitɨ (v) inflate (form bubbles). *See* **pohtohkitɨ**.

muboraʔitɨ (v) bud.

mubɨtsaakatɨ (n) bloom (*lit* blown up, burst).

muhasuarɨ, muhakatsuʔaitɨ K, **muhabuni** W (v) frown.

muhatsi (adj) bright. **Muhatsi̱ku kupi̱takatɨ.** The light is bright.

muhbi, muubi, mubi, mu- (n) nose.

muhibitɨ (v) inhale deeply through nose, breathe through nose.

muhkarɨ W (v) hook something.

muhnemiʔarɨ (v) lead others (as horse leads other horses).

muhnetɨ, muunerɨ (v) proceed ahead, precede someone (be in the lead).

muhpeʔ (n) hoe (heavy type). **Surɨɨ waʔihpɨanɨɨ pɨɨ muhpeʔmaʔai paakɨhu weenu̱.** Those women went down in the water with their hoes (127:6). *See* **toʔtsimuhpeʔ**.

muhpoo kahni wanapɨ K, **muhpoo wanapɨ** W (n) mosquito net.

muhraaʔipɨ, muhraipɨ (n) kiss.

muhrarɨ (v) kiss someone.

muhwitɨ K (v) throw with nose or mouth. *See* **mukwɨbɨarɨ**.

muhyɨ nakwɨ (n) east (cardinal direction) [**muhyɨ** doorway + **nakwɨ** direction] (Comanche dwellings were traditionally oriented to face the rising sun).

muhyɨ (n) doorway. **Surɨkwɨ uhrɨ kahni muhyɨhkutɨ kuʔinɨbuni.** Those two were roasting much out from their teepee door (105:23). *See* **namuhyɨ, natsahtɨmaʔ**.

mukuhparɨ W (v) gore someone.

mukwihterɨ (v) suck on something (one time).

mukwiteʔ (n) lollypop, candy sucker. *See* **mubi̱tsooʔniʔ**.

mukwo (n voc) husband. *See* **kwɨɨhtɨkatɨ**.

Mukwooru (name) Spirit-talker (civil chief who attended the San Antonio Council House meeting in 1840).

mukwubuaru W (v) throw with nose or mouth. *See* **muhwitu**.

mukwuru W, mukwutikuru K (v) gore, butt (as with horns).

mumutsi?, muumutsi? (n) soapweed, yucca, beargrass (roots used as soap and to cure ulcers). *Yucca louisianensis* Trelease.

munaikiyutu W (v) be ahead of. **Sarii tsa? tenahpu? munaikiyutu.** The dog is in front of the man.

munakuaitu (v) poke out nose [**mu-** nose + **na-** (refl) + **kua** come out].

munakwu (adv loc) ahead, in front of. **Sarii tsa? tenahpu? munakwu.** The dog is ahead of the man.

munua? (n) hog, pig (*lit* moves something with nose). *See* **po?ro?**.

muparai habinitu K, muhpa?araitu W (adj) lying facedownward, lying in prone position.

mupitsi (n) giant (mythical hero).

mupitsuha pisahpi W, mupitsapisahpi K (n fungus) mushroom, puffball, devil's snuffbox.

mupitsuha tunowapi W (n) camel (*lit* giant packhorse).

mupihabiitu (adj) bent over.

mupihabiru (v) bend over (as a tree limb).

Mura hunu?bi (n) Pease River (*lit* mule creek).

Mura kwitapu (name) Mule-dung (former Comanche chief).

murora?ipu W, muruhrapu K (n) bud of a plant or tree.

muruahwunuru (v) point out something (with lower lip or chin).

murukaru (v) extinguish (blow out), quench a fire.

muru?itu (v) overflow. **Hunu?bi tsa? muru?i.** The creek overflowed. *See* **paru?itu**.

musasuaru (v) worry (be concerned). *See* **pisukwitaru**.

musoopitu (v) suck on body to draw out pain (as traditionally practiced by Comanche healers).

mutsi- (pfx) point, pointed.

mutsikwà?aa? (n) mosquito (*lit* pointed thing that awkwardly flaps wings).

mutsi atsamukwe? (n) wild grape (winter variety). *See* **natsamukwe?**.

mutsikuni, mutsikahni (n) wigwam (made of curved sticks) [**mutsi** point + **kahni** house].

mutsimuhpe? (n) pick (a tool; *lit* pointed hoe).

mutsipu (n) sharp-pointed object (as an ice pick).

mutsiwahtu, mutsikwahtu (adj) dull (unpointed).

mutsonoo?itu (v) pull someone's beard.

mutsu?itu (v), *pl* **mutsi?itu** dive (as into water).

mutusiberu (v) shave someone.

muunanahwenuru W, muunahweru K (v) hoot (as an owl).

muura? (n) mule.

muutsi, mutsi- (n) point (tapering end). *See* **puha kahni muutsi**.

muu yakenitu (v) moo (as a cow) [**muu** moo + **yake** cry].

muuyaketɇ (v) make music, play a wind instrument. *See* **yaketɇ, muyakeʔ.**

muwainitɇ K (v) root around (as a hog). *See* **ahwenitɇ.**

muwarɇ W (v) follow scent, smell around (as a dog does). *See* **ɇkwịsɇʔninitɇ.**

muwoʔneʔ (n) termites [**mu-** nose + **woʔne-** make holes]. *See* **wobi muwoʔneʔ.**

muyakeʔ (n) music of any kind, sounding of a horn. *See* **muuyaketɇ.**

muyɇɇʔwɇrɇ (v) bend over [**mu-** head + **yɇɇwɇ-** go down].

muʔibuikɇrɇ (v) fill up (*lit* to the mouth fill up, as to fill a bucket).

muʔkwipunaʔ (n) elephant (ref. to trunk).

muʔwoo (n) grown man, adult male.

muʔyạnesuarɇ (v) grin, smile [**mu-** mouth + **yahne-** laugh + **sua-** feel].

mɇa (n) moon, month.

mɇahtabebaʔitɇ (adj) have moonlight.

mɇakatɇ (n) moonlight.

mɇarɇboopɇ (n) calendar (*lit* month paper).

mɇhɇ (pro, 2nd gen du) of you two.

mɇi (pro, 2nd acc pl) you. **Hakani mɇi naahkaku maʔ paroʔịkitɇ.** As you (pl) were continuing, somehow the water rose (122:15).

mɇkwɇ, mɇhɇ (pro, 2nd nom du) you two. **Hina mɇkwɇ?** What do you two (want)?

mɇmi (pro, 2nd acc pl) you.

mɇmɇ, mɇɇ (pro, 2nd gen pl) your. **Mɇmɇmaʔai nɇʔ pisikwa-nuuʔii.** I slid with you (pl).

mɇnitɇ (v) unable (though willing and agreeable). **Pɇɇ muhyi urɇɇ muninɇ.** They were unable to do (open) their door (4:17).

mɇnɇ, mɇnɇ (pro, 2nd nom pl) you. **Mɇnɇkia nɇkɇbɇni?** Are you (pl) dancing? (3:4).

mɇroʔitɇ (v) bob up.

mɇɇ (pro, 2nd gen pl) your. **mɇɇ hipɇ** your things. *Also* **mɇmɇ.**

mɇɇrɇ (v) do to, treat, control someone. **Hakani ɇ mɇɇruʔi?** What shall I do with you?

mɇɇrɇʔikatɇ (v) feel pity. **Tɇtaa marii mɇɇrɇʔikatɇ mɇ.** I feel pity for them.

mɇɇwarɇʔitɇ (v) perplexed (not knowing what to do with something).

N

na- (pfx, reflexive).

naabaitɇ, naahbaihtɇ (num) six.

naabia, nahbiʔa (n) male kinsman.

naahábitɇ (v), *pl* **naahkwabịka-** continue lying down.

naahkarɇ (v) hire, continue doing something.

naanaarɇ, nahnaarɇ (v) grow in height and health.

naapẹ (n) foot, lower leg. *See* **nape-.**

nabaa (n) oil, gasoline. *See* **naʔbukuwàaʔ nábaa, nahyɇ.**

nabaai tokwaaitɇ (n) oil well [**nabaa** oil + **tokwaaitɇ** looked for in ground]. *See* **tukaʔanabaa.**

nabaakạ (n) bullet [**na-** (refl) + **paakạ** arrow].

nabakɇtɇ (v) commit suicide.

Nabakwⱨhtiapⱨ (n), *pl*
  Nabakwⱨhti- apⱨnⱨⱨ Christian,
  baptized one.
nabanaʔaitⱨ (adj) conceited.
nabatai K (n) tributary, creek
  branch. *See* **atąhunubi.**
nabawⱨhtiarⱨ (v) immerse oneself
  in water.
nabehkakⱨrⱨ (v, sg obj), *pl obj*
  nakwⱨsⱨkⱨrⱨ cause to be
  killed.
nabihtawⱨna (n) beginning, start.
nabikapⱨ (n) leather, leather
  harness (*lit* leather item).
nabimarⱨ (adj) covered (having a
  cover).
nabinai tⱨboopⱨ (n) deed or title to
  land.
nabinaihkatⱨ (adj) chosen.
nabinarⱨ (v) choose, pick out.
nabinaʔetⱨ (v) save, store away.
nabisoʔarⱨ (v) puncture oneself
  with something.
nabitⱨkⱨrⱨ (n) war, battle with
  weapons.
nabitⱨbunitⱨ (v) look behind
  oneself.
nabiʔaaikⱨnakarⱨ K, nabiʔaikⱨʔ
  W (n) rocking chair.
nabiʔatsikatⱨ (adj) taboo.
naboo-, naboorⱨ (adj) marked,
  striped, spotted.
naboohmatⱨsohpeʔ W (n) leopard
  (*lit* spotted wildcat). *See* **nabooh
  toyaruhkuʔ, toyaruhkuʔ.**
naboohmuraʔ (n) zebra (*lit* striped
  mule).
Naboohnⱨⱨ (n) Navaho people;
  Athapascans (former enemies of
  the Comanches).
naboohroya ruhkuʔ K (n) leopard
  (*lit* carrying spots underneath).

See **toya ruhkuʔ, nabooh
  matⱨsohpeʔ.**
Naboohroyaʔ N (n) Navaho
  Mountain (named after the
  Navaho people).
naboopⱨ (n) picture [**na-** (refl) +
  poo- write].
naboopⱨha naroʔnikaʔ (n) picture
  frame [**naboopⱨ** picture + **-ha**
  (acc) + **na-** (refl) + **toʔnikaa-**
  put away].
naboopⱨha narⱨso (n) picture
  frame [**naboopⱨ** picture + **-ha**
  (acc) + **naruso** sack].
naboopⱨha pⱨkⱨratoʔnikaʔiʔ (n)
  picture frame.
nabooʔ K (n) pencil, marking
  instrument. *See* **tⱨbooʔ.**
naboʔ (n) marking.
naboʔaa W (n) shingle, siding,
  covering.
**nabuihwⱨnⱨtⱨ W, nabuiʔwⱨnetⱨ
  K** (v) examine oneself, check over
  one's appearance.
nabunitⱨ (v) look at oneself, appear
  (as to dress) [**na-** (refl) + **puni**
  see]. **Nohiʔ tsaa nabuniyu nⱨⱨ.** I
  look very nice (32:12).
nabuniʔ (n) mirror, looking glass
  [**na-** (refl) + **puni-** see].
nabusaʔ (n) chain.
nabusiʔaketⱨ (v) delouse (look for
  head lice on one another).
**nabⱨsa nabikapⱨ, nabusa
  narⱨmuhkⱨ** (n) harness (chain)
  [**nabⱨsaʔ** chain + **narⱨmuhkⱨ**
  harness].
nabⱨsiʔaipⱨ (n) dream.
nabⱨsiʔaitⱨ (v) dream.
nabⱨesⱨ (adv time) early (ahead of
  time). **Nabⱨesⱨ namakaʔ muki!**
  Get ready ahead of time!

nabᵾkapᵾ W, nᵾpᵾkapᵾ K, N (n) grave, burial mound.

nagwee, naʔwée? (n) ford, river crossing. *See* **puʔe nagwe.**

nah (adv) just. **Tanᵾwitsa nah paakᵾhu ma wihinᵾ.** We should just throw him in the water (16:20).

naha-, nah- (pfx, reciprocal) with each other, together.

nahabitᵾtᵾ (v) come onto someone, happen to be somewhere.

nahamuhkᵾ K (n) safety pin, diaper pin, pin. *See* **naʔhᵾmuhkᵾ.**

nahaniitᵾ (v), *pl* **nayᵾkwiitᵾ** continue, go along. **Suni urii nayᵾkwịbᵾniku, ᵾ Oha ahnakatᵾ ᵾrᵾᵾkᵾ bitᵾnᵾ.** They continued much that way; Coyote arrived among them (3:3).

nahapᵾ (n) happening, event.

naharᵾ (v) happen, become, continue (*lit* how did you become?). **Hakani ᵾnᵾ nahánᵾ?** What happened to you? (6:14).

nahawaruʔikatᵾ (adj) needy, hard up.

nahayaʔni (adv compar) worse (when previously not too bad). **Nahayaʔni ma nᵾsukatᵾ.** She is getting worse.

nahimiitᵾ (v) exchange gifts (give gifts to each other).

nahkabaʔitᵾ (adj) rejected, refused (said of a person).

nahkᵾepᵾ K (n) stingy person.

nahkᵾsuaberᵾ (v) understand someone.

nahmakutᵾ (v) compare one thing with another.

nahmaʔai (adv) together (with each other).

nahnamiʔarᵾ (v, anim subj) grow.

nahnapᵾ (n), *pl* **nanᵾnapᵾrᵾᵾ** eldest child, grown son or daughter, adult kinsman.

nahnia (n) name.

nahnia makarᵾ (v) name someone. *See* **nihakᵾrᵾ, makaarᵾ.**

nahnᵾmiitᵾ (v) walk around. **Nᵾ? nahnᵾmiitᵾ.** I have been walking around.

nahohiyaitᵾ (v) hurt oneself. *See* **namarᵾnitᵾ, nahuhyaitᵾ.**

nahorapᵾ (n) hole dug by man.

nahotsaʔma?, nahotsaʔama? (n) horse blanket, saddle blanket.

nahoʔyopịkurᵾ (v) mark inexactly (slightly above or below the proper mark).

nahuahtsitᵾ, nahutsitᵾ W (n) sigh. *See* **nasuawᵾhkitᵾ.**

nahúbiniitᵾ (v) groan. **Surᵾkᵾse? wihnu nahubiniiyᵾ.** Then that one was groaning (5–6:12).

nahubiyaarᵾ (v) sing a song for someone. **Mᵾi nahubiyaaruʔi nᵾ?.** I will sing for you (pl) (3:6).

nahuhyaitᵾ W (v) hurt oneself. *See* **nahohiyaitᵾ, namarᵾnitᵾ.**

nahuu? W, nahhoo? K (n) knife, drawing knife.

nahᵾyatᵾ, naʔᵾyatᵾ N (adj) sloping, slanting.

nahweakᵾtᵾ W (v) burn oneself.

nahyemiʔarᵾ (v) go live with in-laws.

nahyᵾ (n) oil. *See* **naʔbukuwàʔa nahyᵾ.**

naiya (adv time) often, frequently.

naiʔbi, naiʔpị N (n) young woman (to about fifteen years old).

nakaaʔaitᵾ, nakaʔaitᵾ (adj) false, hypocritical.

nakabarʉ (v) reject a person.

nakahanupʉ W (n) unfriendliness. *See* **kwetʉsapʉ.**

nai?bi

nakamabitsiahkatʉ (adj) attentive (paying attention).

nakarʉ W (v) hear. *See* **tʉnakarʉ.**

nakarʉ? W (n) chair. *See* **wobinakarʉ?.**

nakarʉ?karʉ (v) sit down.

nakatsʉhetʉ, nakatseetʉ (v) smoke ritually (to seek medicine).

nakị (n) ear.

nakị hiikatʉ K (v) heed, listen with attention.

nakị kwiitạ (n) K back part of ear cartilage; W ear lobe.

nakị oonạ (n) ear wax (*lit* ear salt).

nakị sarii? (n) hound dog (*lit* ear dog).

nakị tai?, nakị tóone N (n) lizard (long variety; *lit* large earholes).

nakị toonʉkatʉ K, **nakị toona** N (n) pierced ear. *See* **nanakịtonapʉ.**

nakị tsa?nika? (n) earring (*lit* entered into the ear).

nakị wʉnʉkatʉ (adj) have an earache.

nakkuminoorʉ (v) somersault. *See* **anikwitami?arʉ.**

nakkʉtaba?i, na?kʉtabai huuhpi, na?kʉta?i? huuhpi (n) pecan. *Carya illinoensis* [Wang.] K. Koch. (nuts eaten, leaves used in treating ringworm and also as black stain [C & J]).

nakobe matsuma? (n) face towel [**na-** (refl) + **kobe** face + **matsuma?** wiper].

nakobe tsa?nika? (n) halter [**na-** (refl) + **kobe** face + **tsa?nikatʉput** down].

nakohpoopʉ K (n) brand (identifying animal's owner).

nakohpoopʉ W (n) printed material.

nakohtóo? (n) stove (*lit* possession for fire).

nakoo?ipʉ (n) pieces (anything cut into pieces, as dried fruit or nuts) [**na-** (refl) + **koo?i** cut + **-pʉ** (nom)].

nakuhkwarakitʉ (v) steam bathe (take a steam bath).

nakuhkwaraki? K (n) sweat bath, steam bath (steam made by throwing water on hot rocks).

nakutịsi, nakutʉsi (n) gunpowder.

nakutʉkʉna? (n) heated rock (used like heating pad to ease pain).

nakuyaarʉ (n) grass fire, prairie fire, fire.

nakʉahkatʉ (adj) protruding.

nakʉakitʉ (v) appear (come in sight, become visible).

nakʉhkuparʉ (v) eat oneself to death, drink oneself to death.

nakʉmʉʉ?etʉ W (adj) turned.

nakʉhitʉ (v) listen. *See* **tʉnakiitʉ.**

nakʉhoorʉ (v) eavesdrop, overhear.

nakʉhoowaaitʉ (n) eavesdropper, sneaky person.

nakʉkatʉ (adj) attentive, listening.

nakʉnikatʉ waikina, nakʉni waikina (n) covered wagon (*lit* wagon made into a home).

nakʉnʉʉʔmaitʉ (adj) discouraged, tired of something. *See* **narahtokwetʉ, manʉʉʔmai.**

nakʉwiyakʉrʉ K (v) burn oneself.

nakwiita (n) saucer [**na-** (refl) + **kwiita** bottom].

nakwʉsi tsaʔnikaʔ (n) saddle strap (*lit* that which is put on the tail; flank girth, passes under tail of horse).

nakwʉsipʉ (n) dried pumpkin (dried and braided for winter use) [**na-** (refl) + **kwʉsipʉ** braided].

nakwʉsiʔ (n) pumpkin.

nakwʉsukʉrʉ (v, pl) kill several persons. *See* **nabehkakʉrʉ.**

namabeʔahkapʉ (n) part (in the hair).

namabimarʉ (v) put away, hide something (put food in oven).

namabitsiapʉ (n) care for oneself.

namabitsooni sonihpʉ (n) mesquite weed. *Leguminoseae.*

namabitsooʔni (n) mesquite. *Prosopis glandulosa* Torr. (meal from pods eaten; leaves used to neutralize stomach acidity [C & J]; wash mesquite and make sugar from it, mixing with patsokwe; mixture is called patso). *See* **wohiʔhuu, natsohkweʔ.**

namabunitʉ (v) practice something.

namahkaʔmukitʉ (adj) complete, prepared. *See* **namakaʔmukitʉ.**

namahkiapʉ W (n) cut on hand.

namahku (n), acc namahkui, acc pl namahkunii clothes (any wearing apparel), household goods, personal belongings.

namahtowʉnarʉ (v, sg obj), *pl obj* **namahtowʉniʔitʉlean** something. **Huunaroʔiʔ maktu namaahtowʉnʉka.** A ladder stood leaning along it.

namahyaʔ (n) baking powder.

namakaʔmukitʉ (v) prepare oneself (get oneself ready). **Meekuka namakaʔmuki.** Now everyone get ready (70:11–12). *See* **namahkaʔmukitʉ.**

namakupakʉrʉ (v) work someone to death.

namakupʉkatʉ (adj) overworked, worked to death.

namakʉmaʔaipʉ (n) sharpened item.

namakʉnʉmapʉ (n) tired person, sore person.

namakwatubiitʉ (v) fold over, wrap, roll up. *See* **tahkwatúubitʉ, tʉmakwatʉbiʔetarʉ.**

namakweyaipʉ (n) exhausted person or animal.

namaminaitʉ (v) sprain or break hand or lower arm.

namamiʔakʉ (interj, byword) That's life!

namamohkarʉ, nanomohkarʉ (adj) hitched (as animals).

namamʉsurʉ (v) prohibit.

namanahkeetʉ W (v) parade (as Native Americans went from camp to camp in full dress before leaving on a trip). *See* **wʉhabitʉ.**

namanahkitʉ (v) measure oneself.

namanakwʉ K (adv loc) separated by great distance.

namanoke (interj, byword) It is worse!

namanuhkitʉ (v), *pl* **namanuraarʉ** run away afraid, flee from.

namaro?ihkatʉ (n) discarded thing.

namaro?itʉ (v) discard something, escape from somewhere (get rid of something). *See* **tsahwitʉ.**

namarunehtsʉrʉ, namarunetsʉ (v) run to something through fear, flee from.

namarʉkapʉ (n) finished item.

namarʉnitʉ K (v) hurt oneself, to wound. *See* **nahohiyaitʉ, nahuhyaitʉ.**

nama?abʉ (n), *pl* **nama?ʉbʉnʉʉmʉ** sickly person. *See* **kenama ?ʉbʉ?itʉ.**

nama?yʉkwitʉ (v) primp. *See* **ma?yʉkwiitʉ.**

namewatsʉkwitʉ (num) eight.

nami?

nami? (n) younger sister.

namotʉsibetʉ, namutʉsibe (v) shave oneself.

namotʉsibe? (n) handkerchief (*lit* nose wiper).

namo?o kotsetʉ (v) wash hand.

namo?o matsuma? (n) napkin [**mo?o** hand + **matsuma** wipe].

namuhkarʉ (v) fasten on harness.

namuhyʉ (n) doorway. *See* **muhyʉ, natsahtʉma?.**

namutsono?itʉ (v) pull own beard.

namutsora? (n) bridle bit (*lit* object held in mouth).

namuwoo, namʉwoo (n, arch) husband.

namʉsu?netʉ (v) rub hands together.

namʉnewapi (n) leader, important man.

namʉsi (adv) hurriedly, quickly. **Namʉsi kohtoohtsika tai maaka.** Quickly making us a fire, feed us (85:9).

namʉsi buhihwi tekwapʉ (n) telegram (*lit* quick money word).

namʉsohi, namʉsoi (adv time) immediately, right now.

namʉsohitʉ (v) hurry up (make haste). **Namʉsohiika!** Hurry up! (85:11).

namʉsokoopʉ (n) buried person or thing.

namʉsoapʉ (n) clothing, apparel.

namʉsoarʉ (v) change clothes, dress (get dressed).

nana- (pfx) through, throughout.

nanáarʉmu?i tʉboopʉ (n) story- book [**na-** (refl) + **narʉmu?ipʉ** tell story + **tʉboo** paper]. *See* **narʉmu?i tʉboopʉ.**

nanaarʉʉmoa (adj) marvelous, wonderful.

nanabuni saawʉ? (n) window screen.

nanabuni tsahpara? (n) window blind.

nanabuni wanapʉ K (n) curtain (*lit* window cloth).

nanabuni wanatsahpara? W (n) curtain (*lit* window cloth spread out).

nanabuni? (n) window [**nana-** through + **buni** see].

nanahbiso?aitʉ (adv) slow-moving.

nanahtenanʉʉ (n) menfolk, husbands.

nanakatso?arʉ (v) splice (*lit* do through the end).

nanakitonapʉ (n) pierced ear (*lit* pierced through). *See* **nakitoonʉkatʉ**.

nanakukʉtʉ (v) judge (*lit* talk through in behalf of).

nanakuya?arʉ (adj) fearful, odd, queer, strange (*lit* scared through; said of people).

nanakʉhurʉ (v) gamble (*lit* burned through). *See* **wanarohpetitʉ**.

nanakwʉʉhtʉ (v) marry each other (get married). **Nanakwʉʉhtu?i urʉ.** They are getting married.

nanakwʉʉrʉ (v) marry someone (perform the marriage ceremony).

nanakwʉhʉ W, **nanakwʉnʉkwʉ** K (n) married couple.

nanamʉ?aitʉ K, **nanamʉanoorʉ** W (v) stall (delay oneself).

nanamʉsu? (n) in-law.

nananisuyake (adj, pl) pretty.

nananʉʉ?maitʉ (v) tire oneself, exhaust oneself (become exhausted). *See* **narahkupaitʉ**.

nanapunipʉ (n) footprint. *See* **napʉ, narapunipʉ**.

nanarʉna?itʉ (v, arch) run a race.

nanawatsikarʉ (v) misunderstand statement. *See* **kenanawatsitʉ**.

nanawa?ihpʉ?anii (n, acc pl) women.

nanawa?ihpʉ?anʉ W (n), *acc pl* **na?kwa?ihpʉ?a** womenfolk (man speaking).

nana?atahpu na?ha? rʉʉpi (n) diamond (*lit* different flashes rock).

nana?atanaiki, nana?atahpoto K (adv dir) from different directions.

nana?ataputʉ (adj) different kinds. *See* **nanisusumatʉ**.

Nana?butitʉikatʉ mʉa (n) March (*lit* hot-or-cold month).

nana?isa nayʉkwi tʉkwʉ (v) flirt with each other.

nanihkanuitʉ (v) clear throat.

nanihkuparʉ (v), *pl* **nanihtokwe-** laugh heartily.

naníhpana?aitʉ (v) boast, brag on oneself. *See* **nihpana?aitʉ**.

nanihpu?e?aikʉpʉ K (n) pact, treaty, tradition. *See* **pu?e?aikʉpʉ**.

naníhtsawa?itʉ (v) ask for help, request something. *See* **nigwaitʉ**.

nanihtʉbinitʉ (v) ask permission.

nanika?witʉ (v) meet to suggest something.

nanimaa?ʉbʉ?ikʉtʉ (v) ask, plead, beseech.

nanina?ukitʉ (v) rejoice verbally.

nanipu?e?aitʉ, nani?atsiitʉ (v) make an agreement or contract). **Nʉmʉnʉʉ paraibonʉi ʉ?aii nanipu?e?aitʉ.** The Comanches made an agreement with the government.

nanípʉka (n) guess-over-the-hill (game played by boys).

nanitsʉwakatʉ K (adj) quarrelsome, argumentative.

naniyo?naitʉ K (v) riot (have a commotion).

nani?emʉahpʉ aitʉ (v) blaspheme (say what one does not mean).

nani?ookitʉ (v) try (bring to trial as in court).

nani?ooki taiboo? (n) lawyer (*lit* trial white man).

nani?ʉrʉ?aitʉ (v) counsel, advise. *See* **tʉsu?ʉrʉ?.**

nani?wiketʉ W (v) quarrel, argue. **Nani?wiketʉ marʉkwʉ.** They are arguing.

nani?yʉsʉkaitʉ W (n) commotion.

nanisuabeta?aitʉ (v) introduce oneself (make oneself known). *See* **natsahpunitʉ.**

nanisusumatʉ (adj) different kinds. *See* **nana?atapatʉ.**

nanisutaikʉtʉ (v) intercede, pray for someone.

nanisutaitʉ, nanʉsutai (v) pray.

nanisuwʉkaitʉ (n) spirit, marvel, miracle.

nanisuwʉkaitʉ (adj) spirited, marvelous, wonderful (having a spirit). *See* **suyoro?akapʉ.**

nanohmʉnʉ wapi K (n) officer, leader.

nanoomanitʉ (v) harness something (as an animal).

nano?onai (adv dir) from all directions.

nanʉsutsawaitʉ (adj) faithful.

nanʉʉhtʉpʉka? (n) buckle, button, hook. *See* **natsweni?.**

nanʉwokʉ (n) payment of damages (usually paid in horses, guns, blankets, or clothing in the old days).

nanʉso?iitʉ W, **nanʉso?otʉ** K (adj) busy.

nanʉsu?uyaatʉ (adj) laughingstock, ridiculous.

naparʉkitʉ (v) soak oneself in water.

napatawi?aitʉ (adj) wornout (shoes).

napiso?aitʉ (adj) slow [**na-** (refl) + **piso-** angry + **ai-** made to be].

napisarʉ (v) paint oneself, make up oneself (apply make-up).

napiso?akatʉ (adj) punctured (by object, in buttocks area).

napʉ-, nape- (pfx) ref. to foot and lower leg, shoes. *See* **naape.**

napʉ (n) shoe, footprint, trail. *See* **nanapunipʉ.**

napʉ makarʉ (v) give away moccasins.

napʉ narawʉna? (n) shoe nail [**napʉ** shoe + **na-** (refl) + **roobʉna?** stake].

napʉ rahpaana (n) shoe sole [**napʉ** shoe + **tahpaana** sole]. *See* **narahpaana.**

napʉ rʉrawʉna? (n) shoe nail [**napʉ** shoe + **tʉrawʉna?** nail].

napʉ rʉ?eka? (n) shoe polish [**napʉ** shoe + **tʉ?eka?** paint].

napʉ saarʉ (adj) laced, strung.

napʉ soona (n) floor (*lit* shoe quilt).

napʉ tsakwʉsa? (n) shoelace, shoestring [**napʉ** shoe + **tsakwʉsa?** string].

napʉbosarʉ (v) fasten with shoelace.

napʉbosa? (n) shoehook, shoelace.

napʉhu (n) trail.

napʉhu mi?arʉ (v) trail (follow a trail closely).

nara- (pfx) ref. to foot or lower leg.

naraaikʉ? (n) bicycle (*lit* item for feet to make lope). *See* **ta?aikʉtʉ.**

narabee?aitʉ (v) take an oath.

narabʉ (n, voc) old man (familiar joking term).

narahka?witʉ (v) congregate, gather together. *See* **uhoika?wʉtʉ.**

narahki?apʉ (n) a cut on the foot, foot wound.

narahkooni wapi W (n) shepherd.

narahkupaitu (v) exhaust oneself, give up. *See* **nananui u?maitu.**

narahpaana (n) shoe sole. *See* **napurahpaana.**

narahpana? (n) tire (of wheel).

narahpomi?itu (adj) (divided into groups).

narahpunipu (n) footwear tried on, attempt (anything).

narahtokwetu (adj) discouraged, downhearted. *See* **nakunuu?- maitu, ai?bihinuusukatu.**

narahtsukikatu, narahtsukikatu (adj) crowded together (as people in a room).

narahtukii? (n) stirrup (*lit* item to put foot in). *See* **ta?nika?.**

naraketorootu (n) haircut (hair cut short).

narakotseru (v) wash feet.

narakwusakatu napu, narakwisa napi (n) cowboy boots.

naraminaitu K (v) sprain ankle.

naraminaitu W (v) break at joint of foot.

narapunipu (n) footprint. *See* **nanapunipu, napu.**

nararunaru (v) gamble over some type of competition. **Meeku takwu maba?atu nararuuna.** Now let us two run a race over it (to see who will win) (9:8).

narawekwi kahni (n) jail, prison.

narawuhtama? (n) garter (*lit* item one ties on the leg).

narayaakupu (n) pound (unit of weight).

narayaakuru (v) weigh something.

narayaaku? (n) scale (for weighing).

nara?okatu (adj) bunched up, pounded, dried.

nara?uraitu (v) meet, encounter someone.

nara?urakutu (v) learn, find out for oneself.

nara?woru K (v) scratch, rub with foot (as to relieve itch).

narenahpu? (n), *pl* **nanahtenanuu** man's male kinsman.

nariso?aru W (v) give an enema (insert something into rectum).

narohkwuri?etu (adj) spilled.

narohparu (v) fight hand-to-hand, wrestle.

narohtsanaru (adj) hanging, hung up.

narohtuma? (n) can, lid, canned goods.

narominaitu (v) break at joint of body (as elbow or knee).

naromunitu (v) lack (run short of something), outrun someone.

naropusaru (adj), *pl* **naropusi?i** beaded.

naro?ikahni K (n) bathroom (*lit* defecating house).

naro?itu (v) defecate.

naro?i? (n) ladder, stairs.

naro?toneetsi? (n) throwing arrows (up to distance of two hundred yards).

Narua, Nadua (n) Cynthia Ann Parker (white girl captured by Comanches in 1836; after being taken back to the whites, she died grieving for her Comanche family).

narubunitu (v) run a race.

naruituahkaru (v) help one another.

narureru (v) stretch arms or body (as when one has been sitting for a long period).

narutsaʔi (n, voc) old lady (husband's term for wife).

naruahweru (v) confess (tell on oneself).

naruahwuku (n) bride.

narubahkaru , narubaʔeru (v) bet on something.

narubuniʔetuʔ (n) racer (person who races).

naruhkapu (n) partly eaten food.

naruhkaʔ (n) groceries.

naruhkaʔruaru, naruhkaʔrumuu (v) buy or otherwise receive groceries.

naruhkaʔ sokoobi (n) vegetable garden. *See* **tumusua sokobi.**

naruhkaʔtsuʔmaru (v) run out of groceries.

narukitu (adj), *pl* **naruniʔi** placed, put in place.

narukuyunapu (n) tale, fairy story. *See* **narumuʔipu.**

narukuyunu ruboopu (n) history (*lit* story on paper).

narumakaru (v) pay with money.

narumaʔeru (v) exchange.

Narumiʔ (name) Lord, Master (name used for deity).

narumuhku (n) bridle reins, harness.

narumuʔikatu (v) tell, relate. **Ma haitsinii nu narumuʔikatu.** I am telling his friends. *See* **tuʔaweru.**

narumuʔipu (n) story, tale. *See* **narukuyunapu.**

narumuʔi tuboopu (n) newspaper, storybook. *See* **nanáarumuʔi tuboopu.**

narumuuru (v) trade, sell to one another, exchange. **Pu oyoru? ma narumuuru.** They are selling their clothes to one another.

narumuuʔ (n) town, store.

narunoo bapi, narunoo paapi (n) saddle horn.

narunookatu unuu (n) camel [**narunookatu** have a saddle + **unuu** animal].

narunooʔ (n) packsaddle.

narunooʔ namuku (n) saddle strap (that which passes around the girth).

narunooʔroʔyaru, (v) *pl* **narunooʔ rooʔitu** (v) unsaddle a horse.

narunooʔrukitu (v), *pl* **narunooʔ tahniʔru** saddle up.

narurunitu (v, arch) hold races.

naruʔekaru (v) massage, apply medicine. **Natusuʔu naruʔekai nu.** I rubbed medicine (on him). *See* **mabararu.**

naruʔuyapu (adj) mean, dangerous.

naruʔuyu kuhtsuniʔ (n) typhoid fever (*lit* dangerous fever).

naruʔuyu tasiʔa (n) smallpox (*lit* dangerous spots).

naruʔuyu uuʔaʔ (n) chronic sore, cancer, lesion.

naruso, naruso (n) bag, sack.

narusoʔipu (n) tanned hide, process of tanning a hide.

nasaanutoʔitu (v) rust, rust out; *adj* rusted, rusted out.

nasaapu (n) boiled food.

nasaaʔwuʔ K (n) screen door.

nasaaʔwuʔ W (n) bedspring, window screen.

nasanopi K, **nasaanutoʔipu** W (n) rust.

naséka (n) persimmon. *Diospyros virginiana* L. (fruit eaten fresh or dried).

nasiyuukiʔ (n), **kahni siʔyuki** roofing shingles [**na-** (refl) + **siʔyukiʔ** overlap].

nasuawʉhkitʉ K (v) sigh, breathe deeply while awake. *See* **nahuahtsitʉ, ʉsuaketʉ.**

nasukooʔi kahni (n) sweathouse [**nasukooʔi** sweat + **kahni** house].

nasukooʔitʉ (v) steam bathe (take a sauna, sweat bath).

nasukooʔiʔ (n) sweat bath, sauna.

nasupetipʉ K (n) faithful person, dependable person. *See* **nasutsawaitʉ.**

nasupetitʉ (v) hope in, depend on someone.

nasupetiʔ (n) hope.

nasupʉ K (n) ground up object. *See* **tusupʉ.**

nasutamakʉrʉ W (v) remind someone.

nasutamʉ habitʉ (v) rest pensively, lie down and think.

nasutamʉ wʉminaitʉ K (v) break a bone.

nasutamʉ wʉminaitʉ W (v) fall short.

nasutamʉkatʉ tamai, nasutamarʉ (v) think about something, remember. *See* **sukwʉkitʉ.**

nasutarʉ (v) surrender, give up.

nasutsa akwarʉ K (v) show off, act pretentious. **Iima nʉʔ nasutsa akwatuʔi.** I am going to show off with this.

nasutsarʉ (v) display (show off something).

nasutsawaitʉ W (adj) faithful, dependable. *See* **nasupetipʉ.**

nasuwatsi (v) lose something.

nasuwatsipʉ (adj) forgotten.

nasuwatsirʉ (v) forget. **Nʉ nisuwatsipʉha nʉ ninʉsutamakʉbʉni.** You (pl)

remind me a lot of the one I had forgotten (8:43).

nasuwʉhkitʉ (v) lose faith in someone.

nasuyaketʉ (v) covet, wish for, lust for, admire.

nasúyakeʔ K (n) lust.

nasuʔaitʉʔ (n) shame.

nasuʔaitʉ (adj) ashamed, bashful.

nasuʔana (adv compar) terrible, much worse (when previously already bad). **Nasuʔana u nʉsukatʉ.** He is feeling much worse.

nasʉkiʔapʉ (adj) fringed.

nasʉsʉaʔeetʉ, nasʉseetʉ (adj) nasty, dirty, no good. *See* **tuhtsaipʉ.**

Natai (n) Proud (or arrogant) People (Wichita name for the Comanches of Tejas.

natsa (interj) no matter! (related to remonstrance or accusation).

natsaakʉsi, natsaakwʉsi (n) sneezeweed. *Helenium microcephalum* Gray (yellow flowers; to induce sneezing, to cure headache, or expel afterbirth [C & J]).

natsaaturuʔitʉʔ (n) tug-of-war (*lit* pulling against one another).

natsahkiʔapʉ (n) cut, gash.

natsahkiʔarʉ (v) cut oneself, gash oneself, wound oneself.

natsahkupʉkatʉ (v) pull oneself down.

natsahkupʉkatʉ (v) scratch (digging into skin).

natsahkweniitʉ (adj) hung up, hanging.

natsahkweʔyarʉ (v), *pl* **natsah kweʔyuʔitʉ** undress, disrobe. *See* **tsahkweʔyarʉ.**

natsahkwine? (n) automatic pistol (*lit* spins to wound).

natsahkwinu?itu (v, adj) spin around, spun. *See* **kwinu?yaru**.

natsahpunitu (v) test something; introduce oneself (to someone) [**na-** (refl) + **tsah-** hand + **puni** see]. *See* **nanisuabeta?aitu**.

natsahto?itu (v) pull oneself up.

natsahtsiaitu (v) scratch oneself.

natsahtuma? K (n) door, doorway. *See* **namuhyu, muhyu**.

natsahwi?etu (v) open of its own accord. **Punusu tsa? natsahwi-?etu.** It opens itself.

natsaka?uhtu?etu (v) betray someone.

natsaka?uhtu?etu? (n) traitor, betrayer.

natsakwenitu (v) swing back and forth.

natsakwusa? (n) zipper (anything that closes by pulling up on handle).

natsakwusiku? (n) laced object (anything that laces up).

natsamaru (v) accuse someone, complain about someone, exaggerate (woman's word).

natsamarunitu (adj, hum) strained.

natsaminaitu (v) dislocate (pull out of joint of own accord).

natsaminaru (v) disjoint (pull out of joint on purpose).

natsamukwe? (n) wild grape. *Vitis* sp. *See* **mutsinatsamukwe?**.

natsamukwe?a paa (n) wine, grape juice.

natsamukwe?a suuki (n) grapevine.

natsamuritu, natsamurihitu (v) turn over.

natsanahaatu (adj) persistent.

natsanuhku? (n) saddle girth.

natsawenitu (v) hang (suspended off ground), swing. **Kakwohwi tsa? natswenihkatu.** The bell is hanging.

natsaweni? (n) hanger, hook.

natsawo?nitu (v) scratch an itch. *See* **tsakwo?neru**.

natsawunukatu (adj) situated, set in place (as a lamp).

natsawunuru (v) set something in place.

natsayaa ruka? K, **natsayaahkatu tuka?** W (n) lantern, lamp (carried by handle). *See* **tuka?**.

natsayaaru (v) carry by the handle.

                     ✗ wehki'ai

natsa?ani?

natsa?ani? (n) four-wheeled hack, two-seated buggy (*lit* fold back, since top folded back). *See* **wobipuuku**.

natsa?nikaru (v) wear something.

natsihpara? (n) ventilator at top of teepee (opened to allow smoke to escape; closed to keep out the cold).

natsihpe?akaru (v) part hair (using special Comanche instrument for that purpose). **Wa?ipu tsa? natsihpe?akaaru.** The woman parted her hair with the hair-parter.

natsihpe?aka? (n) hair-parter (wooden artifact used by Comanches to part hair).

natsihpᵾsaʔ (n) buckle that is buckled.

natsihtóo miʔarᵾ (v) walk away (using walking cane).

natsihtóo noorᵾ (v) walk with cane.

natsihtóoʔ K (n) cane, staff, crutch. *See* **tᵾʔehkooiʔ.**

natsihtóoʔetᵾ (n) double ball (variation of shinny or lacrosse).

natsihtóoʔitᵾ (v) play lacrosse.

natsihtuʔyeetᵾ (v) comb hair.

natsihtuʔyeʔ (n) comb, hairbrush. *See* **puhihwi natsihtuʔyeʔ.**

natsihtᵾmaʔ (n) padlock. *See* **tᵾtsihtᵾmaʔ.**

natsihtᵾpᵾkaʔ (n) brooch, decorative pin.

natsiminaʔ (n) joint.

natsinaroʔikᵾtᵾ (v) give oneself an enema.

natsinᵾhkᵾrᵾ (v) cram into limited space. *See* **tsinᵾkᵾrᵾ.**

natsiwekwaʔ (n) spur [**na-** (refl) + **tsi** pointed + **wekwa-** jab].

natsohkweʔ (n) mesquite [**na-** (refl) + **tsohkwe-** pound fine]. *See* **namabitsooʔni, wohiʔhuu.**

natsomᵾ (n) dried plum.

natsuwᵾkai (adj) odd, strange (not like others). **Nenahpᵾ tsaʔ natsuwᵾkaiʔarᵾ.** The man is odd.

natsu taiboʔ K (n) medical doctor (*lit* medicine man). *See* **natᵾsuʔupuha raibooʔ.**

natsuwi (n) strength.

natsuwitᵾmakaʔeetᵾ (v) strengthen, encourage. **Taʔahpᵾ tsaʔ natsuwitᵾmakaʔetᵾ.** God gives us strength.

natsuwitᵾ (adj) strong physically. **natsuwitᵾ tenahpᵾʔ** strong man. **Noha u natsuwitᵾ.** He was strong

(previously but not now). He used to be strong.

Natᵾmᵾᵾ paʔi hunaʔ (n) north fork of Red River (at Traders Spring, Okla.; *lit* trading river).

natᵾsuʔᵾ narᵾmᵾᵾʔ (n) drugstore (*lit* medicine store).

natᵾsakᵾna (n) rawhide wardrobe case (envelope-shaped, laced at edges; with fold-over, tie-down flap; the best suit of clothing was kept in this bag).

natᵾsuʔu puha raibooʔ W (n) doctor (*lit* medicine-power man). *See* **natsu taiboʔ.**

natᵾsuʔᵾ (n) medicine. *See* **puha̱.**

natᵾsuʔᵾ kahni (n) hospital, drugstore (*lit* medicine house). *See* **wᵾmi̱naa kahni.**

nawohani (n) maize (cross between Indian corn and white corn). *Zea mays* L.

nawooʔi, nahwooi- (v, pl), *sg* **yaketᵾ** cry.

nawoʔorᵾ (adj) striped.

nawᵾhkobaitᵾ (v) break bone. **Nᵾ ome nawᵾhkobai.** I broke my leg.

Naya (name) Slope (person).

nayaarᵾ, nagyaarᵾ (v) trail a human or an animal. **Tenahpᵾ tsaʔ arᵾkaʔa naayaarᵾ.** The man is trailing the deer. *See* **tᵾnahyarᵾ.**

nayanohitekwarᵾʔ (n) joker (person who jokes frequently).

nayaʔisaʔaitᵾ (n) liar (person who likes to spread stories). *See* **isapᵾʔ.**

nayᵾkwiitᵾ (v, pl), *sg* **nahanitᵾ** continue along, move on. **Suni ʔuri nayᵾkwitᵾ uʔ.** They moved on there.

nayɨɨ wokwe (n) cactus (small species; sometimes difficult to see as it blends with the soil). *Mammalaria* sp.

na?a- (pfx, reciprocal).

na?aa (n) buffalo horn case (used for storing fire-making drills). *See* **aa.**

na?ahnia K, na?ahni̯a N (n) palomino horse (*lit* that which wallows).

na?akɨtɨ (v) meet, come together.

na?anampɨ (n) in-law.

na?anitɨ (v), *pl* **na?ani?itɨ** wallow, roll over or around (animal action).

na?ata W, na?atanakwɨ̯ K (adv loc) separated but in same general area.

na?atsiyaa? (n) seesaw, teeter-totter.

na?a?tsome? (n) dried plum. *See* **kusisɨkɨi.**

na?arurɨɨ? (n) fist fight.

na?arutɨ W (v) fight, hit with fists.

na?beko?arɨ (adj) parted, separated (as clouds part or break up).

na?bukuwàa? (n) automobile [**na-** (refl) + **puku** horse + **waa** horn sound].

na?bukuwáa? kahni̯ (n) garage (*lit* automobile house).

na?bukuwàa?a nábaa (n) gasoline (for automobiles). *See* **nabaa.**

na?bukuwàa?a nahyu̯ (n) motor oil. *See* **nabaa.**

na?bukuwàa?a narahpaana̯ W, na?bukuwà?a tahpaana̯ K (n) automobile tire. *See* **makwɨ?nikɨ.**

na?butikɨmakatɨ tɨɨhka?aa? (n) double-bladed axe. *See* **tɨɨhka?a?.**

na?hɨmuhkɨ W (n) safety pin. *See* **nahamuhkɨ.**

na?isahanitɨ W (v) commit adultery.

na?iyaitɨ (v) watch oneself.

na?isa suakɨtɨ (v) K want to flirt; W flirt with someone.

na?i̯sa yɨkwitɨ̯ K (v) flirt with someone (not reciprocated). **Nai?bi tsa? na?isa yɨkwiitɨ?.** The young woman is flirting (with no response).

na?mahpe?e?, na?mahpee? (n) ball (*lit* object thrown by hand; used to play game of jacks).

na?nia (n) buckskin horse.

na?nohne?eyu? (n) archaic game.

na?nɨbe? (adj) divided evenly.

na?nɨmɨ (n) female kinsman.

na?nɨɨmɨ (n) kinsman, descendant. *See* **nɨhmabina.**

na?okitɨ (v) rejoice.

na?okɨsuarɨ (v) feel happy.

na?omo̯, na?oomo̯ (n) wheel.

na?omo̯ nasɨwɨhki? (n) spoke of wheel.

na?oyorɨmakarɨ K (v) exchange several gift items.

na?raiboo? (n) slave, tenant (*lit* possession of white man).

na?rɨbomitɨ (v) divide, break up under own volition.

na?rɨbomitɨ̯ (adj) divided, broken up.

na?sɨhpee? (n) ball (small, Native-American football) [**na-** (refl) + **sɨh** kick + **pee?** fall].

na?sɨhpe?etɨ (n) Native-American ball game.

na?sɨkia? (n) fringes, shawl with fringes. *See* **pohotɨ̯ na?sɨkia?, tapi na?sɨkia?.**

naʔtsiyaaʔ (n) seesaw, teeter- totter [**na-** (refl) + **tsiyaa-** throw one].

naʔtsiʔaikɨʔ (n) baby buggy.

naʔuhturɨ W (v, sg obj), *pl obj* **hinanahimiitɨ** exchange gifts.

naʔɨyɨbuti W, **naʔɨyɨbetotɨ** K (adv dir) down, downward.

naʔɨyatɨ (adj) slanting, sloping.

naʔwaʔihpɨʔ (n) man's female kinsman. *See* **waʔihpɨʔ.**

naʔweeʔ, nagwee (n) ford, wagon crossing. *See* **puʔe nagwe.**

naʔwekitɨʔ (n) hide-and-seek.

naʔwosa (n) drawer. *See* **ooyorɨ tahna.**

naʔyɨnehtɨʔ W (n) shield.

naʔyɨnetɨ (v, pl), *sg* **yahneetɨ** laugh.

naʔyɨwetɨ (v) play hand games.

nehki wɨhtɨpɨka? (n) belt buckle.

nehki W, **nehkiʔ** K (n) belt.

ni- (pfx) ref. to speech.

nigwaitɨ K, **nikwaitɨ** W (v) request something. *See* **naníhtsawaʔitɨ.**

nigwatsɨkatɨ (v) stutter.

nikwekwitɨ (v, pl), *sg* **niʔikaʔitɨ** invite someone in.

nihakɨrɨ (v) name someone, read (as a book). *See* **nahniamakarɨ.**

nihkwibihbikitɨ (v) tremble in speech (as when about to cry, or when elderly).

nihmakwihtserɨ (v), *pl* **nihmakwih-tseyurɨ** call down, rebuke, scold.

nihpanaʔaitɨ (v) brag on someone, praise someone. *See* **naníhpanaʔaitɨ, panaʔaitɨ.**

nihpitɨkɨrɨ (v) coax someone.

nihpɨʔaitɨ (v) stop talking.

nihtoʔitɨ (v) ban, order to leave. **Pɨhi tuaʔa u nihtoʔitɨ.** He is ordering their son to leave.

nihtoʔitɨ (v) sing a song, sing out.

nihtsamuʔitɨ (v) agree to a proposal, nod the head in agreement. **Tenahpɨ tsaʔ pɨ miaruʔiha uri nihtsamuʔi.** The man promised them that he would go.

nihtunetsarɨ (v) pester someone (keep talking in a manner which disturbs). *See* **nimɨsasuarɨ.**

nihtunetsɨʔitɨ (v) urge on, encourage to go on.

nihtunetsɨkatɨeʔ (n) a bore (one who pesters by talk).

nihtɨbuniorɨ (v) waken by speaking to someone.

niikwiitɨ (v) speak to, address (used with me). **Oha ahnakatɨ, 'Mɨi nahubiyaaruʔi nɨ?,' me urii niikwiiyɨ.** Coyote said to them, 'I will sing for you all.'

niipuni-, nihpunitɨ (v) ask (to persuade someone to do something).

nikwɨkitɨ (v) inquire (ask around to procure information).

nimabunikɨtɨ (v) explain, instruct (tell to do). *See* **nitsɨbunikɨtɨ.**

nimaihkana? (n) called one.

nimaikatɨ (v) call to someone. **Waʔipɨ tsaʔ pɨ kumapɨʔa nimaikatɨ.** The woman called to her husband.

nimakabaitɨ (v) reject someone.

nimakaʔmukitɨ (v) make a plan. *See* **suʔatsitɨ.**

nimakwihtsetɨ (v) say mean things, talk tough, fuss at someone.

nimamɨsukɨtɨ, nimamɨsuitɨ (v) say no to someone, refuse.

nimarɨkaitɨ (v) finish telling.

nimoyaʔekɨrɨ (v) forbid, prohibit (tell not to do).

nimɨɨmiʔarɨ W (v) pass word on, gossip.

nimɨsasuarɨ (v) annoy, harass by chatter, pester by talk. **Tɨepɨrɨ tsaʔ nimɨsasuarɨ.** The child annoyed (us) by his talk. *See* **nihtunetsarɨ.**

ninabitsiarɨ, nimabitsiarɨ (v) order sternly, speak firmly.

ninakabarɨ (v) refuse to accept someone, reject man as husband.

ninakabaʔikɨtɨ (v) prohibit, warn (tell someone not to do something wrong).

ninakabaʔitɨ (n) rejected person.

Ninakabaʔiʔ (name) Refusing (person).

ninakɨakɨrɨ W (v) give notice, tip off.

ninɨkitɨ W (v) compare with something.

ninɨsuabitarɨ K (v) advise, inform (let someone know something).

ninɨsupetitɨ (v) appease, gratify.

ninɨsutamakɨtɨ (v) reminded orally (remember by something someone says).

Nipanɨɨ (n) Eastern Apaches (Ipa's People; fought the Comanches in battle on E. Red River; the Apaches were routed).

nipɨkaaʔeetɨ (n) fortuneteller, shaman. *See* **nɨminipɨkaʔ, mapaanaʔ, tɨnipɨkawapi.**

nipɨkarɨ (v) tell a fortune. **Nɨ nipɨkaai u.** He told my fortune. *See* **nɨnipɨkarɨ.**

nipɨyerɨ (v) sing one song after another (in succession).

nisuabetarɨ (v) K explain something, teach someone something; **W** introduce someone.

nisutaitɨ (v) pet, stroke. **Sariiʔa nisutaiʔi.** He petted his dog. *See* **tohtarakiʔarɨ.**

nisuyakeetɨ (v) tempt by describing something.

nisuʔuyaitɨ W (v) jeer, mock (make fun of). *See* **usúʔuyaʔitɨ.**

nitsɨbahikɨʔitɨ (v) persuade someone to do something, talk someone into something.

nitsɨbunikɨtɨ (v) explain, instruct (cause to know). *See* **nimabunikɨtɨ.**

nitɨsuʔnai wapi (n) mediator, go-between.

niwatsiʔaikɨʔitɨ (v) hold back information, keep quiet.

niwɨnɨrɨ (v, pl), **sg tekwarɨ** talk to someone.

niyakekɨtɨ (v) imitate a cry, make a birdcall. **Huutsuʔa niyakekɨi u.** He imitated the bird cry.

niyukarɨrɨ W, **niyunahkarɨ** K (v) quiet someone (command to neither move nor talk).

niʔatsiwapiʔ (n) commander. *See* **tɨni atsikatɨʔ.**

niʔatsiitɨ (v) advise, order, command.

niʔemɨabɨnitɨ (v) rave, speak irrationally (as when one is delirious or near death).

niʔheʔbunitɨ (v) insult, taunt, berate someone falsely.

niʔikaʔitɨ (v), *pl* **nigwekwitɨ** invite into home or room. **Mari nigwekwi nɨʔ.** I invited them to come in.

niʔtsuʔnarɨ (v) forgive, quiet by speech. *See* **tɨsuʔnarɨ.**

niʔwatsɨkatɨʔ (n) error in speech.

niʔwikerɨ (v) scold someone.

ni?wiketʉ (v) quarrel with someone. **Nani?wiketʉ marʉkwʉ.** The two of them are quarreling.

ni?woso?arʉ (v) berate someone.

ni?yʉsʉkaitʉ (v) disturb, create a commotion, upset people by bad tidings.

nobʉahraitʉ (v) abandon someone, leave someone behind.

noha (adv) nearly, almost, used to. **Noha u? nʉ kwʉhʉru?i.** He almost caught me. (105:28). **Noha nʉ mi?arʉ.** I was going (but did not).

nohabitʉ (n) hen (clucker), setting hen.

nohabi̱ suwaitʉ (v) want to lay an egg. *See* **suwai.**

nohi (adv) very. **nohi tʉtaatʉ taa haitsi̱our** very small friend. *See* **mohatsi̱.**

nohi?nuraarʉ (v) run around and play.

nohitʉetʉ (n) doll (*lit* toy child).

nohiwaikinʉ, nohi wobipuku (n) toy wagon.

nohihtaiboo?nʉʉ (n pl) circus, circus people (*lit* playing white men).

nohitekwarʉ (v) fool someone, joke, pretend, make-believe. *See* **kaasuarʉ.**

nohitʉ (v) play (make fun of), ridicule. **Nahruku nʉmi nohiti.** That one is just playing with us (making fun of us) (8:44). *See* **tʉnimakwihtserʉ.**

nohi? (n) plaything, toy.

nohko aawo? K (n) oven (*lit* biscuit container).

nohko aawo̱ (n) oven for baking biscuits. *See* **pʉkʉra nohko?ena̱.**

nohkopʉ (n) biscuit.

nohkorʉ (v) bake biscuits.

nohrʉna? (n) bedstead.

nohrʉna saawʉ, nohna saawʉ? (n) bedspring.

nohrʉnaarʉ (v) make a bed.

noka?itʉ (v) move off to live separately, camp apart from the main group.

nokimarʉ (v) come moving along. *See* **nora?wʉarʉ.**

Nokoni (n) Comanche band (located between Red River and Peace River).

nomi?arʉ (v), *pl* **sʉmʉnomi?arʉ** move away (change residence).

nomohkarʉ (v) hitch up horses and buggy, hook up doubletrees on buggy. *See* **mahkarʉ.**

nomʉnewapi W (n) officer, leader.

nonanʉʉ (n pl), *sg* **monahpʉ?** sons-in-law.

noo (adv) sure, particular, definite. **Obotika hunu?ruti noo hina puhwaihbʉʉni̱.** Over there along the creek look for a particular thing (6:24).

noo- (pfx) hill, knoll; ref. to hauling.

noohkirʉ (v) haul in. *See* **noopitʉ.**

nookarʉrʉ (n) one hill standing alone. *See* **anáabi.**

Nookoni, Nocona, Peta Nokona (name) Wanderer (Comanche chief, Kwana Parker's father; died in 1860 on Mule Creek).

nookwarʉ, nookwai (v) carry away, haul away.

noomanitʉ (v) carry across.

noona K, noopʉ W (n) load.

noonʉmi?arʉ (v) move from place to place. *See* **noyʉkarʉ.**

noopitʉ (v) haul in, arrive carrying something. *See* **noohkirʉ, pitʉnʉ.**

nooru̱ (v) to haul away. **Ohka tanu̱ tuhkanáai? tenahpu̱?a tu̱mu̱su̱apu̱ kahti noohtsi.** Let's carry off some of that Wichita man's crop (77:7).

nooyo̱ (n) egg.

norawu̱?aitu̱ (v) move away.

nora?wu̱aru̱ W, **noragwu̱aru̱** K (v) go moving along. *See* **nokimaru̱.**

noro?yaru̱ (v), *pl* **noro?itu̱** unhitch a horse. **Pu̱ puukuni? u noro?itu̱.** He unhitched his horses. *See* **to?yaru̱.**

noru̱bakitu̱ (v), *pl* **tu̱bakitu̱** pack. **Noru̱baki u kimai.** She packed and came on.

noru̱naaru̱ (v) make a bed.

noru̱napu̱ (n) bed (made up with linens).

notsa?kaaru̱ (v) take women along, allow women to accompany. **Notsa?kaa mi?aru̱ sa?.** He is taking women along.

notsa?ka? (n) partner, friend, sweetheart, spouse. **Su̱mu̱? tuibihtsi? pu̱ notsa?ka?ma?ai pa?anai urii puni?i.** One young man with his sweetheart saw them (70:21). *See* **tu̱htu̱i?, tu̱u̱?urapu̱.**

noyotso?me̱ tabu? (n) Easter rabbit [**noyotso?me** Easter + **taabu** rabbit].

noyo?na ohapi̱yuna (n) egg yolk.

Noyu̱hkanu̱u̱, Nookoni (n) Roamers, Wanderers (band of middle Comanches; formerly located in Peace River region of Texas; now located between Lawton and Richard's Spur).

noyu̱karu̱ (v) wander from place to place, roam. *See* **noonu̱mi?araru̱.**

noyu̱ka? (n) roamer, vagabond.

no?a-, no?apu̱ (adj) pregnant.

no?a nohkopu̱ (n) pie (*lit* pregnant biscuit).

no?itu̱ (v) pluck out something, pick a bird of its feathers. **pu̱hu̱ no?itu̱** pluck eyebrows.

no?wosaru̱ (adj) hunchback.

no?yaiku̱tu̱ (v) boil, steam. **Huba tai no?yaiku̱.** Boil us some coffee. **Paapasi tu̱ no?yaiku̱u̱tu̱.** The potatoes are boiling.

nuaru̱ (v) slide, move over. **Pu̱nu̱su̱ u? nuai.** He moved over. *See* **pisikwanúu?itu̱.**

nuhkitu̱ (v) run, run away. **Ohaahnakatu̱ makuhpa nuhkínu̱.** Coyote ran ahead of him (10:18). *See* **pu̱anuhkitu̱, wenu?nukimi- ?aru̱.**

nuhtsairu̱ (v) stoop, bend over. **Tenahpu̱ tsa? nuhtsai.** The man is stooped. **Huupi tsa? nuhtsaru̱.** The tree (limb) broke off.

nuhtsaitu̱ (adj) crumbled.

nuhtsapu̱ (adj) bent over, broken (as a fallen tree), stooped (as the elderly). *See* **tumuuru̱.**

nuhya? (n, arch) snake of any species.

nuhyimi?aru̱ W, **nuhyinooru̱** K (v) crawl like a snake.

nuhyu̱yukitu̱, nuhyukitu̱ (v) rotate, change from one position to another. **Wo?aruhkapu̱ha tsa? nuhyu̱yukitu̱.** She poured the rice from one pan to another.

nunurawu̱tu̱ (v) run away one by one. **Nu̱mu̱nu̱u̱ tsa? nunurawu̱tu̱.** The Comanches ran off one by one.

nunura?wu̱?, nunurakwu̱ (n) movie (that which runs and runs).

nuraakitʉ (v) come running. **Situu siʔana nuraakii.** These came running here somewhere.

nʉ (pro, 1st excl gen sg) my.

nʉbawʉhtiawapi (n) baptizer (one who baptizes).

nʉbawʉhtiarʉ (v) baptize someone.

nʉe (pro 1st acc sg) me.

nʉemaitʉ (v) cease blowing, become calm.

nʉena (n) wind. **Ma nʉena tsaʔ aitʉ.** The wind is not good.

Nʉena (name) Wind (person).

Nʉenuhkiki (name) Wind-running-here (woman's name).

nʉepi (n) tornado, wind storm. **Nʉepi tsaʔ tamʉku kimarʉ.** The storm is coming to us.

nʉetʉ (v) blow (as wind). **Kʉhta ma nʉetʉ.** The wind is blowing hard.

Nʉetʉtsi (name) Blowing-wind (person).

nʉetʉ (n) wind, breeze.

nʉhkana W, **nʉhkarʉ** K (n) powwow, dance.

nʉhkarʉ (v) dance. **Tai nʉhka-ruʔika.** Let's dance (3:8).

nʉhkiʔapʉ (n) a cut.

nʉhmabina (n) descendants.

nʉhpopiʔ, nʉhpopiwiyaaʔ (n) jumping rope.

nʉhtsikwarʉ (v) labor in childbirth, body pain. **Nʉ nape tsaʔ nʉhtsowarʉ.** My foot is hurting (paining me). *See* **nʉʉtsikwarʉ.**

nʉkuwʉmiʔarʉ (v) clabber, curdle.

nʉkuʔwʉpʉ (n) clabber. **pitsipʉha nʉkuʔwʉpʉ** clabbered milk. *See* **nʉtsʉʔwʉpa pitsipʉ.**

nʉkʉta (n) goose, *pl* **nʉkʉtanʉʉ** geese.

nʉkʉrʉ (v) dance. **Surʉʉ kʉseʔ nʉkʉbʉniyʉ.** They danced much.

nʉmamoʔoʔ (n) raccoon. *See* **paruukuʔ.**

nʉmi (pro, 1st pl excl acc) us, people.

nʉmi booʔetʉ W (n) camera. *See* **pʉhtu kunʉmʉ tʉbooʔena, kobenaboʔ.**

nʉmi himaʔetʉ (n) policeman, sheriff, lawman (*lit* one who catches us). *See* **tʉʉhtamʉh raiboʔ.**

nʉmi makwinumaʔetʉ pahmu (n) marijuana cigarette.

nʉmi makwinumaʔetʉʔ (n) marijuana (*lit* that which makes us dizzy).

nʉmi nipʉkaʔ K (n) fortuneteller [**nʉmi-** us + **nipʉ-** tell fortunes + **-ʔ** (nom sg)]. *See* **nipʉkaaʔeetʉ.**

nʉmi nooʔetʉ, nʉnʉmi nooʔetʉʉ (n) bus, taxi (*lit* that which carries people on its back).

nʉmi tsaʔʉbʉikʉʔeetʉ (n) ether (*lit* that which makes people sleep).

nʉmirʉ (v), *pl* **yʉkarʉ** able to walk, move around (as a child learning or a person who has been ill).

nʉmʉ (pro, 1st pl excl gen) our; *n* The Comanche People, *pl* **Nʉmʉnʉʉ.** (Whites use the alternate names **Nʉmʉ, Nʉʉmʉ, Nerm, Nimma.**)

nʉmʉ haahkanaʔ (n), *pl* **nʉmʉ nahkanʉʉ** family, relatives.

nʉmʉ hani (n) maize, Indian corn, squaw corn (blue kernel with long, narrow cob). *Zea mays* L. *See* **haniibi.**

nʉmʉ kuhtsuʔ (n) buffalo (*lit* our cow).

nʉmʉ kuhtsuʔ

nʉmʉ maʔtsaʔbahkiʔ (n) lizard (clings to skin).

nʉmʉ narʉmʉʉʔ (n) trading post, Indian store.

nʉmʉ nohkopʉ (n) Indian corncake, biscuit.

nʉmʉ paraiboʔ (n) Indian agent.

nʉmʉ renahpʉʔ (n) Comanche man.

nʉmʉ tsuhni (n) Comanche bones [nʉmʉ our + tsuhni bones].

nʉmʉwahtʉ (n) prairie (open, uninhabited land). See pʉhʉwahtʉ.

nʉmʉ kutsu tʉhkapʉ (n) buffalo meat. **Nʉmʉ kuhtsu tʉhkapʉ tsaʔ tʉhkarʉ.** I eat buffalo meat.

nʉmʉkʉni, nʉmʉ kahni (n) teepee, skins or other covering for teepees (*lit* our dwelling).

nʉmʉnainaʔ (n) life (must occur with possessor). **nʉ nʉmʉnainaʔ** my life, **ta nʉmʉnainaʔ** anyone's life.

nʉmʉnaitʉ (v) acculturate as a Comanche (live as a Comanche).

nʉmʉnakarʉ (v) own a home.

nʉmʉ napʉ (n) moccasin (*lit* our shoe). See taʔseʔyukʉʔ.

nʉmʉnetʉ (v) dwell, live somewhere.

nʉmʉ rekwakʉ wapi (n) interpreter of Comanche. See tekwakʉ wapi.

nʉmʉ ruaitʉ (v) Comanche-born. **Tuinʉhpʉ tsaʔ nʉmʉ ruai.** A Comanche baby boy was born.

Nʉmʉ ruibetsʉ (name) She-invites-her-relatives (person).

nʉmʉ ruibihtsiʔ (n) Comanche young man.

nʉmʉ rʉborapʉ K (n) present generation (present living ones; *lit* our born-ones). See pʉhkʉra nahanʉ, ʉkʉ nʉmʉnʉʉ.

nʉmʉ rʉborarʉ (adj) procreated by us (born of Comanche parents).

nʉmʉ rʉhorapʉ (n) creation (**lit** created from heaven).

nʉmʉ rʉsaasi (n) Comanche perfume plant (leaves are used as perfume). See tʉsaasi.

nʉmʉʔaraʔ (n voc) lover (used between parties to an extra-marital affair).

nʉna wʉhtʉpʉkaʔ (n) buckle.

nʉna karʉkʉʔ K (n) brooch (ornament worn on chest).

Nʉnapi (n) little people similar to elves.

nʉnapʉ (n) chest (of the body).

nʉnatsiʔnikaʔ (n) jewelry (pinned on or with a stickpin).

nʉníhkoonirʉ (v) send word to someone to return.

nʉnipʉkarʉ (v) guess, tell fortunes. See nipʉkarʉ.

nʉnoorʉ (v) carry on back.

nʉnʉ (pro, 1st pl excl nom) we.

nʉnʉ pʉhiʔ, nʉnʉphi (n) midget, troll (lives in rocky hill). See pʉe tʉyaaiʔ.

nʉnʉbetʉ (adj) fit (proper size). **Nʉ napʉ tsaʔ nʉnʉbetʉ.** My shoes fit.

nʉnʉmʉni tʉhtsʉ (adv man) badly, wrong. **Nʉnʉmʉni tʉhtsʉ ʉnʉ** hina haniyu. You really do things wrongly.

nɨnɨʔitɨ (v) stop following someone, slow down what one is doing.

nɨnɨʔyɨwiʔ W, nɨnɨyɨʔwoʔ K (n) alligator (lit that which swallows people).

nɨpetsɨʔ (n) wife. Nɨpetsɨʔa pitɨi u. He brought the girl (wife) home.

nɨpetsɨʔitɨ (v) get engaged to be married, lead away a wife, get married. Orɨ tsaʔ nɨpetsɨi. He is getting married.

nɨpɨkapɨ K, N, W (n) grave.

nɨpɨkapɨ K, W (n) graveyard.

nɨpɨkarɨ (v) bury someone. Nɨ nɨbahaʔa nɨpɨkai. I buried my nephew.

nɨpɨkarɨɨʔ (n) funeral, burial ceremony.

nɨpɨkɨ sokoobi (n) cemetery, graveyard.

nɨrɨaʔwekɨʔ, nɨrɨahwekɨʔ (n) bride (one who has been given away in marriage).

nɨtsɨʔwɨpa pitsipɨ K (n) buttermilk, clabbered milk. See nɨkuʔwɨpɨ.

nɨtɨhyoi wapi, nɨtɨhyɨi wapi (n) messenger, angel.

nɨɨsihwaʔitɨ (v) tear skin.

nɨɨbanikatɨ (v, hum subj) lean against something.

nɨɨhkiʔyuʔitɨ (v) mutilate oneself, hack oneself (self-mutilation in mourning death of a loved one).

nɨɨhkupatɨ (v) trip and fall. See nɨɨhpisiʔmaitɨ.

nɨɨhkwitubitɨ (v) wrap around and around (as yarn on a ball).

nɨɨhpisiʔmaitɨ (v) trip and fall. See nɨɨhkupatɨ.

nɨɨhtamiʔitɨ (adj) wrapped and tied up.

nɨɨhtaʔneerɨ (v) brush something off of oneself.

nɨɨhtokaʔeʔ (n) muscle (lit that of oneself which is cut; refers to ancient custom of self-mutilation for the dead).

nɨɨhtonitɨ (v) strut, display (mating ritual of animals).

nɨɨhtoʔitɨ (v) mount on horseback.

nɨɨhtsiʔaitɨ (v) split of own accord.

nɨɨhtɨmaʔ (n) fence.

nɨɨhtɨpikaʔ (n) button, harness buckle.

nɨɨhtɨʔekaʔ (n) petroleum jelly, personal ointment. See tsiʔwɨnɨɨ tɨʔekaʔ.

nɨɨhɨhtsaʔwɨʔ (n) fan (of any kind; lit that with which to make oneself feel cool).

nɨɨkiʔaitɨ (v) cut oneself.

nɨɨkitseʔ (n) a bruise.

nɨɨkɨnarɨ (v) cover over (place cover over the top of something).

nɨɨkwenitɨ (v) hang oneself.

nɨɨkwitsɨnarɨ (v) twist oneself. See kwitsunairɨ.

nɨɨminaitɨ (v) break bone (arm or leg).

nɨɨmiʔakɨrɨ (v) operate manually (as lawnmower or wheelbarrow). See mamiʔakɨtɨ.

nɨɨmɨ (n) liver (requires possessor). nɨ nɨɨmɨmy liver, u nɨɨmɨ marɨkwɨ two livers.

nɨɨpearɨ (v, sg obj), pl obj nɨɨpiyuʔitɨ chip off (one, many chips).

nuupịtuaʔ (n) sash, band (for supporting baby on back).

nuupurusuanupuru (v) unravel something.

nuupurusuaru (v) unravel of own accord. *See* **purusuʔaru**.

nuuputsapu (n) surgery, surgical operation.

nuusooʔ, nuusoo kahni (n) canvas tent.

nuusooʔetu (v) hang over something, lean over something.

nuusukatu (adj) puny, sickly.

nuutiʔakatu (v) spill of own accord.

nuutiʔaru (v) spill something.

nuutsikwaru K (v) ache, give pain (with aching member as subject). **Nu papi tsaʔ nuutsikwaru.** My head aches (*lit* my head aches). *See* **nuhtsikwaru**.

nuutsukeʔ (n) haircut.

nuutsuketu (v) get a haircut.

nuutsukunaru (adj) tied up.

nuuʔkwipunaru (v) twist oneself around something.

nuuʔmaitu (v) tire out, become lazy.

nuuʔnuaru (v) rise from seated position.

nuuʔwikeetu (v) shake something off. *See* **suutaʔniʔaru**.

nuʔ (pro, 1st nom sg) I.

nuʔunehkị K (n) belt (for waist).

nuʔuhpeeʔ (n) baseball.

nuʔunehkiʔa nanuutupịkaʔ W (n) belt buckle.

nuʔunehkịkatuʔ (adj) belted, sash (*lit* wearing something around the waist).

O

obutuma? (n) upriver.

oha- (pfx) ref. to yellow color.

ohaahnakatu W (n) fox, coyote (*lit* yellow under arms). **Ohaahnakatu uruuku pitunu.** Coyote arrived among them (3:3). *See* **kuʔkwuriaʔ**.

ohaekapitu (adj) orange (*lit* yellow-red). **W** (n) bay horse (light bay color). *See* **ekaohapitu, ohapituu**.

ohaekaʔ K (n) bay horse (light bay color).

ohahuupi (n) osage orange, bois d'arc tree. Maclura pomifera (Raf.) Schneider (bows manufactured from branches; roots used in treatment of eye disease).

ohahukwunikatu, oha huwuni? (adj) early, before dawn, early dawn (*lit* yellow horizon).

ohanunapu W (n) field lark, meadowlark. Sturnella (*lit* yellow breast). *See* **hiitoo?**.

ohawaikịna (n) streetcar, trolley (*lit* yellow wagon).

Ohawasápe (name) Yellow-bear (Comanche chief).

Ohawunu (name) Yellow-steps (person).

ohahkuyaaʔ (n) king in playing-card deck (*lit* yellow head holding; for crown on king's head).

ohahpitu suku?kamatu W (n) lemon (*lit* yellow sour-tasting).

ohahpiyaaʔ (n) bumblebee (*lit* carrying yellow on its back).

ohahpokopi K, ohapitu pokopi W (n) domestic carrot (*lit* yellow fruit).

ohahpuhihwi (n) copper (*lit* yellow metal).

ohahtuhkapu (n) domestic carrot.

ohakuhtsuni (n) yellow fever.

Ohapia (name) Bay-mare (person).

ohapi (adj) yellow.

ohapi, ohape (n, acc) watermelon (yellow variety).

ohapituu, ohapitua pokopi (n) orange (citrus fruit). *See* **ohaekapitu**.

ohápituu?a taka? W (n) grapefruit (*lit* kinsman of orange). *See* **pia ohapitu**.

Ohapitu kwahi (name) Yellow-back (person).

ohasuhuubi (n) black willow. *Salix nigra* Marsh (*lit* yellow willow; for yellow tinge of bark; ashes used to treat sore eyes).

ohayaa? (n) sunflower. *Helianthus* sp. (yellow flower of any kind).

ohinibetutu (adv dir) left (to the left). *See* **tubitsi petutu**.

ohinikatu (adj) left-handed. *See* **tubitsikatu**.

ohininakwu (adv loc) at or to the left side. *See* **tubitsinakwu**.

ohka, ohko (pro dem, dist acc sg) him, her.

ohnáakuno? (n) cradle (*lit* baby container).

ohna?a noruhnaa? (n) baby crib, baby bed.

ohna?a? (n) baby (girl or boy).

ohnitu (v) cough.

ohpepu (n) tear.

ohpeto?ikaru (v) eyes water, tears flow.

ohta- (pfx) ref. to dirt, soil.

ohta kahni W (n) storm cellar, adobe house, cyclone cellar (*lit* dirt house). *See* **sekwikuni**.

ohtakatu (adj) earth-covered (as a cellar).

ohtapii (n) dirt, soil.

ohútuki, ohútukoi (n) flank (animal side; part from which Comanches remove sinew for sewing hides).

oihtuyaitu (v) choke to death by rope around the neck. *See* **tsa?oibehkatu**.

okweetu (v) flow. **Hunu?bi tsa? kuhta okwetu.** The river flowed fast.

okwèetu (n) creek, stream, small river. *See* **hunu?bi?**.

okwehkwatu (v) float away. **Taa tuhkapuruku tsa? okwehkwa?i.** Our meat floated away (123:24). *See* **sumu okwetu**.

omo-, oomo (n) lower leg (from the knee down).

omotoi (n) pipe stem (straight leg bone used as stem).

ona- (pfx) ref. to salt.

Onawai (name) Salt-worn-out (person).

onaabi (n) salt.

ona?aitu (v) salt something (*lit* make to be salty). **Tuhkapuha onaa?aitu nu?.** I salted the food.

Ononuu, Ohnonuu (n) Hill People (Comanche band that lived in area of Cyril, Okla.)

ono?itu (adj), *pl* o?onokawutu crooked. **Pu?e tsa? ono?itu.** The path (is) crooked.

ooibehkaru (v) hang someone with a rope.

ooyoru tahna (n) drawer, dresser drawer. *See* **na?wosa**.

oo?itu (v) vomit.

oo?ru W, **o?yoru** K, N (n), *acc pl* **oo?ri** clothing, apparel, belongings of any type. **Maruu oo?ru o?okwenuna.** Their clothes were floating (122:19).

oo?ru kahni W, **o?yoru kahni** K (n) clothes closet.

oo?ru tani?i?, o?yoru tahna? (n) bureau (for clothes), chest of drawers.

oo?ru tohtsana? W (n) clothes hanger.

oo?ru tutsihtu?ye? W, **o?yoru natsihtuye?** K (n) clothes brush.

oo?ru tohtsani?i?ana huuhpi (n) clothesline pole.

oru (pro dem, 3rd dist nom sg) he, she, it.

otu- (pfx) K beige, brown; W brown. *See* **otupitu.**

otuhtu mapo?akatu (adj) brown-skinned.

otupitu (adj) K beige; W brown.

otu aawo (n) bottle (*lit* brown container).

otu kamaitu (v) bland (taste neither sweet nor sour).

otu kuma? W (n) sorrel horse, chestnut-brown horse.

Otu kwasu (name) Brown-robe (person).

otu kwasukuru (v) brown the food, cook something brown (well done; almost burned).

otu mitsonaa? (n) soapberry (*lit* brown blackberry). *Sapindus Drummondii* H. and A. (stems used for making arrows for aratsi game).

otu nohkopu W (n) cookies (*lit* brown biscuits). *See* **pihná nohkopu.**

otu peena (n) wasp, yellow jacket (*lit* brown sugar-eaters).

otu pihnàa? W (n) brown sugar.

otu suakatu (adj) stingy (*lit* think brown).

otu tohtía? (n) cookie (gingersnap(s); *lit* brown bread).

owóora (n) tree trunk (main body of the tree).

oyo-, oyu, oyètu, oyo?ko (num) all.

oyóotu? (n) parfleche, meat bag (bag made of rawhide).

oyoru tumaru (v) buy clothing.

oyo?ru ka?wekitu (adj) above everything, more than anything.

oyo?rutu (adv loc) throughout a location.

o?oo? (n) owl (horned or long-eared).

o?yu?su (adv time) every time.

P

pa- W (pfx) ref. to water.

paa (n) water. *See* **tuupu.**

paa kua?etu (v) drip water. **Nu pui tsa? paa kua?eetu.** My eye waters (once in a while).

paa ma?ibu?ikutu K (v) fill with water. *See* **ibu?ikuru, pawusa?naitu.**

paa mutsaa? (n) bend in river (*lit* water's elbow).

Paa roponi (name) See-how-deep-the-water-is (person).

paa tsoko (n) otter [**paa** water + **tsoko-** old one].

Paa tsokotubutu (name) Black-otter (person).

Paa tso?ko (name) Otter (*lit* water-old; person).

paa tupunaatu? W, **paa tupunaatu** K (n) island.

paabitsanitʉ (v) strangle on water, choke. *See* **pitsanitʉ**.

paai, pai, bai (n) vein.

paaka, paka (n) arrow.

paakipʉ, pahkipʉ (n) dried cowhide, leather.

paanʉ (n) loaf of bread.

paapasi, papasi (n) wild potato, Irish potato. *Convolvulaceae* (tuber eaten raw or cooked).

paapi (n) head. *See* **papi-**.

paasitsi (n) sleet (*lit* water sailing).

pabiʔ (n) elder brother.

pabo- (pfx) clear, transparent.

pabo taibooʔ (n) white man.

pabo tuhku (n) hindquarter, light meat, thigh meat.

pabokaʔaitʉ (adj) clear (as glass).

paboko, pabokohi (n) large intestine (*lit* light or clear intestine).

paboko aawo (n) drinking glass, jar, vase, bottle.

pabokopitʉ (adj) crystal clear, transparent (free from cloudiness or stain).

pabokoʔai

pabokoʔai (n) lizard (timber variety).

pabopitʉ (adj) blond, light-complected. **Waipʉ tsa? pabopitʉ.** The woman has a light complexion. *name* **Pabopitʉ** Light-complected (person).

paha piahpʉ (n) sister-in-law (of a woman).

pahabitʉ (v), *pl* **pakwabitʉ** bathe, swim. **Pibia kwasinaboo? mawakatu pakwabihkwaina.** Big snakes are swimming around toward her (52:18). *See* **tapʉhabi**.

pahabi aawo (n) bathtub (*lit* swimming container).

pahabi kahni W (n) bathroom.

pahaʔ (n) father's sister; woman's brother's child (either sex).

pahibahtʉ (adj) three separated groups. **Pahibahku nʉ? marahniʔi.** I laid them out in three separate piles.

pahibahtʉnʉnʉ (n) three separate families, three groups of people.

pahihtʉ (adj) three.

pahitʉ (v), *pl* **yumarʉ** fall off, be born, drop off (as leaves from a tree).

pahki wiyaaʔ (n) rawhide rope.

pahkipʉ (n) rawhide ready to use. *See* **ʉhtaayuʔ**.

pahmo namahya (n) sumac (*lit* tobacco mixer). *Anacardiaceae* sp. (mixed with tobacco to smoke; cannot be smoked alone; clears sinuses).

pahmu (n) tobacco.

pahnaʔaitʉ (v) treat with respect. **Sʉmʉʔa pahnaʔaitʉ.** He treats someone with respect.

paho ʉmarʉ, pahoopi (n) hail.

pahorapʉ (n) water well, well.

pahparatsihkweetʉ W (adj) bright, shiny.

pahparatsihkwetʉ tʉʉpi (n) diamond (*lit* shiny stone).

pahpatsohkitʉ (v) drip.

pahtsi (adj) smooth, slick.

pahtsi bapikatʉ K (adj) bald headed (*lit* smooth headed).

pahtsi kaburuu? (n) slick-haired goat (*lit* smooth goat).

Pahtsi ketu (name) Smooth (person).

pahtsi ku?e (n) bald head (*lit* smooth top).

pahtsi kwasi (n) opossum (*lit* slick tail).

pahtsi kwasi tukahpu (n) mulberries (*lit* opossum food).

pahtsi mubitai, paatsi mubitai? (n) hickory (*lit* smooth walnut; used for barbecuing).

pahtsi no?itu (v) pluck a bird clean of feathers. *See* **puhu no?itu.**

pahtsi okwe? (n) clear stream (*lit* clear-flowing; spring-fed stream).

pai (n, acc) water. *See* **paa.**

paihtsi (adj) shrunken. **Paihtsi ma? nahai pumi nu kotsehka.** When I washed it, it shrank.

Pai paka pia huna? (n) Pedernales River (*lit* arrowhead river; riverbed contains flint for making arrowheads).

pai tusi?itu K (v) spit out liquid. *See* **tusitu.**

paiyapi (n) plant with edible fruit (name unknown; grows in Apache, Okla. area; seeds not swallowed; roots roasted or boiled and eaten).

paka tuu?ru? (n) dragonfly (*lit* stretches itself arrow-like).

Pakawa (name) Kills-something (person).

pakawkoko?, pakokoko (n) prairie chicken.

pakeeso, pakeetso (n) purple prairie clover. *Petalostemum purpureum* (Vent.) Rydb. (roots chewed have sweet taste).

Pakekuni, Pake kahni (name) Dry-teepee (person).

pakuyu?atu (adj) lukewarm.

paku?neru (v) duck head under water. *See* **tsahpaaku?nikaru.**

pakunaikatu (adj) foggy. *See* **kwiisuatu.**

pakuuka (n) wild onion, swamp weed (*lit* water onion). *Allium* sp. (bulbs roasted and eaten).

paku?nuapu, pakunaipu (n) fog.

pakusiiwunuru (v) drool.

pakwaruhtukitu W (v) gargle (with water or other liquid). *See* **wuhkwaru?rukitu.**

pakwa?nuaru (v) splash into water.

pakwihtsikuru, pawihtsikuru (v) splash water on, dampen.

pakwu?su?mitu (adj) filled with water by drinking. *See* **wutsu?mitu.**

pamukwaru?rukitu (v) bubble in water, make bubbles.

pamuputso?ni, pamuputsoo?nipu (n) swamp.

panaaitu (v) praise (speak well of; personal object obligatory). *See* **nihpana aitu.**

panaaitu (adj) proud.

panatsayaa? (n) blackberry, raspberry.

panatsitoo? (n) oar, canoe paddle (*lit* water stick).

panihputu mabà?atu (adj) high, tall (*lit* upward long).

panimi?aru (v) take someone home as guest, escort a guest some place. **Sumu?a panimi?ai.** He took someone home.

Papitsimina? (n), *pl* **Papitsimina-nuu** Sioux people.

papi (n) head (including face and hair). **Meekuru nu papiba?a**

to?i. Now climb up on my head
(19:12). *See* **paapi̱.**

papi̱ hʉnʉpoʔa, papi boʔa (n) scalp
(*lit* head skin).

papi̱ kuʔe̱ (n) scalp (*lit* head top).

papi̱ tsaʔnikaʔ (n) wig (*lit* to put on
the head).

papi̱ tsihtʉpʉkaʔ (n) hairpin,
barrette, bobby pin.

papi̱ tsiʔnikaʔ (n) side comb (*lit* to
put in the hair).

papi̱ tsʉnʉʔitʉ (v) tangled hair.

papi̱ wihtʉʔekaʔ (n) hair tonic (*lit*
hair grease).

papi̱ wʉnʉkatʉ (adj) headache.

papi̱ wʉi htamaʔ (n) otter, mink (*lit*
bundled head).

papi̱kamaitʉ (v) have a headache.
Papi̱kamai nʉʔ kʉtʉ. I had a
headache yesterday.

papi̱kamaka natʉsuʔu (n) aspirin
(*lit* headache medicine).

papoosinʉ (adj) soaked thoroughly,
rotting.

papʉsipʉ (adj) rotten. **KokoraʔaР
noyo tsaʔ papʉsipʉ.** The egg was
rotten.

papʉsitʉ (v) rot (become rotten).
Kokoraʔa noyo tsaʔ papʉsituʔi.
The egg will turn rotten.

papʉtsipitʉ (adj) naked.

paraibo (n) peace chief (family
headman who could become
peace chief for the band).

paraibooʔ (n) chief, officer, agent,
chief wife among multiple wives,
stepmother.

paraimoʔo (n) mole (*lit* upside-
down hands).

paratsihkweʔerʉ (v), *pl* **paratsih-
kweyutʉ** glitter, shimmer.

parawa sʉkʉ (n) late-summer plum.

paroʔikitʉ (v) rise, swell (as a
river or creek). **Hunuʔbi tsaʔ
paroʔikitʉ.** The creek is rising.
See **atabaroʔitʉ.**

paruaitʉ (v) flood (cover dry area
with water).

paruhparʉ (v) paddle hands in the
water, dog paddle (*lit* slap water).
See **masuʔwaʔnekitʉ.**

Parukaa, Padouka (n) Comanches
(Siouan name for the Comanche
people).

paruukuʔ, paʔruhkuʔ (n) raccoon,
coon. *See* **nʉmamoʔoʔ.**

Paruwa kuma̱ (name) Bull-elk (war
chief of the Antelope Band).

Paruwa sʉmʉno (name) Ten-elks
(person).

paruʔitʉ (v) flood the riverbank,
overflow the creek bed.
Hunuʔbi tsaʔ paruʔi. The creek
overflowed. *See* **muruʔitʉ.**

parʉa, parʉabi, parʉʉabi (n)
rough-leafed dogwood. *Cornus
asperifolia* Michx. (crossgrain
wood used for making arrow
shafts).

Parʉa kuhma (name) Bull-bear
(strong, fierce man who broke a
black bear's neck with his bare
hands).

parʉa kuhma, parʉʉhya kuhma
(n) bull elk (*lit* male water horse).

parʉa sʉkʉiʔ (n) plum, plum tree.
Prunus sp. (fruit eaten fresh or
dried; dried for later use). *See*
sʉkʉʔi̱, yusʉkʉ.

parʉbooʔ, parʉbooʔa tʉboʔ (n) ink
pen (*lit* water-writer).

parʉbʉʉʔitʉ (v) soak through (as
water through cloth).

parʉhwimiʔarʉ (v) melt away.

parʉhwitʉ (v) melt.

parʉkitʉ (v) soak in water (for period of time).

parʉkwihtsipʉ (n, pl) sg **sʉʉkɪ** switches (as willow twigs, young and tender). **Sitʉ waʔihpʉ? tʉrʉeh parʉkwihtsipʉha u matsʉbakiʔetʉ.** This woman sticks it on a little switch.

parʉtsohpeʔ (n) spring, spring water.

parʉʉtsɪ (n) chin.

pasahòo (n) pigeon, dove, wren. *See* **kuʔe wóoʔ.**

pasahtahtʉkitʉ W (v), *pl* **pasah-tahniʔitʉ** set out to dry, sit in the sun to dry. *See* **mabasahtʉkitʉ.**

pasahtohtsanarʉ (v) hang up to dry.

pasakʉrʉ (v) dry something.

pasanuarʉ (v) recede (go down, as creek after rising).

pasapuni (n) cross-eyed person.

pasapʉ (n) dry object.

pasarʉ (v) dry off body, dry out (as wet clothes). *See* **tʉbitsibasarʉ.**

Pasawío (name) Big-green-frog (Comanche name for one of E. Canonge's daughters).

pasawíʔoo? (n) frog. *See* **pohpi kwáaiʔ, ebi muura yaʔkeʔ.**

pasawiʔooʔa hʉkiʔaiʔ (n) mushroom (*lit* frog shade).

pasi waapɪ (n) sand, fine gravel.

pasibunarʉ (v) sprinkle (rain), shower (light rain).

Pasiwa huunuʔbi, Pasi hunuʔbi (n) Sand Creek.

pasiwanoorʉ (v) haul sand.

pasiwanooʔ W, **pasiwanookatʉ** K (n) sand dune, sand hill.

pasiwona pʉhʉbi, pasiwʉnuʔ bohoobi (n) silvery wormwood.

Artemesia filifolia Torr (velvet-like leaf used as toilet tissue; in bulk used as cushion in teepee or mattress in childbirth).

pasiwʉnʉʉrʉ (v) leak (running in a steady stream).

pasokoʔarʉ (v, sg obj), *pl obj* **pasokooʔitʉ** cover with earth, bury (as in planting potatoes).

pati- (pfx) green.

patiwiaketʉ, patuiwiakeetʉ (adj) green (moss-colored).

patowoʔnepʉ (n) eroded soil, washout.

patowoʔnerʉ (v) wash out earth, erode.

patsahtoʔitʉ (v) pump water (as with a hand pump).

patsahtoʔiʔ (n) windmill, water pump (*lit* make water go up).

patsanuarʉ (v) channel water (by ditches or dam).

patsaʔaikʉ, paatsaʔaikʉ? (n) water pump, pump [**paa** water + **tsaʔaikʉ?** pumper].

patsiketʉ (adj) slick, smooth.

patsiʔ (n) eldest sister. **nʉbatsi** my eldest sister.

patsoʔ, patsokwe (n) mesquite-leaf mixture (mixed with other material having good flavor).

patsoʔitʉ (adj) damp, wet. *See* **paʔɪsoketʉ.**

patʉ tsanitʉ (v), *pl* **patʉ tsaniʔerʉ** snagged (as along water's edge).

patʉrʉyaitʉ (v), *pl* **patʉkooitʉ** drown.

pawahkapʉ (n) herb (name unknown; grows near creeks).

pawobi puukʉ W, **pawobi** K (n) boat, canoe [**paa** water + **wobi** board + **puukʉ** horse].

pawuhpaʔitu (v) splash with water, beat on someone with watery object.

pawuhtia wapi (n) baptizer (one who baptizes).

pawuhtumapu (n) dam (*lit* water banked up).

pawunuaru (v) scrub.

pawunua? (n) mop [**paa** water + **wunuai** sweep].

pawupaʔitu (v) paddle feet in water (as when swimming).

pawuʔweʔniitu (adj) sprayed with water.

pawusaʔnaitu W (v) fill with water. *See* **ibuʔikuru, paa maʔibuʔikutu.**

payaape, payapi (n) aqueous, wild tuber (grows above water, producing rich-flavored, potato-like tubers in clusters, each about three inches long). *See* **ahwepu.**

payunitu (v) water something, pour water on (from container).

payuʔyukatu (adj) softened. *See* **yuʔyukaru.**

paʔa- (pfx) long.

paʔa toyokatu huutsuu? K, paʔati toyopukatu huhtsuu? W (n) crane (bird), stork (*lit* long- neck bird). *See* **kusikwaʔaa?.**

paʔabeʔnuu (n) triplets.

paʔarai, paʔrai (adv loc) upside down, on opposite side, on back.

paʔarai moʔo (n) woodchuck.

paʔa ruyu?, paʔa toʔayo? (n) giraffe (*lit* long neck).

paʔasu, paʔatusu, paʔatsu (adj) shallow (not deep or thick, as depth of chair or height of stairstep).

paʔatu (adj) long, high.

paʔboosi? (n) water lizard, water dog.

paʔekusahpana? (n) sailor (*lit* water soldier).

paʔibuikatu (adj) water-filled.

paʔikaru (v), *pl* **paaʔkwekwi** sink to the bottom in water. **Suru huupi paʔikaai u?.** That log sank.

paʔisokeru (v) sprinkle, dampen (as clothes to iron). *See* **piʔwuʔwenitu.**

paʔitsiʔwunuru (adj) short (in stature; *lit* stand short).

paʔisoketu, paʔisoki (adj) wet, soaked. **Aawo tsa? paʔisoki.** The cup got wet. *See* **mabaʔisokitu, patsoʔitu.**

paʔituhtsi? (adj) short (in length).

paʔkwakume, paa kwakume (n) snapping turtle. *Chelydra serpentina* (lives in rivers and streams). *See* **kwasi nuruuʔwu?.**

paʔmukusuʔaru (v) sprout. **Pihuura tsa? paʔmukusuʔai.** The beans sprouted.

paʔmutsi (n) plant similar to water lily (name unknown; root eaten raw or cooked; have rich, sweet taste).

paʔmutsi?, paʔmutsia (n) saddle (made of animal hip bones covered with wet rawhide which dries to shape; loops gird horse) [**paʔa** high + **mutsi** pointed]. *See* **tumuhku.**

paʔokwetu (v) eyes water heavily, shed many tears. **Nu pui tsa? paʔokweetu.** My eyes are watering heavily.

paʔpuhi tuhka? (n) celery.

paʔraihabiitu (v) lie on back. **Situ tenahpu? pu norunapuka**

pa?araihabiitṳ. This man is lying on his back in his bed (99:10).

pa?sa ponii, pa?sah ponii (n) acorn.

pa?sa ponii huupi (n) oak. *Quercus* sp. (acorns eaten; trunks used for fence posts).

pa?sonipṳ (n) weeds.

pa?sṳno?a?, pa?asṳno?a? (n) kangaroo (*lit* shallow pregnancy).

pa?wṳhtakóo? (n) tadpole.

pa?wṳhtaràa?, pakwṳhtaràa? (n) scaffold (from which to hang water containers).

pa?wṳhtṳma? (n) beaver (*lit* makes dams).

pa?wṳtiarṳ (v, sg obj), **pl obj pawṳ?weniitṳ** baptize (pour water on someone); spray water on something (pour water here and there or in one spot).

pa?wṳtṳ (v) dam up (body of water).

pehe, huupipehe (n) seed.

pehkarṳ (v), *pl* **wasṳpṳ** kill. **Ihka nṳ? tṳhṳye pehkatṳ.** I am killing this horse. *See* **tṳkṳwasṳ?.**

peko?arṳ (v) split open, part (as clouds).

pekwi pṳmata hṳarṳ (n) fish trap.

Pekwi tṳhka (n) Fish Eaters (Comanche band said to have become a separate band around 1200 A.D.)

pekwi tṳhka?, pekwi tṳhka? huutsu (n) kingfisher. *Alcedinidae.*

pekwipṳ (adj) swollen. **kṳ?itsi pekwipṳ** swollen throat. **Nṳ ku?itsi tsa? pekwikatṳ.** My tonsils are swollen.

pekwitṳ (v) swell. **U nape tsa? pekwitu?i.** His feet are going to swell. **Pekwikatṳ ma?.** It is swollen.

pekwitṳ, peekwi (n), *pl* **sootṳ peekwi** fish (general term). **sooka?wṳkatṳ** school of fish. **Pekwi nṳ? tsapietṳ.** I am fishing.

Pena tṳhka (n) Sugar Eaters, Honey Eaters (southern-most Comanche band before and during the migration).

Penanṳṳ (n) Sugar Eaters (Comanche band now at Spur, Okla. and in northern Okla.)

pepịkurṳ (n) casino.

pesotái (n) buttonbush. *Cephalanthus occidentalis* L. (wood used to make lacrosse sticks).

peti- (v) drop (let fall).

petihtarṳ (v) throw away, dispose of. **Ma petihtai nṳ?.** I threw it away. *See* **wihtaitṳ.**

petsṳ kwarṳ (v) invite to go along.

petsṳ mi?arṳ (v) fetch, go to get.

petsṳ pitarṳ (v) go after (to bring back to point of origin).

petṳ toyapṳ K (n) adopted daughter (*lit* daughter to carry).

petṳboopṳ W (n) adopted daughter [**petṳ** daughter + **tṳboopṳ** paper].

petṳ? (n) daughter.

pia (n) mother, mother's sister.

pia (adj) big, large, loud. **Su?ana u pia pṳhṳwahtṳkṳ tṳrikuu?nṳṳ sookṳniba?ị.** Somewhere there in the big prairie, prairie dogs had a town.

pia animui (n) horsefly (*lit* large fly).

pia pṳku rekwarṳ (v) shout (raise voice louder than ordinary speech).

pia utsaatʉ (adv man) piled badly, disorderly in placement. **Itʉ tsa? aiku pia utsaatʉ.** This thing is badly piled.

Pia ʉtsʉ?i mʉa (n) December (*lit* big cold month).

pia baa (n) ocean (*lit* large water).

Pia baa (name) Big-water (Comanche chief who attempted to negotiate prisoner exchange in San Antonio in 1840).

Pia buha rabenḭ (n) Fourth of July (*lit* big Sunday).

piabʉ (n) female animal. **kabʉrʉ?a piabʉ** female goat (a nanny goat).

pia huutsuu? (n) eagle (*lit* large bird).

pia huyubatʉ (adj) oblong. *See* **huyuba?atʉ.**

pia kahúa (n), *pl* **pibia kahúu** rat, field mouse (*lit* large mouse).

pia kuitsi? (n) adam's apple (*lit* big throat). *See* **kuitsḭ tʉkwʉni.**

pia kʉsarʉ (v) open mouth wide.

pia kwihnai (n) eagle. *See* **kwihnai.**

Pia mʉa (n) July (large month; shortened form of name). *See* **Pʉmata pia buhha ra?ena mʉa.**

Pia nʉ?ʉpai?i (n) Big-whip (whip-holder at a dance who had the special privilege of stopping a dance to recite a coup; similar to a master of ceremonies).

pia ohapitʉ K (n) grapefruit (*lit* large yellow). *See* **ohápḭtʉʉ?ataka?.**

Pia opʉ, Pi?opʉ (name) (Chief captured by Coronado in 1540.)

Pia pasi hunu?bi (n) Red River (*lit* large sand creek).

pia pʉhʉ re?tsi (n) tarantula (*lit* large fuzzy brother-in-law). *See* **pʉhʉ re?tsḭ.**

Piana buni?, Piana ronitʉ (name) Big-looking-glass (a former Yapai chief).

piana huwai? (n) big doctoring (Beaver ceremony).

piapʉ (n) giant, large object; *adv* loudly, widely, everywhere.

pia rekwa (v) shout (talk loudly to someone).

pia rʉnikwʉtʉ (v) sing loudly. **Waipʉ tsa? pia rʉnikwʉrʉ.** The woman is singing loudly [**pia** loud + **tʉnikwʉ** sing].

Pia rʉtsima (name) Big-fall-by-tripping (person).

pia rʉ?ewo (n) tablespoon. *See* **tʉe aawo.**

pia tsatuakatʉ (adj) wide open.

pia tsatuarʉ (v) open something wide.

pia tseena? (n) wolf (*lit* large fox).

pia tso?nika? (n) headdress, war bonnet (big hat).

pia tʉbookʉni (n) college. *See* **tʉboo kahni.**

pia wekḭtʉ (adj) wide, roomy.

pia wʉ?utsitʉ (v) pile high, heap up. **Hina ta pia wʉ?utsi?** What shall we pile up high?

Pibia nḭwʉnʉ?nʉʉ (n) Talk Loud (Comanche band).

pihi- (pfx) ref. to heart.

pihikarʉ (adj) satisfied (*lit* the heart is set; have enough of something).

pihima (v, pl obj), *sg obj* **piyarʉ** ride double (carry someone behind on horseback).

pihinaboo? (n) heart (in card game; *lit* heart printed).

pihisi?apʉ (n) cowardly, piker (*lit* heart-chipped-off).

pihiso?ai (adj) vexed, peeved, angry.

pihiso?aitu (adj) disturbed, angry.

pihiso?aiwunuru (v) stand angrily, desire not to be disturbed.

pihitsi (adj) greedy.

pihitsinaina (n) greed.

pihitsituyaru (adj) extremely greedy, hoggish.

pihi?a W, **pihi?anuu** K (n, pl), *sg* **tuinahpu?** boys.

pihi (n) heart.

pihkaru (v), *pl* **pipikutu** drumming, ring a bell (make repetitive sound by striking hollow object).

pihka?aru (v) break loose (something being pulled from behind).

pihka (n) scar.

pihkobaru (v) break something down (as by sitting on it). *See* **pinutsaru**.

pihkuma? K, **pihkumaaru** W (n) hem (bottom edge of something hanging).

pihnaketu, piinakeru (v) itch. **Nu paapi tsa? piinaketui.** My head will itch.

pihnaaketu (adj) itch. **Nu mo?o tsa? pihnaaketu.** My hand itches.

pihnákamaru (adj) taste sweet (have a sweet taste).

pihná nohkopu (n) sweet bread, cake, cookies (*lit* sugar biscuit). *See* **otu nohkopu**.

pihná ruhkaru (v) crave sweets [**pihna?** sweets + **tuhka** eat].

pihná baa (n) soda pop [**pihnaa** sugar + **paa** water].

pihnáa? W (n) sugar, sweets.

pihpárubu?ai (adj) wet seat (of pants or dress soaked from inside to outside).

pihpi, piipi (n) horsefly.

pihpokaaru, piipokaru (adj) uneven, fall short (too short or too long). **Ohka tsa? kwasu piipokame.** The dress is uneven.

pihpóo?, piipóo? (n) water jug (made of hide or stomach of animal; wet hide is stitched with sinew, then air is blown in while it dries). **Pihpóo? tsa? paa ukupayu?iitu.** They carry water in the hide water jug.

pihtsamuu (n) milky-rooted plant.

pihtsaku huupi, waikina pihtsaku huupi (n) singletree.

pihúraa, pihúura? (n) bean.

pihúura huupi (n) catalpa. Catalpa speciosa Warder (*lit* bean tree).

piinaai (n) leftover, remnant saved (as of food or cloth). **wanapu piinaimatu** leftover piece of cloth.

piitsunua? (n) straight pin [**pih-** long + **tsu?nua?** round at end].

pika (n) leather.

pika kwasu? (n) man's buckskin jacket.

pika namusoopu (n) buckskin clothing (for man, woman, or child).

pikapu (n) leather, buckskin, tanned deer hide. *See* **taibo pikapu**.

pikutsekaru (v) crush, mash (as by sitting on something soft).

pikwebuitu (v) turn around quickly. **Sarii tsa? piikwebui.** The dog turned around quickly.

pikwurupuka? W, **pipurupuka?** K (n) diaper (*lit* folded over for the seat).

pikwusii? (n) sulky, buggy (two-wheeled vehicle, singletree). **Uba nu rua pikwusii to?inu.** There

I climbed into the buggy. *See* **sumasunooi.**

pimimi?aru (v) walk backward, step backward, back up.

pimoroo taiboo? (n) cowboy.

pimoroo? (n), *pl* **pimoroo?nuu** cow. **Su?ana piapuhu pimoróo? kimaayu.** A big cow was coming along the edge of the water (19:1).

pimoroo?a korohko? (n) white elm. *Ulmus americana* L.

pimoroo?a kuhma (n) bull.

pimoroo?a piabu (n) cow.

pimoroo?a tua? (n) calf.

pimoroo?a tuyu?wipu (n) cow's cud.

pimoro?a puhi (n) cowhide, animal hide.

pimunikatu (adj) stuck fast (unable to pull something out).

pinai, binai (post) from behind. **Situkuse? kwasinaboo? u pinai u kuhtsianu.** This snake bit him from behind him (27:9).

pinakutsuru, pinakutsuitu (v) tickle someone.

pinakwu, pinaku (post) behind. **Tuinuhpu tsa? kahni pinaku.** The boy is behind the house.

pinutsaru (v) sit on something breaking it to pieces. *See* **pihkobaru.**

Pipiku? (name) Squeaky (short form of name of Elliot Canonge's son). *See* **Kahúu nihkupipikure.**

pipóhtoru (v) pop (make popping sound by sitting on something).

pisahpi (n) powder. *See* **homopu.**

pisaru (v) make up someone (apply make-up). **Nu takana kobe homopisai.** I powdered my sister's face. **homobisai** apply powder.

pisayu?ne? (n) tin or other shiny metal, jingles (shoe ornaments of metal). **Ma pisayu?ne?ai tanu.** Let's make jingles (shoe ornaments) out of it.

pisi (adj) festering, infected. **Ma?u?a tsa? pisi.** The sore is infected.

pisi (n) pus, infection.

pisi ma?rokóo? (n) rainbow (*lit* infected thumb).

pisi mi?aru (v) infecting (becoming infected).

Pisi narumuu? (n) Cache, Okla. (*lit* rotten store).

pisi wa?kóo? W (n) oyster [**pisi** pus + **wa?kóo?** shell].

pisi wa?rokóo? K (n) oyster [**pisi** smelly + **wa?rokóo?** seashell].

pisibuni? (n) cattail, cat's tail. *Typha latifolia* L.

pisiko?i (v) ride seated on a sled. **Nu kako tsa? pisikooinu.** Grandma went on a sled ride.

pisikwanúu?itu (v) slide down. **Wihnu suru pisikwanúu?inu.** Then that one slid down (5:11). *See* **nuaru.**

pisikwanúu?i? (n) slide.

pisona?aitu (v) build a nest. *See* **huupiso?na?aitu.**

pisoonaru (v) put down something to sit on.

pisóona (n) quilt, 3' by 6' pallet used during peyote meeting.

piso?aru (v) prick someone with something.

Pisu kwá?na? (n) Smeller (somewhat derogatory name given northern band by other bands).

pisukwitaitu (v) squirm, move nervously.

pisukwitak<u>u</u>r<u>u</u> (v) interrupt someone because of worry.

pisukwitar<u>u</u> (v) fret, worry, suffer on deathbed. **P<u>u</u> tuabaat<u>u</u> pisukwitai.** She is worried about her boy. *See* **musasuar<u>u</u>**.

pisunar<u>u</u> (v) drag something spread on flat surface. **T<u>u</u>?ehwaikina pisunaar<u>u</u> n<u>u</u>?.** I am dragging the small wagon.

pisuníi? K (n) skunk (*lit* constant bad odor). *See* **pohni?ats<u>i</u>**.

pisuni?eey<u>u</u> (n) skunk (*lit* casts off bad odor).

pisu?net<u>u</u> (v) rub against something, scratch rear or back against something. **Pimoróo? tsa? pisu?net<u>u</u>.** The cow is rubbing her rear.

pisu?ni? (n) nest. **kahúa pisu?ni** rat nest.

pis<u>u</u>t<u>u</u>kit<u>u</u> (v) pace (as a horse). **T<u>u</u>h<u>u</u>ya tsa? pis<u>u</u>t<u>u</u>kit<u>u</u>.** The horse is pacing (along).

pitsa mi?ar<u>u</u> (v) return, go back (moving away from speaker).

pitsa múu, pihtsa múu? (n) legume. *Camote de ratán, Hoffmanseggia Jamesii* T. and G. (*lit* milky roots; tubers eaten).

pitsa naboo? K (n) calico horse (*lit* spotted on the hips). *See* **tosanaboò**.

pitsa <u>u</u>kwakatu kimar<u>u</u> (v) back up, come backwards (movement with back toward speaker).

pitsákar<u>u</u> (v) pull something behind (as a trailer).

pitsaka? (n) trailer (anything pulled behind). *See* **t<u>u</u>biyaak<u>u</u>?**.

pitsanit<u>u</u>, pits<u>u</u>hanit<u>u</u> (v) choke. **Tehahp<u>u</u> tsa? pitsanikat<u>u</u>.** The man choked. *See* **paabitsanit<u>u</u>**.

pitsan<u>u</u> t<u>u</u>yait<u>u</u> (v) choke to death. **Pitsanu t<u>u</u>yaihumiar<u>u</u> ma?.** He is choking to death.

pitsi makat<u>u</u> (v) wean a baby. **N<u>u</u> r<u>u</u>?eti n<u>u</u>? pitsi makat<u>u</u>.** I weaned my baby.

pitsi p<u>u</u>ha n<u>u</u>ku?w<u>u</u>p<u>u</u> (n) clabber, clabbered milk. **N<u>u</u>ku?kw<u>u</u>?ima?.** It is sour.

pitsi tora, pitsi tohra (n) prickly poppy. *Argemone intermedia* Sweet (used for treating sore eyes).

pitsii?, p<u>i</u>tsam<u>u</u> (n) woman's breast.

pitsimai (adj) weaned.

pitsip<u>u</u>, pitsip<u>a</u> (n) milk.

pitsip<u>u</u> pimoróo? W (n) milk cow.

pitsip<u>u</u> wihtua (n) milk bucket, milk can.

pitsip<u>u</u>ha po?aa (n) cream (*lit* milk's covering).

pitsohka kwaba W, pitsoko kwaa?ba? W (n) turtle (alligator snapping, large water turtle). *Macroclemys temmincki.*

pitsohkor<u>u</u> (v) put on trousers. **Tenahp<u>u</u> tsa? pitsohkor<u>u</u>.** The man put on his trousers.

pits<u>u</u>kwina? (n) apron (worn by Indian women).

pit<u>u</u>s<u>u</u> (adv dir) back. **Pit<u>u</u>s<u>u</u> mi?ar<u>u</u> n<u>u</u>?.** I am going back. **Pit<u>i</u>s<u>u</u> u yaai.** He took it back.

pit<u>u</u>s<u>u</u> nu?ye? W (n) woodpecker.

pit<u>u</u>wet<u>u</u> (v) limp (of human or of hind leg of animal). **Tenahp<u>u</u> tsa? pit<u>u</u>wet<u>u</u>.** The man is limping. *See* **mat<u>u</u>wet<u>u</u>**.

pit<u>u</u>n<u>u</u> (v) arrive, approach someone. **Wakare?ee? mawaka pit<u>u</u>ni.** Turtle came up to him. **Oha ahnakat<u>u</u> ur<u>uu</u>k<u>u</u> pit<u>u</u>ni.**

Coyote arrived among them. *See*
noopituͅ.

pituͅbaruͅ (v) crack something by
sitting on it.

pituͅsohko̱?, pitsohko̱? (n)
trousers.

piwokami?aruͅ (v) drag something
along. **Suͅmuͅ? tenahpuͅ? puͅ kahni
wuͅhpiwokuͅkatuͅ.** One man is
dragging his teepee (123:21).

piwokaruͅ (v) drag something. *See*
wuͅhpiwokaruͅ.

piwo?sa wuͅnaruͅ (v) ache in lower
back, have a backache.

piwo?sa wuͅnuͅkatuͅ (v) have a
backache in lower back.

piwo?sa̱, piwo?se (n, acc) hip,
lower back, tailbone. **Nuͅ biwose
nuͅ? mahruͅni.** I hurt my hip.

piyaruͅ, piyami?aruͅ (v), *pl*
pihimacarry someone behind on
horseback, ride double.

pi?isuͅtuͅ (n) pacer (type of horse).
Tuͅhuͅya tsa? pi?isuͅtuͅ. The horse
is a pacer.

**pi?nakwuͅ buͅetsuͅ, pi?nakuͅ
puͅetsuͅkuͅ** (adv) day after
tomorrow.

pi?nu?a mi?aruͅ, pignu?a mi?aruͅ
(v) go backwards, go back and
forth or from side to side (as in
wagon).

pi?nu?a? (n) crab (*lit* goes
backward).

pi?onuͅ suakuͅtuͅ (adj) angry.

**Pi?opuͅ paruͅba tuͅyo, Peope
Padiva, Taoyo, Tuyo** (name)
Boy (very young chief of the Fish
Eaters band in earlier years).

pi?to, pi?to?na?i (adj) bobtailed.
Sarii tsa? pi?to. The dog is
bobtailed. **Suͅsuͅmuͅ? kwasinaboo?**

pi?to?na?i̱. Some snakes are
bobtailed (36:16).

pi?tohtsía? W (n) white-tailed deer
(*lit* bob-tailed white spot).

pi?to?aruͅ, pi?to?na?ituͅ (v) bob a
tail, cut off short.

pi?weesu?ru?ituͅ (v) swing sitting
down.

pi?weke mi?aruͅ (v) walk swinging
hips.

pi?wesurúu?i̱? (n) playground
swing [pi? backside +
weesuru?uͅi swing].

pi?wuͅ?wenituͅ (v) spill, sprinkle.
Pai u? pi?wuͅ?wenimi?aruͅ. It is
going along sprinkling water (as
city water-sprinkler truck). *See*
pa?isokeruͅ.

pi?wuͅriaruͅ (v) spill something (by
sitting on or beside it).

pi?yuͅpuͅ káa?i̱ W (n) railroad
handcar [**pi?yuͅpuͅ** pumping
motion + **kaa?i** that which does].
See **kuͅ?wuͅnuͅbaa?i̱.**

pohbituͅ, popituͅ (v), *pl* **pohbiaruͅ**
jump. **Situͅ oha ahnakatuͅ
hunu?matuͅ pohpínuͅ.** This coyote
jumped into the creek (14:18, 19).

pohituͅ (adj) stretched (as a hide).

pohkóo? (n) burrowing owl.

pohni?atsi̱ (n, arch) skunk.
Pohni?atsi̱ha nuͅ? uͅkwi. I smell a
skunk. *See* **pisuníi?.**

pohóobi, pohho nuͅkwuͅ (n)
sagebrush, quinine weed.
Artemisia tridentata Nutt.

pohotatuͅ (adj) thick. **Esiwana tsa?
pohotatuͅ.** The blanket is thick.

pohotuͅ na?suͅkía? (n) heavy shawl.
See **na?suͅkia?.**

pohpi kwáai? W (n) frog (*lit*
jumping goes). *See* **pasawi?oo?.**

pohtohkikatʉ (adj) bloated (swelled up from air or gas inside). **Sarii tsaʔ pohtohkikatʉ.** The dog is bloated.

pohtokitʉ (v) puff up, bloat, swell up, rise (as bread dough). **Tohtia tsaʔ pia pohtokii.** The bread rose high (large). *See* **mubohtohkitʉ.**

pohtokʉrʉ (v) inflate [**pohto** burst + **-ku** (cause)]. *See* **mubohtohkirʉ.**

pohtoʔitʉ (v) burst (break open with a bang).

pohyamiʔarʉ (v) run slowly, walk fast, trot. *See* **aimiʔarʉ.**

poiya (n) fever plant (plant whose leaves are used in treatment of fever).

pokarʉ (v) play poker.

poko rʉhkaʔ (n) cucumber (large variety).

pokopi tuarʉ (v) bear fruit.

pokopi (n) berries, fruit, nuts.

pokopi masʉapʉ (n) orchard, garden.

pomapʉ (n) picked berries, harvested crop, produce.

pomarʉ (v) pick fruit, harvest a crop. **Panatsaya nʉʔ pomarʉ.** I am picking berries. *See* **tʉbomarʉ.**

poohkatʉ, poorʉ (adj) scattered around (scattered here and there, piece by piece). **Amawóo tsaʔ poohkatʉ.** The apples are scattered around. *See* **tsahpoʔarʉ.**

poosubʉhkaitʉ (v) go crazy, have an evil spirit.

poosubʉkʉkaitʉ (adj) berserk, crazed (gone crazy).

Pooʔaikʉ (name) Blow-it-away (person).

pooʔsaʔ (n) crazy person. **Tenahpʉ tsaʔ pooʔsaʔ.** The man is crazy. *See* **poʔsa.**

popʉtsanawʉtʉ (adj) bumpy (as a road).

porokarʉ (v) crack (make cracking sound, as knuckles).

porokitʉ (v) snap (emit snapping sound as of fingers).

posaaki (n) bridge.

Positsʉ mʉa (n) February (*lit* sleet month).

poyohkarʉ (adj) made to trot.

poʔarʉ (v) spread legs out.

poʔayaahkwarʉ (v) blow away. **Nʉetʉ tsaʔ u poʔayaakʉʔi.** The wind is blowing it away (49:29).

poʔayaakʉtʉ (v) blow away.

poʔayaʔeetʉ (n) thistle (*lit* many blown around). *Cirsium undulatum* Nutt., Spreng.

poʔaʔ (n) bark, cover, skin. *See* **huupi poʔaʔ, hʉnʉ poʔaʔ, amawoʔaʔ poʔaʔ, sonaboʔa.**

poʔhibahpakitʉ, poʔahibahpakitʉ (v) wave, flap (in the wind).

poʔhimarʉ, poʔahimarʉ (v) winnow (as to clean grain).

poʔoyaʔ (n) blown-away object.

poʔro tʉhkapʉ K (n) pork. *See* **mubipoʔroo rʉhkapʉ.**

poʔro tʉhtʉmapʉ (n) fence of hog pen.

poʔropʉnʉʉ (n, pl), *sg* **hookị** hogs.

poʔroʔ (n), *pl* **poʔroʔnʉkwʉ,** *du* **poʔroʔnʉʉpig,** hog, swine. *See* **munuaʔ, hookị.**

poʔsa (adj) crazy.

poʔsa baa (n) whisky (*lit* crazy water).

poʔsa baa kahni (n) saloon.

poʔsabihiʔa (adj) mischievous.

Pua paatsoko (name) Medicine-
otter (person).

puha bahmuʔitɯ (v) smoke during
religious ceremony.

puha kahni (n) church, peyote
teepee (*lit* medicine house).

puha kahni muutsi̱ (n) steeple. *See*
muutsi̱.

puha nabisarɯ (v) anoint (apply
medicine paint).

puha namakaʔmukipɯ (n) medicine outfits (paraphernalia for
peyote ceremony; herbs, rattles,
gourds). **Situɯ sɯmɯʔoyetɯ
pɯɯ puha namakaʔmukipɯha
himanṵ.** All these ones got their
medicine outfits (70:18).

puha natsu W (n) red false mallow
(used for reducing swelling).
Malvastrum coccineum [Pursh.] A.
Gray. *See* **yokanatsuʔu.**

puha niwɯnɯrɯɯ K, **puha
niwɯnɯrɯ** W (n) church service.

Puha rabeni (n) Sunday (holy day).

puha raibooʔ W, **puha
rekwi̱raibooʔ** K (n) preacher,
medicine man.

Puha rakatɯ (n) Sunday (*lit* holy
rest).

puha rekwarɯ W, **puha rekwṵtsitɯ**
K (v) preach (*lit* speak with
power).

Puha rɯpaanɯ (n) Lawton, Okla.

Puha rɯpanaabi̱ (n) Medicine Bluff

Puha rɯboopɯ (n) Bible (*lit* holy
writings).

puha tenahpɯ (n) medicine man,
medicine doctor.

puha wɯhtitɯ, puha kwɯhtirɯ (v)
bewitch someone.

puhakatɯ (n) heal-all plant (acts as
a stimulant). *Prunella caroliniana*

Mill.; *adj* K **puhakatɯ,** W
puha namahkukatɯ having
supernatural power.

Puhawi (name) Medicine-woman
(person).

puhaʔaitɯ (n) shaman.

puhaʔaitɯ (n) prepared medicine,
curing ceremony.

puhaʔarɯ (v) prepare medicine,
hold a curing ceremony for
someone.

puha̱ (n) medicine, supernatural
power. *See* **natɯsuʔu.**

puhi (n) leaf.

puhi huuba̱ (n) dry tea (*lit* leaf
coffee). *See* **puhi tuhpaa.**

puhi hɯɯki̱ (n) brush arbor (*lit* leaf
shade). **Puhi hɯɯki̱ puha niwɯnɯ
urɯɯ.** They had a brush-arbor
meeting.

puhi kooʔipɯ (n) dead grass
(burned by the sun).

Puhi mɯa, Puhhi mɯa (n) June
(leaf month).

puhi taitɯ (n) K clump of grass; W
bush. *See* **puhi topi̱ka.**

puhi taʔaraʔ, puhi taʔraabɯ
(n) poison ivy (*lit* leaf poison).
Anacardiaceae.

puhí tsawooʔ (n) cultivator (*lit*
grass scratcher).

puhi tubi, puhi tuhpa K (n)
bush clover (beverage made
from leaves acts as stimulant).
Lespedeza capitata Michx.

puhi tuhpaa W (n) liquid tea. *See*
puhi huuba̱.

puhi tɯhkapɯ (n) lettuce (*lit* leaf
food).

puhi tɯmakwatubiʔ (n) leaf
wrappers for cigarettes. *See*
tɯmakwatui.

puhi tɨrɨhka? (n) mistletoe. **Viscum Foradendron** sp. (*lit* leaf thief).

puhi tɨyaitɨ (v), *pl* **puhi koo?i** choke out, kill by growing over.

puhi tɨyaitɨ (n) dead grass.

puhi yɨkwitɨ (v) hoe soil.

puhi yɨkwitɨ? (n) hoe (implement).

puhi bihnáa? (n) watermelon.

puhihwi (n) money, gold (*lit* shiny leaf). **Sitɨ kɨse? wihnu ma kwɨhɨ sooti puhihwipa?i.** This then his wife had much money (47:7). *See* **ekapuhihwi.**

puhihwi kahni (n) financial bank (*lit* money house).

puhihwi narɨso W (n) pocketbook, wallet, coin purse (*lit* money sack). *See* **puhihwi wosa.**

puhihwi natsihtu?ye? (n) metal comb, wire brush. *See* **natsihtu?ye?.**

puhihwi paraiboo? (n) banker (*lit* money boss).

puhihwi tekwapɨhana huupi (n) telephone pole (*lit* money talk pole).

puhihwi tekwapɨ (n) telephone (*lit* money talk).

puhihwi tuarɨ (v) get, have money.

puhihwi tɨboopɨ (n) check, bank draft (for transfer of money).

puhihwi tɨɨhtɨmarɨ (v) put up a barbed wire fence.

puhihwi tɨɨhtɨma? (n) barbed wire (*lit* money fence).

puhihwi wehki (v) look for money. *See* **wehkinitɨ.**

puhihwi wosa K (n) woman's purse, pocketbook. *See* **puhihwi narɨso.**

puhihwi yaarɨ (v), *pl* **puhihwɨ himarɨ** cash a check (receive money in exchange).

puhihwimaka (v) give money to someone.

puhihwi ta ahweetɨ (n) treasure (*lit* gold dug up).

puhipɨ (n) leaf (from tree or bush).

Puhipɨha pɨma oha to?i?ena mɨa, Puhipɨha (n) October (leaf fall month).

puhitookatɨ (v) graze on turkey grass.

puhitóo? K (n) turkey.

puhitóo? (n) turkey grass.

puhitopɨka (n) bush. *See* **puhitaitɨ.**

puhkapɨ (adj) ripped, torn.

puhkarɨ (v) tear something, rip something.

puhkarɨ (adj) burst open (as a cloud).

puhnuketɨ (adj) slick, smooth, slippery.

puhwaaitɨ (v) look for, search carefully for (search with the eyes). **Obotika hunu?ruti noo hina puhwaihbɨɨni.** Look for something over the creek (6:24).

puhyɨnukitɨ (v) glide, move slowly (as train moves along track).

pui (n) eye.

pui hwai (adj) blind (sightless).

pui narɨso, pui naso (n) eyelid.

pui tsaseni, puitsasena? (n) rye grass (sharp-edged, used in cutting cataract from the eye). *Elymus* sp.(?)

pui tsa?nika? (n) eyeglasses.

puibɨɨtɨ (v) be sleepy-eyed (have eyes heavy with sleep).

puibɨɨtɨtɨ (adj) sleepy.

puih tsahtsurɨ (v) wink (*lit* squeeze the eye).

puihtsara? W (n) flank of animal.

puihtsita? K (n) rib area of animal.

puikɨso (n) chigger, redbug.

puiwɨnɨrɨ (v) examine, look over. *See* **tsaʔatsitɨ.**

puiʔ (n) temple (upper side of the head).

puitɨsii, puʔtɨsii (n) eyelash.

puku, puukɨ (n), acc puki horse. **Tai puku tsakakɨ kwatuʔi nɨʔ.** I will go to lead the horse for us (43:25). **Sitɨ kɨseʔ ma kumahpɨʔ pɨhɨ puki toʔyanɨ.** This her husband unhitched their horse (48:17).

puku hibikɨʔ (n) water trough.

puku kahni, pukukɨni (n) stable. *See* **kahni.**

puku tsakami̱ʔarɨ, K puku tsakɨkarɨ (v) lead a horse.

puku rúaʔ (n) colt (*lit* horse child).

puku rɨhkaʔ, puku tɨhkaʔ (n) nosebag.

Pukutsi (n) Crazy Warriors (men who did everything backward; similar to the Koshare of Eastern Pueblo).

Pukuʔa tuaʔ (name) Colt (*lit* horse child).

puni kwarɨ (v) visit (go to see). **Uhka tai puni kwatuʔika.** We will (let's) go to see that one (7:36).

punitɨ (v) see, look at. **Sitɨ pia tɨrahyapɨ ma puninɨ.** This big meatball saw it (23:29).

Punitɨ (name) Looking (person).

pupɨkatɨ (adj) threadbare (thin cloth).

puruarɨ (v) splatter. **Yuhu tsaʔ puruanɨ.** The lard splattered. **Orɨ tsaʔ waipɨʔ ma puruʔai.** That woman splattered it. *See* **kuhpuruʔairɨ.**

pusiaketɨ (v) search for head lice, delouse.

pusiʔa natsihtuʔyeʔ (n) fine-toothed comb (*lit* head louse comb).

pusi̱ʔa, pusiʔa̱ (n) head louse. *See* **yupusia.**

putsi kwɨtsɨbaitɨ (v) sing high pitched (as does a woman).

putsi tɨnikwɨyɨ K (adj) high pitched.

putsi waipɨ (n) trunk of a white, dead tree. **Siʔana putsi waipɨha soho bokóoʔa wɨnɨku.** Here where a white, dead mulberry tree is standing (16:13).

puuhkikatɨ (adj) blown out, extinguished (as a candle).

puuhkitɨ (v) blow breath (blow on a person in a curing ritual).

puuyaketɨ (n) buzzing sound (made by a mosquito).

puʔe nagwe (n) wagon crossing. *See* **nagwe.**

Puʔekatɨ (n) Christian (*lit* one who has a path). *See* **tɨipuʔe.**

puʔeyarɨ (v) follow a road.

puʔeʔaikɨpɨ W (n) tradition. *See* **nanihpuʔeʔaikɨpɨ.**

puʔeʔarɨ (v) construct a road, clear a path.

puʔe̱ (n) road, trail, path. **Puʔetu nɨʔ miʔarɨ.** I am going through the road. *See* **tɨipuʔe.**

puʔiʔ (n) gall bladder.

puʔiʔwɨnɨrɨ (adj) suffer gall-bladder pain.

pɨ (pro coref, 1st gen sg) his, her, its.

Pɨ tua wɨni kwai (name) Been-to-see-his-son (person).

Pɨa kwarɨ (n) Desert-in-large-group (Comanche band now in Walters

area; so named by other group
because a large group deserted
together).

p̶a mi?ar̶ (v) leave someone for
good.

p̶a nuhkit̶ (v) run away from
somewhere, desert. *See* **nuhkit̶.**

p̶a watsi (n) wild stallion, horse.

p̶ah kwar̶ (v) separate in
marriage, leave a spouse.

p̶ah tait̶ (v) forsake someone,
desert.

p̶ah taikat̶ (adj) divorced,
separated in marriage.

p̶ar̶ (v) turn loose, quit
something, cease doing. **Ma
p̶aru?i n̶?.** I will let go of him.
P̶ pahmu?ina u? p̶ai. He quit
smoking. *See* **tohp̶ar̶.**

p̶e, p̶es̶ (adv time) already.

p̶e n̶m̶ roop̶n̶̶ (n) forefathers
(past generations).

p̶e t̶yaai?, p̶eh t̶yaai? (n)
ghost, evil spirit (spirit of someone
long deceased, invisible but can
be heard). *See* **n̶n̶p̶hi?.**

p̶esúube? K (n) velvet cloth, work-
type handkerchief.

p̶esúube? W (n) nursling, young
(as pony, chick, kitten).

p̶ets̶ku, p̶ets̶kus̶ (adv)
early morning (before sunup).
**Sit̶̶k̶se? u p̶ets̶ku sooyot̶
pit̶s̶ t̶as̶ uk̶hu mi?an̶.**
These ones (who) are many that
morning went back again (28:24).

p̶ets̶kunakw̶sa (n, arch)
morning.

p̶et̶p̶ (n) elderly woman.

p̶ewatsi (adj) wild, untamed.

p̶ewatsi k̶̶ka (n) wild onion. *See*
k̶htsuts̶̶?ni?.

p̶het̶, p̶hhet̶ (adv man) fast,
quick.

p̶himataka (adv man) barely.
P̶himataka ok̶ pitai. They
barely arrived (in time).

p̶hkai (v) stop crying, hush.

p̶hkaikat̶ (adj) hushed,
comforted.

**p̶hkait̶niit̶ W, p̶hkoot̶nit̶
K** (v) comfort an adult (help
someone stop crying).

p̶hkit̶ (v) stop raining. **P̶hkip̶
̶man̶.** It stopped raining.

p̶hk̶ra nahan̶ W (n) present
generation. *See* **n̶m̶ r̶borap̶.**

**p̶hkwinu?it̶ W, p̶kwitsunit̶
K** (v, nonhum subj) squirm,
wriggle.

p̶htsap̶ (adj) broken, burst, blown
out (as a tire).

p̶htsar̶, p̶ts̶har̶ (v) burst,
explode (as a balloon). **Sur̶ ur̶̶
hanip̶ p̶ts̶hán̶.** Their charge
exploded (29:28).

p̶htsa?et̶? (n) dynamite,
explosive. **Sit̶̶k̶se? suhka
p̶htsa?eti uk̶hu hanin̶.** These
ones prepared there that explosive
(29:26).

p̶htuku n̶m̶, t̶boo?ena
(n) camera. *See* **t̶boo?et̶,
kobenabo?.**

p̶ht̶ (adj) heavy.

p̶h̶ kab̶r̶̶? (n) sheep (*lit* woolly
goat).

p̶h̶ ku?kwe?ya? (n) lion (*lit* head
covered with hair).

p̶h̶ kw̶su?̶ (n) fur coat.

p̶h̶ n̶nap̶ (n) hairy chest, chest
hair.

p̶h̶ pusia (n) crab louse (*lit* hair
louse). *See* **suhposía.**

pɨhɨ tsahkweʔyarɨ (v) skin an animal. *See* **wɨsiboʔarɨ.**

pɨhɨ tsoʔnikaʔ (n) fur hat.

pɨhɨwahtɨ (n) prairie. *See* **nɨmɨwahtɨ.**

pɨhɨ natsu (n) medicinal herb (grows in Mexico; medicinal use to ease pain, lower fever, cure kidney disease).

pɨhɨ noʔitɨ (v) pluck a bird clean. *See* **pahtsi noʔitɨ.**

pɨhɨ rasoona (n) rug, carpet (*lit* fuzzy floor).

pɨhɨ reʔtsi (n) brother-in-law, spider (*lit* fuzzy brother-in-law). *See* **pia pɨhɨ reʔtsi, tetsi.**

pɨhɨ rɨmuihpaaʔ (n) fur cap. *See* **tɨmuihpaaʔ.**

pɨhɨ rɨʔsaasi, pɨhɨ rɨtsaasi (n) medicinal herb (has roots with hairs similar to wool; used in mixture for purifying blood).

pɨhɨsɨʔkɨi (n) peach (fuzzy plum).

pɨhɨʔ (n) hair fuzz, animal hide, shee wool, hairy vegetation (*lit* hair fuzz).

pɨka (v) bury (animals or humans).

pɨkapɨ (n) lap (of a seated person).

Pɨkɨra totsiyaaʔaiʔeka (n) Decoration Day [**pɨkɨ-** field + **-ra** (gen) + **totsiyaaʔ** flowers + **ai** do + **eka** day]. *See* **Totsiyaaih tabenihtɨ.**

pɨkɨhu, pɨkhu (n) place known by speaker and hearer. **Pɨkɨhu nɨʔ nɨminɨ.** I have been there (speaker and hearer know where).

pɨkɨra nohkoʔena W (n) oven (*lit* place in which one bakes biscuits). *See* **nohko aawo.**

pɨkɨra yɨkwiʔena W (n) parlor, livingroom (*lit* place in which to sit). *See* **yɨkwi kahni.**

pɨmata nookoina (n) wheat flour.

Pɨmata pia buhha raʔena mɨa (n) July (Fourth-of-July month; long form). *See* **Pia mɨa.**

Pɨmata waahimaʔena mɨa, Pɨmata wahi mɨa (n, month) December (*lit* gift month).

Pɨmata wanohiʔema mɨa (n) December (**lit** Christmas-gift month).

pɨnɨsɨ (pro, refl) oneself. **pɨnɨsɨ habinɨ** go to bed oneself.

pɨpaʔakura tɨbòoʔena W (n) desk (*lit* place on which to write). *See* **tɨboorɨhkaʔ.**

pɨpaʔakura tɨrahkwɨʔneʔena (n) ironing board (*lit* place on which one irons).

pɨpeʔ (adj) complete, fulfilled.

pɨrɨsɨʔarɨ (v) uncoil, unwind, unravel. *See* **wɨhpɨkɨsuarɨ, tsahkwɨmarɨ.**

pɨɨ (pro coref, 3rd gen pl) their.

pɨɨ- (pfx) ref. to blood.

pɨɨokwetɨ (v) bleed, hemmorhage.

pɨɨhibirɨ (v) partake of Communion.

pɨɨhibituʔitɨ (n), *pl* **pɨɨhibituʔinɨnɨ** Communion (sacrament), Mass (sacrament). *See* **tohtíarɨhkapɨ.**

pɨɨhpi (n) blood.

pɨɨpi (n) Communion wine.

pɨɨra (n) arm.

pɨɨyɨ namanahkepɨ (n) decoy duck (*lit* duck-parading item).

pɨɨyɨ (n) duck.

Pɨʔna petɨ (name) Only-daughter (person).

pɨʔɨne W, **pɨʔne** K (adv num) only. **pɨʔne pɨɨyɨ** only (one) duck.

S

saa huubạ (n) soup (boiled tree-water).

saabara (n) bedsheet, sheet for bed.

saabe busia (n) body louse (*lit* sleeve louse).

saah totsi baa (n) beer, hard cider (intoxicating drink of any type that foams up; anything that boils up or bubbles up as solder on a hot iron) [**saa-** boil + **totsi** square + **paa** water].

saahtotsitoʔikatɨ (adj) fermented, foaming, frothing at the mouth.

saahtotsitoʔiʔ (n) foam.

saapɨ (n) boiled meat.

saatitamakatɨ (adj), *pl* **tsatsatita-makatɨ** loose tooth, chattering teeth.

saatotsiya (n) flowering plant (*lit* boiling flower).

saatotsiyapɨ (n) potted plant.

saatɨ (v) boil.

saawihtua (n) cooking pot, cauldron (*lit* bucket for boiling).

saaʔarɨ (v) cause to boil.

saaʔwɨ (n) ref. to holes.

saaʔwɨ tɨkɨmaʔaiʔ (n) lace (perforated trimmed edge).

saaʔwɨtɨ (adj) holey (full of holes).

saaʔwɨʔ (n) mesh, sieve, screening.

saaʔwɨ hɨaʔ (n) fishnet.

saaʔwɨ napɨ (n) sandals (*lit* perforated shoes). *See* **waraatsi**.

sahkị (n) canoe.

sahpáanaʔ (n) side of stomach or abdomen (on surface).

sakwɨsikɨtɨ (v) tangle, *adj* tangled. *See* **kwisihkarɨ**.

samohpɨʔ (n), nom *pl* **samonɨɨ**, acc *pl* **samonii** sibling, brother, sister.

sanahkena W, **sanahpị** K (n) sap (of a tree or plant).

sanahkoo kɨyuʔnetɨ (v) chew gum.

sanahkooʔ W, (n) gum; **sanahkooʔa kɨtsɨkwetɨ** K chewing gum. **Usɨ pɨnihku nɨmɨ sanahkóoʔaiʔenạ.** That's the way (we) made our gum (110:21).

Sanah pia (name) (Comanche medicine woman).

Sanah pia ariba (name) (Comanche female chief).

sanahtuʔreʔ (n) snail (*lit* sticky leech).

sanarɨ (v) adhere, stick to.

sanaweha (n) broomweed, mormon tea. *Gutierrezia dranunculoides* [D.C.] Blake (used for making brooms and to cure kidney or bladder trouble and influenza).

Santanta (name) (Comanche chief; mother was Wapɨsoni; went to Washington, D.C.; in 1847, signed German peace treaty).

sapɨ (n) stomach. **Sitɨ kɨseʔ oha ahnakatɨ ma sapɨka ikanụ.** This coyote entered into her stomach (20:22).

sapɨ (n) ref. to stomach.

sapɨ nɨɨtsikwarɨ (n) stomach ache.

sapɨ wɨnɨkatɨ (n) baby colic, extreme stomach pain.

saraa (adv dir) across (meaning uncertain). **Surɨ kɨseʔ, 'Hinatsa nɨʔ panoo saraa saraa saraa?'** That one said, 'What shall I carry across?' (19:3).

Saria Tɨhka, Sata Teichas (n) Dog Eaters (Comanche band that split cir. 1300 A.D. from the Teichas; what is now Texas).

Sarii Tᵾhka? (n), *pl* **Sarii Tᵾhka?nᵾᵾ** Cheyenne, Arapaho (**lit** dog eaters).

sarii? (n), *pl* **sarii?nᵾᵾ**, *pl* **accsarii?nii** dog. **Sitᵾᵾ kᵾse? ma sarii?nᵾᵾ tᵾnayaarᵾ.** These his dogs are trailing (91:3). **Sitᵾ kᵾse? pᵾ sarii?nii pianimaiᵾ.** This one loudly called (to) his dogs (92:19).

Sata Tejas I, Saria Tᵾhka I (name) **Sata Tejas I** (Dog Eaters chief cir. 1689–1693).

Sata Tejas II, Saria Tᵾhka II (name) **Sata Tejas II** (Dog Eaters chief cir. 1873–1889).

sekwi (n) ref. to mud.

sekwi bii? (n) second stomach of cow (*lit* mud stomach).

sekwikᵾni, sekwᵾ kahni K (n) cellar, storm cellar (*lit* mud house). *See* **ohta kahni, sokokᵾni.**

sekwi nuyu?itᵾ (adj) mud-covered. **Sekwi nuyu?itᵾ ᵾnᵾ.** You are covered with mud.

sekwi sᵾhkai, sekwikᵾ sᵾhkai (adj) stuck in the mud. **Nabukuwaa tsa? sekwi kᵾsᵾhkai.** The car is stuck in the mud. *See* **yubu tsᵾhkatᵾ.**

sekwipᵾ (n) mud.

sekwitsipuhitsi (n) mud-men (clowns; masked dancers).

seni (adv man) different ways, various ways.

senihtᵾhtsi? (n) pitiful, undependable person.

setᵾᵾ (pro dem, scattered nom pl) those.

seyᵾyuki?, ehyᵾyuki? (n) ash. *Fraxinus* sp. (name refers to seed pods that rattle in the wind).

sia- (pfx) ref. to feather.

sia sona rᵾbaki? (n) feather mattress.

sia tsohpe (n) feather pillow.

siba huupi, siiba huupi K (n) flowering dogwood. *Cornus florida.*

sibepᵾ (n) shaving, scraping.

sibe?nikiyutᵾ (adv time) from now on. **Tahᵾ puhiwihta takwᵾ sibe?nikiyutᵾ puhihwikahnikᵾ tahni?i?etu?i.** From now on we'll put our money in the bank (49:33).

sie (n, acc) feather. **Sie nᵾbuni.** I see a feather.

Sihka tabe ke isopᵾ (name) This-midday-sun-does-not-tell-a-lie (person).

sihkupᵾ W (n) collarbone. *See* **huuku.**

sihkutᵾ (adv) from here.

sihwapi (n) torn object.

sihwarᵾ (v) tear something. **Ma tsa? sihwa nᵾ.** I tore it.

siibarᵾ K (v) harrow. *See* **tsatᵾsukitᵾ.**

siibetᵾ (v) shave, scrape off. **Huupita siibetᵾ ma?.** He scraped the stick. *See* **wᵾhsibetᵾ.**

siiko, sikoo? W (n) wild hyacinth. *Camassia esculenta* [Ker.] Robinson? (roots eaten raw [C & J]).

siikᵾ (n) navel.

siipᵾ? (n) urine.

siitᵾ (v) urinate. **Siitu?i nᵾ.** I am going to urinate.

sikusarᵾ (v) steal. *See* **tᵾrᵾhkarᵾ.**

simuhtarᵾ (v) suck through nose (as elephant sucks water, or as insect sucks nectar).

sinihku (adv man) manner (in this way). **Ketaʔ kwasikʉ sinihku atʉhʉna nohiʔa yaarʉ.** Next time don't take in this way a stranger's toy (83:32).

situkwʉ (pro, 3rd prox nom du) these two.

siʔarʉ (v) chip off.

siʔana (pro, 2nd prox acc sg) you.

siʔanetʉ (adv loc, prox) at this point.

siʔbaʔ (n) arrow [**si** feather + **pa** arrow].

soho bokopi (n) hackberry. **Celtis reticulat** Torry.

soho boʔkooʔ W (n) mulberry. **soho boʔkóoʔ** mulberry tree. *Morus rubra* L. (fruit eaten; wood used for making bows). **Huuhkaba soho bokóoʔ wʉnʉrʉ.** In the timber, there is a mulberry tree (16:10).

soho kʉaʔetʉ totsiyaaʔ (n) morning glory (*lit* climbing flower). *Convolvulaceaesp.*

soho obi (n) cottonwood. *Populus deltoides* Marsh (thin skin next to bark peeled off and fed to horses to give them endurance).

soho roʔitʉ (v), *pl* **soho kʉa** climb up.

soho weerʉ (v, pl) climb down.

soko (n) land.

sokobaʔaihtʉ (n) nations.

soko bookʉtʉ (n) title deed, deed (title to land).

soko kimarʉ (v), *pl* **soko nʉmitʉ** come walking (come on foot).

soko naboopʉ W (n) map (*lit* land picture).

soko rahkaʔmiitsaʔ (n) cucumber (*lit* ground wart; small, introduced domestic plant).

soko rʉboopʉ (n) geography, map [**soko** land + **tʉboopʉ** paper].

soko rʉmanahkepʉ (n) quarter section [**soko** land + **tʉmanahke**-measure]. *See* **sokotsihkaʔapʉ.**

soko rʉmʉrʉ (v) lease land.

soko rʉtsʉpʉ (n) mile.

soko sikʉsa (n) dandelion (*lit* ground-stealing plant). *Taraxacum officinale* Wiggins (medication for respiratory problems).

soko sikʉsatotsiyaʔ (n) dandelion flower.

soko tsatʉwarʉ (v) open country to settlement. **kesʉ ta soko tsatiwaku** before our country was opened.

soko tsihkaʔapʉ (n) quartersection of land [**soko** land + **tsihkaʔa** cut off]. *See* **soko rʉmanahkepʉ.**

soko yʉʔyʉmuhkurʉ (v) quake of earth, tremor of earth.

soko yʉʔyʉmuhkutʉ (n) earthquake.

sokobi paa tʉbinaatʉ W (n) island (*lit* land in the middle of water).

sokokʉni, soko kahni (n) cellar, storm cellar. *See* **sekwikʉni.**

sokomiʔarʉ (v) go walking (go on foot). **Sokomiʔarʉ nʉʔ.** am walking (going on foot).

sokoobi (n) land, earth.

sona (n) cloth cover.

sona boʔa (n) quilt top.

sona rʉbakiʔ, sonana rʉbakiʔ (n) mattress (*lit* stuffed quilt) [**soona** quilt + **tʉbaki**- stuff].

soni (n) grass.

soni bihnáaʔ (n) sugar cane.

soni hʉʉki (n) brush arbor, arbor. *See* **hʉkiʔaitʉ.**

soni narúa?, soni narui? (n) oats.

soni narʉso? (n) towsack, gunny sack [**soni** grass + **narʉso** sack].

soni nʉʉhtama? K, sonipʉha nʉʉhtama? W (n) baling wire [**sonipʉ** grass + **-ha** (acc) + **nʉʉhtama?** tying thing].

soni sokoobi (n) pasture (open grassland).

soni tooru (v) graze on grass.

soni tsiyaa? (n) pitchfork [**soni** grass + **tsiyaa?** to pitch].

soni tso?nika? (n) straw hat, hat [**soni** grass + **tso?nika?** hat].

soni tʉhtʉmapʉ (n) fenced pasture [**soni** grass + **tʉhtʉma-** fence + **pʉ** (nom sg)].

soni wiyaa? (n) twine, clothesline rope; arch split root used for weaving baskets.

soni wokweebi (n) grass burr [**soni** grass + **wokweebi** thorn].

soni wʉhpomarʉ (v) mow grass, cut weeds or grass (with hoe or sickle) [**soni** grass + **wʉhpoma** cut down].

soni wʉhpoma? (n) sickle.

soni wʉhtʉmapʉ (n) pasture, feeding lot (around haystack) [**soni** grass + **wʉhtʉmapʉ** fenced place].

soni wʉhtʉma?, soni tʉhtʉma? (n) baling wire, wire [**soni** grass + **wʉhtʉmaa?** bale].

soni wʉtsʉkerʉ (v) mow grass (with lawnmower or tractor).

soni wʉtsʉke? K (n) scythe, lawnmower. *See* **tuutsʉke?.**

sonipʉ (n) grass.

sonitsiima?, sonitsihima? (n) pitchfork [**soni** grass + **tsi** (nom) + **hima** take].

soo (num) many, much.

soo be?sʉ, soo be?sʉkʉ (adv time) many years ago, long ago. **Soo be?sʉkʉ tsa? tʉa su?ana tʉ?rikuu?nʉʉ soo kʉniba?i.** It is said that long ago the prairie dogs had a town somewhere.

soo huuhpi (n) woods, forest (*lit* many trees). *See* **huukabatʉ.**

Soo kʉni? (n) Lawton, OK (*lit* many houses, town; so named by Cache Comanches).

soo mo?o? (n) centipede (*lit* many hands).

soo naahkwetʉ (adj) distant (*lit* a long way off).

soo naboo? (n) printed material [**soo** many + **na** (nom) + **boo** print].

Soo pitenʉ (name) Comes-often (person).

soo tuku, soo tukukʉ (n) flank of animal (*lit* much meat).

soo tʉhimarʉ? (n) coon can, kick-the-can (*lit* many rations).

soo yake? W (n) mockingbird, locust (*lit* always chirping). *See* **tʉnimanahke huutsu?.**

sookʉni, soo kahni (n) town, village. **Tʉ?rʉkuu?nʉʉ sookʉniba?i.** The prairie dogs had a town.

soomo (n) lung.

soona (n) quilt, cloth cover.

sootʉ, sooti (num indef) many, much. **Sooti kʉse? surʉ tʉrʉe?tʉpa?i.** That one had many children (15:2). **Sitʉ kʉse? pimoróo? sootʉkʉhu paakʉhu weenʉ.** This cow went down to much water (20:23).

soro?rokitʉ (v) purr (as a cat).

so?o narʉbaki?, soo narʉbaki? (n) shotgun (*lit* cheek to put [shells] in).

so?o ruhkʉ (n) gums (of teeth) [**so?o** cheek + **tuhkʉ** flesh]. *See* **tamaruhkʉ.**

so?o tsuhni (n) cheekbone [**so?o** cheek + **tsuhni** bone].

so?ǫ (n) cheek, cheekbone.

sua, suarʉ (n) mind, breath, soul, thought.

sua kwanạ (n) breath odor. **aisua kwanạ** bad breath. **tsaa suakwanạ** good-scented breath.

sua soyurapeʉ (v) allow to rest or cool off.

sua watsikatʉ (v) faint, become comatose. *See* **esitʉyaitʉ, kwinumạ suarʉ.**

sua watsikʉ (adj) unconscious, comatose.

sua watsitʉ (v) become insane (lose mind).

sua yurahpitʉ (v) rest, relax.

suaabe, suabi (n) cross (Christian symbol).

suabetaikatʉ (adj) conscious, revived (after being knocked out).

suabetaikʉrʉ (v) teach, train someone. *See* **tʉnị suabetarʉ.**

suabetaitʉ, suabetarʉ (v) recognize. **Nʉ suabetainụ urʉa.** He recognized me. *See* **masuabetaitʉ.**

Suabi puharaibo (n) Catholic person, priest, nun (*lit* holy people of the cross).

suahkenạ (n) breath.

suahketʉ (v) breathe. **Kehtaku ma? suahketʉ.** He is breathing heavily.

suakʉtʉ (v) think good thoughts (think well of someone). **Tsaa u suakʉtʉ.** He thinks well of him.

suakʉtʉaitʉ (v) sympathize (feel for someone; think of someone a lot).

suana (n) will, soul, thoughts.

suapʉ (n) thought, sense.

suapʉwahtʉ (adj) stupid, senseless. **Urʉ tsa? sarii suapʉwahtʉ.** That dog is stupid.

suatʉtʉ (v) think.

sua?sua?miarʉ (v) breathe heavily, pant.

sua?su?maitʉ (v) unable to breathe, out of breath, dead. **Suatsu?mai ma?.** He is dead (quit breathing).

sua?su?makatʉ (adj) breathless, dying one. **Suatsu?makatʉ ma?.** He is dying (breathing his last).

sube? (conj) both.

sube?sʉ (adv time) immediately, since then. **Sube?sʉ kʉse? suni uhka u mʉʉhka, sʉsʉmʉ? kwasinaboo? pi?to?na?i.** Since then when he acted on him that way, some snakes are bobtailed (36:16).

sube?tʉ, sube?tʉ (interj) That's all (narrative-closing; end of story). **Tanʉ usʉ tsihákwitso?ainụ. Subetʉ.** We were saved from hunger by that. That's all (18:36, 37).

suhkapʉ (n dem, dist acc sg) that one.

Suhta? (n), *pl* **Suhta?nʉʉ** Sioux people.

suhu posía (n) crab louse. *See* **pʉhʉ pusia.**

suhurʉkitʉ (v) snort.

sukuupʉ (n) elderly man (over 70 years).

sukwʉkitʉ (v) think about, reason. *See* **nasutamakatʉ.**

suni (adv man) that way. **Keta? kwasikʉ ʉ puhiwihta suni**

mʉʉrʉ. Next time don't treat your money that way (49:33).

suniyutʉ (adv) because (for that reason).

sunihku (adv man) thus.

supanaʔitʉ (adj) knowledgeable, knowing. **Maʔnoo nʉ tʉrʉeʔtʉhtsinʔʉʉ supanaʔitʉ.** I wonder what he knows about my children (15:9).

supewaitʉ (adj) carefree, leisurely.

supi̱kaahkatʉ (adj) perceptive, aware.

surʉ (pro dem, dist nom sg) he, she, it.

surʉʉ (pro dem, dist nom pl) those.

sutaaitʉ (v) bless someone, have mercy.

sutaitʉ (adj) blessed.

sutena (adv man) forcefully.

sutena betsʉmiarʉ (v) lead off by force.

sutena betʉ (v) take someone by force.

sutena ikʉrʉ (v) enter by force. *See* **ikarʉ.**

sutena karʉrʉ (v) force to sit down.

sutenapʉ (n) stubborn person.

sutsamurʉ (v) promise.

sutuuʔarʉ (v) find out, notice.

suuta? (n) jack (in playing cards).

suwaitʉ (v) want, desire, need. **Kahni nʉʔ suwaaitʉ.** I need a house. **Tsaa nʉʔ naboori kwasuʔi suwaaitʉ.** I want a nice, designed coat (32:8). *See* **nohabi̱ suwaitʉ.**

suwʉkaitʉ (adj) amazing.

suwʉʔkai (v) be amazed.

suyoroʔakapʉ (adj) wonderful. *See* **nani̱suwʉkaitʉ.**

suyoroʔarʉ (v) wonder at.

suʔahri (adv loc) along there. **Oha ahnakatʉ suʔahri tʉpanakʉhi tsaʔwoʔnetʉ.** Coyote is scratching along there in the bank (16:16).

suʔakʉtʉ (v) like someone, admire someone. *See* **tokwetʉtuarʉ.**

suʔatsitʉ (v) think about something, make a plan. *See* **nimakaʔmukitʉ.**

suʔatʉ (pro indef) another one (not this one).

suʔmakʉtʉ (v) spend money. **Tenahpʉ tsaʔ puhiwihta suʔmakʉi.** The man is spending money.

suʔurarʉ (v) recall, ponder, search the mind in effort to remember [**su** think + **ura** find].

suʔuyaaʔarʉ (v) laugh at, deride. *See* **tʉni̱ suʔuyaʔeetʉ.**

suʔuyaʔiʔ (n) laughingstock. *See* **usúʔyaʔitʉ.**

sʉatʉ (v) grow (increase), bloom (bud open), augment in number. **Sonipʉ tsaʔ suahkatʉ.** The grass is growing. **Pimoroonʉʉ tsaʔ sʉanʉ.** The herd of cattle is growing.

sʉhkwibitʉ, sʉhkwibiʔbikitʉ (v) shiver, tremble, quiver. *See* **kʉhkwibikitʉ.**

sʉhtorokitʉ W, sʉwiʔnoʔnoʔkitʉ K (v) shiver (from the cold). *See* **tsihturuarʉ.**

sʉhtʉyaitʉ (v), *pl* **sʉhkooi** freeze to death, die of the cold.

sʉhʉ, sʉhʉʉbi (n) willow. *Salix* sp.

sʉhʉ aawo (n) basket (woven of willow).

sʉhʉ mupitsʉ (n) screech owl (*lit* willow giant) [**sʉhʉʉbi** willow + **mupitsi̱** giant].

suhu tsitsina?, suutsununi (n) willow twigs, arch potato [**suhu** willow + **tsitsina?** root].

suku- (pfx) ref. sour.

suku ka?ma? (n) lemon [**suku** sour + **kama-** taste].

sukubuninitu (v) make a wry face (as from eating something sour or bitter).

suku?i (n) plum (a particular wild variety). *Prunus* spp. **suku?i huuhpi** plum tree. *See* **yusuku, parawa suku, kusi suku, natsomu, parua sukui?.**

sukwe naisu (n) side of an object (front or back).

sukwe tuyai (adj) paralyzed (*lit* nerves dead). *See* **ma?itsa?bukatu.**

sukwe tuyaipu (n) paralyzed person.

sukweebi? (n) fifty cents, half-dollar.

sukweru (adj) half, *n* **sukweebi** end of row or nerve.

sumasu nooi K, **sumu?a noo?, suma noo?** (n) one-horse buggy, horse-drawn sulky. *See* **pikwusii?.**

Sumonu kuhtsu paa (n) Nueces River (*lit* river of ten buffalo; name derived from a hunting expedition in which ten buffalo were killed).

sumu (num) one; *adv* completely, thoroughly.

sumu kuhtsumai (adj) eaten up completely.

sumu makukatu (adj) complete, thorough.

sumu okwetu (v) float away. *See* **okwehkwatu.**

sumu nokimaru (v, pl), *sg* **kimaru** come (as a group).

sumu nomi?aru (v, pl), *sg* **nomi?aru** move away as a group (abandon a location).

sumu oyetu (pro indef) everyone.

sumu rayu?neru (v) pound completely (as pounding meat).

sumu ruhkaru (v) devour, eat most of something.

sumu sihwaru (v) tear off, rip completely.

sumu susunitu (adj) homogeneous throughout (all the same). *See* **suunitu.**

sumu uhtsumitu (v, pl), *sg* **uhtsumaru** close everyone's eyes (require everyone to close eyes completely).

sumu? (pro indef) one, someone, people. *acc* **sumu?a. sumu?a ka?wikatu** gathering of people, congregation.

sumusu (adv) once, one time.

suroonitu, tasuroonitu (v) bristle (hair), stand hair on end. **Sariia tsa? puhu suroonitu.** The dog's fur bristled.

susuatu (adj) cool, chilly.

susumu? (num indef) one at a time, some. *See* **su?sumu?nuku.**

susu?ana (adv time) sometimes, once in a while.

susu?nikatu (adj) numbness.

susu?nitu (v) numb, feel numb, asleep. *See* **tasusu?nitu, masusu?nitu.**

suu (adv accom) together (said of a group).

suu aniru (v) kick (causing object to bounce away).

suu awo (n) tin cup.

suu potseru (v) kick something away. *See* **suuhpotsukatu.**

suuhkwuhtitu (v) kick.

suuhkwuhtukuru (v) kick something.

suuhpotsukatu (adj) kicked away, discarded by kicking. *See* **suupotseru.**

suuki (n), *pl* parukwihtsipu twig, switch.

suukoitu, suhkoitu K (v) freeze (solids). **Tomatu tsa? suhkoi.** The tomatoes froze.

suuku (adj) sour, acidic.

suukutsa?noo (adv doubt) perhaps, maybe. *See* **kia.**

suumaru, suumanuru (num) ten.

suuma?aitu (v) gather together, congregate. *See* **narahka?witu.**

suuma?okaru (v) call together many people, invite to congregate.

suumu?oku (n) group of people, crowd of people.

suunitu (adj) homogeneous, alike. *See* **sumu susunitu.**

suupetu, suuhpetu (adj) level, even, flattened. **Sokobi tsa? suupetu.** The earth is level.

suuta?ni?aru (v) kick off, shake something off. *See* **nuu?wikeetu.**

suutsunitu (v) chill (have chills), tremble with cold. *See* **suhkwibitu.**

su?sumu?nuku (adv) one at a time. *See* **susumu?.**

T

ta (unspecified subject or possessor).

ta-, tah- (pfx) ref. to foot; ref. to sound *tah* (as in pounding or cracking).

taa (pro, 1st gen du) of us two.

taa- (pfx) ref. to morning.

taabu?kina noyo (n) Easter egg (*lit* rabbit egg).

taahkatu (adj) morning, daytime [*ta* morning + -katu have].

taahkitu (adj) dawn. *See* **huwuni.**

taaitu (n) hole (in the ground).

taamahkaru (v) prepare breakfast for someone [**taa-** morning + **mahka** make for].

taama (n) tooth.

taaruhkapu (n) pancakes, cereal [**taa-** morning + **tuhkapu** food].

taaruhkaru (v) eat breakfast (*lit* morning eating).

taatsa, tatsatu (adj) summer season.

taatsukwitu (num) seven.

taayutsutu (v), *pl* taayoritu arise (get up in the morning). **Itu tsa? tenahpu? puetsuku taayutsunu.** This man got up early.

tabahko (n) Indian tobacco. *Rubella Nicotiana rustica* L. (roots cooked with fat to make soup [C & J]; medicinal use to cure asthma, liver ailment, kidney malfunction, influenza, and fever).

tabakoitu (v) split (cause to split). **Ma rabakoi!** Split it! (expression accompanied by blowing toward storm cloud to avoid having storm).

tabe-, taabe (n) sun, day, clock, wristwatch.

Tabe kwi?ne (name) Sun-eagle (Comanche war chief about 1759).

tabe mo?o (n) hour hand (on clock or watch).

Tabe nanika (name) Hears-the-sunrise, Voice-of-the-sunrise (Comanche chief living in 1872).

tabe narumuhku (n) watch chain [**tabe** watch + **narumuhku** harness].

tabetotsiyaa (n) fleabane daisy, clock flower. **Erigeron tenuis** T. and G. (root used as medicine).

tabe wenuakʉʔ (n) watch chain [**tabe** watch + **wenuakʉʔ** hanging down object].

Tabe wʉnʉrʉ (name) Standing-sun (person).

tabe wʉnʉʔitʉ (v) stand in the sun, stand just above the horizon (said of the sun before it sets).

tabe kusʉwehkatʉ (adj) hot day, scorching day.

tabéni̱ (adv) today, morning.

tabe rʉhkapʉ W (n) dinner, lunch.

tabe rʉhkarʉ K (v) eat dinner or lunch [**tabe** sun + **tuhka-** eat].

tabe toʔikitʉ W (adj), **tabe toiʔ** K (n) sunrise, sunup.

tabe ʉhpʉitʉ (v), *pl* **tabe ʉhkoorʉ** nap (take a nap) [**tabe-** day + **ʉhpʉi** sleep].

tabe ʉhyʉhʔ K, **tabe ʉhyʉihka** W, **tabe ʉhʉyi** (adv) afternoon.

tabéʔaitʉ (v) swear (take an oath), vow (as in court).

tabeʔehi (adv time) late in the day.

tabeʔikai K (n), **tabeʔikarʉ** W (adj) evening, sunset, sundown.

tabeʔikamiʔarʉ (v) sun goes down (setting of the sun).

tabeʔikʉnakwa̱ʔ (n) west (*lit* where the sun goes down).

tabúʔkina̱ʔ (n) rabbit. **Soobeʔsʉ kʉtsaʔ rʉa piarabúʔkina̱ʔ kahníba̱ʔi̱.** Long ago it is said a big rabbit had a home (15:1).

tabʉikatʉ (n) grief, sadness.

tah- (pfx) foot. *See* **ta-.**

tahbaitʉ (v) break in pieces. *See* **tahtabaʔitʉ.**

tahhanitʉ (v) pound on something, hammer something (*lit* make a *tah* noise).

tahhimaʔerʉ (v) catch (with claws), grab (with claws).

tahhomonutsarʉ W (v) crumble to powder with the foot [**tah-** foot + **homo** powder + **nutsa** crumble]. *See* **mahomonutsarʉ.**

tahi, tahhibatʉ W, **tahi̱bi** K (adj with inanimate nouns) flat, thin, lightweight. **Tʉsoona tsaʔ tahibi.** The plate is flat.

tahipʉ pekwi (n) flounder (*lit* flat fish). *Pleuronectes genus.*

tahka- (pfx) ref. to ice or snow.

tahka aawo (n) refrigerator, icebox.

Tahka hunuʔbi (n) Colorado River (*lit* ice creek).

tahkaaitʉ (v) cut out of the herd, divide.

tahkabi (n) ice, snow.

tahkamʉrʉ (v) stand waiting (for someone or something).

tahkanaʔ (n) spear. *See* **tʉtsiwaiiʔ.**

Tahkapʉ (name) Poor-one (person).

tahka weʔwenukaʔ (n) icicle (*lit* ice hanging down).

tahkaʔ (n) arrowhead (*lit* divided, broken).

tahkaʔikatʉ (adj) frozen.

tahkaʔimiarʉ (v) freeze (be in the process of freezing).

tahkaʔʉmarʉ (v) snowfall (*lit* snow rains or falls).

tahkitemiʔarʉ (v) slip standing up, slide standing up, skate [**tah-** feet + **kite-** slide + **miʔa-** go]. *See* **tasikoʔiʔmiʔarʉ.**

tahkobarʉ, tahkobakatʉ (v) break off, snap off (with the foot).

tahkoonikaru (v) round up, herd, rustle (as to steal cattle).

tahkoonitu (v) domineer, stop someone by force.

tahkuya?aru (v) frighten, make threatening movements (with the foot, as in kicking toward someone).

tahkuaru (v) drive out, force (encourage) to leave (animate subj).

tahkuaru (v) drive away, force away (with the foot).

tahkuma?aitu (v) sharpen (using a treadle grindstone) [**tah-** foot + **kuma?aa-** sharpen].

tahkwatúubitu (v) fold (with the foot) [**tah-** foot + **kwatuubituto** fold]. *See* **namakwatubiitu.**

tahkwe?yaru (v), *pl* **tahkwe?yu?i-** take off a shoe.

tahkwineru W (v) wipe (with the foot or lower end of something).

tahkwumaru (v), *pl* **tahkwumi?i-** unwrap something (with the foot) [**tah-** foot + **kwuma** unwrap].

tahkwu?neru (v) iron, press (as of clothing; *lit* rub with a foot).

tahkwuriaru (v) spill something (with foot) [**tah-** foot + **kwuriaru** spilled].

tahma (n), *adj* **tahma ro?ikatu** spring season, summer.

tahmai napu (n) deer meat, dried meat, summer-dried meat (butchered and dried in the summer) [**tahma** summer + **inapu** dried meat].

Tahma mua, Kurahmaru mua (n) April (*lit* new-spring month).

Tahma uhuyi (n) August.

tahma yokake? (n) popcorn [**tahma** spring + **yokake?** spongy + **?** (nom sg)].

tahma ro?itu (v) become spring.

tahnaaru (v) plant seeds, sow seeds.

tahnikatu (v) keep an orphan as foster child.

tahni?aru (v) defeat, overcome, win in a contest against someone. *See* **kwakuru.**

tahnutsa?eru K (v) crumble (with the foot). *See* **manutsa?aru.**

tahpáana (n) sole of foot [**tah** foot + **paana** palm].

tahpai (adj) cracked of own accord.

tahpana?aaru (v) sole shoes (put soles on shoes) [**tah-** foot + **pana-** sole + **?a-** (V)].

tahpapu (n) broken object (as a dish or glass).

tahpararu (v) soften something by trampling on it (Comanches put rawhide or dried meat on a flat surface, covered it, then tramped on it to soften it).

tahpara?itu (v) align spine, stand on someone's back to ease pain.

tahparu (v) crack something, break something. *See* **tapearu, wutubaru.**

tahpiko? (n) heel of shoe.

tahpomi?itu (v, pl), *sg* **tsahkokaru** break.

Tahpooku mua (n) March (*lit* cotton-ball month).

tahpooku? (n) cottonwood. *See* **we?yuku sohoobi.**

tahporooru (v) break in pieces, shatter.

tahpunitu (v) try on shoes [**tah-** foot + **puni-** see].

tahtaba?itu (v) cause to break in pieces. **Keta? ma rahtaba?itu.** Don't break it to pieces. *See* **tahbaitu.**

tahta?nitʉ (v) shake the foot (as to shake off dust or dirt). *See* **ta?wikitʉ.**

tahta?yʉtʉ, W (v) jerk the lower leg [**tah-** foot + **taa?yʉ-** jerk]. *See* **ta?yʉrʉhkitʉ.**

tahtokoo? (n) big toe [**tah-** foot + **to?koo?** grandfather].

tahtoorʉ (v) put on shoes.

tahto?itʉ (v) let out (allow to leave, as by opening gate).

tahtsaitʉ (v) catch up with, overtake.

tahtsanitʉ (v) stumble [**tah-** foot + **tsani-** hang].

tahtsarʉ (v) raise one leg.

tahtsiarʉ (v) scratch someone (with foot or toes) [**tah-** foot + **tsia-** scratch].

tahtsukitʉ (v) erase, wipe away (using foot).

tahtsumarʉ K (v) wipe something off.

tahtsʉkitʉ (adj) crowded while standing (*lit* crowded foot, as in tight shoes).

tahtúa? (n) little toe (*lit* foot child). *See* **tʉeh tahtua?.**

tahtunaabarʉ (v) straighten something wrinkled (using the foot).

tahtʉbunitʉ (v) waken (cause to wake up with heavy steps or noisy walking) [**tah-** foot + **tʉbuni-** wake up]. *See* **tʉbunitʉ.**

tahtʉkarʉ (v), *pl* **tahni?itʉ** put away, drill in (as seed), keep something. *See* **tʉkarʉ.**

tahtʉkitʉ (v) take away something live.

tahtʉki?i? (n) stool, footstool.

tahtʉkwarʉ (v), *pl* **tahpa?itʉ-** throw at something.

tahtʉmarʉ (v) close up (nail shut, cover over).

tahtʉpinaa? (n) middle toe [**tah** foot + **tʉpinaa (weki)** middle].

tahuhkuwʉnʉrʉ (v) raise dust by walking [**ta-** foot + **huhku-** dust + **wʉnʉ-** stand].

tahu?nerʉ (v) crawl on knees [**ta-** on knees + **hune-** crawl]. *See* **mahu?netʉ, wʉhu?nerʉ.**

tahʉ (1st pers pl poss pro) our.

tahʉʉki?aikʉ (n) brush arbor, arbor (*lit* planted shade). *See* **hʉʉki?aitʉ.**

tahwikarʉ (v) earn something. *See* **tʉrahwikatʉ.**

tai (1st pers pl obj pro) us.

taibo bihnaa? (n) cantaloupe (*lit* white man's sugar). **Surʉʉ kʉse? taiboo? bihnáa?a tʉrʉní?inʉ.** Those ones planted cantaloupes (77:2).

taibo ekʉsahpana? (n) soldier (white man) [**taibo-** white man + **ekʉsahpana?** red-chested]. *See* **ekasahpana?.**

taibo huutsuu? (n) pigeon (*lit* white man bird). *See* **ku?ewóo?.**

taibo na?seeka? (n) date (*lit* white man persimmon).

taibo pikapʉ (n) leather (commercially prepared; *lit* white man leather). *See* **pikapʉ.**

taibo sʉkʉ?i (n) domestic plum (usually a hybrid) [**taibo-** white man + **sʉ?kʉ?i** wild plum].

taiboo? (n) non-Indian, white person. **Sitʉʉ taiboo?nʉʉ tʉbehkapʉha sʉmʉ noohtsi, pʉ kahnikʉhu mi?anʉ.** Carrying off these white men's game, he went home (97:33).

taina (n) hole, cave, room.

takahpʉ (n) poor person.

taka?aitʉ (adj) duplicate (*lit* made a sibling).

taka?arʉ (v) copy, duplicate (*lit* make a sibling).

taka?katʉ (adj) having a sibling (brother, sister, mate).

takoosahpʉ? W, takootsapʉ? K (n) a mix, batter allowed to become set, dough-like batter (as cornmeal, plaster, blacktop road).

takotserʉ (v) wash feet (of someone or something else).

takuhtʉyaaihumi?arʉ (v) thirst to death, die of thirst (suffer great thirst).

takʉsito?itʉ, takwʉsito?itʉ (v) perspire, sweat.

takʉsuaitʉ (adj) thirst (feel thirsty) [**takʉ** dry + **sua-** feel].

takwainitʉ (v) go on foot to look for [**ta-** foot + **kwai-** go away + **ni** walk].

takwekwitʉ (v, pl obj), *sg obj* **ta?ikʉrʉ** imprison.

takwi- (pfx), *adj* **takwikatʉ** wrinkled. **takwikoobe** wrinkled face; **takwimo?o** wrinkled hand.

takwikakwo?apʉ (n) wrinkled all over.

takwikakwo?arʉ (v) wrinkle something.

takwipʉ (n) person of delicate health, sickly person.

takwitsoo?nimi?arʉ (v) wither, wilt, droop.

takwi?oobitʉ (v) gather (as in sewing).

takwokarʉ W (v) drag something (with the foot).

takwʉkitʉ (v) throw (throw at the foot of something, throw at a line).

takwʉperʉ (v) crease (with the foot). *See* **makwipunarʉ**.

takwʉsaitʉ (v) loosen (with the foot).

takwʉsarʉ (adj) loosened by foot.

takwʉsipʉ (n) perspiration, sweat.

takwʉsiskʉrʉ (v) tangle (with the foot).

tama- (pfx) tooth. *See* **taama**.

tamakotse? (n) toothpaste [**taama** tooth + **kotse?** washer].

tamakwita (n) roots of the teeth [**taama** tooth + **kwiita** bottom].

tamamatsuma? (n) toothbrush [**taama** tooth + **matsuma** wiper].

tamatsa?nika? (n) false teeth, dentures [**taama** tooth + **tsa?nika** put on].

tamanahkerʉ (v) measure (by stepping off a distance) [**ta-** foot + **manahke** measure].

tamanikarʉ (v) drive across (as drive cattle across).

tamanʉʉtsikwatʉ, tamanʉʉsukatʉ (v) suffer from a toothache [**taama** teeth + **nʉʉsukaa** feel].

tamaruhkʉ (n) gums of teeth [**taama** teeth + **tuhkʉ** flesh]. *See* **so?oruhkʉ**.

tamarʉkarʉ (v) graduate (finish high school or college).

tamarʉkʉkatʉ (adj) completed, graduated person.

tamihtsi?benihtsi? (n, voc) dear little brothers (an expression of endearment). **Tamihtsi?benihtʉhtsi?nʉʉ, hina mʉnʉ hanibʉì ni?** Dear little brothers, what are you doing so much? (5:3).

taminaitʉ (v) break at the joint (cause to be broken).

tamiʔ (n) younger brother.

tamu, tamʉ (n) sinew (taken from muscle of beef). **nʉmʉ ramu** Comanche thread.

tamunaikʉmiʔarʉ (v) go on foot to meet someone, meet someone by going on foot.

tamutsoʔi K, tamutʉsoʔi (n) greenbriar. *Smilax bonanox* (leaves used as cigarette wrappers).

Tamutʉsoʔi hunuʔbi (n) Briar Creek.

tamʉkʉrʉ (v) drive animals by force. **Tʉhʉye tamʉkʉ.** Drive the horses up.

tana, tanapʉ (n) knee.

tanatookarʉtʉ (v), *pl* **tanatooyʉkwitʉ** kneel down sitting back on heels. *See* **wʉnʉhkarʉrʉ.**

tanaʔ kuʔe (n) kneecap [**tana** knee + **kuʔe** top].

Taninʉʉ (n) Liver Eaters (band of middle Comanches in Texas located south of the Peace River).

tanisiʔ W, tanʉniʔ K (n) king (in card game).

Tanoyoʔtsoʔmeʔe (n) Easter [**ta-** (unspec) + **noyoʔ** egg + **tsoʔmeʔ** gather].

tanuarʉ (v) push, move something, rake together (with foot).

tanuraakʉtʉ (v) chase away.

tanʉkikʉtʉ (v) shoo (cause to fly away in some way, as to frighten chickens). *See* **manʉkikʉrʉ.**

tanʉʉhkupaitʉ (v) trip someone [**ta-** with foot + **nʉʉhkupai-** made fall].

tanʉʔyʉkitʉ (v) tread heavily, stomp (make sound of running, heavy footsteps).

tanʉkʉtʉ K (v) tamp down (with the feet).

tapearʉ (v) crack something. *See* **tahparʉ.**

taperʉ (v) push, make fall using foot (as push soil into a hole).

tapi wanapʉ K (n) dry goods (*lit* thin cloth, as opposed to sturdy, hand-woven material or buffalo hide). *See* **tarʉwanapi.**

tapi naʔsʉkiaʔ (n) lightweight shawl [**tapi** flat, thin + **naʔsʉkia** shawl]. *See* **pohotʉ naʔsʉkiaʔ.**

tapisoʔaitʉ W (adj) angered, enraged.

tapikoʔ (n) heel of the foot.

tapitʉhtsi (adj) thin (tissuelike), sheer. *See* **hʉnʉketʉ.**

tapʉnukeerʉ W, tapinuketʉ K (v) polish (slick, smooth). *See* **mapʉnukeerʉ.**

tapʉ K, tapʉhʉ W (n) leg hair [**ta-** foot + **pʉhʉ** fuzz].

tapʉhabi (v, sg obj), *pl obj* **tahpakwabi** make swim. *See* **pahabitʉ.**

tapʉherʉ (v, sg obj), *pl obj* **tayu miʔitʉdrop** (let fall), remove, take off (with claws or foot).

tapʉtsaitʉ (v) break open (with the foot), burst (with the foot).

tarʉwanapi W (n) dry goods, material possessions. *See* **tapiwanapʉ.**

tasarʉ (v) step over something (lift foot to step over something).

tasakwʉʉhkiʔ (n) toes.

tasiito (n) toenail, claw, hoof.

tasikoʔiʔmiʔarʉ (v) skate (slide on something while standing on feet). **Kahnikuhu tasiko?imi?a-ru.** He skated to the house. *See* **tahkitemi?aru.**

tasitotsaru W (v) scratch, rub (with foot, as to relieve an itch).

tasi?a? W, **tasi?akoobe** K (n) smallpox, freckles, rash on skin. *See* **tutusa?wutu.**

tasi?kwairu (v) tear with the foot [ta- foot + si?kwa tear].

tasi?kwaitu (adj) torn by a foot.

tasi?womi?aru (v) walk dragging one foot (as when injured or lame).

tasoni (n, acc) floor, carpet, rug.

tasoona (n, nom) floor, carpet, rug [ta- foot + soona quilt].

tasukaru (v) touch, feel with foot.

Tasúra (n) That's It, Water Horse Band (a Comanche band).

tasu?netu (v) wipe feet, rub feet [ta- foot + su?ne rub].

tasukupunitu (v) squint, peep (look through squinted eyes). **Sumu? kuse? uruumatu tasukupuni.** One of them peeped (4:13). *See* **wihtekatu.**

tasukumitu (v) have cold feet [ta- feet + sukumi become cold].

tasusu?nitu (v) numb, asleep. **Nu napema nu? karu u tasusu?ni.** Sitting on my foot, it became numb. *See* **susu?nitu.**

tatsatu (adj), *n* **taatsa** summertime.

Tatsatu mua, Tatsa mua (n) August (*lit* summer month).

tatsii? (n) nits, lice eggs. **Ma papikuku nu? tatsii punii.** I saw, found lice eggs in her hair.

tatsinuupi (n) star. **Tatsinuupi tsa? tsitsirapuutu.** The star is twinkling, sparkling.

tatsipu (n) sumac (foul, ill-smelling), skunkbush. **Rhus trilobata** Nutt. (bark used in treating colds).

Tatsiwóo (name) Buffalo (person).

tatsukweru (v) mash, crush, smash.

tatuwetu (v) limp (person only). *See* **wihnaitu.**

tatubaru (v) break something. **Ohnaa tsa? nu tusone tatubai.** The baby broke my dish.

tatuke?neru, tanukunuru (v) press something down (with foot) [ta- foot + take?ne press down].

tawekwitu (adj) penned up, driven into ground (one end). *See* **ta?ikukatu.**

tawiaru W, **turawi?iaru** K (v) wear out shoes.

tawohho (n) enemy tribe (*lit* our enemies). *See* **wohho-.**

tawo?i? K (n) gun (any type), pistol, rifle.

tawunaru (v), *pl* **tawuni?itu** stake down, nail down. **Numukahni u? tawuni?itu.** He staked down the teepee (using several stakes).

tayu?maru (v), *pl* **tayumi?i-** knock something down.

tayu?nekaru (v) pound food. **U sumutayu?netsi, u maroponi?inu.** Completely pounding it, (they) made balls of it (grapes) (116:17).

tayu?neru (v) crush, pound with a pestle (cause to be crushed). **Hanibihta u? tayu?netu.** She pounded the corn (with a pestle).

tayutsuru (v) awaken someone by shouting, speaking (cause someone to get out of bed by shouting or speaking).

Ta?ahpu (name) Our Father, Great Spirit (deity).

ta?ahpu?a tekwawapi K (n) prophet (one who tells forth a message).

ta?aikutu (v) pedal (cause to roll by pushing with feet as in pedaling a bicycle) [**ta-** foot + **ai** lope + **ku** (caus)]. *See* **naraaikutu.**

ta?aikutu (n) bicycle. *See* **naraaiku?.**

ta?ikukatu (adj) imprisoned, locked up. *See* **tawekwitu.**

ta?ikuru (v), *pl* **takwekwitu** pen up animal, lock up someone.

ta?itsa?buru W (v) have leg cramp.

ta?ka? (n), *pl* **ta?ka?nuu** kinsman of either sex.

ta?ka?miitsa? (n) wart.

ta?ki? (n) kidney.

ta?kubuu? W, tahkabuu? K (n) slingshot.

ta?nika? W, tahtukii? K (n) stirrup [**ta-** foot + NIKA? put through]. *See* **narahtukii?.**

ta?nikutu (v) insert (put through), nail something.

ta?okitu (adj) spilled by someone.

ta?ookitu (v) drive together, round up (get together as cattle).

ta?oo? (n) meat (dried and pounded).

ta?se?yuku?, ta?si?yuki? (n) man's moccasin (named for the rattle or jingle of tin decorations on buffalo-hide moccasin as man walked). *See* **numunapu.**

ta?si?wooru (v) paw the earth, scratch up earth.

ta?siwoo ruhkapu W (n) buffalo meat.

ta?si?woo?

ta?siwoo wana?uhu W, ta?siwoo uhu K (n) buffalo blanket (soft, tanned hide).

ta?si?woo? (n) buffalo [**ta-** foot + **si?woo** paw earth]. **Ta?si?wóo?a muu tubitsi yuhuwehki?ha tai tubehkaku.** Kill us a buffalo that you find (is) really fat (69:4).

ta?uraru (v) meet someone. **O tsa? wa?ihpu? pu kumahpu?a ra?uranu.** That woman met her husband.

ta?urukaru K (v) own something. **oyo?ko bu ta?urukanaall** she owns.

ta?urukaru W (v) deserve, merit. **U ra?urukatu ?u.** He deserves it.

ta?wahkóo? W, ta?bahkóo K (n) edible tuber. *See* **ahwepu.**

ta?wairu (v) locate something (by feeling around with the foot).

ta?wiitsa (n), *du* **taa?witsanuku** calf of leg [**ta-** foot + **wiitsa** leg].

ta?wikitu (v) shake foot. *See* **tahta?nitu.**

ta?witsa roponiitu K (v) have leg cramp (in calf of leg). *See* **toponitu.**

ta?wokinae?ree eka K (n) swamp rabbit. *See* **ekae?ree.**

ta?wo?ekaru (v), *pl* **ta?kwubai-** shoot a gun repeatedly (as a rifle or machine gun).

ta?wo?i? (n), acc ta?wo?i? a
  gunshot. Ta?wo?i?a nʉ? nakai. I
  heard a gunshot. See tsatʉkarʉ.
ta?yaami?arʉ (v) carry in the claws.
ta?yaahkana? W, ta?yaahkatʉ
  K (n) something carried in the
  claws.
ta?yʉrʉhkitʉ K (v) jerk the leg. See
  tahta?yʉtʉ.
tebuunitʉ (v) recover from illness,
  improve in health. Tʉepʉrʉ tsa?
  tebuuni. The child got better.
tekwawapi (n) speaker, spokesman.
tekwakʉwapi W, tekwawapi
  K, (n) interpreter. Taibo? nʉʉ
  u? nʉmʉ tekwawapi. He was
  the interpreter of Comanche
  for the white man. See nʉmʉ
  rekwakʉwapi.
tekwakʉtʉ (v) interpret (lit to help
  to speak; speak for someone).
  Taibo?nii u? tekwakʉtʉ. He
  interpreted for the white men.
tekwapʉ (n) word, speech.
tekwapʉ rʉboopʉ (n) grammar (lit
  words on paper).
tekwarʉ (v), pl niwʉnʉrʉ speak,
  talk to someone. See yʉkwitʉ.
Tekwitsi M (name) Skinny-and-
  wrinkled (person).
tekwʉniwapi (n) a brave, Indian
  brave, town crier. Paraibo tsa? u
  tekwʉniwapi?ai. The chief made
  him a brave.
tekwʉnitʉ (v) announce (as town
  crier gives news). Paraibo?a
  kimana?u tekwʉni?i. He
  announced the chief's coming.
tenahpʉ? W, tʉnahpʉ? K (n) man,
  pl tananʉʉ, tenanʉʉ men. Urʉ
  tsa? tʉnahpʉ? nʉʉmʉ. That man
  is a Comanche.

tenahpʉ?a kwasu?ʉ (n) man's shirt.
  See kwasu?ʉ.

tenahpʉ?

Tenebeka, Tʉnʉbekʉ (name) Gets-
  to-be-middle-aged-man (a man
  who lived in 1872).
tetsi (n) man's brother-in-law. See
  pʉhʉre?tsi.
te?animui (n) biting fly.
timʉihʉ? (n) snake root, church
  root (from Mexico). Liatris Schreb.
  (for curing asthma, emphysema;
  rub on legs or feet to repel
  rattlesnakes). See itsa.
Tinawa, Tenawa, Tehnahwah
  (n) Those-who-stay-downstream
  (Comanche band formerly
  northeast of the Brazos River and
  northwest of the present Dallas-
  Fort Worth area).
tiro?woko (n) throwing arrows.
tobo?ihupiitʉ (v) stop (come to a
  stop). Kuyuníi?nʉʉ si?ana maba?a
  tobo?ihupiitʉ. The turkeys came
  to a stop here somewhere by him
  (8:41). See wʉnʉhupiitʉ.

tobo?ikatʉ (v) stand.

toh- (pfx) ref. to push (with the fist, hand).

tohhobinitʉ, tohnobinitʉ (v) hurt (cause to groan by hitting with fist).

tohhomonutsarʉ W, **tuhhumunutsarʉ** K (v) crumble, crush in pieces (with fist).

tohkobi?itʉ (v) break something up. **Huupita ma? tohkobi?itʉ.** He is breaking up the wood (into sticks).

tohkonarʉ (v) dig a hole in the ground (as with crowbar or pole).

tohkʉarʉ (v, sg obj), *pl obj* **tohto-?itʉ** help to mount. *See* **to?itʉ.**

tohkwe?yarʉ (v) take off, disassemble, remove (as part from an object).

tohkwʉmarʉ (v) pry open, pound on to open, open forcibly.

toh-, tohmapʉ (n) year.

Tohmʉa (n) January (year month, for beginning a new year) [**tohmapʉ** year + **mʉa** month].

tohoobe̱, tohobe (n) hindquarter, thigh (from knee up), foreleg. *See* **kotsana.**

tohpaaku?netʉ W (adj) pushed under water.

tohpakurʉ (v, pl), *sg* **topʉkaarʉ** chisel something, split something.

tohparaarʉ W (v) soften by pounding. *See* **tsohkwe.**

tohpa?itʉ (v), *pl* **tohtʉkwarʉ** hit with fist, slap with palm of hand, punch. **Ma kobetohpa?itʉ u?.** He hit him on the face.

tohpa?i̱sokitʉ W (adj) sprinkled.

tohporoorʉ (v) scatter by force. **Haniibita u? tohporo?ai.** He scattered the corn.

tohpotsotsii (n) nightshade. *Sola- num* sp [C & J] (used in general tonic and in tuberculosis remedy).

tohpunitʉ (v) test, try out, bargain, make a deal (as in buying or bartering).

tohpʉarʉ (v) stop hitting with fist or palm of hand. *See* **pʉarʉ.**

tohpʉtsa?itʉ (v) make burst (as a bag). **Wose u? tohpʉtsa?i.** He burst the bag.

tohpʉsakʉrʉ K (v) dab to wipe or erase, erase. *See* **tohtsomarʉ.**

tohtani?itʉ (v) carry and put down.

tohtarakiitʉ (v) pet, stroke.

tohtarakitʉ (v) clap hands [**toh-** hand + **tara-** (sound) + **ki-** say].

tohtaraki?arʉ (v) knock on door, pet or stroke. *See* **nisutaitʉ.**

tohtía masʉa? (n) wheat (grain).

tohtía narʉmʉʉ? (n) bakery (*lit* bread store).

tohtía narʉso̱ (n) flour sack.

tohtía sonipʉ (n) wheat plant (*lit* bread grass).

tohtía sonipʉha taka? (n) rye, barley (*lit* mate to wheat).

tohtía tsasa?wʉki? (n) flour sifter.

tohtía? (n) bread, tortilla, pancake.

tohtía?arʉ (v) bake, make bread.

tohtía? rʉhkapʉ (n) Communion (sacrament), Mass (sacrament). *See* **pʉʉhibitu?itʉ.**

tohtoponitʉ (adj) round, spherical. *See* **maropo?ni?pʉ.**

tohtopo?narʉ (v) roll up with something.

tohto?itʉ (v, pl), *sg* **tohkʉarʉ** exit forcibly. *See* **to?itʉ, kʉarʉ.**

tohtsanarʉ (v), *pl* **tohtsani?i** hang up something.

tohtsatsaru (v) move from side to side (as a snake before attack).

tohtsiyuʔitu (v) scrape meat from a hide, chisel or split with an axe. *See* **topukaaru.**

tohtsiʔaru (v) K chisel wood; W hit with knuckle or fist.

tohtsomaru W (v) dab to wipe or erase. *See* **tohpusakuru.**

tohtubuʔitu (v) drill a hole with an instrument (as into wood or leather with a drill).

tohtukiʔaru (v) put something back in place.

tohtukwaru (v, pl), *sg* **tohpaʔitu** slap or punch repeatedly.

tohtumapu (adj) closed off, stopped up.

tohtumaru (v), *pl* **tohtumiʔitu** stop flow (as of liquid by putting lid on opening).

tohturooniitu W (adj) braced, supported. *See* **marurooniitu.**

tohturuʔaru W (v) rip something. *See* **wuhturuʔaru.**

tohtuwaru (v) open something (using an instrument).

tokaru (v) pull off, knock off. *See* **wuhtokaru.**

tokiaru (v) peel off (as tree bark).

tokoboʔniitu K (adj) calm, quiet.

tokoʔ (n), *acc* **tokoʔa** maternal grandfather, man's uterine grandchild.

tokusuakutu (v) trust someone, believe in someone. **U rokusuakutu nu?.** I believe in him.

tokwaitu (v) excavate, explore for oil, dig (searching in soil).

tokwetabeni (n) noon, midday.

tokwetukan (n), *adj* **tokwehtukanihtu** midnight (at the stroke of midnight).

tokwetukatu (adj) agreeable, approving. **Tokwetukatu u? Cachekahtu miʔaruʔi.** She agreed to go to Cache.

tokwetuparu (v) listen (pay attention), obey orders.

tokwetutuaru (v) admire, agree with someone. *See* **suʔakutu.**

tokwetu (adj) exact, proper. **Nu napu tsa? tohtokwetu.** My shoes fit just right.

tokwitetu (v) peep into.

tokwuriaitu (v) spill something on purpose.

tokwusikutu (v) tangle something (with the hands).

tokwusuakuna (n) belief, faith.

tokwusuakutu (v) believe something or someone.

tokwukiʔaru (v) pitch, throw (something long, as a spear).

tokwuriaru (v) spill out on something, pour on. **Pitsipuha u tokwuriaru.** He poured the milk on it.

tomakwuyetu W (v) chase on horseback.

tominaru (v) break at joint of body.

tomo- (pfx) ref. to sky, cloud.

tomobaʔatu (n) sky, heavens [**tomo** cloud + **paʔatu** above].

tomohtoopu W (n) two-year-old item. *See* **wahatomopu.**

tomohtootu W (adj) two years old.

tomoobi (n) clouds, heavens.

tomooru (adj) winter. **Utsui tomooru maʔ.** It was a cold winter.

tomopu (n) year. **tomoopu** K (n) cloud, winter, year.

tomotsiaru W (v) sharpen to a point.

tomoyaketu (v) thunder. **Pia tomoyaketu.** It thundered loudly [**tomo-** cloud + **yake** cry].

Tomo?a tua? (name) Sky-child (person).

tomoakatʉ W (adj) cloudy. **Tomoakatʉ ma?.** It was a cloudy day. **Tomookati nʉ? puni.** It is clouded up I see.

tomo?akitʉ (v) cloud up.

tomʉsiketʉ K (adj) tangled up. **Nʉ paapi tsa? tomʉsiketʉ.** My hair is tangled up.

tonarʉ (v), *pl* **towaka-** insect sting, stab, pierce. **Ʉnʉbihnaa nʉ tona?i.** The bee stung me.

tona? (n) stinger of an insect.

tonʉkʉrʉ (v) tamp down (with instrument, as with crowbar or pole).

tookaatso̱, tohkaatso (n) toe.

tooniitʉ (v), *pl* **tooyʉhkatʉ** graze from place to place. **Pimoroonʉʉ tsa? nana?atanaiki̱ tooyʉhka-tʉʉ.** The cows are grazing in different pastures.

toorʉ W (v) graze.

too?itʉ (v, pl), *sg* **to?yarʉ** unhitch.

Tope (name) Quanah Parker's wife, Tope (died in 1962 at over ninety years of age).

Topehtsi, Topache (name) Pass-it-on (outstanding deacon; a strong Christian man).

topohtʉ (adj) round (ball-like), spherical.

toponi- (pfx) ref. to ball-like.

toponibihuura? (n) pea [**toponi (htʉ)** round + **pihuura?** bean].

toponitʉ K (v) have muscle cramp or spasm (describes knot formed when muscle cramps). **Nʉtawʉ tsa? toponi.** My foot muscle cramped. *See* **ta?witsaroponiitʉ.**

toponiweki̱ (adj) circular.

Topʉsana (name) Flower (baby of Cynthia Ann Parker; the baby died of white man's disease after being captured with her mother by whites).

topʉ (n), *acc* **topʉha** shield. **Topa u?yarʉ.** He took a shield.

topʉkaarʉ (v), *pl* **tohpakurʉ, tohpaku?itʉ** chisel, split (as to split wood). *See* **tohtsiyu?itʉ.**

topʉsarʉ (v) bead something (do beadwork on an article). **Nʉmʉnapʉha u? topʉsarʉ.** She beaded the moccasin.

toro?ihtʉkitʉ (adj) isolated, separated from others.

tosa- (pfx) white, silver.

tosa ekapi̱tʉ W (adj) pink (lit white-red).

tosa hʉwʉnikatʉma?, tosa hʉ?wʉnikitʉ (adv) early, before dawn (lit white horizon). *See* **hʉwʉni, tsaa nabuni.**

tosa kwana?hʉ W, **tosa wanahʉ** K (n) bedsheet [**tosa** white + **kwana?hʉ** blanket].

tosa kwiisu? (n) black bird with white wings.

tosa naboo? (n) K horse (calico); W horse (paint; white patches on chest and rump) [**tosa** white + **naboo** painted]. *See* **pitsa naboo?**

tosa nabunitʉ (v) appear to be white [**tosa-** white + **na** (refl) + **puni** see].

tosa nakaai (n) hawk [**tosa** white + **nakaai** hear].

tosa nʉʉbaai? (n) frost, dew (short form) [**tosa** white + **nʉʉbaa?i̱** dew].

tosa nʉʉbaikatʉ (n) frost. **Tosa nʉʉbaikatʉ ma?.** There is frost.

tosa ohapitʉ (adj) cream colored (*lit* white-yellow).

tosaraiʔ (n) devil's horse (insect).

tosahpuhihwi̱ (n) silver money, coins [**tosa** white + **puhihwi̱** money].

tosahtukaʔ W (n) candle [**tosa** white + **tuka** light].

tosahwi̱ (n) silver.

tosapi̱ K (n), *adj* **tosapi̱tʉ** W white, silver.

tosa rohtiyaʔ (n) cracker [**tosa** white + **tohtiyaʔ** bread].

tosa seyuʔyukiʔ (n) ash tree. *Fraxinus americana* L.

tosa tukanai huupi (n) white oak.

tosa wahtsuki (n) horseweed.

tosa waikina̱ (n) hack (white two-seated buggy). *See* **tuwaikina̱.**

tosa yuhu rukaiʔ K (n) candle [**tosa** white + **yuhhu** lard + **tukai** light].

tosaʔ   ⸸ wehki'ai

tosaʔ (n) white horse.

tosiite (n), *acc* **tosíito̱** hoof (as of cow or horse).

tosiʔkwarʉ (v) tear something (using an instrument, as a knife). **Tʉhanitʉ u pʉhi tosikwai.** He tore the hide he is skinning.

tosoʔnetʉ (v) rub off, scrape off.

tosoʔwaitʉ (v) try or want to hit with fist.

totohtʉ (n) edible tuber. *See* **ahwepʉ.**

totsiyaa aawo̱ (n) vase (*lit* flower container).

Totsiyaaih tabenihtʉ W, **Totsi yaarabeni̱htʉ** K (n) Decoration Day, Memorial Day (**lit** flower day). *See* **Pʉkʉra totsiyaaʔaiʔeka.**

Totsiyaa mʉa (n) May (*lit* flower month).

totsiyaa papihtsipʉ (n) stamen of flower.

totsiyaa patʉpi̱naatʉ, totsiyaa puhhipʉ (n) flower petal (*lit* flower leaf).

totsiyaa tsakwʉnaʔ (n) flower vase (*lit* flowers set out). *See* **tsakwʉnarʉ.**

totsiyaaʔ, totsiyaapʉ (n) flower. **Tsaati nʉʔ totsiyaaʔa puni.** I see a pretty flower.

totsiyaaʔa sʉʉki̱ (n) vine, stem of plant.

totsiyaitʉ (v) bloom, blossom out.

totsiyakatʉ (adj) blooming.

totsʉbakitʉ (v) hang up. **Nabooʔa u totsʉbakii uʔ.** He hung the picture.

totʉbihkurʉ (v) beat on, knock on, make galloping sound. **Tʉhʉi nʉʔ totʉbihkunʉ nahkai.** I hear the horses galloping.

toya, toyaabi̱ (n) mountain.

toyaarʉkitʉ W, **toyaakatʉ** K (v) carry (hold something in lap while riding). **Ohnaaʔa u toyaarʉkitʉ.** He is holding the baby in his lap.

toyaketʉ (v) make cry by hitting [**to-** hit + **yake-** cry].

toya ruhku? (n) leopard (*lit* mountain meat). *See* **nabooh roya ruhku?**.

toyaru (v), *pl* **tohimaru** adopt a child, lift up, carry in arms. **Ohnáa?a ma? toyaai.** She carried the baby (in her arms). **Puu ohna?nii maruu tohimau.** They carried their babies. *See* **tuetunabinaru**.

toyo (n) neck.

toyo kwabaru (v) hug (around neck) [**toyo** neck + **kwabe** hug]. **Nu kaku tsa? nu toyokwabai.** My grandmother hugged me. *See* **kwabaru**.

toyo tahka?miitsa (n) sweetbreads (*lit* neck wart).

toyo tsihka?aru (v), *pl* **toyo tsihpomaru** behead (cutting, as with knife). **Kokora?a?a toyo tsihka?ai.** He cut off the chicken's head.

toyo wuhka?aru (v) behead (chopping, as with axe).

toyopu, tooyo (n), *acc* **toyopuna** neck. **Nu toyopu tsa? nuutsikwaru.** My neck hurts.

toyusekaitu (v) excite, stir up excitement.

toyusukai (adj) exciting.

to?aikuru (v) roll to start something, start (cause to operate with the hand).

to?itu (v, pl), *sg* **kuaru** appear, come out. *See* **tohto?itu**.

to?i (n), *acc* **to?iha** pipe (for smoking). **Pu to?iha u? pahumu?itu.** He is smoking his pipe.

to?ibitu (v), *pl* **kiahbitu** come out at particular place.

to?nikaru K (v) put away for safekeeping. *See* **turubaki?aru**.

to?nikaru W (v), *pl* **tubakitu** load into a container. **maro?nikatu** put food into mouth.

to?pu (n) shield. *See* **topu**.

to?roponii? (n) beetlike tuber. *See* **ahwepu**.

to?tsimuhpe? (n) mattock, pick for scraping hides (with short cedarwood handle and heavy metal blade). [**to?tsi** chisel + **muhpe** hoe]. *See* **muhpe?**.

to?uraru (v) meet someone, find something being looked for. **Pai to?uraai u?.** He found water.

to?wuminaitu (v) fail to reach, fall short.

to?wu?wenitu (v, pl), *sg* **wuhtiaru** empty into, dump into (pour into different containers).

to?yabaitu (v) prick up the ears. **Tuhuya tsa? to?yabahkatu.** The horse is pricking up its ears.

to?yaru W (v), *pl* **too?itu** unhitch an animal. **Pu puuki u to?yaru.** He unhitched his horse. *See* **noro?yaru**.

tsaa (adj) good, well. **Suruse? tsaa kamanu.** That tasted good (110:15). **Tsaa nu? u muui.** I made him well, healed him.

tsaa kamaru (v) taste good.

tsaa manusuru (v) please someone (make someone happy, be happy).

tsaa manusu?itu (adj) pleased.

tsaa marabetoikatu K (adj) bright, shiny.

tsaa naahkatu (adj) rich. **Oru tsa? tunahpu tsaa naahkatu.** That (he) is a rich man.

tsaa nabuni (adv) dawn. *See* **tosa huwunikatuma?, huwuni**.

tsaa nabunitʉ (v) dawn (light enough to see). **Tsaa nabunikitʉ maʔ.** It is getting light enough to see.

tsaa nʉʉsukatʉ (adj) happy, rejoicing.

Tsaa tenayakeʔ (name) Good-crier (person).

Tsaa tsopaʔ (name) Easy-to-break (person).

tsaana, tsanani (adv) futilely, emptily (in vain, to no avail).

tsaanahapʉ (n), *acc* **tsaanahapʉha** riches, treasure.

tsaati tamakatʉ W, **tsatsati tamakatʉ** (v) chatter (teeth), quiver (lips).

tsaatʉ (adj) good.

tsaatʉ narʉmuʔipʉ (n) gospel, good news.

tsah- (pfx) ref. to pull (forward or up by hand).

tsahhanitʉ, tsahaniitʉ (v) drive a car or team by hand.

tsahhomonutsarʉ (v) crush, crumble (with both hands).

tsahhorarʉ (v) dig (with the hands). *See* **mahorarʉ.**

tsahhuhyarʉ (v) hurt someone by accident.

tsahhʉkwʉʔniitʉ W, **tsahhʉwʉʔniʔarʉ** K (v) lift up (as to see underneath).

tsahimarʉ (v, pl obj), *sg obj* **tsayarʉ** carry a container by the handle.

tsahkarʉkʉrʉ (v, sg obj), *pl obj* **tsayʉkwikʉ-** set upright, right something.

tsahkaʔarʉ (v, sg obj), *pl obj* **tsah pomiʔitʉ** pull apart, break off (sever a flexible object by hand). **Puibihnáa nʉʔ tsahpomiʔituʔi.** I

am going to pull watermelons (off the vine).

tsahkítoʔarʉ (v) shell something by hand, peel something. **Ohapitʉa uʔ tsahkitoʔai.** He peeled the orange (with fingers).

tsahkiʔaitʉ (v) cut someone to wound, scratch using an instrument.

tsahkobarʉ (v, sg obj), *pl obj* **tsahkobiʔitʉ** break off, snap off (sever something stiff with hands).

tsahkokarʉ (v, sg obj), *pl obj* **tahpomiʔitʉ** break something up (into fine pieces with foot) [**tah-** foot + **pomi-** break up].

tsahkooʔitʉ (v) cause to return, cause to turn around and come back.

tsahkʉarʉ (v, pl obj), *sg obj* **tsahtoʔitʉ** pull up, force out, take out.

tsahkʉnarʉ (v) sew (primarily by hand though could be by machine).

tsahkwanitʉ (v) claw at something, tear at something.

tsahkwaʔnuʔitʉ (v) throw down a person (as in wrestling).

tsahkweʔyarʉ (v, sg obj), *pl obj* **tsahkweʔyuʔitʉ** undress, disrobe, pull something off or out. *See* **natsahkweʔyarʉ.**

tsahkwitsoʔarʉ (v) save someone's life (by pulling him out of something).

tsahkwʉmarʉ (v, sg obj), *pl obj* **tsahkwʉmiʔitʉ** unwrap, unwind, unlace, loosen, unroll. **Nʉ nahposa nʉʔ tsahkwʉmarʉ.** I am unlacing my shoe. *See* **pʉrʉsuʔarʉ, tsahpekoʔarʉ.**

tsahkwʉnunúukitʉ (v) unwind (as thread or yarn). **Nʉ wanaramị u? tsahkwʉnanukị.** He unwound my thread.

tsahkwʉrʉ?arʉ (v) skin animal, take off layer. **Arʉka?a nʉ? tsahkwʉrʉ?arʉ.** I am skinning the deer. *See* **pʉhʉ tsahkwe?yarʉ.**

tsahnʉarʉ (v) lift from a prone position. **Tenahpʉ tuinahpʉ?a tsa?nʉai.** The man helped the boy get up.

tsahpaaku?nikarʉ (v) duck someone, push someone under water. **Ohka u tsahpaaku?nikatʉ.** He is ducking her. *See* **paku?nerʉ.**

tsahpakitʉ (v) adhere (stick on), cling to.

tsahpako?arʉ (v) split, tear apart. **Amawo?a tsahpa?ko?i nʉ?.** I split the apple in two (with hands).

tsahpakʉkarʉ (v) attach (as a postage stamp). **Tsa? tʉboopʉ tsahpakʉkatʉkwʉ.** The two pieces of paper are stuck together.

tsahpararʉ (v) spread out something (as piece of cloth). **Tosakʉni nʉ? tsahpararʉ.** I am stretching out a canvas (on the ground).

tsahparʉ (v) pull down. **Sooni nʉ? tsahpe.** I pulled my blanket down.

tsahparʉ W (v) release (allow someone to go) [**tsah-** pull + **pʉa?** let loose].

tsahpeko?arʉ (v) unwrap an object. **Nʉe tamasursai?a tsahpeko?ai.** I unwrapped my gift. *See* **tsahkwʉmarʉ.**

tsahperʉ (v, sg obj), *pl obj* **tsayuma** tear down (as a building); scatter bundled items (throw groups of items here and there).

tsahpetitʉ (adj) scattered (bundled items).

tsahpiso?arʉ (v) anger. **Nʉ naami? nʉ? tsahpiso?ai.** My younger sister made me angry.

tsahpitsoorʉ (v) wring out with hands (as in washing clothes). **Wa?ihpʉ? tsa? oyo?ri tsahpitsooni.** The woman wrung out the clothes.

tsahpi?erʉ (v) fish, pull out (fish). **Pekwina nʉ? tsahpi?eru?i.** I will fish. **Orʉ tsa? tʉepʉ paapasi oko tsahpi?epʉniitʉ.** That child is pulling potatoes out of that container.

tsahpohtoorʉ (v) burst by pulling [**tsah-** pull + **pohto-** burst].

tsahpomi?itʉ (v, pl) break, pull apart. *See* **tsahka?arʉ.**

tsahporakitʉ (v) crack knuckles. **Pʉ mo?ai u? tsahporakiitʉ.** He is cracking his knuckles.

tsahporʉ (v) mark off, make a mark on something. **Ohka nʉ? sokobitʉ tsahporu?i.** I am going to mark off that land.

tsahpo?arʉ, tsahpo?akatʉ (v) scatter something. **Tuinapʉ tsa? amawoo?a tsahpo?akatʉ.** The boy scattered the apples around. *See* **poohkatʉ.**

tsahpo?tsarʉ (v, inan obj) jerk something toward oneself, pull a bouncy object [**tsah-** pull + **po?tsa** jerk].

tsahpunitʉ (v) show someone something (make known to

someone) [**tsah-** pull + **puni**
see]. **Pꭒ naboohpꭒ tsahpunii.**
She is showing her picture.

tsahpꭒarꭒ W (v) release (allow
someone to go) [**tsah-** pull + **pꭒa**
let loose].

**tsahpꭒkꭒsuʔarꭒ W, tsahpꭒsuʔarꭒ
K** (v) unfold, take apart, unroll.
tsahpꭒsuʔaitꭒ unfolded (as
cloth).

tsahpꭒyerꭒ (v) pull out of
container. **Siʔanetꭒ ma
kwasimaku marii tsapꭒyénꭒ.** At
this place he pulled them out by
their tails (10:20).

tsahpꭒherꭒ, tsaapꭒherꭒ (v), *pl*
tsayumiʔi take down off of
something, unload. **Nꭒ soona
tsahpꭒhe.** I pulled down, took
down my blanket (off shelf). *See*
tsapꭒyetꭒ.

tsahtaaikatꭒ (adj) holey (having
hole or holes).

tsahtaikꭒtꭒ (v) dig, make a hole
with hands. **Orꭒ tsaʔ waʔipꭒ
ohta wanahpꭒ u tsahtaikꭒtꭒ.**
She is making a hole through the
material (cloth).

tsahtobarꭒ (v) uproot (pull up by
the roots). **Sꭒmꭒruku tsaʔ ma
tsahtoba ohka tamꭒsuaka.**
Someone uprooted that plant. **Pꭒ
itꭒmꭒsꭒapꭒ uʔ tsahtoba- katꭒ.**
She is uprooting her plant.

tsahtokoʔarꭒ (v) pull bones out of
joint.

tsahtopoʔnarꭒ (v), *pl* **tsahtoponi-
ʔitꭒ** roll into a ball (make round).

tsahtoʔarꭒ K, tsahtokoʔarꭒ W
(v) unseal something, pry up,
pull off. **U kuʔe tsahtoʔarꭒ.** He
is unsealing the top. **U kuʔe uʔ**

tsahtoʔakatꭒ. He is pulling the
top off.

tsahtoʔirꭒ (v, sg obj), *pl obj*
tsapꭒyetꭒ bring out, take out,
pull up. **Orꭒ tsahtoʔi kahnikꭒ-
kꭒ.** That man brought that baby
out of the house.

tsahtoʔitꭒ (adj), *pl* **tsahkꭒarꭒ**
forced out, pulled up.

tsahtsiʔarꭒ (v) scratch leaving a
mark. **Waʔooʔ nꭒ tsahtsiʔai.** The
cat scratched me.

tsahtsukitꭒ (v) close (as to shut a
window). **Narabuni uʔ tsahtsuki.**
He closed the window.

tsahtsuʔmarꭒ (v) deplete a supply.
Kobe matsumaʔ tsah- tsuʔmai.
He took the last towel.

tsahtukarꭒ (v) unplug to extinguish,
to disconnect (as an electric cord).
W snuff fire with fingers.

tsahtunaabarꭒ (v) straighten (lay
out straight). **Ohka nꭒʔ huupina
tsahtunaabaruʔi.** I am going to
straighten that wood.

tsahtunehtꭒ (adj) stretched (as a
bow), straightened (as an arrow).

tsahturerꭒ (v, sg obj), *pl obj*
tsah- tunehtsꭒtꭒ pull with full
strength, stretch (make tense, as a
bow).

tsahturꭒ (v) stretch something out
(as a rope).

tsahtꭒwarꭒ, tsaatꭒwarꭒ (v,
sg obj), *pl obj* **tsahtꭒwaʔitꭒ**
open something (as a box or
trunk), take down a teepee. **Ma
tsaatꭒwa.** Open it. **Mutsikꭒni
uʔ tsahtꭒwai.** He took down the
tent.

tsahtꭒbunitꭒ (v) wake someone.
Orꭒ tsaʔ tenahpꭒʔ tꭒeʔpꭒri

tsahtʉbuni. That man woke the baby. *See* **tʉbunitʉ.**

tsahtʉkitʉ (v, sg obj), *pl obj* **tsahtanuhiʔitʉ, tsahtahini** W, *pl* **tsahtaniʔitʉ** K set down, put down in place.

tsahtʉmarʉ (v) close (as to close a door). **Tenahpʉ tsahtʉmaruʔi.** The man will close the door.

tsahtʉrʉʔarʉ (v) rip with fingers (as threads or seams).

tsahtʉʔokiʔ K (n) rake. *See* **tʉtsanuaʔ.**

tsahwitʉ (v) open, discard (toss aside). **Ma tsahwituʔi nʉʔ.** I am going to open it. **Ohko tʉboopʉ narʉbakina hunapʉ tsahwi.** He threw that bag of paper trash outside. *See* **namaroʔitʉ.**

tsaiʔwarʉ K (v) tear something (with hands into small pieces).

tsakamiʔarʉ (v, sg obj), *pl obj* **umamiʔarʉ** lead along. **Tʉhʉyʉ uʔ tsakamiʔarʉ.** He led the horse along. *See* **matsaaihkakurʉ.**

tsakarʉ (v) lead a person or an animal.

tsakaʔuhrʉ (v) betray, lead astray.

tsakitsetʉ (v) crush or squash (with the fingers).

tsakʉbitʉkitʉ (v) arrive home (leading a person or an animal).

tsakʉhunitʉ (v, sg obj), *pl obj* **tsakʉhuyʉkʉrʉ** lead up a horse.

tsakwatʉ (v) feel around, grope around (as for something as in the dark). **Pʉ wiyaʔa uʔ tsakwai.** He felt around for his rope.

tsakwenitʉ (v) hang something.

tsakwerʉ (v) help down (as by holding hand). **Waikinbaku uʔ**

tsakwee. He helped her off the wagon.

tsakwipunarʉ (v), *pl* **tsaʔkwitsuniʔitʉ** twist something, screw something in.

tsakwoʔnerʉ (v) scratch an itch. **Nʉ pʉʉrʉ tsakwoʔnetʉ.** I am scratching my arm (where it itches). *See* **natsawoʔnitʉ.**

tsakwʉhburʉ (v) cause to turn something around.

tsakwʉhwitʉ (v) caused to turn around.

tsakwʉnarʉ (v, sg obj), *pl obj* **tsawʉniʔitʉ** set down carefully, lay out (as food on a table). **Iki ma tsakwʉna.** Set it here. *See* **totsiyaa tsakwʉnaʔ.**

tsakwʉkatʉ (v) shoot (let fly with force as a gun or an arrow). *See* **wʉhkikatʉ, tsatʉkarʉ.**

tsakwʉriarʉ (v) knock over and spill accidentally.

tsakwʉsarʉ W, **tsikwʉsarʉ** K (v) lace up.

tsakwʉsikʉkatʉ K (v) tangle. **Tamu uʔ tsakwusikʉkatʉ.** She is tangling the thread.

tsakwʉʔikʉrʉ W (v) tangle something. **Tamʉ natsakwʉsikʉ.** The thread is tangled.

tsamanirʉ (v) carry across. **Ohka puʔetʉ ma tsamani. He carried it across the road. Sʉmʉ tsamani etʉtsi.** Each having carried everything across.

tsamarʉkarʉ (v) finish. **Pʉ tʉtsawo uʔ tsamarʉkai.** He finished plowing. *See* **marʉkarʉ.**

tsaminarʉ (v) disjoint (pull something out of joint). **U moʔi uʔ**

tsaminaru?i. He will pull his
hand out of joint.

tsami?akʉrʉ (v) help someone
walk. Ukʉ wa?ihpʉ tsami?akʉ-
tu?i nʉ?. I will help that woman
to walk.

tsamuhraikʉtʉ (v) cause (two
others) to kiss. Orʉ tsa?
tenahpʉ ohka tuinʉhpa?a ma
tsamuhraikʉi. The man made the
young man kiss her.

tsamukʉsitʉ (v) blow the nose.

tsamupʉsitʉ W (v) cause to sneeze.
See tsa?akʉsitʉ.

tsamʉsasuakatʉ (adj) worried,
caused to worry. Nʉ ruapʉ nʉ
tsamʉsasuakatʉ. My boy has got
me worried.

tsamʉrikarʉ (v) turn something over.

tsanamʉsohnitʉ (v) hurry, cause to
hurry.

tsanikatʉ (v) hang suspended. Nʉ
kwasu tsa? tsanikatʉ iima. My
dress is hung on, by this thing.

tsanoorʉ (v) pull, pluck (by hand,
something growing). Sonipa u?
tsanoo?i. He pulled the grass.
Kokora?a pʉhi tsanoo?itu?i. He
will pluck the chicken's feathers.

tsanuarʉ (v) move by hand, pull on
something. Pʉ kune u? tsanuaru?i.
He is going to move his firewood.

tsanutsarʉ (v) break into pieces,
break off a piece. Tohtiya u?
tsanutsai. He broke off a piece of
bread.

tsanʉmaitʉ (v) lazy.

tsanʉnʉrʉ (v) cause to stop (rein
in a horse, wave down a car). *See*
tʉtsanʉnʉ?itʉ.

tsanʉkʉrʉ (v) buckle or tighten
something. Narʉmuhki u?

tsanʉkʉi. He buckled (or
tightened) the harness.

tsapeherʉ, tsaperʉ (v, sg obj), *pl
obj* yumarʉ jerk down, pull down
(make someone fall). Orʉ tsa? nʉ
tsaperʉ. That person made me
fall down.

tsapʉsikʉ (n) sensitive briar.
Schrankia Nutt. (dc.)

tsapʉhesuwarʉ, tsaphesuwarʉ (v)
tempt to turn aside (attempt to
throw off someone from a goal or
purpose).

tsapʉkarʉ, tsasi?arʉ W (v) split,
cut in half. Huupita nʉ? tsapʉ-
karu?i. I will split the wood.

tsapʉtsarʉ (v) burst (by applying
pressure). Orʉ tsa? nʉ mubohto-
ki?. That person burst my balloon.

tsapʉyetʉ (v, sg obj), *pl obj*
tsayumi?i unload (take down
from). Waikinakahku nasoki
u? tsapʉyeetʉ. He took the
sack down from the wagon. *See*
tsahpʉherʉ.

tsasa?wʉkitʉ (v) sift. Homopʉha
nʉ? tsasa?wʉkiitʉ. I am sifting
flour.

tsasa?wʉki? K, tsasa?kwʉki? W (n)
sieve, flour sifter.

tsasikwaitʉ (adj) torn up
completely.

tsasinʉkaarʉ, tsasinakatʉ (v) pull
back, scrape, skin. Nʉ mo?i nʉ?
tsasinʉkatʉ. I scraped my hand.

tsaso?arʉ (v) strain out something.

tsasukarʉ (v) feel something,
examine (with fingers).

tsasukwarʉ (v) grab for, snatch,
sieze. Ohko puhihwita
tsasuwai. He grabbed for that
man's money.

tsasuʔatsitʉ (v) help decide, convince someone. **Nʉ peta nʉʔ tsasuʔatsituʔi u hanituʔiha.** I am trying to help my girl make up her mind what to do.

tsasuʔnerʉ (v) scrape, smooth, soften (as a hide). **Ohka pahkipa tsasuʔne.** He scraped the hide.

tsasʉsʉʔnikatʉ (adj) numb (from cutting off the blood supply). **Nʉ moʔe ʉnʉ masʉsʉʔnikʉkatʉ.** You made my hand numb. **Tsasʉsʉʔni u?.** It was numb from squeezing. *See* **sʉsʉʔnitʉ.**

tsatsia? (n) splinter (as of wood).

tsatsubihkurʉ (adj) rattled, rattling.

tsatsʉbipʉkurʉ (v) make something rattle. **Tʉboopʉa u? tsatsʉbipʉkurʉ.** He is rattling the paper.

tsatʉkarʉ (v) shoot, propel (as a gun or arrow). **Taʔwoʔa u? tsatʉkai.** He shot the gun. *See* **tsakwʉkatʉ, taʔwoʔekarʉ.**

tsatʉkaʔkarʉ (v) shoot a repeating gun. **Taʔwoʔa u? tsatʉkaʔkaruʔi.** He will shoot the repeating rifle. *See* **taʔwoʔekarʉ.**

tsatʉsukitʉ (v) harrow, till (loosen soil). **Pʉ sokobita u? tsatʉsukii- tʉ.** He is harrowing his ground. *See* **tʉtsatʉsukitʉ, siibarʉ.**

tsawehkwatʉ (v) haul off. **Nah nʉʔ mʉʉ kahnikʉhu ʉ tsaweeh-kwatuʔi.** I will just haul you off to your camp (39:35).

tsayaketʉ (v) cause to ring. **Kawohwiʔa nʉʔ tsayaketʉ.** I am ringing the bell. *See* **tuʔtsayaketʉ, kawohwitʉ.**

tsayarʉ (v, sg obj), *pl obj* **tsahima-rʉ** carry a container by the handle (as by a strap usually on top).

tsayoritʉ (v) rouse, wake up someone.

tsayumarʉ (v) throw down.

tsayumiʔi (v, pl obj), *sg* **tsapʉyetʉ** take down, unload, remove (such as roasted meat from coals). *See* **tsahpʉherʉ.**

tsayʉkwikʉ (v, pl obj), *sg obj* **tsahkarʉkʉrʉ** set up straight.

tsayʉkwitʉ (v) sit straight.

-tsaʔ (enclitic, declarative mode). **Kohtopʉtsaʔ tukamiʔarʉ.** The fire is going out. **itsaʔ nʉ kahni.** This is my house.

tsaʔaikʉrʉ (v) pump (as water). **Pai u? tsaʔaikʉtʉʔ paa tsaʔaikʉrukʉ.** He is pumping water from the pump.

tsaʔaikʉrʉ (v) make (animal) lope. **Pʉ puuki u? tsaʔaikʉi.** He made his horse lope.

tsaʔakʉsitʉ K (v) sneeze.

tsaʔatsitʉ (v) inspect. **Tʉhʉye u? tsaʔatsi.** He inspected the horse. *See* **puiwʉnʉrʉ.**

tsaʔikarʉ (v, sg obj), *pl obj* **tsaʔwekwitʉ** admit (allow to enter). **Urii nʉmʉni tsaʔwekwi.** Let those Comanches in.

tsaʔnika?, tsaʔanika? (n) underwear, G-string, loincloth, jock strap. *See* **kohinehki?.**

tsaʔnikoorʉ (v) put something down.

tsaʔnikʉkatʉ (adj) have underwear on. **Tuinapʉ tsaʔnikʉkatʉ.** The boy is wearing underwear.

tsaʔohkwerʉ (v) drain a liquid (by hand, as by opening a faucet).

Pai nʉʔ tsaʔohkweruʔi. I will drain the water out. **Pai nʉʔ tsaʔohkwetʉ.** I am draining the water.

tsaʔoibehkatʉ (adj) strangled (outside cause, not food). *See* **oihtʉyaitʉ.**

tsaʔokʉrʉ (v) strangle (person or animal).

tsaʔokwetʉ (v) drain. **Paa tsaʔ orʉ tsaʔokwetʉ.** The water is draining.

tsaʔonutsai (adj) bent. **Paka tsaʔ tsaʔonutsai.** The arrow is bent.

tsaʔonutsarʉ (v) bend. **Pʉ pake uʔ tsaʔonutsai.** He bent his arrow.

tsaʔookitʉ (v) bunch up. **Sonipʉ tsaʔookituʔi.** The grass is going to bunch up. **Sonipʉ tsaʔoohkitʉ.** The grass has been raked up.

tsaʔoorʉ (v) rake up, bunch up. **Sonipʉha uʔ tsaʔooruʔi.** He is going to rake the grass. **Sonipʉha uʔ tsaʔookitʉ.** He is raking the grass.

tsaʔrurʉ (v) give (in hanging container).

tsaʔwenitʉ, tsahkwenitʉ W (v) hang up something on a nail or hook.

tsaʔwikiitʉ (v) shake something. **Nʉ saria nʉʔ tsaʔwikiitʉ.** I am shaking my dog.

tsaʔwʉminarʉ (v) fail to reach something. **Tuinapʉ tsaʔ tʉhka? tsaʔwʉmihnai.** The little boy cannot reach the table (top).

tseenaʔ K (n) gray fox, coyote (short form). *See* **ekatseenaʔ, kʉʔtseena.**

tsihakooihkatʉ (v) have famine, drought.

tsihakwitsoʔarʉ (v) save (from starvation). **Sariiʔa nʉʔ tsihamakwitsoʔai.** I saved the dog from starvation.

tsiharʉyaitʉ (v, sg), *pl* **tsihakoorʉ** starve to death. **Tsiharʉyaai humiʔarʉ nʉʔ.** I am about to die of hunger. **Tenahpʉʔ tsaʔ tsiharʉyaai.** The man died of hunger.

tsihasiʔapʉ (n) ravenously hungry person (hungry all the time). **Tuinʉhpʉ tsaʔ tsihasiʔapʉ.** That boy is hungry all the time.

tsihasuarʉ (v) hunger, have an appetite (feel hungry).

tsihhabʉhkamapʉ (n) menopausal woman. **Pʉ tsihabʉhkamapʉ ai.** She has gone through menopause.

tsihhabʉhkamarʉ, tsihhabʉhketʉ (v) menstruate.

tsihimarʉ (v, pl obj), *sg obj* **tsiʔyarʉ** carry something on a stick.

tsihkaʔarʉ (v) cut with a knife. **Tʉhkapa uʔ tsihkaʔarʉ.** She is cutting the meat (with knife).

Tsihkoba, Chikoba (n) Breaks Something (Antelope band).

tsihkwinumai (adj) weak, faint (from hunger).

tsihpeʔakarʉ (v) part hair.

tsihpoma (v, sg obj), *pl obj* **tsihpomiʔitʉ** cut up into pieces, slice. *See* **tʉtsihpomiʔipʉ.**

tseenaʔ

tsihpooru (v) mark something, draw line (using pointed object). **Tuboopuha ma? tsihpooru.** He marked the paper (with pointed object). *See* **kohpooru.**

tsihpuraru (v) ventilate (set up ventilator at top of teepee).

tsihtabo?ikutu (v, pl obj), *sg obj* **wunukuru** insert, set out, transplant. **Kuuke u? tsihtabo?ikutu.** He set out onion plants.

Tsihtara (name) Short-dress (person).

tsihtararu (adj) tall, high up (as a short dress).

tsihto?aru W, **tsihtu?waru** K (v) pry open. **U tsihto?aai u.** He pried it open.

tsihtsirahputu (adj) shiny, sparkling. **Taahka tsihtsirahputu.** The icicle is shiny.

tsihturuaru K (adj, anim) be stiff (inan obj must have **ta-** or **nara-**). **Ma tatsuturua.** Get it stiff. **Tenahpu?a kwasu?u tsa? naratsuturuapu.** The shirt is stiff.

tsihturuaru W (v) shiver from cold, shake from cold. **Tsihturuaru nu?.** I am shivering. *See* **suhtorokitu.**

tsihtu?yeru (v) comb hair, curry animal fur. **Tuewa?ihpu?a nu? tsihtu?yeetu.** I am combing the little girl's hair.

tsihtupukaru (v) pin together. **Wanapunihiu? nahma tsihtupukai.** She pinned the cloth together.

tsihturooru (v) support something (to keep it upright). **Huuhpima u? tsihturooni.** He supported it with a stick.

tsihtu?aweru (v) point (in a direction).

tsihtuwaru (v) unlock. **Natsahtuma ma? tsihtuwai.** He unlocked the door.

tsiikuwitehka? K, **tsikwitehka?** W (n) petroleum jelly (*lit* chapping oil). *See* **tsi?wunuu tu?eka?, nuuhtu?eka?.**

tsiira? (n) chili pepper. **Tsire?a ma? tuhkai.** He ate chili pepper.

tsii?wuweniitu (v) dredge, scoop, shovel out. **Huuhkupa u? tsii?wu?weniitu.** He is shoveling out the dirt.

tsikwainitu, tsiwainitu (v) probe (feel around with something sharp or with a pole).

tsiminaru, tsimino?itu (v) disjoint (separate bones at joint).

tsimi?akuru (v) miss doing (nearly accomplish; almost acquire but lose). **Tuhuye u? tsimiakui.** He almost hit the horse. *See* **awi-.**

tsimuami?aru (v) stagger when walking.

tsinuku (adj) crammed into limited space, squeezed tight, crowded (inanimate item).

tsinukuru (v) cram (crowd something into a limited space). **Pihuura?a kurohkuaawoku u? tsinukui.** He crowded the beans into the jar. *See* **natsinuhkuru.**

tsiperu, tsipeheru (v) unseat, unhorse (cause to fall off, as to unhorse with a spear or lance).

tsisu?waru (v, sg obj), *pl obj* **tsisu?kwa?nekitu** poke, jab.

tsiyaketu (v) hurt someone (make someone cry).

tsiyunaru (v) shovel (carry material on end of something, as a shovel).

Huuhkupa uʔ tsiyunaʔi. He is shoveling the dirt (moving it from one location to another).

tsiʔaikɄrɄ (v) push something that rolls (as a baby buggy). *See* **maʔaikɄrɄ.**

tsiʔnikarɄ (v) insert into something. **OrɄ tsaʔ aawokɄ wanapɄha tsiʔnikai.** He stuck a rag in a bottle.

tsiʔwapɄ, tsiiʔwa (adj) chapped (as rough or cracked skin).

tsiʔwapɄ W (n) rough skin, cracked skin.

tsiʔwaʔitɄ, tsiʔkwaʔitɄ (v) chap (become rough or cracked). **NɄ hɄnɄpoʔa tsaʔ tsiʔkwaʔi.** My skin is chapped.

tsiʔwɄnɄɄ tɄʔekaʔ W (n) petroleum jelly [**tsiʔwaʔi-** chap + **wɄnɄ-** skin **tɄʔeka-** paint]. *See* **tsiikɄwitehkaʔ, nɄɄhtɄʔekaʔ.**

tsiʔyarɄ (v, sg), *pl* **tsihimarɄ** carry something (object is hanging off the end, as of a stick). **Huuhpima uʔ wanapɄha tsiʔyai.** He carried the cloth on the end of a stick.

tsobokitɄ (v) shake vigorously.

tsohkwe K (v) soften by pounding. *See* **tohparaarɄ.**

tsohkweʔ (n) pestle (wooden, with hole in center). **NɄ tsohkweʔa nɄʔ watsikɄi.** I lost my wooden pestle.

tsohpe takwɄnarɄ (v) pound pillowsticks into ground.

tsohpe tawɄnaʔ (n) pillowsticks (two forked sticks pounded into ground at head of the bed for hanging belongings).

tsohpe tɄhkaʔaaʔ W, tsohpi tɄhkaʔaaʔ K (n) hatchet (as for chopping bones or tent stobs). **Tsohpi tɄhkaʔaaʔ tsaʔ kɄhmapɄ.** The hatchet is sharp.

tsohpe̞ (n) pillow. **Tsohpe tsaʔ kahpebaʔatɄ.** The pillow is on the bed.

tsohponiitɄ (v) try on headwear.

tsohtɄkikatɄ (v) lay the head down on something. **Tsohpeba- ʔa maʔ tsohtɄkikatɄ.** He lay his head down on the pillow.

tsokwɄkɄɄnaʔ W, tsoʔkɄnaʔ K (n) scarf, bandana. *See* **wɄhtsohkɄnaʔ.**

tsomo-, tsoomɄ (n) bead.

tsomo korohko (n) bead necklace [**tsoomo** bead + **korohko** necklace]. **Tsomo korohkoʔai nɄʔ.** I made a necklace.

tsonikarɄ (v, sg obj), *pl obj* **tsowekwatɄ** have a hat. **Sooti maʔ tsowekwakatɄ.** She owns many hats.

tsoohpa tsuuni W, tsoo tsuuni K (n) shoulder bone.

tsooʔ (n) great grandparent, great grandchild.

tsopekwiiyu W, tsopewiiyɄ K (n) cockscomb (crest on rooster's head).

tsotsomarɄ (v) wipe something with the head.

tsotsooʔni (n) meningitis. **WaʔihpɄ tsaʔ tsotsoʔni hanikatɄ.** The woman is ill with meningitis.

tsotsoʔneetɄ (v) rub head against something. **Kahni tɄbanaakɄ tsotsoneetɄ.** He rubbed his head against the wall.

tsoʔaahpɄʔ (n) granddaughter's husband.

tsoʔapiaʔ (n) grandson's wife.

tso?apʉ (n) shoulder. **Nʉ tso?apʉ tsa? nʉʉtsikwarʉ.** My shoulder hurts.

tso?meetʉ (v) gather, pick (harvest plant product). **Naakʉtabai?a nʉ? tso?meetʉ.** I am gathering pecans.

tso?mepʉ (n) harvest (picked or gathered items). **Nʉ tso?mepʉ ma?.** That is what I picked (my harvest).

tso?nikarʉ (v) wear a hat, poke head into something (put on a hat). **Tso?nikarʉ ma?.** He is wearing a hat. **Aawokʉ nʉ? tso?nikaai.** I poked my head in a can. *See* tʉtso?nikarʉ.

tso?nika? (n), *pl* tsowekwa? hat.

tso?nʉarʉ (v) lift head, raise head.

tso?wiketʉ (v) shake the head no, oppose something (indicating negative feeling).

tso?yaarʉ (v) carry something on the head. **Otʉaawe tso?yaarʉ.** She is carrying a jar on her head.

tso?yaa? (n) head of hair, hair.

tsuh (interj) yes, now, ready.

tsuhitʉ (v) unable to do something. *See* kemahpʉ?arʉ.

Tsuhni (name) Bone (person).

tsuhni, tsuhni? (n) bone. **Tsuhnipʉ tsa? kohpapʉ.** The bone is broken.

tsuhni bunitʉ, tsuuni bunitʉ (v) glare at (with hateful expression; *lit* bone look).

tsuhni karʉ (v) sit down quickly (*lit* bone sit).

tsuhni kwʉnʉrʉ K, tsuhnisihkwetʉ W (v) stop suddenly.

tsuhni muyake?, tsuhni pʉmayake? (n) whistle (originally only of bone; now also of wood).

tsuhni tekwarʉ (v, sg), *pl* tsuhni niwʉnʉtʉ curse (*lit* bone talk; talk mean or rough).

tsuhni wʉminahkatʉ (adj) rheumatic.

tsuhni wʉminakatʉ? (n) rheumatism (*lit* bone illness).

tsuhnipʉ (n) skull.

tsukuhpʉ? (n) old object, elderly male. **Tsukuhpʉ? tsa? ainʉʉsukatʉ.** The elderly man is ill.

tsunisʉ, tsunʉsʉ (n) certain plant with edible tuber.

tsuwíhnu (expr) doubt the truth of a statement.

tsu?ma, tsu?makʉtʉ (v) finish, use up. **Pihuura tsa? sʉmʉ tsu?mai.** The beans are all gone.

tsʉhkarʉ (v) stuck down in (animate subj). **Tsʉhkai nʉnʉ.** We're stuck. **Tsʉhkami?arʉ nʉnʉ.** We became stuck.

tsʉhkikatʉ (v) crowd with people, fill with people. **Kahni tsa? tsʉhki.** The house is crowded (by many people).

tsʉkikatʉ (adj) crowded into narrow place, stuck between two things.

tsʉmʉkikatʉ (adj) calm spirit, quiet spirit, peaceful spirit.

tsʉʉ?tsʉki? (n) whooping cough.

tsʉ?nitʉ (v) stay late, delay. **Ʉi u? tsʉ?nii.** He stayed too late (longer than he should have).

tsʉ?tsʉkitʉ (v) whoop (cough), cough hard.

tu-, tuh- (pfx) black, dark.

tua boopʉ W (n) adopted son [**tua** son + **boopʉ** paper].

tuakatʉ (v) be in labor, give birth.

tua? (n) son. **Hina ʉnʉ tua??** What son are you? (13:3).

tubokóo (n) thornapple, black haw
(local term) [**tu** black + **pokóoʔ**
fruit] *Crataegus* sp. (sweet fruit
eaten; inner bark chewed as gum).

tubupokoo (n) chippaberry (black
fruit; threshed down from the
nine-foot tree; the leaf is about
an inch long and thorny; the bark
used as chewing gum).

tuhani̱ (n) shadow.

tuhbanatsaya, tuu panatsaya (n)
blackberry bush. *Rosaceae* sp.

tuhhu (n) shinbone.

tuhhu rʉhkapʉ (n) bone marrow
[**tuhhu** bone + **tʉhkapʉ** meat].

tuhhu rʉhkarʉ (v) eat bone marrow.

tuhhuuʔ (n) stick for hand game,
poker chip.

tuhkanaai kwasuʔʉ (n) undershirt.

tuhkatʉ (adj) deep, down,
downward (a hole in ground).

tuhkaʔnaai rekwarʉ (v) speak
Wichita language.

Tuhkaʔnaaiʔ (n), *pl* **Tuhkaʔnaiʔ-
nʉʉ.** Wichita people.

tuhkaʔnaaiʔ niwʉnʉ (n) Speakers
of Wichita language.

tuhkohhi̱ W, **tuhkoihi̱** (n) intestine.

tuhku tsaʔnikapʉ (n) sausage
(Kiowa dish of intestine stuffed
with meat and juice, then boiled).

tuhkʉ (n) flesh, body, meat.

tuhkʉni, tuukʉni (n) black cradle.

Tuhkwasi taibooʔ (n) Satan, devil.
See **ketokwe hina haniitʉ.**

tuhmeko̱ (n) cricket.

tuhmubitai (n) black walnut.
Juglans nigra L. (nuts eaten; leaves
used for treating ringworm and as
an insecticide).

tuhnaséka (n) Mexican persimmon.
Brayodendron texanum Scheele

(small tree; fruits eaten; serves as
opossum or raccoon food).

tuhnatsoʔmeʔ, tuu natsoʔmeʔa (n,
acc) prune (*lit* black dried plums).
Tuu natsoʔmeʔa nʉ tʉhkai. I ate
prunes.

tuhparokooʔ, tuu parokoʔ (n)
water moccasin (snake) [tuh-
black + **paa** water + **ro** through
+ **ko** cutter]. **Tuhparokooʔ tsaʔ
ma kʉhtsiai.** A water moccasin
bit him.

tuhpihhínabooʔ (n) spade (in card
game) [**tu** black + **pihhi** heart +
naboʔ printed].

tuhpui, tuhpuui (n) pupil of eye.
Tuhpuuiha nʉʔ mahrʉni. I hurt
the pupil of my eye.

**tuhtahkanabooʔ, tuu tahkana-
booʔ** (n) spade (in card game)
[**tuu** black + **tahka** arrow +
naboʔ printed].

tuhtaibooʔ W, **tuhtenahpʉ** K (n)
black person.

tuhtsaipʉ (n) dirty object (unclean).
Wanapʉ tsaʔ tuhtsaipʉ. The
cloth is dirty. *See* **nasʉsʉaʔeetʉ.**

tuhtseenaʔ (n) wolf [**tuh** black +
tseenaʔ coyote].

**tuhu rekwarʉ, tuhu rʉkweerʉ,
tuhu rekwaitʉ** (v) jerk and slam
things in anger, talk rough, act
angry (human), growl in anger
(animal).

tuhu suʔaitʉ (v) feel anger, feel
rage.

tuhu yʉkwiitʉ (v) rave (rave madly
at someone in anger).

tuhubʉkʉkatʉ (v) become angry
at a person. **Pʉ patsia uʔ
tuhubʉkʉkatʉ.** She became
angry at her sister.

tuhupi (adj) black. **Tuhupitu
kwasu.** It is a black dress.
Tuhupiti nu kwasukatu. I have a
black dress.

tuhupu (n) mean person or animal
(easily angered).

tuhuupi, tuhu huupi (n) blackjack
oak, barren oak. **Quercus
marilandica** Muench (acorns
eaten; leaves used as cigarette
wrappers [C & J]).

tuhupu (n) hide, raw skin.

tuibihtsi? (n) young man, Indian
brave (warrior).

tuinuhpu?

tuinuhpu? W (n), *pl* **pihi?anuu** K
boy. *See* **pihi?a.**

tuka uhyui (adv) night, early
morning (from midnight to
dawn).

tukaani, tukani (adv) evening,
night. **Tukani humi?aru.** It is
getting dark (82:13).

tukami?aru (v) go out, die out
(said of fire). **Kohtopu tsa?
tukami?aru.** The fire is going out.
See **wuhtukaru.**

Tukanai (n) Caddo people (*lit* night
hunter).

tukanikatu (adj) dark (without
light), unlighted.

tukanitu (adj) be night.

tukaru (v) extinguish (put out a fire
or flame). **Nu?kohtopuha tukai.** I
put out the fire. *See* **wuhtukaru.**

tuka? (n) lamp, light. *See* **kupita?,
natsayaa ruka?.**

tuka?a nabaa (n) kerosene, coal oil,
oil well [**tuka?a** lamp + **nabaa**
oil]. *See* **nabaai tokwaaitu,
keto?kapaa.**

tuka?a nahhuupi (n) lamppost (*lit*
lamp wood).

tuka?a naku?e W, **tuka naku?e** K
(n) lamp chimney, chimney. **Oru
tsa? tuka naku?e puuhtsai.** The
lamp chimney broke (cracked).

tuka?a nawanapi (n) lamp wick.

tuka?ekapitu (adj) red (dark).

tuka?yuwu W (adj) purple.

tukuhputu (adv dir) upward
(limited in distance; not as high
as sky).

tukumakwuyetu? W,
tukuwekwikatu K (n) rodeo. *See*
kuhtsu taibo nohhiitu.

tukunu natsu, tuka natsu (n)
purple coneflower. *Echinacea* sp.
(roots used in treating sore throat
and toothache [C & J]).

tumuukatu (adj) bent down,
stooped.

tumuuru (v) bend down, stoop. *See*
nuhtsapu.

tuna, tunaa (adj) straight. tuna
wunukatu stand straight.

tuna wosa (n) war-bonnet bag
(also held feathers, war paint,
brush, and mirror; was of tubular

shape and worn hanging from the waist).

tunehtsʉrʉ (v) go on, run to something. **Meeku tunehtsʉru?i takwʉ.** Now we two will run (9:13).

tunʉhaa (n) cymopterus plant. *Cymopterus acaulis* (Pursh.) Rydberg (rootstocks eaten [C & J]).

tupisinawoni? (n) dusk (after sundown).

tupisi kʉma? (n) bay horse.

tupisibitʉ (adj) dark color.

tupʉsʉnarʉ (adj) dusk, evening.

turetʉ (v) stretch.

turuarʉ (v) bear offspring, lay eggs (give birth to many young).

turuawapi (n) hen, laying hen (as leghorn).

Tusa Kahni (n) Black Houses (name for Wichita people because of black inside fire pits and dark purple color of tents).

tusanahpi (n) tar [**tu-** black + **sanahpʉbi** sap].

tusi, tusipʉ (n) saliva. *See* **kʉpisi?**.

tusi aawo (n) spittoon, ashtray [**tusi (pʉ)** spit + **aawo** container].

tusitʉ (v) expectorate, spit. **Sokoko urúsiitʉ.** He spit on the ground. *See* **paitusi?itʉ**.

tusohó? (n) elm [**tu-** black + **soho** cottonwood + **?** (nom sg)] *Ulmus fulva* Michx.

Tusoho?okwe? (n) Washita River [**tusoho** elm + **okwe?** river]. **Tusoho?okwe? tsa? paru?ikitʉ.** The Washita River is rising.

Tusokwe? K, Tusoho?kwe? W (n) Anadarko, Okla. [**tusoho** elm + **kwe?** place].

tusupʉ W (n) pulverized or grated object, grounds. *See* **nasupʉ**.

tusurʉ (v) grind, thresh. **Pʉ haniibita tusurʉ.** He ground his corn.

tutupitʉ (n) wild tuber (dark-skinned root; white inside; grows in field or along pond). *See* **ahwepʉ**.

tutʉsawʉ koobe (n) freckled face (*lit* spotted face).

tutʉsa?wʉtʉ W, tutʉsa kawo?arʉ (adj) freckled. **Sooti ma? tutʉsa?wʉtʉ.** He has many freckles. *See* **tasi?a?**.

tutʉtsaai wahtʉ (adj) clean, spotless, pure (in mind and soul; *lit* without spots).

tuu- (pfx) water (in container).

tuuhuniitʉ W, tuuniitʉ K (v, sg), *pl* **tuuhuyʉkarʉ, tuuyukarʉ** fetch water.

tuukʉmi?arʉ (v) fetch water for someone.

tuume?so (n) young catfish.

tuumo?tso? (n) fullgrown catfish [**tuu** water + **mo?tso?** whiskers].

tuupʉ (n) water (in container, having been brought in). *See* **paa**.

tuurʉ (v) draw water. **Hunu?bikitʉ u ruurʉ.** He is drawing water at the stream. **Tuumi?ai u?.** He went to draw water.

tuusanahpitʉ (v) pave a road; adj blacktopped. **Tuusanahpitʉ ma? pu?e?aitʉ.** He is putting tar on the road.

tuu?etʉ, tuuwapi (n) water boy (one who fetches water).

tuu?re napʉ (n) galoshes, rubber boots.

tuu?re tahpiko?, (n) rubber heel.

tuʉnʉʉ? (n) june bug, black beetle [**tu-** black + **ʉnʉʉ** bug].

tuwaikina (n) hack, carriage (black top, two-seater). **Tuwaikinapa nʉ? too?i.** I unhitched the black carriage. *See* **tosa waikina.**

tuwikaa?, tuhwikaa? (n) raven, crow, blackbird.

tuwokwe (n) goathead (vine with thorns) [**tu-** black + **wokwe** thorn].

tu?amowoo, tʉrʉi amawoo (n) thorn apple, red haw (local popular term). *Crataegus* sp. (fruits eaten [C & J]).

tu?anikuura? (n) wood ant (*lit* black ant).

tu?ebipitʉ (adj) K dark blue; W purple.

Tu?paapi (name) Black-head (person).

tu?re?, tuu?re? (n) leech, rubber band.

tu?runaasʉ (adj) straighter-than-straight [**tu-** (redup) + **tunaa** straight + **sʉ**].

Tu?runaasʉ (name) Straighter-than-straight (person).

tu?rʉmetʉ (adj) wasted.

tu?tsayaketʉ (v) ring something (as a bell). *See* **tsayaketʉ.**

tʉ- (pfx, unspecified object).

tʉa, -rʉa (quotative adv) it is said that, they say that.

tʉanóo (conj) or.

tʉapako?itʉ (v) split into two parts.

tʉahpi (n) Chickasaw plum. *Prunus angustifolia* Marsh (fruits eaten fresh or stored [C & J]; grown around Anadarko).

tʉasʉ (conj) also, and, again. **Tʉasʉ tʉ?ahwe.** Tell it again.

tʉbakitʉ (v, pl obj), *sg obj* **norʉbakitʉ** load items (as into wagon, gun, sack).

tʉbanaa rʉbopʉ (n) wallpaper.

tʉbanaa? (n) wall, edge, cliff. *See* **kahni tʉbanaa.**

tʉbawʉhtia wapi (n) baptizer (one who baptizes) [**tʉ-** (unspec) + **pa** water + **wʉhtia-** put under + **wapi** (nom)].

tʉbehkapʉ (n), *pl* **tʉkwʉsʉ** animal killed or butchered for food.

tʉbehkarʉ (v, sg obj), *pl obj* **tʉkwʉsʉrʉ** butcher an animal. **Pimoroo?a urʉ tʉbehkai.** They butchered the cow. *See* **tʉhaniitʉ.**

tʉbehyaarʉ (v) accuse someone falsely, find fault with someone.

tʉbekwipʉ, tʉbekwi (n) mumps [**tʉ-** (unspec) + **pekwi** swell]. **Tʉbekwikatʉ u.** He has the mumps.

tʉbinaa?wekitʉ (adj) divided in half.

tʉbinaa?weki (adv) middle. **Pia kwasinaboo? suhka sekwikʉni tʉbinaa?weki habitʉ.** A big snake was lying in the middle of that cellar (51:6). num half. **Pʉ puhiwihta ma? tʉbinaa?wekiti narohtumakʉ tʉkinu.** She put half her money in a can (48:10).

tʉbinaa?werʉ (v) divide in half.

tʉbinarʉ (v, sg obj), *pl obj* **tʉrʉbinitʉ** question someone. **U rʉbini u.** He questioned him.

tʉbinitʉ (v) ask a question, question someone. **Nʉsu?a tsa? sʉmʉ?a mʉi tʉbinitu?i.** I will ask you one question.

tʉbitsi (adv intens) really, surely. **Tʉbitsiku nʉ? mi?apa su waitʉ.** I really want to go. **Tʉbitsi ʉtsʉi kwihne ma?.** It was really a cold winter.

tʉbitsi basapʉ (adj) dried, dry. *See* **pasapʉ.**

tʉbitsi basarʉ (v) dry something. *See* **pasarʉ.**

tʉbitsikatʉ (adj) right-handed. *See* **ohinikatʉ.**

tʉbitsi petutʉ (adv dir) to the right. *See* **ohinibetutʉ.**

tʉbitsi suarʉ (v) decide, intend.

tʉbitsinakʉkʉrʉ K (v) listen carefully.

tʉbitsinakwʉ (adv loc) right side. *See* **ohininakwʉ.**

tʉbiyaakʉ? W (n) trailer (anything hanging at rear of vehicle). *See* **pitsaka?, kahni tʉbitsika?.**

tʉbitabu?itʉ (adj) blind (unable to see clearly).

tʉbitsiyu (adj) true.

tʉbomarʉ, tʉbumarʉ (v) gather in (as garden produce). *See* **pomarʉ.**

tʉboo kahni (n) school house, building [**tʉboo** writing + **kahni** house]. *See* **pia tʉbookʉni.**

Tʉboo renahpʉ makwe kwi?ena mʉa (n) September (*lit* paper man hand enter month). *See* **Kwi?ena mʉa.**

tʉboo tahni? (n), *pl* **tʉboo tahni?i** postman, mailman (*lit* letter deliver).

tʉboo wapi (n) male teacher (middle and high-school grades).

tʉboo bia? (n) teacher [**tʉboo** write + **pia?** mother].

tʉboo hima?eetʉ K, tʉboo parahni?i?eetʉ W (n) postman, mailman [**tʉboo** letter + **hima** take + **?e** (rep)].

tʉboopʉ (n) letter, paper.

tʉboopʉ kʉni (n) post office (*lit* letter house).

tʉboopʉ wosa W, tʉboo wosa K (n) mailbox. *See* **wosa.**

tʉboorʉ (v) write **Pʉ haitsiha tʉboo?i.** He wrote to his friend.

tʉboo rʉhka? (n) desk (*lit* writing table). *See* **pʉpa?akura tʉbòo?ena.**

tʉboorʉʉ pia? (n) female teacher [**tʉboorʉʉ** students + **pia?** mother] (teaches in elementary grades).

tʉboo? (n) pencil. **Tʉboo?a u? nʉ uhtʉnʉ.** He gave me a pencil. *See* **naboo?.**

tʉboo?etʉ W (n) camera. *See* **kobenabo?**

tʉbora, tʉborakatʉ (adj) born, originated.

tʉbunitʉ (v) wake up, awaken. *See* **tahtʉbunitʉ, tsahtʉbunitʉ.**

tʉbuuhki? (n) bellows, blacksmith's blower.

tʉe (adj) little, small. **Tʉe huupita nʉ? masʉai.** I planted a little tree.

tʉe aawo (n) spoon, teaspoon [**tʉe** little + **aawo** container]. *See* **piarʉ?ewo.**

tʉe amawóo? (n), *pl* **tʉrʉe amawóo?** crab apple. *Pyrus coronaria* L. *See* **eka amawoo?.**

tʉe tʉmakupa? (n) bobcat [**tʉe** little + **tʉmakupa?** panther].

tʉe basuu? W (n) quail. *See* **kuyúusi?, tʉrʉe basuu.**

Tʉe buakʉtʉ (name) Little-medicine (person).

Tʉeh buha rabeni (n) Saturday.

tʉehmahtua? W (n) little finger [**tʉe-** little + **ma** hand + **tua?** child].

tʉehna matsuma? (n) washcloth [**tʉe-** little + **na** (nom) + **matsuma?** wiper].

tɨehpɨʔrɨ (n) child.

tɨeh tahtua? (n) little toe [tɨe little + tah- foot + tua? child]. *See* tahtúa?.

tɨe kahuu? (n) mouse.

Tɨe kuhtsu (name) Little-buffalo (led a large number of N. Comanches in 1864 attacking in Texas near the Brazos River on Elm Creek, near Fort Belknap; died Oct. 13, 1864; Fehrenbach 1974:453).

tɨe kuyúutsi K (n) quail, partridge (small variety) [tɨe- little + kuyúutsi quail]. *See* tɨrɨe kuʔyuutsi.

tɨetekwɨni wapi (n) Indian brave, brave young man.

tɨetɨnabinarɨ (v) adopt a child. *See* toyarɨ.

tɨetɨtaatɨ kɨɨka (n) wild onion. *Allium* sp. (small, strong like garlic, grows in pastures).

tɨe waikina (n) single buggy (one-seated buggy).

tɨe anikuura? (n) sugar ant (*lit* small ant).

tɨe esi ɨnɨɨ (n) gnat [tɨe little + esi gray + ɨnɨɨ bug].

tɨeʔtɨ (n) child, little one (must have possessor). Nɨ tɨeʔtɨ tsa? tɨboo? kwai. My child went to school.

tɨhaniitɨ (v) butcher (cut up in pieces). Pimorooʔa uʔ tɨhaniitɨ. He is cutting up the cow. *See* tɨbehkarɨ.

tɨhaʔwokatɨ (adj) hollow.

tɨhhorarɨ (v) dig a hole. tɨɨhtɨmaʔa tɨhhorapɨ dug fencepost hole.

tɨhimana W, tɨhimarɨ K (n) rations. Ke tsa? soohi tɨhimarɨ. There were not many rations.

tɨhimaʔetɨ (v) get rations. Tɨhimakwai uʔ. He went to get rations.

tɨhima rabeni (n) ration day (day on which rations were distributed).

tɨhkamarɨ (v) eat up (finish eating completely). Pihuura nɨ? tɨhkamai. I finished eating beans. Pihuuratsa? kɨhtsuʔmai nɨ. I ate up all the beans.

tɨhkanɨmiitɨ (v, sg), *pl* tɨhkayɨkarɨ graze (move about eating).

tɨhkapa (n, acc) meat, food.

tɨhkapa nakoopɨ (n) steak.

tɨhkapa narɨsupɨ W, tɨhkapa nasupɨ K (n) ground meat.

tɨhkapɨ (n) meat, food. Setɨ seʔ nɨɨmɨ? wihnu tɨhkapɨ tuaʔetɨ. Those Comanche people then got meat (130:13).

tɨhkarɨ (v) eat. Tɨhkaruʔi tanɨ! Let's eat! Ɨ tɨhkaruʔi tanɨ! Eat your food!

tɨhka? (n) fork, table fork.

tɨhkaʔena (n) food.

tɨhkupa? (n) billy club.

tɨhnearɨ W, tɨniarɨ K (v) read. Tsaa tɨhneanu. You spoke well (made a speech). Ohka tɨboo pɨha tsaa tɨhnearɨ. You read that letter well.

tɨhoitɨ (v) hunt game. Tabuʔkina nɨ? tɨhoitɨ. I am hunting rabbits.

tɨhorarɨ (v) dig (with a tool). *See* wɨhhorarɨ, horarɨ.

tɨhora?, tɨhhora? (n) crowbar, posthole digger. *See* tɨkɨh kweʔya?.

tɨhpetɨ (adj, sg), *pl* tɨtɨbetɨ full and running over, overflowing. Aawo tsa? tɨhpetɨ. The cup is running over. **Paa tsaʔ aawo tutubetu.** The jars are full of water.

tuhpoʔtseʔ (n) ball bat [**tuh-** (unspec) + **poʔtseʔ** bouncer].

tuhraniitu K, **tuhhanitu** W (v) pound, hammer. **Ihka nuʔ tuhraniitu.** I am hammering.

tuhtsohpeʔaipu (n) Comanche butter. *See* **tuutsohpepu.**

tuhtsohpeʔaru (v) render an animal carcass; make Comanche butter (by boiling crushed bones).

tuhtuiʔ (n) girl friends, partners. *See* **notsaʔkaʔ.**

tuhtukitu (v, sg), *pl* **turuniʔitu** plant seed (using a dibble stick).

tuhuya, tuhuuya (n) horse. **Tuhuuya.** I see a horse. **Tuhuhya tsaʔ toonitu.** The horse is grazing.

tuhuya karu, tuhuya karunitu K (v, sg), *pl* **tuhuya yukwitu** ride horseback. *See* **kuayukaʔetu.**

tuhuya

tuhuya natsihtuʔyeʔ, tuhhuya tsihtuʔyeʔ, tuuya tsihtuʔyeʔ (n) currycomb, horse brush. **Oka tuhuya tsihtuʔyeʔ nu uhtu.** Give me that currycomb.

Tuhuyana kwahipu (name) Horseback (Comanche chief).

tuhuya roʔitu (v), *pl* **tuhuya kuaru** climb on horseback (get on a horse; more general term than mount). *See* **tuya toʔyeru.**

tuhuyena puni W, **tuhuyena napuni** K (n) horse tracks, hoofprints. **Tuhuyena napuanaai putu nuʔ miʔai.** I followed the horse tracks.

tuhubu, tuhpu (n) hide (raw skin).

tuhwaitu (v) come open (when not tightly closed). **Natsahtu matuhwai.** The door came open.

tuhwaru (v) open something. *See* **matuhwaru.**

tuhyetu (v) mail a letter or package, send something or someone. **Ihkana nuʔ tuhyetuʔi.** I am going to send this.

tuhyu (n) motor oil (petroleum). **Nuʔ tuhyuʔuku hani.** I put oil in my car.

tuituaru (v) help someone. **Pu piaʔa uʔ tuituai.** She helped her mother.

tuiʔ (n) friend (of a woman).

tukamuru, tukamukatu (v) ambush (those who lie in wait; source of name Tucumcari, NM). *See* **makamukaru.**

tukaru (v, sg), *pl* **tahniʔitu** put away, put in place, bury. **U tukii nuʔ oku.** I put it up there. *See* **tahtukaru.**

tukarukupu (n) cloth patch, stewed food. *See* **kohtsáaʔ.**

tukarukuru (v) patch something, cook food, stew food. **Tahpani tukarukui uʔ.** He patched the tire.

tukaʔ (n) light, lamp.

tukeh kooʔ, tukoh kooʔ (n) scissors [**tukeh-** cut + **kooʔ** cutter]. *See* **wanakooʔ.**

tɨkerɨ (v) hunt (several days from main camp). **Ma tua? tɨkenɨ.** Her son hunted several days from the main camp.

tɨkiihkarɨ (v) board someone, care for needs of someone, keep an orphan as foster child.

tɨkiitɨ K, tɨkɨhnetɨ W (v) lay something down. **Ma tɨɨki!** Put it down!

tɨkohpoopɨ (n) brand.

tɨkohpoo? (n) branding iron [tɨ- (unspec) + koh- heat + poo? marker]. **Tɨkohpoo?a nɨ? tɨmai.** I bought a branding iron.

tɨkotse? K, tɨkotse?eetɨ W (n) washing machine [tɨ- (unspec) + kotse wash + ?e (rep)].

tɨkɨ (n) ref. to food.

tɨkɨ ahwerɨ (v) dig edible roots. **Pɨetsɨkusɨ nɨ? tɨkɨ ahwenɨ.** Early this morning I dug something to eat.

tɨkɨ himarɨ (v, pl), *sg* tɨkɨ yaarɨ receive food.

tɨkɨ mahnitɨ, tɨkɨ mɨhanitɨ (v) cook for someone (prepare a meal). **Marii tɨɨmahyakɨ!** Cook for them!

tɨkɨ mahya? (n) pepper.

tɨkɨ manipɨ (n) meal (prepared food). **Orɨ tsa? nɨ tɨkɨ manipɨ nɨ yuni.** Let that person bring my meal to me.

tɨkɨ maniwapɨ (n) hired cook (person known for cooking).

tɨkɨ masɨa sokoobi W (n) garden patch, vegetable garden plot. *See* tɨmɨsɨa sokobi.

tɨkɨ noopɨ (n), *acc* tɨkɨ noopana lunch (food carried along). **Nɨ rɨkɨ noopana hanikɨi.** She prepared a lunch for me.

tɨkɨ noorɨ (v) carry food (take a lunch along). **Tɨkɨ noo kwatu?i nɨ?.** I am going to take food along.

tɨkɨ soona (n) tablecloth [tɨkɨ food + soona quilt]. **Tɨkɨ soona tɨmɨi nɨ?.** I bought a tablecloth.

tɨkɨ to?ipɨ (n) leftover food [tɨkɨ- food + to?ipɨ left over]. **Tɨkɨ to?ipɨha nɨnɨ tɨhkai.** We ate the leftover food.

tɨkɨ tsuhmarɨ (v) exhaust food supply, run out of food. **Sɨmɨ tɨkɨ tsuhmai nɨnɨ?.** We are all out of food.

tɨkɨ tusupɨ (n) sausage, ground food of any type.

tɨkɨ tusu? (n) food grinder, grinder.

tɨkɨ tɨmɨɨpɨ (n) groceries, store-bought food. **Tɨkɨ tɨmɨɨrui nɨ?.** I am going to buy some store food.

tɨkɨ wasɨ? (n, sg), *pl* wasɨpɨ game (animals killed in the hunt). **Tɨkɨ wasɨi tsa? tɨ oorɨ.** That person killed some game. *See* pehkarɨ

tɨkɨ wesipɨ (n) crumbs, scraps (leftovers after a meal) [tɨkɨ food + wesipɨ toasted]. *See* tɨkɨ yɨmapɨ.

tɨkɨ wɨhpara? K, tɨkɨ kwɨhpara? W (n) apron. **Nɨ tɨkɨ wɨhpara?a nɨ uhta!** Give me my apron!

tɨkɨ wɨhpomi?, tɨkɨ wɨhpoma? (n) cleaver (*lit* food cutter). **Tɨkɨ wɨhpoma? nɨ? su?waitɨ.** I want a cleaver.

tɨkɨ yaarɨ (v, sg), *pl* tɨkɨ himarɨ K eat (partake of food); W take to eat.

tɨkɨ yɨmapɨ (n), *pl* tɨkɨ yɨmi?ipɨ crumbs. **Sarii tsa?**

ohka **tɨkɨ yumapɨha tɨhkai.**
The dog ate those crumbs. *See*
tɨkɨ wesipɨ.

tɨkɨh kaʔaʔ (n) wire pincers
[**tɨkɨh-** bite + **kaʔa-** break off].

tɨkɨh kweʔyaʔ (n) pliers, pincers,
crowbar [**tɨkɨh-** bite + **kweʔyaʔ**
pull out]. *See* **tɨhoraʔ.**

tɨkɨh pehkarɨ (v, sg), *pl* **tɨkɨ**
wasɨrɨ bag game. **Tɨkɨ pehka**
kwai uʔ. He went to bag game.

tɨkɨh pomaʔ (n) wire cutter, pincer
[**tɨkɨh-** bite + **puma-** break in
little pieces].

tɨkɨmaʔai (n) ribbon, bias tape (*lit*
edge trim).

tɨkɨmaʔaitɨʔ (n) ambusher; cloth
edged with ribbon or lace.

tɨkɨrɨ (v) cut (with teeth or sharp
edge).

tɨkɨ kahni (n) restaurant, eating
place. **Okɨ nɨʔ tɨkɨ kahnikɨ**
tɨhkaruʔi. I am going to eat over
at that restaurant.

tɨkɨ soonarɨ (v) spread a tablecloth. **Nɨ bia tsaʔ tɨkɨ soonai.**
My mother spread a tablecloth.
Situɨ kɨseʔ tɨkɨ sonɨtsi pɨɨ
tɨkɨh manipɨha tsawɨniʔinɨ.
These ones spreading a cloth, set
out their cooked things (128:17).

tɨkwibukiitɨ (v) switch, whip (as to
whip a horse while riding). **Nɨrua**
nɨʔ kwibuki. I switched my boy.
See **kwibukitɨ.**

tɨkwita (n) base, bottom. **kahni**
tɨkwitaku to the base of the
teepee. **Ohka tɨkwita tsaa**
nabuni. The base of that thing
looks good.

tɨkwitsunaʔ (n) elephant (described
by its trunk).

tɨkwɨrɨ (v) shoot, propel. **Paka**
mɨa tɨkwɨi uʔ. He shot an arrow.
See **tsatɨkarɨ, wɨhkikatɨ.**

tɨkwɨsiitɨ (v) braid, weave. **Kakuʔ**
tsaʔ aawo tɨkwɨsiitɨ. Grandma
is weaving a basket.

tɨkwɨsɨkupɨʔ (n) roasted meat.
See **kuʔinapɨ.**

tɨkwɨsɨkɨrɨ (v) roast meat (or any
other food in live coals or on a grill).

tɨkwɨsɨrɨ (v, pl), *sg* **tɨbehkarɨ**
kill, butcher.

tɨmabarɨ (v) knead. **Pɨ tohtía maʔ**
tɨmabaarɨ. She kneaded her
bread. *See* **mabarɨ.**

tɨmabekarɨ (v) pay something
to medicine man. **Pahmui ma**
tɨmabekakɨ! Give him (pay him)
tobacco now! *See* **mabekakɨrɨ.**

tɨmabisoʔaitɨ (adj) hateful,
troublesome, ornery.

tɨmabukweʔ (n) screwdriver [**tɨ-**
(unspec) + **mabɨkwerotate**].
Tɨmabukweʔ maʔ yaakatɨ. He
has a screwdriver.

tɨmabunikɨrɨ (v) demonstrate,
show how (to do something).
Pɨniku ra tɨrapɨsaʔena ma
tɨmabunikɨ. Show him how to
do beadwork.

tɨmahkupaʔ (n) panther [**tɨma-**
clench + **kupa** smother].
Tɨmahkupaʔ tsaʔ narɨʔyatɨ. A
panther is dangerous.

tɨmahyokɨrɨ (v) agree to a
statement, listen to someone.

tɨmakarɨ, tɨmaakarɨ (v) pay
debts. **Pɨ tɨbopɨ ma rɨmakatɨ.**
He is paying his bills.

tɨmakotsetɨ (v) wash dishes. **Nɨ**
biaʔ tsaʔ aawo tɨmakotsetɨ. My
mother is washing the dishes.

tɨmakɨmaʔaaiʔ (n) stone, whetstone, sandpaper. *See* **tɨpi tɨmatsuneʔ.**

tɨmakɨmaʔarɨ (v) hone, sharpen something.

tɨmakwatuiʔ, tɨmɨkɨtubiʔ, tɨmakwatɨbiʔ (n) cigarette-wrapper plant (when used as cigarette wrappers, odor of burning leaves is sweet, similar to marijuana odor).

tɨmakwatɨbiʔetarɨ (v) roll up, wrap up (as wrap a package). *See* **namakwatubiitɨ.**

tɨmanahketɨ (v) measure something. **Ika nɨʔ huupita tɨmanahketɨ.** I am measuring this tree. *See* **manahkerɨ.**

tɨmanahkeʔ (n) ruler, tape measure, any device used for measuring. **Ohka tɨmanahke nɨ uhtɨ.** Give me that ruler.

tɨmanɨkuʔwetɨ (n) cottage cheese.

tɨmaramiitɨ (v) share in, chip in, join in (partnership). **Wahatina ɨ ma tɨmaramituʔi.** I am going to chip in two dollars.

tɨmarɨ (v) W fill something; K cover up (put a lid on). **Ma yaatsi marɨma.** Take it and put a cover on it.

tɨmarɨkarɨ (v) finish (complete a task). **Tabeni nɨnɨ tɨmarɨka-rɨʔi.** We will finish at noon.

tɨmarɨmaʔ K (n) lid. *See* **tɨrohtɨmaʔ.**

tɨmarɨɨmaatɨ (num) many, much. **Tɨmarɨɨmaatɨ naʔkɨtabai.** There are many pecans. **Paa tsaʔ tɨmarɨɨmaatɨ.** There is a lot of water.

tɨmatsukiʔ (n) screw [tɨ- (unspec) + matsuki- go out of sight].

Tɨmatsukiʔa nɨʔ watsikɨi. I lost the screw. *See* **tɨtsipɨsaʔ.**

tɨmatsumaʔ W, **tɨratsukiʔ** K (n) dishtowel, dustcloth, cloth for wiping [tɨ- (unspec) + matsuma-wipe].

tɨmatsunarɨ (v) file a surface, rasp a surface. **Huupita u tɨmatsunarɨ.** He filed the wood.

tɨmatsuneʔ W, **tɨmatsunaiʔ** K (n) file, rasp. **Pɨ tɨmatsunaiʔ watsikɨi.** He lost his file.

tɨmaya huupi (n) smooth sumac (*lit* mix together). *Rhus glabra* L. (fruit eaten by children; leaves mixed with tobacco for smoking).

tɨmayokɨrɨ (v) trust, obey. **Ohka tɨmayokɨkatɨ nɨʔ.** I am trusting that person. **Marɨmayokɨkɨ!** Obey him!

tɨmaʔniikarɨ K (v) **tɨmaʔnika- ʔetɨ** W (v) insert hand (as into pocket). **Nɨ moʔe nɨ kwasu tɨmaʔnikai.** I put my hand in my pocket.

tɨmaʔokwetɨ (v) milk a cow. **Pɨetsɨkusɨ nɨʔ tɨmaʔookwe.** Early this morning I milked the cow. *See* **maʔokwerɨ.**

tɨmerɨ (v) gamble. **Nɨʔ tɨme-miʔarɨ.** I am going to gamble. *See* **wanarohpetitɨ.**

tɨmoʔo wɨhtamaʔ (n) hobble for a horse (rope or other material to be tied on as hobble).

tɨmuhku (n) Indian-type saddle. **Tɨmuhkukatɨ nɨʔ.** I have an Indian saddle. *See* **paʔmutsiʔ.**

tɨmuihpaaʔ W, **tɨʔmepaaʔ** K (n) cap (billed, as baseball cap). *See* **pɨhɨ rɨmuihpaaʔ.**

tɨmuʔnikatɨ (adj) caught (stuck inside something as in a hole or sack). **Sarii tsaʔ mubita tumuʔ-nikatu.** The dog's nose is caught.

tumuuru (v) buy, trade. **Kwasuʔu tumuumiʔaru nuʔ.** I am going to buy a dress. **Oyoʔru tumuuru nuʔ.** I am buying clothing.

Tumubo, Timbo (name) Son-of-bull-bear (kindhearted; known for saying, 'If you ever have grandchildren, never let them go hungry.')

tumusua sokobi K (n) garden patch, vegetable garden. **Nu tumusua sokobita unu hanikutui.** You are going to prepare a garden spot for me. *See* **tukumasua sokoobi.**

tumusuapu (n) garden crop, garden product. **Nu rumusuapu tsaa nabuni suakatu.** My crops are growing and looking good.

tumusuaru (v) plant crops, raise a garden. **Tumusuʔai u.** It grew (of plants). **Tumusuru nuʔ.** I am raising a garden. *See* **tukumasua sokoobi.**

tunahyaru (v) trail something. **Arukaʔa tunahyaa miʔaru.** He is going along trailing a deer. *See* **nayaaru.**

tunakaru (v) listen, hear something. **Ohka nuʔ tunakaʔruʔi.** I am going to hear what he is saying. *See* **nakaru.**

tunakatu (n) hearing (having ability to hear).

tunakatu (adj) obedient. *See* **ketunakatu.**

tunakiitu (v) listen, pay attention. **Tunaki kima.** I came to listen. *See* **nakuhi.**

tuni-, tuniru (pfx) authority, rule (govern).

tuniatsikatuʔ (n) commander. **Tai tuniʔatsikatu uʔ.** He is our commander. *See* **niʔatsiwapiʔ.**

tunikepisaʔ (n) spokesman, elocutionist (speaker who strengthens others by his talk). **Taahpuʔ tsaʔ nu tunikepisaʔ.** Our Father (God) is my strength.

tunihpararu (v) plead. **Miʔapuha tunihparaa.** She pleaded to go.

tunikukekitu K, **tuninukekutu** W (v) announce (speak loud and clear).

tunikwuru (v) sing a song. **Puhakuniku uʔ tunikwuuru.** He is singing in church.

tunimakwihtseru (v) criticize, ridicule (make fun of). *See* **nohitu.**

tunimanahke huutsuʔ K (n) mockingbird (repeating bird). *See* **soo yakeʔ.**

tunipukawapi W (n) fortuneteller (person with extrasensory perception). *See* **nipukaaʔeetu.**

tunisuatu (adj) noisy. **Turuʔepuru tumaku tunisuatu.** The children are noisy.

tuniwaitu (v) collect money, dun (to collect payment). **U runiwai kwaú!** Go and collect (the money)!

tuniwaituʔ (n) tax collector, bill collector.

tuniʔatsiku (n) counselor, adviser (one who gives advice and direction).

tuniʔatsitu (v) advise, counsel. **Nu ahpuʔ tsaʔ nu tuniʔatsituʔi.** My father will give me counsel (my father counsels me).

tunisuabetai wapi W, **tunisua wapi** K (n) teacher.

tunisuabetaru (v) teach something to someone. *See* **suabetaikuru.**

tunisuʔuyaitu, tunisuʔuyaʔeetu (v) mock, laugh at, jeer at (make fun of). **Turueʔpuruu ohka tenahpu sukuhpa tunisuʔuyaitu.** The children are making fun of that man. *See* **usuʔuyaʔitu.**

tunoo kuna waikina K, tuunooh kuna kwaikina W (n) freight train [**tuunoo** haul + **kuuna** fire + **waikina** wagon].

tunookatu? (n) camel.

tunoona bukuwaʔ (n) truck (for hauling).

tunoo wapi (n) pack-animal leader. **Nu tunoo wapi tsaʔ tsaa numi muʔheetu.** My pack horse is a good leader.

tunoo waikina (n) truck, wagon [**tunoo** haul + **waikina** wagon].

tunookuru (v) load up (an animal or a vehicle). **Na bukuwaa tunookutu uruu.** They are loading up a car.

tunoomiʔaru (v) pack a load on foot.

tunoopu W, tunooku K (n) pack for an animal (loaded and ready to go).

tunooru (v) carry load (on back). **Huupitoo uʔ tunooru.** He is carrying a load of firewood. **Pu ohnaa waakune tunooru.** She is carrying her baby on her back.

tunooʔ (n) saddlebag (double satchel thrown over saddle to carry bedding or food for travel).

Tuoyobisesu (name) Chief Comanche-dog-soldiers.

Tupanai (name) Cliff (person).

tupánaʔ (n) creek bank, incline.

tupe (n) mouth, lips. *See* **tuupe.**

tupe tsahkweʔyaru (v) unbridle a horse (take off bridle and bit).

tupe tsaʔnikaru (v) bridle a horse.

tupe tsaʔnikaʔ (n) bridle [**tupe-** mouth + **tsaʔnikaʔ** hook on].

tupe wihtuaʔ (n) bucket with spout [**tupe-** mouth + **wihtuaʔ** bucket].

tupehemiʔaru (v, an subj) fall off. *See* **tupuheru.**

tupi (n) stone, rock. *See* **tuupi.**

tupi aawo (n) crock, jug (stone container). **Nu tupi aawo tsaʔ soo toomoopu.** My crock is very old.

tupi kuni (n) stone or brick house, jail, prison [**tuupi** stone + **kahni** house].

Tupi kuniʔ (name) Stonehouse (person).

tupi natsu (n) medicinal plant (*lit* rock medicine; a bug mixes sunflower rosin with a secretion, then leaves it on the fork of this weed; the rosin mixture was put in a buckskin amulet and worn to keep one from having bad dreams or to keep evil spirits away from a baby). *See* **kunanatsu.**

tupi pabokoʔaai W, tupi paboko K (n) rock lizard [**tuupi** stone + **paboko** clear].

tupi táhparu (v, sg), *pl* tupi táhpaʔitu stone someone (throw stones at someone or something). **U rupi tahpaʔi uʔ.** They stoned him.

tupi tumatsuneʔ (n) whetstone, sandpaper. *See* **tumakumaʔaaiʔ.**

Tupi wunu (name) Rocky-creek (person).

tupi puʔe (n) surfaced road (gravel or concrete). *See* **puʔe.**

tʉpi simuhta? (n) moth (large species) [**tʉpi-** rock + **simuhta** nose].

tʉpi sokoobi W, tʉpi sokoona K (n) rocky ground.

tʉpunirʉ (v) look at, watch (as at a show). *See* **watsi puniitʉ.**

tʉpuuni (n) picture.

tʉpuuni yʉ?yʉmuhku? K (n) movie [**tʉpuuni** picture + **yʉyʉmuhku?** move].

tʉpʉherʉ W, tʉpeherʉ, tʉpherʉ K (v) fall off or away from. *See* **tʉpehemi?arʉ.**

tʉpʉnaatʉ (adv loc) middle, center (in the middle).

tʉpʉsi kʉma? (n) sorrel horse (of yellowish or reddish-brown color).

tʉrah kwʉ?nerʉ K (v) iron clothing (*lit* rub with foot).

tʉrah kwʉ?ne? (n) iron, flatiron (for ironing clothes).

tʉrahnai?itʉ (v) drill a field (plant a field by machine).

tʉrahnarʉ (v) plant by hand (sow crops or garden by hand).

tʉrahnirʉ (v) cut down (as to fell a tree).

tʉrahtsuki? K (n) eraser [**tʉra-** press + **tsuki-** rub].

tʉrahwikatʉ (v) win a prize, earn something. *See* **tahwikarʉ.**

tʉrahyapʉ (n) meatball (Comanche-style; prepared of dry, pounded meat mixed with grease and sugar).

tʉrahyarʉ (v) meatball preparation (mix sugar, grease, and pounded meat together forming meatballs). **Nʉ bia? tsa? tʉrahyarʉ.** My mother is making meatballs.

tʉraka?aitʉ (adj) increasing numerically, augmenting in quantity.

tʉrana (n) *pl* **tʉrananai** root.

tʉrana?ipʉ (n) marrow (cooked out from bones).

tʉrana?itʉ (v) cook out marrow from bones.

tʉrana (n) leg bones, marrow bones (marrow is taken to make meatballs eaten at peyote breakfast).

tʉranʉ (n) breadroot, Indian bread.

tʉrape suwaitʉ (v) tempt one to sin.

tʉrapehekatʉ (n) sinner (fallen one).

tʉrapʉtsarʉ W (v) puncture a tire, blow out a tire.

tʉrawʉnarʉ K, tʉrakwʉnarʉ W (v) stake something, nail something. **Wobita u tawʉnai.** He nailed the board.

tʉrawʉna? K, tʉrakwʉna? W (n) tent pin, stake, nail. **Tʉrawʉna-?a tso?me.** Pick up the stake.

tʉrayaa sarii (n) bloodhound. **Tʉrayaa sarii u hipʉkatʉ.** He has a bloodhound.

tʉrayu?nepʉ (n) pounded meat.

tʉrayu?nerʉ (v) pound meat.

tʉrayu?ne?, tʉraiyu?ne? (n) wooden pestle (made of hardwood tree knot, used for pounding meat or corn). **Pʉʉ tʉrayu?ne?a yaahtsi, uma u tayu?nenʉ.** Taking their pestle, with it they pounded it (116:16).

tʉroh paku?i? (n) wedge.

tʉrohtsanitʉ (v) hang something (with a clothespin or on a hook).

tʉrohtsani?i? (n) clothesline, hook, nail.

tʉrohtʉbʉʔiʔ (n) auger bit, bit used for boring holes (as in a hide).

tʉrohtʉmapʉ (n) canned food. **Sʉʉkʉi tohtʉmapa nʉʔ suʔwaitʉ.** I want (a jar of) canned plums.

tʉrohtʉmaʔ (n) lid (*lit* close the neck). *See* **tʉmarʉmaʔ.**

tʉrohtʉwaʔ (n) can opener [**tʉro-** lid + **tohtʉwa-** open by punching].

tʉrokuriapʉ K (n) garbage. *See* **tʉtsakwʉriapʉ.**

tʉrokwʉsuakʉtʉ (adj) believer. **Ta Ahpʉʔa u tʉrokwʉsuakʉtʉ.** She believes in Our Father God.

tʉropʉsapʉʔ (n) beadwork.

tʉropʉsarʉ (v) bead something. **Nʉmʉ napʉha tʉropʉsai.** She beaded the moccasins.

tʉroʔnikarʉ (v) put something into the mouth.

tʉrʉbakiʔarʉ (v) load into. **Waikina u tʉrʉbaki.** He loaded the wagon. *See* **toʔnikarʉ.**

tʉrʉbinitʉ (v) ask a question.

tʉrʉe, tʉrʉeʔtʉ, tʉrʉeʔti (n, acc) child.

tʉrʉe kuʔyuutsi (n) quail. *See* **tʉe kuyúutsi.**

tʉrʉe basuu K (n) quail. **Lophortyx** sp. *See* **tʉe basuu.**

tʉrʉehpʉ (n), nom *pl* **tʉrʉehpʉʔrʉʉ,** *acc pl* **tʉrʉehpʉʔrii** child, children.

tʉrʉetʉparʉ (v) have children.

tʉrʉetʉsuarʉ (v) care for child (like a mother).

tʉrʉhkarʉ (v) steal. **Puhihwihta u tʉrʉhkai.** He stole the money. *See* **sikusarʉ.**

tʉrʉhkaʔ (n) thief.

tʉrʉkʉ kahni (n) den of thieves, house of thieves.

tʉrʉkwobamʉ (n) sneezeweed. *Helenium autumnale L.* (used in bath to treat fever [C & J]).

tʉrʉnirʉ (v) ask for something. **Kokoraʔa u tʉrʉni.** He asked for a chicken.

tʉrʉtsʉpʉ (n) number, group of figures (Arabic numerals).

tʉrʉtsʉrʉ (v) count something (unspecified) [**tʉ** (unspec) + **tʉtsʉ** count].

tʉrʉʔai waipʉ (n) working woman.

tʉrʉʔai wapi (n) workman, servant, renter, hired hand, clerk, disciple.

tʉrʉʔaipʉʔ (n) work.

tʉrʉʔaitʉ, tʉrʉʔarʉ (v) do work. **Lawtontsa tʉrʉʔaitʉ.** He is working in Lawton.

tʉrʉʔawe wapi W (n) prophet (one who proclaims a message).

tʉrʉʔekarʉ (v) paint something, *adj* painted.

tʉrʉʔekaʔ (n) paint. *See* **tʉʔekaʔ.**

tʉrʉhaniʔ W, tʉhraniʔ K (n) hammer. **Nʉrʉhaniʔa nʉ yaanʉki.** You must bring back my hammer.

tʉrʉnapʉ (n) planted crops.

tʉrʉnarʉ (v) plant (sow seed using a planting machine).

tʉrʉnaʔ (n, sg), *pl* **tʉrʉniʔiʔ** planter, seeder (machine for sowing seed).

tʉrʉniʔitʉ (v, pl), *sg* **tʉhtʉkitʉ** plant seed (using a dibble stick).

tʉsáarʉ (v) dye something (nonspecific color). **Wanapa tʉsaarʉ.** She dyed the cloth. **U rʉsaai u.** He dyed it. **ekʉsaʔarʉ** dye red, **ebisaʔarʉ** dye blue.

tɨsaasi̱ (n) Indian perfume plant, sage. **Tɨsaasi̱kinɨ nɨ himinɨ̱.** Give me some sage. *See* **nɨmɨ rɨsaasi̱.**

tɨsaaʔ (n) dye (nonspecific color). **Ekatɨsaaʔ nɨʔ suʔwitɨ̱.** I want red dye.

tɨsibetɨ (v) plane something smooth. **Huupihta tɨsibeʔi tsaakɨ̱.** He planed the wood good (smooth).

tɨsibeʔ (n) carpenter's plane (tool for smoothing wood).

tɨsoona, tɨsoona̱ (n), *acc* tɨso- one pan, dishpan, plate. **Tɨsoone nɨʔ kotse.** I washed the pan.

tɨsoyuni (n) grinding stone, sifter.

tɨsoʔarɨ (v) tan a hide.

tɨsoʔipɨʔ (n) tanned hide.

tɨsutaibitsi̱ (n) mercy, pity, meekness. **Tɨsutaibitsi̱ maʔoorɨ.** That person is merciful.

tɨsutaikatɨ (v) pity, befriend (treat with kindness). **Tsukuhpa ohka tɨsutaikatɨ uʔ.** He has pity on that old man.

tɨsuwaʔitɨ (adj) jealous (of husband or wife, unspec object).

tɨsuʔatsipɨ (n) judicial power, power, will, authority.

tɨsuʔatsi̱katɨ̱ (v) think about something. **Nɨ biaʔ nɨʔ tɨsuʔatsi̱katɨ̱.** I am thinking about my mother. **Tɨsuʔatsi nɨʔi miʔarɨ.** I think I will go.

tɨsuʔatsi̱tɨ (v) have authority, have power. **Tsaa u tɨsuʔatsitɨ.** He has good power.

tɨsuʔnarɨ (v) forgive, pardon. **Nɨ tɨsuʔnai uʔ.** He forgave me. *See* **niʔtsuʔnarɨ.**

tɨsuʔnarɨ (v) quiet down, calm down (become quiet).

tɨsuʔɨrɨ (v) give counsel, advise. **Nɨroko tsaʔ tsaa tɨsuʔɨrɨ.** Grandpa gives good advice. *See* **naniʔɨruʔaitɨ.**

tɨsuʔɨrɨʔ (n) wisdom, counsel, kind thoughts.

tɨtaatɨ (adj) small size, unworthy, pitied. **Tɨtaatɨwe u!** She's pitiful!

tɨtaatɨ (num, indef) small quantity. *See* **huitsi.**

tɨtsahkɨnarɨ (v) sew (on a sewing machine). **Pɨ tɨtsahkɨna ɨhtukɨ̱ uʔ.** She sewed through it.

tɨtsahkɨnaʔ (n) sewing machine.

tɨtsahtɨʔoorɨ (v) rake something.

Tɨtsakana (n) Sewers (derogatory group name).

tɨtsakɨnaha yuhu (n) sewing machine oil.

tɨtsakwoo raibooʔ (n) white farmer. **Nɨ ahpɨʔ tɨtsakwo raiboeetɨ.** My father farmed for a living.

tɨtsakwoopɨ (n) plowed field.

tɨtsakwɨɨriapɨ W (n) garbage. *See* **tɨrokuriapɨ.**

tɨtsakwɨriapɨ K (n) trash.

Tɨtsanoo yehkɨ (n) Comanche band.

tɨtsanuaʔ (n) rake (garden tool). *See* **tsahtɨʔokiʔ.**

tɨtsanunɨʔitɨ (v, adj) stop (as a team of horses); stopped, halted (from a buggy or from horseback). *See* **tsanɨnɨrɨ.**

tɨtsapara huupi (n) clothesline pole.

tɨtsatɨkiʔ (n) harrow (cultivating implement).

tɨtsatɨsukitɨ (v, adj) harrow, harrowed (break up or pulverize soil). *See* **tsatɨsukiitɨ̱.**

tɨtsaʔookiʔ (n) hay rake (farm implement).

tʉtsaʔwooʔ K, tʉtsakwooʔ W (n)
plow.

tʉtsaʔworʉ, tʉtsakworʉ (v, unspec
obj) plow soil. **Pʉ sokoni u
tsaʔwoi.** He plowed his ground.

tʉtsihkaʔarʉ (v, sg obj), *pl obj*
tʉtsihpomiʔitʉ cut off, cut up.
Pʉ paapi uʔ tsihpomai. She cut
her hair. **Tʉtsipomiʔi uʔ.** She cut
them (the hairs).

tʉtsihpetiʔ (n) spade (garden tool).

tʉtsihpomiʔipʉ (n) object cut into
pieces. *See* **tsihpoma.**

tʉtsihtsukaʔ (n) index finger.

tʉtsihtʉmaʔ (n) key, lock (*lit* close
with something pointed).

tʉtsihtʉrʉ (v) padlock something.

tʉtsikwʉsarʉ (v) swindle, cheat
(take against someone's will).
Naiʔbihta uʔ tʉtsikwʉsai. He
beat him out of that girl.

tʉtsipʉsaʔ, tʉʉhtsipʉsaʔ (n) screw.
See **tʉmatsukiʔ.**

tʉtsiwaiiʔ K, tʉtsikwaiiʔ W (n)
spear, sword [**tʉ-** (unspec) +
tsiʔwai- probe with long pole].
See **tahkanaʔ.**

tʉtsiyaaʔ W (n) pitchfork [**tʉ-**
(unspec) + **tsiya-** pick up with
long pole].

tʉtsiyunarʉ (v, unspec obj) shovel
something. **Tʉtsiyunarʉ uʔ.** He is
shoveling (unspec object).

tʉtsiyunaʔ (n) shovel. *See* **kusiyunaʔ.**

tʉtsiyunaʔ K (n) spade.

tʉtsiyuʔiʔ (n) chisel (tool).

tʉtsoʔnikarʉ (v) poke head into
something (unspec obj) [**tʉ-**
(unspec) + **tsoʔnika** poke head
in]. **Tʉtsoʔnikaai uʔ.** He poked
his head into something. *See*
tsoʔnikarʉ.

tʉtsuʔmapʉ (n) broke financially,
penniless.

tʉtsu-, tʉhtsu (adj) cruel, mean,
ugly, bad. *See* **kesuatʉ, aitʉ.**

tʉtsu narʉmiʔitʉ (v) gossip, tell
off-color stories [**tʉtsu-** bad +
narʉmu- tell story].

tʉtsu puhaʔ (n) witch doctor
[**tʉtsu-** bad + **puha** medicine].
Tʉtsu puha uʔ umikwai. He
went to see a witch doctor.

tʉtsʉrʉ (v) count definite objects.

tʉtsʉhanitʉ (v, unspec obj) drive,
handle, manage (as to drive
a vehicle or ride a horse) [**tʉ-**
(unspec) + **tsahani** handle].

tʉtʉbetʉ (adj, pl), *sg* **tʉhpetʉ** full.

tʉtʉsuana (n) evil spirit, unclean
spirit.

tʉʉhkaʔarʉ (v, sg), *pl* **tʉʉhpo-
miʔitʉ** chop. **Tʉʉhkaʔama uʔ
tʉʉhkaʔarʉ.** He is chopping with
an axe.

tʉʉhkaʔaʔ (n) axe. *See* **naʔbuti-
kʉmakatʉ tʉʉhkaʔaaʔ.**

tʉʉhkonarʉ (v, unspec obj)
sharpen a cutting edge, croak (as
of a frog). **Tʉʉhkonaai uʔ.** He
sharpened it something. **Pasawio
tsaʔ tʉʉhkonarʉ.** The frog
croaked.

tʉʉhkoʔneʔ (n) a steel tool (as
implement for sharpening knives).

tʉʉhtamaʔ (n) string, yarn, ties.
Tʉʉhtama nʉʔ. I saw some yarn.
See **wʉhtamaʔ.**

tʉʉhtamʉh raiboʔ, tʉʉhtʉmʉ
raibooʔ, tʉhtamʉ raiboʔ (n)
policeman, sheriff (*lit* man who
ties us up). **Tʉʉhtamʉh raibooʔ
tsaʔ pite.** The policeman drove
up. *See* **nʉmi himaʔetʉ.**

tɨɨhtsohpeʔ (n) congealed bone marrow. **Tɨɨhtsohpe tɨsai uʔ.** She cooked congealed bone marrow (prepared it).

tɨɨhtɨmapɨha tɨrawɨnaʔ (n), *pl* **tɨɨtɨmapa narawɨniʔi** fence staples.

tɨɨhtɨmapɨ K (n) fence. **tɨɨhtɨmapɨ nahhuupi** fence post.

tɨɨhtɨmarɨ (v, unspec) fence something. **Tɨɨhtɨmai uʔ.** He fenced something. *See* **wɨhtɨmarɨ.**

tɨɨmooi, tɨɨmoanɨ (adj) surprised, amazed.

tɨɨnoo ɨnɨɨʔ K (n) camel. *See* **ɨnɨʔa pɨnɨsɨ narɨnooʔ- katɨ.**

tɨɨnua (n) broom grass. *Gramineae* (one of the kinds of grasses used to make brooms).

tɨɨnuarɨ (v, unspec obj) sweep something. **Tɨɨnuaʔi uʔ.** She swept. *def obj* **Tasoneʔ wɨɨnuarɨ.** She is sweeping the floor.

tɨɨnuaʔ (n) broom. **Tɨɨnua tɨmɨi nɨʔ.** I brought a broom.

tɨɨnuaʔ, tɨɨnua masɨaʔ (n) broom corn. *Sorghum vulgare* Pers. [**tɨɨnua-** sweep + **masɨaʔ** corn].

tɨɨpe (n) mouth, lips. **Nɨ tɨɨpe tsaʔ tsiiwa.** My lips are chapped.

tɨɨpi (n) stone, rock. **Tɨɨpiʔa u wihi.** He threw a stone. *See* **tɨpi.**

tɨɨtsohpepɨ (n) Indian butter (skimmed grease).

tɨɨtsɨkeʔ W (n) lawnmower, scythe. *See* **soniwɨtsɨkeʔ.**

tɨɨtsɨkɨnarɨ (v, unspec obj) tie up a horse (particular horse unspecified). **Tɨɨtsɨkɨnai uʔ.** He tied up a horse.

tɨɨyɨ mutsoraʔ K (n) bridle bit.

tɨɨʔurapɨ W, K (n) sweetheart, lover, boy friend (of a woman). *See* **notsaʔkaʔ.**

tɨwoorɨ W (v) go hunting (go on a hunting trip involving the whole camp).

tɨyaaitɨ (v, sg), *pl* **kooitɨ** die. **Tenahpuʔ tsaʔ tɨyaai.** The man died.

tɨyai waikina K (n) hearse.

tɨyaipɨ kohno (n) casket (*lit* death box).

tɨyaipɨ, tɨyaiʔ K (n) corpse, dead body. **Tɨyaipɨ tsaʔ puʔekɨ habiitɨ.** The corpse was lying in the road.

tɨyaipɨha nooʔeeʔtɨ (n) W hearse, K undertaker. **tɨyaipɨ nooetɨʔ** K hearse.

tɨyatoʔyerɨ (v) mount a horse. *See* **tɨhɨyaroʔitɨ.**

tɨyumarɨ (v) fall into something. **Ɨmapakɨ tɨyumai.** He fell into the pond.

tɨyuwarɨ (v) swallow something. **Pai u tɨyuwi.** He swallowed water.

tɨyɨkwipɨ (n) actions (behavior). **Suni uʔ tɨyɨkwitɨ.** That is the way she behaves.

tɨʔaape (n) voice.

tɨʔape nanakarɨ (v) echo. **Hapanitɨkɨtɨ tɨʔape nanakaʔi uʔ.** It echoed in the valley.

tɨʔasɨitɨ (v) freeze (liquid). **Paa tsaʔ tɨʔasɨi.** The water froze.

tɨʔawetɨ (v) tell. **Hakɨ surɨ pokopi ɨ tɨʔawenaʔ** Where is that fruit you told of? (16:12). *See* **narɨmuʔikatɨ.**

tɨʔawekɨɨkarɨ (v) answer. **Nɨ tɨʔawekɨɨka.** Answer me.

tɨʔehkooiʔ W (n) walking cane, walking stick, rod, shepherd's crook. *See* **natsihtóoʔ.**

tɨʔekarɨ (v) paint something, anoint, grease something. **Kahni nɨʔ tɨʔekaruʔi.** I will paint the house. *See* **wihi̱ tɨʔekarɨ.**

tɨʔekaʔ W (n) paint. *See* **turɨʔekaʔ.**

tɨʔíiʔ (n) sandpiper.

tɨʔinakɨrɨ (v) jerk meat for someone.

tɨʔinawɨnɨrɨ (v) have pneumonia. *See* **amawɨnɨtɨ.**

tɨʔiyaʔi wapi̱ (n) watchman, watchdog.

tɨʔi̱katɨ (adj) resemble someone (appearance or personality). **Pɨ pia̱ʔ u tɨʔi̱katɨ.** He is like his mother.

tɨʔnooʔ (n) travel carrier made of teepee poles, *travois* (for carrying children or bedding).

tɨʔoibɨkɨrɨ (v) be ill, suffer an illness.

tɨʔoikatɨ (adj) ill for a long time.

tɨʔoipɨ (n) long illness, invalid. *See* **wɨhmina nɨɨmɨ.**

tɨʔonaaʔ (n) weakness.

tɨʔonaapɨ, tɨʔohnaabɨ (n) weak person or animal. **Itɨ tɨhɨɨya̱ tɨʔonaabɨ.** This horse is weak.

ᚥ wehki'ai

tɨʔrɨkúuʔ

tɨʔrɨkúuʔ W, **turɨkúuʔ** K (n), *acc* **tɨʔrikuuʔa,** *pl* **tɨʔrikúuʔnɨɨ** prairie dog. **Suʔana turikúuʔnɨɨ sookɨniba̱ʔi̱.** There the prairie dogs had a town (3:1).

Tɨʔsinaʔ (name) Hanging-from-the-belt (ref. to items usually hung from the belt, such as tobacco, knife, or pick to make moccasins).

tɨʔɨyatɨ (v) frighten. **Sariia nɨʔ tɨʔɨyatɨ.** The dog will scare (a person).

U

u (pro, 3rd dist nom sg) he, she, it.

ubitakuhtsiʔa (adv man) slowly. **Nabukuwaa tsaʔ ubitakuhtsiʔa miʔarɨ.** The car moved slowly.

ubitɨkɨɨtɨ, ubitɨkɨrɨ (v) flirt (pursue opposite sex). **Naiʔbi tsaʔ ubitɨkɨɨtɨ.** The girl is chasing him (but he does not respond).

uhka (pro dem, dist acc sg) him, her, it.

uhoi kaʔwɨtɨ (v) congregate, crowd many people together. *See* **narahkaʔwitɨ.**

uhúntɨkɨ (adj) be ill, sickly.

umamiʔarɨ (v, pl) *sg* **tsakamiʔarɨ** lead.

umarhnitɨ (v) hurt someone.

unahrɨ (v) move across (be on the other side). **Hunuʔbi unahrɨ uʔ.** He is on the other side of the river.

urahkarɨ (v) learn something new (do something for the first time).

urarɨ (v), *pl* **uʔɨruhkurɨ** find something. **Wanɨseʔa uʔ urai.** She found a penny. *See* **maʔurarɨ.**

urii (pro dem, dist acc pl) them.

urɨ (pro dem, dist nom sg), he, she, it; *pl* **urɨɨ** they.

usúni̱ (adv) always, forever. **Usúni̱ nɨʔ sɨme suatɨ.** I always think like that.

usú?uya?itʉ W, unisu?uyaa?aitʉ K (v) mock, deride, laugh at. *See* tʉnị su?uyaitʉ, nisu?uyaitʉ.

utʉkatʉ (v), *pl* himikatʉ give (something). Pʉ tua?a hina utʉkatʉ. She is giving her nephew one thing. Pʉ tua?a u? kiano himikatʉ. She is giving her nephew many things.

uwíhị (n), *acc* uwihi spear, sword (arch long knife). *See* tahkana?, tʉtsiwaii?.

ʉ

ʉbia (interj) oh! oh my! (exclamation of surprise used by women only). Ʉbia, kimarʉ marʉ. Oh my! They're coming. *See* ha?íi, yaa.

ʉhpʉitʉ (v), *pl* ʉhkooitʉ sleep. Ohnaa tsa? ʉhpʉikatʉ. The baby is asleep. Kahnikuhpatʉ tsa? sʉmʉ ʉhkoihkatʉ. Everyone in the house is asleep. *See* yuu?ʉhpʉitʉ.

ʉhtaarʉ (v) stake down tightly (as a hide being stretched). Pʉhi u? ʉhtaarʉ. He is staking down the hide.

ʉhtaayu? (n) rawhide (being stretched). *See* pahkipʉ.

ʉhtamakʉ?atʉ (v) yawn. Orʉ tsa? nʉ? ʉhtamakʉ?etʉ. That makes me yawn.

ʉhta?etʉ (adj) staked-down object.

ʉhtsumarʉ (v), *pl* sʉmʉʉhtsumitʉ close the eyes.

ʉhʉ (n) blanket (without fringes, as a beaver blanket). Ma ʉhʉ nohina?suyakinu. Her blanket is beautiful.

ʉhʉkatʉ (v) cover oneself.

ʉhʉkʉrʉ (v) cover (someone). Ma ʉhʉkʉ. She covered him up.

ʉi (adv time) too late, past the time (beyond help). Ʉi ma? tsʉnipʉ. It is too late.

ʉkʉ (adv time) recently (just now), still. Ʉkʉ pitʉi ma?. He just now came in.

ʉkʉ- (pfx) young.

ʉkʉ nʉmʉ roopʉnʉ K (n) youngest generation.

Ʉkʉ tomopʉ (n) New Year's Day.

ʉkʉbitsị (adj) young. Ʉkʉbitsị ma? orʉ nai?bi. That girl is young.

Ʉkʉi yʉba mʉa (n) August (*lit* new fall month).

ʉkʉnaa (adv order) first. Ʉkʉnaa ma iikʉ. Let him in first.

ʉkʉnanakatʉ (adj) young, youthful. Tuinʉhpʉ? tsa? urʉ ʉkʉnanakatʉ. The boy is just young.

ʉkʉ nʉmʉnʉʉ, ʉkʉ nʉmʉ roopʉ- nʉʉ (n) younger generation (generation of young Comanches). Ʉkʉ nʉmʉnʉʉ tsa? hina tʉahwitʉ. The younger generation expresses itself plainly. *See* nʉmʉ rʉborapʉ.

Ʉkʉ tooma mʉa (n) January (*lit* new year month).

ʉkʉsʉ (adv time) still, yet. Ʉkʉsʉ u? karʉʉrʉ. It is still sitting there.

ʉkwihkatʉ (v) sniff an odor, smell something. Ma ʉʉkwi?. Smell this (as one holds out a flower). Totsiyaa?a nʉ? ʉkwihkatʉ. I smell the flower.

ʉkwịsʉ?ninitʉ K (v) sniff around, smell around (as a dog does). *See* muwarʉ.

138

ukwụsụ?nitụ (v) smell something
from a distance (get a whiff of
something).

umakahni, umakụni (n) rain
shelter (lit rain house; summer
shelter of buckskin hung outside
the teepee to deflect rain from
coming through the teepee top or
opening). See yu?a umakụni.

umaarụ (v) rain. Imarụ ma?. It's
raining. Soo umaarụ. It's raining
heavily. Ụmahkụti na puni nụ?.
I see the rain coming.

umahpaa? (n), obj umahpai rain
water, pond, lake. Ụmahpai nụ?
hibi. I drank some rainwater.
Ụmahpai nụ puni. I see a pond.

umapụ (n) rain. Ụmapụ ma?
wụesụ. It already rained.

unụ (2nd pers sg dat pro) to you.

unụ bihnaa (n) honey [unụụ insect
+ pihnaa sugar]. Ụnụ bihnaa
urai nụ. I found some honey.

unụ bihnaa kahni K (n) honeycomb
(lit honey house).

unụụ? ruu? (n) honey sieve (to
separate honey from honeycomb)
[unụụ insect + tuu- through].

unụì ? (n), pl unụụ? bug,
insect, creature. Ụnụì ? tsa?
tụmarụmá- atụ. There are sure
a lot of bugs.

unụ?a punụsụ narụnoo?katụ W (n)
camel (lit creature that carries its
own saddle). See tụụnoo unụụ?.

upinakwụ (adv loc) behind.

ura (adv) thank you. Ụrahkokị.
Thank you very much. See ahó.

Ụrụi mụa (n) July (hot month).

urụụ (excl) ouch! it burns.

urụ? (adj, n) meek, kind, good-
hearted. Ụrụ ma? orụ. She is a

kind person. Orụ tsa? ụrụ?. That
one (over there) is kind.

urụ?itụ (n) dry season, drought,
hot weather. Ụhkitsi tabenima
urụ?itụ. Today is a hot day.

usorokiitụ (v) snore. Sarii tsa?
usorokiitụ. The dog is snoring.

usuaketụ (v) breathe deeply in
sleep. See nasuawụhkitụ.

utsụ?itụ (adj, n) cold. Tụbitsi
utsụ?itụ. It's really cold.

u?a?, u?e (n) wound, sore. Ụ?e nụ?
puni. I see a sore. Ụ?akatụ ma?
pụ napekụ. She has a sore on her
feet.

u?bụi? (n) cocoon. Ori u?bụi?nii
puni. Look at those cocoons.

W

waa- (pfx) cedar. See waapị.

waahimarụ (v), pl waanohi?itụ
celebrate Christmas (lit to take a
cedar tree).

waahima? (n) Christmas.

Waahkusi okwe? (n) Beaver Creek
(lit gray flowing cedar creek;
river which flows through present
Wichita Falls, TX).

Waahunu?bi (n) Canadian River (lit
cedar creek; near Anadarko, OK).

waahuupị (n) teepee pole (made of
cedar).

waaitụ (v) dry up.

Waakakwa (name) Trotter
(Laughing-John; person).

waakohno, waakụne (n) cradleboard, day cradle (made of
two cedar boards four inches
wide, covered with buckskin
sewed on with hood to cover the

baby's head; laced up in front).
Waakŭno ma? waruhtarŭ. The
baby is laced in the day cradle.
See **habikŭno?.**

wehki'ai

waakohno

waani K, **waa?ne?** W (n) fox.
Waani tsa? aimaiaa?arŭ. The fox
is loping.

waapi (n), *acc* **waapita** cedar.
waapi huupi cedar trunk;
wahuupi cedar lumber. **Waapi
tsaa kwanarŭ.** Cedar smells good.

waata, waahta (n), *pl* **waatanii**, *obj*
waate teepee pole (cedar- wood
teepee pole located apart from
the teepee). **Isa haka waatana?**
Whose poles are these?

waatsŭ K (n), *acc* **waatsŭna** rib. **Pŭ
waatsi u? wŭhkobaia.** She broke
her rib.

waa?akitŭ (v) yell, wahoo. **Urii
wa?akikŭ!** Yell at them!

waha- (pfx) two, double.

wahabahti (num) doubles (two
separate items, two pairs, two
groups). **Wahabahti nŭ? wana
napŭkatŭ.** I have two pairs of

socks. **Wahabahkŭ u? nŭmihimi.**
He counted them out two-by-two.
See **wa?wa?.**

wahabisuatŭ (adj) undecided,
doubtful (*lit* think two ways). **Uku
nŭ? wahabisuatŭ.** I can't decide
(am undecided) about that.

wahati, wahatŭ (num) two. **Wahati
ma? tuakatŭ.** She has two boys.

wahatomopŭ K (n) two-year-old.
Itŭ tsa? wahatomopŭ. He is a
two-year-old. **Waha ma? tomopŭ.**
The child is two years old. *See*
tomohtoopŭ.

Wahi mŭa, Wahima mŭa (n)
December (evergreen month; a
memorial day celebrated before
the coming of the white man;
winter solstice celebration).

wahkami?arŭ (v, pl) *sg* **aimi?arŭ**
lope (as a horse with rider or a
pack load).

wahta (n) pole, club.

wahtóorŭ (v) club someone,
something [**wahta** pole, club +
oo do]. *See* **wŭhtokwŭrŭ.**

waikina, waikina (n) wagon, truck,
train, streetcar.

waikina nakwŭŭki (n) spokes (of
a wagon wheel; *lit* wagon spread-
like-a-fan).

waikina na?oomo (n) wagon wheel.
**Waikina naa?oomi tsa?sekwikŭ
tsŭkŭkatŭ.** The wagon wheel is
stuck in the mud.

waipa wananapŭ (n) ladies hosiery.
See **wananapŭ.**

wakarée? K, **waka?ré?ee?** W
(n) turtle. **Wakare?ee? tsa?
mahimi?ai.** Turtle went to war.
**Surŭ kŭse? wakare?ee?, 'Ke
nŭ? tunehtsŭwa?i naahkatŭ,'**

waikina

me yukwiiyu. That turtle said, 'I can't run' (9:9).

Wakaréʔe (name) Turtle (name of one of E. Canonge's daughters).

wakarukatu (v) aim something (as a gun or arrow). U wakarukatu nu?. I am aiming at him.

wakuʔwutu (adj, n) zigzag, rickrack, jagged item. Tuupi tsa? wakuʔwutu. The rock is jagged. Wakuʔwuti ma? matsahkunai. She sewed rickrack on it.

wana- (pfx) cloth. See Wanapu.

wana atsi?, waná atsi? (n), acc waná atsi?a playing cards. Waná atsikatu nu?. I have playing cards.

wana buhihwi (n), acc wana buhiwita paper money (lit cloth money: money for trade goods).

wana hu K, wana uhu W (n), acc wana hi cotton blanket, shawl.

wana koo? (n, arch) scissors (lit cloth cutter). See tukehkoo?.

wana kotse aawo (n) washtub.

wana kotse tsahparaa? K, wana kwiyaa? W (n) clothesline rope.

wana kotse? (n) soap [wana cloth + kotse washer].

wana napu (n) stockings, socks. See waipa wana napu.

wana ramu, wana ramuna (n), acc wana rame thread, crochet thread (lit cotton sinew).

wana rohpetiru (v) gamble, play cards (lit throw down yard goods). Wana rohpeti?etu ma?. He gambles a lot. Tenahpu? tsa? wana rohpetiru?i. The man is going to gamble. See nana kuhuru, tumeru.

wana soona (n), acc wana soone cotton quilt.

wana tsahkuna? (n) needle [wana cloth + tsahkuna sew].

wana tsihparaa? (n) bracing stick (holds up a cloth for shade).

wana tsiyaa? (n) flag [wana cloth + tsiyai hold on a pole].

wana tsiyaa?a náhuupi (n) flagpole.

wanama suapuha pokopi W, wana sona pokóopi K (n) cotton boll (lit cotton fruit).

wanapu K (n), acc wanapuha, wanapha W cloth, clothes, trade goods. Wanapha tumui hnu. I brought some trade goods.

Wanarɨ (name) Quanah Parker's daughter.

wanasihtaraaʔ W (n) lizard (striped) [**wa-** reptile + **natsihtaraaʔ** standing high].

wanatsihtaraaʔ (adj) striped, multi-colored.

waraatsi (n) sandals (fr. Span. huarache). *See* **saaʔwɨnapɨ**.

warɨʔikatɨ (v) miss (fail to find or locate), lack (fail to make connections). **Nɨ ruaʔa nɨ? warɨʔikatɨ.** I am missing my son (since his death). **Ke hina warɨʔinɨ.** He did not lack anything.

wasápe pɨmata kwɨhɨrɨʔ (n) bear trap (used for bears or other animals).

wasápeʔa tɨhkapɨ (n) pear (*lit* bear's food).

wasápe (n), *acc* **wasápeʔa** bear.

wasɨpɨ (n, pl), *sg* **tɨkɨwasɨʔ** bagged game.

wasɨrɨ (v, pl), *sg* **pehkatɨ** kill. **Kokoráʔanii uʔ wasɨrɨ.** He is killing the chickens. **Wasápeʔa uʔ pehkai.** He is killing a bear.

watasi (n) ace (in game of cards).

watsi ikatɨ (v) sneak in. **Kahnikɨ watsi ikai uʔ.** He sneaked into the house.

watsi iyarɨ (v) spy on someone secretly (*lit* secretly watching).

watsi miʔarɨ (v) leave secretly, sneak away.

watsi punitɨ (v) watch someone, spy on someone. **watsih punikatɨ** person spied upon. **Sitɨ kɨseʔ wakaréʔee u watsih punihka.** This turtle is hiding watching him (10:24). *See* **tɨpunitɨ**.

watsih nikwɨnɨrɨ (v) whisper, speak softly.

watsih tekwarɨ (v) **du watsihtawɨkɨ** whisper gossip, tell (tip off someone). **Watsih tɨawɨkɨi uʔ, ta miʔaruʔi.** He whispered to him that we are going.

watsikɨrɨ (v) lose something. **Hina nɨʔ watsikɨi.** I lost something. **Nɨ wana napɨha nɨʔ watsikɨi.** My sock is lost.

watsikwarɨ (v) going to get lost.

watsitɨ, watsikatɨ (v, adj) lose way, lost (become lost). **Huukukɨ uʔ watsii.** He is lost in the woods.

watsitɨkitɨ K, watsih tahtɨkitɨ W (v), *pl* **watsih tahniʔitɨ** hide (put away secretly; *lit* cause to be made secret). **Suhka pɨ kuʔina- pɨha tsayumiʔitsi u watsih tahniʔinɨ.** Taking off that, his roasted meat, (he) put it away in hiding (7–8:39). **Nɨ puhwihtɨ nɨʔ watsih tɨkituʔi.** I am going to hide my money.

watsiʔarɨ (v) keep secret (*lit* hide something in the mind). **watsi-ʔaitɨ** secretive, secret. **Naya nɨʔ hina watsiʔaitɨ.** I like to keep things secret.

watsi habiitɨ (v) hide, secret oneself away. **Tɨeʔpɨ orɨ tsaʔ watsi habiitɨ.** The child is hiding.

waʔihpɨʔ (n) woman's female kinsman. **Waʔihpɨʔ tsaʔ tɨmɨ-miʔarɨ.** The woman is going shopping. *See* **naʔwaʔihpɨʔ**.

waʔkooʔ W (n) clam, oyster (any shellfish).

waʔkooʔ K (n) shell of any shellfish.

waʔooʔ, waʔóʔa (n) cat.

wa?ihpɨ?

wa?roo koyáa? (n), *acc* **wa?ro kɨya?a.** W crawfish, crawdad (*lit* grabs and pinches).

Wa?sáasi? (n), *pl* **Wa?sáasinɨɨ** Osage people.

wa?wa? (n, du) twins, two-by-two, two apiece. **Wa?wahkɨ nɨmi himii.** They handed them out two-by-two. *See* **wahabahti.**

weehtsitɨ (v), *pl* **weerɨ** go down, get off (as of car or wagon). **Weeka!** Get off! **Surɨ kɨse? makɨhu weehtsi, u yaanɨ.** That one, going down to it, took it (7:28). **Waikinabai urɨɨ wee.** They are getting down off the wagon.

wehhari tuka?eetɨ (n) fireman.

wehkinitɨ (v) search (look around for). **Hina ɨnɨ wehkíniina?** What are you looking around for? (15:6). *See* **puhihwi wehki.**

wehkitɨ (v) look for. **Pɨ kwɨhi ma? wehkitɨ.** He is looking for his wife.

wehuru?i (n) thin person, emaciated person. **Nama? wehuru?ikatɨ nɨ?.** I am reducing.

wekɨbupɨ, wɨkɨbubi (n) bullroarer.

wekwiitɨ (v, pl), *sg* **ikarɨ** enter.

wekwimi?arɨ (v, pl) enter.

wenuarɨ (v), *pl* **wekwenuarɨ** hang something. **U kwasu?ɨ tsa? wehnuatɨ.** Her dress is hanging there.

wenu?nukimi?arɨ (v) run downhill, get off running. *See* **nuhkitɨ.**

wepɨkaitɨ (v) dangle, swing (swing from side to side or back and forth).

wesi- (pfx) burned, curled.

wesibaapi (n) curly hair [**wesi-** burned + **paapi** hair].

wesibapi?arɨ (v) curl hair, wave hair (give a permanent wave).

wesikatɨ (adj) burnt, scorched, toasted, browned.

wesikitɨ, wesiketɨ (adj) curly, curled. **U paapi wesiketɨ.** Her hair is curled.

wesikɨrɨ (v) burn something up, scorch, toast bread, brown food.

we?haki? (n), *acc* **wehari** flame, fire.

we?harɨ (v) burn, flame. **wehhakatɨ** burn oneself; **wehakɨárɨ** burn someone. **Ma? nɨ wehahkatɨ.** It's burning me.

we?kwiyanorɨ (adj v caus) shiny, iridescent. **Wanapɨ tsa? we?kwiyanorɨ.** The cloth is iridescent.

we?kwiyanutɨ tɨɨpi, wekwiyanu rɨɨpi (n) diamond (*lit* flashing stone).

we?kwiyanuutɨ (v) gleam, shine, flash. **Kahnikɨ we?kwiyanuutɨ.** The house is shining.

we?yɨkɨ sohoobi K (n) cottonwood. *See* **tahpookɨ?.**

wia? (n) mestizo (Native American having hispanic blood).

Wia?nʉʉ (n) Comanche band of Walters area (called Worn-away People by other bands).

wihirʉ (v) throw. **Tahkana? u? wihi.** He threw the spear. **Ma wihi!** Throw it (here)!

wihi̱ (n) melted grease.

wihi̱ tʉ?ekarʉ (v) lubricate, grease something. **Ta waikina na?omi wihi̱ tʉ?ekʉ.** Grease the wagon wheels. *See* **tʉ?ekarʉ.**

wihi̱ kamatʉ (v) taste oily or greasy.

wihnai mi?arʉ (v) walk lamely, limp (in walking; only hind legs of animals). **wihnai mi?arʉ** move along, walk limping. **Pʉ kahnibetu u? wihnai mi?arʉ.** He went home limping.

wihnaitʉ (adj) crippled. *See* **tatu̱wetʉ.**

wihnu (adv time) then. **Urʉʉkʉhʉ u yuhuwehkipʉ wihnu surʉ pisikwanúu?inʉ.** Then that one, the fattest to be found of them, slid down (5:11).

wihtaitʉ (v) throw away. **Ika nʉ? tʉboopʉi?a wihtaitu?i.** I am going to throw this paper away. *See* **petihtarʉ.**

wihtekatʉ (v, adj) peep, peer through, peeping. **Tʉetʉ tsa? wihtekatʉ.** The child is peeping out. *See* **tasʉkʉpunitʉ.**

wihto?aitʉ (v, adj) disintegrate, disintegrated, worn out (wear out of own accord).

wihto?arʉ (v) wear something out. **wʉkwi?aitʉ** wear out clothes; **takwiarʉ** wear out shoes;

tsokwiarʉ wear out hat. *See* **wʉkwi?arʉ.**

wihtua? (n), *acc* **wihtuai** bucket, container. **Wihtuai u? wʉhtʉkwai.** He hit the bucket.

wihtʉ?eka? (n) cream, grease.

wiiyʉ (n) awl, ice pick, any sharp-pointed implement for punching holes through which sinews pass (as in making moccasins).

Witawoo?ooki (name) Barking-buttocks (person).

Witsapaai? (n), *pl* **Witsapaainʉʉ** Pawnee (ref. to tuft of hair on head or to witchcraft they practiced).

wiyaa? (n), *acc* **wiya?a** rope.

wi?hikoyo?itʉ (v) skip.

wi?nʉʉpi (n) plum bush (not the fruit). **Okʉ tsa? wi?nʉataitu ukika sʉ?kʉia humakwa̱.** There are a lot of plum trees over there; go and get some plums.

wobi (n) ref. to wood.

wobi aawo̱ (n) trunk (container), box, chest (for personal belongings), barrel [**wobi** wood + **aawo̱** container].

wobi ka̱hni, wobi kʉ̱ni (n) frame house [**wobi** wood + **kahni** house].

wobi muwo?ne? K (n) termite(s). *See* **muwo?ne?.**

wobi nakarʉ? (n) wooden bench, wooden chair. *See* **nakarʉ?.**

wobi narʉmʉ? (n) lumberyard (*lit* lumber store).

wobi pihnaa ʉnʉʉ? (n) honeybee. *Apis mellifera.*

wobi pi̱hnaa? (n) K honey; W honeycomb [**wobi** wood + **pihnaa** sugar].

wobi puuku̱ (n) buggy, hack (*lit* wood horse). *See* **natsaʔani.**

wobi tohtaraki̱ K (n) woodpecker.

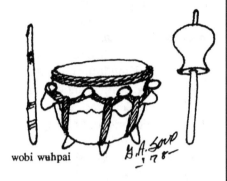

wobi wu̱hpai

wobi wu̱hpai K, **wobi wihtua** W (n) wooden drum (container), bucket.

wohho (n) ref. to enmity.

wohho namakaʔmukiʔaru̱ (v) warpath (prepare for war).

wohho napu̱saru̱ (v) apply war paint.

wohho suaru̱ (v) deride, oppose.

wohho tu̱ikwu̱pitu̱ K (n) war songs, songs of victory.

wohhohpu̱ʔ (n), *pl* **wohhonu̱u̱** enemy, rival provoking jealousy. **Nu̱ wohhonu̱u̱ tsaʔ kimaru̱.** My enemies are coming. *See* **tawohho.**

wohiʔhuu, wohihu̱ (n) mesquite. *See* **natsohkweʔ.**

wohkaʔniʔ (n) young unmarried man, bachelor.

wohtsawu̱kitu̱ (v) shake, bounce. **wohtsawiki miʔaru̱** go bouncing along.

wohtsaʔwu̱tu̱ (adj) rough terrain, uneven land.

wohya (n) row (series of items lined up). **Nu̱ paapasi tsaʔ wohyaku̱ naru̱hnikatu̱.** My potatoes are planted in a row.

woinu (n) bugle, any wind instrument. *See* **aamuyakeʔ.**

woko, wokóobi (n) pine. **wokóobi huupi̱** pine tree.

wokoohwi (n) tree squirrel (*lit* turns fast).

woko̱ huutsu̱ (n) parrot, parakeet (*lit* pine tree bird; parakeets used to be common in the wild in the U.S.).

woku̱ huupi̱ (n) thorn tree, honey locust. *Gleditschia triacanthos* (?) (thorns used as needles by early Comanches).

wokweebi̱

wokwe, wokweebi̱ (n) peyote plant or button, thorn, thistle. *Lophophora* Williamsii Lem. Coulter (peyote used strictly in religious ritual in curing or in conjunction with spirit power).

wokwe kahni (n) peyote teepee (used for peyote religious service).

wokwéesi (n) barrel cactus (commonly called *big-leaf cactus*; edible red berries). *Echinocereus Baileyi.*

wokwéesi (n) prickly pear cactus. *Opuntia* sp. (fruits eaten: burn off thorns, then eat to stop diarrhea [C & J]).

wokwekatʉ amakwooʔ (n) pineapple (*lit* thorny apple).

wokwekatʉ huupi (n) thorn apple, black haw (local term). *Crateagus* sp. (sweet fruits eaten; inner bark chewed as gum).

wokwesonipʉ (n) thorny weed (general term), sunburst (a specific thorny plant).

wokwetʉhkarʉ (v) eat peyote, conduct a peyote meeting.

woobi (n) board, wood, lumber.

woohpʉnitʉ (v) howl, moan.

woorʉ (v) howl, moan. **U woona nʉʔ nakai.** I heard it howling.

wooʔetʉ (n) a howl.

worʉrokʉ (n) esophagus, windpipe.

wosa aʔraʔ (n) grasshopper (large species) [**wosa** bag + **aaʔraʔ** uncle].

wosa (n), *acc* **wose** box, suitcase, bag. *See* **tʉboopʉ wosa.**

woʔa-, woʔarʉ (pfx) wormy.

woʔaabi (n), *acc* **woʔabita** maggot, worm.

woʔanatsuʔ (n) western ragweed (*lit* dried worms). **Ambrosia psilostachya** D.C. (used to kill screw worms and to cure influenza or bad cold [C & J]).

woʔarʉhkapʉ (n) rice (*lit* worm food, because of resemblance to larvae).

woʔataama (n), *acc* **woʔarami** decayed tooth (*lit* wormy tooth). **woʔaramakatʉ** have a decayed tooth.

woʔnerʉ (v) perforate (make holes).

woʔnokatʉ (n) ditch. **Urʉ tsaʔ tamumunakʉ woʔnokatʉ.** There is a ditch in front of us.

woʔrohtsarʉ (adj) have a stiff neck.

woʔrooookiʔ W, woʔrorai K (n) windpipe.

woʔwoʔkitʉ (v) bark (as an animal barks; *lit* say **woʔwo**).

wʉ- (pfx) flitter (nonhuman), force (human).

wʉanuraitʉ K (v) run away from something.

wʉapaʔarʉ (v) beat up.

wʉhabitʉ K, wʉkwaitʉʉ W (v) parade. **Nʉmʉnʉʉ tsaʔ wʉhabitʉ.** The Comanches are in parade. *See* **namanahkeetʉ.**

wʉhbuikatʉ W, wʉhhwikatʉ K (v) turn, turn away from. **Tʉhʉya tsaʔ muhyupetu wʉhwikatʉ.** The horse is turning around. **Kahnikʉ nʉʔ pitsʉ wʉhhwi.** I turned back home.

wʉhhabiʔarʉ (v) defeat, force to lie down wielding a weapon.

wʉhhanirʉ (v) cultivate, chop up (with instrument).

wʉhhaʔwokarʉ (v) make hollow (with instrument).

wʉhhomonutsaʔarʉ (v) crumble, break into small pieces (with instrument).

wʉhhorarʉ (v) dig (with hoe or pick). *See* **tʉhorarʉ.**

wʉhhubinitʉ (v) hurt (cause to groan or cry as by hitting).

wʉhibiʔ (n) cup, drinking glass, spoon.

wʉhkarʉ (v), *pl* **wʉhpomiʔitʉ** chop down, cut down.

wʉhkikatʉ (v) shoot a gun, let an arrow fly. *See* **tsatʉkarʉ.**

wʉhkitsuʔtsukitʉ (v) rattle (make rattling noise).

wʉhkitsuʔtsukiʔ (n) rattle (sound-producing organ on rattlesnake).

wᵾhki?arᵾ (v) cut (as with a knife).

wᵾhkobarᵾ (v), *pl* **wᵾhkobi?itᵾ** break up (with instrument). **Huupita nᵾ? wᵾhkobi?itᵾ.** I am breaking up the wood.

wᵾhkonarᵾ (v) chop a hole. **Huupita wᵾhkonai.** He chopped a hole in the tree [**wᵾh-** (instr) + **ko-** chop + **na-** do].

wᵾhkuparᵾ, wᵾkuparᵾ (v), *pl* **wᵾhtokwetᵾ** kill with a weapon. **Sariia wᵾhkupa.** Kill that dog.

wᵾhkurᵾ (v) sight to shoot, aim a gun. **Ta?wo?i wᵾhkurᵾ urᵾᵾ.** They are shooting with a gun.

wᵾhkuya?arᵾ (v) frighten, scare. *See* **wᵾ?yᵾrᵾhkikatᵾ, wᵾᵾyoritᵾ.**

wᵾhkᵾnai, wᵾhkᵾnᵾkatᵾ (adj) covered (any object).

wᵾhkᵾnarᵾ (v) cover something (put its cover on a dish or other container). **Tᵾhkapa nᵾ? wᵾhkᵾnaru?i.** I will cover the food. **Aawe nᵾ wᵾhkᵾnarᵾ nᵾ.** I am covering the dish. *See* **hᵾhkᵾnarᵾ.**

wᵾhkwabikᵾrᵾ (v) knock down (with instrument). **Huuma u wᵾhkwikᵾi.** He knocked them down with a stick.

wᵾhkwarᵾ?rᵾkitᵾ K (v) gargle. *See* **pakwarᵾhtᵾkitᵾ.**

wᵾhkwatubi (v) wind, wrap, or coil (something).

wᵾhkwe?yarᵾ (v) unscrew, unbolt.

wᵾhkwinarᵾ (v) swab out, clean the inner part.

wᵾhkwitso?arᵾ (v) rescue (save by using an instrument). *See* **kwitso?arᵾ.**

wᵾhkwitsunarᵾ (v) wag (as to wag tail).

wᵾhkwitubikatᵾ (v) roll up to itself.

wᵾhkwitunarᵾ (v) wrap up, wrap around.

wᵾhkwᵾmarᵾ (v) explode, open (come apart by force).

wᵾhkwᵾnetᵾ (v) scrape outer side, dehair a hide, cut fat off surface. **Kaku tsa? wᵾhkwᵾneyᵾ.** Grandma is dehairing it (the hide).

wᵾhminanᵾᵾmᵾ (n), *pl* **wᵾ?mina?nᵾᵾmᵾ** invalid. *See* **tᵾ?oipᵾ.**

wᵾhpaaku?nerᵾ (v) hit and push under water [**wᵾh** (instr) + **paa** water **-ku** in + **ne-** push].

wᵾhpararᵾ (v) stretch out something, spread out something. **Wanapᵾha u wᵾhparai.** She spread out the cloth.

wᵾhpa?itᵾ (v, pl), *sg* **wᵾhtᵾkwarᵾ** beat, hit repeatedly (with instrument). **Nᵾᵾpa?ima u wᵾhpa?itᵾ.** I am whipping with a whip.

wᵾhpekwitᵾ (v) bruise (raise a bump, cause to swell using an instrument).

wᵾhpetsᵾrᵾ (v) wave (wave down; wave hand). **Pᵾ haitsa u wᵾhpetsᵾrᵾ.** He is waving to his friend.

wᵾhpitᵾ (v) overtake, catch up with, approach (reach a destination). **Na?ᵾ nᵾ ma wᵾhpi- tᵾ?i.** You will catch up some day (elder says to younger person). **ᵾ wᵾhpitᵾi nᵾ?.** I caught up with you.

wᵾhpiwokarᵾ (v) drag by force. *See* **piwokarᵾ.**

wᵾhpohto?itᵾ (v) strike out, pop (as crack a whip).

wᵾhpomarᵾ (v) cut down, mow. **Puhhipa nᵾ? wᵾhpomarᵾ.** I am weeding the garden.

wɯhpomiʔitɯ (v, pl), *sg* **wɯhkarɯ**
chop down, cut down.

wɯhpoʔtserɯ K, **kwɯhpoʔtserɯ** W
(v) knock something, jerk something (with an instrument). **Huma
nɯʔ u wɯhpoʔtse.** I knocked it
with a stick.

wɯhpɯkɯsuarɯ (v) unwind, uncoil
something. *See* **pɯrɯsuʔarɯ.**

wɯhsibetɯ (v) shave (as shave
face). *See* **siibetɯ, wɯsiberɯ.**

wɯhtabarɯ (v) smash (break to
pieces with an instrument).

wɯhtakɯmiitɯ (v) partially
sun-dry. **Tɯhkapa inapɯ urɯ
wɯhtakɯmituʔi.** The jerked meat
will be dried in the sun.

wɯhtamarɯ (v) bundle together,
tie something, bale something.
Wanapɯ wɯhtamarɯ. The cotton
is baled.

wɯhtamaʔ (n) string (any item with
which to tie). *See* **tɯɯhtamaʔ.**

wɯhtarakiitɯ (v) pound something,
tap on something. **Pɯ inapa wɯhtarakiitɯ.** He is pounding his
meat (to keep it from spoiling).

wɯhtaráaʔ (n) camp bed
(framework of sticks covered
by dry grass; nine forked sticks
are pounded into ground, long
crosspoles are placed through
forks, and branches or grass are
placed on frame).

wɯhtiarɯ (v), *pl* **toʔwɯʔwenitɯ**
pour out, spill, dump into, empty
into (pour into different containers). **Pai u wɯhtiaai.** He poured
out the water. **Sitɯkwɯ kɯseʔ
pɯhɯ pomapɯha toʔwɯʔwenimi-
miʔa̱.** These two kept dumping
their pickings (115:7).

wɯhtikɯrɯ, kwɯtikɯrɯ (v) shoot,
fire on (fire a weapon, shoot at
someone or something). **Arɯkaʔa
kwɯhtikɯ urɯ.** He is over there
shooting a deer. **Tenahpɯʔa u
kwɯhtii.** He shot at the man.

wɯhtokarɯ (v) knock off something
hanging (with instrument).

wɯhtokweetɯ (v) kill with a
weapon.

wɯhtokweʔ (n, pl) clubbed ones
(those that are clubbed to death).

wɯhtokwɯrɯ, wɯhtóorɯ (v) club
someone or something. **Surɯ
kɯseʔ urii wɯhtokwɯkina̱.** That
one came clubbing them. *See*
wahtóorɯ.

wɯhtokwɯtɯ (v) club something.

wɯhtopoʔnitɯ (v) wind into a ball.

wɯhtopɯʔnoorɯ (v) tie in round
bundle or round knot.

wɯhtoʔyarɯ (v) turn loose, untie.
Ohka tɯhɯyɯ wɯhtoʔyai. She
untied the horse.

wɯhtsabeyaaʔ (n) gourd rattle
(used in peyote ceremony).

wɯhtsabeyakatɯ W, **wɯhtsaya
kwasinabooʔ** K (n) rattlesnake.
See **kwasinaboo wɯhkitsuʔ-
tsuʔikatu.**

wɯhtsamɯhkitɯ (v) becalm (stop
blowing). **Nɯetɯ tsaʔ wɯhtsamɯhkitɯ.** The wind has stopped
blowing.

wɯhtsamɯɯhkikatɯ (adj) calm
(wind or weather).

wɯhtsanitɯ (v) hang up carelessly
(throw over a line or pole).

wɯhtsiboʔarɯ (v) peel off (using
an instrument). **Huupita u
wɯhtsiboʔarɯ.** He is peeling bark
off the tree.

wᵾhtsinetᵾ (v) scrape (as in curing a hide; scrape inner side of flat object with instrument). **Pimoro?a pᵾhi u wᵾhtsinetᵾ.** He is scraping the hide.

wᵾhtsito?arᵾ (v) pare, peel. **Nahuma paapasi wᵾhtsito?arᵾ.** She is peeling the potato with a knife.

wᵾhtsi?arᵾ (v) shave off, cut off pieces (with instrument). **Huupita u wᵾhtsi?aru?i.** He will cut off wood shavings.

wᵾhtsobokitᵾ (v) blink, wink [wᵾh- eye + tsoboki- roll].

wᵾhtsohkᵾna? (n) bandana, scarf. *See* **tsokwᵾkᵾᵾna?, yu?a korohkọ.**

wᵾhtsu?marᵾ (v) scrape until clean, wipe off completely. **Nahuma nᵾ? ma wᵾhtsumarᵾ.** I am scraping it with a knife.

wᵾhtsᵾkᵾnarᵾ (v) tie. **Wiya?a u wᵾhtsᵾkᵾnai.** He tied the rope.

wᵾhtuitᵾ (v) wait (for someone or something to catch up from behind). **Si?ana pu?ekᵾ ma pia? ma wᵾhtúuihkatᵾ.** Here somewhere in the trail his mother is waiting for him (83:31).

wᵾhtukarᵾ K, kwᵾhtukatᵾ W (v) extinguish a fire (put out a fire or flame). **Wehari nᵾ? wᵾhtu- karᵾ.** I am putting out a fire. *See* **tukarᵾ.**

wᵾhturu?aipᵾ (n) windbreak (constructed outside teepees, of braided cane to protect from cold wind).

wᵾhturu?arᵾ (v) make a windbreak.

wᵾhtᵾbunitᵾ (v) wake someone by pounding.

wᵾhtᵾkwaitᵾ (v) fall down.

wᵾhtᵾkwarᵾ (v), *pl* **wᵾhpa?itᵾ** hit something, beat on someone. Surᵾ kᵾse? wihnu okᵾhu paa- kᵾhu wᵾhtᵾi kwanᵾ. Then that one hit there in the water (5–6:12). **Wᵾhtᵾkwaru?i nᵾ?.** I am going to hit (beat) you.

wᵾhtᵾmarᵾ (v) fence up, bank up, clog up. *See* **tᵾᵾhtᵾmarᵾ.**

wᵾhtᵾpᵾkarᵾ (v) button up, fasten, pin together.

wᵾhtᵾpᵾka? (n) buckle, button.

wᵾhtᵾroonitᵾ (v) brace with some- thing. **Huuma ma wᵾhtᵾrooni.** He braced it with a pole.

wᵾhtᵾru?arᵾ K (v) rip something. **Wanapa ukʔ wᵾhtᵾru?ai.** She ripped the cloth. *See* **tohtᵾru?arᵾ.**

wᵾhu?nerᵾ (v) creep, scoot, crawl (stretched out on the stomach). *See* **mahu?netᵾ, tahu?nerᵾ.**

wᵾhᵾwᵾ?niitᵾ (v) trim (to shape a tree), prune (to shape a tree). **Huupita u wᵾhᵾwᵾ?niitᵾ.** He is trimming (pruning) the tree. *See* **wᵾ?yᵾkwitᵾ, kᵾhpomarᵾ.**

wᵾkᵾtsarᵾ (v) switch (as a tail).

wᵾkᵾtserᵾ (v) crush, mash (with an instrument). **Paapasi nᵾ? wᵾkᵾtse.** I mashed my potatoes.

wᵾkweniitᵾ K, kwᵾkwenitᵾ W (v) hang up. **Pia kwᵾsu?e wᵾkweni.** Hang up your coat.

Wᵾkwiya, Wekwaa?a (name) Jesus-man (Comanche born around 1861).

wᵾkwi?arᵾ (v) wear out clothes. **Nᵾ kwasui wᵾkwiai.** I am wearing out my dress. *See* **wihto?arᵾ.**

wᵾkwᵾbihkurᵾ (v) beat on, rattle. **Huuma nᵾ? wᵾkwᵾbihki.** I made noise with a stick.

wʉkwʉsarʉ (v) sprain a joint of the body. **Pʉ napi u wʉkwʉsai.** He sprained his ankle.

wʉmetʉ (v) overcome pain, bear pain. **Mohatsi̱ nʉʉtsikwari u wʉme.** He overcame severe pain.

wʉminahkatʉ (adj) ill for a long time, invalid. **Monʉʔohni uʔ wʉmi̱nahkatʉ.** He was ill with tuberculosis for a long time.

wʉminarʉ (v) break or reach something (with instrument). *See* **maʔwʉminarʉ.**

wʉmiʔakʉrʉ K (v) force to go. **Nʉ wʉmiʔakʉi uʔ.** He made me leave (says woman because husband beat her). **Ma wʉmiʔakʉi nʉʔ.** I made it go (as by winding a clock).

wʉmiʔarʉ W (v, inan obj) cause to run, move, go. **U wʉmiʔarʉ uʔ.** He is winding it.

wʉmi̱naaʔ (n) illness.

wʉmi̱natʉ (num) nine.

wʉmupʉsitʉ (v) cause to blow nose (by force, as by hitting) [wʉ force + mupʉsi- blow nose].

wʉmutsiakatuʔi (adj) keep sharpened.

wʉmutsiarʉ K (v) sharpen to a point (with instrument). **Pʉ wiiyʉ wʉmutsiai.** He is sharpening his pick.

wʉmʉʉrihkatʉ (adj) turned over, shaped.

wʉmʉʉrʉ (v) turn something over, shape or change something (with instrument). **Nʉ tasoni wʉmʉʉri.** I turned over my rug.

wʉnekʉrʉ (v) fan (as to fan the fire). **Ohka uʔ wehari wʉnekʉtʉ.** He is fanning the fire.

wʉnekʉtʉʔ K (n) fan for fire. *See* **wʉʔʉnenihkuʔ.**

wʉnikarʉ (v) insert into something.

wʉnoʔitʉ (v) chop down, cut. **Soonipa nʉʔ wʉnoʔitʉ̱.** I am cutting the grass (roots and all).

wʉnoʔkarʉrʉ (v) hill up (as soil). *See* **maʔohtaʔaitʉ.**

wʉnoʔyaitʉ (adj) stirred. **Pʉ kooʔ tsaʔ wʉnoʔyaitʉ.** Her mush is stirred.

wʉnoʔyarʉ (v) stir. **U wʉnoʔyaai uʔ.** She stirred it.

wʉnuarʉ (v) sweep. **Pʉ tasooni wʉnuarʉ.** She is sweeping the floor.

wʉnutsarʉ (v) shatter, break into pieces (with instrument).

wʉnʉhkarʉrʉ W (v) squat. *See* **kwanuʔitʉ, wʉtahkarʉrʉ.**

wʉnʉkʉtʉ (v) transplant (set out a plant). *See* **tsihtaboʔikʉtʉ.**

wʉnʉrʉ (adj) standing. **Inakwʉ tsaʔ sohobokooʔ wʉnʉrʉ.** In this direction a mulberry tree is standing.

wʉnʉʉhkuparʉ (adj) knocked down.

wʉnʉʉkuparʉ (v) knock down by force.

wʉnʉʔyʉʔitʉ, wʉnʉʔyʉruʔitʉ (v) hit by surprise (causing a thud). **Orʉ ohko wʉnʉʔyʉʔtuʔi.** He is going to hit him by surprise (causing a thud).

wʉnʉ hupiitʉ (v), *pl* tobooi hupiitʉ stop movement toward something. **Hunakʉ wʉnʉhupiitʉ uʔ.** He stopped in front. *See* **toboʔi hupiitʉ.**

wʉnʉkʉtʉ (v) tighten, turn, wind.

wʉpitapuʔni (n) war club, battle axe with flintstone handle.

wupitooru (v) tie a child to back.

wupiyaru (v) core something, remove item by item. **Amawoo?a wupiye u?.** He cored the apple.

wupunukeru (v) scrape (make smooth as to scrape a road).

wupuheru W, wupheru K (v), *pl* **wuyumi?itu** flail, knock off with an instrument, be thrown forcibly from a horse.

wupuhoikutu (v) prosper.

wupukaru (v) cut open.

wupukoi? (n) woodpecker (large species no longer native to Oklahoma). *Picidae.*

wuputsaru (v) cut open, perform surgery.

wura? (n) panther, mountain lion.

wusa?maru W, wuhtsa?nakuru K (v) protrude (stick out). **Huupi wusa?maaru.** The tree is sticking out (as when stripped of leaves). **Ma paapi wuhtsa?naku.** His hair is sticking out (every direction).

wusibepu (n) wood shaving.

wusiberu K (v) shave off, brush off. *See* **wuhsibetu, kwusiberu.**

wusibo?aru (v) skin an animal (take off hide when butchering). *See* **tsahkwuru?aru.**

wusi?kwaru (v) cut a strip.

wusóoru (v) hang a long object on a line.

wusuabetaitu (v) restore circulation (get feeling back after being numb).

wusukatu (v) experience something (feel in body or soul).

wusukwaru W, wusu?waru K (v) attempt to hit with a weapon.

wusuwarukiitu (v) give up waiting for someone.

wusu?naru (v) scrape (with instrument, as a hide with a knife).

wutahkaruru K (v) squat (sit on heels). *See* **wunuhkaruru.**

wutsupai (adj) witchy.

wutsu?mi (adj) full stomach (as a result of gluttony).

wutsu?mitu (adj) satisfied with sufficient food, filled up. *See* **pakwu?sumitu.**

wutsukaru (v) cut, shear, mow.

wutsukitu (v) crowd, shove. **U wutsuki u?.** He crowded him. adj tight, ill-fitting. **Pu nape wutsukitu.** His shoes are tight. *See* **ma?wikaru.**

wutsukunaru (v) tie a knot. **Nu napuna nu? wutsukunaru.** I am tying my shoes. **Situkwu kuse? ma napema ma wutsukuì nanu.** These two tied it on his leg (9:12).

wutukwaru (v), *pl* **wuhpa?itu** beat.

wutubaru (v) crack something, break by dropping. **Kupita?a ma? wutubai.** He broke that lamp. *See* **tahparu.**

wutuki?netu (v) pound flat, smooth down (cause to be smooth). **Hanibitu wutuki?netu.** He is pounding the corn.

wuuyoritu, wuyoritu (v) disturb, startle, scare (causing to fly or jump up). **Huutsuni ma wiyori.** He scared up the birds (into flight). *See* **wuhkuya?aru.**

wuyakeetu W, wuyakitu K (n) songs of youth (special type sung at night by young Comanches going from camp to camp).

wuyaketu (v) cause to cry (by whipping, threatening, rattling something). **Wutsabiya? wuyakeyu.** He is rattling the gourd.

wuyaru (v) lift (with instrument, as a pole).

wuyumi?ipu (n) flailed material (as fruit or nuts knocked from tree).

wuyumi?itu (v, pl), *sg* **wupuheru** flail, knock off.

wuyupa?nitu (v) quiet down, calm down.

wu?aikuru (v) crank, row (with oars). *See* **ma?aikuru.**

wu?aniru (v) chop down, swat down. **Huupita u wu?ani.** He chopped down the tree.

wu?kuru (n) archery game (first man shoots arrow to place mark; each man shoots four arrows; closest to mark wins).

wu?ku?buu? (n) hummingbird [**wu-** flitter + **ku?buu?** say boo]. *Trochilidae.*

wu?kwuriaru (v) throw out of something.

wu?mina?nuumu (n, hum pl), *sg* **wuhminanuumu** invalids, handicapped persons.

wu?nikaru (v), *pl obj* W **wuwe-kwuru,** K **wukwekwuru** bolt down, screw in. **Meeku ma wu?niku.** Now bolt it together. **Pu nabukuwa?a ma? natsawe wukweku.** The doors are screwed on his car.

Wu?rabiahpu (name) Swift-moving (person).

wu?rabiaru (v) move quickly, act speedily.

wu?tsikwaru (adj) weary, tired of something. *See* **manuu?mai.**

wu?uraru (v) find something (with instrument). **Pu pokweti u wu?u-rai.** They found their canoe (with stick, poking in water).

wu?utsitu (v) pile up (cause to be lined up). **Huupita u wu?utsitu.** He is stacking his wood.

wu?uaru?aru (v) crack something (with an instrument). **Aawo huupima wu?uaruakatu.** He is cracking the cup with a stick.

wu?unenihku? W (n) fan for fire. *See* **wunekutu?.**

wu?wenitu K, **kwu?kwenitu** W (v) empty out, pour out. **U kwu?-kweni u.** He emptied it.

wu?yukwitu K, **kwu?yukwitu** W (v) trim, prune (as to shape a tree). **Tsaa u wu?yukwitu.** He is trimming it well. *See* **kuhpomaru, wuhuwu?niitu.**

wu?yuruhkikatu (adj) scared, afraid. *See* **makuya?aitu, kuya?akatu.**

wu?yuruhkitu (v) frighten someone with something, scare.

wuminaa kahni (n) hospital [**wuminaa** illness + **kahni** house]. *See* **natusu?u kahni.**

Y

yaa (interj) Oh! (used by women only). *See* **ha?ii, ubia.**

yaahuyaru (v), *pl* **yaahunitu** fetch, scrounge for.

yaakuru (v, sg obj), *pl obj* **himaki- tu** return an item, bring something back to someone.

yaapu (n) object or item taken.

yaaru (v, sg obj), *pl obj* **hima?aru** take one or several things. **Ihka yaa.** Take this.

yahihpu? (n) parent-in-law (of woman).

yahkatʉ (v) hold, have something in hand.

yahneetʉ (v), *pl* **naʔyʉnetʉ** laugh.

yahnena (n) laughter.

yaketʉ (v), *pl* **nawooʔi, nahwooitʉ** cry (make noise). *See* **muuyaketʉ, muyakeʔ.**

yakeyʉkarʉ (v) crying walking around (as mooing, bleating, etc.)

yanawoʔiʔ (n) cannon.

Yapai tʉhka (n), *pl* **Yapai nʉaʉ** Yap-eaters. (Shoshones name for Comanches—probably the last band to leave Shoshonean traditions; northernmost band located in Medicine Park, Meers, Elgin, Fletcher, Cyril, Apache, Boone counties of Oklahoma).

yee (interj) Oh, no! (used by men only, with appropriate negative intonation). Oh, good! (used by men only, with appropriate positive intonation).

yohyakatʉ K (v) hurry.

yohyaku (adv man) hastily, hurriedly (in a hurry).

yoka, yokapʉ (n) phlegm, juice (heavy liquid).

yokabahmʉ (n) chewing tobacco, snuff, tobacco [**yoka-** phlegm + **pahmʉ** smoke].

yokake, yokaketʉ (adj) spongy, soggy, soft.

yokanatsuʔu K (n) red false mallow (taboo term used only by medicine men). *See* **puhanatsu.**

yorimiʔarʉ (v, pl), *sg* **yʉtsʉrʉ** fly up, rise up.

yoʔmitsaitʉ (v) stir around, move around. **Ʉ ʉnʉbihnaa yoʔmitsai-tʉ.** The honey bees are stirring around.

yubutsʉhkatʉ (v) stuck in the mud, bogged down. *See* **sekwi sʉhkai.**

yuhhu K (n) lard, grease, fat. **Sʉsʉmʉʔ kʉseʔ pʉmʉ u yuhukʉ u kwasʉi kʉnʉ.** Some (themselves) fried it in that fat (127:12). *See* **yuhukarʉka.**

yuhibitsipʉ K (n) buttermilk.

yuhnukarʉ (v) hold something (in a container).

yuhnunimiʔarʉ (v) carry something (in a container).

yuhu (n) ref to fat.

yuhu bitsipʉ (n) butter [**yuhu** lard + **pitsipʉ** milk].

yuhu bʉhkaitʉ (v) gain weight, fatten.

yuhu nohkopʉ (n) fried bread, frybread.

yuhu nohkorʉ (v) make frybread.

yuhu rʉkʉhmanipʉ (n) fried meat, meat.

yuhu wehkipʉ (n) fattest one. **Urʉʉkʉhʉ u yuhu wehkipʉ wihnu surʉ pisikwanúuʔinʉ.** Then that one, the fattest to be found of them, slid down (5:11).

yuhukarʉ (v) render lard. *See* **ku- ʔokwerʉ, kuhpitsʉniʔarʉ, kuhpawikʉʔitʉ.**

yuhukarʉka W (n) lard. *See* **yuhhu.**

yuhukarʉkarʉ (adj) rendered (as lard).

yukahnibarʉ (v) live unconcerned.

yukarʉrʉ (v), *pl* **yuuyʉkwitʉ** sit still.

yumarʉ (v, pl), *sg* **pahitʉ** fall, be born, drop off.

yunaharʉ (v) calm (continue having calm breeze or wind).

yunahkatʉ (adj) quiet, still (without movement). **Yunaahkạ!** Be still!

yunar (v) separate milk from cream, skim from the surface. **Pitsiuyuhina atahpu u yuna.** Skim the cream off.

yunir, yuniit (v) give something (in a container). **Aawokunu u yuni nu?.** I gave it to her in a cup.

yunumit (v), *pl* **yuyukar** live well, be well behaved (be good).

yupusia, yuposia (n) head louse. *See* **pusi?a.**

yupu (n) fat person.

yurahpet (v) shrink, heal (stop swelling).

yusuat, yuusua (adj) right (proper), normal (thinking good thoughts, *lit* fat-thinker). **Hakaniyuta unu ke yuusua?** Why don't you think right?

yusuhubi (n) weeping willow. *Salix* sp.

yusuku, yuu sukui (n) early plum (*lit* fat plum; fresh fruit eaten, dried fruit stored for use later). *Prunus* sp. *See* **parua sukui?, kusisukui.**

yuu sonipu (n) prairie clover, common grass. *Leguminosae.*

yuu habíitu (v), *pl* **yuu kwabitu** lie still.

yuu taibo? (n), *pl* **yuu taibonu** Mexican (*lit* fat white man).

yuu wunuru, yuu kwunuru (v), *pl* **yuutoboru** stand still (be unconcerned).

yuu uhpuitu (v) sleep unconcerned. **Ituu yu uhkoiku.** They slept on (in spite of noise). *See* **uhpuitu.**

yu?a, yu?atu (adj) warm.

yu?a korohko (n) scarf (*lit* warm necktie). *See* **tsokwukuuna?, korohko.**

yu?a kwusu?u (n) sweater (*lit* warm blouse, shirt).

yu?a nakohtoo? (n) heater (*lit* warming stove).

yu?a namusooru (v) wear warm clothing.

yu?a nue kahpi?nakwu (n) southwest.

yu?a umakuni (n) rain shelter for winter (a teepee lining made of buckskin or rawhide used to keep out cold and rain). *See* **uma kahni.**

yu?anee (n) south wind, summer wind.

yu?anube nakwubu (n) south (*lit* warm-wind direction).

yu?anue muhyunakwubu (n) southeast.

yu?a?itu (v) warm up.

yu?naitsi K, **yu?nai tuhtsi** W (adv man) easy, easily. **Yu?naitsi ma nahaniitu.** It is easily made.

yuba (n) fall season.

Yuba mua (n) October (*lit* fall month).

yubaru (v) past the peak (movement in time).

Yuba uhi mua (n) November (*lit* levelling-toward-winter month).

yuhnu (n) porcupine. *See* **huunu?.**

yuhnu wokweebi? (n) porcupine quill (*lit* porcupine thorn).

yuihka (adv) this evening.

yuihtuhkatu (v) eat supper.

yuihtuhka? (n) supper (evening meal).

yuitu (adj) evening.

yukaru (v, pl), *sg* **numi** walk, move about.

yukwi kahni K (n) parlor (*lit* sitting room). *See* **pukura yukwi?ena.**

yukwiku (v, pl), *sg* **karukuru** set up teepees.

yukwimi?aru (v, pl), *sg* **karuru** sit down, stay. *See* **karukatu**.

yukwitu (v), *pl* **niwunuru** say. **Sume mayukwiitu.** He said it. *See* **tekwaru**.

yumuhkitu (v) move, change position.

yuruhkitu (v) startle, frighten. **Aawo pahitsi nu mayuruhkinu.** The cup falling frightened me.

yutsuru (v), *pl* **yorimi?aru** rise up, go up, fly up.

yutsu? (n) airplane.

yuwimi?aru (v) descend, go down (go out of sight). **Tu?rikuu tsa? pu kahni taikuku yuwimi?ai.** The prairie dog went down into his hole.

yuwitu W (v) swallow something.

yuyukaru (v, pl), *sg* **yunumitu** live well, be good, well behaved.

yu?bana?itu (v) sway, rocking way of walking (keep in time with music by body movement; chiefly said of women).

yu?yukaru (adj) be soft, softened. *See* **payu?yukatu**.

yu?yukaru (v) soften.

yu?yumuhkumi?aru W (v) live, move around (keep moving). **Tsaaku mahpuutu yu?yumuh-kumi?a.** He is living this good life.

yu?yumuhkuna (n) life.

yu?yumuhku? W (n) movies, moving pictures.

yu?yuturu (v) twitch, bodily jerk (with obligatory prefix indicating area of body jerking). **mayu?yu-tu jerking hand.**

Appendix A: Fauna

Animals

arʉkaʔ deer
awonoʔoʔ armadillo
ebimuura yaʔkeʔ bullfrog
ekaeʔree (W) swamp rabbit
ekakúuraʔ buffalo calf
ekakʉmaʔ reddish brown horse, bay
ekapiaʔ sorrel mare
ekatseenaʔ red fox
ekaʉnʉʉʔa tʉhkaʔeetʉ anteater
esikʉhmaʔ gray male horse
esimuuraʔ gray mule
esipiaʔ slate gray mare
esiʉnʉʉʔ elephant
ewa kʉʉpiʔ ground squirrel
haʔnii beaver
hookị hog
huunaʔ groundhog, woodchuck
hʉnʉbi pokaaʔ bat
hʉʉnʉʔ porcupine
kaawosạ fox, jackal
kabʉrʉʉʔ sheep
kabʉrʉʉʔa tua lamb
kahuúʔ mouse
kuhtsu tʉbiniʔ toad, horned toad
kuhtsuʔ cow, cattle

kusimuura donkey
kutsiʔwobiʔ donkey
kuura pack rat
kʉhtsayaʔyaʔkeʔ coyote
kʉʔkwʉriaʔ fox, coyote
kʉʔtseena fox, wolf, coyote
kwasi taibooʔ monkey
kwipʉsiapʉ palomino horse
matʉsohpeʔ wildcat
maʔnʉ sariiʔ dachshund
motso sariiʔ poodle
mubị sariiʔ greyhound
munuaʔ hog, pig
mupitsʉha tʉnowapị camel
muuraʔ mule
muʔkwipunaʔ elephant
naboohmatʉsohpeʔ (W) leopard
naboohmuraʔ zebra
naboohroya ruhkuʔ leopard
nakị sariiʔ hound dog
narʉnookatʉ ʉnʉʉ camel
naʔahnia (K), naʔahnịa (N)
   palomino, horse
naʔnia buckskin horse
noyotsoʔmẹ tabuʔ rabbit (Easter)
nʉmamoʔoʔ coon, raccoon
nʉmʉ kuhtsuʔ buffalo
ohaahnakatʉ (W) fox, coyote

155

ohaeka?, ohaekapitʉ light brown horse, bay horse
otʉ kʉma? (W) sorrel horse (male)
paa tsoko otter
pahtsi kabʉrʉʉ? slickhaired goat
pahtsi kwasi possum
papiwʉi htama? otter, mink
paraimo?o mole
paruuku?, pa?ruhku? coon, raccoon
parʉa kuhma bull elk
pasawí?oo? frog
pa?a ruyu?, pa?a to?yo? giraffe
pa?arai mo?o woodchuck
pa?sʉnó?a? kangaroo
pa?wʉhtakóo? tadpole
pa?wʉhtʉma? beaver
pia kahúa rat, field mouse
pia tseena? wolf
pimoroo?, pimoroo?a piabʉ cow
pimoroo?a kuhma bull
pimoroo?a tua? calf
pisuni?eeyʉ, pisuníi? skunk
pitsa naboo? (K) calico horse
pitsipʉ pimoróo? milk cow
pi?isʉtʉ pacer
pi?tohtsía? (W) white tailed deer
pohni?atsi skunk
pohpi kwáai? (W) frog
po?ro? pig, hog, swine
puku rúa? colt
pʉa watsi wild stallion
pʉhʉ kabʉrʉʉ? sheep
pʉhʉ ku?kwe?ya? lion
sanahtu?re? snail
sarii? dog
ta?si?woo? buffalo
ta?wokinae?ree eka swamp rabbit
tosa naboo? paint horse, calico horse
tosa? white horse
toya ruhku? leopard

tseena? gray fox, coyote
tuhtseena? wolf
tupisi kʉma? bay horse
tu?kina?, tabú?kina? rabbit
tʉe kahuu? mouse
tʉe tʉmakupa? bobcat
tʉhʉya horse (general)
tʉkwitsuna? elephant
tʉmahkupa? panther
tʉnookatʉ? (K) camel
tʉpʉsi kʉma? sorrel horse
tʉrayaa sarii bloodhound
tʉʉnoo ʉnʉʉ? (K) camel
tʉ?rʉkúu? prairie dog
waani (K), **waa?ne?** (W) fox
wasápe bear
wa?oo? cat
wokoohwi tree squirrel
wʉra? panther, mountain lion
yʉhnʉ, hʉʉnʉ? porcupine

Birds

ebihuutsuu? bluejay, bluebird
ebikuyuutsi? chaparral, roadrunner
ekabapi red headed buzzard
ekahuutsu? cardinal, redbird
hiitoo? (K, N) meadowlark
huhmara?, huumara? falcon
huutsúu bird (general)
kokáa? guinea fowl
kokorá?a chicken
kusikwa?aa? crane
kusikwi?ii? (W) type of bird
kusisai? small gray bird
kuyu?nii? turkey
kuyúutsi? quail
ku?e wóo? dove, pigeon
kʉkʉbʉraakwa?si? scissortail, fork tailed flycatcher
kwihnai eagle

nohabitʉ hen
nʉkʉta goose
ohanʉnapʉ (W) meadowlark, field lark
oʔooʔ horned owl
pakawkokoʔ, pakokokoʔ prairie chicken
pasahòo pigeon, dove, wren
paʔa toyokatʉ huutsuuʔ crane, stork
pekwi tʉhkaʔ kingfisher
pia huutsuuʔ eagle
pia kwihnai eagle
pitʉsʉ nuʔyeʔ (W) woodpecker
pohkóoʔ burrowing owl
puhitóoʔ turkey/turkey gobbler
pʉʉyʉ duck
soo yakeʔ mocking bird
sʉhʉ mupitsʉ screech owl
taibo huutsuuʔ pigeon
tosa kwiisuʔ black bird (white wings)
tosa nakaai hawk
turuawapͅi laying hen, leghorn
tuwikaaʔ raven, crow, blackbird
tʉe basuuʔ (W) quail
tʉe kuyúutsi (K) partridge, quail (small)
tʉnimanahke huutsuʔ (K) mockingbird
tʉrʉe basuu (K) quail
tʉrʉe kuʔyuutsi quail
tʉʔiiʔ sandpiper
wobi tohtarakͅi (K) woodpecker
wokͅo huutsʉ parrot, parakeet
wʉpʉkoiʔ woodpecker (large sp.)
wʉʔkʉʔbuuʔ hummingbird

Reptiles

ebimuutarooʔ mountain boomer
ebipabokoʔaiʔ (P) mountain boomer

kʉhtáa nuʔyaʔaʔ (W) racer snake
kwasi nʉrʉʉʔwʉʔ snapping turtle
kwasinaboo wʉhkitsuʔtsuʔikatʉ rattle snake
kwasinabooʔ snake (general)
nakͅi taiʔ, nakͅi tóone (N) long sp. lizard
nuhyaʔ snake, any species
nʉmʉ maʔtsaʔbahkiʔ clinging lizard
nʉnʉʔyʉwiʔ (W) alligator
pabokoʔai timber lizard
paʔboosiʔ water lizard, water dog
paʔkwakʉme snapping turtle
pitsohka kwaba (W) alligator, snapping turtle
tuhparokooʔ water moccasin
tʉpi pabokoʔai rock lizard
wakaréeʔ (K), **wakaʔréʔeeʔ** (W) turtle
wanatsihtaraaʔ (W) striped lizard
wʉhtsabeyakatʉ (W) rattlesnake

Fish

hʉato fish (unknown sp.)
kwasinaboo pekwi eel
pekwͅi fish
tahipʉ pekwi flounder
tuumeʔsͅo young catfish
tuumoʔtsoʔ full grown catfish
tuʔreʔ leech
waʔroo koyáaʔ crawfish, crayfish

Insects

ahtakii grasshopper (small sp.)
ahtamuu jumbo grasshopper
anͅikuuraʔ ant
anͅimuͅi housefly

ekapusi?a flea

ekaunuu red ant

kahni busi?a bedbug

ka?ra?áa? tick

kuna na?mahpee? lightning bug

kwasi tona? scorpion

kwita maropona doodlebug,
  sowbug

mutsikwù?aa? mosquito

muwo?ne? termite

ohahpiyaa? bumblebee

otu peena wasp

paka tuu?ru? dragonfly

pia animui horsefly

pihpi horsefly

puikuso redbug, chigger

pusi?a head louse

puhu pusia crab louse

saabe busia body louse

soo mo?o? centipede

soo yake? locust

te?animui biting fly

tosarai? devil's horse

tuhmeko cricket

tuunuu? Junebug, black beetle

tu?anikuura? wood ant

tue anikuura? sugar ant

tue esi unuu gnat

tupi simuhta? moth (long sp.)

unú? bug, insect, creature

wobi muwo?ne? (K) termite

wobi pihnaa unuu? honeybee

wosa a?ra? grasshopper (long sp.)

yupusia head louse

Appendix B: Flora

Trees

ekamurora?i huupi̱ redbud tree

etɨhuupi̱ osage orange, hedge apple, bois d'arc

huupi̱, huuhpi̱ tree (general)

kunanatsu prickly ash, toothache tree

kɨhtáa mubitai? hickory

kɨrahúu?, kɨ?ra?húu? hackberry

kwe?yɨkɨ sohóobi silver maple

mitsonaa? southern hackberry

mubitai, mu?bitai walnut

namabitsoo?ni mesquite

naséka persimmon

natsohkwe? mesquite

na?kɨta?i? huuhpi̱ pecan tree

ohahuupi̱ osage orange, bois d'arc

ohasɨhɨɨbi willow, black

otɨ mitsonaa? soapberry tree

pahtsi mubitai hickory

parɨa, parɨabi dogwood (rough leaf)

pa?sa ponii huupi̱ oak

pihúura huupi catalpa

pimoroo?a korohko? elm, white elm

seyɨyuki? ehyu̱yuki? ash tree

siba huupi̱ dogwood (flowering variety)

soho bokopi̱ hackberry

soho bo?koo? huupi̱ mulberry tree

soho obi̱ huupi̱ cottonwood tree

sɨhɨɨbi willow

sɨkɨ?i huuhpi̱ plum tree

tosa seyu?yuki? white ash

tosa tukanai huupi white oak

tubokóo huuhpi black haw (local term), thornapple

tuhmubitai black walnut

tuhnaséka Mexican persimmon

tuhuupi, tuhu huupi blackjack oak

tusohó? elm

tɨe amawoo? crabapple

tɨmaya huupi smooth sumac

waapi̱ cedar

we?yɨkɨ sohoobi (K) cottonwood

wohi?huu mesquite

wokóobi pine

wokɨ huupi̱ thorn tree, honey locust

wokwekatɨ huupi̱ thornapple, black haw

yusɨhɨbi weeping willow

yusɨkɨ yuu sɨkɨi early plum

Plants

aakáa? devil's horn/devil's claw
anakwanare? gourd
atabitsɨnoi button snakeroot
ebitotsiya? Texas thistle
ekahkoni Indian breadroot
ekamitsaa? cactus
ekanatsɨ eriogonum root
ekapokopi yaupon holly
ekapo? mescal bean
ekasonipɨ little bluestem
ekatsiira? red pepper
ekawoni smartweed
esinɨɨhparabi loco weed
hani- maize, corn
hi?ookwana? sunflower
huutsú?a tɨahkapɨ sumac
kabitsi cabbage
kahnitueka Indian paintbrush
kamúuta? sweet potato
kapisi namaya croton weed
kuhtsu pokàa? cocklebur, burr
kumiitsanatsu milkweed
kusinɨɨhparabi gray colored plant
kusiwɨɨnɨ sage like shrub
kɨhtsɨtsɨɨ?ni? poisonous wild
   onion
kɨriata yellow pond lily
kɨrɨ?atsi yellow lotus
kɨɨkanarɨhka?, kɨɨka wild onion
kwasinabo?a tɨahkapɨ tomato,
   goat's rue
mumutsi? soapweed, yucca,
   beargrass
mutsi natsamukwe? wild grape
nakwɨsi? pumpkin
namabitsooni sonipɨ mesquite
   weed
natsaakɨsi sneeze weed
natsamukwe?a sɨɨki grapevine
nayɨɨ wokwe cactus

nɨmɨ rɨsaasi Indian perfume plant
ohahpokopi, ohahtɨkapɨ domestic
   carrot
ohapi watermelon, yellow
ohayaa? sunflower
paapasi wild potato
pahmo namahya sumac
pahmu tobacco
paiyapi wild plant with edible fruit
pakeeso purple prairie clover
pakɨɨka wild onion, swamp weed
panatsayaa? blackberry bush,
   raspberry bush
pasiwona pɨhɨbi silvery
   wormwood
pawahkapɨ herb (name unknown)
payaape aqueous wild tuber
pa?mutsi water lilylike plant
pa?puhi tɨhka? celery
pa?sonipɨ weeds
pesotái buttonbush
pihtsamuu milky rooted plant
pihúraa bean plant
pisibuni? cattail
pitsa múu legume with edible
   tubers
pitsi tora prickly poppy
pohóobi sagebrush, quinine weed
poiya feverplant
poko rɨhka? cucumber
po?aya?eetɨ thistle
puha natsu red false mallow
puhakatɨ heal all plant
puhi bihnáa? watermelon
puhi ta?ara? poison ivy
puhi topika bush
puhi tubi bush clover
puhi tɨhkapɨ lettuce
puhi tɨmakwatubi? cigarette
   wrapper leaf
puhi tɨrɨhka? mistletoe
pui tsaseni rye grass

puewatsi kuuka wild onion

puhu natsu, puhu ru?saasi medicinal herb

saatotsiya flowering plant

sanaweha broomweed, mormon tea

siiko wild syacinth

simuihu? snakeroot, church root

soho kua?etu totsiyaa? morning glory

soko rahka?miitsa? cucumber

soko sikusa dandelion

soni bihnáa? sugar cane

soni narúa oats

soni wokweebi grass burrs

sonipu grass

suhu tsitsina? potato

tabetsotsiyaa fleabane daisy, clock flower

taibo bihnaa? cantaloupe

taibo suku?i domestic plum

tamutso?i greenbriar

tatsipuu sumac, skunkbush

tohpotsotsii nightshade

tohtía sonipu wheat plant

tohtía sonipuha taka? rye

toponibihuura? peas

tosa wahtsuki horseweed

totohtu edible tuber

to?roponii? beetlike tuber

tsapusiku sensitive briar

tsiira? chili pepper

tsunisu edible tuber

tuhbanatsaya blackberry bush

tukunu natsu purple coneflower

tunuhaa cymopterus plant

tutupipu wild tuber

tuwokwe goathead vine

tu?amowoo thornapple, blackhaw

tuahpi Chickasaw plum

tuetutaatu kuuka wild onion

tumakwatui? cigarette wrapper plant

tupi natsu medicinal plant

turanu breadroot, Indian bread

tusaasi Indian perfume plant, sage

tuunua broomgrass

tuunua? broom corn

wokweebi peyote plant, thorn, thistle

wokwesonipu thorny weed, sunburst plant

wokeéesi barrel cactus, prickly pear

wo?anatsu? western ragweed

yokanatsu?u red false mallow

yuu sonipu prairie clover, common grass

Appendix C: Body Parts

ahna side of chest, underarm, armpit
ahnapʉ pubic hair, underarm hair
ahnatukate armpit
ahrapʉ (Y, P) jaw
eekǫ tongue
ekotʉwʉni? glottis
e?rée forehead
hekwi? spleen
huhkʉ collarbone
hʉnʉpo?a? human skin
kasạ wing
katsonakwʉ end, rear, back part
ka?i forehead
ka?ibʉhʉ eyebrow
kiipʉ elbow
kohhi? small intestine, waist, abdomen
koobẹ face
kotsana flank of living animal, hindquarter
kuitsị throat
kuitsịtʉkwʉni adam's apple
kupịsi, kubịsi brain
kutsi?omo shin, shinbone
kʉʉtsị wisdom tooth
kwahi back of person/animal
kwahi kupịsi spinal cord (excluding bones)

kwahinupʉ spine
kwahiporopʉ spinal column
kwahitsuhnị vertebra (one)
kwahiwo?oraa spine, backbone
kwahtsʉ (Y), kwahtsʉna rib
kwasị tail of animal
kwiita buttocks
kwitatsị large intestine
mahtokoo? thumb
mahtua? (K) little finger
mahtʉpịnáa? (K) middle finger
makwe back of the hand, hand
mapaanạ palm of hand
mapó?a? human skin
mapʉhʉ hair on arm/wrist
masiitǫ fingernail
masʉwʉhki? (K) fingers (including the thumb)
mawaatsạ rib
ma?wiítsạ wrist
miihtsị ankle
mitʉko?o roof of mouth
motsǫ beard
mo?o mo?e hand
muubi nose
naapẹ foot, lower leg
nakị ear
nakị kwiitạ ear lobe, back of ear

natsimina? joint of the body
nunapu chest of the body
nuuhtoka?e? muscle
nuumu liver
ohutuki flank of animal
oomo leg (from knee down)
paai vein
paapi, papi head (including face)
pabokohi large intestine
papi hunupo?a scalp of head
paruutsi chin
pihi heart
pitsii?, pitsamu breast of woman
piwo?sa hip, lower back
pui eye
pui naruso eyelid
puihtsara? (Y) flank of animal
puihtsita? (K) rib area of animal
pui? temple
puitusii eyelash
pu?i? gall bladder
pukapu lap
puura arm
sahpáana? side of stomach or
    abdomen
sapu stomach
sekwi bii? second stomach
    of a cow
sia feather
sihkupu (Y) collar bone
siiku navel
soo tuku flank of animal
soomo lung
so?o ruhku gums of teeth
so?o tsuhni cheekbone
so?o cheek, cheekbone

taama tooth
tahpáana sole of foot
tahtokoo? big toe
tahtúa? little toe
tahtupinaa? middle toe
tamakwita roots of the teeth
tamaruhku gums of the teeth
tamu sinew
tanapu knee
tana? ku?e kneecap
tapiko? heel of foot
tapu, tapuhu hair of leg
tasakwuuhki? toes
tasiito toenail, claw, hoof
ta?ki? kidney
ta?wiitsa calf of the leg
tohoobe thigh, from the knee up
tookaatso toe
toyo tahka?miitsa sweetbreads
toyopu neck
tsoohpa tsuuni shoulder bone
tso?apu shoulder
tso?yaa? head of hair
tsuhnipu skull
tsuhni? bone
tuhhu shin/shinbone
tuhkohhi (Y) intestine
tuhku body, flesh
tuhpui pupil of the eye
tupe mouth, lips
turana bones of leg, marrow bones
tutsihtsuka? index finger
waatsu rib
woruroku esophagus, windpipe
wo?rorooki (Y) windpipe
    múu lúf H

Appendix D: Months of the Year

January

Toh mᵾa 'year month'
ᵾkᵾrooma mᵾa 'middle month'

February

Positsᵾ mᵾa 'sleet month'

March

Nana?butitᵾikatᵾ mᵾa 'hot or cold month'
Tahpookᵾ mᵾa 'cottonball month'

April

Tahma mᵾa 'new spring month'

May

Totsiyaa mᵾa 'flower month'

June

Puhi mᵾa 'leaf month'

July

Pᵾmata piabuhhara?ena mᵾa 'Fourth of July month'
Pia mᵾa 'large month'
ᵾrᵾi mᵾa 'hot month'

August

Tahma ᵾhᵾyi, Tatsatᵾ mᵾa 'summer month'
ᵾkᵾiyuba mᵾa 'new fall month'

September

Tᵾboo renahpᵾmakwe kwi?ena mᵾa 'paper man enters school'
Kwi?ena mᵾa 'back to school month'

October

Yᵾbamᵾa 'fall month'

November

Yᵾbaᵾhi mᵾa 'leveling toward winter month'
Aho tabenihtᵾ mᵾa 'Thanksgiving month'

December

Pia ᵾtsᵾ?i mᵾa 'big cold month'
Pᵾmata wahi mᵾa, Pᵾmata waa hima?ena mᵾa 'gift month'
Wahimᵾa 'evergreen month'
Pᵾmata wanohi?ema mᵾa 'Christmas gift month'

165

Appendix E: Personal Names

Arʉka paaʔ Deer water
Atakʉni, Ata kahni Lone tipi
Atsabiʔ Creator, Holy Spirit
Eka kura Red buffalo
Ekamurawa Red crooked nose
Ekawokani Red young man
Esahibi Wolf drinking
Esatai Little wolf
Esihabiitʉ Gray streak, Gray flat
   lying object
Esikono Gray box
Esitamiʔ Ase tammy
Esʉnapʉ Asenap
Hiitooʔ Meadowlark
Huuhwiya Refuse to come
Huuwʉhtʉkwaʔ Take a stick and
   hit someone
Hʉkiyani Carrying her sunshade
Hʉwʉni Dawn
Hʉʔnipitʉ Hiccough daughter
Isananakaʔ, Isʉnanika Howling
   coyote, Echo of the wolf's howl
Isatekwa Liar, Lie talk
Isawʉra Crazy bear
Ishatai Coyote droppings
Kaatʉ, Katinʉ God
Kahpewai No bed

Kahúu nihku pipịkurẹ, Pipịkuʔ
   Squeaky like a mouse
Kaʔmʉtʉhiʔ, Kamʉrʉʔiʔ Looking
   from side to side
Ke tokwe hina haniitʉ Satan
Kebakoweʔ Coyote
Kehaitsipaapị Bald
Ketse nabʔbo Painted feather
Kiyu Horseback
Kohi Narrow gut
Kohitʉ seʔtanʉkʉ Sitting bear
Kuhiyai Peeping from behind tree
Kuhtsu kwiʔta Cow dung
Kuhtsuna kwapipʉ Buffalo hump
Kuhtsunu kwahipʉ One who rides
   buffalo
Kuhtu Coals in a fire
Kukapʉ Cooks dried meat
Kurupitsoni Looks brown
Kʉtsʉkwipʉ Chew up
Kwahira Robe on his back
Kwana Quanah Parker
Kwasia Eagle tail feather
Kwihne tosabitʉ White eagle
Mooʔwetʉ No hand
Mopai Owl
Mota, Tatseni Lee Motah
Moʔpi tsokopʉ Old owl

167

Mukwooru Spirit talker
Mura kwitapu Mule dung
Nabakwutiapu Christian
Narua, Nadua Cynthia Ann Parker
Narumi? Lord, Master
Naya Slope
Ninakaba?i? Refusing
Nookoni, Nocona, Peta Nokona Wanderer
Nuenuhkiki Wind running here
Nuetutsi Blowing wind
Numu ruibetsu She invites her relatives
Ohapia Bay mare
Ohapitu kwahi Yellow back
Ohawasápe Yellow bear
Ohawunu Yellow steps
Onawai Salt worn out
Otu kwasu Brown robe
Paa roponi *See* How deep the water is
Paa tsokotubutu Black otter
Paa tso?ko Otter
Pabopitu Light complexion
Pahtsi ketu Smooth
Pakawa Kills something
Pakekuni, Pake kahni Dry teepee
Paruwa kuma Bull elk
Paruwa sumuno Ten elks
Parua kuhma Bull bear
Pasawío Big green frog
Pia baa Big water
Pia nu?upai?i Big whip
Pia rutsima Big fall by tripping
Pia opu, Pi?opu Pia?opu
Piana buni?, Piana ronitu Big looking glass
Pipiku? Squeaky
Pisu kwá?na? Smeller
Pi?opu paroba tuyo, Peope Padiva, Taoyo, Tuyo Boy
Poo?aiku Blow it away

Pua paatsoko Medicine otter
Puhawi Medicine woman
Puku?a tua? Colt
Punitu Looking
Pu?ekatu Christian
Pu tua wuni kwai Been to see his son
Pu?na petu Only daughter
Sanah pia Sanahpia
Sanah pia ariba Sanahpia ariba
Santanta Santanta
Sata Tejas I, Saria Tuhka I Sata Tejas I
Sata Tejas II, Saria Tuhka II Sata Tejas II
Sihka tabe ke isopu This midday sun does not tell a lie
Soo pitenu Comes often
Tabe kwi?ne Sun eagle
Tabe nanika Hears the sunrise, Voice of the sunrise
Tabe wunuru Standing sun
Tahkapu Poor one
Tatsiwóo Buffalo
Ta?ahpu Our Father, Great Spirit
Tekwitsi Skinny and wrinkled
Tenebeka, Tunubeku Gets to be middle aged man
Tomo?a tua Sky child
Tope Tope
Topehtsi, Topache Pass it on
Topusana Flower
Tsaa tenayake? Good crier
Tsaa tsopa? Easy to break
Tsihtara Short dress
Tsuhni Bone
Tuhkwasi taiboo? Satan
Tu?paapi Black head
Tu?runaasu Straighter than straight
Tue buakutu Little medicine
Tue kuhtsu Little buffalo

Tɨhɨyana kwahipɨ Horseback

Tɨmɨbo, Timbo Son of bull bear

Tɨoyobisesɨ Chief Comanche dog soldiers

Tɨpanai Cliff

Tɨpi kɨniʔ Stonehouse

Tɨpi wɨnɨ Rocky creek

Tɨʔsinaʔ Hanging from the belt

Waakakwa Trotter (Laughing John)

Wakaréʔe Turtle

Wanarɨ Wanarɨ

Witawooʔooki Barking buttocks

Wɨkwiya, Wekwaaʔa Jesus man

Wɨʔrabiahpɨ Swift moving

Part II

English-Comanche Lexicon

English-Comanche Lexicon

A a

abandon someone nobuahraitu
abdomen kohi̱
abdomen, side of stomach or
  sahpáana?
abdominal pain, suffer kohikamutu
able to walk numiru
about, move yukaru
about, think sukwu̱kitu
about something, think
  nasutamu̱katu tamai, su?atsitu,
  tu̱su?atsi̱katu̱
above everything oyo?ru ka?weki̱tu
_above the horizon, stand just tabe
  wunu?itu
accept someone, refuse to
  ninakabaru
accident, die in anitu
accident, hurt someone by
  tsahhuhyaru
accidentally, knock over and spill
  tsakwu̱riaru
accidentally, spilled
  makwuri?aikatu
accompany, allow women to
  notsa?kaaru

accord, open of its own
  natsahwi?etu
accord, spill of own nuuti?akatu
accord, split of own nuuhtsi?aitu
accord, unravel of own
  nuupuru̱suaru
acculturate (as a Comanche)
  numu̱naitu
accuse someone natsamaru
accuse someone falsely
  tu̱behyaaru
accuse someone of being gray-
  faced (in making fun of
  someone) etu̱sikawo?aru W
ace (in game of cards) watasi̱
ache manuutsikwa? W,
  nuutsikwaru K
ache, have a head- papi̱kamaitu
ache, head- papi̱ wunu̱katu
ache, stomach kohikamu̱katu, sapu̱
  nuutsikwaru
ache tree, tooth- kunanatsu
ache in lower back piwo?sa
  wunaru
acid mohakamaru
acidic moha-, suuku̱
acorn pa?sa ponii
across saraa

173

across, drive tamanikarʉ
across, move unahrʉ
act angry tuhu rekwarʉ
act pretentious nasutsa akwarʉ K
act speedily wʉʔrabiarʉ
act without self-dignity eʔmʉarʉ
actions tʉyʉkwipʉ
adam's apple kuitsitʉkwʉni, pia kuitsiʔ
address (speak to) niikwiitʉ
adhere sanarʉ, tsahpakitʉ
admire nasuyaketʉ, tokwetʉtuarʉ
admire someone suʔakʉtʉ
admit tsaʔikarʉ
adobe house ohta kahni W
adopt a child toyarʉ, tʉetʉnabinarʉ
adopted daughter petʉ toyapʉ K, petʉboopʉ W
adopted son tua boopʉ W
adult kinsman nahnapʉ
adult male muʔwoo
adultery, commit naʔisahanitʉ W
advise naniʔʉrʉʔaitʉ, ninʉsuabitarʉ K, niʔatsiitʉ, tʉniʔatsitʉ, tʉsuʔʉrʉ
adviser tʉniʔatsikʉ
afflict makwihtserʉ
afraid kuyaʔakatʉ, wʉʔyʉrʉhkikatʉ
afraid, run away namanuhkitʉ
A-frame, meat-drying inakwata
after, go petsʉ pitarʉ
after, run miakʉrʉ
after another, sing one song nipʉyerʉ
afternoon tabe ʉhyʉh? K
again tʉasʉ
against someone, win in a contest tahniʔarʉ
against something, lean nʉʉbanikatʉ
against something, rub pisuʔnetʉ
against something, rub head tsotsoʔneetʉ

against something, scratch rear or back pisuʔnetʉ
-against, Those-who-are-always Komanche
agent itsiną, paraibooʔ
agent, Indian itsiną, nʉmʉ paraiboʔ
agnatic grandchild, man's kʉnuʔ
agnatic grandnephew, man's kʉnuʔ
agnatic grandchild, woman's huutsi
ago, long soo beʔsʉ
ago, many years soo beʔsʉ
agree to a proposal nihtsamuʔitʉ
agree to a statement tʉmahyokʉrʉ
agree with someone tokwetʉtuarʉ
agreeable tokwetʉkatʉ
agreement or contract, make an nanipuʔeʔaitʉ
agreement, nod the head in nihtsamuʔitʉ
ahead munakwʉ
ahead of, be munaikiyutʉ W
ahead, proceed muhnetʉ
aim (a gun) wʉhkurʉ
aim, miss awi-
aim (something) wakarʉkatʉ
airplane yʉtsʉʔ
alcoholic beverage, drink hibikʉtʉ
align spine tahparaʔitʉ
alike sʉʉnitʉ
all oyo-
all, That's subeʔtu
all over, wrinkled takwikakwoʔapʉ
alligator nʉnʉʔyʉwiʔ W
allow to rest or cool off sua soyuraperʉ
allow women to accompany notsaʔkaarʉ
almost noha
alone, leave person kekʉnabeniitʉ
alone, one hill standing nookarʉrʉ

along (or away), drive
  mahkʉsuwaitʉ
along, farther miibeʔtʉ
along, go nahaniitʉ
along, go moving noraʔwʉarʉ W
along, lead matsaaihkakurʉ,
  tsakamiʔarʉ
along, roll anikwita miʔarʉ
along, take women notsaʔkaarʉ
along the edge of kʉma?
along there suʔahri
alongside kʉmaʔrʉ
already pʉe
also tʉasʉ
always usúni̱
-always-against, Those-who-are
  Komanche
amazed tʉʉmoo|bi|r
amazed, be suwʉʔkai
amazing suwʉkaitʉ
ambush makamʉkarʉ, tʉkamʉrʉ
ambushed mahooikatʉ
ambusher tʉkʉmaʔaitʉ?
Anadarko, Okla Tusokweʔ K
and tʉasʉ
angel kasaráibooʔ, nʉtʉhyoi wapi̱
anger tsahpisoʔarʉ
anger, feel tuhu suʔaitʉ
anger, jerk and slam things in
  tuhu rekwarʉ
anger someone kʉpisoʔaitʉ K,
  mahrubʉhkaitʉ
angered mabisoʔàitʉ, tapisoʔaitʉ W
angrily, stand pihisoʔaiwʉnʉrʉ
angry mabisoʔàitʉ, pihisoʔai,
  pihisoʔaitʉ, piʔonʉ suakʉtʉ
angry, act tuhu rekwarʉ
angry, become (at a person)
  tuhubʉkʉkatʉ
animal (or person), exhausted
  namakweyaipʉ
animal, female piabʉ

animal, flank of puihtsaraʔ W, soo
  tuku
animal, flank of living kotsana
animal, hobble an moʔo
  wʉhtamarʉ
animal, lead a person or an
  tsakarʉ
animal, male kuuma
animal, mean person or tuhupʉ
animal, leader, pack- tʉnoo wapi̱
animal, pack for an tʉnoopʉ W
animal, pen up taʔikʉrʉ
animal, rib area of puihtsitaʔ K
animal carcass, render an
  tʉhtsohpeʔarʉ
animal, skin an pʉhʉ
  tsahkweʔyarʉ, wʉsiboʔarʉ
animal, tame an masuyuʔikarʉ K
animal, trail a human or an
  nayaarʉ
animal, unhitch an toʔyarʉ W
animal, water an hibikʉtʉ
animal, weak person or tʉʔonaapʉ
animal hide pimoroʔa pʉhi, pʉhʉ?
animal hole itsaraitʉ ʉnʉa kahni
animal horn aa
animal horn comb aanatsihtuyeʔ
animal killed or butchered for
  food tʉbehkapʉ
animal tail kwasi-, kwasi̱
animals, drive by force tamʉkʉrʉ
animals, drive in mahkʉkitʉ K
animals, drive up mahkʉrʉ W
ankle miihtsi̱
ankle, sprain naraminaitʉ K
announce tekwʉnitʉ, tʉnikʉkekitʉ K
annoy kʉpisoʔaitʉ K, nimʉsasuarʉ
anoint puha nabisarʉ, tʉʔekarʉ
another ata-
another, help one naruituahkarʉ
another, sing one song after
  nipʉyerʉ

another one su?atᵾ
another way, doing atapu
answer tᵾ?awekᵾᵾka̠rᵾ
ant an̤ikuura?
ant, red ekaᵾnᵾᵾ
ant, sugar tᵾe anikuura?
ant, wood tu?anikuura?
anteater ekaᵾnᵾᵾ?a tᵾhka?eetᵾ
Antelope Eaters Kwahari tᵾhka
any shellfish, shell of wa?koo? K
any species, snake of nuhya?
anything, more than oyo?rᵾ
  ka?weki̠tᵾ
Apaches, Eastern Nipanᵾᵾ
apart, pull tsahka?arᵾ, tsahpomi?itᵾ
apart, take tsahpᵾkᵾsu?arᵾ W
apiece, two wa?wa?
apparel namᵾsoapᵾ, oo?rᵾ W
apart, tear tsahpako?arᵾ
appear kunakᵾarᵾ K, kuro?itᵾ W,
  nabunitᵾ, nakᵾakitᵾ, to?itᵾ
appear gray esinabuniitᵾ
appear to be white tosa nabunitᵾ
appearance, check over one's
  nabuihwᵾnᵾtᵾ W
appearance, gray esitsᵾnᵾ?iitᵾ
appease ninᵾsupetitᵾ
appetite, have an tsihasuarᵾ
applaud (clap hands) tohtarakitᵾ
apple amawóo
apple, crab ekaamawoo?, tᵾe
  amawóo?
apple, hedge etᵾhuupi
apple, thorn tu?amowoo,
  wokwekatᵾ huupi
apple, thorn- tubokóo
apple juice amawóo?a pàa
apple skin amawo?a? po?a?
apply medicine narᵾ?ekarᵾ
apply powder to oneself
  homonabi̠sakatᵾ
apply war paint wohho napᵾsarᵾ

applying pressure with the hands,
  rub masu?nerᵾ
approach wᵾhpitᵾ
approach someone pitᵾnu̠
approving tokwetᵾkatᵾ
April Tahma mᵾa
apron pitsᵾkwina?, tᵾkᵾ
  wᵾhpara? K
aqueous payaape̠
Arapaho Sarii Tᵾhka?
arbor soni hᵾᵾki, tahᵾᵾki?aikᵾ
arbor, brush hᵾᵾki?aitᵾ, puhi
  hᵾᵾki̠, soni hᵾᵾki, tahᵾᵾki?aikᵾ
arbor, poles for constructing
  brush hᵾᵾkina huupi̠
arch potato sᵾhᵾ tsitsina?
archaic game na?nohne?eyu?
archery game wᵾ?kᵾrᵾ
-are-always-against, Those-who
  Komanche
area, separated but in same
  general na?ata W
area, waist kohi̠
argue nani?wiketᵾ W
argumentative nanitsᵾwakatᵾ K
arise taayᵾtsᵾtᵾ
arm pᵾᵾra̠
arm or hand, hair on lower
  mapᵾhᵾ
arm, sprain or break hand or
  lower namaminaitᵾ
arm, stretch out maruru?arᵾ
arm, under- ahna, ana-
arm hair, under- anapᵾhᵾ
arm to waist, under- ama-
armadillo awono?o?
armpit ahna, ana-, anatukate
arms, carry in toyarᵾ
arms, carry in the kwabarᵾ
arms or body, stretch narurerᵾ
army officer eka̠sahpana? paraiboo?
around, feel makwarᵾ, tsakwatᵾ

around, feel (with hand) mawa-
around, grope tsakwatʉ
around, kid kaasuarʉ
around, move nʉmirʉ, yoʔmitsaitʉ, yʉʔyʉmuhkumiʔarʉ W
around, roll maropoʔnarʉ
around, roll over or naʔanitʉ
around and play, run nohiʔnuraarʉ
around, scattered poohkatʉ
around something, slip a rope kuʔnikarʉ
around, smell muwarʉ W, ʉkwisʉʔninitʉ K
around, sneak hoʔaniitʉ
around, sniff ʉkwisʉʔninitʉ K
around, spin kwinuʔyarʉ, natsahkwinuʔitʉ
around, stir yoʔmitsaitʉ
around, turn koonitʉ, kooniʔetʉ, kwinuʔyarʉ
around quickly, turn pikwebuitʉ
around something, twist oneself nʉʉʔkwipunarʉ
around, walk nahnʉmiitʉ
around the neck, wear something korohkọrʉ
around the waist, wear something kohinehkitʉ
around, wrap wʉhkwitunarʉ
around and around, wrap nʉʉhkwitubitʉ
arrest kwʉhʉrʉ
arrive pitʉnụ
arrive (carrying something) noopitʉ
arrive home tsakʉbitʉkitʉ
arrow paakạ, siʔbaʔ
arrow fly, let an wʉhkikatʉ
arrowhead tahkaʔ
arrows, throwing naroʔtoneetsiʔ, tiroʔwoko
article of clothing, own an kwasuʔukatʉ K

Asenap Esʉnapʉ
Asetammy Esitamiʔ
ash seyʉyuki?
ash, prickly kunanatsu
ash tree tosa seyuʔyuki?
ashes, color of (gray) kusi-
ashamed nasuʔaitʉ
ashes etʉsipʉ, kusipʉ
ashes, roast in kusiwʉhpima W
ashtray tusi aawọ
aside, tempt to turn tsapʉhesuwarʉ
ask nanimaaʔʉbʉʔikʉtʉ, niipuni-
ask a question tʉbinitʉ, tʉrʉbinitʉ
ask for help naníhtsawaʔitʉ
ask for something tʉrʉnirʉ
ask permission nanihtʉbinitʉ
asleep sʉsʉʔnitʉ, tasʉsʉʔnitʉ
aspirin papịkamaka natʉsuʔu
assemble, dis- tohkweʔyarʉ
astray, lead tsakaʔʉhrʉ
at, glare tsuhni bunitʉ
at, laugh suʔuyaaʔarʉ, tʉnisuʔuyaitʉ, usúʔuyaʔitʉ W
at, look punitʉ, tʉpunirʉ
at oneself, look nabunitʉ
at a time, one sʉsʉmʉ?, sʉʔsʉmʉʔnʉku
at, peep kuhiyarʉ
at last haya kwasikʉ
at or to someone or something maaitʉ
at or to the left side ohininakwʉ
at this point siʔanetʉ
at top of teepee, ventilator natsihparaʔ
Athapascans Naboohnʉʉ
attach tsahpakʉkarʉ
attempt narahpunipʉ
attempt to hit with a weapon wʉsukwarʉ W
attention, listen with nakị hiikatʉ K

attention, pay tᵾnakiitᵾ

attentive nakamabitsiahkatᵾ, nakᵾkatᵾ

auger bit tᵾrohtᵾbᵾ?i?

augment in number sᵾatᵾ

augmenting in quantity tᵾraka?aitᵾ

August Tahma ᵾhᵾyi, Tatsatᵾ mᵾa, Ʉkᵾi yᵾba mᵾa

aunt (father's sister) paha?

aunt, maternal great kaku?

authority tᵾni-, tᵾsu?atsipᵾ

authority, have tᵾsu?atsitᵾ

automatic pistol natsahkwine?

automobile na?bukuwàa?

automobile tire na?bukuwàa?a narahpaana W

awaken tᵾbunitᵾ

awaken someone by shouting tayᵾtsᵾrᵾ

aware supᵢkaahkatᵾ

away, drive tahkᵾarᵾ

away (or along), drive mahkᵾsuwaitᵾ

away from (or off), fall tᵾpᵾherᵾ W

away, far manakwᵾ K

away, float okwehkwatᵾ, sᵾmᵾ okwetᵾ

away, force tahkᵾarᵾ

away, haul nookwarᵾ

away, kick something sᵾᵾ potserᵾ

away, kicked sᵾᵾhpotsᵾkatᵾ

away a wife, lead nᵾpetsᵾ?itᵾ

away, melt parᵾhwimi?arᵾ

away, move nomi?arᵾ, norawᵾ?aitᵾ

away (as a group), move sᵾmᵾ nomi?arᵾ

away, push mahbotsetᵾ

away, put namabimarᵾ, tahtᵾkarᵾ, tᵾkarᵾ

away for safekeeping, put to?nikarᵾ K

away, run nuhkitᵾ

away afraid, run namanuhkitᵾ

away from something, run wᵾanuraitᵾ K

away from somewhere, run pᵾa nuhkitᵾ

away one by one, run nunurawᵾtᵾ

away, secret oneself watsi habiitᵾ

away, shoo manᵾkikᵾrᵾ

away, sneak watsi mi?arᵾ

away, store nabina?etᵾ

away something live, take tahtᵾkitᵾ

away, throw petihtarᵾ, wihtaitᵾ

away, to haul noorᵾ

away from, turn wᵾhbuikatᵾ W

away, walk natsihtóo mi?arᵾ

away, wipe tahtsukitᵾ

a while, once in sᵾsᵾ?ana

awl wiiyᵾ

axe tᵾᵾhka?a?

axe, battle (with flintstone handle) wᵾpitapu?ni

axe, chisel or split with an tohtsiyu?itᵾ

axe, double-bladed na?butikᵾmakatᵾ tᵾᵾhka?aa?

B b

baby ohna?a?

baby, wean a pitsi makatᵾ

baby bed ohna?a norᵾhnaa?

baby buggy na?tsi?aikᵾ?

baby colic sapᵾ wᵾnᵾkatᵾ

baby crib ohna?a norᵾhnaa?

bachelor wohka?ni?

back kwahi, pitᵾsᵾ

back, ache in lower piwo?sa wᵾnarᵾ

back, carried on manookatᵾ

back, carry on nɨnoorɨ
back, carry on the kwahi noorɨ
back, come koʔitɨ
back, go pitsa miʔarɨ
back and forth, go (or from side to side) piʔnuʔa miʔarɨ
back, hunch- noʔwosarɨ
back on heels, kneel down sitting tanatookarɨtɨ
back, lie on paʔraihabiitɨ
back, lower piwoʔsa̲
back, on paʔarai
back, pull tsasinɨkaarɨ
back in place, put something tohtɨkiʔarɨ
-back, Robe-on-his Kwahira
back against something, scratch rear or pisuʔnetɨ
back to ease pain, stand on someone's tahparaʔitɨ
back and forth, swing natsakwenitɨ
back, tie a child to wɨpi̲toorɨ
-back, Yellow Ohapi̲tɨ kwahi
back of the hand makwe
back part (of ear cartilage) K naki̲ kwiita̲
back up hupi̲miʔarɨ, pimimiʔarɨ, pitsa ɨkwakatu kimarɨ
backache, have a piwoʔsa wɨnarɨ
backache, have a (in lower back) piwoʔsa wɨnɨkatɨ
backbone kwahinupɨ, kwahiporopɨ
backpack kwahi noorɨ
backward, step pimimiʔarɨ
backward, walk pimimiʔarɨ
backwards, come pitsa ɨkwakatu kimarɨ
backwards, go hupi̲miʔarɨ, piʔnuʔa miʔarɨ
bad aitɨ, tɨtsɨ-
bad odor, have kwanarɨ

bad tidings, upset people by niʔyɨsɨkaitɨ
badly nɨnɨmɨni̲ tɨhtsɨ
badly, piled pia utsaatɨ
bag narɨso̲, wosa̲
bag, nose puku rɨhkaʔ
bag, war-bonnet tuna wosa
bag game tɨkɨh pehkarɨ
bagged game wasɨpɨ
bake tohtíaʔarɨ
bake biscuits nohkorɨ
bakery tohtía narɨmɨɨʔ
baking biscuits, oven for nohko aawo̲
baking powder namahyaʔ
Bald Kehaitsipaapi̲
bald head pahtsi kuʔe
bald headed pahtsi bapikatɨ K
bale something wɨhtamarɨ
baling wire soni nɨɨhtamaʔ K, soni wɨhtɨmaʔ
ball naʔmahpeʔeʔ, naʔsɨhpeeʔ
ball, puff- mupitsɨha pisahpi̲ W
ball, roll into a tsahtopoʔnarɨ
ball, wind into a wɨhtopoʔnitɨ
ball bat tɨhpoʔtseʔ
ball game, Native-American naʔsɨhpeʔetɨ
ball-like toponi-
balloon mubohtohkipɨ
ban nihtoʔitɨ
banana aakaaʔ
band nɨɨpi̲tuaʔ
band, Comanche Kwarɨ, Nokoni, Tɨtsanoo yehkɨ
band, Comanche (of Walters area) Wiaʔnɨɨ
band, rubber tuʔreʔ
Band, Water Horse Tasúra
bandana tsokwɨkɨɨnaʔ W, wɨhtsohkɨnaʔ
bank, creek tɨpánaʔ

bank (financial) puhihwi kahni
bank, river ekatotsa̱
bank (of stream) ekatotsa̱
bank draft puhihwi tɨboopɨ
bank up wɨhtɨmarɨ
banker puhihwi paraiboo?
baptize pa?wɨtiarɨ
baptize by sprinkling ku?e naba wɨhtia
baptize someone nɨbawɨhtiarɨ
baptized mabáaku?neetɨ
baptized one Nabakwɨhtiapɨ
baptizer nɨbawɨhtiawapi̱, pawɨhtia wapi̱, tɨbawɨhtia wapi̱
barbecue kuhtu tɨkɨmanirɨ K, ku?inarɨ
barbecue grate ku?inawaata̱
barbed wire puhihwi tɨɨhtɨma?
barbed wire fence, put up a puhihwi tɨɨhtɨmarɨ
bare, thread- pupu̱katɨ
barely himataaka, pɨhimataka
bargain tohpunitɨ
bark po?a?, wo?wo?kitɨ
bark, tree huupi po?a?, huupita po?a
Barking-buttocks Witawoo?ooki
barley tohtía sonipɨha taka?
barrel huu aawo, wobi aawo̱
barrel cactus wokwéesi
barren oak tuhuupi
barrette papi̱ tsihtɨpɨ̱ka?
base tɨkwita
baseball nɨ?ɨhpee?
bashful nasu?aitɨ̱
basket sɨhɨ aawo
bat hɨnɨbi pokaa?
bat, ball- tɨhpo?tse?
bath, steam nakuhkwaraki? K
bath, take a steam kuhkwarɨkitɨ
bath, sweat nakuhkwaraki? K, nasukoo?i?

bathe pahabitɨ
bathe, steam nakuhkwarakitɨ, nasukoo?itɨ
bathed kuhkwarɨkitɨ
bathroom naro?ikahni K, pahabi̱ kahni W
bathtub pahabi̱ aawo̱
batter kasamawɨrɨ
batter (allowed to become set) takoosahpɨ? W
battered kasamawɨrɨ
battered tree huupi kasamawɨ
battle axe with flintstone handle wɨpitapu?ni
battle with weapons nabitɨkɨrɨ
bay horse ekakɨma?, ohaeka? K, tupi̱si kɨma?
bay horse W ohaekapitɨ
Bay-mare Ohapia
be ahead of munaiki̱yutɨ W
be amazed suwɨ?kai
be born pahitɨ, yumarɨ
be carried away by wind mabo?ayarɨ
be cold kwihnerɨ
be feverish kuhtsɨni̱tɨ
be good yɨyɨkarɨ
be hard and brittle koobetɨ
be ill tɨ?oibɨkɨrɨ, uhúntɨkɨ
be in deep water kenawɨnɨrɨ
be in labor tuakatɨ
be made dizzy makwi?numaitɨ
be married kuumabaitɨ
be missing kehewa?itɨ
be night tukani̱tɨ
be sleepy-eyed puibɨɨtɨ̱
be soft yɨ?yɨkarɨ
be stiff tsihturuarɨ K
be straight kewesi̱ketɨ̱
be tempted masuyakerɨ
be well-behaved yunɨmitɨ
bead tsomo-
bead necklace tsomo korohko

bead something topꙮsarꙮ,
  tꙮropꙮsarꙮ
beaded naropꙮsarꙮ
beadwork tꙮropꙮsapꙮ?
bean pihúraa
bean, mescal ekapo?
bear wasápe̱
-bear, Sitting Kohitꙮ se?tanꙮkꙮ
-bear, Son-of-bull Tꙮmꙮbo
-bear, Yellow Ohawasápe
bear fruit pokopi tuarꙮ
bear offspring turuarꙮ
bear pain, to wꙮmetꙮ
bear trap wasápe pꙮmata kwꙮhꙮrꙮ?
beard motso̱
beard, pull own namutsono?itꙮ
beard, pull someone's
  mutsonoo?itꙮ
bearded white man motso taiboo?
beargrass mumutsi?
beat wꙮhpa?itꙮ, wꙮtꙮkwarꙮ
beat on totꙮbihkurꙮ, wꙮkwꙮbihkurꙮ
beat on someone wꙮhtꙮkwarꙮ
beat on someone (with watery
  object) pawꙮhpa?itꙮ
beat up wꙮapa?arꙮ
beaver ha?nii, pa?wꙮhtꙮma?
Beaver Creek Waahkusi okwe?
becalm wꙮhtsamꙮhkitꙮ
because suniyutꙮ
become naharꙮ
become angry at a person
  tuhubꙮkꙮkatꙮ
become calm nꙮemaitꙮ
become comatose sua watsikatꙮ
become insane sua watsitꙮ
become lazy nꙮꙮ?maitꙮ
become Spring tahma ro?itꙮ
bed kahpe, norꙮnapꙮ
bed, baby ohna?a norꙮhnaa?
bed, camp- wꙮhtaráa?
bed, make a nohrꙮnaarꙮ, norꙮnaarꙮ

bed, No- Kahpewai
bed, overflow the creek paru?itꙮ
bed, sheet for saabara
bedbug kahni busi̱?a
bedroom habikꙮni
bedsheet saabara, tosa kwana?hꙮ W
bedspring nasaa?wꙮ? W, nohrꙮna
  saawꙮ
bedstead nohrꙮna?
bee, bumble- ohahpiyaa?
bee, honey- wobi pihnaa ꙮnꙮꙮ?
Been-to-see-his-son Pꙮ tua wꙮni
  kwai
beer saah totsi baa
beetlike tuber to?roponii?
before hunakꙮ
before dawn ohahꙮkwꙮnikatꙮ, tosa
  hꙮwꙮnikatꙮma?
befriend tꙮsutaikatꙮ
beg marꙮꙮ?nitꙮ
beginning nabihtawꙮna
behaved, be well- yunꙮmitꙮ
behaved, well yꙮyꙮkarꙮ
behead toyo tsihka?arꙮ, toyo
  wꙮhka?arꙮ
behind pinakwꙮ, ꙮpinakwꙮ
behind, from pinai
behind, leave someone
  nobꙮahraitꙮ
behind oneself, look nabitꙮbunitꙮ
behind, pull something pitsákarꙮ
beige koropitꙮ
beige K otꙮ-, otꙮpitꙮ
belch akwarꙮtꙮ, akwarꙮ?
belief tokwꙮsuakꙮna
believe in someone tokꙮsuakꙮtꙮ
believe (something or someone)
  tokwꙮsuakꙮtꙮ
believe (pretend), make-
  nohitekwarꙮ
believer tꙮrokwꙮsuakꙮtꙮ
bell kawohwi̱?

bellows tʉbuuhki?
belonging to hipʉ
belongings (of any type) oo?rʉ W
belongings, personal namahku
beloved kamakʉna̱ W
belt kohinehki?, nehki̱ W,
　nʉ?ʉnehki̱ K
belt buckle nehki wʉhtʉpʉka?,
　nʉ?ʉnehki?a nanʉʉtʉpi̱ka? W
belted nʉ?ʉnehki̱katʉ?
bench, wooden huunakarʉ?, wobi
　nakarʉ?
bend tsa?onutsarʉ
bend down tumuurʉ
bend (in river) paa mutsaa?
bend over mupi̱habirʉ,
　muyʉʉ?wʉrʉ, nuhtsairʉ
bent tsa?onutsai
bent down tumuukatʉ̱
bent over mupi̱habiitʉ, nuhtsapʉ̱
berate someone ni?woso?arʉ
berate someone falsely
　ni?he?bunitʉ̱
berries pokopi̱
berries, picked pomapʉ̱
berry, chippa- tubupokoo
berry, hack- kʉrahúu? K, soho
　bokopi̱
berry, huckle- huwabo?kóo?
berry, soap- otʉ̱ mitsonaa?
berry, southern hack- mitsonaa?
berserk poosubʉkʉkaitʉ
beseech nanimaa?ʉbʉ?ikʉtʉ
beside kʉma?, kʉma?kʉ̱
bet on something narʉbahkarʉ
betray tsaka?uhrʉ
betray someone kaanatsaka?uhturʉ,
　natsaka?uhtu?etʉ
betrayer natsaka?uhtu?etʉ?
betrays, one who
　kaanatsaka?uhtupʉ̱
between, go- nitʉ̱su?nai wapi̱

between, two things, stuck tsʉki̱katʉ
beverage, drink alcoholic hibikʉtʉ
bewitch someone puha wʉhtitʉ
bias tape tʉkʉma?ai
Bible Puha rʉboopʉ̱
bicycle naraaikʉ?, ta?aikʉtʉ
big pia
big doctoring piana huwai?
big toe tahtokoo?
Big-fall-by-tripping Pia rʉtsima
Big-green-frog Pasawío
Big-looking-glass Piana buni?
Big-water Pia baa
Big-whip Pia nʉ?ʉpai?i
bill collector tʉniwaitʉ?
billy club tʉhkupa?
bird huutsúu
bird, blue- ebihuutsuu?
bird, humming- wʉ?kʉ?buu?
bird, mocking- soo yake? W,
　tʉnimanahke huutsu? K
bird, red- eka̱huutsu?
bird of its feathers, pick a no?itʉ̱
bird (small gray) kusisai?
bird clean, pluck a pʉhʉ no?itʉ
bird clean of feathers, pluck a
　pahtsi no?itʉ
bird, small gray kusisai?
bird nest huutsú?a kàhni̱, huutsú?a
　pisoo?ni̱
birdcall, make a niyakekʉtʉ̱
birdhouse huutsú?a kàhni̱
birth, give tuakatʉ
biscuit nohkopʉ̱, nʉmʉ nohkopʉ̱
biscuits, oven for baking nohko
　aawo̱
bit, auger tʉrohtʉbʉ?i?
bit, bridle namutsora?, tʉʉyʉ
　mutsora?
bit, little hʉitsi
bit (used for boring holes)
　tʉrohtʉbʉ?i?

bite kɨhtsiarɨ, kɨnabenitɨ

bite into (and not turn loose)
kɨhkarɨkatɨ

bite off kɨhkaʔarɨ

bite off kɨhpomiʔitɨ K

bite to death kɨhkobarɨ

bite together kɨhkarɨʔitɨ,
kɨtsɨbakitɨ

biting fly teʔanimui

bitter moha-, mohakamarɨ

black tu-, tuhupi

black beetle tuɨnɨɨʔ

black bird (with white wings) tosa
kwiisuʔ

black cradle tuhkɨni

black haw tubokóo, wokwekatɨ
huupi

Black Houses Tusa Kahni

black person tuhtaibooʔ W

black walnut tuhmubitai

black willow ohasɨhɨɨbi

Black-head Tuʔpaapi

Black-otter Paa tsokotubɨtɨ

blackberry panatsayaaʔ

blackberry bush tuhbanatsaya

blackbird tuwikaaʔ

blackjack oak tuhuupi

blacksmith's blower tɨbuuhkiʔ

blacktopped, paved a road
tuusanahpitɨ

blame manímɨarɨ

bland otɨ kamaitɨ

blanket esiwanaʔɨhɨ, ɨhɨ

blanket, buffalo taʔsiwoo
wanaʔɨhɨ W

blanket, cotton wana hɨ K

blanket, horse nahotsaʔmaʔ

blanket, Mexican kusikwiʔiiʔ

blanket, saddle kwahitɨkiʔ,
nahotsaʔmaʔ

blaspheme naniʔemɨahpɨ aitɨ

bleed pɨɨokwetɨ

bless someone sutaaitɨ

blessed sutaitɨ

blind pui hwai, tɨbitabuʔitɨ

blind, window nanabuni tsahparaʔ

blink wɨhtsobokitɨ

blister ekawɨkwiapɨ

bloat pohtokitɨ

bloated pohtohkikatɨ

blond pabopitɨ

blood pɨɨ-, pɨɨhpi

bloodhound tɨrayaa sarii

bloom mubɨtsaakatɨ, totsiyaitɨ

blooming totsiyakatɨ

blossom out totsiyaitɨ

blow nɨetɨ

blow away poʔayaahkwarɨ,
poʔayaakɨtɨ

blow (breath) puuhkitɨ

blow (dust) huhkukwɨnɨrɨ,
huukukwɨmɨrɨ, huukunatsirɨ,
huukunɨetɨ

blow (hard) kɨhtáanɨetɨ

blow heat toward one kusɨwetɨ

blow out (a tire) tɨrapɨtsarɨ W

blow (the nose) mubisitɨ,
tsamukɨsitɨ

blower, blacksmith's tɨbuuhkiʔ

Blow-it-away Pooʔaikɨ

blowing, cease nɨemaitɨ

Blowing-wind Nɨetɨtsi

blown out puuhkikatɨ, pɨhtsapɨ

blown-away object poʔoyaʔ

blue ebi-, eebi

blue, dark tuʔebipitɨ K

blue, light ebipitɨ, kusipi W,
kusiebipitɨ K

blue-gray ebipitɨ

bluebird ebihuutsuuʔ

bluejay ebihuutsuuʔ

bluestem, little ekasonipɨ

board woobi

board, cradle- waakohno

board, ironing pɨpaʔakura tɨrahkwɨʔneʔenạ

board someone tɨkiihkarɨ

boast naníhpanaʔaitɨ

boat pawobi puukụ W

bob a tail piʔtoʔarɨ

bob up kunakɨarɨ K, kuroʔitɨ W, mɨroʔitɨ

bobby pin papị tsihtɨpɨkaʔ

bobcat tɨe tɨmakupaʔ

bobtailed piʔto

bodily jerk yɨʔyɨturɨ

body tuhkụ

body, break at joint of narominaitɨ, tominarɨ

body, dead tɨyaipɨ

body, dry off pasarɨ

body, powder the homopisarɨ

body, rub medicine on mabararɨ

body, sprain a joint of the wɨkwɨsarɨ

body, stretch arms or narurerɨ

body (to draw out pain), suck on musoopitɨ

body on the ground, throw kwanuʔitɨ K

body, twist the kwitsunairɨ

body louse saabe busia

body pain nɨhtsikwarɨ

bogged down yubutsɨhkatɨ

boil kuhnuʔitɨ W, noʔyaikɨtụ, saatɨ

boil, cause to saaʔarɨ

boil food karɨkɨrɨ

boiled kuhnuʔitɨ W

boiled food nasaapɨ

boiled meat saapɨ

bois d'arc tree ohahuupi

bois d'arc wood etɨhuupi

bois d'arc wood for archery bows eetɨ

boll, cotton wanama sɨapɨha pokopị W

bolt, un- wɨhkweʔyarɨ

bolt down wɨʔnikarɨ

bone tsuhni

Bone Tsuhni

bone, break nawɨhkobaitɨ, nɨɨminaitɨ

bone, break a kɨminarɨ, nasutamɨ wɨmịnaitɨ K

bone, cheek- soʔo tsuhnị, soʔọ

bone, collar huukụ, sihkupɨ W

bone, shin or shin kutsiʔomo

bone, shin- tuhhu

bone, shoulder tsoohpa tsuuni W

bone, tail piwoʔsạ

bone marrow tuhhu rɨhkapɨ

bone marrow, congealed tɨɨhtsohpeʔ

bone marrow, eat tuhhu rɨhkarɨ

bones, Comanche nɨmɨ tsuhni

bones, leg tɨranạ

bones, marrow tɨranạ

bones out of joint, pull tsahtokoʔarɨ

bonnet, war pia tsoʔnikaʔ

-bonnet bag, war tuna wosa

book, pocket- puhihwi narɨsọ W, puhihwi wosa K

book, story- nanáarɨmuʔị tɨboopɨ, narɨmuʔi tɨboopɨ

boomer, mountain ebimuutarooʔ, ebipabokoʔaiʔ P

boots, cowboy kuhtsu taibo napɨ, narakwɨsakatɨ napɨ

boots, rubber tuuʔre napɨ

bore nihtunetsɨkatɨeʔ

born tɨbora

born, be pahitị, yumarɨ

born, Comanche- nɨmɨ ruaitɨ

both subeʔ

bottle otɨ aawọ, paboko aawo

bottom kwiita, tɨkwita

bottom in water, sink to the paʔikarɨ

-bought food, store tuku tumuupu
bounce wohtsawukitu
bouncy object, pull a tsahpo?tsaru
bow (for shooting arrows) eetu
box koono, wosa
box, ice- tahka aawo
boy tuinuhpu? W
Boy Pi?opu paruba tuyo
boy, water tuu?etu
boy friend tuu?urapu W, K
boys pihi?a W
brace maruroonitu
brace (with something)
  wuhturoonitu
braced marurooniitu K,
  tohturooniitu W
bracelet ma?witsohko
bracing stick wana tsihparaa?
brag (on oneself) naníhpana?aitu
brag (on someone) nihpana?aitu
braid aawusipu, aawusitu, kwisikatu
  K, tukwusiitu
braided kwusipu W
brain kupisi
brains, rub with kupisi?aru
branch mooka
branch, creek nabatai K
branch of a creek atahunubi
branch out mookusuaitu
brand kohpooru, nakohpoopu K,
  tukohpoopu
branding iron tukohpoo?
brave tekwuniwapi
brave, Indian tekwuniwapi,
  tuibihtsi?, tuetekwuni wapi
brave young man tuetekwuni wapi
bread tohtía?
bread, corn haninookopu
bread, fried yuhu nohkopu
bread, fry- yuhu nohkopu
bread, Indian turanu
bread, loaf of paanu

bread, make tohtía?aru
bread, sweet pihná nohkopu
bread, toast wesikuru
breadroot turanu
breadroot, Indian ekahkoni
breads, sweet toyo tahka?miitsa
break tahpomi?itu, tsahpomi?itu
break (a bone) kuminaru, nasutamu
  wuminaitu K
break (a horse) masuyu?ikaru K
break (a taboo) mahyaru
break (at joint of body)
  narominaitu, tominaru
break (at joint of foot)
  naraminaitu W
break (at the joint) taminaitu
break bone nawuhkobaitu,
  nuuminaitu
break (by dropping) wutubaru
break, Easy-to- Tsaa tsopa?
break hand or lower arm, sprain
  or namaminaitu
break, wind- wuhturu?aipu
break in pieces, (cause to)
  tahtaba?itu
break in pieces tahbaitu,
  tahporooru
break into pieces tsanutsaru,
  wunutsaru
break into small pieces
  wuhhomonutsa?aru
break loose pihka?aru
break off tahkobaru, tsahka?aru,
  tsahkobaru
break off a piece tsanutsaru
break open maputsaru, taputsaitu
break open (with the teeth)
  kuputsaru
break or reach something
  wuminaru
break or sever (with the teeth)
  kuhkobaru

break something kʉminarʉ, tahparʉ, tatʉbarʉ

break something down pihkobarʉ

break something up tohkobiʔitʉ, tsahkokarʉ

break up kohparʉ, manutsaʔarʉ W, wʉhkobarʉ

break up (under own volition) naʔrʉbomitʉ

break up (with the teeth) kʉnutsarʉ

breakfast, eat taarʉhkarʉ

breakfast for someone, prepare taamahkarʉ

breaking it to pieces, sit on something pinutsarʉ

Breaks Something Tsihkoba

breast, woman's pitsii?

breath sua, suahkena̱

breath odor sua kwana̱

breath, out of suaʔsuʔmaitʉ

breathe suahketʉ

breathe (deeply in sleep) ʉsuaketʉ

breathe (deeply while awake) nasuawʉhkitʉ K

breathe heavily hehékitʉ, suaʔsuaʔmiarʉ

breathe through nose muhibitʉ

breathe, unable to suaʔsuʔmaitʉ

breathless suaʔsuʔmakatʉ

breeze nʉetʉ

brew coffee huba aikʉtʉ

Briar Creek Tamutʉsoʔi̱ hunuʔbi̱

briar, sensitive tsapʉsikʉ

brick, red ekatʉʉpi̱

brick house, stone or tʉpi kʉni

bride narʉahwʉkʉ, nʉrʉaʔwekʉ?

bridge posaaki

bridle arai, tʉpe tsaʔnika?

bridle a horse tʉpe tsaʔnikarʉ

bridle bit namutsora?, tʉʉyʉ mutsora? K

bridle reins narʉmuhkʉ̱

bright muhatsi, pahparatsihkweetʉ W, tsaa marabetoikatʉ K

bright red mohatsʉkuekapi̱tʉ

brim, filled to the ibuʔitʉ

bring back firewood kono honiitʉ

bring in firewood konóorʉ

bring out tsahtoʔirʉ

bring something back (to someone) yaakʉrʉ

bristle sʉroonitʉ

broke financially tʉtsuʔmapʉ̱

broken nuhtsapʉ̱, pʉhtsapʉ̱

broken object kohpapʉ̱, tahpapʉ̱

broken up makoobikatʉ̱, naʔrʉbomitʉ̱

brooch natsihtʉpʉ̱ka?, nʉna karʉkʉ? K

broom tʉʉnua?

broom corn tʉʉnua?

broom grass tʉʉnua

broomweed sanaweha

brother samohpʉ?

brother, elder pabi?

brother, younger tami?

brother-in-law pʉhʉ reʔtsi̱

brother-in-law, man's tetsi̱

brothers, dear little tamihtsiʔbenihtsi?

brother's child, woman's paha?

brown koropi̱tʉ, otʉ-, otʉpi̱tʉ W

brown, cook something otʉ kwasʉkʉrʉ

brown, looks- kurupitsoni

brown food wesikʉrʉ

brown sugar otʉ pihnàa? W

brown the food otʉ kwasʉkʉrʉ

Brown-robe Otʉ kwasu

brown-skinned otʉhtʉ mapoʔakatʉ

browned wesikatʉ

bruise nʉʉki̱tse?

bruise wʉhpekwitʉ

brush arbor hʉʉki?aitʉ, puhi hʉʉki̲, soni hʉʉki, tahʉʉki?aikʉ

brush arbor, poles for constructing hʉʉkina huupi̲

brush, clothes oo?rʉ tʉtsi̲htu?ye? W

brush, hair- natsihtu?ye?

brush, horn aanatsihtuye?

brush, horse tʉhʉya natsihtu?ye?

brush, tooth- tamamatsuma?

brush, wire puhihwi natsihtu?ye?

brush off kwʉsiberʉ W, wʉsiberʉ K

brush something off (of oneself) nʉʉhta?neerʉ

bubble mubohtohkipʉ

bubble in water pamukwarʉ?rʉkitʉ

bubbles, make pamukwarʉ?rʉkitʉ

buck arʉkáa kuhma, arʉka? nʉkuhma

buck off ku?e wʉnʉrʉ

bucket wihtua?, wobi wʉhpai K

bucket, milk pitsipʉ wihtua

bucket (with spout) tʉpe wihtua?

buckle nanʉʉhtʉpʉka?, nʉna wʉhtʉpʉka?, wʉhtʉpʉka?

buckle, harness nʉʉhtʉpi̲ka?

buckle (or tighten something) tsanʉkʉrʉ

buckle (that is buckled) natsihpʉsa?

buckskin pikapʉ

buckskin clothing pika namʉsoopʉ

buckskin horse na?nia

buckskin jacket, man's pika kwasu?

bud mubora?itʉ

bud (of a plant or tree) murora?ipʉ W

bud, red- ekamurora?i huupi

buckle, belt- nehki wʉhtʉpʉka?, nʉ?ʉnehki?a nanʉʉtʉpi̲ka? W

buffalo nʉmʉ kuhtsu?, ta?si?woo?

Buffalo Tatsiwóo

-buffalo, Red Eka kura

buffalo blanket ta?siwoo wana?ʉhʉ W

buffalo calf ekakúura?

Buffalo Eaters Kuhtsu tʉhka

buffalo horn case na?aa

buffalo meat nʉmʉ kutsu tʉhkapʉ, ta?siwoo rʉhkapʉ W

Buffalo-hump Kuhtsuna kwahipʉ

buffalo, One-who-rides- Kuhtsunu kwahipʉ

bug ʉnʉ́?

bug, doodle- kwita maropona

bug (of any kind), house kahni busi̲?a

bug, june tuʉnʉʉ?

bug, lightning kuna na?mahpee?

bug, red- puikʉso

bug, sow- kwita maropona

buggy pikwʉsii?, wobi puukʉ

buggy, baby na?tsi?aikʉ?

buggy, hitch up horses and nomohkarʉ

buggy, hook up doubletrees on nomohkarʉ

buggy, one-horse sʉmasʉ nooi K

buggy, single tʉe waikina̲

buggy, two-seated natsa?ani?

bugle woinu

build a fire kohtóorʉ

build a house kahni?aitʉ

build a nest pisona?aitʉ

builder, fire- kohtoo wapi̲

building tʉboo kahni

bull pimoroo?a kuhma̲

-bull-bear, Son-of Tʉmʉbo

bull elk parʉa kuhma

Bull-bear Parʉa kuhma

Bull-elk Paruwa kumá̲

bullet nabaaka̲

bullfrog ebimuura ya?ke?

bullroarer wekʉbupʉ

bumblebee ohahpiyaa?
bumpy popᵤtsanawᵤtᵤ
bunch up tsa?ookitᵤ, tsa?oorᵤ
bunched up nara?okatᵤ
bundle or round knot, tie in round wᵤhtopᵤ?noorᵤ
bundle together wᵤhtamarᵤ
bureau oo?rᵤ tani?i?
burial ceremony nᵤpᵤkarᵤᵤ?
burial mound nabᵤkapᵤ W
buried person or thing namᵤsokoopᵤ
burn kutsi̲tonarᵤ, we?harᵤ
burn down kuhtsu?marᵤ
burn oneself nahweakᵤtᵤ W, nakᵤwi̲yakᵤrᵤ K
burn oneself to death kuhtᵤyarᵤ
burn red ekawehaarᵤ
burn something up kuhtsahwirᵤ, wesikᵤrᵤ
burn to death accidentally kuhkuparᵤ
burned wesi-
Burned Meat Ihtata?o
burned out tree trunk kuwo?nepᵤ
burns, ouch! It ᵤrᵤᵤ
burnt wesikatᵤ
burp akwarᵤtᵤ, akwarᵤ?
burr kuhtsu pokàa?
burr, grass soni wokweebi
burrow kahnitaikᵤ
burrowing owl pohkóo?
burst pohto?itᵤ, pᵤhtsapᵤ, pᵤhtsarᵤ, tsapᵤtsarᵤ
burst by pulling tsahpohtoorᵤ
burst from overheating kupᵤtsarᵤ
burst, make tohpᵤtsa?itᵤ
burst open mapᵤtsarᵤ, puhkarᵤ
burst with the mouth kᵤhpohtorᵤ
bury pasoko?arᵤ, pᵤka, tᵤkarᵤ
bury someone nᵤpᵤkarᵤ
bus nᵤmi noo?etᵤ

bush puhitopi̲ka
bush W puhi taitᵤ
bush, blackberry tuhbanatsaya
bush, button- pesotái
bush clover puhi tubi
bush, plum wi?nᵤᵤpi̲
bush, skunk- tatsipᵤ
busy nanᵤso?iitᵤ W
butcher tᵤhaniitᵤ, tᵤkwᵤsᵤrᵤ
butcher an animal tᵤbehkarᵤ
butt mukwᵤrᵤ W
butter yuhu bitsipᵤ
butter, Comanche tᵤhtsohpe?aipᵤ
butter, Indian tᵤᵤtsohpepᵤ
butter, make Comanche tᵤhtsohpe?arᵤ
buttermilk nᵤtsᵤ?wᵤpa̲ pitsipᵤ K, yuhibitsipᵤ K
buttocks kwiita
button nanᵤᵤhtᵤpᵤka?, nᵤᵤhtᵤpi̲ka?, wᵤhtᵤpᵤka?
button, peyote plant or wokwe
button snakeroot atabitsᵤnoi
button up wᵤhtᵤpᵤkarᵤ
buttonbush pesotái
buy tᵤmᵤᵤrᵤ
buy an article of clothing kwasu?ᵤ tᵤmᵤᵤrᵤ
buy clothing oyorᵤ tᵤmarᵤ
buy (for oneself) mahípᵤrᵤmᵤrᵤ
buy or otherwise receive groceries narᵤhka?ruarᵤ
buy something marᵤ́mᵤrᵤ
buzzard, redheaded ekabapi̲
buzzing sound puuyaketᵤ
by describing something, tempt nisuyakeetᵤ
by force, take someone sutena betᵤ
by going on foot, meet someone tamunaikᵤmi?arᵤ
by hand, shell something tsahkíto?arᵤ

by pounding, soften tohparaarɨ W,
tsohkwe K

**by trampling on it, soften
something** tahpararɨ

-by-two, two waʔwaʔ

by someone, spilled taʔokitɨ

by a foot, torn tasiʔkwaitɨ

by speaking to someone, waken
nihtɨbuniorɨ

by cheating, win in a contest
kaakwakurɨ

C c

cabbage kabitsi̱

cache kuupɨ̱, kuurɨ

Cache, Okla Pisi narɨmɨɨʔ

cactus ekamitsáaʔ, husi̱,
nayɨ́wokwe

cactus, prickly pear wokwéesi

Caddo people Tukanai

cake pihná nohkopɨ̱

calendar mɨarɨboopɨ̱

calf pimorooʔa tuaʔ

calf, buffalo ekakúuraʔ

calf (of leg) taʔwiitsa̱

calico horse pitsa nabooʔ K

call down nihmakwihtserɨ

call (to someone) nimaikatɨ̱

call together many people
sɨɨmaʔokarɨ

called one nimaihkanaʔ

calm kesósoorɨ, tokoboʔniitɨ̱ K,
wɨhtsamɨɨhkikatɨ̱, yunaharɨ

calm, become nɨemaitɨ

calm down tɨsuʔnarɨ, wɨyupaʔnitɨ

calm spirit tsɨmɨki̱katɨ̱

camel mupitsɨ̱ha tɨnowapi̱ W,
narɨnookatɨ ɨnɨɨ, tɨnookatɨʔ,
tɨɨnoo ɨnɨɨʔ K, ɨnɨʔa pɨnɨsɨ
narɨnooʔkatɨ W

camera kobe naboʔ K, nɨmi booʔetɨ
W, pɨhtuku nɨmɨ, tɨbooʔetɨ W

camp (apart from the main group)
nokaʔitɨ̱

camp bed wɨhtaráaʔ

can narohtɨmaʔ

can, coon soo tɨhimarɨʔ

can, kick-the- soo tɨhimarɨʔ **can,
milk** pitsipɨ̱ wihtua

can opener kɨmapɨ̱, tɨrohtɨwaʔ

Canadian River Waahunuʔbi

cancer narɨʔɨyɨ̱ ɨɨʔaʔ

cancerous moonɨʔɨakatɨ

candle tosahtukaʔ W, tosa yuhu
rukaiʔ K

candy sucker mubi̱ tsooʔniʔ,
mukwiteʔ

cane natsihtóoʔ K

cane, sugar huupi̱hnàa, soni
bihnáaʔ

cane, walk with natsihtóo noorɨ

cane, walking tɨʔehkooiʔ W

canned food tɨrohtɨmapɨ̱

canned goods narohtɨmaʔ

cannon yanawoʔiʔ

canoe pawobi puukɨ̱ W, sahki̱

canoe paddle panatsitooʔ

cantaloupe taibo bihnaaʔ

canvas tent nɨɨsooʔ

cap tɨmuihpaaʔ W

cap, fur pɨhɨ rɨmuihpaaʔ

cape, mourning kuʔnikaʔ

cape, nurse kuʔhibooʔ

captive kwɨhɨpɨ̱

capture kwɨhɨrɨ

**captured by the Comanches,
Mexicans** Esitoyanɨɨ

car, hand- kɨʔwonɨhɨbai

car or team, drive a (by hand)
tsahhanitɨ

car, railroad kunawaikinɨ,
kunawobipuukɨ̱

car, street- ohawaikina, waikina
carcass, render an animal
tuhtsohpeʔaru
card deck, king in playing-
ohahkuyaaʔ
card game, full house in
manekihtu?
cardinal ekahuutsu?
cards, play wana rohpetiru
cards, playing wana atsi?
care for mabitsiaru,
mananaaʔwaihkaru
care for (child) turuetusuaru
care for (needs of someone)
tukiihkaru
care for (oneself) namabitsiapu
carefree supewaitu
carefully, listen tubitsinakukuru K
carefully for, search puhwaaitu
carefully, set down tsakwunaru
carelessly, hang up wuhtsanitu
carpenter's plane tusibe?
carpet puhu rasoona, tasoni, tasoona
carriage tuwaikina
carried on back manookatu
carrier made of teepee poles,
travel tuʔnoo?
carrot, domestic ohahpokopi K,
ohahtuhkapu
carry manooru, toyaarukitu W
carry a container by the handle
tsahimaru, tsayaru
carry a stick huuyaaru
carry (across) noomanitu,
tsamaniru
carry (and put down) tohtaniʔitu
carry away nookwaru
carry (by the handle) natsayaaru
carry food tuku nooru
carry in himaʔikaru
carry in arms toyaru
carry in the arms kwabaru

carry in the claws taʔyaamiʔaru
carry load tunooru
carry on back nunooru
carry on the back kwahi nooru
carry on the head kuyaaru
carry someone behind on
horseback piyaru
carry something tsiʔyaru,
yuhnunimiʔaru
carry something on a stick
tsihimaru
carry something on the head
tsoʔyaaru
Carrying-her-sunshade Hukiyani
case, buffalo horn naʔaa
case, rawhide wardrobe
natusakuna
cash a check puhihwi yaaru
casino pepikuru
casket tuyaipu kohno
cat waʔoo?
cat, wild- matusohpe?
cat's tail pisibuni?
catalpa pihúura huupi
catch kwuhuru, tahhimaʔeru
catch something with the mouth
kuhtsakaru
catch up with tahtsaitu, wuhpitu
catfish, fullgrown tuumoʔtso?
catfish, young tuumeʔso
Catholic person Suabi puharaibo
cattail pisibuni?
cattle kuutsu? K
cattleman kuhtsu taibo?
caught tumuʔnikatu
cauldron saawihtua
cause to kiss tsamuhraikutu
cause to be killed nabehkakuru
cause to blow nose wumupusitu
cause to boil saaʔaru
cause to break in pieces tahtabaʔitu
cause to cry wuyaketu

cause to hurry tsanamʉsohnitʉ
cause to protrude manakʉarʉ
cause to return tsahkooʔitʉ
cause to ring tsayaketʉ
cause to run wʉmiʔarʉ W
cause to sneeze tsamupʉsitʉ W
cause to stop tsanʉnʉrʉ
cause to tangle kwisihkarʉ
cause to turn around and come
   back tsahkooʔitʉ
cause to turn something around
   tsakwʉhburʉ
caused to turn around
   tsakwʉhwitʉ
caused to worry tsamʉsasuakatʉ
cave kahni tai, taina
cease blowing nʉemaitʉ
cease doing pʉarʉ
cedar waa-, waapi
cedar, red ekawaapi
celebrate Christmas waahimarʉ
celery paʔpuhi tʉhka?
cellar sekwikʉni, sokokʉni
cellar, cyclone (tornado) ohta
   kahni W
cellar, storm ohta kahni W,
   sekwikʉni, sokokʉni
cement mawoʔaʔaiyʉ
cemetery nʉpʉkʉ sokoobi
cemetery (or graveyard) nʉpʉkapʉ
   K, W, nʉpʉkʉ sokoobi
center tʉpʉnaatʉ
centipede soo moʔo?
cents, fifty sʉkweebi?
cereal taarʉhkapʉ
cereal, cooked kohtsáa?
ceremony, burial nʉpʉkarʉʉ?
ceremony, curing puhaʔaitʉ
ceremony (for someone), hold a
   curing puhaʔarʉ
ceremony, smoke during religious
   puha bahmuʔitʉ

certain plant (with edible tuber)
   tsunisʉ
chain nabusa?
chain, watch tabe narʉmuhkʉ, tabe
   wenuakʉ?
chair nakarʉ? W
chair, rocking nabiʔaaikʉnakarʉ K
chair, wooden wobi nakarʉ?
change clothes namʉsoarʉ
change from one position to
   another nuhyʉyukitʉ
change position yʉmʉhkitʉ
change something, shape or
   wʉmʉʉrʉ
channel water patsanuarʉ
chap tsiʔwaʔitʉ
chaparral cock ebikuyuutsi?
chapped tsiʔwapʉ
charcoal kuhtuubi K
charcoal, cook over kuhtu
   tʉkʉmanirʉ K
chase miakʉrʉ, miakʉtʉ K
chase away tanuraakʉtʉ
chase on horseback tomakwʉyetʉ W
chase someone makwiyetʉ
chased makwiyetʉ
chatter tsaati tamakatʉ W
chatter, harass by nimʉsasuarʉ
chatter the teeth kʉʉhtarakiitʉ
chattering teeth saatitamakatʉ
cheat kaabehkarʉ, kaahaniitʉ,
   tʉtsikwʉsarʉ
cheat, intend to deceive or
   kaasuarʉ
cheater kaayʉkwitʉ
cheating, defeat by kaakwakurʉ
cheating, win in a contest by
   kaakwakurʉ
check puhihwi tʉboopʉ
check, cash a puhihwi yaarʉ
check over one's appearance
   nabuihwʉnʉtʉ W

cheek so?o̱
cheekbone so?o tsuhni̱, so?o̱
cheese ko?abitsi̱pu̱
cheese, cottage tu̱manu̱ku?wetu̱
chest nu̱napu̱
chest, hairy pu̱hu̱ nu̱napu̱
chest, side of ahna, ama-
chest hair pu̱hu̱ nu̱napu̱
chest of drawers oo?ru̱ tani?i̱?
chest pain, suffer amawu̱nu̱tu̱
chestnut-brown horse otu̱ ku̱ma? W
chew ku̱tsu̱kwetu̱, ku̱yu?netu̱
chew gum sanahkoo ku̱yu?netu̱
chew up fine W ku̱hpomi?itu̱
Chew-up Ku̱tsu̱kwipu̱
chewing gum ku̱tsu̱we?,
   sanahkoo? W
chewing tobacco yokabahmu̱
Cheyenne Sarii Tu̱hka?
Chickasaw plum tu̱ahpi̱
chicken kokorá?a
chicken, prairie pakawkoko?
chicken coop kokorá?a kahni
chicken egg kokorá?a nooyo̱,
   kokorá?a atùapu̱
chicken hawk kokorá?a
   aràhima?etu̱
chicken pox kokorá?a tasi?a
chicken wire kokorá?a aru̱htu̱ma?
chief paraiboo?
Chief Comanche-dog-soldiers
   Tu̱oyobisesu̱
chief, peace paraibo
chief wife among multiple wives
   paraiboo?
chigger puiku̱so
child tu̱ehpu?ru̱, tu̱e?tu̱, tu̱ru̱e,
   tu̱ru̱ehpu̱ children tu̱ru̱ehpu̱
child, care for tu̱ru̱etu̱suaru̱
child, eldest nahnapu̱
child, keep an orphan as foster
   tahnikatu̱, tu̱kiihkaru̱

child, rear a manu̱aru̱
-child, Sky Tomo?a tua?
child to back, tie a wu̱pitooru̱
child, woman's brother's paha?
childbirth, labor in nu̱htsikwaru̱
children tu̱ru̱ehpu̱
children, have tu̱ru̱etuparu̱
chili pepper tsiira?
chill su̱u̱tsu̱nitu̱
chilly su̱suatu̱
chimney tuka?a naku?e W
chimney, lamp tuka?a naku?e W
chin paru̱u̱tsi̱
Chinese Ku?e kwu̱sih taibo?
chip, poker tuhhuu?
chip in tu̱maramiitu̱
chip off nu̱u̱pearu̱, si?aru̱
chippaberry tubupokoo
chips kunapi̱so?ni̱
chisel topu̱kaaru̱, tu̱tsiyu?i?
chisel or split with an axe
   tohtsiyu?itu̱
chisel something tohpakuru̱
chisel wood tohtsi?aru̱ K
choke paabitsanitu̱, pitsanitu̱
choke out puhi tu̱yaitu̱
choke to death pitsanu̱ tu̱yaitu̱
choke to death by rope around the
   neck oihtu̱yaitu̱
choked makuhpu̱katu̱
choose nabinaru̱
chop koo?itu̱, tu̱u̱hka?aru̱
chop a hole wu̱hkonaru̱
chop down wu̱hkaru̱, wu̱hpomi?itu̱,
   wu̱no?itu̱, wu̱?aniru̱
chop firewood kuhkeru̱
chop up wu̱hhaniru̱
chosen nabinaihkatu̱
Christian Nabakwu̱htiapu̱, Pu?ekatu̱
Christmas waahima?
Christmas, celebrate waahimaru̱
chronic moonu̱?u̱akatu̱

chronic sore narʉʔʉyʉ ʉʉʔaʔ

chuck, wood- huunaʔ, paʔarai moʔo

church puha kahni

church root itsa, timʉihʉʔ

church service puha niwʉnʉrʉʉ K

cider, hard saah totsi baa

cider, sweet amawóoʔa pàa

cigarette, marijuana nʉmi makwinumaʔetʉ pahmu

cigarette-wrapper plant tʉmakwatuiʔ

cigarettes, leaf wrappers for puhi tʉmakwatubiʔ

circles, go in mahoinitʉ

circular toponiwekí

circulation, restore wʉsuabetaitʉ

circus nohihtaibooʔnʉʉ

circus people nohihtaibooʔnʉʉ

clabber nʉkuwʉmiʔarʉ, nʉkuʔwʉpʉ, pitsi pʉha nʉkuʔwʉpʉ

clabbered milk nʉtsʉʔwʉpa̱ pitsipʉ K, pitsi pʉha nʉkuʔwʉpʉ

clack the teeth kʉhkwitsitʉ

claim it!, I aahe

clam waʔkooʔ W

clap hands tohtarakitʉ

claw tasiito̱

claw, devil's aakáaʔ

claw at something tsahkwanitʉ

claws, carry in the taʔyaamiʔarʉ

clean tutʉtsaai wahtʉ

clean, scrape until wʉhtsuʔmarʉ

clean the inner part wʉhkwinarʉ

clear kenanawatsitʉ, pabo-, pabokaʔaitʉ

clear a path puʔeʔarʉ

clear, crystal pabokopi̱tʉ

clear stream pahtsi okweʔ

clear throat nanihkanuitʉ

cleaver tʉkʉ wʉhpomiʔ

clerk tʉrʉʔai wapi̱

click kʉtubarʉ W

cliff tʉbanaaʔ

Cliff Tʉpanai

climb down soho weerʉ

climb on horseback tʉhʉya roʔitʉ

climb out kʉarʉ

climb up soho roʔitʉ

cling to tsahpaki̱tʉ

clock tabe-

clock flower tabetotsiyaa

clog up wʉhtʉmarʉ

close marʉmarʉ, tsahtsukitʉ, tsahtʉmarʉ

close everyone's eyes sʉmʉ ʉhtsumitʉ

close someone's hand mahtsukitʉ

close the eyes ʉhtsumarʉ

close the hand mahtsokaitʉ

close the mouth kʉhtsuukarʉ

close up mamárʉmarʉ, tahtʉmarʉ

close up with hand marohtʉmarʉ

closed off tohtʉmapʉ

cloth matsumaʔ, wana-, wanapʉ K

cloth, dust- tʉmatsumaʔ W

cloth, table tʉkʉ soona̱

cloth, velvet pʉesúubeʔ K

cloth, wash- tʉehna matsumaʔ

cloth (edged with ribbon or lace) tʉkʉmaʔaitʉʔ

cloth (for wiping tʉmatsumaʔ) W

cloth cover sona, soona̱

cloth patch tʉkarʉkʉpʉ

clothes namahku, wanapʉ K

clothes, wear out wʉkwiʔarʉ

clothes brush ooʔrʉ tʉtsi̱htuʔyeʔ W

clothes closet ooʔrʉ kahni W

clothes hanger kwasuʔu sakweni, ooʔrʉ tohtsanaʔ W

clothesline tʉrohtsaniʔiʔ

clothesline pole ooʔrʉ tohtsaniʔiʔana huuhpi, tʉtsapara huupi

clothesline rope soni wiyaaʔ, wana kotse tsahparaaʔ K

clothing namusoapu, oo?ru W
clothing, buckskin pika namusoopu
clothing, buy oyoru tumaru
clothing, buy an article of kwasu?u
  tumuuru
clothing, iron turah kwu?neru K
clothing, opening in kuruupe
clothing, own an article of
  kwasu?ukatu K
clothing, wear warm yu?a
  namusooru
cloud tomo-, tomopu 2
cloud up tomo?akitu
clouds tomoobi
cloudy tomoakatu W
clover, bush puhi tubi
clover, prairie yuu sonipu
clover, purple prairie pakeeso
club kasamaaru, wahta
club, billy tuhkupa?
club, war wupitapu?ni
club someone wahtóoru
club someone (or something)
  wuhtokwuru
club something wuhtokwutu
clubbed ones wuhtokwe?
cluck kokorá?a yaketu K
clump of grass K puhi taitu
clump of trees huukabatu
clumsily, waddle or move
  masu?wa?nekitu
coal kutuhuubi W
coal mine kutuhubihtaa ohweetu
coal oil tuka?a nabaa
coal shovel kutuhuyuna? W
Coals-in-a-wood-fire Kuhtu
coat kwasu?u
coat, fur puhu kwusu?u
coax someone nihpitukuru
cob, corn- haniwo?ora K
cock, chaparral ebikuyuutsi?
cocklebur kuhtsu pokàa?

cockscomb tsopekwiiyu W
coconut kwasi taiboo?a
  na?kuhtabai, kwasi taiboo?a
  tuhkapu
cocoon u?bui?
coffee huba, huuba?
coffee, brew huba aikutu
coffee, drink hubebitu
coffee, make huba aitu
coffeepot huba aawo?
coil maropo?naru
coil, or wuhkwatubi
coil, un- purusu?aru
coil something, un- wuhpukusuaru
coin purse puhihwi naruso W
coins ekapuhihwi, tosahpuhihwi
cold utsu?itu
cold, be kwihneru
cold, die of the suhtuyaitu
cold feet, have tasukumitu
cold, shake from tsihturuaru W
cold, shiver from tsihturuaru W
cold, tremble [shiver] with
  suutsunitu
cold, turn kwihneru
colic, baby sapu wunukatu
collarbone huuku, sihkupu W
collect money tuniwaitu
collector, bill tuniwaitu?
collector, tax tuniwaitu?
college pia tubookuni
Colorado River Tahka hunu?bi
color, dark tupisibitu
color, gold ekahwi
color, red eka-
color, slate esipitu
color of ashes (gray) kusi-
color, yellow oha-
colored, cream tosa ohapitu
colored, dust- koropitu
colored, multi- wanatsihtaraa?
colt puku rúa?

Colt Puku?a tua?

column, spinal kwahiporopʉ

Comanche, interpreter of nʉmʉ rekwakʉ wapi

Comanche band Kwarʉ, Nokoni, Tʉtsanoo yehkʉ

Comanche band of Walters area Wia?nʉʉ

Comanche bones nʉmʉ tsuhni

Comanche butter tʉhtsohpe?aipʉ

Comanche butter, make tʉhtsohpe?arʉ

Comanche man nʉmʉ renahpʉ?

Comanche perfume plant nʉmʉ rʉsaasi

Comanche young man nʉmʉ ruibihtsi?

Comanche-born nʉmʉ ruaitʉ

Comanches Parukaa

Comanches, Mexicans captured by the Esitoyanʉʉ

Comanches of Tejas), Proud People (Wichita name for Natai

comatose sua watsikʉ

comatose, become sua watsikatʉcomb natsihtu?ye?

comb natsihtu?ye?

comb, animal horn aanatsihtuye?

comb, curry- tʉhʉya natsihtu?ye?

comb, fine-toothed pusi?a natsihtu?ye?

comb, honey- ʉnʉ bihnaa kahni K, wobi pihnaa? W

comb, metal puhihwi natsihtu?ye?

comb, side papi tsi?nika?

comb, wooden huunatsihtu?ye?

comb hair natsihtu?yeetʉ, tsihtu?yerʉ

comb someone's hair matsíhtuyeetʉ P

come kimarʉ, sʉmʉ nokimarʉ

-come, Refuse-to Huuhwiya

come back ko?itʉ

come backwards pitsa ʉkwakatu kimarʉ

come moving along nokimarʉ

come onto someone nahabitʉtʉ

come open tʉhwaitʉ

come out kʉarʉ, to?itʉ

come out (at a particular place) kiahbitʉ, to?ibitʉ

come running nuraakitʉ

come slowly mahuinoorʉ

come this way ibʉniitʉ

come together na?akʉtʉ

come walking soko kimarʉ

Comes-often Soo pitenʉ

comfort an adult pʉhkaitʉniitʉ W

comforted pʉhkaikatʉ

command hanitʉnirʉ, ni?atsiitʉ

commander ni?atsiwapi?, tʉniatsikatʉ?

commit adultery na?isahanitʉ W

commit suicide nabakʉtʉ

common grass yuu sonipʉ

commotion nani?yʉsʉkaitʉ W

commotion, create a ni?yʉsʉkaitʉ

Communion pʉʉhibitu?itʉ, tohtía? rʉhkapʉ

Communion, partake of pʉʉhibirʉ

Communion wine pʉʉpi

compare (one thing with another) nahmakutʉ

compare with something ninʉkitʉ W

competition, gamble over some type of nararʉnarʉ

complain about someone natsamarʉ

complected, light- pabopitʉ

complete namahka?mukitʉ, pʉpe?, sʉmʉ makʉkatʉ

completed tamarʉkʉkatʉ

completely (adv) sʉmʉ

completely, pound sʉmʉ rayu?nerʉ

completely, rip sᵼmᵼ sihwarᵼ
completely, torn up tsasikwaitᵼ
completely, wipe off wᵼhtsu?marᵼ
conceited nabana?aitᵼ
conduct a peyote meeting
  wokwetᵼhkarᵼ
coneflower, purple tukunᵼ natsu̠
confess narᵼahwerᵼ
congealed bone marrow
  tᵼᵼhtsohpe?
congregate narahka?witᵼ,
  sᵼᵼma?aitᵼ, uhoi ka?wᵼtᵼ
congregate, invite to sᵼᵼma?okarᵼ
conscious suabetaikatᵼ
conscious, un- sua watsikᵼ
construct a house (or other
  building) kahni?aitᵼ
construct a road pu?e?arᵼ
constructing brush arbor, poles
  for hᵼᵼkina huupi̠
container aawo, awo-, koono̠,
  wihtua?
container, carry a (by the handle)
  tsahimarᵼ, tsayarᵼ
container, load into a to?nikarᵼ W
container, pull out of tsahpᵼyerᵼ
contest against someone, win in a
  tahni?arᵼ
contest by cheating, win in a
  kaakwakurᵼ
continue nahaniitᵼ, naharᵼ
continue along nayᵼkwiitᵼ
continue doing something
  naahkarᵼ
continue lying down naahábitᵼ
continue uncontrollably
  kenaninabenitᵼ
contract, make an agreement or
  nanipu?e?aitᵼ
control someone mᵼᵼrᵼ
convince someone tsasu?atsitᵼ
convulse esikooitᵼ, esitᵼyaitᵼ

cook karᵼkᵼrᵼ, kohtsáarᵼ, kwasᵼtᵼ
-cook corn soup, quick atakwá?sᵼ?
cook food tᵼkarᵼkᵼrᵼ
cook for someone tᵼkᵼ mahnitᵼ
cook, hired tᵼkᵼ maniwapᵼ
cook out marrow from bones
  tᵼrana?itᵼ
cook over charcoal kuhtu
  tᵼkᵼmanirᵼ K
cook something brown otᵼ
  kwasᵼkᵼrᵼ
cooked cereal kohtsáa?
cooked food kwasᵼkᵼpᵼ
cookie otᵼ tohtía?
cookies otᵼ nohkopᵼ W, pihná
  nohkopᵼ
cooking pot saawihtua
Cooks-dried-meat Kukapᵼ
cool sᵼsuatᵼ
cool, feel hᵼhtsawᵼkatᵼ
cool off hᵼᵼkatᵼ, hᵼᵼtsa?wetᵼ
cool off, allow to rest or sua
  soyuraperᵼ
coon paruuku?, pa?ruhku?
coon can soo tᵼhimarᵼ?
coop, chicken kokorá?a kahni
copper ohahpuhihwi
copy taka?arᵼ
cord, spinal kwahi kupi̠si̠
core something wᵼpiyarᵼ
corn hani-, haníibi̠
corn, broom tᵼᵼnua?
corn, ear of hani-, haníibi̠
corn, ground hanitusupᵼ
corn, Indian nᵼmᵼ hani
corn, parch kukᵼmerᵼ
corn, parched kukᵼmepᵼ
corn, pop- kuhmito?ai?, tahma
  yokake?
corn, quick-dried atakwa?sᵼ?aipᵼ
corn, roast atakwa?sᵼ?aitᵼ,
  hanikwasᵼkᵼrᵼ

corn, roasted atakwaʔsʉʔaipʉ
corn, squaw nʉmʉ hani
corn, toast hanikwasʉkʉrʉ
corn bread haninookopʉ
corn leaves hani buhipʉ
Corn People Hanitaibo
corn shucks hani buhipʉ
corn soup hanisahoba
corn soup, quick-cook atakwáʔsʉʔ
corncake, Indian nʉmʉ nohkopʉ
corncob haniwoʔora K
corner kii
cornmeal hanitusupʉ
cornmeal mush hanikotsapʉ, kooʔ
corpse tʉyaipʉ
cottage cheese tʉmanʉkuʔwetʉ
cotton blanket wana hʉ K
cotton boll wanama sʉapʉha pokopi W
cotton quilt wanạ soonạ
cottonwood soho obị, tahpookʉʔ, weʔyʉkʉ sohoobi K
cough ohnitʉ
cough, whooping tsʉʉʔtsʉkiʔ
cough hard tsʉʔtsʉkitʉ
council, hold kaʔwitʉ
counsel naniʔʉrʉʔaitʉ, tʉniʔatsitʉ, tʉsuʔʉrʉʔ
counsel, give tʉsuʔʉrʉ
counselor tʉniʔatsikʉ
count definite objects tʉtsʉrʉ
count something tʉrʉtsʉrʉ
country, foreign atʉsokoobi
country to settlement, open soko tsatʉwarʉ
couple, married nanakwʉhʉ W
cousin, same-sex haitsị
cover mamárʉmarʉ, marʉmarʉ, poʔaʔ, ʉhʉkʉrʉ
cover, cloth sona, soonạ
cover oneself ʉhʉkatʉ
cover over nʉʉkʉnarʉ

cover something hʉhkʉnarʉ, wʉhkʉnarʉ
cover something over W manaʔkoroomitʉ
cover the head K manaʔkoroomitʉ
cover up K tʉmarʉ
cover with earth pasokoʔarʉ
covered nabimarʉ, wʉhkʉnai, wʉhkʉnʉkatʉ
covered, earth- ohtakatʉ
covered, mud- sekwi nuyuʔịtʉ
covered wagon nakʉnikatʉ waikinạ
covering naboʔaa W
covering for teepees, skins or other nʉmʉkʉni
covet kwahisiʔa, nasuyaketʉ
covetous person kwahisiapʉ
cow kuhtsuʔ W, kuutsuʔ K, pimorooʔ, pimorooʔa piabʉ
cow, milk pitsipʉ pimoróoʔ W
cow, milk a tʉmaʔokwetʉ
cow, second stomach of sekwi biiʔ
Cow-dung Kuhtsu kwiʔta
cow's cud pimorooʔa tʉyʉʔwipʉ
cowardly pihisiʔapʉ
cowboy kuhtsu taiboʔ, pimoroo taibooʔ
cowboy boots kuhtsu taibo napʉ, narakwʉsakatʉ napʉ
cowhide pimoroʔa pʉhi
cowhide, dried paakipʉ
coyote kʉhtsayaʔyaʔkeʔ, kʉʔkwʉriaʔ, kʉʔtseena, ohaahnakatʉ W, tseenaʔ K
Coyote Kebakoweʔ
Coyote-droppings Ishatai
crab piʔnuʔaʔ
crab apple ekaamawooʔ, tʉe amawóoʔ
crab louse pʉhʉ pusia, suhu posía
crack porokarʉ
crack knuckles tsahporakitʉ

crack something marátụbaitụ, tahparụ, tapearụ, wụtụbarụ, wụ?ụaru?arụ

crack something by sitting on it pitụbarụ

crack something with hands marụbarụ

crack with the teeth kụtụbarụ

cracked of own accord tahpai

cracked skin tsi?wapụ W

cracker tosa rohtiya?

crackle kuhporákitụ, kukụbihkutụ

cradle koonọ, ohnáakụno?

cradle, black tuhkụni

cradle, day waakohno

cradleboard waakohno

cradleboard, day habikụno?

cram tsinụkụrụ

cram into limited space natsinụhkụrụ

crammed into limited space tsinụkụ

cramp, have (in hand) ma?wụtsa ro?ponitụ

cramp, have leg ta?itsa?bụrụ W, ta?witsa roponiitụ K

cramp (or spasm), have muscle toponitụ K

cramped hand ma?itsa?bụkatụ

crane kusikwa?aa?, pa?a toyokatụ huutsuu? K

crank wụ?aikụrụ

crave sweets pihná rụhkarụ

crawdad wa?roo koyáa?

crawfish wa?roo koyáa?

crawl wụhu?nerụ

crawl like a snake nuhyimi?arụ W

crawl on hands and knees mahu?netụ

crawl on knees tahu?nerụ

crazed poosubụkụkaitụ

crazy po?sa

crazy, go e?mụarụ, poosubụhkaitụ

crazy person poo?sa?

Crazy Warriors Pukutsi

Crazy-bear Isawụra

creak kụtsu?tsu?kitụ

cream pitsipụha po?aa, wihtụ?eka?

cream, face kobe kiihtụ?eka? W

cream, separate milk from yunarụ

cream colored tosa ohapitụ

crease takwụperụ

crease with the hands makwipunarụ K

create a commotion ni?yụsụkaitụ

creation nụmụ rụhorapụ

Creator Atsabi?

creature ụnú?

creek hunu?bị, okwèetụ

-creek, Rocky Tụpi wụnụ

Creek, Sand Pasiwa huunu?bi

Creek, Timber Huuhunu?bị

creek bank tụpána?

creek bed, overflow the paru?itụ

creek branch nabatai K

creep wụhu?nerụ

cremate kuhkuparụ

crib, baby ohna?a norụhnaa?

cricket tuhmekọ

crier, town tekwụniwapị

crippled wihnaitụ

criticize manímụarụ, tụnimakwihtserụ

croak tụụhkonarụ

crochet thread wana ramụ

crock tụpi aawo

crook, shepherd's tụ?ehkooi? W

crooked ono?itụ

-crooked-nose, Red Ekamurawa

crop, garden tụmụsụapụ

crop, harvest a pomarụ

crop, harvested pomapụ

crops, plant tụmụsụarụ

crops, planted tụrụnapụ

cross suaabe
cross over manitʉ
cross-eyed person pasapuni
crossing, river nagwee
crossing, wagon naʔwee?, puʔe
nagwe
croton weed kupisinamaya
crow tuwikaa?
crowbar tʉhora?, tʉkʉh kweʔya?
crowd wʉtsʉkitʉ
crowd many people together uhoi
kaʔwʉtʉ
crowd of people sʉʉmʉʔokʉ
crowd with people tsʉhkikatʉ
crowded tsinʉkʉ
crowded into narrow place
tsʉkikatʉ
crowded together narahtsʉkikatʉ
crowded while standing tahtsʉkitʉ
cruel tʉtsʉ-
crumble homonutsaitʉ,
manutsaʔarʉ W, tahnutsaʔerʉ
K, tohhomonutsarʉ
W, tsahhomonutsarʉ,
wʉhhomonutsaʔarʉ
crumble to powder mahomonutsarʉ
crumble to powder (with the foot)
tahhomonutsarʉ W
crumbled nuhtsaitʉ
crumbs tʉkʉ wesipʉ, tʉkʉ yumapʉ
crush pikʉtsekarʉ, tatsukwerʉ,
tayuʔnerʉ, tsahhomonutsarʉ,
wʉkʉtserʉ
crush (in pieces)
tohhomonutsarʉ W
crush (or squash) tsakitsetʉ
crushed (into small pieces)
mabisukiitʉ
crutch natsihtóo? K
cry hubiyaarʉ, nawooʔi, yaketʉ
cry by hitting, make toyaketʉ
cry, cause to wʉyaketʉ

cry, imitate a niyakekʉtʉ
cry loudly hubiyaa piayakeetʉ
cry out hubinitʉ
crying, stop pʉhkai
crying (walking around)
yakeyʉkarʉ
crystal clear pabokopitʉ
cucumber poko rʉhka?, soko
rahkaʔmiitsa?
cud, cow's pimorooʔa tʉyʉʔwipʉ
cultivate wʉhhanirʉ
cultivator puhí tsawoo?
cup aawo, awo-, hibikahti, wʉhibi?
cup, drinking hibiawo
cup, tin sʉʉ awo
cupboard aworahna
curdle nʉkuwʉmiʔarʉ
cure partially through touch
marebunitʉ
curing ceremony puhaʔaitʉ
curing ceremony (for someone),
hold a puhaʔarʉ
curl hair wesibapiʔarʉ
curled wesi-, wesikitʉ
curly wesikitʉ
curly hair wesibaapi
currant, wild huwaboʔkóo?
curry animal fur tsihtuʔyerʉ
currycomb tʉhʉya natsihtuʔye?
curse aikurekwatʉ, tsuhni tekwarʉ
curtain nanabuni wanapʉ K,
nanabuni wanatsahpara? W
cut ko-, natsahkiʔapʉ, tʉkʉrʉ,
wʉhkiʔarʉ, wʉnoʔitʉ, wʉtsʉkarʉ
nʉhkiʔapʉ
cut, hair- naraketorootʉ, nʉʉtsʉke?
cut, hair- (get a) nʉʉtsʉketʉ
cut a strip wʉsiʔkwarʉ
cut down tʉrahnirʉ, wʉhkarʉ,
wʉhpomarʉ, wʉhpomiʔitʉ
cut fat off surface wʉhkwʉnetʉ
cut in half tsapʉkarʉ

cut into pieces, object
tʉtsihpomiʔipʉ
cut off tʉtsihkaʔarʉ
cut off pieces wʉhtsiʔarʉ
cut off short piʔtoʔarʉ
cut on hand namahkiapʉ W
cut on the foot narahkiʔapʉ
cut oneself natsahkiʔarʉ, nʉʉkiʔaitʉ
cut open wʉpʉkarʉ, wʉpʉtsarʉ
cut out of the herd tahkaaitʉ
cut someone (to wound)
tsahkiʔaitʉ
cut something kiʔarʉ
cut someone down kuparʉ
cut up tʉtsihkaʔarʉ
cut up into pieces tsihpoma
cut up something kooʔitʉ
cut weeds or grass soni wʉhpomarʉ
cut with a knife tsihkaʔarʉ
cutter, wire tʉkʉh pomaʔ
cutting edge, sharpen a
tʉʉhkonarʉ
cyclone cellar ohta kahni W
cymopterus plant tunʉhaa
Cynthia Ann Parker Narua

D d

dab to wipe or erase tohpʉsakʉrʉ
K, tohtsomarʉ W
dachshund maʔnʉ sariiʔ
daisy, fleabane tabetotsiyaa
dam pawʉhtʉmapʉ
dam up paʔwʉtʉ
damages, payment of nanʉwokʉ
damp patsoʔitʉ
dampen pakwihtsikʉrʉ, paʔisokerʉ
dampened mabaʔisokitʉ
dance nʉhkana W, nʉhkarʉ, nʉkʉrʉ
dandelion soko sikʉsa
dandelion flower soko sikʉsatotsiyaʔ

dangerous narʉʔʉyapʉ
dangle wepʉkaitʉ
dark ketunabunitʉ, tu-, tukanikatʉ
dark blue tuʔebipitʉ K
dark color tupisibitʉ
darken ketunabunitʉ
dart kwiitsʉbaʔitʉ
date taibo naʔseekaʔ
daughter petʉʔ
daughter, adopted petʉ toyapʉ K,
petʉboopʉ W
daughter or son (offspring),
grown nahnapʉ
-daughter, Only Pʉʔna petʉ
daughter-in-law huutsi piahpʉʔ,
huutsi piahpʉ
dawn hʉwʉni, kʉhʉwʉnʉkatʉ,
taahkitʉ, tsaa nabuni, tsaa
nabunitʉ
dawn, before ohahʉkwʉnikatʉ, tosa
hʉwʉnikatʉmaʔ
dawn, early ohahʉkwʉnikatʉ
Dawn Hʉwʉni
day tabe-
day after tomorrow piʔnakwʉ
bʉetsʉ
day cradle waakohno
day cradleboard habikʉnoʔ
day, hot tabe kusʉwehkatʉ
day, late in the tabeʔehi
day, ration tʉhima rabeni
day, scorching tabe kusʉwehkatʉ
day, Sun Puha rabeni, Puha rakatʉ
daytime taahkatʉ
dead suaʔsuʔmaitʉ
dead body tʉyaipʉ
dead grass puhi kooʔipʉ, puhi
tʉyaitʉ
dead person kooipʉ
dead, play kaabehkarʉ
dead tree putsi waipʉ
deaf ketʉnakatʉ

deal, make a tohpunitᵾ
dear friend haitsíi
dear little brothers
    tamihtsiʔbenihtsiʔ
death, choke to pitsanᵾ tᵾyaitᵾ
**death, choke to (by rope around
    the neck)** oihtᵾyaitᵾ
death, drink oneself to
    nakᵾhkuparᵾ
death, eat oneself to nakᵾhkuparᵾ
death, freeze to sᵾhtᵾyaitᵾ
death, prevent someone's
    makwitsoʔaitᵾ
death, starve to tsiharᵾyaitᵾ
death, thirst to
    takuhtᵾyaaihumiʔarᵾ
death, work someone to
    namakupakᵾrᵾ
death, worked to namakupᵾkatᵾ
death wail hubiya piayakeetᵾ
deathbed, suffer on pisukwitarᵾ
debts, pay tᵾmakarᵾ
decay eʔbootsiarᵾ, eʔbootsiaʔ
decayed tooth woʔataamą
deceitful emᵾahkatᵾ
deceive kaabehkarᵾ, kaahaniitᵾ
deceive, to emᵾahkatᵾ
deceive or cheat, intend to
    kaasuarᵾ
December Pia ᵾtsᵾʔi mᵾa, Pᵾmata
    waahimaʔena mᵾa, Pᵾmata
    wanohiʔema mᵾa, Wahi mᵾa
deceptive emᵾahkatᵾ
decide tᵾbitsi̱ suarᵾ
decide, help tsasuʔatsitᵾ
decided, un- wahabi̱suatᵾ
deck, king in playing-card
    ohahkuyaaʔ
Decoration Day Pᵾkᵾra
    totsiyaaʔai̱ʔeka, Totsiyaaih
    tabenihtᵾ W
decorative pin natsihtᵾpᵾka?

decoy duck pᵾᵾyᵾ namanahkepᵾ
deed soko bookᵾtᵾ
deed, title soko bookᵾtᵾ
deed or title to land nabinai
    tᵾboopᵾ
deep tuhkatᵾ
deer arᵾka?
deer, white-tailed piʔtohtsíaʔ W
deer food K, O arᵾkáa rᵾhkapᵾ
deer meat arᵾka tuhku K, O, P,
    arᵾkáa rᵾhkapᵾ, tahmai napᵾ
Deer-water Arᵾka páaʔ
defeat kwakurᵾ K, tahniʔarᵾ,
    wᵾhhabiʔarᵾ
defeat by cheating kaakwakurᵾ
defecate naroʔitᵾ
deficient ketokwetᵾ
defile mahyarᵾ
definite noo
dehair a hide wᵾhkwᵾnetᵾ
delay tsᵾʔnitᵾ
delayed mamamᵾekatᵾ
delicate health, person of takwipᵾ
delouse nabusiʔaketᵾ, pusiaketᵾ
demonstrate tᵾmabunikᵾrᵾ
den itsaraitᵾ ᵾnᵾa kahni
den of thieves tᵾrᵾkᵾ kahni
dentures tamatsaʔnika?
depend on someone nasupetitᵾ
dependable nasutsawaitᵾ W
dependable person nasupetipᵾ K
dependable person, un-
    senihtᵾhtsiʔ
deplete a supply tsahtsuʔmarᵾ
deride suʔuyaaʔarᵾ, usúʔuyaʔitᵾ W,
    wohho suarᵾ
descend yᵾwimiʔarᵾ
descendant naʔnᵾumᵾ
descendants nᵾhmabina
describing something, tempt by
    nisuyakeetᵾ
desert pᵾa nuhkitᵾ, pᵾah taitᵾ

Desert-in-large-group Pꞟa kwarꞟ

deserve taʔurꞟkarꞟ W

desire suwaitꞟ

desire not to be disturbed pihisoʔaiwꞟnꞟrꞟ

desk pꞟpaʔakura tꞟbòoʔena̱ W, tꞟboo rꞟhkaʔ

destroy aibuniitꞟ

destruction], self-immolate [self-sacrifice or kuhtꞟyarꞟ

detained mamamꞟekatꞟ

device used for measuring, any tꞟmanahkeʔ

devil Ketokwe hina haniitꞟ, Tuhkwasi taibooʔ

devil's claw aakáaʔ

devil's horn aakáaʔ

devil's horse tosaraiʔ

devil's snuffbox mupitsꞟha pisahpi̱ W

devour sꞟmꞟ rꞟhkarꞟ

dew tosa nꞟꞟbaaiʔ

diamond kiinaboo, nanaʔatahpu naʔhaʔ rꞟꞟpi̱, pahparatsihkwetꞟ tꞟꞟpi̱, weʔkwi̱yanutꞟ tꞟꞟpi̱

diaper pikwꞟrꞟpꞟkaʔ W

diaper pin nahamuhkꞟ K

dice game awonohiʔ

die tꞟyaaitꞟ

die, to kooitꞟ

die in accident anitꞟ

die of the cold sꞟhtꞟyaitꞟ

die of thirst takuhtꞟyaaihumiʔarꞟ

die out tukamiʔarꞟ

different ata-, atꞟrꞟ, ebu

different kinds nanaʔataputꞟ, nani̱susumatꞟ

different ways seni

differently, doing atapu

dig mahorarꞟ, tokwaitꞟ, tsahhorarꞟ, tsahtaikꞟtꞟ, tꞟhorarꞟ, wꞟhhorarꞟ

dig a fire hole kutꞟhorarꞟ

dig a hole horarꞟ, tꞟhhorarꞟ

dig a hole in the ground tohkonarꞟ

dig edible roots tꞟkꞟ ahwerꞟ

dig up awerꞟ

digger, posthole tꞟhoraʔ

dignity, act without self- eʔmꞟarꞟ

dinner tabe rꞟhkapꞟ W

dinner or lunch, eat tabe rꞟhkarꞟ K

direction, this ibu, inakwꞟ

directions, from all nanoʔonai

directions, from different nanaʔatanaiki̱

directions, various ebu

dirt ohta-, ohtapi̱i̱

dirty nasꞟsꞟaʔeetꞟ

dirty object tuhtsaipꞟ

disagreement, shake head in kaʔwitsetꞟ K

disassemble tohkweʔyarꞟ

discard tsahwitꞟ

discard something namaroʔitꞟ

discarded by kicking sꞟꞟhpotsꞟkatꞟ

discarded thing namaroʔihkatꞟ

discharge a flash of lightning ekakwitseʔerꞟ

disciple tꞟrꞟʔai wapi̱

disconnect, to tsahtukarꞟ

discouraged aiʔbihinꞟꞟsukatꞟ, nakꞟnꞟꞟʔmaitꞟ, narahtokwetꞟ

disgust, expression of ai

dishes, wash awomakotserꞟ, tꞟmakotsetꞟ

dishonest person kaawosa̱

dishpan tꞟsoona

dishtowel awomatsumaʔ, tꞟmatsumaʔ W

dishwasher awomakotse

disintegrate wihtoʔaitꞟ

disintegrated wihtoʔaitꞟ

disjoint natsaminarꞟ, tsaminarꞟ, tsiminarꞟ

dislike kemabanaʔitꞟ

dislocate natsaminaitʉ
disobedient ketʉnakatʉ
disorderly in placement pia utsaatʉ
disown a friend haitsi̱ wihtaitʉ
display nasutsarʉ, nʉʉhtonitʉ
dispose of petihtarʉ
disrobe natsahkwe?yarʉ, tsahkwe?yarʉ
distance, separated by great namanakwʉ̱ K
distance), smell something (from a ʉkwʉsʉ?nitʉ
distant soo naahkwetʉ̱
distraught kenaninabenitʉ
disturb ni?yʉsʉkaitʉ̱, wʉʉyoritʉ
disturbed pihiso?aitʉ
disturbed, desire not to be pihiso?aiwʉnʉrʉ
ditch wo?nokatʉ̱
dive mutsʉ?itʉ
divide na?rʉbomitʉ, tahkaaitʉ
divide in half tʉbinaa?werʉ
divided na?rʉbomitʉ̱
divided evenly na?nʉbe?
divided in half tʉbinaa?wekitʉ
divided into groups narahpomi?itʉ̱
divorced pʉah taikatʉ
dizzy kwinumakatʉ
dizzy, be made makwi?numaitʉ
dizzy, make kwinumarʉ
do hani̱tʉ
do something, fail to kemahpʉ?arʉ
do something, persuade someone to nitsʉ̱bahikʉ?itʉ
do something, unable to kemahpʉ?arʉ, tsuhitʉ
do to mʉʉrʉ
do work tʉrʉ?aitʉ
doctor natʉ̱su?u puha raiboo? W
doctor, medical natsu̱ taibo? K
doctor, medicine puha tenahpʉ̱

doctor, witch tʉtsʉ puha?
doctoring, big piana huwai?
does-not-tell-a-lie, This-midday-sun- Sihka tabe ke isopʉ
dog sarii?
Dog Eaters Saria Tʉhka
Dog hero Makutabai
dog, hound- naki̱ sarii?
dog, prairie tʉ?rʉkúu? W
dog, watch- tʉ?iya?i wapi̱
dog, water pa?boosi?
dog paddle masu?wa?nekitʉ, paruhparʉ
dog-soldiers, Chief Comanche- Tʉoyobisesʉ
dogwood, flowering siba huupi
dogwood, rough-leafed parʉa
doing another way atapu
doing, cease pʉarʉ
doing something, continue naahkarʉ
doing, slow down what one is nʉnʉ?itʉ
doing differently atapu
doing, miss tsimi?akʉrʉ
doll nohitʉetʉ
doll up someone ma?yʉkwiitʉ
dollar, half- sʉkweebi?
domestic carrot ohahpokopi K, ohahtʉhkapʉ̱
domestic plum taibo sʉkʉ?i
domestic tree humasʉapʉ̱
domineer tahkoonitʉ
Don't! keta?
donkey kusimuura, kutsihpʉ̱?, kutsi?wobi?
doodlebug kwita maropona
door natsahtʉma? K
door, knock on tohtaraki?arʉ
door, screen nasaa?wʉ? K
doorway muhyʉ̱, namuhyʉ̱, natsahtʉma? K

double waha-

double, ride pihima, piyaru

double ball natsihtóoʔetu

double-bladed axe
  naʔbutikumakatu tuuhkaʔaa?

doubles wahabahti

doubletrees, hook up (on buggy)
  nomohkaru

doubt the truth of a statement
  tsuwíhnu

doubtful wahabisuatu

doubtless kewáhabahku

dough-like batter takoosahpu? W

dove kuʔe wóoʔ, pasahòo

down naʔuyubuti W, tuhkatu

down, fall wuhtukwaitu

down, force to sit sutena karuru

down, go weehtsitu, yuwimiʔaru

down, help tsakweru

down, hold (with hand) makunaitu

down, jerk tsapeheru

down (sitting back on heels),
  kneel tanatookarutu

down, knock wuhkwabikuru

down (by force), knock
  wunuukuparu

down, knock something tayuʔmaru

down, knocked wunuuhkuparu

down, lay something tukiitu K

down on something, lay the head
  tsohtukikatu

down, lie haahpitu 2, habiitu,
  kwabitu

down and think, lie nasutamu
  habitu

down, lying haahpi

down, nail tawunaru

down, pant with tongue hanging
  hehekubuniitu

down, press mabararu

down with hands to expel water,
  press mabitsooru

down, press something tatukeʔneru

down, pressed manukutu

down, pull tsahparu, tsapeheru

down, pull oneself natsahkupukatu

down in place, put tsahtukitu

down, put something tsaʔnikooru

down something to sit on, put
  pisoonaru

down, quiet tusuʔnaru,
  wuyupaʔnitu

down, set tsahtukitu

down carefully, set tsakwunaru

down, sit karukatu 1, nakaruʔkaru,
  yukwimiʔaru

down quickly, sit tsuhni karu

down, slide pisikwanúuʔitu

down (what one is doing), slow
  nununʔitu

down, smooth wutukiʔnetu

down, stake tawunaru

down tightly, stake uhtaaru

down object, staked- uhtaʔetu

down in, stuck tsuhkaru

down, sun goes tabeʔikamiʔaru

down, swat wuʔaniru

down, swing sitting
  piʔweesuʔruʔitu

down, take tsayumiʔi

down a teepee, take tsahtuwaru

down off of something, take
  tsahpuheru

down, tamp tanukutu K, tonukuru

down, tear tsahperu

down, throw tsayumaru

down a person, throw
  tsahkwaʔnuʔitu

down, upside paʔarai

downhearted aiʔbihinuusukatu,
  narahtokwetu

downhill, run wenuʔnukimiʔaru

-downstream, Those-who-stay
  Tinawa

downward na?ʉyʉbuti W, tuhkatʉ

downward, lying face- muparai habinitʉ K

draft, bank puhihwi tʉboopʉ

drag by force wʉhpiwokarʉ

drag something kʉwokarʉ, piwokarʉ, takwokarʉ W

drag something along piwokami?arʉ

drag something spread on flat surface pisunarʉ

dragging one foot, walk tasi?womi?arʉ

dragonfly paka tuu?ru?

drain tsa?okwetʉ

drain a liquid tsa?ohkwerʉ

draw line tsihpoorʉ

draw out pain, suck on body to musoopitʉ

draw water tuurʉ

drawer na?wosa, ooyorʉ tahna

drawer, dresser ooyorʉ tahna

drawing knife nahuu? W, nahhoo? K

drawknife huusibe?

dream nabʉsi?aipʉ, nabʉsi?aitʉ

dredge tsii?wʉweniitʉ

dress kwasu?ʉ, namʉsoarʉ

-dress, Short Tsihtara

dress, un- natsahkwe?yarʉ, tsahkwe?yarʉ

dresser, (chest of drawers) oo?rʉ tani?i?

dresser drawer ooyorʉ tahna

dribble kʉ?kwʉriarʉ

dribble from the mouth kʉ?okwetʉ

dried nara?okatʉ, tʉbitsi basapʉ

-dried corn, quick atakwa?sʉ?aipʉ

dried cowhide paakipʉ

dried meat esi inapʉ, tahmai napʉ

-dried meat, summer tahmai napʉ

dried plum natsomʉ, na?a?tsome?

dried pumpkin nakwʉsipʉ

drill a field tʉrahnai?itʉ

drill a hole with an instrument tohtʉbʉ?itʉ

drill in tahtʉkarʉ

drink hibitʉ

drink alcoholic beverage hibikʉtʉ

drink coffee hubebitʉ

drink oneself to death nakʉhkuparʉ

-drinking, Wolf Esahibi

drinking cup hibiawo

drinking glass paboko aawo, wʉhibi?

drip pahpatsohkitʉ

drip water paa kʉa?etʉ

drive tʉtsʉhanitʉ

drive a car or team by hand tsahhanitʉ

drive across tamanikarʉ

drive along or away mahkʉsuwaitʉ

drive animals by force tamʉkʉrʉ

drive away tahkʉarʉ

drive in animals mahkʉkitʉ K

drive out tahkʉarʉ

drive together ta?ookitʉ

drive up animals mahkʉrʉ W

driven into ground tawekwitʉ

driver, screw- tʉmabukwe?

drool pakʉsiiwʉnʉrʉ

droop takwitsoo?nimi?arʉ

drop peti-, tapʉherʉ

dropping, break by wʉtʉbarʉ

drop off pahitʉ, yumarʉ

drought tsihakooihkatʉ, ʉrʉ?itʉ

drown patʉrʉyaitʉ

drugstore natʉsu?ʉ narʉmʉʉ?, natʉsu?ʉ kahni

drum, wooden wobi wʉhpai K

drumming pihkarʉ

drunk hibipʉ, kwinumapʉ

drunk, made makwi?numaitʉ

drunk person hibipʉ

dry tʉbitsi basapʉ

dry (by heating) kupisarʉ

dry, hang meat up to ina?etʉ
dry, hang up to pasahtohtsanarʉ
-dry, partially sun wʉhtakʉmiitʉ
dry it for jerky), roast meat over fire (or ku?inarʉ
dry, set out to pasahtahtʉkitʉ W
dry, sit in sun to mabasahtʉkitʉ K
dry, sit in the sun to pasahtahtʉkitʉ W
dry goods tapi wanapʉ K, tarʉwanapi W
dry object pasapʉ
dry off body pasarʉ
dry out pasarʉ
dry season ʉrʉ?itʉ
dry something pasakʉrʉ, tʉbitsi basarʉ
dry tea puhi huuba
dry up kuwaaitʉ, waaitʉ
Dry-teepee Pakekʉni
drying, A-frame, meat- inakwata
duck pʉʉyʉ
duck, decoy pʉʉyʉ namanahkepʉ
duck head under water paku?nerʉ
duck someone tsahpaaku?nikarʉ
dug (by man), hole nahorapʉ
dug (in soil), hole hoora
dull kʉmakwa?i, mutsiwahtʉ
dulled kemakʉmapʉ
dulled edge kemakʉmapʉ
dumb ketekwa
dump into to?wʉ?wenitʉ, wʉhtiarʉ
dun tʉniwaitʉ
dune, sand pasiwanoo? W
duplicate taka?aitʉ, taka?arʉ
during religious ceremony, smoke puha bahmu?itʉ
dusk tupisinawoni?, tupʉsʉnarʉ
dust huhku-, huhkupʉ, huukupʉ
dust, raise huukuhʉnʉrʉ
dust by walking, raise tahuhkuwʉnʉrʉ

dust, saw- huupita homoketʉ, huupita pisoni, huutusupʉ W
dust, stir up huukuhʉnʉrʉ
dust off huukunatsirʉ
dust off by hand huukumatsumarʉ
dust storm huhkukwʉnʉrʉ, huukuhʉnʉrʉ
dust-colored koropitʉ
dustcloth tʉmatsuma? W
dusty huukukatʉ
dwell nʉmʉnetʉ
dye tʉsaa?
dye something tʉsáarʉ
dying one sua?su?makatʉ
dynamite pʉhtsa?etʉ?

E e

dying one sua?su?makatʉ
dynamite pʉhtsa?etʉ?
eagle kwihnai, pia huutsuu?, pia kwihnai
-eagle, Sun Tabe kwi?ne
-eagle, White Kwihne tosabitʉ
Eagle-tail-feather Kwasia
ear naki
ear cartilage, back part of K naki kwiita
ear lobe W naki kwiita
ear of corn hani-, haníibi
ear, pierced naki toonʉkatʉ K, nanakitonapʉ
ear wax naki oona
earache, have an naki wʉnʉkatʉ
early nabʉesʉ, ohahʉkwʉnikatʉ, tosa hʉwʉnikatʉma?
early dawn ohahʉkwʉnikatʉ
early morning pʉetsʉku, tuka ʉhyʉi
early plum yusʉkʉ
earn something tahwikarʉ, tʉrahwikatʉ

earring naki̱ tsaʔnikaʔ
ears, prick up the toʔyabaitʉearth sokoobi̱
earth sokoobi̱
earth, cover with pasokoʔarʉ
earth, paw the taʔsiʔwoorʉ
earth, quake of soko yʉʔyʉmuhkurʉ
earth, scratch up taʔsiʔwoorʉ
earth [or earthquake], tremor of soko yʉʔyʉmuhkurʉ
earth, wash out patowoʔnerʉ
earth-covered ohtakatʉ
earthquake soko yʉʔyʉmuhkutʉ
ease pain, stand on someone's back to tahparaʔitʉ
easily yuʔnaitsi K
east muhyʉ nakwʉ̱
east, north- kwihne muhyʉnakwʉ̱
east, south- yuʔanʉe muhyʉnakwʉ̱bu
Easter Tanoyoʔtsoʔmeʔe̱
Easter egg taabuʔkina noyo
Easter rabbit noyotsoʔme̱ tabuʔ
Eastern Apaches Nipanʉʉ
easy yuʔnaitsi K
Easy-to-break Tsaa tsopaʔ
eat tʉhkarʉ
eat K tʉkʉ yaarʉ
eat, take to W tʉkʉ yaarʉ
eat bone marrow tuhhu rʉhkarʉ
eat breakfast taarʉhkarʉ
eat dinner or lunch tabe rʉhkarʉ K
eat most of something sʉmʉ rʉhkarʉ
eat oneself to death nakʉhkuparʉ
eat peyote wokwetʉhkarʉ
eat supper yʉihtʉhkatʉ
eat up kʉhtsuʔmarʉ, tʉhkamarʉ
eaten food, partly narʉhkapʉ̱
eaten up completely sʉmʉ kʉhtsumai

Eaters, Sugar Pena tʉhka, Penanʉʉ
-eaters, Yap Yapai tʉhka
eating, finish off by kʉhtsuʔmarʉ
eating place tʉkʉ kahni
Eating-tribe Marʉhke
eavesdrop nakʉhoorʉ
eavesdropper nakʉhoowaaitʉ̱
echo tʉʔape nanakarʉ
edge tʉbanaaʔ
Echo-of-the-wolf-howl Isananakaʔ
edge tʉbanaaʔ
edge, dulled kemakʉmapʉ̱
edge, knife kʉmapʉ̱
edge, sharpen a cutting tʉʉhkonarʉ
edge, sharpen an makwʉmutsiarʉ
edge, sharpened kʉmapʉ̱
edged, cloth (with ribbon or lace) tʉkʉmaʔaitʉʔ
edible fruit, plant with paiyapi̱
edible roots, dig tʉkʉ ahwerʉ
edible tuber taʔwahkóoʔ W, totohtʉ
eel kwasinaboo pekwi
effort to remember, search the mind in suʔurarʉ
egg kokoráʔa pokopi̱, nooyo̱
egg, chicken kokoráʔa nooyo̱, kokoráʔa atùapʉ̱
egg, Easter taabuʔkina noyo
egg, want to lay an nohabi̱ suwaitʉ̱
egg yolk noyoʔna ohapi̱yuna
eggs, lay turuarʉ
eight namewatsʉkwi̱tʉ̱
either sex, kinsman of taʔkaʔ
elbow kiipʉ̱
elder brother pabiʔ
elderly male tsukuhpʉ̱ʔ
elderly man sukuupʉ̱
elderly woman hʉbi tsiitsiʔ, pʉetʉpʉ̱
eldest child nahnapʉ̱
eldest sister patsiʔ

elephant esiᵻnᵾᵾ?, mu?kwipuna?, tᵾkwitsuna?

elk, bull parᵾa kuhma

elm tusohó?

elm, white pimoroo?a korohko?

elocutionist tᵾnikepịsa?

elves, little people similar to Nᵾnapi

emaciated person wehuru?i

emptily tsaana

empty into to?wᵾ?wenitᵾ, wᵾhtiarᵾ

empty out wᵾ?wenitᵾ K

encircle mahoinitᵾ

encounter someone nara?uraitᵾ

encourage kebisa?makarᵾ, natsᵾwitᵾmaka?eetᵾ

encourage to go on nihtunetsᵾ?itᵾ

end, stand hair on sᵾroonitᵾ

end of row or nerve sᵾkwerᵾ

enema, give an nariso?arᵾ W

enema, give oneself an natsinaro?ikᵾtᵾ

enemy wohhohpᵾ?

enemy tribe tawohho

engaged to be married, get nᵾpetsᵾ?itᵾ

enmity wohho

enough, not good ketokwetᵾ

enraged tapiso?aitᵾ W

enter wekwiitᵾ, wekwimi?arᵾ

enter by force sutena ikᵾrᵾ

entertain mananaa?waihkarᵾ, ma?yᵾneetᵾ

envy another person kwahisi?a

erase tahtsukitᵾ, tohpᵾsakᵾrᵾ K

erase, dab to wipe or tohpᵾsakᵾrᵾ K, tohtsomarᵾ W

eraser tᵾrahtsuki? K

eriogonum root ekanatsᵾ

erode patowo?nerᵾ

eroded soil patowo?nepᵾ

error in speech ni?watsᵾkatᵾ?

escape kᵾarᵾ

escape from somewhere namaro?itᵾ

escort a guest some place panimi?arᵾ

esophagus worᵾrokᵾ

ether nᵾmi tsa?ᵾbᵾikᵾ?eetᵾ

even sᵾᵾpetᵾ

even, un- ho?yopịpᵾ, pihpokaarᵾ

even land, un- wohtsa?wᵾtᵾ

evenly divided na?nᵾbe?

evening tukaanị, tupᵾsᵾnarᵾ, yᵾitᵾ

evening, this yᵾihkạ

event nahapᵾ

every time o?yᵾ?sᵾ

everyone sᵾmᵾ oyetᵾ

everywhere piapᵾ 2

evil aitᵾ

evil spirit pᵾe tᵾyaai?, tᵾtᵾsuana

evil spirit, have an poosubᵾhkaitᵾ

exact tokwetᵾ

exaggerate natsamarᵾ

examine puiwᵾnᵾrᵾ, tsasukarᵾ

examine oneself nabuihwᵾnᵾtᵾ W

excavate tokwaitᵾ

exchange narᵾma?erᵾ, narᵾmᵾᵾrᵾ

exchange gifts hinanahimitᵾ, nahimiitᵾ, na?uhturᵾ W

exchange one item for another mabihtᵾ?uyarᵾ

exchange several gift items na?oyorᵾmakarᵾ K

excite manᵾᵾsukaarᵾ, toyᵾsekaitᵾ

excitement, stir up toyᵾsekaitᵾ

exciting toyᵾsᵾkai

excrement kwitapᵾ

exhaust food supply tᵾkᵾ tsuhmarᵾ

exhaust oneself nananᵾᵾ?maitᵾ, narahkupaitᵾ

exhaust supply kehewa?itᵾ

exhausted, give up anitᵾ

exhausted person or animal namakweyaipᵾ

exit forcibly tohto?itʉ

expectorate tusitʉ

expel water, press down with hands to mabitsoorʉ

experience, know by masuabetaitʉ

experience, learn by masuabetaitʉ

experience something wʉsukatʉ

explain nimabunikʉtʉ, nitsʉbunikʉtʉ

explain something nisuabetarʉ K

explode pʉhtsarʉ, wʉhkwʉmarʉ

explode from heat kupʉtsarʉ

explore for oil tokwaitʉ

explosive pʉhtsa?etʉ?

expression of disgust ai

extend hospitality to a guest mananaa?waihkarʉ

extinguish murukarʉ, tukarʉ

extinguish, unplug to tsahtukarʉ

extinguish a fire wʉhtukarʉ K

extinguished puuhkikatʉ

extreme stomach pain sapʉ wʉnʉkatʉ

extremely greedy pihitsituyarʉ

eye pui

eye, pupil of tuhpui

eyebrow ka?ibʉhʉ

eyeglasses pui tsa?nika?

eyelash puitʉsii

eyelid pui narʉso

eyes, close everyone's sʉmʉ ʉhtsumitʉ

eyes, close the ʉhtsumarʉ

eyes water ohpeto?ikarʉ

eyes water heavily pa?okwetʉ

F f

face kobe

face, false kobe tsa?nika?

face, freckled tutʉsawʉ koobe

face, gray esikakwo?a

face, make a wry sʉkʉbuninitʉ

face cream kobe kiihtʉ?eka? W

face- downward, lying muparai habinitʉ K

face powder homobi saapi

face towel kobe matsuma?, nakobe matsuma?

fail to do something kemahpʉ?arʉ

fail to reach to?wʉminaitʉ

fail to reach something tsa?wʉminarʉ

faint esituyaitʉ, sua watsikatʉ, tsihkwinumai

faint, feel kwinumasuarʉ

faint repeatedly esikooitʉ

fairy story narʉkuyunapʉ

faith tokwʉsuakʉna

faith in someone, lose nasuwʉhkitʉ

faithful nanʉsutsawaitʉ, nasutsawaitʉ W

faithful person nasupetipʉ K

falcon huumara?

fall yumarʉ

fall using foot, make taperʉ

fall, snow- tahka?ʉmarʉ

fall, trip and nʉʉhkupatʉ, nʉʉhpisi?maitʉ

fall down wʉhtʉkwaitʉ

fall into something tʉyumarʉ

fall off pahitʉ, tʉpehemi?arʉ

fall off or away from tʉpʉherʉ W

fall plum kusisʉkʉi

fall season yʉba

fall short nasutamʉ wʉminaitʉ W, pihpokaarʉ, to?wʉminaitʉ

false nakaa?aitʉ

false face kobe tsa?nika?

false mallow, red puha natsu W, yokanatsu?u K

false teeth tamatsa?nika?

falsely, accuse someone tʉbehyaarʉ

families, three separate
 pahibahtᵼnᵼnᵼ
family nᵼmᵼ haahkana?
famine, have tsihakooihkatᵼ
fan nᵼᵼhᵼhtsa?wᵼ?, wᵼnekᵼrᵼ
fan for fire wᵼnekᵼtᵼ? K,
 wᵼ?ᵼnenihku? W
fantasy, (fairy story) narᵼkuyunapᵼ
far away manakwᵼ K
farmer, white tᵼtsakwoo raiboo?
farther along miibe?tᵼ
fast pᵼhetᵼ
fast, stuck pimᵼnikatᵼ
fast, walk pohyami?arᵼ
fasten wᵼhtᵼpᵼkarᵼ
fasten on harness namuhkarᵼ
fasten with shoelace napᵼbosarᵼ
fat yuhhu K
fat, cut off surface wᵼhkwᵼnetᵼ
fat, fry out kuhpitsᵼni?arᵼ W
fat, ref to yuhu
fat person yupᵼ
father ahpᵼ?
Father, Our Ta?ahpᵼ
father's sister paha?
fatten yuhu bᵼhkaitᵼ
fattest one yuhu wehkipᵼ
fault, find manímᵼarᵼ
fault, find (with someone)
 tᵼbehyaarᵼ
fear, run to something through
 namarunehtsᵼrᵼ
fearful nanakuya?arᵼ
feather sia-, sie
-feather, Painted Ketse na?bo
feather mattress sia sona rᵼbaki?
feather pillow sia tsohpe
feathers, pick a bird of its no?itᵼ
feathers, pluck a bird clean of
 pahtsi no?itᵼ
February Positsᵼ mᵼa
feces kwitapᵼ

feed makaarᵼ
feed, tell to makahtᵼnikatᵼ
feeding lot soni wᵼhtᵼmapᵼ
feel masukaarᵼ
feel anger tuhu su?aitᵼ
feel around makwarᵼ, tsakwatᵼ
feel around with hand mawa-
feel cool hᵼhtsawᵼkatᵼ
feel faint kwinumasuarᵼ
feel happy na?okᵼsuarᵼ
feel numb susᵼ?nitᵼ
feel pity mᵼᵼrᵼ?ikatᵼ
feel rage tuhu su?aitᵼ
feel something tsasukarᵼ
feel with foot tasukarᵼ
feet, have cold tasᵼkᵼmitᵼ
feet in water, paddle pawᵼpa?itᵼ
feet, standing on hind
 manawᵼnᵼkatᵼ
feet, wash narakotserᵼ, takotserᵼ
feet, wipe tasu?netᵼ
female animal piabᵼ
female kinsman na?nᵼmᵼ
female kinsman, man's
 na?wa?ihpᵼ?
female kinsman, woman's
 wa?ihpᵼ?
female teacher tᵼboorᵼᵼ pia?
fence nᵼᵼhtᵼma?, tᵼᵼhtᵼmapᵼ K
fence, hog mubi po?roo
 rᵼhtᵼma? W
fence, hog-pen hooki tᵼᵼhtᵼmapᵼ
fence, put up a barbed wire
 puhihwi tᵼᵼhtᵼmarᵼ
fence of hog pen po?ro tᵼhtᵼmapᵼ
fence something tᵼᵼhtᵼmarᵼ
fence staples tᵼᵼhtᵼmapᵼha
 tᵼrawᵼna?
fence up wᵼhtᵼmarᵼ
fenced pasture soni tᵼhtᵼmapᵼ
fermented saahtotsito?ikatᵼ
festering pisi

fetch petsʉ miʔarʉ, yaahuyarʉ
fetch firewood kono miʔarʉ
fetch water tuuhuniitʉ W
fetch water for someone
  tuukʉmiʔarʉ
fever kuhtsʉni?
fever, typhoid narʉʔʉyʉ kuhtsʉni?
fever, yellow ohakuhtsʉni
feverish, be kuhtsʉnịtʉ
fever plant poiya
few hʉitsi, hʉʉ
few times hʉʉsʉ
field, drill a tʉrahnaiʔitʉ
field, plowed tʉtsakwoopʉ
field lark hiitoo? K, N,
  ohanʉnapʉ W
field mouse pia kahúa
Field-lark Hiitoo? K, N
fifty cents sʉkweebi?
fight naʔạrutʉ W
fight, fist naʔạrurʉʉ?
fight hand-to-hand narohparʉ
figures, group of tʉrʉtsʉpụ
file tʉmatsune? W
file a surface tʉmatsunarʉ
fill ibuʔikʉrʉ
fill something W tʉmarʉ
fill up muʔibuikʉrʉ
fill with people tsʉhkịkatʉ
fill with water paa maʔibuʔikʉtʉ K,
  pawʉsaʔnaitʉ W
-filled, water paʔibuikatʉ
filled to the brim ibuʔitʉ
filled up wʉtsʉʔmitʉ
filled with water by drinking
  pakwʉʔsʉʔmitʉ
finally (or at last) haya kwasikʉ
financial bank puhihwi kahni
financially, broke tʉtsuʔmapʉ
find fault manímʉarʉ
find fault with someone
  tʉbehyaarʉ

find out sutuuʔarʉ
find out for oneself naraʔurakʉtʉ
find room for someone or
  something haakarʉ
find something urarʉ, wʉʔurarʉ
find something being looked for
  toʔurarʉ
find something with the hand
  maʔurarʉ
fine gravel pasi waapị
fine-toothed comb pusiʔa
  natsihtuʔye?
finger, index tʉtsihtsuka?
finger, little mahtua?,
  tʉehmahtua? W
finger, middle mahtʉpịnáa? K,
  masʉwʉhki? W
finger ring maʔnika?, moʔo
  tsiʔnika?
fingernail masiitọ
fingers masʉwʉhki?
fingers, rip with tsahtʉrʉʔarʉ
fingers, snap mabohto
fingers, snuff fire with W
  tsahtukarʉ
finish marʉkarʉ, tsamarʉkarʉ,
  tsuʔma, tʉmarʉkarʉ
finish off by eating kʉhtsuʔmarʉ
finish telling nimarʉkaitʉ
finished item namarʉkapʉ
fire kohtoopʉ, nakuyaarʉ, weʔhaki?
fire, build a kohtóorʉ
fire, extinguish a wʉhtukarʉ K
fire, fan for wʉnekʉtʉ? K,
  wʉʔʉnenihku? W
fire, grass nakuyaarʉ
fire, heat of kohtoopʉ
fire, light a lamp or kupịtarʉ
fire, prairie nakuyaarʉ
fire, quench a murukarʉ
fire (or dry it for jerky), roast
  meat over kuʔinarʉ

fire, set on kutsitonarʉ
fire with fingers, snuff W
  tsahtukarʉ
fire, stir up kuma?omerʉ,
  ma?omerʉ
fire, throw into the kuhtsahwirʉ
fire hole kutʉhorapʉ W
fire hole, dig a kutʉhorarʉ
fire on wʉhtikʉrʉ
fire poker kutsani
fire-builder kohtoo wapi
fire-tender (in a peyote meeting)
  momʉsaka
fireman kohtoo rʉnahpʉ, wehhari
  tuka?eetʉ
fireplace kutʉhorapʉ W
firewood kono-, kuna-
firewood, bring back kono honiitʉ
firewood, bring in konóorʉ
firewood, chop kuhkerʉ
firewood, fetch kono mi?arʉ
firmly, speak ninabitsiarʉ
first ʉkʉnaa
fish ekwi, hʉato, pekwitʉ, tsahpi?erʉ
fish, to hʉarʉ
Fish Eaters Pekwi tʉhka
fish hook hʉa? W
fish or fishing hʉa-
fish trap pekwi pʉmata hʉarʉ
fisherman hʉawapi
fishing pole hʉahuupi
fishnet saa?wʉ hʉa?
fist, hit with tohpa?itʉ
fist, hit with knuckle or W
  tohtsi?arʉ
**fist or palm of hand, stop hitting
  with** tohpʉarʉ
fist, try or want to hit with
  toso?waitʉ
fist fight na?arurʉʉ?
fists, hit with na?arutʉ W
fit nʉnʉbetʉ

five mo?obe?
fix hanitʉ
fix up ma?yʉkwiitʉ
flag wana tsiyaa?
flagpole wana tsiyaa?a náhuupi
flail wʉpʉherʉ W, wʉyumi?itʉ
flailed material wʉyumi?ipʉ
flame we?haki?, we?harʉ
flank ohútuki
flank of animal puihtsara? W,
  soo tuku
flank of living animal kotsana
flap po?hibahpakitʉ
flap wings kasabipikurʉ
flash kuhtabearʉ, kwiitsʉba?itʉ,
  we?kwiyanuutʉ
flash, lightning ekakwitse?e
flash of lightning, discharge a
  ekakwitse?erʉ
flashlight kupita?
flat tahi
flat, long and huyuba?atʉ
flat, pound wʉtʉki?netʉ
flatiron tʉrah kwʉ?ne?
flatten something marʉki?netʉ
flattened sʉʉpetʉ
flea ekapusi?a
fleabane daisy tabetotsiyaa
flesh tuhkʉ
flicker kwiitsʉba?itʉ
flirt ubitʉkʉʉtʉ
flirt, want to K na?isa suakʉtʉ
flirt with each other nana?isa
  nayʉkwi tʉkwʉ
flirt with someone na?isa yʉkwitʉ K,
  na?isa suakʉtʉ W
flitter wʉ-
float away okwehkwatʉ, sʉmʉ
  okwetʉ
flood paruaitʉ
flood the riverbank paru?itʉ
floor napʉ soona, tasoni, tasoona

flounder tahipᵾ pekwi
flour homo-, homopisarᵾ, homopᵾ
flour, packaged homorohtía?
flour, wheat pᵾmata nookoina
flour sack tohtía narᵾso
flour sifter tohtía tsasa?wᵾki?,
tsasa?wᵾki? K
flow okweetᵾ
flow, stop tohtᵾmarᵾ
flow, tears ohpeto?ikarᵾ
flower totsiyaa?
Flower Topᵾsana
flower, clock tabetotsiyaa
flower, dandelion soko
sikᵾsatotsiya?
flower, purple cone- tukunᵾ natsᵾ
flower, stamen of totsiyaa
papihtsipᵾ
flower, sun- ohayaa?
flower head, sun- hi?oopitaohayaa
flower salve, sun- hi?ookwana?
flower stalk or plant, sun- hi?oopi
flower petal totsiyaa patᵾpinaatᵾ
flower vase totsiyaa tsakwᵾna?
flowering dogwood siba huupi
flowering plant saatotsiya
flowers, sun hi?oo-
flu ebi wᵾmina?
flu, intestinal kohikamᵾkatᵾ
fly, horse- pia animui, pihpi
fly, house- animui
fly, let an arrow wᵾhkikatᵾ
fly spray animui wasᵾ
fly up yorimi?arᵾ, yᵾtsᵾrᵾ
flycatcher, fork-tailed
kᵾkᵾbᵾraakwa?si?
flyswatter animui wᵾhtokwe?a?
foam saahtotsito?i?
foaming saahtotsito?ikatᵾ
fog pakᵾnnᵾapᵾ
foggy kwiisuatᵾ W, pakᵾnaikatᵾ
fold tahkwatúubitᵾ

fold, un- marᵾpisu?arᵾ W,
tsahpᵾkᵾsu?arᵾ W
fold over namakwatubiitᵾ
folded makwatubiitᵾ
folk, women- nanawa?ihpᵾ?anᵾ W
follow a road pu?eyarᵾ
follow scent muwarᵾ W
following someone, stop nᵾnᵾ?itᵾ
food tᵾhkapa, tᵾhkapᵾ, tᵾhka?ena,
tᵾkᵾ
food, animal killed or butchered for
tᵾbehkapᵾ
food, boil karᵾkᵾrᵾ
food, boiled nasaapᵾ
food, brown wesikᵾrᵾ
food, brown the otᵾ kwasᵾkᵾrᵾ
food, canned tᵾrohtᵾmapᵾ
food, carry tᵾkᵾ noorᵾ
food, cook tᵾkarᵾkᵾrᵾ
food, cooked kwasᵾkᵾpᵾ
food, deer K, O arᵾkáa rᵾhkapᵾ
food (of any type), ground tᵾkᵾ
tusupᵾ
food, leftover kᵾhtᵾkᵾto?ipᵾ, tᵾkᵾ
to?ipᵾ
food, partly eaten narᵾhkapᵾ
food, pound tayu?nekarᵾ
food, prepared hanipᵾ
food, receive tᵾkᵾ himarᵾ
food, roast kwasᵾkᵾrᵾ
food, run out of tᵾkᵾ tsuhmarᵾ
food, satisfied with sufficient
wᵾtsᵾ?mitᵾ
food, stew tᵾkarᵾkᵾrᵾ
food, stewed kohtsáa?, tᵾkarᵾkᵾpᵾ
food, store-bought tᵾkᵾ tᵾmᵾᵾpᵾ
food grinder tᵾkᵾ tusu?
food supply, exhaust tᵾkᵾ tsuhmarᵾ
fool kaabehkarᵾ, kaahaniitᵾ
fool someone nohitekwarᵾ
foot naape, ta-, tah-
foot, break at joint of naraminaitᵾ W

foot, crumble to powder with the tahhomonutsaru̶ W
foot, cut on the narahki?apu̶
foot, feel with tasukaru̶
foot, go on (to look for) takwainitu̶
foot, go on (to meet someone) tamunaiku̶mi?aru̶
foot, heel of the tapi̱ko?
foot, loosened by takwu̱saru̶
foot, make fall using taperu̶
foot, meet someone by going on tamunaiku̶mi?aru̶
foot, pack a load on tu̶noomi?aru̶
foot, rub with nara?woru̶ K
foot, shake ta?wikitu̶
foot, shake the tahta?nitu̶
foot, sole of tahpáana̱
foot, tear with the tasi?kwairu̶
foot, torn by a tasi?kwaitu̶
foot, walk dragging one tasi?womi?aru̶
foot and lower leg napu̶|b-|r
foot or lower leg nara-
foot wound narahki?apu̶
footprint nanapunipu̶, napu̶, narapunipu̶
footstool tahtu̶ki?i?
footwear tried on narahpunipu̶
for, look ho?aniitu̶, puhwaaitu̶, wehkitu̶.
for money, look puhihwi wehki
for, lust nasuyaketu̶
for, prepare maka?mukitu̶
for safekeeping, put away to?nikaru̶ K
for someone, prepare breakfast taamahkaru̶
for, reach makwu̶bu̶tsu̶ru̶ W, maruru?aru̶
for, scrounge yaahuyaru̶
for, search carefully puhwaaitu̶

for teepees, skins or other covering nu̶mu̶ku̶ni
for someone, wait makamaitu̶
for, watch iyaa?itu̶
for, wish nasuyaketu̶
forbid nimoya?eku̶ru̶
force tahku̶aru̶
force, by (knock down) wu̶nu̶u̶kuparu̶
force, drag by wu̶hpiwokaru̶
force, drive animals by tamu̶ku̶ru̶
force, enter by sutena iku̶ru̶
force, lead off by sutena betsu̶miaru̶
force, scatter by tohporooru̶
force, stop someone by tahkoonitu̶
force, take someone by sutena betu̶
force away tahku̶aru̶
force out tsahku̶aru̶
force to go wu̶mi?aku̶ru̶ K
force to lie down wielding a weapon wu̶hhabi?aru̶
force to sit down sutena karu̶ru̶
forced out tsahto?itu̶
forcefully sutena
forcibly exit tohto?itu̶
forcibly, open tohkwu̶maru̶
ford nagwee, na?wee?
forefathers pu̶e nu̶mu̶ roopu̶nu̶u̶
forehead e?rée, ka?i
foreign country atu̶sokoobi
foreigner atabitsi̱ W, atana?i 1
foreleg tohoobe̱
forest soo huuhpi̱
forever usúni̱
forget nasuwatsiru̶
forgive ni?tsu?naru̶, tu̶su?naru̶
forgotten nasuwatsipu̶
fork tu̶hka?
fork of Red River, north Natu̶mu̶u̶ pa?i huna?
fork of a stream atahunubi

fork, pitch- soni tsiyaaʔ, sonitsiimaʔ, tʉtsiyaaʔ W
fork, table tʉhkaʔ
fork-tailed flycatcher kʉkʉbʉraakwaʔsiʔ
form into a point manutsiarʉ W
formed to a point mamámutsiakatʉ
former friend haitsi ihtaipʉ
forsake someone pʉah taitʉ
forth, swing back and natsakwenitʉ
fortune, tell a nipʉkarʉ
fortunes, tell nʉnipʉkarʉ
fortuneteller mapaanaʔ, nipʉkaaʔeetʉ, nʉmi nipʉkaʔ K, tʉnipʉkawapi W
foster child, keep an orphan as tahnikatʉ, tʉkiihkarʉ
four hayarokwetʉ
four-wheeled hack natsaʔaniʔ
Fourth of July Pia buha rabeni
fowl, guinea kokáaʔ
fox kaawosa, kʉʔkwʉriaʔ, kʉʔtseena, ohaahnakatʉ W, waani K
fox, gray tseenaʔ K
fox, red ekatseenaʔ
frame house wobi kahni
frame, picture naboopʉha naroʔnikaʔ, naboopʉha narʉso, naboopʉha pʉkʉratoʔnikaʔiʔ
freckled tutʉsaʔwʉtʉ W
freckled face tutʉsawʉ koobe
freckles tasiʔaʔ W
freeze sʉʉkoitʉ, tahkaʔimiarʉ, tʉʔasʉitʉ
freeze (or die of the cold) sʉhtʉyaitʉ
freeze to death sʉhtʉyaitʉ
freight train tʉnoo kuna waikina K
frequently naiya
fret pisukwitarʉ
fried bread yuhu nohkopʉ
fried meat yuhu rʉkʉhmanipʉ

friend notsaʔkaʔ, tʉiʔ
friend, dear haitsíi
friend, disown haitsi wihtaitʉ
friend, former haitsi ihtaipʉ
friends, girl- tʉhtʉiʔ
friend, same-sex haitsi
friendliness, un- nakahanupʉ W
friendly, un- kwetʉsapʉ
frighten kuyaʔarʉ, tahkuyaʔarʉ, tʉʔʉyatʉ, wʉhkuyaʔarʉ, yʉrʉhkitʉ
frighten someone with something wʉʔyʉrʉhkitʉ
frightened kuyaʔakatʉ, makuyaʔaitʉ
fringed nasʉkiʔapʉ
fringes naʔsʉkiaʔ
fringes, shawl with naʔsʉkiaʔ
frog pasawíʔooʔ, pohpi kwáaiʔ W
frog, bull- ebimuura yaʔkeʔ
(from a distance), smell something ʉkwʉsʉʔnitʉ
from a hide, scrape meat tohtsiyuʔitʉ
from a toothache, suffer tamanʉʉtsikwatʉ
from, turn away wʉhbuikatʉ W
from all directions nanoʔonai
from behind pinai
from cold, shake tsihturuarʉ W
from cold, shiver tsihturuarʉ W
from different directions nanaʔatanaiki
from hands, release mabʉarʉ
from heat, shrivel up kuhtakwitsooʔnitʉ W
from here sihkutʉ
from now on sibeʔnikiyutʉ
from seated position, rise nʉʉʔnʉarʉ
from something, run away wʉanuraitʉ K
from somewhere, run away pʉa nuhkitʉ

from the surface, skim yunarʉ

(from place to place), wander noyʉkarʉ

front of, in hunakʉ, munakwʉ

frost tosa nʉʉbaai?, tosa nʉʉbaikatʉ

frothing at the mouth saahtotsito?ikatʉ

frown muhasuarʉ

frozen tahka?ikatʉ

fruit pokopi

fruit, bear pokopi tuarʉ

fruit, pick pomarʉ

fruit, plant with edible paiyapi

fry meat or vegetables kwasʉkʉrʉ

fry out fat kuhpitsʉni?arʉ W

frybread yuhu nohkopʉ

frybread, make yuhu nohkorʉ

fulfilled pʉpe?

full tʉtʉbetʉ

full and running over tʉhpetʉ

full house in card game manekihtʉ?

full stomach wʉtsʉ?mi

full strength, pull with tsahturerʉ

fullgrown catfish tuumo?tso?

funeral nʉpʉkarʉʉ?

funeral (burial ceremony) nʉpʉkarʉʉ?

fur, curry animal tsihtu?yerʉ

fur cap pʉhʉ rʉmuihpaa?

fur coat pʉhʉ kwʉsu?ʉ

fur hat pʉhʉ tso?nika?

fuss at someone nimakwihtsetʉ

futilely tsaana

fuzz, hair pʉhʉ?

G g

G-string kohinehki?, tsa?nika?

gag kuitsitsiwoirʉ W

gag oneself kuitsikwaitʉ K

gain weight yuhu bʉhkaitʉ

gall bladder pu?i?

gall-bladder pain, suffer pu?i?wʉnʉrʉ

galloping sound, make totʉbihkurʉ

galoshes tuu?re napʉ

gamble nanakʉhurʉ, tʉmerʉ, wana rohpetirʉ

gamble over some type of competition nararʉnarʉ

game tʉkʉ wasʉ?

game, archaic na?nohne?eyu?

game, dice awonohi?

game, hunt tʉhoitʉ

game, Native-American ball na?sʉhpe?etʉ

games, play hand na?yʉwetʉ

game, stick for hand tuhhuu?

game, wheel aratsi?

garage na?bukuwáa? kahni

garbage tʉrokuriapʉ K, tʉtsakwʉʉriapʉ W

garden pokopi masʉapʉ

garden, raise a tʉmʉsuarʉ

garden, vegetable narʉhka? sokoobi, tʉmʉsʉa sokobi K

garden crop tʉmʉsʉapʉ

garden patch tʉkʉ masʉa sokoobi W, tʉmʉsʉa sokobi K

garden plot, vegetable tʉkʉ masʉa sokoobi W

garden product tʉmʉsʉapʉ

garden product, home-grown masʉapʉ W

garden product, raise masʉarʉ W

gargle pakwarʉhtʉkitʉ W, wʉhkwarʉ?rʉkitʉ K

garter narawʉhtama?

gash natsahki?apʉ

gash oneself natsahki?arʉ

gasoline nabaa, na?bukuwàa?a nábaa

gather takwi?oobitʉ, tso?meetʉ

gather in tʉbomarʉ
gather together ka?witʉ, narahka?witʉ, sʉʉma?aitʉ
gathered, hand matsi?okwʉkatʉ
geese nʉkʉta
general area, separated but in same na?ata W
generation, present nʉmʉ rʉborapʉ K, pʉhkʉra nahanʉ W
generation, younger ʉkʉ nʉmʉnʉʉ
generation, youngest ʉkʉ nʉmʉ roopʉnʉ K
gentle kesósoorʉ
geography soko rʉboopʉ
get puhihwi tuarʉ
get a haircut nʉʉtsʉketʉ
get engaged to be married nʉpetsʉ?itʉ
get, go to petsʉ mi?arʉ
get married nʉpetsʉ?itʉ
get off weehtsitʉ
get off running wenu?nukimi?arʉ
get rations tʉhima?etʉ
Gets-to-be-middle-aged-man Tenebeka
ghost pʉe tʉyaai?
giant mupitsi, piapʉ
gift-exchanging partner hinanahimitʉ waipu
gifts, exchange hinanahimitʉ, nahimiitʉ, na?uhturʉ W
giraffe pa?a ruyu?
girl friends tʉhtʉi?
girth, saddle natsanʉhkʉ?
give tsa?rurʉ, utʉkatʉ
give an enema nariso?arʉ W
give away moccasins napʉ makarʉ
give birth tuakatʉ
give counsel tʉsu?ʉrʉ
give money to someone puhihwimaka

give notice ninakʉakʉrʉ W
give oneself an enema natsinaro?ikʉtʉ
give pain nʉʉtsikwarʉ K
give sensation manʉʉsukaarʉ
give several objects himiitʉ
give something yunirʉ
give up narahkupaitʉ, nasutarʉ
give up exhausted anitʉ
give up waiting for someone wʉsuwarʉkiitʉ
glare at tsuhni bunitʉ
glass, drinking paboko aawo, wʉhibi?
glass, looking nabuni?
gleam we?kwiyanuutʉ
glide puhyʉnukitʉ
glitter paratsihkwe?erʉ
glory, morning soho kʉa?etʉ totsiyaa?
glottis ekotʉwʉni?
glove mo?o narʉso
glued matsʉbakikatʉ
gnat tʉe esi ʉnʉʉ
go miarʉ, wʉmi?arʉ W
go after petsʉ pitarʉ
go along nahaniitʉ
go along, invite to petsʉ kwarʉ
go back pitsa mi?arʉ
go back and forth or from side to side pi?nu?a mi?arʉ
go backwards hupimi?arʉ, pi?nu?a mi?arʉ
go crazy e?mʉarʉ, poosubʉhkaitʉ
go down weehtsitʉ, yʉwimi?arʉ
go, force to wʉmi?akʉrʉ K
go hunting tʉwoorʉ
go in circles mahoinitʉ
go live with in-laws nahyemi?arʉ
go moving along nora?wʉarʉ W
go on tunehtsʉrʉ
go on foot to look for takwainitʉ

go on foot to meet someone
 tamunaikʉmiʔarʉ

go on vacation hʉʉtsaʔwʉ miʔarʉ

go on warpath mahimiʔarʉ

go out tukamiʔarʉ

go to get petsʉ miʔarʉ

go up yʉtsʉrʉ

go visiting kahni miʔa

go walking sokomiʔarʉ

go-between nitʉsuʔnai wapi

goat, slick-haired pahtsi kabʉrʉʉ?

goathead tuwokwe

God Kaatʉ

goes down, sun tabeʔikamiʔarʉ

going on foot, meet someone by
 tamunaikʉmiʔarʉ

going to get lost watsikwarʉ

gold ekapuhihwi, puhihwi

gold color ekahwi

good tsaa, tsaatʉ

good, be yʉyʉkarʉ

good, leave someone for pʉa
 miʔarʉ

good enough, not ketokwetʉ

good news tsaatʉ narʉmuʔipʉ

good, no nasʉsʉaʔeetʉ

good!, Oh, yee

good, taste tsaa kamarʉ

good thoughts, think suakʉtʉ

Good-crier Tsaa tenayake?

good-hearted ʉrʉ?

goods, canned narohtʉma?

goods, dry tapi wanapʉ K,
 tarʉwanapi W

goods, household namahku

goods, trade wanapʉ K

goose nʉkʉta

gore mukwʉrʉ W

gore someone mukuhparʉ W

gospel tsaatʉ narʉmuʔipʉ

gossip isananarʉmuʔipʉ?,
 nimʉʉmiʔarʉ W, tʉtsʉ narʉmiʔitʉ

gossip, whisper watsih tekwarʉ

gossips, one who isanaramuʔitʉ?

gourd anakwanare?

gourd rattle wʉhtsabeyaa?

gown, night- habikwasuu**grab for**
 tsasukwarʉ

graduate tamarʉkarʉ

graduated person tamarʉkʉkatʉ

grammar tekwapʉ rʉboopʉ

grandchild, man's agnatic kʉnu?

grandchild, man's uterine toko?

grandchild, woman's agnatic
 huutsi

grandchild, woman's uterine kaku?

granddaughter's husband
 tsoʔaahpʉ?

grandfather, maternal toko?

grandfather, paternal kʉnu?

grandmother, maternal kaku?

grandmother, paternal huutsi

grandnephew, man's agnatic
 kʉnu?

grandson's wife tsoʔapia?

grape, wild mutsi atsamukwe?,
 natsamukwe?

grape juice natsamukweʔa paa

grapefruit ohápitʉʉ?a taka? W, pia
 ohapitʉ K

grapevine natsamukweʔa sʉʉki

grasp matsarʉ W

grass ekasonipʉ, soni, sonipʉ

grass, broom tʉʉnua

grass, clump of puhi taitʉ K

grass, common yuu sonipʉ

grass, cut weeds or soni
 wʉhpomarʉ

grass, dead puhi kooʔipʉ, puhi
 tʉyaitʉ

grass, graze on soni toorʉ

grass, graze on turkey puhitookatʉ

grass, mow soni wʉhpomarʉ, soni
 wʉtsʉkerʉ

grass, rye pui tsaseni
grass, turkey puhitóo?
grass burr soni wokweebi
grass fire nakuyaarʉ
grasshopper aatakíi?, aatamúu?,
   wosa a?ra?
grated object, pulverized or
   tusupʉ W
gratify ninʉsupetitʉ
grave nabʉkapʉ W, nʉpʉkapʉ
   K, N, W
gravel, fine pasi waapi
graveyard nʉpʉkapʉ K, W, nʉpʉkʉ
   sokoobi
gray esi-, esipitʉ, kusipi W
gray, appear esinabuniitʉ
gray appearance esitsʉnʉ?iitʉ
gray bird, small kusisai?
gray (color of ashes) kusi-
gray face esikakwo?a
gray-faced, accuse someone of
   being (used in making fun of
   someone) etʉsikawo?arʉ W
gray fox tseena? K
gray mare esipia?
gray mountain esitoyaabi
Gray-box Esikono
gray-colored plant kusinʉʉhparabi
Gray-flat-lying-object Esihabiitʉ
Gray-streak Esihabiitʉ
graze kʉnorʉ, toorʉ W,
   tʉhkanʉmiitʉ
graze (from place to place)
   tooniitʉ
graze (on grass) soni toorʉ
graze (on turkey grass)
   puhitookatʉ
grease wihtʉ?eka?, yuhhu K
grease, melted wihi
grease something tʉ?ekarʉ, wihi
   tʉ?ekarʉ
greasy, taste oily or wihi kamatʉ

great aunt, maternal kaku?
great distance, separated by
   namanakwʉ K
great grandchild tsoo?
great grandparent tsoo?
great uncle, paternal kʉnu?
Great Spirit Ta?ahpʉ
greater than ka?wekitʉ
greed pihitsinaina
greedy pihitsi
greedy, extremely pihitsitʉyarʉ
green pati-, patiwiaketʉ
greenbriar tamutso?i K
greyhound mubi sarii?
grief tabʉikatʉ
grill ku?inawaata
grin mu?yanesuarʉ
grind kʉhpitsoonitʉ, tusurʉ
grind, hand makitsarʉ
grind the teeth kʉhporokitʉ
grinder tʉkʉ tusu?
grinder, food tʉkʉ tusu?
grinding stone tʉsoyuni
grit the teeth kʉhkwitsitʉ,
   kʉhporokitʉ
groan hubinitʉ, nahúbiniitʉ
groceries narʉhka?, tʉkʉ tʉmʉʉpʉ
groceries, buy (or otherwise
   receive) narʉhka?ruarʉ
groceries, run out of
   narʉhka?tsu?marʉ
grope around tsakwatʉ
ground corn hanitusupʉ
ground, dig a hole in the tohkonarʉ
ground, driven into tawekwitʉ
ground, pound pillowsticks into
   tsohpe takwʉnarʉ
ground, rocky tʉpi sokoobi W
ground, throw body on the
   kwanu?itʉ K
ground food of any type tʉkʉ
   tusupʉ

ground meat tᵾhkapa narᵾsupᵾ W

ground squirrel ekwakᵾᵾpi?, ewa kᵾᵾpi?

ground up object nasupᵾ K

groundhog huuna?

grounds tusupᵾ W

group of figures tᵾrᵾtsᵾpᵾ

group of people sᵾᵾmᵾ?okᵾ

groups, divided into narahpomi?itᵾ

groups of people, three pahibahtᵾnᵾnᵾ

groups, three separated pahibahtᵾ

grow nahnami?arᵾ, sᵾatᵾ

grow in height and health naanaarᵾ

growing over, kill by puhi tᵾyaitᵾ

grown man mu?woo

grown son or daughter nahnapᵾ

guess nᵾnipᵾkarᵾ

guess-over-the-hill nanípᵾka

guest, escort a (some place) panimi?arᵾ

guest, extend hospitality to a mananaa?waihkarᵾ

guest, take someone home as panimi?arᵾ

guinea fowl kokáa?

gum sanahkoo? W

gum, chew sanahkoo kᵾyu?netᵾ

gum, chewing kᵾtsᵾwe?, sanahkoo? W

gums so?o ruhkᵾ

gums of teeth tamaruhkᵾ

gun tawo?i? K

gun, aim a wᵾhkurᵾ

gun, shoot a wᵾhkikatᵾ

gun repeatedly, shoot a ta?wo?ekarᵾ

gun, shoot a repeating tsatᵾka?karᵾ

gun, shot- so?o narᵾbaki?

gunny sack soni narᵾso?

gunpowder nakutisi

gunshot ta?wo?i?

H h

hack tosa waikina, tuwaikina, wobi puukᵾ

hack, four-wheeled natsa?ani?

hack oneself nᵾᵾhki?yu?itᵾ

hackberry kᵾrahúu? K, soho bokopi

hackberry, southern mitsonaa?

hail paho ᵾmarᵾ, pahoopi

hair tso?yaa?

hair, chest pᵾhᵾ nᵾnapᵾ

hair, comb natsihtu?yeetᵾ, tsihtu?yerᵾ

hair, comb someone's matsíhtuyeetᵾ P

hair, curl wesibapi?arᵾ

hair, curly wesibaapi

hair, head of tso?yaa?

hair, leg tapᵾ K

hair, part natsihpe?akarᵾ, tsihpe?akarᵾ

hair on end, stand sᵾroonitᵾ

hair, tangled papi tsᵾnᵾ?itᵾ

hair, underarm anapᵾhᵾ

hair, wave wesibapi?arᵾ

hair fuzz pᵾhᵾ?

hair on lower arm or hand mapᵾhᵾ

hair tonic papi wihtᵾ?eka?

hair-parter natsihpe?aka?

hairbrush natsihtu?ye?

haircut naraketorootᵾ, nᵾᵾtsᵾke?

haircut, get a nᵾᵾtsᵾketᵾ

-haired goat, slick pahtsi kabᵾrᵾᵾ?

hairpin papi tsihtᵾpᵾka?

hairy chest pᵾhᵾ nᵾnapᵾ

hairy vegetation pᵾhᵾ?

half sᵾkwerᵾ

half-dollar sɨkweebi?
halter nakobe tsa?nika?
hammer tɨhraniitɨ K, tɨrɨhani? W
hammer something tahhanitɨ
hand mo?o
hand, back of the makwe
hand, close someone's mahtsukitɨ
hand, close the mahtsokaitɨ
hand, close up with marohtɨmarɨ
hand, cramped ma?itsa?bɨkatɨ
hand, cut on namahkiapɨ W
hand, find something with the
    ma?urarɨ
hand (or lower arm), hair on
    mapɨhɨ
hand, have cramp in ma?wɨtsa
    ro?ponitɨ
hand, have something in yahkatɨ
hand, hired tɨrɨ?ai wapi
hand, hold down with makɨnaitɨ
hand, hour tabe mo?o
hand, insert tɨma?niikarɨ K 2
hand or wrist, lose something
    from ma?kwe?yarɨ
hand, move by tsanuarɨ
hand, No- Moo?wetɨ
hand, numb the masɨsɨ?nitɨ
hand, offer mahiyaitɨ
hand, open the makwɨsaitɨ
hand, palm of mapaana
hand, paralyzed ma?itsa?bɨkatɨ
hand, plant by tɨrahnarɨ
hand games, play na?yɨwetɨ
hand, polish by mapɨnukeerɨ
hand, quench by marukarɨ
hand, shell something by
    tsahkíto?arɨ
hand, slap with palm of tohpa?itɨ
hand or lower arm, sprain or
    break namaminaitɨ
hand, squeeze matsáhtsurɨ
hand, game, stick for tuhhuu?

hand, stop hitting with fist or
    palm of tohpɨarɨ
hand, tangled by makwɨsikɨkatɨ
hand, throw over- kwihitɨ
hand, touch lightly with the
    makwɨ?netɨ
hand, wash namo?o kotsetɨ
hand. wipe off with the
    makwineetɨ
hand gathered matsi?okwɨkatɨ
hand grind makitsarɨ
hand jerk mayɨ?yɨrɨ
hand lotion makwɨrɨ?eka? W,
    mo?o kwitɨ?eka? K
hand-to-hand, fight narohparɨ
hand twitch mayɨ?yɨrɨ
handcar kɨ?wonɨhɨbai
handcar, railroad kɨ?wɨnɨbaa?i,
    pi?yɨpɨ káa?i W
handcuff a person mo?o wɨhtamarɨ
-handed, left ohinikatɨ
-handed, right tɨbitsikatɨ
handicapped persons
    wɨ?mina?nɨɨmɨ
handkerchief namotɨsibe?
handkerchief, work-type
    pɨesúube? K
handle tɨtsɨhanitɨ
handle, carry by the natsayaarɨ
handle, carry (a container by the)
    tsahimarɨ, tsayarɨ
hands, clap tohtarakitɨ
hands, crack something with
    marɨbarɨ
hands, crease with the
    makwipunarɨ K
hands and knees, crawl on
    mahu?netɨ
hands, hold mo?o tsaaitɨ
hands, loosen with mahkwɨmarɨ
hands, make a hole with
    tsahtaikɨtɨ

hands in the water, paddle
paruhparu

**hands to expel water, press down
with** mabitsooru

hands, release from mabuaru

**hands, rub applying pressure with
the** masu?neru

hands together, rub namusu?netu

hands, wring out with tsahpitsooru

handsaw mo?o huutsihka?a?

hand saw, two-man huutsihkaa?

hang natsawenitu

hang a long object on a line wusóoru

**hang (choke to death by rope
around the neck)** oihtuyaitu

hang meat up to dry ina?etu

hang oneself nuukwenitu

hang over something nuusoo?etu

hang someone with a rope
ooibehkaru

hang something tsakwenitu,
turohtsanitu, wenuaru

hang suspended tsanikatu

hang up totsubakitu, wukweniitu K

hang up carelessly wuhtsanitu

hang up something tohtsanaru

**hang up something on a nail or
hook** tsa?wenitu, tsahkwenitu W

hang up to dry pasahtohtsanaru

hanger natsaweni?

hanger, clothes kwasu?u sakweni,
oo?ru tohtsana? W

hanging narohtsanaru,
natsahkweniitu

hanging, knock off something
wuhtokaru

hanging down, pant with tongue
hehekubuniitu

Hanging-from-the-belt Tu?sina?

happen naharu

happen to be somewhere
nahabitutu

happening nahapu

happy tsaa nuusukatu

happy, feel na?okusuaru

harass by chatter nimusasuaru

hard kuhtáatu, kutáatu

hard (and brittle), be koobetu

hard cider saah totsi baa

hard up nahawaru?ikatu

harness nabusa nabikapu,
narumuhku

harness, fasten on namuhkaru

harness, leather nabikapu

harness buckle nuuhtupika?

harness something nanoomanitu

harrow siibaru K, tsatusukitu,
tutsatuki?, tutsatusukitu

harrowed tutsatusukitu

harvest koho?aaitu, tso?mepu

harvest a crop pomaru

harvested crop pomapu

hastily yohyaku

hat soni tso?nika?, tso?nika?

hat, fur puhu tso?nika?

hat, have a tsonikaru

hat, straw soni tso?nika?

hat, wear a tso?nikaru

hatchet tsohpe tuhka?aa? W

hateful tumabiso?aitu

haul away nookwaru

haul away, to nooru

haul in noohkiru, noopitu

haul in a vehicle manooru

haul off tsawehkwatu

haul sand pasiwanooru

hauling noo-

have a backache piwo?sa wunaru

have a backache in lower back
piwo?sa wunukatu

have a hat tsonikaru

have a headache papikamaitu

have a husband kuumabaitu

have a sore throat kuitsisuatu

have a stiff neck woʔrohtsaru
have an appetite tsihasuaru
have an earache naki wunukatu
have an evil spirit poosubuhkaitu
have authority tusuʔatsitu
have bad odor kwanaru
have children turuetuparu
have cold feet tasukumitu
have cramp (in hand) maʔwutsa
  roʔponitu
have famine tsihakooihkatu
have hope kuʔuru
have leg cramp taʔitsaʔburu W,
  taʔwitsa roponiitu K
have mercy sutaaitu
have money puhihwi tuaru
have moonlight muahtabebaʔitu
have muscle cramp or spasm
  toponitu K
have odor kwanaru
have pneumonia tuʔinawunuru
have power tusuʔatsitu
have something in hand yahkatu
have underwear on tsaʔnikukatu
having a sibling takaʔkatu
having supernatural power
  puhakatu
haw, black tubokóo, wokwekatu
  huupi
haw, red tuʔamowoo
hawk tosa nakaai
hawk, chicken kokoráʔa
  aràhimaʔetu
hay rake tutsaʔooki?
he maʔ, oru, suru, u, uru
head paapi, papi
head, carry on the kuyaaru
head, carry something on the
  tsoʔyaaru
head, cover the manaʔkoroomitu K
head, duck under water
  pakuʔneru

head down (on something), lay
  the tsohtukikatu
head, lift tsoʔnuaru
head in agreement, nod the
  nihtsamuʔitu
head in disagreement, shake
  kaʔwitsetu K
head into something, poke
  tsoʔnikaru, tutsoʔnikaru
head, raise tsoʔnuaru
head against something, rub
  tsotsoʔneetu
head no, shake the tsoʔwiketu
head, squeeze to a maʔokweru
head lice, search for pusiaketu
head, sunflower hiʔoopitaohayaa
head, wipe something with the
  tsotsomaru
head louse pusiʔa, yupusia
head of hair tsoʔyaaʔ
headache papi wunukatu
headache, have a papikamaitu
headdress pia tsoʔnikaʔ
-headed buzzard, red ekabapi
headwear, try on tsohponiitu
heal yurahpetu
heal-all plant puhakatu
health, improve in tebuunitu
health, person of delicate takwipu
healthy kehoʔyopitu,
  kenamaʔubuʔitu
heap up pia wuʔutsitu
hear nakaru W
hear or make noise in timber
  huukisaakitu
hear, over- nakuhooru
hear something tunakaru
hearer, place known by speaker
  and pukuhu
hearing tunakatu
Hears-the-sunrise Tabe nanika
hearse tuyai waikina K

hearse tᵾyaipᵾha nooʔeeʔtᵾ W
heart pihi-, pihinabooʔ, pihi̱
heart, sweet- notsaʔkaʔ,
   tᵾᵾʔurapᵾ W, K
hearted, good- ᵾrᵾʔ
heartily, laugh nanihkuparᵾ
hearth kutᵾhorapᵾ W
heat, explode from kupᵾtsarᵾ
heat, kill with kuhkuparᵾ
heat, radiate kusᵾwetᵾ
heat, shrivel up from
   kuhtakwitsooʔnitᵾ W
heat of fire kohtoopᵾ
heat something kuhtsᵾnikurᵾ
heated rock nakutᵾkᵾnaʔ
heater yuʔa nakohtooʔ
heating, dry by kupisarᵾ
heavens tomobaʔatᵾ, tomoobi̱
heavily, pant hehekᵾbᵾniitᵾ
heavily, tread tanᵾʔyᵾkitᵾ
heavy pᵾhtᵾ
heavy shawl pohotᵾ naʔsᵾkíaʔ
hedge apple etᵾhuupi
heed naki̱ hiikatᵾ K
heel, rubber tuuʔre tahpikoʔ
heel of shoe tahpi̱koʔ
heel of the foot tapi̱koʔ
heels, kneel down sitting back on
   tanatookarᵾtᵾ
height and health, grow in
   naanaarᵾ
held matsokatᵾ
hello ahó
help, ask for naníhtsawaʔitᵾ
help decide tsasuʔatsitᵾ
help down tsakwerᵾ
help, offer someone masutsarᵾ
help one another naruituahkarᵾ
help someone tᵾituarᵾ
help someone walk tsamiʔakᵾrᵾ
help to mount tohkᵾarᵾ
help up matsáyᵾtsᵾrᵾ

help up from sitting to standing
   position matsákwᵾnᵾkᵾrᵾ
hem pihkᵾmaʔ K
hemmorhage pᵾᵾokwetᵾ
hen nohabitᵾ, turuawapi̱
hen, laying turuawapi̱
hen, setting nohabitᵾ
her ma, mahka, ohka, ohko,
   pᵾ, uhka
herb pawahkapᵾ
herb, medicinal pᵾhᵾ natsu, pᵾhᵾ
   rᵾʔsaasi
herd marᵾa, tahkoonikarᵾ
herd, cut out of the tahkaaitᵾ
here iki̱
here (at this point) siʔanetᵾ
here, from sihkutᵾ
here, right makᵾ
-here, Wind-running Nᵾenuhkiki
hiccough hᵾʔniipᵾʔ, hᵾʔniitᵾ
Hiccough-daughter Hᵾʔnipitᵾ
hickory kᵾhtáa mubitaiʔ, pahtsi
   mubitai, paatsi mubitaiʔ
hide tuhᵾpᵾ, tᵾhᵾbᵾ, watsitᵾkitᵾ K,
   watsi̱ habiitᵾ
hide, animal pimoroʔa pᵾhi, pᵾhᵾʔ
hide, cow pimoroʔa pᵾhi
hide, dehair a wᵾhkwᵾnetᵾ
hide, process of tanning a
   narᵾsoʔipᵾ
hide, raw- ᵾhtaayuʔ
hide ready to use, raw- pahkipᵾ
hide rope, raw- pahki wiyaaʔ
hide, scrape meat from a
   tohtsiyuʔitᵾ
(hide oneself), secret oneself away
   watsi̱ habiitᵾ
hide, tan a kwiipᵾsiarᵾ, tᵾsoʔarᵾ
hide, tanned narᵾsoʔipᵾ, tᵾsoʔipᵾʔ
hide, tanned deer pikapᵾ
hide something namabimarᵾ
hide-and-seek naʔwekitᵾʔ

hides, pick for scraping
to?tsimuhpe?

high panihputʉ mabà?atʉ, pa?atʉ

high pitched putsi tʉnikwʉyʉ K

high pitched, sing putsi
kwʉtsʉbaitʉ

high up tsihtararʉ

hill keno, ku?ebi, noo-

hill, guess-over-the- nanípʉka

hill, one anáabi

hill standing alone, one nookararʉrʉ

hill, sand pasiwanoo? W

Hill People Ononʉʉ

hill up ma?ohta?aitʉ, wʉno?karʉrʉ

hillside keno

him ma, mahka, ohka, ohko, uhka

hind feet, standing on
manawʉnʉkatʉ

hindquarter kotsana, pabo tuhku,
tohoobe

hip piwo?sa

hips, walk swinging pi?weke mi?arʉ

hire naahkarʉ

hired cook tʉkʉ maniwapʉ

hired hand tʉrʉ?ai wapi

his pʉ

history narʉkuyunʉ rʉboopʉ

hit, attempt to (with a weapon)
wʉsukwarʉ W

-hit-someone, Take-a-stick-and
Huuwʉhtʉkwa?

hit and push under water
wʉhpaaku?nerʉ

hit by surprise wʉnʉ?yʉ?itʉ

hit repeatedly wʉhpa?itʉ

hit something wʉhtʉkwarʉ

hit with fist tohpa?itʉ

hit with fist, try or want to
toso?waitʉ

hit with fists na?arutʉ W

hit with knuckle or fist
tohtsi?arʉ W

hitch, un- too?itʉ

hitch a horse, un- noro?yarʉ

hitch an animal, un- to?yarʉ W

hitch up mahkarʉ W

hitch up horses and buggy
nomohkarʉ

hitched namamohkarʉ

hitting, make cry by toyaketʉ

**hitting with fist or palm of hand,
stop** tohpʉarʉ

hobble mo?o wʉhtama?

hobble an animal mo?o wʉhtamarʉ

hobble for a horse tʉmo?o
wʉhtama?

hoe kuwʉhora?, muhpe?, puhi
yʉkwitʉ?

hoe soil puhi yʉkwitʉ

hog hooki, mubi po?roo?, munua?,
po?ro?

hog fence mubi po?roo rʉhtʉma? W

hog-pen fence hooki tʉʉhtʉmapʉ

hog pen, fence of po?ro tʉhtʉmapʉ

hoggish pihitsitʉyarʉ

hogs po?ropʉnʉʉ

hold yahkatʉ

**hold a curing ceremony for
someone** puha?arʉ

hold back information
niwatsi?aikʉ?itʉ

hold council ka?witʉ

hold down with hand makʉnaitʉ

hold hands mo?o tsaaitʉ

hold races narʉrʉnitʉ

hold something yuhnukarʉ

hole taaitʉ, taina

hole, animal itsaraitʉ ʉnʉa kahni

hole, chop a wʉhkonarʉ

hole, dig a horarʉ, tʉhhorarʉ

hole, dig a fire kutʉhorarʉ

hole, dig a (in the ground)
tohkonarʉ

hole digger, post- tʉhora?

hole, drill a (with an instrument)
tohtʉbʉʔitʉ

hole, fire kutʉhorapʉ W

hole with hands, make a
tsahtaikʉtʉ

hole, smoke kahkuʔe, kahni kuʔe

hole dug by man nahorapʉ

hole dug in soil hoora

holes saaʔwʉ

holey saaʔwʉtʉ, tsahtaaikatʉ

hollow haʔwoʔitʉ, kuwoʔnepʉ,
tʉhaʔwokatʉ

hollow, make wʉhhaʔwokarʉ

holly, yaupon ekapokopi

Holy Spirit Atsabiʔ

home kah-, kahni

home, (to) arrive tsakʉbitʉkitʉ

home or room, invite into
niʔikaʔitʉ

home, own a nʉmʉnakarʉ

home as guest, take someone
panimiʔarʉ

home-grown garden product
masʉapʉ W

homogeneous suunitʉ

homogeneous throughout sʉmʉ
susʉnitʉ

hone tʉmakʉmaʔarʉ

honey ʉnʉ bihnaa

Honey Eaters Pena tʉhka

honey K wobi pihnaaʔ

honey locust wokʉ huupi

honey sieve ʉnʉʉʔ ruuʔ

honeybee wobi pihnaa ʉnʉʉʔ

honeycomb ʉnʉ bihnaa kahni K,
wobi pihnaaʔ W

honor mabitsiarʉ

honored maritsiakatʉ

hoof tasiito, tosiite

hoofprints tʉhʉyena puni W

hook nanʉʉhtʉpʉkaʔ, natsaweniʔ,
tʉrohtsaniʔiʔ

hook, fish hʉaʔ W

hook, shoe- napʉbosaʔ

hook something muhkarʉ W

hook up doubletrees on buggy
nomohkarʉ

hoot muunanahwenurʉ W

hope nasupetiʔ

hope, have kʉʔurʉ

hope in nasupetitʉ

horizon, stand just above the tabe
wʉnʉʔitʉ

horn aamuyakeʔ

horn, animal aa

horn, devil's aakáaʔ

horn, saddle narʉnoo bapi

horn, sounding of a muyakeʔ

horn brush aanatsihtuyeʔ

horned toad kuhtsu tʉbiniʔ

horse esikʉhmaʔ, puku, pʉa watsi,
tʉhʉya, tosa nabooʔ K

horse, bay ekakʉmaʔ, ohaekaʔ K,
tupisi kʉmaʔ, W ohaekapitʉ

horse, be thrown forcibly from a
wʉpʉherʉ W

horse, break a masuyuʔikarʉ K

horse, bridle a tʉpe tsaʔnikarʉ

horse, buckskin naʔnia

horse, calico pitsa nabooʔ K

horse, chestnut-brown otʉ kʉmaʔ W

horse, devil's tosaraiʔ

horse, hobble for a tʉmoʔo
wʉhtamaʔ

horse, lead a puku tsakamiʔarʉ

horse, lead up a tsakʉhunitʉ

horse, mount a tʉyatoʔyerʉ

horse, palomino kwipʉsiapʉ,
naʔahnia K

horse, sorrel otʉ kʉmaʔ W, tʉpʉsi
kʉmaʔ

horse, tie up a tʉʉtsʉkʉnarʉ

horse, unbridle a tʉpe
tsahkweʔyarʉ

horse, unhitch a noro?yarʉ
horse, un- tsiperʉ
horse, unsaddle a narʉnoo?ro?yarʉ
Horse Band, Water Tasúra
horse, white tosa?
horse blanket nahotsa?ma?
horse brush tʉhʉya natsihtu?ye?
horse buggy, one- sʉmasʉ nooi K
horse tracks tʉhʉyena puni W
horse-drawn sulky sʉmasʉ nooi K
Horseback Kiyu, Tʉhʉyana kwahipʉ
horseback, carry someone behind on piyarʉ
horseback, chase on tomakwʉyetʉ W
horseback, climb on tʉhʉya ro?itʉ
horseback, mount on nʉʉhto?itʉ
horseback, ride kʉayʉka?etʉ W, tʉhʉya karʉ
horsefly pia animui, pihpi̱
horses and buggy, hitch up nomohkarʉ
horseweed tosa wahtsuki
hosiery, ladies waipa wananapʉ
hospital natʉsu?u̱ kahni, wʉmi̱naa kahni
hospitality, extend to a guest mananaa?waihkarʉ
hot day tabe kusʉwehkatʉ
hot, turn red ekawehaarʉ
hot weather ʉrʉ?itʉ
hound dog naki̱ sarii?
hound, blood- tʉrayaa sarii
hour hand tabe mo?o
house kah-, kahni, kahni
house, build a kahni?aitʉ
house, construct a (or other building) kahni?aitʉ
house, adobe ohta kahni W
house, bird- huutsú?a kàhni̱
house, frame wobi ka̱hni
house, rooming kwaabih kahni

house, school tʉboo kahni
house, Stone- Tʉpi kʉni?
house, stone or brick tʉpi kʉni
house, sweat nasukoo?i kahni
house, trailer kahni tʉbitsika? K
house bug (of any kind) kahni busi̱?a
house mouse kahúu?
house of thieves tʉrʉkʉ kahni
house paint kahni̱ ebi̱ K
housefly animui̱
household goods namahku
housetop kahni ku?e
how many? hʉʉ
how many? how much? hipeka?i, hipetʉ
how? hakai, hakani
how, show tʉmabunikʉrʉ
how?, what way? hakaniiku
howl woo?etʉ
howl woohpʉnitʉ, woorʉ
Howling-coyote Isananaka?
huckleberry huwabo?kóo?
hug kwabarʉ, toyo kwabarʉ
human or an animal, trail a nayaarʉ
human skin hʉnʉpo?a?, mapó?a?
humble kesósoorʉ
hummingbird wʉ?kʉ?buu?
hunchback no?wosarʉ
hung up narohtsanarʉ, natsahkweniitʉ
hunger tsihasuarʉ
hungry person, ravenously tsihasi?apʉ
hunt ho?aitʉ, tʉkerʉ
hunt game tʉhoitʉ
hunting, go tʉwoorʉ W
hurriedly namʉsi, yohyaku
hurry tsanamʉsohnitʉ, yohyakatʉ K
hurry, cause to tsanamʉsohnitʉ
hurry up namʉsohitʉ

hurt tohhobinitʉ, wʉhhubinitʉ

hurt oneself nahohiyaitʉ,
   nahuhyaitʉ W, namarʉnitʉ K

hurt someone mawʉmerʉ,
   tsiyaketʉ, umarhnitʉ

hurt someone by accident
   tsahhuhyarʉ

husband kumahpʉ?, mukwo,
   namuwoo

**husband, granddaughter's
   (grandson-in-law)** tso?aahpʉ?

husband, have a kuumabaitʉ

husband, reject man as ninakabarʉ

husbands nanahtenanʉʉ

hush pʉhkai

hushed pʉhkaikatʉ

hyacinth, wild siiko

hymn hubiya?

hypocritical nakaa?aitʉ

I i

I nʉ?

I claim it! aahe

ice tahkabi

ice or snow tahka-

ice pick wiiyu̲

icebox tahka aawo

icicle tahka we?wenuka?

ignore kwetʉsuakʉrʉ W

ill ho?yopitʉ, ho?yopi̲

ill, be tʉ?oibʉkʉrʉ, uhúntʉkʉ̲

ill for a long time tʉ?oikatʉ̲,
   wʉminahkatʉ

illness hubʉhka?, wʉmi̲naa?

illness, long tʉ?oipʉ

illness, recover from tebuunitʉ

illness, suffer an tʉ?oibʉkʉrʉ

imitate a cry niyakekʉtʉ̲

immediately kihtsi?, namʉsohi,
   sube?sʉ

immerse oneself in water
   nabawʉhtiarʉ

-immolate (sacrifice/destroy), self
   kuhtʉyarʉ

**implement for punching holes
   (through which sinews pass)**
   wiiyu̲

important man namʉnewapi̲

imprison takwekwitʉ

imprisoned ta?ikʉkatʉ

improve in health tebuunitʉ

in, gather tʉbomarʉ

in, haul noohkirʉ, noopitʉ

in a vehicle, haul manoorʉ

in, hope nasupetitʉ

in ashes, roast kusiwʉhpima W

in, screw wʉ?nikarʉ

in, screw something tsakwipunarʉ

in, share tʉmaramiitʉ

in, sneak watsi ikatʉ

in, stuck down tsʉhkarʉ

in agreement, nod the head
   nihtsamu?itʉ

in disagreement, shake head
   ka?witsetʉ K

in front of hunaku̲, munakwʉ̲

in sun to dry, sit mabasahtʉkitʉ K

in the mud, stuck sekwi sʉhkai,
   yubutsʉhkatʉ

in the mouth, take something
   kʉhyaarʉ

in-law nanamʉsu?, na?anampʉ

-in-law, brother pʉhʉ re?tsi

-in-law, daughter huutsi piahpʉ?,
   huutsi̲ piahpʉ

-in-law, parent yahihpʉ?

-in-law, sister paha piahpʉ

-in-law, son monahpʉ?

-in -law, sons nonanʉʉ

in-laws, go live with nahyemi?arʉ

in place, put narʉkitʉ̲, tʉkarʉ

in place, set natsawʉnʉkatʉ

in place, set something
natsawʉnʉrʉ

in the sun to dry, sit
pasahtahtʉkitʉ W

in water, sink to the bottom
paʔikarʉ

in water, soak parʉkitʉ

in water, soak oneself naparʉkitʉ

incite to rear up manáawʉnʉʔetʉ

incline tʉpána?

increasing numerically
tʉrakaʔaitʉ

index finger tʉtsihtsuka?

Indian agent itsina, nʉmʉ paraibo?

Indian brave tekwʉniwapi,
tuibihtsi?, tʉetekwʉni wapi

Indian bread tʉranʉ

Indian breadroot ekahkoni

Indian butter tʉʉtsohpepʉ

Indian corn nʉmʉ hani

Indian corncake nʉmʉ nohkopʉ

Indian, non- taiboo?

Indian paintbrush kahnitʉeka

Indian perfume plant tʉsaasi

Indian store nʉmʉ narʉmʉʉ?

Indian tobacco tabahko

Indian-type saddle tʉmuhku

inexact hoʔyopipʉ

inexactly, mark nahoʔyopikurʉ

infected pisi

infecting pisi miʔarʉ

infection pisi

inflate mubohtohkirʉ,
mubohtohkitʉ, pohtokʉrʉ

influenza ebi wʉmina?

inform ninʉsuabitarʉ K

information, hold back
niwatsiʔaikʉʔitʉ

inhale deeply through nose
muhibitʉ

ink pen parʉboo?

inquire nikwʉkitʉ

insane, become sua watsitʉ

insect ʉnú?

insect, stinger of an tona?

insect sting tonarʉ

insert taʔnikʉtʉ, tsihtaboʔikʉtʉ

insert hand tʉmaʔniikarʉ K 2

insert into something tsiʔnikarʉ,
wʉnikarʉ

inspect tsaʔatsitʉ

instruct nimabunikʉtʉ,
nitsʉbunikʉtʉ

instrument, any wind woinu

instrument, drill a hole with an
tohtʉbʉʔitʉ

instrument, knock off with an
wʉpʉherʉ W

instrument, marking naboo? K

instrument, play mayaketʉ

instrument, play a wind
muuyaketʉ

instrument, scratch using an
tsahkiʔaitʉ

insult niʔheʔbunitʉ

intend tʉbitsi suarʉ

intend to deceive or cheat
kaasuarʉ

intercede nanisutaikʉtʉ

interpret tekwakʉtʉ

interpreter tekwakʉwapi W

interpreter of Comanche nʉmʉ
rekwakʉ wapi

**interrupt someone (because of
worry)** pisukwitakʉrʉ

intestinal flu kohikamʉkatʉ

intestine tuhkohhi W

intestine, large kwitatsi, paboko

intestine, small kohi

into, dump toʔwʉʔwenitʉ, wʉhtiarʉ

into, empty toʔwʉʔwenitʉ,
wʉhtiarʉ

into, load tʉrʉbakiʔarʉ

into a container, load toʔnikarʉ W

into small particles, mash
mahomonutsarʉ

into, peep tokwi̱tetʉ

into something, poke head
tsoʔnikarʉ, tʉtsoʔnikarʉ

into the mouth, put something
tʉroʔnikarʉ

into two parts, split tʉapakoʔitʉ

into the fire, throw kuhtsahwirʉ

into a ball, wind wʉhtopoʔnitʉ

intoxicated hibipʉ, makwiʔnumaitʉ

intoxicated person hibipʉ,
kwinumapʉ

introduce oneself nani̱suabetaʔaitʉ,
natsahpunitʉ

introduce someone nisuabetarʉ W

invalid tʉʔoipʉ, wʉhminanʉʉmʉ,
wʉminahkatʉ

invalids wʉʔminaʔnʉʉmʉ

invite into home or room
niʔikaʔitʉ

invite someone in nikwekwitʉ

invite to congregate sʉʉmaʔokarʉ

invite to go along petsʉ kwarʉ

-invites-her-relatives, She Nʉmʉ
ruibetsʉ

iridescent weʔkwi̱yanorʉ

Irish potato paapasi̱

iron tahkwʉʔnerʉ, tʉrah kwʉʔneʔ

iron, branding tʉkohpooʔ

iron, flat- tʉrah kwʉʔneʔ

iron clothing tʉrah kwʉʔnerʉ K

ironing board pʉpaʔakura
tʉrahkwʉʔneʔena̱

irrationally, speak niʔemʉabʉnitʉ

island paa tʉpʉnaatʉʔ W, sokobi
paa tʉbi̱naatʉ W

isolated toroʔihtʉkitʉ

it ma, mahka, maʔ, orʉ, surʉ, u,
uhka, urʉ

it is said that tʉa

It is worse! namanoke

itch pihnaketʉ, pihnaaketʉ

itch, scratch an natsawoʔnitʉ,
tsakwoʔnerʉ

item, exchange one for another
mabihtʉʔuyarʉ

item, finished namarʉkapʉ

item, jagged wakʉʔwʉtʉ

item, return an yaakʉrʉ

item by item, remove wʉpi̱yarʉ

item, sharpened namakʉmaʔaipʉ

item taken (or object) yaapʉ

item, tested marʉmabunipʉ

item, tried marʉmabunipʉ

item, two-year-old tomohtoopʉ W

items, exchange several gift
naʔoyorʉmakarʉ K

items, load tʉbakitʉ

its pʉ

itself, roll up to wʉhkwitubikatʉ

up with something, roll
tohtopoʔnarʉ

ivy, poison puhi taʔaraʔ

J j

jab tsisuʔwarʉ

jack ekakuyáaʔ, suutaʔ

jackal kaawosa̱

jacket, man's buckskin pika
kwasuʔ

jacket, yellow otʉ peena

jagged item wakʉʔwʉtʉ

jail narawekwi̱ kahni, tʉpi kʉni

January Tohmʉa, Ʉkʉ tooma mʉa

jar paboko aawo

jaw ahra, arapʉ

jealous tʉsuwaʔitʉ

jealousy, rival provoking
wohhohpʉʔ

jeer nisuʔuyaitʉ W

jeer at tʉni̱suʔuyaitʉ

jelly ekayʉʔyʉʔkaʔ
jelly, petroleum nʉʉhtʉʔekaʔ, tsiikṳwitehkaʔ K, tsiʔwṵnʉʉ tʉʔekaʔ W
jerk and slam things in anger tuhu rekwarʉ
jerk, bodily yʉʔyʉturʉ
jerk, hand mayʉʔyʉrʉ
jerk down tsapeherʉ
jerk meat inaʔetʉ
jerk meat for someone tʉʔinakʉrʉ
jerk something wʉhpoʔtserʉ K
jerk something toward oneself tsahpoʔtsarʉ
jerk the leg taʔyʉrʉhkitʉ K
jerk the lower leg tahtaʔyʉtʉ
jerked meat inapṳ, inarʉ
jerky esi inapṳ, inapṳ
jerky, meat inarʉ
jerky), roast meat over fire (or dry it for kuʔinarʉ
Jesus-man Wʉkwiya
jewelry nʉnatsiʔnikaʔ
jingles pisayuʔneʔ
jock strap tsaʔnikaʔ
join in tʉmaramiitʉ
joint natsiminaʔ
joint, break at the taminaitʉ
joint. pull bones out of tsahtokoʔarʉ
joint of the body, sprain a wʉkwṵsarʉ
joke nohitekwarʉ
joker nayanohitekwarʉʔ
jowl meat aratuhku
judge nanakukʉtʉ
judicial power tʉsuʔatsipṳ
jug tʉpi aawo
jug, water pihpóoʔ
juice yoka
juice, grape natsamukweʔa paa

July Pia mʉa, Pʉmata pia buhha raʔena mʉa, Ʉrʉi mʉa
jump pohbitʉ
jumping rope nʉhpopiʔ
June Puhi mʉa
june bug tuʉnʉʉʔ
juniper ekawaapi
just nah
just above the horizon, stand tabe wʉnʉʔitʉ

K k

kangaroo paʔsʉnoʔaʔ
kebob, shish kutsiyaapʉ
keep an orphan as foster child tahnikatʉ, tʉkiihkarʉ
keep quiet niwatsiʔaikʉʔitʉ
keep secret watsiʔarʉ
keep sharpened wʉmutsiakatuʔi
keep something tahtʉkarʉ
kerosene ketoʔkapaa, tukaʔa nabaa
key tʉtsihtʉmaʔ
khaki koropitṵ
kick sʉʉ anirʉ, sʉʉhkwʉhtitʉ
kick off sʉʉtaʔniʔarʉ
kick something sʉʉhkwʉhtʉkurʉ
kick something away sʉʉ potserʉ
kick-the-can soo tʉhimarʉʔ
kicked away sʉʉhpotsʉkatʉ
kicking, discarded by sʉʉhpotsʉkatʉ
kid around kaasuarʉ
kidney taʔkiʔ
kill pehkarṳ, tʉkwṵsʉrʉ, wasʉrʉ
kill by growing over puhi tʉyaitʉ
kill several persons nakwṵsʉkʉrʉ
kill with a weapon wʉhkuparʉ, wʉhtokweetʉ
kill with heat kuhkuparʉ
killed, cause to be nabehkakʉrʉ

Kills-something Pakawa
kind ᵾruʔ
kind thoughts tᵾsuʔᵾruʔ
kinds, different nanaʔataputᵾ,
  nanịsusumatᵾ
king tanisiʔ W
king in playing-card deck
  ohahkuyaaʔ
kingfisher pekwi tᵾhkaʔ
kinsman naʔnᵾᵾmᵾ
kinsman, adult nahnapᵾ
kinsman, female naʔnᵾmᵾ
kinsman, man's female naʔwaʔihpᵾʔ
kinsman, male naabia, nahbiʔa
kinsman, man's male narenahpᵾʔ
kinsman, woman's female
  waʔihpᵾʔ
kinsman of either sex taʔkaʔ
Kiowa people Kaaiwanᵾᵾ
kiss muhraaʔipᵾ
kiss, cause to tsamuhraikᵾtᵾ
kiss someone muhrarᵾ
knead mabarᵾ W, tᵾmabarᵾ
knee tana
kneecap tanaʔ kuʔe
kneel down sitting back on heels
  tanatookarᵾtᵾ
knees, crawl on tahuʔnerᵾ
knife nahuuʔ W, nahhooʔ K
knife, cut with a tsihkaʔarᵾ
knife, drawing nahuuʔ W,
  nahhooʔ K
knife, draw- huusibeʔ
knife edge kᵾmapᵾ
knock down wᵾhkwabikᵾrᵾ
knock down by force
  wᵾnᵾᵾkuparᵾ
knock off tokarᵾ, wᵾyumiʔitᵾ
knock off something hanging
  wᵾhtokarᵾ
knock off with an instrument
  wᵾpᵾherᵾ W

knock on totᵾbihkurᵾ
knock on door tohtarakiʔarᵾ
knock over and spill accidentally
  tsakwᵾriarᵾ
knock something wᵾhpoʔtserᵾ K
knock something down
  tayuʔmarᵾ
knocked down wᵾnᵾᵾhkuparᵾ
knocked over mahuihkatᵾ
knoll noo-
knot, tie a wᵾtsᵾkᵾnarᵾ
knot, tie in round bundle or round
  wᵾhtopᵾʔnoorᵾ
know by experience masuabetaitᵾ
knowing supanaʔitᵾ
knowledge of, lack kemabanaʔitᵾ
knowledgeable supanaʔitᵾ
known by speaker and hearer,
  place pᵾkᵾhu
knuckles, crack tsahporakitᵾ

L l

labor, be in tuakatᵾ
labor in childbirth nᵾhtsikwarᵾ
lace saaʔwᵾ tᵾkᵾmaʔaiʔ
lace, shoe- napᵾ tsakwᵾsaʔ,
  napᵾbosaʔ
lace, un- tsahkwᵾmarᵾ
lace up tsakwᵾsarᵾ W
laced napᵾ saarᵾ
laced object natsakwᵾsikᵾʔ
lack naromᵾnitᵾ
lack knowledge of kemabanaʔitᵾ
lacrosse, play natsihtóoʔitᵾ
ladder huunaroʔiʔ, naroʔiʔ
ladies hosiery waipa wananapᵾ
lady, old narutsaʔi
lake ᵾmahpaaʔ
lamb kabᵾrᵾᵾʔa tua
lamely, walk wihnai miʔarᵾ

lamp kupiṭa?, natsayaa ruka? K, tuka?, tʉka?

lamp or fire, light a kupiṭarʉ

lamp chimney tuka?a naku?e W

lamp wick tuka?a nawanapi̱

lamppost tuka?a nahhuupi̱

land soko, sokoobi̱

land, deed or title to nabinai tʉboopʉ

land, lease soko rʉmʉrʉ

land, quarter-section of soko tsihka?apʉ

land, uneven wohtsa?wʉtʉ

language, sign mootekwo?pʉ

language, speak Wichita tuhka?naai rekwarʉ

language, Speakers of Wichita tuhka?naai? niwʉnʉ

lantern natsayaa ruka? K

lap pʉkapʉ

lap with the tongue ka?amoorʉ

lard yuhhu K, yuhukarʉka W

lard, render kuhpitsuni?arʉ W, ku?okwerʉ W, yuhukarʉ

large pia

large intestine kwitatsi̱, paboko

large object piapʉ 1

lariat moowi?

lark, field hiitoo? K, N, ohanʉnapʉ W

lark, meadow- hiitoo? K, N, ohanʉnapʉ W

lash kwibukitʉ

last kwasikʉ

late keyu K, keyu?u

late, stay tsʉ?nitʉ

late, too ʉi

late in the day tabe?ehi

late-summer plum parawa sʉkʉ

laugh na?yʉnetʉ, yahneetʉ

laugh at su?uyaa?arʉ, tʉni̱su?uyaitʉ, usú?uya?itʉ W

laugh heartily nanihkuparʉ

laughingstock nanʉsu?uyaatʉ, su?uya?i?

laughter yahnena

lavender esiebipi̱tʉ

lavender W kusiebipi̱tʉ

law mahyarʉ

-law, in nanamʉsu?, na?anampʉ

-law, brother-in pʉhʉ re?tsi̱

-law, daughter-in huutsi piahpʉ?, huutsi̱ piahpʉ

-law, parent-in yahihpʉ?

-law, sister-in paha piahpʉ

-law, son- in monahpʉ?

-law, sons-in nonanʉʉ

laws, go live with in- nahyemi?arʉ

lawman nʉmi hima?etʉ

lawnmower soni wʉtsʉke? K, tʉʉtsʉke? W

Lawton, OK Soo kʉni?

Lawton, Okla Puha rʉpaanʉ

lawyer nani?ooki̱ taiboo?

lay an egg, want to nohabi̱ suwaitʉ

lay eggs turuarʉ

lay out tsakwʉnarʉ

lay something down tʉkiitʉ K

lay the head down on something tsohtʉkikatʉ

layer, take off tsahkwʉrʉ?arʉ

laying hen turuawapi̱

lazy tsanʉmaitʉ

lazy, become nʉʉ?maitʉ

lead umami?arʉ

lead a horse puku tsakami̱?arʉ

lead a person or an animal tsakarʉ

lead along matsaaihkakurʉ, tsakami?arʉ

lead astray tsaka?uhrʉ

lead away a wife nʉpetsʉ?itʉ

lead off by force sutena betsʉmiarʉ

lead others muhnemi?arʉ

lead up a horse tsakʉhunitʉ

leader namɨnewapi̠, nanohmɨnɨ wapi̠ K, nomɨnewapi̠ W

leader, pack-animal tɨnoo wapi̠

leaf puhi, puhipɨ

leaf mixture, mesquite- patso?

leaf wrappers for cigarettes puhi tɨmakwatubi?

leak pasiwɨnɨɨrɨ

lean against something nɨɨbani̠katɨ

lean on something mahtokwɨnaitɨ K

lean over something nɨɨsoo?etɨ

lean something namahtowɨnarɨ

learn nara?urakɨtɨ

learn by experience masuabetaitɨ

learn something new urahkarɨ

lease land soko rɨmɨrɨ

leather nabikapɨ, paakipɨ, pika, pikapɨ, taibo pikapɨ

leather harness nabikapɨ

leave a spouse pɨah kwarɨ

leave, order to nihto?itɨ

leave person alone kekɨnabeniitɨ

leave secretly watsi mi?arɨ

leave someone behind nobɨahraitɨ

leave someone for good pɨa mi?arɨ

leaves, corn hani buhipɨ

leaving a mark, scratch tsahtsi?arɨ

Lee Motah Mota

leech tu?re?

left ohinibetutɨ

left side, at or to the ohininakwɨ

left-handed ohinikatɨ

leftover piinaai

leftover food kɨhtɨkɨto?ipɨ, tɨkɨ to?ipɨ

leg bones tɨrana̠

leg, calf of ta?wiitsa̠

leg, foot and lower napɨ|b-|r

leg, foot or lower nara-

leg, fore- tohoobe̠

leg cramp, have ta?itsa?bɨrɨ W, ta?witsa roponiitɨ K

leg hair tapɨ K

leg, jerk the ta?yɨrɨhkitɨ K

leg, jerk the lower tahta?yɨtɨ

leg, lower naape̠, omo-

leg, raise one tahtsarɨ

legs out, spread po?arɨ

legume pitsa múu

leisurely supewaitɨ

lemon ohahpitɨ sɨkɨ?kamatɨ W, sɨkɨ ka?ma?

leopard naboohmatɨsohpe? W, naboohroya ruhku? K, toya ruhku?

lesion narɨ?ɨyɨ ɨɨ?a?

let an arrow fly wɨhkikatɨ

let out tahto?itɨ

letter tɨboopɨ

letter or package, mail a tɨhyetɨ

lettuce puhi tɨhkapɨ

level sɨɨpetɨ

level valley haapane

liar isapɨ, kaawosa̠, naya?isa?aitɨ

Liar Isatekwa

lice, search for head pusiaketɨ

lice eggs tatsii?

lick ekwɨsibeniitɨ

lid narohtɨma?, tɨmarɨma? K, tɨrohtɨma?

lie isapɨ, isa?aitɨ

lie down haahpi̠tɨ, habiitɨ, kwabitɨ

lie down and think nasutamɨ habitɨ

lie down , force to (wielding a weapon) wɨhhabi?arɨ

lie on back pa?raihabiitɨ

Lie-talk Isatekwa

-lie, This-midday-sun-does-not-tell-a Sihka tabe ke isopɨ

life nɨmɨnaina?, yɨ?yɨmuhkuna̠

life, save someone's tsahkwitso?arʉ
life!, That's namami?akʉ
lift wʉyarʉ
lift from a prone position tsahnʉarʉ
lift head tso?nʉarʉ
lift up toyarʉ, tsahhʉkwʉ?niitʉ W
light kupita?, tuka?, tʉka?
light on something, throw a
    kupitarʉ
light a lamp or fire kupitarʉ
light blue ebipitʉ, kusipi W
    kusiebipitʉ K
light, flash- kupita?
light meat pabo tuhku
light-complected pabopitʉ
lighted, un- tukanikatʉ
lightly, rub makwʉ?netʉ
lightly with the hand, touch
    makwʉ?netʉ
lightning bug kuna na?mahpee?
lightning, discharge a flash of
    ekakwitse?erʉ
lightning flash ekakwitse?e
lightweight tahi
lightweight shawl tapi na?sʉkia?
-like-a-mouse, Squeaky Kahúu
    nihku pipikurẹ
like someone su?akʉtʉ
lily, plant similar to water
    pa?mutsi
lily, yellow pond kʉriata
limb, tree huupita mooka
limited space, cram into
    natsinʉhkʉrʉ
limited space, crammed into
    tsinʉkʉ
limp matʉwetʉ, pitʉwetʉ, tatʉwetʉ,
    wihnai mi?arʉ
line, clothes- tʉrohtsani?i?
line, draw tsihpoorʉ
line, hang a long object on a
    wʉsóorʉ

lion pʉhʉ ku?kwe?ya?
lion, mountain wʉra?
lips tʉpe, tuupe
liquid, drain a tsa?ohkwerʉ
liquid, spit out pai tusi?itʉ K
liquid tea puhi tuhpaa W
listen nakʉhitʉ, tokwetʉparʉ,
    tʉnakarʉ, tʉnakiitʉ
listen carefully tʉbitsinakʉkʉrʉ K
listen to someone tʉmahyokʉrʉ
listen with attention nakị hiikatʉ K
listening nakʉkatʉ
little tʉe
little bit hʉitsi
little bluestem ekasonipʉ
little finger mahtua?,
    tʉehmahtua? W
little one tʉe?tʉ
little people similar to elves
    Nʉnapi
little toe tahtúa?, tʉeh tahtua?
Little-buffalo Tʉe kuhtsu
Little-medicine Tʉe buakʉtʉ
Little-wolf Esatai
live kahtʉ, yʉ?yʉmuhkumi?arʉ W
live separately, move off to
    noka?itʉ
live, take away something
    tahtʉkitʉ
live somewhere nʉmʉnetʉ
live unconcerned yukahnibarʉ
live well yunʉmitʉ, yʉyʉkarʉ
live with in-laws, go nahyemi?arʉ
liver nʉʉmʉ
Liver Eaters Taninʉʉ
livingroom pʉkʉra yʉkwi?ena W
lizard nakị tai?, nʉmʉ
    ma?tsa?bahki?, paboko?ai,
    wanasihtaraa? W
lizard, rock tʉpi paboko?aai W
lizard, water pa?boosi?
load noona K

load, carry tɨnoorɨ
load into tɨrɨbaki?arɨ
load into a container to?nikarɨ W
load items tɨbakitɨ
load on foot, pack a tɨnoomi?arɨ
load, un- tsahpɨherɨ, tsapɨyetɨ,
  tsayumi?i
load up tɨnookɨrɨ
loaf of bread paanɨ
lobe, ear W nakɨ kwiita
locate something ta?wairɨ
location, throughout a oyo?rɨtu
lock tɨtsihtɨma?
lock, pad- natsihtɨma?
lock something, pad- tɨtsihtɨrɨ
lock, un- tsihtɨwarɨ
lock up someone ta?ikɨrɨ
locked up ta?ikɨkatɨ
loco weed esinɨɨhparabi
locust soo yake? W
locust, honey wokɨ huupɨ
loincloth tsa?nika?
lollypop mukwite?
Lone-tipi Atakɨni
long pa?a-, pa?atɨ
long ago soo be?sɨ
long and flat huyuba?atɨ
long illness tɨ?oipɨ
long time, ill for a tɨ?oikatɨ,
  wɨminahkatɨ
look at punitɨ, tɨpunirɨ
look at oneself nabunitɨ
look behind oneself nabitɨbunitɨ
look for ho?aniitɨ, puhwaaitɨ,
  wehkitɨ
look for, go on foot to takwainitɨ
look for money puhihwi wehki
look over puiwɨnɨrɨ
Looking Punitɨ
looking glass nabuni?
Looking-from-side-to-side
  Ka?mɨtɨhi? W

Looks-brown Kurupitsoni
loose hagwoitɨ W, ha?wo?itɨ
loose, break pihka?arɨ
loose, turn pɨarɨ, wɨhto?yarɨ
loose tooth saatitamakatɨ
loosen takwɨsaitɨ, tsahkwɨmarɨ
loosen with hands mahkwɨmarɨ
loosened by foot takwɨsarɨ
lope aimi?arɨ, wahkami?arɨ
lope, make tsa?aikɨrɨ
Lord Narɨmi?
lose way watsitɨ
lose faith in someone nasuwɨhkitɨ
lose something nasuwatsi,
  watsikɨrɨ
lose something from hand or wrist
  ma?kwe?yarɨ
lost watsitɨ
lost, going to get watsikwarɨ
lot, feeding soni wɨhtɨmapɨ
lotion, hand makwɨrɨ?eka? W,
  mo?o kwitɨ?eka? K
lotus, yellow kɨrɨ?atsɨ
loud pia
Loud, Talk Pibia nɨwɨnɨ?nɨɨ
loudly piapɨ
loudly, cry hubiyaa piayakeetɨ
loudly, sing pia rɨnikwɨtɨ
louse, body saabe busia
louse, crab pɨhɨ pusia, suhu posía
louse, de- nabusi?aketɨ, pusiaketɨ
louse, head- pusi?a, yupusia
love kamakɨrɨ
loved one kamakɨna W
lover nɨmɨ?ara?, tɨɨ?urapɨ W, K
lower arm, sprain or break hand
  or namaminaitɨ
lower back piwo?sa
lower leg naape, omo-
lower leg, foot and napɨ|b-|r
lower leg, foot or nara-
lubricate wihɨ tɨ?ekarɨ

lukewarm pakuyu?atʉ
lumber woobi̱
lumberman huuyʉkkwi?
lumberyard huunarʉmʉʉ?, wobi narʉmʉ̱?
lunatic emʉahkatʉ̱
lunch tabe rʉhkapʉ̱ W, tʉkʉ noopʉ̱
lunch or dinner, eat tabe rʉhkarʉ K
lung soomo̱
lust nasúyake? K
lust for nasuyaketʉ
lye isawasʉ̱ wanakotse?
lying down haahpi̱
lying down, continue naahábitʉ
lying face-downward muparai habinitʉ K
lying in prone position muparai habinitʉ K
lying somewhere haahpi̱tʉ

M m

machine, sewing tʉtsahkʉna?
machine, washing tʉkotse? K
machine oil, sewing tʉtsakʉnaha yuhu
made drunk makwi?numaitʉ
made of teepee poles, travel carrier tʉ?noo?
made to trot poyohkarʉ
maggot wo?aabi̱
mail a letter or package tʉhyetʉ
mailbox tʉboopʉ̱ wosa W
mailman tʉboo tahni?, tʉboo hima?eetʉ̱ K
maize hani-, haníibi̱, nawohani, nʉmʉ hani
maize, toasted kukʉ̱mepʉ̱
make kwisihkarʉ
make lope tsa?aikʉrʉ

make a bed nohrʉ̱naarʉ, norʉ̱naarʉ
make a bird nest huupiso?na?aitʉ
make a birdcall niyakekʉtʉ̱
make a deal tohpunitʉ
make a hole with hands tsahtaikʉtʉ
make a mark on something tsahporʉ
make a plan nimaka?mukitʉ̱, su?atsitʉ
make a windbreak wʉhturu?arʉ
make a wry face sʉkʉbuninitʉ
make (an agreement or contract) nanipu?e?aitʉ
make bread tohtía?arʉ
make bubbles pamukwarʉ?rʉkitʉ
make burst tohpʉtsa?itʉ
make coffee huba aitʉ
make Comanche butter tʉhtsohpe?arʉ
make cry by hitting toyaketʉ
make dizzy kwinumarʉ
make fall using foot taperʉ
make frybread yuhu nohkorʉ
make galloping sound totʉ̱bihkurʉ
make hollow wʉhha?wokarʉ
make music muuyaketʉ
make noise, pull to matsáapikaarʉ
make noise yelling hubiyairʉ
make pointed mamutsiarʉ
make popping noise kuhporákitʉ̱
make round with the mouth kʉhtoponarʉ W
make something rattle tsatsʉ̱bipʉ̱kurʉ
make swim tapʉ̱habi
make threatening movements tahkuya?arʉ
make up oneself napi̱sarʉ
make up someone pisarʉ
make-believe nohitekwarʉ
male kuhma

male, adult muʔwoo
male, elderly tsukuhpʉʔ
male animal kuuma
male kinsman naabia, nahbiʔa
male kinsman, man's narenahpʉʔ
male teacher tʉboo wapi
mallet, wooden huutʉrohpakoʔiʔi
mallow, red false puha natsu W,
  yokanatsuʔu K
mallet, wooden huutʉrohpakoʔiʔi
mallow, red false puha natsu W,
  yokanatsuʔu K
man kuhma, tenahpʉʔ W
man, bearded white motso taibooʔ
man, brave young tʉetekwʉni wapi
man, Comanche nʉmʉ renahpʉʔ
man, Comanche young nʉmʉ
  ruibihtsiʔ
man, elderly sukuupʉ
man, grown muʔwoo
man, hole dug by nahorapʉ
man, important namʉnewapi
man, marry a kuumarurʉ
man, medicine puha raibooʔ W,
  puha tenahpʉ
man, old narabʉ
man, pay medicine mabekakʉrʉ W
man, pay something to medicine
  tʉmabekarʉ
man, police nʉmi himaʔetʉ,
  tʉʉhtamʉh raiboʔ
man, post- tʉboo tahniʔ, tʉboo
  himaʔeetʉ K
-man, Red-young Ekawokani
man as husband, reject ninakabarʉ
man, spokes- tekwawapi,
  tʉnikepisaʔ
-man hand saw, two huutsihkaaʔ
man, watch- tʉʔiyaʔi wapi
man, white huuyʉkkwiʔ, pabo
  taibooʔ
man, work- tʉrʉʔai wapi

man, young tuibihtsiʔ
man, young unmarried wohkaʔniʔ
man's agnatic grandchild kʉnuʔ
man's agnatic grandnephew kʉnuʔ
man's brother-in-law tetsi
man's buckskin jacket pika kwasuʔ
man's female kinsman
  naʔwaʔihpʉʔ
man's male kinsman narenahpʉʔ
man's moccasin taʔseʔyukʉʔ,
  taʔsiʔyukiʔ
man's shirt tenahpʉʔa kwasuʔʉ
man's uterine grandchild tokoʔ
manage tʉtsʉhanitʉ
mane ania
manner sinihku
manually, operate mamiʔakʉtʉ,
  nʉʉmiʔakʉrʉ
many soo, sootʉ, tʉmarʉʉmaatʉ
many?, How hʉʉ
many?, How (how much?)
  hipekaʔi, hipetʉ
many tears, shed paʔokwetʉ
many years ago soo beʔsʉ
map soko naboopʉ W, soko rʉboopʉ
maple, silver kweʔyʉkʉ sohóobi
March Nanaʔbutitʉikatʉ mʉa,
  Tahpookʉ mʉa
mare, gray esipiaʔ
mare, sorrel ekapiaʔ
marijuana nʉmi makwinumaʔetʉʔ
marijuana cigarette nʉmi
  makwinumaʔetʉ pahmu
mark, scratch leaving a tsahtsiʔarʉ
mark inexactly nahoʔyopikurʉ
mark off tsahporʉ
mark on something, make a
  tsahporʉ
mark something tsihpoorʉ
marked naboo-
marking naboʔ
marking instrument nabooʔ K

marriage, propose kwʉhʉniwaitʉ

marriage, separate in pʉah kwarʉ

marriage, separated in pʉah taikatʉ

marriage of uncle and niece arakwʉʔʉtʉ

married kwʉʉhtʉkatʉ W, K

married, be kuumabaitʉ

married, get nʉpetsʉʔitʉ

married, get engaged to be nʉpetsʉʔitʉ

married couple nanakwʉhʉ W

marrow tʉranaʔipʉ

marrow, bone tuhhu rʉhkapʉ

marrow, cook out (from bones) tʉranaʔitʉ

marrow, eat bone tuhhu rʉhkarʉ

marrow bones tʉranạ

marry kuhmaru, kwʉʉhturʉ

marry a man kuumarurʉ

marry each other nanakwʉʉhtʉ

marry someone nanakwʉʉrʉ

marvel nanịsuwʉkaitʉ

marvelous nanaarʉʉmoa, nanịsuwʉkaitʉ

mash makịtsarʉ, makʉtserʉ, pikʉtsekarʉ, tatsukwerʉ, wʉkʉtserʉ

mash in the mouth kʉhkihtserʉ K

mash into small particles mahomonutsarʉ

mash up something mapịtserʉ

mashed makịtsetʉ

mask kobe tsaʔnika?

massage mabararʉ, narʉʔekarʉ

Master Narʉmi?

match huukuna?

material, flaile wʉyumiʔipʉ

material possessions tarʉwanapi W

material, printed nakohpoopʉ W, soo naboo?

maternal grandfather toko?

maternal grandmother kaku?

maternal great aunt kaku?

matter!, no natsa

mattock kuwʉhora?, toʔtsimuhpe?

mattress sona rʉbaki?

mattress, feather sia sona rʉbaki?

May Totsiyaa mʉa

maybe kia, sʉʉkʉtsaʔnoo

me nʉe

meadowlark hiitoo? K, N, ohanʉnapʉ W

Meadowlark Hiitoo? K, N

meal tʉkʉ manipʉ

meal, corn- hanitusupʉ

mean kesuatʉ, narʉʔʉyapʉ, tʉtsʉ-

mean person or animal tuhupʉ

mean things, say nimakwihtsetʉ

measles ekatasia

measure manahkerʉ, tamanahkerʉ

measure oneself namanahkitʉ

measure something tʉmanahketʉ

measure, tape tʉmanahke?

measuring, any device used for tʉmanahke?

meat taʔoo?, tuhkụ, tʉhkapa, tʉhkapʉ, yuhu rʉkʉhmanipʉ

meat (animal killed or butchered for food) tʉbehkapʉ

meat bag oyóotʉ?

meat, boiled saapʉ

meat, buffalo nʉmʉ kutsu tʉhkapʉ, taʔsiwoo rʉhkapʉ W

meat, deer arʉka tuhku K, O, P, arʉkáa rʉhkapʉ, tahmai napʉ

meat, dried esi inapʉ, tahmai napʉ

meat, fried yuhu rʉkʉhmanipʉ

meat (or vegetables), fry kwasʉkurʉ

meat, ground tʉhkapa narʉsupʉ W

meat up to dry, hang inaʔetʉ

meat, jerk inaʔetʉ

meat, jerk (for someone)
tᵿ?inakᵿrᵿ

meat, jerked inapᵾ, inarᵿ

meat jerky inarᵿ

meat, jowl aratuhku

meat, light pabo tuhku

meat, pound tᵿrayu?nerᵿ

meat, pounded tᵿrayu?nepᵾ

meat, roast tᵿkwᵾsᵿkᵿrᵿ

meat over fire (or dry it for jerky), roast ku?inarᵿ

meat, roasted ku?inapᵾ, tᵿkwᵾsᵿkᵿpᵾ?

meat from a hide, scrape tohtsiyu?itᵿ

meat, summer-dried tahmai napᵾ

meat, thigh pabo tuhku

meat-drying A-frame inakwata

meatball tᵿrahyapᵾ

meatball preparation tᵿrahyarᵿ

mediator nitᵿsu?nai wapi

medical doctor natsᵾ taibo? K

medicinal herb pᵿhᵿ natsu, pᵿhᵿ rᵿ?saasi

medicinal plant tᵿpi natsu

medicine natᵿsu?ᵾ, puha

medicine, apply narᵿ?ekarᵿ

medicine, prepare puha?arᵿ

medicine, prepared puha?aitᵾ

medicine on body, rub mabararᵿ

Medicine Bluff Puha rᵿpanaabi

medicine doctor puha tenahpᵾ

medicine man puha raiboo? W, puha tenahpᵾ

medicine man, pay mabekakᵿrᵿ W

medicine man, pay something to tᵿmabekarᵿ

medicine outfits puha namaka?mukipᵾ

Medicine-otter Pua paatsoko

Medicine-woman Puhawi

meek ᵿrᵿ?

meekness tᵿsutaibitsi

meet nara?uraitᵿ, na?akᵾtᵿ

meet someone ta?urarᵿ, to?urarᵿ

meet someone by going on foot tamunaikᵿmi?arᵿ

meet someone, go on foot to tamunaikᵿmi?arᵿ

meet to suggest something nanika?witᵿ

meeting, conduct a peyote wokwetᵿhkarᵿ

meeting, pallet used during peyote pisóona

melon, water- ohapi, puhi bihnáa?

melt parᵿhwitᵿ

melt away parᵿhwimi?arᵿ

melt something kuhpawikᵿ?itᵿ

melted kuhparᵿ

melted grease wihi

Memorial Day Totsiyaaih tabenihtᵿ W

men tenahpᵾ? W

men, mud- sekwitsipuhitsi

menfolk nanahtenanᵿᵿ

meningitis tsotsoo?ni

menopausal woman tsihhabᵿhkamapᵾ

menstruate tsihhabᵿhkamarᵿ

mercy tᵿsutaibitsi

mercy, have sutaaitᵿ

merit ta?urᵿkarᵿ W

mescal bean ekapo?

mesh saa?wᵿ?

mesquite namabitsoo?ni, natsohkwe?, wohi?huu

mesquite weed namabitsooni sonihpᵿ

mesquite-leaf mixture patso?

messenger nᵿtᵿhyoi wapi

mestizo wia?

metal, tin or other shiny pisayu?ne?

metal comb puhihwi natsihtuʔye?

Mexican yuu taiboʔ

Mexican blanket kusikwiʔiiʔ

Mexican persimmon tuhnaséka

Mexicans captured by the Comanches Esitoyanʉʉ

midday tokwetabeni

-midday-sun-does-not-tell-a-lie, This Sihka tabe ke isopʉ

middle tʉbinaaʔwekị, tʉpʉnaatʉ

middle finger mahtʉpịnáaʔ K, masʉwʉhkiʔ W

middle toe tahtʉpinaaʔ

middle-aged woman hʉbi

midget nʉnʉ pʉhiʔ

mildew eʔbootsiarʉ, eʔbootsiaʔ

mile soko rʉtsʉpʉ

milk pitsipʉ

milk a cow tʉmaʔokwetʉ

milk bucket pitsipʉ wihtua

milk, butter- nʉtsʉʔwʉpạ pitsipʉ K, yuhibitsipʉ K

milk, clabbered nʉtsʉʔwʉpạ pitsipʉ K, pitsi pʉha nʉkuʔwʉpʉ

milk from cream, separate yunarʉ

milk can pitsipʉ wihtua

milk cow pitsipʉ pimoróoʔ W

milk something maʔokwerʉ

milkweed kumiitsanatsu

Milky Way Esitohiʔ

milky-rooted plant pihtsamuu

mill, wind- patsahtoʔiʔ

mind sua

mind in effort to remember, search the suʔurarʉ

mine, coal kutʉhubihtaa ohweetʉ

mink papị wʉ́htamaʔ

miracle nanịsuwʉ̣kaitʉ

mirror nabuniʔ

mischievous emʉahkatʉ̣, poʔsabihiʔa

miss warʉʔikatʉ

miss aim awi-

miss doing tsimiʔakʉrʉ

missing, be kehewaʔitʉ

mistletoe puhi tʉrʉhkaʔ

misunderstand statement nanawatsikarʉ

mix mabarʉ W

mix takoosahpʉʔ W

mixture, mesquite-leaf patsoʔ

moan woohpʉnitʉ, woorʉ

moccasin nʉmʉ napʉ

moccasin, man's taʔseʔyukʉʔ, taʔsiʔyukiʔ

moccasins, give away napʉ makarʉ

moccasin (snake), water tuhparokooʔ

mock nisuʔuyaitʉ W, tʉnịsuʔuyaitʉ, usúʔuyaʔitʉ W

mockingbird soo yakeʔ W, tʉnimanahke huutsuʔ K

moisten in the mouth kʉhparoʔaitʉ K

moistened mabáaʔaitʉ

molasses huupịhnàa

mole paraimoʔo

money ekapuhihwi, puhihwi

money, collect tʉniwaitʉ

money, give (to someone) puhihwimaka

money, have puhihwi tuarʉ

money, look for puhihwi wehki

money, paper wana buhihwị

money, pay with narʉmakarʉ

money, silver tosahpuhihwị

money, spend suʔmakʉtʉ

monkey kwasi taibooʔ

month mʉa

moo muu yakenitʉ

moon mʉa

moonlight mʉakatʉ

moonlight, have mʉahtabebaʔitʉ

mop pawʉnuaʔ

more than anything oyo?rʉ ka?wekịtʉ

mormon tea sanaweha

morning pʉetsʉkunakwʉsa, taa-, taahkatʉ, tabénị

morning, early pʉetsʉku, tuka ʉhyʉi

morning glory soho kʉa?etʉ totsiyaa?

mortar huaawo, huu aawo

mosquito mutsikwà?aa?

mosquito net muhpoo kahni wanapʉ K

moth tʉpị simuhta?

mother pia

mother, step- paraiboo?

mother's sister pia

motion, move in slow aimi?arʉ

motor oil na?bukuwàa?a nahyʉ, tʉhyu

mound, burial nabʉkapʉ W

mount a horse tʉyato?yerʉ

mount, help to tohkʉarʉ

mount on horseback nʉʉhto?itʉ

mountain toya

mountain, gray esitoyaabị

Mountain, Navaho Naboohroya? N

mountain boomer ebimuutaroo?, ebipaboko?ai? P

mountain lion wʉra?

mountains east of El Paso, Texas Esitoya?

mourning cape ku?nika?

mouse tʉe kahuu?

mouse, field pia kahúa

mouse, house kahúu?

-mouse, Squeaky-like-a Kahúu nihku pipịkurẹ

mousetrap kahúu pʉmata hʉarʉ?

mouth tʉpe, tʉʉpe

mouth, catch something with the kʉhtsakarʉ

mouth, close the kʉhtsuukarʉ

mouth, dribble from the kʉ?okwetʉ

mouth, frothing at the saahtotsito?ikatʉ

mouth, make round with the kʉhtoponarʉ W

mouth, mash in the kʉhkihtserʉ K

mouth, moisten in the kʉhparo?aitʉ K

mouth wide, open pia kʉsarʉ

mouth, open the kʉsarʉ

mouth, pop with the kʉhpohtorʉ

mouth, put something into the tʉro?nikarʉ

mouth, roll in the kʉhkwatuubirʉ K

mouth, roof of mitʉko?o

mouth, take something in the kʉhyaarʉ

mouth, throw with nose or muhwitʉ K, mukwʉbʉarʉ W

mouth, unwrap something with the kʉhto?yarʉ K

move wʉmi?arʉ W, yʉmʉhkitʉ

move about yʉkarʉ

move across unahrʉ

move around nʉmirʉ, yo?mitsaitʉ, yʉ?yʉmuhkumi?arʉ W

move away nomi?arʉ, norawʉ?aitʉ

move away as a group sʉmʉ nomi?arʉ

move by hand tsanuarʉ

move clumsily, waddle or masu?wa?nekitʉ

move from place to place noonʉmi?arʉ

move from side to side tohtsatsarʉ

move in slow motion aimi?arʉ

move nervously pisukwitaitʉ

move off to live separately noka?itʉ

move on nayʉkwiitʉ

move over nuaṟʉ
move quickly wʉʔrabiarʉ
move slowly puhyʉnukitʉ
move something tanuarʉ
move something with the mouth
 kʉnuaitʉ
movement toward something,
 stop wʉnʉ hupiitʉ
movements, make threatening
 tahkuyaʔarʉ
movie nunuraʔwʉʔ, tʉpuuni
 yʉʔyʉmuhkuʔ K
movies yʉʔyʉmuhkuʔ W
moving, rope someone or
 something while kuʔnikakʉrʉ
-moving, slow nanahbisoʔaitʉ
-moving, Swift Wʉʔrabiahpʉ
moving pictures yʉʔyʉmuhkuʔ W
mow wʉhpomarʉ, wʉtsʉkarʉ
mow grass soni wʉhpomarʉ, soni
 wʉtsʉkerʉ
mower, lawn- soni wʉtsʉkeʔ K,
 tʉʉtsʉkeʔ W
much soo, sootʉ, tʉmarʉʉmaatʉ
much?, How many?, How
 hipekaʔi, hipetʉ
much worse nasuʔana
mud sekwi, sekwipʉ
mud, stuck in the sekwi sʉhkai,
 yubutsʉhkatʉ
mud-covered sekwi nuyuʔitʉ
mud-men sekwitsipuhitsi
mulberries pahtsi kwasi tʉkahpʉ
mulberry huwaboʔkóoʔ, soho
 boʔkooʔ W
mule esimuuraʔ, muuraʔ
Mule-dung Mura kwitapʉ
multi-colored wanatsihtaraaʔ
mumble esipipikuurʉ
mumps tʉbekwipʉ
murmur esipipikuurʉ
muscle nʉʉhtokaʔeʔ

muscle cramp or spasm, have
 toponitʉ K
mush kooʔ
mush, cornmeal hanikotsapʉ, kooʔ
mushroom mupitsʉha pisahpi W,
 pasawiʔooʔa hʉkiʔaiʔ
music, make muuyaketʉ
music (of any kind) muyakeʔ
mutilate oneself nʉʉhkiʔyuʔitʉ
mutton kabʉrʉʉ tʉhkapʉ
my nʉ
my!, Oh, haʔíi
my!, Oh! Oh ʉbia

N n

nail tʉrawʉnaʔ K, tʉrohtsaniʔi
nail, shoe napʉ narawʉnaʔ, napʉ
 rʉrawʉnaʔ
nail, toe- tasiito
nail down tawʉnarʉ
nail something taʔnikʉtʉ,
 tʉrawʉnarʉ K
naked papʉtsipitʉ
name nahnia
name for the Comanches of Tejas),
 Proud People (Wichita Natai
name someone nahnia makarʉ,
 nihakʉrʉ
nap tabe ʉhpʉitʉ
napkin namoʔo matsumaʔ
Narrow-gut Kohi
narrow place, crowded into
 tsʉkikatʉ
nasty nasʉsʉaʔeetʉ
nations sokobaʔaihtʉ
Native-American ball game
 naʔsʉhpeʔetʉ
natural windbreak huukonoʔitʉ
Navaho Mountain Naboohroyaʔ N
Navaho people Naboohnʉʉ

navel siiku̱

near miitu̱tsi

nearly noha

neck toyo, toyopu̱

neck, have a stiff wo?rohtsaru̱

neck, wear something around the korohko̱ru̱

necklace, bead tsomo korohko

necktie korohko̱

need suwaitu̱

needle wana tsahku̱na?

needy nahawaru?ikatu̱

negative ke-

neighbor kahtu̱i?

nerve, end of row or su̱kweru̱

nervously, move pisukwitaitu̱

nest pisu?ni?

nest, bird huutsú?a kàhni̱, huutsú?a pisoo?ni̱

nest, build a pisona?aitu̱

nest, make a bird huupiso?na?aitu̱

net, fish- saa?wu̱ hu̱a?

net, mosquito muhpoo kahni wanapu̱ K

never Kesu̱

new, learn something urahkaru̱

New Year's Day U̱ku̱ tomopu̱

news, good tsaatu̱ naru̱mu?ipu̱

newspaper naru̱mu?i tu̱boopu̱

next time kwasiku̱

nibble ku̱?kwiyaru̱

niece, marriage of uncle and arakwu̱?u̱tu̱

night tuka u̱hyu̱i, tukaani̱

night, be tukani̱tu̱

nightgown habikwa̱suu

nightshade tohpotsotsii

nine wu̱mi̱natu̱

nits tatsii?

no ke-

no!, Oh, yee

no good nasu̱su̱a?eetu̱

no matter! natsa

No-bed Kahpewai

No-hand Moo?wetu̱

no to someone, say nimamu̱suku̱tu̱

no, shake the head tso?wiketu̱

nod the head in agreement nihtsamu?itu̱

noise (in timber), hear or make huukisaakitu̱

noise, make popping kuhporákitu̱

noise yelling, make hubiyairu̱

noise, pull to make matsáapikaaru̱

noisy tu̱nisuatu̱

non-Indian taiboo?

noon tokwetabeni

north kwihnenakwu̱

north fork of Red River Natu̱mu̱u̱ pa?i huna?

north star kemi?aru̱tatsino

northeast kwihne muhyu̱nakwu̱

northwest kwihne kahpinakwu̱

nose mu-, muhbi

nose, blow the mubi̱situ̱, tsamuku̱situ̱

nose, cause to blow wu̱mupu̱situ̱

nose, inhale deeply through muhibitu̱

nose, poke out munaku̱aitu̱

-nose, Red-crooked Ekamurawa

nose, suck through simuhtaru̱

nose or mouth, throw with muhwitu̱ K, mukwu̱bu̱aru̱ W

nosebag puku ru̱hka?

not good enough ketokwetu̱

not-tell-a-lie, This-midday-sun-does Sihka tabe ke isopu̱

nothing kehe

notice sutuu?aru̱

notice, give ninaku̱aku̱ru̱ W

November Ahotabenihtu̱ mu̱a, Yu̱ba u̱hi mu̱a

now (or at this point) si?anetu̱

now on, from sibeʔnikị̲yutʉ
now, right meeku, namʉsohi
now kihtsiʔ, tsuh
nudge matsurʉ
Nueces River Sʉmonʉ̲ kuhtsu paa
numb sʉsʉʔnitʉ, tasʉsʉʔnitʉ,
　tsasʉsʉʔnikatʉ
numb, feel sʉsʉʔnitʉ
numb the hand masʉsʉʔnitʉ
number tʉrʉtsʉpʉ
number, augment in sʉatʉ
numbness sʉsʉʔnikatʉ
numerically, increasing
　tʉrakaʔaitʉ
nun Suabi puharaibo
nurse cape kuʔhibooʔ
nursling pʉesúubeʔ W
nuts pokopi̲

O o

oak paʔsa ponii huupi
oak, blackjack tuhuupi
oak, white tosa tukanai huupi
oar panatsitooʔ
oath, take mahiyarʉ
oath, take an narabeeʔaitʉ
oats soni narúaʔ
obedient tʉnakatʉ̲
obey tʉmayokʉrʉ
obey orders tokwetʉparʉ
object, broken kohpapʉ̲, tahpapʉ̲
object cut into pieces
　tʉtsihpomiʔipʉ̲
object, dirty tuhtsaipʉ̲
object, dry pasapʉ̲
object, ground up nasupʉ̲ K
object (on a line), hang a long
　wʉsóorʉ
object, laced natsakwʉ̲sikʉʔ
object, large piapʉ̲

object, old tsukuhpʉ̲ʔ
object, pull a bouncy tsahpoʔtsarʉ
object, pulverized or grated
　tusupʉ̲ W
object, round maropoʔni̲ʔipʉ̲
object, sharp-pointed mutsipʉ̲
object, side of an sʉkwe naisʉ
object, staked down - ʉhtaʔetʉ̲
object, torn sihwapi̲
object, unwrap an tsahpekoʔarʉ
object (or item) taken yaapʉ̲
objects, count definite tʉtsʉrʉ
objects, give several himiitʉ
objects, pick up several himaʔarʉ
objects, take several himaʔarʉ
oblong huyubaʔatʉ̲, mahuyubakatʉ̲,
　pia huyubatʉ̲
ocean pia baa
October Puhipʉ̲ha pʉma oha
　toʔi̲ʔena mʉa, Yʉba mʉa
odd nanakuyaʔarʉ, natsuwʉkai
odor, breath sua kwana̲
odor, have kwanarʉ
odor, have bad kwanarʉ
odor, sniff an ʉkwihkatʉ
of two of them mahrʉ
of us two taa
of you two mʉhʉ
off, drop pahitʉ, yumarʉ
off, dust huukunatsirʉ
off, dust (by hand) huukumatsumarʉ
off, fall pahitʉ, tʉpehemiʔarʉ
off (or away from), fall tʉpʉherʉ W
off, get weehtsitʉ
off running, get wenuʔnuki̲miʔarʉ
off, haul tsawehkwatʉ
off, kick sʉʉtaʔniʔarʉ
off, knock tokarʉ, wʉyumiʔitʉ
off, knock something hanging
　wʉhtokarʉ
off, knock (with an instrument)
　wʉpʉherʉ W

off by force, lead sutena betsᵤmiarᵤ
off, mark tsahporᵤ
off, peel kwᵤrᵤʔarᵤ, tokiarᵤ,
     wᵤhtsiboʔarᵤ
off skin, peel kiboʔarᵤ
off, pitch kuʔe wᵤnᵤrᵤ
off, pull tokarᵤ, tsahtoʔarᵤ K
off or out, pull something
     tsahkweʔyarᵤ
off, rub tosoʔnetᵤ
off, scrape siibetᵤ, tosoʔnetᵤ
off, shake something nᵤᵤʔwikeetᵤ,
     sᵤᵤtaʔniʔarᵤ
off, shave wᵤhtsiʔarᵤ, wᵤsiberᵤ K
off, show nasutsa akwarᵤ K
off, snap tahkobarᵤ, tsahkobarᵤ
off, strip makwiteerᵤ
off of something, take down
     tsahpᵤherᵤ
off, take maboʔayarᵤ, tohkweʔyarᵤ
off a shoe, take tahkweʔyarᵤ
off layer, take tsahkwᵤrᵤʔarᵤ
off, tear sᵤmᵤ sihwarᵤ
off, tip ninakᵤakᵤrᵤ W
off completely, wipe wᵤhtsuʔmarᵤ
off with the hand. wipe
     makwineetᵤ
off, wipe something tahtsumarᵤ K
offer hand mahiyaitᵤ
offer someone help masutsarᵤ
office, post tᵤboopᵤ kᵤni
officer nanohmᵤnᵤ wapi K,
     nomᵤnewapi W, paraibooʔ
officer, army ekasahpanaʔ
     paraibooʔ
offspring, bear turuarᵤ
offspring (son or daughter),
     grown nahnapᵤ
often naiya
Oh, good! yee
Oh, my! haʔíi
Oh, no! yee

Oh! yaa
oh! oh my! ᵤbia
oil nabaa, nahyᵤ
oil, coal tukaʔa nabaa
oil, explore for tokwaitᵤ
oil, motor naʔbukuwàaʔa nahyᵤ,
     tᵤhyu
oil, sewing machine tᵤtsakᵤnaha
     yuhu
oil well nabaai tokwaaitᵤ, tukaʔa
     nabaa
oily or greasy, taste wihi kamatᵤ
ointment, personal nᵤᵤhtᵤʔekaʔ
-old, two-year wahatomopᵤ K
-old item, two-year tomohtoopᵤ W
old, two years tomohtootᵤ W
old lady narutsaʔi
old man narabᵤ
old object tsukuhpᵤʔ
Old-owl Moʔpi tsokopᵤ
on back paʔarai
on, fire wᵤhtikᵤrᵤ
on, go tunehtsᵤrᵤ
on foot, go (to look for) takwainitᵤ
on foot, go (to meet someone)
     tamunaikᵤmiʔarᵤ
on, have underwear tsaʔnikᵤkatᵤ
on, knock totᵤbihkurᵤ
on door, knock tohtarakiʔarᵤ
on, move nayᵤkwiitᵤ
on, pour tokwᵤriarᵤ
on, pour water payunitᵤ
on a sled, ride seated pisikoʔi
on deathbed, suffer pisukwitarᵤ
on fire, set kutsitonarᵤ
on purpose, spill something
     tokwᵤriaitᵤ
on, tried marahpunihkatᵤ
on, urge nihtunetsᵤʔitᵤ
on, wait mananaaʔwaihkarᵤ
on opposite side paʔarai
on shoes, put tahtoorᵤ

on someone or something, with or maa

on something, lean mahtokwᵾnaitᵾ K

on something, pull tsanuarᵾ

on something, rest mahtokwᵾnaitᵾ K

on something, suck mukwihterᵾ

on something, tap wᵾhtarakiitᵾ

on top of kuʔe

on trousers, put pitsohkorᵾ

on vacation, go huᵾtsaʔwᵾ miʔarᵾ

on warpath, go mahimiʔarᵾ

on what? hipaʔa

on what?, with what? himakų

once sᵾmᵾsᵾ

once in a while sᵾsᵾʔanạ

one sᵾmᵾ, sᵾmᵾʔ

one, dying suaʔsuʔmakatᵾ

one, fattest yuhu wehkipᵾ

one, little tᵾeʔtᵾ

one another, help naruituahkarᵾ

one, loved kamakᵾnạ W

one another, sell to narᵾmᵾᵾrᵾ

one, that suhkapᵾ

one, wrong atᵾrᵾ

one at a time sᵾsᵾmᵾʔ, sᵾʔsᵾmᵾʔnᵾku

one by one, run away nunurawᵾtᵾ

one hill anáabi

one hill standing alone nookarᵾrų

one is doing), slow down (what nᵾnᵾʔitᵾ

one leg, raise tahtsarᵾ

one song after another, sing nipᵾyerᵾ

one or several things, take yaarᵾ

one to sin, tempt tᵾrape suwaitᵾ

one foot, walk dragging tasiʔwomiʔarᵾ

one time sᵾmᵾsᵾ

one who betrays kaanatsakaʔuhtupᵾ

one who gossips isanaramuʔitᵾ?

one-horse buggy sᵾmasᵾ nooi K

One-who-rides-buffalo Kuhtsunu kwahipᵾ

oneself pᵾnᵾsᵾ

oneself, cut natsahkiʔarᵾ, nᵾᵾkiʔaitᵾ

oneself, examine nabuihwᵾnᵾtᵾ W

oneself, exhaust nananᵾᵾʔmaitᵾ, narahkupaitᵾ

oneself, gag kuitsịkwaitᵾ K

oneself, gash natsahkiʔarᵾ

oneself, hack nᵾᵾhkiʔyuʔitᵾ

oneself, hang nᵾᵾkwenitᵾ

oneself, hurt nahohiyaitᵾ, nahuhyaitᵾ W, namarųnitᵾ K

oneself, immerse (in water) nabawᵾhtiarᵾ

oneself, introduce nanịsuabetaʔaitᵾ, natsahpunitᵾ

oneself, jerk something toward tsahpoʔtsarᵾ

oneself, look at nabunitᵾ

oneself, look behind nabitᵾbunitᵾ

oneself, make up napịsarᵾ

oneself, measure namanahkitᵾ

oneself, mutilate nᵾᵾhkiʔyuʔitᵾ

oneself, paint napịsarᵾ

oneself, prepare namakaʔmukitᵾ

oneself down, pull natsahkupᵾkatᵾ

oneself up, pull natsahtoʔitᵾ

oneself with something, puncture nabisoʔarᵾ

oneself, scratch natsahtsiaitᵾ

oneself away, secret watsị habiitᵾ

oneself, shave namotᵾsibetᵾ

oneself in water, soak naparᵾkitᵾ

oneself, tire nananᵾᵾʔmaitᵾ

oneself, twist nᵾᵾkwitsᵾnarᵾ

oneself around something, twist nᵾᵾʔkwipunarᵾ

oneself, watch naʔiyaitᵾ

oneself, wound natsahki?arʉ

onion, poisonous wild
kʉhtsʉtsʉʉ?ni?

onion, wild kʉʉkanarʉhka?,
kʉʉka̱, pakʉʉka̱, pʉewatsi kʉʉka̱,
tʉetʉtaatʉ kʉʉka̱

Onion Creek, Texas Kuna?itʉ?

only pʉ?ʉne W

Only-daughter Pʉ?na petʉ

onto someone or something, up to
or maatu

open tsahwitʉ, wʉhkwʉmarʉ

open, break mapʉtsarʉ, tapʉtsaitʉ

open, break (with the teeth)
kʉpʉtsarʉ

open, burst mapʉtsarʉ, puhkarʉ

open, come tʉhwaitʉ

open, cut wʉpʉkarʉ, wʉpʉtsarʉ

open, pound on to tohkwʉmarʉ

open, pry tohkwʉmarʉ,
tsihto?arʉ W

open, split peko?arʉ

open, wide pia tsatuakatʉ

open country to settlement soko
tsatu̱warʉ

open forcibly tohkwʉmarʉ

open mouth wide pia kʉsarʉ

open of its own accord
natsahwi?etʉ

open something matʉhwarʉ,
tohtʉwarʉ, tsahtʉwarʉ, tʉhwarʉ

open something wide pia tsatuarʉ

open the hand makwʉsaitʉ

open the mouth kʉsarʉ

opened mahʉrʉhwakatʉ

opener, can kʉmapʉ, tʉrohtʉwa?

opening in clothing kurʉʉpe

openly maihtʉkʉ

operate manually mami?akʉtʉ,
nʉʉmi?akʉrʉ

operation, surgical nʉʉpʉtsapʉ

opossum pahtsi kwasi

oppose wohho suarʉ

oppose something tso?wiketʉ

opposite-sex sibling-in-law haipia?

opposite side, on pa?arai

or tʉanóo

or coil wʉhkwatubi

orally, reminded ninʉsutamakʉtʉ

orange ekaohapi̱tʉ, ohaekapi̱tʉ,
ohapi̱tʉʉ

orange, osage etʉhuupi, ohahuupi

orchard pokopi̱ masʉapʉ

order hani̱tʉni̱rʉ, ni?atsiitʉ

order sternly ninabitsiarʉ

order to leave nihto?itʉ

orders, obey tokwetʉparʉ

originated tʉbora

ornery tʉmabiso?aitʉ

orphan as foster child, keep an
tahnikatʉ, tʉkiihkarʉ

osage orange etʉhuupi, ohahuupi

Osage people Wa?sáasi?

other ata-

other, marry each nanakwʉʉhtʉ

other covering for teepees, skins
or nʉmʉkʉni

other shiny metal, tin or
pisayu?ne?

other, with each naha-

others atʉrʉʉ

others, lead muhnemi?arʉ

others, separated from
toro?ihtʉkitʉ

otter paa tsoko, papi̱ wʉhtama?

Otter Paa tso?ko

ouch! aná

ouch! it burns ʉrʉʉ

our nʉmʉ, tahʉ

Our Father Ta?ahpʉ

out. come (at a particular place)
kiahbitʉ, to?ibitʉ

out, drive tahkʉarʉ

out, dry pasarʉ

out, empty wʉʔwenitʉ K
out, find sutuuʔarʉ
out, find (for oneself) naraʔurakʉtʉ
out, force tsahkʉarʉ
out. forced tsahtoʔitʉ
out, go tukamiʔarʉ
out, lay tsakwʉnarʉ
out, let tahtoʔitʉ
out, pick nabinarʉ
out something, pluck noʔitʉ
out something, point
  muruahwʉnʉrʉ
out nose, poke munakʉaitʉ
out, pour wʉhtiarʉ, wʉʔwenitʉ K
out, pull tsahpiʔerʉ
out of breath suaʔsuʔmaitʉ
out of container, pull tsahpʉyerʉ
out of joint, pull bones
  tsahtokoʔarʉ
out, reach mahiyaitʉ
out and touch, reach
  maʔwʉminarʉ
out of food, run tʉkʉ tsuhmarʉ
out of groceries, run
  narʉhkaʔtsuʔmarʉ
out, rust nasaanutoʔitʉ
out, set tsihtaboʔikʉtʉ
out to dry, set pasahtahtʉkitʉ W
out, shovel tsiiʔwʉweniitʉ
out, sing nihtoʔitʉ
out, snuff marukarʉ
out on something, spill tokwʉriarʉ
out, spit W kʉhkihtserʉ
out liquid, spit pai tusiʔitʉ K
out, spread legs poʔarʉ
out something, spread tsahpararʉ,
  wʉhpararʉ
outer side, scrape wʉhkwʉnetʉ
out something, strain tsasoʔarʉ
out, stretch haahpitʉ 2
out arm, stretch maruruʔarʉ
out something, stretch wʉhpararʉ

out, stretch something tsahturʉ
out, strike wʉhpohtoʔitʉ
out pain, suck on body to draw
  musoopitʉ
out, swab wʉhkwinarʉ
out, take tsahkʉarʉ, tsahtoʔirʉ
out of something, throw
  wʉʔkwʉriarʉ
out, tire kweʔyʉkatʉ, nʉʉʔmaitʉ
out, try kʉhpunitʉ, tohpunitʉ
out, wash- patowoʔnepʉ
out earth, wash patowoʔnerʉ
out clothes, wear wʉkwiʔarʉ
out shoes, wear tawiarʉ W
out, wear something wihtoʔarʉ
out, worn wihtoʔaitʉ
out, worn- napatawiʔaitʉ
out with hands, wring tsahpitsoorʉ
outfits, medicine puha
  namakaʔmukipʉ
outrun someone naromʉnitʉ
outside hunakʉ, hunakʉ
oval huyuni
oven nohko aawoʔ K, pʉkʉra
  nohkoʔena̱ W
oven for baking biscuits nohko
  aawo̱
over, cross manitʉ
over, fold namakwatubiitʉ
over, kill by growing puhi tʉyaitʉ
over, knock (and spill
  accidentally) tsakwʉriarʉ
over, knocked mahuihkatʉ
over something, lean nʉʉsooʔetʉ
over, look puiwʉnʉrʉ
over. move nuarʉ
over, pushed mahuihkatʉ
over fire (or dry it for jerky), roast
  meat kuʔinarʉ
over or around, roll naʔanitʉ
over something, step tasarʉ
over, turn natsamʉritʉ

over, turn something tsamʉrikarʉ, wʉmʉʉrʉ

over, turned wʉmʉʉrihkatʉ

over someone, win kwakurʉ K

over, wrinkled all takwikakwo?apʉ

overcome tahni?arʉ

overcome pain wʉmetʉ

overflow ata?okwetʉ, muru?itʉ

overflow the creek bed paru?itʉ

overflowing tʉhpetʉ

overhand, throw kwihitʉ

overhear nakʉhoorʉ

overheating, burst from kupʉtsarʉ

overtake tahtsaitʉ, wʉhpitʉ

overworked namakupʉkatʉ

owl o?oo?

Owl Mopai

owl, burrowing pohkóo?

owl, Old- Mo?pi tsokopʉ

owl, screech sʉhʉ mupitsʉ

own hipʉkatʉ

own accord, open of its
    natsahwi?etʉ

own accord, spill of nʉʉti?akatʉ

own accord, split of nʉʉhtsi?aitʉ

own accord, unravel of
    nʉʉpʉrʉsuarʉ

own a home nʉmʉnakarʉ

own an article of clothing
    kwasu?ukatʉ K

own beard, pull namutsono?itʉ

own something ta?urʉkarʉ K

owned hipʉ

oyster pisi wa?kóo? W, pisi
    wa?rokóo? K, wa?koo? W

P p

pace pisʉtʉkitʉ

pacer pi?isʉtʉ

pack norʉbakitʉ

pack a load on foot tʉnoomi?arʉ

pack for an animal tʉnoopʉ W

pack rat kuura

pack-animal leader tʉnoo wapi

package, mail a letter or tʉhyetʉ

packaged flour homorohtía?

packed in tightly manʉkʉtʉ

packsaddle narʉnoo?

pact nanihpu?e?aikʉpʉ K

paddle, canoe panatsitoo?

paddle, dog masu?wa?nekitʉ,
    paruhparʉ

paddle feet (in water) pawʉpa?itʉ

paddle hands (in the water)
    paruhparʉ

paddle water masu?wa?nekitʉ

padlock natsihtʉma?

padlock something tʉtsihtʉrʉ

pain manʉʉtsikwa? W

pain, body nʉhtsikwarʉ

pain, extreme stomach sapʉ
    wʉnʉkatʉ

pain, give nʉʉtsikwarʉ K

pain, overcome wʉmetʉ

pain, stand on someone's back to
    ease tahpara?itʉ

pain, suck on body to draw out
    musoopitʉ

pain, to bear wʉmetʉ

pain, suffer abdominal kohikamʉtʉ

pain, suffer chest amawʉnʉtʉ

pain, suffer gall-bladder
    pu?i?wʉnʉrʉ

paint tʉrʉ?eka?, tʉ?eka? W

paint, house K kahni ebi

paint oneself napisarʉ

paint something tʉrʉ?ekarʉ,
    tʉ?ekarʉ

painted tʉrʉ?ekarʉ

Painted-feather Ketse na?bo

paintbrush, Indian kahnitʉeka

pajamas habikwasuu

pale pink esiekapi̲tu̲

pallet used during peyote meeting pisóona̱

palm of hand mapaana̱

palm of hand, slap with tohpaʔitu̲

palm of hand, stop hitting with fist or tohpu̲aru̲

palm reader mapaana?

palomino horse kwipu̲siapu̲, naʔahnia K

pan tu̲soona

pancake tohtía?

pancakes taaru̲hkapu̲

pant hehéki̲tu̲, suaʔsuaʔmiaru̲

pant heavily heheku̲bu̲niitu̲

pant with tongue hanging down heheku̲bu̲niitu̲

panther tu̲mahkupa?, wu̲ra?

paper tu̲boopu̲

paper, sand- tu̲maku̲maʔaai?, tu̲pi tu̲matsune?

paper, wall- kahni̲ tu̲boopu̲, tu̲banaa ru̲bopu̲

paper money wana buhihwi̲

parade namanahkeetu̲ W, wu̲habitu̲ K

parakeet woko̲ huutsu̲

paralyzed su̲kwe tu̲yai

paralyzed hand maʔitsaʔbu̲katu̲

paralyzed person su̲kwe tu̲yaipu̲

parch corn kuku̲meru̲

parched corn kuku̲mepu̲

pardon tu̲suʔnaru̲

pare wu̲htsitoʔaru̲

parent-in-law yahihpu̲?

parfleche oyóotu̲?

Parker, Quanah Kwana

Parker's daughter, Quanah Wanaru̲

Parker's wife, Quanah Tope

parlor pu̲ku̲ra yu̲kwiʔena̱ W, yu̲kwi kahni K

parrot woko̲ huutsu̲

part namabeʔahkapu̲, pekoʔaru̲

part, clean the inner wu̲hkwinaru̲

part hair natsihpeʔakaru̲, tsihpeʔakaru̲

partake of Communion pu̲u̲hibiru̲

parted mabeʔakatu̲ W, naʔbekoʔaru̲

parter, hair- natsihpeʔaka?

partially sun-dry wu̲htaku̲miitu̲

particles, mash into small mahomonutsaru̲

particular noo

partly eaten food naru̲hkapu̲

partner notsaʔka?

partner, gift-exchanging hinanahimitu̲ waipu̲

partners tu̲htu̲i?

partridge tu̲e kuyúutsi K

parts, split into two tu̲apakoʔitu̲

pass word on nimu̲u̲miʔaru̲ W

Pass-it-on Topehtsi

past the peak yu̲baru̲

past the time u̲i

paste, tooth- tamakotse?

pasted matsu̲bakikatu̲

pasture soni sokoobi, soni wu̲htu̲mapu̲

pasture, fenced soni tu̲htu̲mapu̲

patch, cloth tu̲karu̲ku̲pu̲

patch, garden tu̲ku̲ masu̲a sokoobi̲ W, tu̲mu̲su̲a sokobi K

patch something tu̲karu̲kuru̲

paternal grandfather ku̲nu?

paternal grandmother huutsi̲

paternal great uncle ku̲nu?

path puʔe̱

path, clear a puʔeʔaru̲

pave a road tuusanahpitu̲

paved a road (blacktopped) tuusanahpitu̲

paw the earth taʔsiʔwooru̲

Pawnee Witsapaai?

pay attention tɨnakiitɨ
pay debts tɨmakarɨ
pay medicine man mabekakɨrɨ W
pay something to medicine man
 tɨmabekarɨ
pay with money narɨmakarɨ
payment of damages nanɨwokɨ
pea toponibihuura?
pea, sensitive huutsú?a kàhnị
peace chief paraibo
Peace River Kutsiokwe
peaceful spirit tsɨmɨkịkatɨ
peach pɨhɨsɨ?kɨị
peak ku?ebi
peak, past the yɨbarɨ
pear wasápe?a tɨhkapɨ
pear, cactus, prickly wokwéesi
Pease River Mura hunu?bi
pecan kɨhtabai, nakkɨtaba?i
pecker, wood- pitụsɨ nu?ye? W,
 wobi tohtarakị K, wɨpụkoi?
Pecos River Kusiokwe
pedal ta?aikɨtɨ
Pedernales River Pai pakạ pia
 huna?
peel wɨhtsito?arɨ
peel off kwɨrɨ?arɨ, tokiarɨ,
 wɨhtsibo?arɨ
peel off skin kibo?arɨ
peel something tsahkíto?arɨ
peeling tool huusibe?
peep tasɨkɨpunitɨ, wihtekatɨ
peep at kuhiyarɨ
peep into tokwịtetɨ
peeping wihtekatɨ
Peeping-from-behind-tree Kuhiyai
peer through wihtekatɨ
peeved pihiso?ai
pen, ink parɨboo?
pen up animal ta?ikɨrɨ
pencil naboo? K, tɨboo?
penned up tawekwitɨ

penniless tɨtsu?mapɨ
pensively, rest, nasutamɨ habitɨ
people nɨmi, sɨmɨ?
people, Caddo Tukanai
people, Corn Hanitaibo
people, circus nohihtaiboo?nɨɨ
people, crowd of sɨɨmɨ?okɨ
people, crowd with tsɨhkịkatɨ
people, fill with tsɨhkịkatɨ
people, group of sɨɨmɨ?okɨ
People, Hill Ononɨɨ
people, Kiowa Kaaiwanɨɨ
people similar to elves, little
 Nɨnapi
people, Navaho Naboohnɨɨ
people, Osage Wa?sáasi?
(people), Pawnee Witsapaai?
People, Proud (Wichita name for
 the Comanches of Tejas) Natai
people, Sioux Papitsimina?, Suhta?
people, three groups of
 pahibahtɨnɨnɨ
People, Timber Huuh?inɨɨ
people by bad tidings, upset
 ni?yɨsɨkaitɨ
people, Wichita Tuhka?naai?
pepper tɨkɨ mahya?
pepper, chili tsiira?
pepper, red ekatsiira?
perceptive supịkaahkatɨ
perforate wo?nerɨ
perform surgery wɨpɨtsarɨ
perfume plant, Indian tɨsaasị
perhaps kia, sɨɨkɨtsa?noo
permission, ask nanihtɨbinitɨ
perplexed mɨɨwarɨ?itɨ
persecute makwihtserɨ
persimmon naséka
persimmon, Mexican tuhnaséka
persistent natsanahaatɨ
person alone, leave kekɨnabeniitɨ
person, black tuhtaiboo? W

person, covetous kwahisiapʉ
person, crazy poo?sa?
person, cross-eyed pasapuni
person, dead kooipʉ
person, dependable nasupetipʉ K
person, dishonest kaawosa̱
person, drunk hibipʉ
person, emaciated wehuru?i
person, envy another kwahisi?a
person, faithful nasupetipʉ K
person, fat yupʉ
person, graduated tamarʉkʉkatʉ
person, handcuff a mo?o wʉhtamarʉ
person, intoxicated hibipʉ,
   kwinumapʉ
person, paralyzed sʉkwe tʉyaipʉ
person, poor takahpʉ
person, ravenously hungry
   tsihasi?apʉ
person, reject a nakabarʉ
person, rejected ninakaba?itʉ
person, sickly nama?abʉ, takwipʉ
person, sneaky nakʉhoowaaitʉ
person, sore namakʉnʉmapʉ
person, stingy nahkʉepʉ K
person, stubborn sutenapʉ
person, thin kanabʉʉtsi?, wehuru?i
person, throw down a
   tsahkwa?nu?itʉ
person, tired namakʉnʉmapʉ
person, tongue-tied ekotʉyaipʉ
person, undependable senihtʉhtsi?
person or animal, weak tʉ?onaapʉ
person, white taiboo?
person, wounded kwʉhti?
person of delicate health takwipʉ
person or thing, buried
   namʉsokoopʉ
person or animal, exhausted
   namakweyaipʉ
person or an animal, lead a
   tsakarʉ

person or animal, mean tuhupʉ
personal belongings namahku
personal ointment nʉʉhtʉ?eka?
persons, handicapped
   wʉ?mina?nʉʉmʉ
persons, kill several nakwʉsʉkʉrʉ
perspiration takwʉsipʉ
perspire takʉsito?itʉ
persuade someone to do
   something nitsʉbahikʉ?itʉ
pester by talk nimʉsasuarʉ
pester someone nihtunetsarʉ
pesticide isawasʉ?
pestle tsohkwe?
pestle, pound with a tayu?nerʉ
pestle, wooden tʉrayu?ne?
pet nisutaitʉ, tohtarakiitʉ
pet or stroke tohtaraki?arʉ
petal, flower totsiyaa patʉpi̱naatʉ
petroleum jelly nʉʉhtʉ?eka?,
   tsiikʉwitehka? K, tsi?wʉnʉʉ
   tʉ?eka? W
peyote, eat wokwetʉhkarʉ
peyote meeting, conduct a
   wokwetʉhkarʉ
peyote meeting, pallet used
   during pisóona̱
peyote plant or button wokwe
peyote teepee puha kahni, wokwe
   kahni
phlegm yoka
physically, strong natsʉwitʉ
piano mayake?
pick mutsimuhpe?, tso?meetʉ
pick a bird of its feathers no?itʉ
pick for scraping hides
   to?tsimuhpe?
pick fruit pomarʉ
pick, ice wiiyu̱
pick out nabinarʉ
pick up several objects hima?arʉ
picked berries pomapʉ

picture naboopʉ, tʉpuuni

picture frame naboopʉha
naroʔnikaʔ, naboopʉha narʉso,
naboopʉha pʉkʉratoʔnikaʔiʔ

pictures, moving yʉʔyʉmuhkuʔ W

pie noʔa nohkopʉ

piece, break off a tsanutsarʉ

pieces nakooʔipʉ

pieces, break in tahbaitʉ,
tahporoorʉ

pieces, break into tsanutsarʉ,
wʉnutsarʉ

pieces, break into small
wʉhhomonutsaʔarʉ

pieces, crush in
tohhomonutsarʉ W

pieces, crushed into small
mabisukiitʉ

pieces, cut off wʉhtsiʔarʉ

pieces. cut up into tsihpoma

pieces, object cut into
tʉtsihpomiʔipʉ

pieces, sit on something breaking
it to pinutsarʉ

pierce tonarʉ

pierced ear nakị toonʉkatʉ K,
nanakịtonapʉ

pig mubị poʔrooʔ, munuaʔ, poʔroʔ

pigeon kuʔe wóoʔ, pasahòo, taibo
huutsuuʔ

piker pihisiʔapʉ

pile high pia wʉʔutsitʉ

pile up wʉʔutsitʉ

piled badly pia utsaatʉ

pillow tsohpę

pillow, feather sia tsohpę

pillowsticks tsohpe tawʉnaʔ

pillowsticks into ground, pound
tsohpe takwʉnarʉ

pimple mohtoʔa K

pin nahamuhkụ K

pin, bobby- papị tsihtʉpʉkaʔ

pin, decorative natsihtʉpʉkaʔ

pin, diaper nahamuhku K

pin, hair- papị tsihtʉpʉkaʔ

pin, safety nahamuhku K,
naʔhʉmuhku W

pin, straight- piitsʉnʉaʔ

pin together tsihtʉpʉkarʉ,
wʉhtʉpʉkarʉ

pincer tʉkʉh pomaʔ

pincers tʉkʉh kweʔya?

pincers, wire tʉkʉh kaʔaʔ

pinch masitotsarʉ W, matsurʉ

pine woko

pineapple wokwekatʉ amakwooʔ

pink ekaʔotʉ, tosa ekapitʉ W

pink, pale esiekapitʉ

pipe toʔị

pipe stem omotoi

piper, sand- tʉʔíiʔ

pistol tawoʔiʔ K

pistol, automatic natsahkwineʔ

pitch tokwʉkiʔarʉ

pitch off kuʔe wʉnʉrʉ

pitched, high putsi tʉnikwʉyʉ K

pitchfork soni tsiyaaʔ, sonitsiimaʔ,
tʉtsiyaaʔ W

pitied tʉtaatʉ

pitiful senihtʉhtsiʔ

pity tʉsutaibitsị, tʉsutaikatʉ

pity, feel mʉʉrʉʔikatʉ

place, eating tʉkʉ kahni

place, put down in tsahtʉkitʉ

place, put in narʉkitʉ, tʉkarʉ

place, put something back in
tohtʉkiʔarʉ

place, resting koonọ

place, set in natsawʉnʉkatʉ

place, set something in
natsawʉnʉrʉ

place known by speaker and
hearer pʉkʉhu

place to place, graze from tooniitʉ

place to place, move from
noonumi?aru
place to place, wander from
noyukaru
placed narukitu
plain kenanawatsitu
plainly maihtuku
plan, make a nimaka?mukitu,
su?atsitu
plane, carpenter's tusibe?
plane, wood huusibe?
plane something smooth tusibetu
plant turunaru
plant by hand turahnaru
plant, certain (with edible tuber)
tsunisu
plant, cigarette-wrapper
tumakwatui?
plant, Comanche perfume numu
rusaasi
plant, cymopterus tunuhaa
plant, fever poiya
plant, flowering saatotsiya
plant, gray-colored kusinuuhparabi
plant, heal-all puhakatu
plant, Indian perfume tusaasi
plant, medicinal tupi natsu
plant, milky-rooted pihtsamuu
plant (or button), peyote wokwe
plant, potted saatotsiyapu
plant, stem of totsiyaa?a suuki
plant, sunflower stalk or hi?oopi
plant, wheat tohtía sonipu
plant crops tumusuaru
plant seed tuhtukitu, turuni?itu
plant seeds tahnaaru
plant similar to water lily pa?mutsi
plant with edible fruit paiyapi
planted crops turunapu
planter turuna?
plaster ebikahni
plaster W kahni ebi

plate tusoona
play nohitu
play, run around and nohi?nuraaru
play a wind instrument muuyaketu
play cards wana rohpetiru
play dead kaabehkaru
play hand games na?yuwetu
play instrument mayaketu
play lacrosse natsihtóo?itu
play poker pokaru
playground swing pi?wesurúu?ii?
playing-card deck, king in
ohahkuyaa?
playing cards wana atsi?
plaything nohi?
plead nanimaa?ubu?ikutu,
tunihpararu
please someone tsaa manusuru
pleased tsaa manusu?itu
pliers tukuh kwe?ya?
plot, vegetable garden tuku masua
sokoobi W
plow tutsa?woo? K
plow soil tutsa?woru
plowed field tutsakwoopu
pluck tsanooru
pluck a bird clean puhu no?itu
pluck a bird clean of feathers
pahtsi no?itu
pluck out something no?itu
plug to extinguish, un- tsahtukaru
plum parua sukui?, suku?i
plum, (Chickasaw) tuahpi
plum, domestic taibo suku?i
plum, dried natsomu, na?a?tsome?
plum, early yusuku
plum, fall kusisukui
plum, late-summer parawa suk
plum bush wi?nuupi
plum tree parua sukui?
pneumonia, have tu?inawunuru
pocket amawosa

pocketbook puhihwi narųsọ W,
puhihwi wosa K

point mutsi-, muutsi̱, tsihtu?aweru

point, form into a manutsiaru W

point, formed to a mamámutsiakatų

point, sharpen to a tomotsiaru W,
wumutsiaru K

point, sharpened to a
mamutsiakatu

point out something
muruahwunuru

pointed mutsi-

pointed, make mamutsiaru

-pointed object, sharp mutsipų

poison isawasu?

poison ivy puhi ta?ara?

poisonous wild onion
kuhtsutsuu?ni?

poke tsisu?waru

poke head into something
tso?nikaru, tutso?nikaru

poke out nose munakuaitu

poker chip tuhhuu?

poker, fire kutsani

poker. play pokaru

pole wahta

pole, clothesline oo?ru
tohtsani?i?ana huuhpi, tutsapara
huupi

pole, fishing huahuupi̱

pole, flag- wana tsiyaa?a náhuupi̱

pole, teepee huutsiyaa?, waahuupi̱,
waata̱

pole, telephone puhihwi
tekwapuhana huupi

**poles, travel carrier made of
teepee** tu?noo?

poles for constructing brush arbor
huukina huupi̱

policeman numi hima?etų,
tuuhtamųh raibo?

polish tapųnukeeru W

polish by hand mapųnukeeru

pond umahpaa?

pond lily, yellow kuriata

ponder su?uraru

pony tail kuwikųsii

poodle motso sarii?

poor person takahpu

Poor-one Tahkapų

pop kukųbihkutu, pipóhtoru,
wuhpohto?itu

pop, soda pihná baa

pop on someone kuhpuru?airu

pop with the mouth kuhpohtoru

popcorn kuhmito?ai?, tahma
yokake?

poppy, prickly pitsi tora

porch kahni nahuuki

porcupine huunu?, yuhnu

porcupine quill yuhnu wokweebi?

pork mubi̱ po?roo ruhkapų W, po?ro
tuhkapų K

pork rind mubi̱ po?ro?a po?aa W

position, change yumuhkitu

**position, change (from one to
another)** nuhyųyukitu

**position, help up from sitting to
standing** matsákwunukuru

position, lift from a prone
tsahnuaru

position, lying in prone muparai
habinitu K

position, prone haahpi̱

position, rise from seated
nuu?nuaru

possess hipųkatu, huuyaaru,
mahípurumuru, mahípurumutu

possess sticks huuhimaru

possessed hipų

possession, regain mako?itu

possessions, material tarųwanapi̱ W

post, trading ekanarumuu?, numu
narumuu?

post office tᵾboopᵾ kᵾni
posthole digger tᵾhora?
postman tᵾboo tahni?, tᵾboo
  hima?eetᵾ K
pot, cooking saawihtua
potato, arch sᵾhᵾ tsitsina?
potato, Irish paapasi̱
potato, sweet kamúuta?
potato, wild paapasi̱
potted plant saatotsiyapᵾ
pound narayaakᵾpᵾ, tᵾhraniitᵾ K
pound completely sᵾmᵾ rayu?nerᵾ
pound flat wᵾtᵾki̱?netᵾ
pound food tayu?nekarᵾ
pound meat tᵾrayu?nerᵾ
pound on something tahhanitᵾ
pound on to open tohkwᵾmarᵾ
pound pillowsticks into ground
  tsohpe takwᵾnarᵾ
pound something wᵾhtarakiitᵾ
pound with a pestle tayu?nerᵾ
pounded nara?okatᵾ
pounded meat tᵾrayu?nepᵾ
pounding, soften by tohparaarᵾ W,
  tsohkwe K
pounding, wake someone by
  wᵾhtᵾbunitᵾ
pour on tokwᵾriarᵾ
pour out wᵾhtiarᵾ, wᵾ?wenitᵾ K
pour water on payunitᵾ
powder homo-, homopᵾ, pisahpi̱
powder (apply to oneself)
  homonabi̱sakatᵾ
powder, crumble to
  mahomonutsarᵾ
powder, crumble to (with the
  foot) tahhomonutsarᵾ W
powder, face homobi saapi̱
powder, gun- nakuti̱si̱
powder, talcum homoroso?yoki?
powder something homopisarᵾ
powder the body homopisarᵾ

powdery homoketᵾma?
power tᵾsu?atsipᵾ
power, have tᵾsu?atsi̱tᵾ
power, having supernatural
  puhakatᵾ
power, judicial tᵾsu?atsipᵾ
power, supernatural puha̱
powwow nᵾhkana W
pox, chicken kokorá?a tasi?a
pox, small- narᵾ?ᵾyᵾ tasi?a̱,
  tasi?a? W
practice something namabunitᵾ
prairie nᵾmᵾwahtᵾ, pᵾhᵾwahtᵾ
prairie chicken pakawkoko?
prairie clover yuu sonipᵾ
prairie clover, purple pakeeso
prairie dog tᵾ?rᵾkúu? W
prairie fire nakuyaarᵾ
praise panaaitᵾ
praise someone nihpana?aitᵾ
pray nani̱sutaitᵾ
pray for someone nani̱sutaikᵾtᵾ
prayer of thanks ahotabeni̱htᵾ
preach puha rekwarᵾ W
preacher puha raiboo? W
precede someone muhnetᵾ
pregnant no?a-
preparation, meatball tᵾrahyarᵾ
prepare breakfast for someone
  taamahkarᵾ
prepare for maka?mukitᵾ
prepare medicine puha?arᵾ
prepare oneself namaka?mukitᵾ
prepared namahka?mukitᵾ
prepared food hanipᵾ
prepared medicine puha?aitᵾ
present generation nᵾmᵾ rᵾborapᵾ
  K, pᵾhkᵾra nahanᵾ W
press tahkwᵾ?nerᵾ
press down mabararᵾ
press down with hands to expel
  water mabitsoorᵾ

press something down tatuke?neru
pressed down manukutu
pressure with the hands, rub applying masu?neru
pretend kaasuaru, nohitekwaru
(pretend) make-believe nohitekwaru
pretentious, act nasutsa akwaru K
pretty nananisuyake
prevent someone's death makwitso?aitu
prick someone with something piso?aru
prick up the ears to?yabaitu
prickly ash kunanatsu
prickly pear cactus wokwéesi
prickly poppy pitsi tora
priest Suabi puharaibo
primp nama?yukwitu
print, foot- nanapunipu, napu, narapunipu
printed material nakohpoopu W, soo naboo?
prints, hoof- tuhuyena puni W
prison narawekwi kahni, tupi kuni
prize, win a turahwikatu
probe tsikwainitu
proceed ahead muhnetu
process of tanning a hide naruso?ipu
procreated by us numu ruboraru
produce pomapu
product, garden tumusuapu
product, home-grown garden masuapu W
product, raise garden masuaru W
prohibit makuetu W, namamusuru, nimoya?ekuru, ninakaba?ikutu
prohibited mamusuakatu K
promise sutsamuru
prone position haahpi
prone position, lift from a tsahnuaru

prone position, lying in muparai habinitu K
propel tsatukaru, tukwuru
proper tokwetu
prophet ta?ahpu?a tekwawapi K, turu?awe wapi W
propose marriage kwuhuniwaitu
prosper wupuhoikutu
protrude kunakuaru K, kuro?itu W, wusa?maru W
protrude, cause to manakuaru
protruding nakuahkatu
proud panaaitu
Proud People (Wichita name for the Comanches of Tejas Natai
provoking jealousy, rival wohhohpu?
prune kuhpomaru, kumakooru, tuhnatso?me?, wu?yukwitu K
pry open tohkwumaru, tsihto?aru W
pry up tsahto?aru K
puff up pohtokitu
puffball mupitsuha pisahpi W
pull tsah-, tsanooru
pull a bouncy object tsahpo?tsaru
pull apart tsahka?aru, tsahpomi?itu
pull back tsasinukaaru
pull bones out of joint tsahtoko?aru
pull down tsahparu, tsapeheru
pull off tokaru, tsahto?aru K
pull on something tsanuaru
pull oneself down natsahkupukatu
pull oneself up natsahto?itu
pull out tsahpi?eru
pull out of container tsahpuyeru
pull own beard namutsono?itu
pull someone's beard mutsonoo?itu
pull something behind pitsákaru
pull something off or out tsahkwe?yaru
pull to make noise matsáapikaaru

pull up tsahkᵾarᵾ, tsahto?irᵾ
pull with full strength tsahturerᵾ
pulled up tsahto?itᵾ
pulling, burst by tsahpohtoorᵾ
pulverized or grated object
    tusupᵿ W
pump patsa?aikᵾ, tsa?aikᵾrᵾ
pump water patsahto?itᵾ
pump, water patsahto?i?,
    patsa?aikᵾ
pumpkin nakwᵿsi?
pumpkin, dried nakwᵿsipᵿ
punch tohpa?itᵾ
punch repeatedly (or slap)
    tohtᵾkwarᵾ
puncture a tire tᵾrapᵿtsarᵾ W
puncture oneself with something
    nabiso?arᵾ
punctured napiso?akatᵿ
puny nᵾᵾsukatᵾ
pupil of eye tuhpui
pure tutᵿtsaai wahtᵿ
purple tuka?yuwᵾ W
purple coneflower tukunᵾ natsᵿ
purple prairie clover pakeeso
purple W tu?ebipiṯᵿ
purpose, spill something on
    tokwᵾriaitᵾ
purr soro?rokitᵾ
purse, coin puhihwi narᵿsọ W
purse, woman's puhihwi wosa K
pus pisi
push ma?wikarᵾ, tanuarᵾ,
    taperᵾ, toh-
push away mahbotsetᵾ
push someone under water
    tsahpaaku?nikarᵾ
push something that rolls
    ma?aikᵾrᵾ, tsi?aikᵾrᵾ
push under water, hit and
    wᵾhpaaku?nerᵾ
pushed over mahuihkatᵿ

pushed under water
    tohpaaku?netᵾ W
put away namabimarᵾ, tahtᵾkarᵾ,
    tᵾkarᵾ
put away for safekeeping
    to?nikarᵾ K
put down in place tsahtᵾkitᵾ
put down something to sit on
    pisoonarᵾ
put in place narᵾkitᵿ, tᵾkarᵾ
put on shoes tahtoorᵾ
put on trousers pitsohkorᵾ
put something back in place
    tohtᵾki?arᵾ
put something down tsa?nikoorᵾ
put something into the mouth
    tᵾro?nikarᵾ
put up a barbed wire fence
    puhihwi tᵾᵾhtᵾmarᵾ

Q q

quail kuyúusi?, tᵾe basuu? W, tᵾe
    kuyúutsi K, tᵾrᵾe ku?yuutsi, tᵾrᵾe
    basuu K
quake of earth soko yᵾ?yᵾmuhkurᵾ
Quanah Parker Kwana
Quanah Parker's daughter
    Wanarᵾ
Quanah Parker's wife Tope
quantity, augmenting in
    tᵾraka?aitᵾ
quantity, small tᵾtaatᵾ
quarrel nani?wiketᵾ W
quarrel with someone ni?wiketᵿ
quarreling, stop kekᵾnabeniitᵾ
quarrelsome nanitsᵿwakatᵿ K
quarter section soko rᵾmanahkepᵿ
quarter-section of land soko
    tsihka?apᵿ
quarters, sleeping habikᵿni

queer nanakuya?arʉ
quench a fire murukarʉ
quench by hand marukarʉ
question, ask a tʉbinitʉ, tʉrʉbinitʉ
question someone tʉbinarʉ,
   tʉbinitʉ
quick pʉhetʉ
quick-cook corn soup atakwá?sʉ?
quick-dried corn atakwa?sʉ?aipʉ̱
quickly namʉ̱si
quickly, move wʉ?rabiarʉ
quickly, sit down tsuhni karʉ
quickly, turn around pikwebuitʉ
quiet kebayʉmʉkitʉ, tokobo?niitʉ̱ K,
   yunahkatʉ
quiet by speech ni?tsu?narʉ
quiet down tʉsu?narʉ,
   wʉyupa?nitʉ
quiet, keep niwatsi?aikʉ?itʉ̱
quiet someone niyukarʉrʉ̱ W
quiet spirit tsʉmʉki̱katʉ̱
quill, porcupine yʉhnʉ wokweebi?
quilt pisóona̱, soona̱
quilt, cotton wana̱ soona̱
quilt top sona bo?a
quinine weed pohóobi
quit something pʉarʉ
quiver kʉhkwibikitʉ̱, sʉhkwibitʉ

R r

rabbit tabú?kina?
rabbit, Easter noyotso?me̱ tabu?
rabbit, swamp ekae?ree W,
   ta?wokinae?ree eka K
raccoon nʉmamo?o?, paruuku?,
   pa?ruhku?
race, run a nanarʉna?itʉ,
   narubunitʉ
racer narʉbuni?etʉ?
racer snake kʉhtáa nu?ya?a W

races, hold narʉrʉnitʉ
radiate heat kusʉwetʉ
rage, feel tuhu su?aitʉ
ragweed, western wo?anatsu?
railroad car kunawaikinʉ,
   kunawobipuuku̱
railroad handcar kʉ?wʉnʉbaa?i̱,
   pi?yʉpu̱ káa?i̱ W
railroad tracks kunawaikina pu?e
rain ʉmaarʉ, ʉmapʉ̱
rain shelter ʉmakahni
rain shelter for winter yu?a
   ʉmaky̱ni
rain water ʉmahpaa?
rainbow pisi ma?rokóo?
raining, stop pʉhkitʉ
raise a garden tʉmʉ̱sʉarʉ
raise dust huuku̱hʉnʉrʉ
raise dust by walking
   tahuhkuwʉnʉrʉ
raise garden product masʉarʉ W
raise head tso?nʉarʉ
raise one leg tahtsarʉ
raise someone manʉarʉ
rake tsahtʉ?oki? K, tʉtsanua?
rake, hay tʉtsa?ooki?
rake something tʉtsahtʉ?oorʉ
rake together manuarʉ W,
   marʉ?okitʉ K, tanuarʉ
rake up tsa?oorʉ
rash on skin tasi?a? W
rasp tʉmatsune? W
rasp a surface tʉmatsunarʉ
raspberry panatsayaa?
rat pia kahúa
rat, pack kuura
ration day tʉhima̱ rabeni
rations tʉhimana W
rations, get tʉhima?etʉ
rattle wʉhkitsu?tsukitʉ,
   wʉhkitsu?tsuki?, wʉkwʉ̱bihkurʉ
rattle, gourd wʉhtsabeyaa?

rattle, make something
tsatsɨbipɨkurɨ

rattled tsatsubihkurɨ

rattlesnake kwasinaboo
wɨhkitsuʔtsuʔikatɨ,
wɨhtsabeyakatɨ W

rattling tsatsubihkurɨ

rattrap kahúu pɨmata hɨarɨ?

rave niʔemɨabɨnitɨ, tuhu yɨkwiitɨ

ravel, un- pɨrɨsuʔarɨ

ravel of own accord, un-
nɨɨpɨrɨsuarɨ

ravel, something, un-
nɨɨpɨrɨsuanɨpurɨ

raven tuwikaaʔ

ravenously hungry person
tsihasiʔapɨ

raw skin tuhɨpɨ

rawhide ɨhtaayuʔ

rawhide ready to use pahkipɨ

rawhide rope pahki wiyaaʔ

rawhide wardrobe case natɨsakɨna

reach, fail to toʔwɨminaitɨ

reach something, fail to
tsaʔwɨminarɨ

reach (or break) something
wɨminarɨ

reach for makwɨbɨtsɨrɨ W,
maruruʔarɨ

reach out mahiyaitɨ

reach out and touch maʔwɨminarɨ

read nihakɨrɨ, tɨhnearɨ W

reader, palm mapaanaʔ

ready tsuh

ready to use, rawhide pahkipɨ

really tɨbitsi

rear katsonakwɨ

rear a child manɨarɨ

**rear or back against something,
scratch** pisuʔnetɨ

rear up, incite to manáawɨnɨʔetɨ

reared up manawɨnɨkatɨ

reason sukwɨkitɨ

rebuke nihmakwihtserɨ

recall suʔurarɨ

recede pasanuarɨ

receive food tɨkɨ himarɨ

recently ɨku

recognize suabetaitɨ

recover kwitsoʔaitɨ

recover from illness tebuunitɨ

red ekapi̱, tukaʔekapi̱tɨ

red, shine ekakuhtabearɨ

red ant ekaɨnɨɨ

red brick ekatɨɨpi̱

red cedar ekawaapi̱

red color eka-

red false mallow puha natsu W,
yokanatsuʔu K

red fox ekatseenaʔ

red haw tuʔamowoo

red hot, turn ekawehaarɨ

red pepper ekatsiiraʔ

Red River Ekahohtɨpahi hunuʔbi,
Pia pasi hunuʔbi

Red River, north fork of Natɨmɨɨ
paʔi hunaʔ

red rock ekatɨɨpi̱, ekwipi̱saʔ

red soil ekahuukupɨ, ekasokoobi

red store ekanarɨmɨɨ?

Red-buffalo Eka kura

Red-crooked-nose Ekamurawa

Red-young-man Ekawokani

redbird eka̱huutsuʔ

redbud ekamuroraʔi huupi

redbug puikɨso

redheaded buzzard ekabapi̱

ref to fat yuhu

refrigerator tahka aawo

refuse makɨetɨ W, nimamɨsukɨtɨ

refuse to accept someone
ninakabarɨ

Refuse-to-come Huuhwiya

refused nahkabaʔitɨ

Refusing Ninakaba?i?

regain possession mako?itʉ

reins, bridle narʉmuhkʉ

reject kemabana?itʉ, kwetʉsuakʉrʉ W

reject a person nakabarʉ

reject man as husband ninakabarʉ

reject someone kemenikwitʉ W, nimakabaitʉ

rejected kemenikwitʉ W, nahkaba?itʉ

rejected person ninakaba?itʉ

rejoice na?okitʉ

rejoice verbally nanina?ukitʉ

rejoicing tsaa nʉʉsukatʉ

relate narʉmu?ikatʉ

relatives nʉmʉ haahkana?

-relatives, She-invites-her Nʉmʉ ruibetsʉ

relax sua yurahpitʉ

relaxed kesósoorʉ

release tsahparʉ W, tsahpʉarʉ W

release from hands mabʉarʉ

religious ceremony, smoke during puha bahmu?itʉ

remember nasutamʉkatʉ tamai

remember, search the mind in effort to su?urarʉ

remind someone nasutamakʉrʉ W

reminded orally ninʉsutamakʉtʉ

remnant saved piinaai

remove tohkwe?yarʉ, tsayumi?i

remove item by item wʉpiyarʉ

render an animal carcass tʉhtsohpe?arʉ

render lard kuhpitsʉni?arʉ W, ku?okwerʉ W, yuhukarʉ

rendered yuhukarʉkarʉ

renter tʉrʉ?ai wapi

repair hanitʉ

repeatedly, faint esikooitʉ

repeatedly, hit wʉhpa?itʉ

repeatedly, shoot a gun ta?wo?ekarʉ

repeatedly, slap (or punch) tohtʉkwarʉ

repeating gun, shoot a tsatʉka?karʉ

request (ask for something) tʉrʉnirʉ

request something naníhtsawa?itʉ, nigwaitʉ K

rescue kwitso?arʉ, makwitso?aitʉ, wʉhkwitso?arʉ

resemble someone tʉ?ikatʉ

respect mabitsiarʉ

respect, treat with pahna?aitʉ

respect someone marʉhnikatʉ

respected maritsiakatʉ

rest sua yurahpitʉ

rest, allow to (or cool off) sua soyuraperʉ

rest on something mahtokwʉnaitʉ K

rest pensively nasutamʉ habitʉ

restaurant tʉkʉ kahni

resting place koono

restore circulation wʉsuabetaitʉ

return ko?itʉ, pitsa mi?arʉ

return (an item_ yaakʉrʉ

return, cause to tsahkoo?itʉ

return, send word to someone to nʉníhkoonirʉ

return (from warpath) mahiko?itʉ

revived suabetaikatʉ

rheumatic tsuhni wʉmɪnahkatʉ

rheumatism tsuhni wʉmɪnakatʉ?

rib kwahtsʉ W, mawaatsa, waatsʉ K

rib area of animal puihtsita? K

ribbon tʉkʉma?ai

rice wo?arʉhkapʉ

rich tsaa naahkatʉ

riches tsaanahapʉ

rickrack wakʉ?wʉtʉ

ride double pihima, piyarʉ

ride horseback kʉayʉka?etʉ W, tʉhʉya karʉ

ride seated on a sled pisiko?i

-rides-buffalo, One-who Kuhtsunu kwahipʉ

ridicule nohitʉ, tʉnimakwihtserʉ

ridiculous nanʉsu?uyaatʉ

rifle tawo?i? K

right yusuatʉ

right, to the tʉbitsi petutʉ

right here makʉ

right now meeku, namʉsohi

right side tʉbitsinakwʉ

right something tsahkarʉkʉrʉ

right-handed tʉbitsikatʉ

rind, pork mubi po?ro?a po?aa W

ring kawohwitʉ

ring (a bell) pihkarʉ

ring, cause to tsayaketʉ

ring, finger- ma?nika?, mo?o tsi?nika?

ring something tu?tsayaketʉ

Rio Frio Kwana pekwasʉ

Rio Grande Kwana kuhtsu paa?

riot naniyo?naitʉ K

rip completely sʉmʉ sihwarʉ

rip something puhkarʉ, tohtʉrʉ?arʉ W, wʉhtʉrʉ?arʉ K

rip with fingers tsahtʉrʉ?arʉ

ripe kwasʉpʉ

ripped puhkapʉ

ripsaw mo?o huutsihka?a?

rise atabaro?itʉ, paro?ikitʉ, pohtokitʉ

rise from seated position nʉʉ?nʉarʉ

rise up yorimi?arʉ, yʉtsʉrʉ

ritually, smoke nakatsʉhetʉ

rival provoking jealousy wohhohpʉ?

River, north fork of Red Natʉmʉʉ pa?i huna?

River, Nueces Sʉmonʉ kuhtsu paa

River, Peace Kutsiokwe

River, Pease Mura hunu?bi

River, Pecos Kusiokwe

River, Pedernales Pai pakạ pia huna?

River, Red Ekahohtʉpahi hunu?bi, Pia pasi hunu?bi

river, small okwèetʉ

river, up obutʉma?

River, Washita Tusoho?ọkwe?

river bank ekatotsạ

riverbank, flood the paru?itʉ

river crossing nagwee

road pu?ẹ

road, construct a pu?e?arʉ

road, follow a pu?eyarʉ

road, pave a tuusanahpịtʉ

road, paved a- (blacktopped) tuusanahpịtʉ

road, surfaced tʉpi pu?e

roadrunner ebikuyuutsi?

roam noyʉkarʉ

roamer noyʉka?

Roamers Noyʉhkanʉʉ

roast corn atakwa?sʉ?aitʉ, hanikwasʉkʉrʉ

roast food kwasʉkʉrʉ

roast in ashes kusiwʉhpima W

roast meat tʉkwʉsʉkʉrʉ

roast meat over fire (or dry it for jerky) ku?inarʉ

roast on a stick kuhtsiyarʉ

roast on sticks ku?tsiyaarʉ

roasted corn atakwa?sʉ?aipʉ

roasted meat ku?inapʉ, tʉkwʉsʉkʉpʉ?

Robe-on-his-back Kwahira

rock tʉpi, tʉʉpi

rock, heated nakutʉkʉna?

rock, red ekatʉʉpi, ekwipisạ?

rock lizard tʉpi paboko?aai W

rocking chair nabiʔaaikɨnakarɨ K

rocking way of walking
yɨʔbanaʔitɨ

rocky ground tɨpi̱ sokoobi W

Rocky-creek Tɨpi wɨnɨ

rod tɨʔehkooiʔ W

rodeo kuhtsu taibo nohhiitɨ W,
tukumakwɨyetɨʔ W

roll, un- tsahkwɨmarɨ,
tsahpɨkɨsuʔarɨ W

roll along anikwita miʔarɨ

roll around maropoʔnarɨ

roll in the mouth kɨhkwatuubirɨ K

roll into a ball tsahtopoʔnarɨ

roll over or around naʔanitɨ

roll to start something toʔaikɨrɨ

roll up namakwatubiitɨ,
tɨmakwatɨbiʔetarɨ

roll up to itself wɨhkwitubikatɨ

roll up with something
tohtopoʔnarɨ

rolled matsobokɨkatɨ

rolled up makwatubiitɨ

rolls, push something that
maʔaikɨrɨ, tsiʔaikɨrɨ

roof of mouth mitɨkoʔo

room kah-, kahni, kahni tai, taina

**room, find (for someone or
something)** haakarɨ

room, invite into home or
niʔikaʔitɨ

room, living- pɨkɨra yɨkwiʔena̱ W

rooming house kwaabih kahni

roomy pia weki̱tɨ

rooster kokoráʔa kuhma W

root tɨrana

root, church itsa, timɨihɨʔ

root, eriogonum ekanatsɨ̱

root, snake itsa, timɨihɨʔ

root, tree huupita tɨrahna̱

root, up tsahtobarɨ

root around ahweniitɨ, muwainitɨ K

roots, dig edible tɨkɨ ahwerɨ

roots of the teeth tamakwita̱

rope wiyaaʔ

rope, clothesline soni wiyaaʔ, wana
kotse tsahparaaʔ K

rope, hang someone with a
ooibehkarɨ

rope, jumping nɨhpopiʔ

rope, rawhide pahki wiyaaʔ

rope around something, slip a
kuʔnikarɨ

**rope someone or something while
moving** kuʔnikakɨrɨ

rosin huupitan pihnàa

rot eʔbootsiarɨ, eʔbootsiaʔ, papɨsitɨ

rotate nuhyɨyukitɨ

rotten papɨsipɨ

rotting papoosinu̱

rouge ekawɨpi̱si̱ K, ekapi̱saʔ

rough kesuatɨ

rough, talk tuhu rekwarɨ

rough skin tsiʔwapɨ W

rough terrain wohtsaʔwɨtɨ

rough-leafed dogwood parɨa

round tohtoponitɨ, topohtɨ

**round bundle or round knot, tie
in** wɨhtopɨʔnoorɨ

round object maropoʔniʔipɨ

round up tahkoonikarɨ, taʔookitɨ

round with the mouth, make
kɨhtoponarɨ W

rouse tsayoritɨ

row maʔaikɨrɨ, wohya, wɨʔaikɨrɨ

row or nerve, end of sɨkwerɨ

rub tasitotsarɨ W

rub against something pisuʔnetɨ

**rub applying pressure with the
hands** masuʔnerɨ

rub feet tasuʔnetɨ

rub hands together namɨsuʔnetɨ

rub head against something
tsotsoʔneetɨ

rub lightly makwʉ?netʉ

rub medicine on body mabararʉ

rub off toso?netʉ

rub the wrong way masu?naitʉ K, masʉroonitʉ

rub with brains kupịsi?arʉ

rub with foot nara?worʉ K

rubber band tu?re?

rubber boots tuu?re napʉ

rubber heel tuu?re tahpiko?,

rug pʉhʉ rasoona̱, tasoni, tasoona̱

rule tʉni-

ruler tʉmanahke?

rump katsonakwʉ

run nuhkitʉ

run a race nanarʉna?itʉ, narubunitʉ

run after miakʉrʉ

run around and play nohi?nuraarʉ

run away nuhkitʉ

run away afraid namanuhkitʉ

run away from something wʉanuraitʉ K

run away from somewhere pʉa nuhkitʉ

run away one by one nunurawʉtʉ

run, cause to wʉmi?arʉ W

run downhill wenu?nukịmi?arʉ

run out of food tʉkʉ tsuhmarʉ

run out of groceries narʉhka?tsu?marʉ

run short kehewa?itʉ

run slowly pohyami?arʉ

run to something tunehtsʉrʉ

run to something through fear namarunehtsʉrʉ

runner, road- ebikuyuutsi?

running, come nuraakitʉ

running, get off wenu?nukịmi?arʉ

running over, full and tʉhpetʉ

-running-here, Wind Nʉenuhkiki

rust nasaanuto?itʉ, nasanopi K

rust out nasaanuto?itʉ

rustle tahkoonikarʉ

rye tohtía sonipʉha taka?

rye grass pui tsaseni

S s

sack narʉsọ

sack, flour tohtía narʉsọ

sack, gunny soni narʉso?

sack, tow soni narʉso?

sacrifice or destroy oneself, self-immolate kuhtʉyarʉ

saddle pa?mutsi?

saddle, Indian-type tʉmuhku

saddle, pack- narʉnoo?

saddle a horse, un- narʉnoo?ro?yarʉ

saddlebag tʉnoo?

saddle blanket kwahitʉki?, nahotsa?ma?

saddle girth natsanʉhkʉ?

saddle horn narʉnoo bapi

saddle strap nakwʉsi tsa?nika?, narʉnoo? namʉkʉ

saddle up narʉnoo?rʉkitʉ

sadness tabʉikatʉ

safekeeping, put away for to?nikarʉ K

safety pin nahamuhkʉ K, na?hʉmuhkʉ W

sage esipohoobi, tʉsaasị

sagebrush pohóobi

said that, it is tʉa

sailor pa?ekʉsahpana?

saliva hʉʉtsipʉ, kʉpịsi?, tusi

saloon po?sa baa kahni

salt ona-, onaabị

salt something ona?aitʉ

Salt-worn-out Onawai

salve, sunflower hi?ookwana?

same general area, separated but in na?ata W

same-sex cousin haitsi̱

same-sex friend haitsi̱

sand pasi waapi̱

sand, haul pasiwanooru̱

Sand Creek Pasiwa huunu?bi

sand dune pasiwanoo? W

sand hill pasiwanoo? W

sandals saa?wu̱ napu̱, waraatsi̱

sandpaper tu̱maku̱ma?aai?, tu̱pi tu̱matsune?

sandpiper tu̱?íi?

sap sanahkena W

sash nu̱u̱pi̱tua?, nu̱?u̱nehki̱katu̱?

Sata Tejas I (Dog Eaters chief cir. 1689-1693) Sarua Tu̱hka I, Sata Tejas I

Sata Tejas II (Dog Eaters chief cir. 1873-1889) Sarua Tu̱hka I, Sata Tejas II

Satan Ketokwe hina haniitu̱, Tuhkwasi taiboo?

satisfied pihikaru̱

satisfied with sufficient food wu̱tsu̱?mitu̱

Saturday Tu̱eh buha rabeni

saucer nakwiita̱

sauna nasukoo?i?

sausage tuhku tsa?nikapu̱, tu̱ku̱ tusupu̱

save kwitso?aru̱, nabina?etu̱, tsihakwitso?aru̱

save someone makwitso?aitu̱

save someone's life tsahkwitso?aru̱

saved, remnant piinaai

saw, hand- mo?o huutsihka?a?

saw, rip- mo?o huutsihka?a?

saw, see- na?atsiyaa?, na?tsiyaa?

saw, two-man hand- huutsihkaa?

saw something with a saw huutsika?aru̱

sawdust huupita homoketu̱, huupita pisoni̱, huutusupu̱ W

say yu̱kwitu̱

say mean things nimakwihtsetu̱

say no to someone nimamu̱suku̱tu̱

say that, they tu̱a

scaffold pa?wu̱htaràa?

scale narayaaku̱?

scalp ku?e tsasimapu̱, papi̱ hu̱nu̱po?a, papi̱ ku?e̱

scalp someone ku?e tsasimaru̱

scar pihka̱

scare wu̱hkuya?aru̱, wu̱u̱yoritu̱, wu̱?yu̱ru̱hkitu̱

scared kuya?akatu̱, wu̱?yu̱ru̱hkikatu̱

scarf tsokwu̱ku̱u̱na? W, wu̱htsohku̱na?, yu?a korohko̱

scatter by force tohporooru̱

scatter something tsahpo?aru̱

scattered tsahpetitu̱

scattered around poohkatu̱

scent, follow muwaru̱ W

school house tu̱boo kahni

scissors tu̱keh koo?, wana koo?

scissortail ku̱ku̱bu̱raakwa?si?

scold nihmakwihtseru̱

scold someone ni?wikeru̱

scoop tsii?wu̱weniitu̱

scoop up mahoraru̱

scoot wu̱hu?neru̱

scorch wesiku̱ru̱

scorched wesikatu̱

scorching day tabe kusu̱wehkatu̱

scorpion kwasi tona?

scrape tsasinu̱kaaru̱, tsasu?neru̱, wu̱htsinetu̱, wu̱pu̱nukeru̱, wu̱su?naru̱

scrape meat from a hide tohtsiyu?itu̱

scrape off siibetu̱, toso?netu̱

scrape outer side wu̱hkwu̱netu̱

scrape until clean wu̱htsu?maru̱

scraping sibepu̱

scraping hides, pick for to?tsimuhpe?

scraps tʉkʉ wesipʉ

scratch naraʔworʉ K, natsahkupʉkatʉ, tasitotsarʉ W

scratch an itch natsawoʔnitʉ, tsakwoʔnerʉ

scratch leaving a mark tsahtsiʔarʉ

scratch oneself natsahtsiaitʉ

scratch rear or back against something pisuʔnetʉ

scratch someone tahtsiarʉ

scratch up earth taʔsiʔwoorʉ

scratch using an instrument tsahkiʔaitʉ

screech owl sʉhʉ mupitsʉ

screen, window nanabuni saawʉʔ, nasaaʔwʉʔ W

screen door nasaaʔwʉʔ K

screening saaʔwʉʔ

screw tʉmatsukiʔ, tʉtsipʉsaʔ

screw, un- wʉhkweʔyarʉ

screw in wʉʔnikarʉ

screw something in tsakwipunarʉ

screwdriver tʉmabukweʔ

scrounge for yaahuyarʉ

scrub pawʉnuarʉ

scythe soni wʉtsʉkeʔ K, tʉʉtsʉkeʔ W

seal something, un- tsahtoʔarʉ K

sealed matsʉbakikatʉ

search wehkinitʉ

search carefully for puhwaaitʉ

search for head lice pusiaketʉ

search the mind in effort to remember suʔurarʉ

season, dry ʉrʉʔitʉ

season, fall yʉba

season, summer taatsa̱

seat, un- tsiperʉ

seat, wet pihpárʉbʉʔai

seated on a sled, ride pisikoʔi

seated position, rise from nʉʉʔnʉarʉ

-seated buggy, two natsaʔaniʔ

second stomach of cow sekwi biiʔ

secret, keep watsiʔarʉ

secret oneself away watsi̱ habiitʉ

secretly, leave watsi miʔarʉ

secretly, spy on someone watsi iyarʉ

section, quarter soko rʉmanahkepʉ

section of land, quarter- soko tsihkaʔapʉ

see punitʉ

See-**how-deep-the-water-is** Paa roponi

seed pehe

seed, plant tʉhtʉkitʉ, tʉrʉniʔitʉ

seeder tʉrʉnaʔ

seeds, plant tahnaarʉ

seeds, sow tahnaarʉ

seek anahabiniitʉ

seek, hide-and- naʔwekitʉʔ

seesaw naʔatsiyaaʔ, naʔtsiyaaʔ

self-immolate (sacrifice/destroy) kuhtʉyarʉ

sell to one another narʉmʉʉrʉ

send kʉmiʔakʉrʉ

send something or someone tʉhyetʉ

send word to someone to return nʉníhkoonirʉ

sensation, give manʉʉsukaarʉ

sense suapʉ

senseless suapʉwahtʉ

sensitive briar tsapʉsikʉ

sensitive pea huutsúʔa kàhni̱

separate families, three pahibahtʉnʉnʉ

separate in marriage pʉah kwarʉ

separate milk from cream yunarʉ

separated naʔbekoʔarʉ

separated but in same general area naʔata W

separated by great distance
namanakwʉ K

separated from others
toroʔihtʉkitʉ

separated groups, three pahibahtʉ

separated in marriage pʉah taikatʉ

separately, move off to live
nokaʔitʉ

September Tʉboo renahpʉ makwe
kwiʔena̱ mʉa, Kwiʔena̱ mʉa

servant tʉrʉʔai wapi̱

service, church puha niwʉnʉrʉʉ K

set down tsahtʉkitʉ

set down carefully tsakwʉnarʉ

set in place natsawʉnʉkatʉ

set on fire kutsi̱tonarʉ

set out tsihtaboʔikʉtʉ

set out to dry pasahtahtʉkitʉ W

set something in place
natsawʉnʉrʉ

set the table awotsawʉniʔitʉ

set up karʉkʉrʉ, maʔyʉkwiitʉ

set up straight tsayʉkwikʉ

set up teepees yʉkwikʉ

set upright tsahkarʉkʉrʉ

setting hen nohabitʉ

settlement, open country to soko
tsatu̱warʉ

seven taatsʉkwi̱tʉ

sever, or break (with the teeth)
kʉhkobarʉ

several objects, pick up himaʔarʉ

several objects, take himaʔarʉ

several,persons, kill nakwʉsʉkʉrʉ

several things, take one or yaarʉ

sew tsahkʉnarʉ, tʉtsahkʉnarʉ

Sewers Tʉtsakana

sewing machine tʉtsahkʉna?

sewing machine oil tʉtsakʉnaha
yuhu

sex, kinsman of either taʔka?

-sex sibling-in-law, opposite haipia?

-sex cousin, same haitsi̱

-sex friend, same haitsi̱

shade hʉkikʉ, hʉʉki̱

shade, night- tohpotsotsii

shaded hʉkitʉ

shadow hʉhkiapʉ, hʉʉkiaʔ, tuhani̱

shake wohtsawʉkitʉ

shake foot taʔwikitʉ

shake from cold tsihturuarʉ W

shake head in disagreement
kaʔwitsetʉ K

shake something kʉʔwikeetʉ,
tsaʔwikiitʉ

shake something off nʉʉʔwikeetʉ,
sʉʉtaʔniʔarʉ

shake the foot tahtaʔnitʉ

shake the head no tsoʔwiketʉ

shake vigorously tsobokitʉ

shallow paʔasʉ

shaman nipʉkaaʔeetʉ, puhaʔaitʉ

shame nasuʔaitʉ?

shape or change something
wʉmʉʉrʉ

shaped wʉmʉʉrihkatʉ

share in tʉmaramiitʉ

sharp-pointed implement for
punching holes (through which
sinews pass) wiiyu̱

sharp-pointed object mutsipʉ

sharpen tahkʉmaʔaitʉ

sharpen a cutting edge tʉʉhkonarʉ

sharpen an edge makwʉmutsiarʉ

sharpen something tʉmakʉmaʔarʉ

sharpen to a point tomotsiarʉ W,
wʉmutsiarʉ K

sharpened makʉmaʔaitʉ

sharpened edge kʉmapʉ

sharpened item namakʉmaʔaipʉ

sharpened, keep wʉmutsiakatuʔi

sharpened to a point mamutsiakatʉ

shatter tahporoorʉ, wʉnutsarʉ

shave siibetʉ, wʉhsibetʉ

shave off wʉhtsiʔarʉ, wʉsiberʉ K
shave oneself namotʉsibetʉ
shave someone mutʉsiberʉ
shaving sibepʉ
shaving, wood wʉsibepʉ
shavings, wood kunapiso?ni
shawl wana hʉ K
shawl, heavy pohotʉ na?sʉkía?
shawl, lightweight tapi na?sʉkia?
shawl with fringes na?sʉkia?
she ma?, orʉ, surʉ, u, urʉ
She-invites-her-relatives Nʉmʉ ruibetsʉ
shear wʉtsʉkarʉ
shed kwe?yarʉ
shed many tears pa?okwetʉ
sheep kabʉrʉʉ?, pʉhʉ kabʉrʉʉ?
sheep wool kabʉrʉʉ?a pʉhʉ
sheer tapitʉhtsi
sheet for bed saabara
sheet, bed- saabara, tosa kwana?hʉ W
shell of any shellfish wa?koo? K
shell something by hand tsahkíto?arʉ
shellfish, shell of any wa?koo? K
shelter, rain ʉmakahni
shelter for winter, rain yu?a ʉmakʉni
shepherd kabʉrʉ?a tahkoni wapi, narahkooni wapi W
shepherd's crook tʉ?ehkooi? W
sheriff nʉmi hima?etʉ, tʉʉhtamʉh raibo?
shield na?yʉnehtʉ? W, topʉ, to?pʉ
shimmer paratsihkwe?erʉ
shin or shin bone kutsi?omo
shinbone tuhhu
shine we?kwiyanuutʉ
shine red ekakuhtabearʉ
shingle kahni nasiyuuki? K, nabo?aa W

shiny ekahwi, pahparatsihkweetʉ W, we?kwiyanorʉ, tsaa marabetoikatʉ K, tsihtsirahputʉ
shirt kwasu?ʉ
shirt, man's tenahpʉ?a kwasu?ʉ
shirt, under- tuhkanaai kwasu?ʉ
shish kebob kutsiyaapʉ
shiver sʉhkwibitʉ, sʉhtorokitʉ W
shiver from cold tsihturuarʉ W
[shiver] with cold, tremble sʉʉtsʉnitʉ
shoe napʉ
shoe, heel of tahpiko?
shoe, take off a tahkwe?yarʉ
shoe nail napʉ narawʉna?, napʉ rʉrawʉna?
shoe polish napʉ rʉ?eka?
shoe sole napʉ rahpaana, narahpaana
shoehook napʉbosa?
shoelace napʉ tsakwʉsa?, napʉbosa?
shoelace, fasten with napʉbosarʉ
shoes napʉ|b-|r
shoes, put on tahtoorʉ
shoes, sole of tahpana?aarʉ
shoes, try on tahpunitʉ
shoes, wear out tawiarʉ W
shoestring napʉ tsakwʉsa?
shoo tanʉkikʉtʉ
shoo away manʉkikʉrʉ
shoot tsakwʉkatʉ, tsatʉkarʉ, tʉkwʉrʉ, wʉhtikʉrʉ
shoot, sight to wʉhkurʉ
shoot a gun wʉhkikatʉ
shoot a gun repeatedly ta?wo?ekarʉ
shoot a repeating gun tsatʉka?karʉ
shoot something kwʉʉhtikʉrʉ
short pa?itsi?wʉnʉrʉ, pa?itʉhtsi?
short, cut off pi?to?arʉ
short, fall nasutamʉ wʉminaitʉ W, pihpokaarʉ, to?wʉminaitʉ

short, run kehewaʔitʉ
Short-dress Tsihtara
shot, gun- taʔwoʔiʔ
shotgun soʔo narʉbakiʔ
shot, sling- taʔkʉbuuʔ W
shoulder tsoʔapʉ
shoulder bone tsoohpa tsuuni W
shout pia pʉku rekwarʉ, pia rekwa
shouting, awaken someone by
    tayʉtsʉrʉ
shove maʔwikarʉ, wʉtsʉkitʉ
shovel kusiyunaʔ, tsiyunarʉ,
    tʉtsiyunaʔ
shovel, coal kutʉhuyunaʔ W
shovel out tsiiʔwʉweniitʉ
shovel something tʉtsiyunarʉ
show how tʉmabunikʉrʉ
show off nasutsa akwarʉ K
show someone something
    tsahpunitʉ
shrink yurahpetʉ
shrivel up from heat
    kuhtakwitsooʔnitʉ W
shrub kusiwʉʉnʉ
shucks, corn hani buhipʉ
shrunken paihtsi
shyster kaawosa
sibling samohpʉʔ
sibling, having a takaʔkatʉ
sibling-in-law, opposite sex
    haipiaʔ
sick, be tʉʔoibʉkʉrʉ, uhúntʉkʉ
sickle soni wʉhpomaʔ
sickly hoʔyopi, hoʔyopitʉ,
    nʉʉsukatʉ, uhúntʉkʉ
sickly person namaʔabʉ, takwipʉ
side comb papi tsiʔnikaʔ
side of an object sʉkwe naisʉ
side of chest ahna, ama-
side of stomach or abdomen
    sahpáanaʔ
side, on opposite paʔarai

side, right tʉbitsinakwʉ
side, scrape outer wʉhkwʉnetʉ
side to side, go from (or back and forth) piʔnuʔa miʔarʉ
side-to-side, looking from
    kaʔmʉtʉhiʔ W
side to side, move from tohtsatsarʉ
siding naboʔaa W
sieve saaʔwʉʔ, tsasaʔwʉkiʔ K
sieve, honey ʉnʉʉʔ ruuʔ
sieze tsasukwarʉ
sift tsasaʔwʉkitʉ
sifter tʉsoyuni
sifter, flour tohtía tsasaʔwʉkiʔ,
    tsasaʔwʉkiʔ K
sigh nahuahtsitʉ, nasuawʉhkitʉ K
sight to shoot wʉhkurʉ
sign language mootekwoʔpʉ
silver tosa-, tosahwi, tosapi,
    tosahpuhihwi
silver maple kweʔyʉkʉ sohóobi
silver money tosahpuhihwi
silvery wormwood pasiwona
    pʉhʉbi
similar to elves, little people
    Nʉnapi
similar to water lily, plant
    paʔmutsi
sin aihinahanitʉ
sin, tempt one to tʉrape suwaitʉ
since then subeʔsʉ
sinew tamu
sing a song nihtoʔitʉ, tʉnikwʉrʉ
sing a song for someone
    nahubiyaarʉ
sing high pitched putsi kwʉtsʉbaitʉ
sing loudly pia rʉnikwʉtʉ
sing one song after another
    nipʉyerʉ
sing out nihtoʔitʉ
single buggy tʉe waikina
singletree pihtsakʉ huupi

sink to the bottom in water
paʔikarʉ

sinner tʉrapehekatʉ

Sioux people Papitsiminaʔ, Suhtaʔ

sister samohpʉʔ

sister, eldest patsiʔ

sister, father's pahaʔ

sister, mother's pia

sister, younger namiʔ

sister-in-law paha piahpʉ

sit kahtʉ

sit down karʉkatʉ 1, nakarʉʔkarʉ,
yʉkwimiʔarʉ

sit down, force to sutena karʉrʉ

sit down quickly tsuhni karʉ

sit in sun to dry mabasahtʉkitʉ K

sit in the sun to dry
pasahtahtʉkitʉ W

sit on, put down something to
pisoonarʉ

**sit on something (breaking it to
pieces)** pinutsarʉ

sit still yukarʉrʉ

sit straight tsayʉkwitʉ

sitting back on heels, kneel down
tanatookarʉtʉ

Sitting-bear Kohitʉ seʔtanʉkʉ

sitting down, swing
piʔweesuʔruʔitʉ

sitting on it, crack something by
pitʉbarʉ

situated haahpitʉ 1, natsawʉnʉkatʉ

six naabaitʉ

size, small tʉtaatʉ

sizzle kukʉbihkutʉ

skate tahkitemiʔarʉ,
tasikoʔiʔmiʔarʉ

skillet kukʉmeʔawe

skim from the surface yunarʉ

skin hʉnʉpoʔaʔ, kiboʔarʉ, poʔaʔ,
tsasinʉkaarʉ, tsahkʉrʉʔarʉ

skin, animal tsahkwʉrʉʔarʉ

skin an animal pʉhʉ tsahkweʔyarʉ,
wʉsiboʔarʉ

skin animal tsahkwʉrʉʔarʉ

skin, cracked tsiʔwapʉ W

skin, human hʉnʉpoʔaʔ, mapóʔaʔ

skin, peel off kiboʔarʉ

skin, rash on tasiʔaʔ W

skin, raw tuhʉpʉ

skin, rough tsiʔwapʉ W

skin, tear nʉʉsihwaʔitʉ

skin something kiboʔarʉ

skinned, brown- otʉhtʉ mapoʔakatʉ

Skinny-and-wrinkled Tekwitsi M

skins or other covering for teepees
nʉmʉkʉni

skip wiʔhikoyoʔitʉ

skull tsuhnipʉ

skunk pisuníiʔ K, pisuniʔeeyu,
pohniʔatsi

skunkbush tatsipʉ

sky tomo-, tomobaʔatʉ

Sky-child Tomoʔa tuaʔ

slam things in anger, jerk and
tuhu rekwarʉ

slander moyaʔitʉ

slanting nahʉyatʉ, naʔʉyatʉ

slap (or punch repeatedly)
tohtʉkwarʉ

slap (with palm of hand) tohpaʔitʉ

slate color esipitʉ

slave naʔraibooʔ

sled, ride seated on a pisikoʔi

sleep habiitʉ, ʉhpʉitʉ

sleep unconcerned yuu ʉhpʉitʉ

sleeping quarters habikʉni

sleepy mitsokokʉkatʉ, puibʉʉtʉ,
puibʉʉtʉtʉ

sleepy-eyed, be puibʉʉtʉ

sleet paasitsi

sleeve makwʉsàʔ

slender huutubuʔitʉ W,
huutunaakatʉ K

slender, tall and kanaba?aitʉ,
  kʉbʉráatạ

slice koo?itʉ, tsihpoma

slick pahtsi, patsiketʉ, puhnuketʉ

slick-haired goat pahtsi kabʉrʉʉ?

slide nuarʉ, pisikwanúu?i?

slide down pisikwanúu?itʉ

slide standing up tahkitemi?arʉ

slingshot ta?kʉbuu? W

slip a rope around something
  ku?nikarʉ

slip standing up tahkitemi?arʉ

slippery puhnuketʉ

slobber kʉ?okwetʉ

Slope Naya

sloping nahʉyatʉ, na?ʉyatʉ

slow napiso?aitʉ

slow down (what one is doing)
  nʉnʉ?itʉ

slow motion, move in aimi?arʉ

slow-moving nanahbiso?aitʉ

slowly ubitakuhtsi?a

slowly, come mahuinoorʉ

slowly, move puhyʉnukitʉ

slowly, run pohyami?arʉ

small tʉe

small gray bird kusisai?

small intestine kohị

small particles, mash into
  mahomonutsarʉ

small quantity tʉtaatʉ

small river okwèetʉ

small size tʉtaatʉ

smaller than inaarʉ

smallpox narʉ?ʉyʉ tasi?ạ, tasi?a? W

smartweed ekawoni

smash tatsukwerʉ, wʉhtabarʉ

smell around muwarʉ W,
  ʉkwịsʉ?ninitʉ K

smell something ʉkwihkatʉ

smell something (from a distance)
  ʉkwʉsʉ?nitʉ

Smeller Pisu kwá?na?

smile mu?yạnesuarʉ

smoke kwipʉ

smoke during religious ceremony
  puha bahmu?itʉ

smoke hole kahku?e, kahni ku?e

smoke ritually nakatsʉhetʉ

smooth makwʉ?nikutʉ K, pahtsi,
  patsiketʉ, puhnuketʉ, tsasu?nerʉ

Smooth Pahtsi ketʉ

smooth down wʉtʉkị?netʉ

smooth, plane something tʉsibetʉ

smooth sumac tʉmaya huupi

snagged patụ tsanitʉ

snail sanahtu?re?

snake kwasinaboo?

snake, crawl like a nuhyimi?arʉ W

snake, racer kʉhtáa nu?ya?a W

snake, rattle- kwasinaboo
  wʉhkitsu?tsu?ikatʉ,
  wʉhtsabeyakatʉ W

(snake), water moccasin
  tuhparokoo?

snake of any species nuhya?

snake root itsa, timʉihʉ?

snakeroot, button atabitsʉnoi

Snakes Idahi

snap kʉtubarʉ W, porokitʉ

snap fingers mabohto

snap off tahkobarʉ, tsahkobarʉ

snapping turtle kwasi nʉrʉʉ?wʉ?,
  pa?kwakʉme

snatch tsasukwarʉ

sneak around ho?aniitʉ

sneak away watsi mi?arʉ

sneak in watsi ikatʉ

sneaky person nakʉhoowaaitʉ

sneeze aakwʉsitʉ, tsa?akʉsitʉ K

sneeze, cause to tsamupʉsitʉ W

sneezeweed natsaakʉsi,
  tʉrʉkwobamʉ

sniff an odor ʉkwihkatʉ

sniff around ᵾkwi̱sᵾʔninitᵾ K
snore ᵾsorokiitᵾ
snort suhurᵾkitᵾ
snow tahkabi
snow, ice or tahka-
snowfall tahkaʔᵾmarᵾ
snuff yokabahmᵾ
snuff fire with fingers W
tsahtukarᵾ
snuff out marukarᵾ
snuffbox, devil's mupitsᵾha
pisahpi̱ W
soak in water parᵾkitᵾ
soak oneself in water naparᵾkitᵾ
soak through parᵾbᵾᵾʔitᵾ
soaked paʔi̱soketᵾ
soaked thoroughly papoosinᵾ
soap wana kotse?
soapberry otᵾ mitsonaa?
soapweed mumutsi?
socks wana napᵾ
soda pop pihná baa
soft yokake
soft, be yᵾʔyᵾkarᵾ
soften tsasuʔnerᵾ, yᵾʔyᵾkarᵾ
soften (by pounding) tohparaarᵾ
W, tsohkwe K
**soften (something by trampling
on it)** tahpararᵾ
softened payᵾʔyᵾkatᵾ, yᵾʔyᵾkarᵾ
softly, speak watsih nikwᵾnᵾrᵾ
soggy yokake
soil ohta-, ohtapi̱i̱
soil, eroded patowoʔnepᵾ
soil, hoe puhi yᵾkwitᵾ
soil, hole dug in hoora
soil, plow tᵾtsaʔworᵾ
soil, red ekahuukupᵾ, ekasokoobi
soldier ekasahpana?, taibo
ekᵾsahpana?
soldiers, Chief Comanche- dog-
Tᵾoyobisesᵾ

sole of foot tahpáanḁ
sole of shoes tahpanaʔaarᵾ
sole, shoe napᵾ rahpaanḁ,
narahpaanḁ
some sᵾsᵾmᵾ?
someone sᵾmᵾ?
someone, club wahtóorᵾ
someone (or something), club
wᵾhtokwᵾrᵾ
someone, doll up maʔyᵾkwiitᵾ
someone, duck tsahpaakuʔnikarᵾ
someone, encounter naraʔuraitᵾ
someone, fetch water for
tuukᵾmiʔarᵾ
**someone (or something), find
room for** haakarᵾ
someone, flirt with naʔi̱sa yᵾkwitᵾ
K, naʔi̱sa suakᵾtᵾ W
someone, fool nohitekwarᵾ
someone, forsake pᵾah taitᵾ
**someone, frighten (with
something)** wᵾʔyᵾrᵾhkitᵾ
someone, fuss at nimakwihtsetᵾ
someone, give money to
puhihwimaka
someone, give up waiting for
wᵾsuwarᵾkiitᵾ
someone, go on foot to meet
tamunaikᵾmiʔarᵾ
someone, gore mukuhparᵾ W
someone, hang (with a rope)
ooibehkarᵾ
someone, help tᵾituarᵾ
someone walk, help tsamiʔakᵾrᵾ
**someone, hold a curing ceremony
for** puhaʔarᵾ
someone, hurt mawᵾmerᵾ,
tsiyaketᵾ, umarhnitᵾ
someone, hurt (by accident)
tsahhuhyarᵾ
**someone, interrupt (because of
worry)** pisukwitakᵾrᵾ

someone, introduce nisuabetarʉ W

someone in, invite nikwekwitʉ

someone, jerk meat for tʉ?inakʉrʉ

someone, kiss muhrarʉ

someone behind, leave nobʉahraitʉ

someone for good, leave pʉa mi?arʉ

someone, like su?akʉtʉ

someone, listen to tʉmahyokʉrʉ

someone, lock up ta?ikʉrʉ

someone, lose faith in nasuwʉhkitʉ

someone, make up pisarʉ

someone, marry nanakwʉʉrʉ

someone, meet ta?urarʉ, to?urarʉ

someone by going on foot, meet tamunaikʉmi?arʉ

someone, name nahnia makarʉ, nihakʉrʉ

someone help, offer masutsarʉ

someone, outrun naromʉnitʉ

someone to do something, persuade nitsʉbahikʉ?itʉ

someone, pester nihtunetsarʉ

someone, please tsaa manʉsurʉ

someone, pop on kuhpuru?airʉ

someone, praise nihpana?aitʉ

someone, pray for nanisutaikʉtʉ

someone, precede muhnetʉ

someone, prepare breakfast for taamahkarʉ

someone with something, prick piso?arʉ

someone, question tʉbinarʉ, tʉbinitʉ

someone, quiet niyukarʉrʉ W

someone, raise manʉarʉ

someone, refuse to accept ninakabarʉ

someone, reject kemenikwitʉ W, nimakabaitʉ

someone, remind nasutamakʉrʉ W

someone, resemble tʉ?ikatʉ

someone, respect marʉhnikatʉ

someone or something while moving, rope ku?nikakʉrʉ

someone, save makwitso?aitʉ

someone, say no to nimamʉsukʉtʉ

someone, scalp ku?e tsasimarʉ

someone, scratch tahtsiarʉ

someone, send something or tʉhyetʉ

someone to return, send word to nʉníhkoonirʉ

someone, shave mutʉsiberʉ

someone something, show tsahpunitʉ

someone, sing a song for nahubiyaarʉ

someone, spilled by ta?okitʉ

someone, spy on kuhiyarʉ, watsi punitʉ

someone secretly, spy on watsi iyarʉ

someone, stone tʉpi táhparʉ

someone, stop following nʉnʉ?itʉ

someone by force, stop tahkoonitʉ

someone, strangle kuitsimarʉkʉtʉ

someone, surrender manʉsuta?aitʉ

someone by force, take sutena betʉ

someone home as guest, take panimi?arʉ

-someone, Take-a-stick-and-hit Huuwʉhtʉkwa?

someone into something, talk nitsʉbahikʉ?itʉ

someone, talk to niwʉnʉrʉ, tekwarʉ

someone something, teach nisuabetarʉ

someone, teach something to tʉnisuabetarʉ

someone, tempt or test mabunihkarʉ

someone, tickle pinakʉtsʉrʉ

someone or something, toward mawakatu

someone, train suabetaikʉrʉ

someone, trip tanʉʉhkupaitʉ

someone, trust tokʉsuakʉtʉ

someone, understand nahkʉsuaberʉ

someone or something, up to or onto maatu

someone, wait for makamaitʉ

someone, wake tsahtʉbunitʉ

someone by pounding, wake wʉhtʉbunitʉ

someone, wake up tsayoritʉ

someone, waken by speaking to nihtʉbuniorʉ

someone, watch watsi punitʉ

someone, win in a contest against tahni?arʉ

someone, win over kwakurʉ K

someone or something, with or on maa

someone to death, work namakupakʉrʉ

someone's death, prevent makwitso?aitʉ

someone's beard, pull mutsonoo?itʉ

someone's life, save tsahkwitso?arʉ

someone's back to ease pain, stand on tahpara?itʉ

some place, escort a guest panimi?arʉ

somersault nakkuminoorʉ

something wahtóorʉ

something carried in the claws ta?yaahkana? W

something, club wʉhtokwʉtʉ

something, drag kʉwokarʉ, piwokarʉ, takwokarʉ W

something, drag along piwokami?arʉ

something, drag (spread on flat surface) pisunarʉ

something, dry pasakʉrʉ, tʉbitsi basarʉ

something, dye tʉsáarʉ

something, earn tahwikarʉ, tʉrahwikatʉ

something, eat most of sʉmʉ rʉhkarʉ

something, experience wʉsukatʉ

something, explain nisuabetarʉ K

something, fail to do kemahpʉ?arʉ

something, fall into tʉyumarʉ

something, feel tsasukarʉ

something, fence tʉʉhtʉmarʉ

something, fill tʉmarʉ W

something, find urarʉ, wʉ?urarʉ

something, find (being looked for) to?urarʉ

something, find (with the hand) ma?urarʉ

something (or someone), find room for haakarʉ

something, flatten marʉki?netʉ

something, grease tʉ?ekarʉ, wihi tʉ?ekarʉ

something, hammer tahhanitʉ

something, hang tsakwenitʉ, tʉrohtsanitʉ, wenuarʉ

something, hang over nʉʉsoo?etʉ

something, hang up tohtsanarʉ

something, hang up (on a nail or hook) tsa?wenitʉ, tsahkwenitʉ W

something, harness nanoomanitʉ

something in hand, have yahkatʉ

something, hear tʉnakarʉ

something, heat kuhtsʉnikʉrʉ

something, hide namabimarʉ

something, hit wʉhtʉkwarʉ

something, hold yuhnukarʉ

something, hook muhkarʉ W

something, insert into tsiʔnikarʉ, wʉnikarʉ

something, jerk wʉhpoʔtserʉ K

something, jerk (toward oneself) tsahpoʔtsarʉ

something, keep tahtʉkarʉ

something, kick sʉʉhkwʉhtʉkurʉ

something away, kick sʉʉ potserʉ

something hanging, knock off wʉhtokarʉ

something, knock wʉhpoʔtserʉ K

something down, knock tayuʔmarʉ

something down, lay tʉkiitʉ K

something, lay the head down on tsohtʉkikatʉ

something, lean namahtowʉnarʉ

something, lean against nʉʉbanikatʉ

something, lean on mahtokwʉnaitʉ K

something, lean over nʉʉsooʔetʉ

something new, learn urahkarʉ

something, locate taʔwairʉ

something, lose nasuwatsi, watsikʉrʉ

something from hand or wrist, lose maʔkweʔyarʉ

something, make a mark on tsahporʉ

something rattle, make tsatsʉbipʉkurʉ

something, mark tsihpoorʉ

something, mash up mapitserʉ

something, measure tʉmanahketʉ

something, meet to suggest nanikaʔwitʉ

something, melt kuhpawikʉʔitʉ

something, milk maʔokwerʉ

something, move tanuarʉ

something (with the mouth), move kʉnuaitʉ

something, nail taʔnikʉtʉ, tʉrawʉnarʉ K

something, open matʉhwarʉ, tohtʉwarʉ, tsahtʉwarʉ, tʉhwarʉ

something wide, open pia tsatuarʉ

something, oppose tsoʔwiketʉ

something, own taʔurʉkarʉ K

something, padlock tʉtsihtʉrʉ

something, paint tʉrʉʔekarʉ, tʉʔekarʉ

something, patch tʉkarʉkurʉ

something, peel tsahkítoʔarʉ

something, persuade someone to do nitsʉbahikʉʔitʉ

something smooth, plane tʉsibetʉ

something, pluck out noʔitʉ

something, point out muruahwʉnʉrʉ

something, poke head into tsoʔnikarʉ, tʉtsoʔnikarʉ

something, pound wʉhtarakiitʉ

something, pound on tahhanitʉ

something, powder homopisarʉ

something, practice namabunitʉ

something down, press tatʉkeʔnerʉ

something, prick someone with pisoʔarʉ

something, pull on tsanuarʉ

something behind, pull pitsákarʉ

something off or out, pull tsahkweʔyarʉ

something, puncture oneself with nabisoʔarʉ

something that rolls, push maʔaikʉrʉ, tsiʔaikʉrʉ

something back in place, put tohtʉkiʔarʉ

something down, put tsaʔnikoorʉ

something into the mouth, put tʉroʔnikarʉ

something to sit on, put down pisoonarʉ

something, quit puaru

something, rake tutsahtu?ooru

something, request naníhtsawa?itu, nigwaitu K

something, rest on mahtokwunaitu K

something, right tsahkarukuru

something, ring tu?tsayaketu

something, rip puhkaru, tohturu?aru W, wuhturu?aru K

something, roll to start to?aikuru

something, roll up with tohtopo?naru

something while moving, rope someone or ku?nikakuru

something, rub against pisu?netu

something, rub head against tsotso?neetu

something, run away from wuanuraitu K

something, run to tunehtsuru

something through fear, run to namarunehtsuru

something, salt ona?aitu

something with a saw, saw huutsika?aru

something, scatter tsahpo?aru

something, scratch rear or back against pisu?netu

something in, screw tsakwipunaru

something or someone, send tuhyetu

something in place, set natsawunuru

something, shake ku?wikeetu, tsa?wikiitu

something off, shake nuu?wikeetu, suuta?ni?aru

something, shape or change wumuuru

something, sharpen tumakuma?aru

something by hand, shell tsahkíto?aru

something, shoot kwuuhtikuru

something, shovel tutsiyunaru

something, show someone tsahpunitu

something breaking it to pieces, sit on pinutsaru

something, skin kibo?aru

something, slip a rope around ku?nikaru

something, smell ukwihkatu

something (from a distance), smell ukwusu?nitu

something by trampling on it, soften tahpararu

something, spill out on tokwuriaru

something on purpose, spill tokwuriaitu

something, split tohpakuru

something, spread out tsahpararu, wuhpararu

something, stake turawunaru K

something, step over tasaru

something, stop movement toward wunu hupiitu

something, straighten kuhpararu

something wrinkled, straighten tahtunaabaru

something, strain out tsaso?aru

something, stretch out wuhpararu

something out, stretch tsahturu

something, suck on mukwihteru

something, support tsihturooru

something, swallow tuyuwaru, yuwitu W

something, sweep tuunuaru

something live, take away tahtukitu

something, take down off of tsahpuheru

something in the mouth, take kuhyaaru

something, talk someone into
nitsʉbahikʉʔitʉ

something, tangle tokwʉsikʉtʉ,
tsakwʉʔikʉrʉ W

something, tap on wʉhtarakiitʉ

something, teach someone
nisuabetarʉ

something to someone, teach
tʉnisuabetarʉ

something, tear puhkarʉ, sihwarʉ,
tosiʔkwarʉ, tsaiʔwarʉ K

something, tear at tsahkwanitʉ

something, tempt by describing
nisuyakeetʉ

something, test natsahpunitʉ

something, think about
nasutamʉkatʉ tamai, suʔatsitʉ,
tʉsuʔatsikatʉ

something, throw a light on
kupitarʉ

something, throw at tahtʉkwarʉ

something, throw out of
wʉʔkwʉriarʉ

something, tie wʉhtamarʉ

something, tire of manʉʉʔmaitʉ

something, tired of
nakʉnʉʉʔmaitʉ, wʉʔtsikwarʉ

something, toward someone or
mawakatu

something, trail tʉnahyarʉ

something over, turn tsamʉrikarʉ,
wʉmʉʉrʉ

something, twist tsakwipunarʉ

something, twist oneself around
nʉʉʔkwipunarʉ

something, unable to do
kemahpʉʔarʉ, tsuhitʉ

something, uncoil wʉhpʉkʉsuarʉ

something, unravel
nʉʉpʉrʉsuanʉpurʉ

something, unseal tsahtoʔarʉ K

something, unwrap tahkwʉmarʉ

**something with the mouth,
unwrap** kʉhtoʔyarʉ K

**something, up to or onto someone
or** maatu

something, water payunitʉ

something, wear natsaʔnikarʉ

something around the neck, wear
korohkọrʉ

something around the waist, wear
kohinehkitʉ

something out, wear wihtoʔarʉ

something, weigh narayaakʉrʉ

something off, wipe tahtsumarʉ K

something with the head, wipe
tsotsomarʉ

**something, with or on someone
or** maa

something, wrinkle
takwikakwoʔarʉ

sometimes sʉsʉʔanạ

somewhere iʔa

somewhere, escape from
namaroʔitʉ

somewhere, happen to be
nahabitʉtʉ

somewhere, live nʉmʉnetʉ

somewhere, lying haahpitʉ 1

somewhere, run away from pʉa
nuhkitʉ

son tua?

son, adopted tua boopʉ W

son-in-law monahpʉ?

Son-of-bull-bear Tʉmʉbo

**son or daughter (offspring),
grown** nahnapʉ

song hubiya?

song, sing a nihtoʔitʉ, tʉnikwʉrʉ

song after another, sing one
nipʉyerʉ

song for someone, sing a
nahubiyaarʉ

songs, war wohho tʉikwʉpitʉ K

songs of victory wohho tꞟikwꞟpitꞟ K
songs of youth wꞟyakeetꞟ W
sons-in-law nonanꞟꞟ
soon kemarꞟkwisꞟ
sore ꞟʔaʔ
sore, chronic narꞟʔꞟyꞟ ꞟꞟʔaʔ
sore person namakꞟnꞟmapꞟ
sore throat, have a kuitsisꞟatꞟ
sorrel horse otꞟ kumaʔ W, tꞟpꞟsi kumaʔ
sorrel mare ekapiaʔ
soul sua, suana
sound tah ta-
sound, buzzing puuyaketꞟ
sound, make galloping totꞟbihkurꞟ
sounding of a horn muyakeʔ
soup saa huuba
soup, corn hanisahoba
soup, quick-cook corn atakwáʔsꞟʔ
sour moha-, sꞟkꞟ-, sꞟꞟkꞟ
sour, taste mohakamarꞟ
south yuʔanꞟbe nakwꞟbu
south wind yuʔanee
southeast yuʔanꞟe muhyꞟnakwꞟbu
southern hackberry mitsonaaʔ
southwest yuʔa nꞟe kahpiʔnakwꞟ
sow seeds tahnaarꞟ
sowbug kwita maropona
space, cram into limited natsinꞟhkꞟrꞟ
space, crammed into limited tsinꞟkꞟ
spade tuhpihhínabooʔ, tuhtahkanabooʔ, tꞟtsihpetiʔ, tꞟtsiyunaʔ K
sparkling tsihtsirahputꞟ
spasm, have muscle cramp or toponitꞟ K
speak tekwarꞟ
speak firmly ninabitsiarꞟ
speak irrationally niʔemꞟabꞟnitꞟ

speak softly watsih nikwꞟnꞟrꞟ
speak to niikwiitꞟ
speak Wichita language tuhkaʔnaai rekwarꞟ
speaker tekwawapi
speaker and hearer, place known by pꞟkꞟhu
Speakers of Wichita language tuhkaʔnaaiʔ niwꞟnꞟ
speaking tayꞟtsꞟrꞟ
speaking to someone, waken by nihtꞟbuniorꞟ
spear tahkanaʔ, tꞟtsiwaiiʔ K, uwíhi
species, snake of any nuhyaʔ
speech ni-, tekwapꞟ
speech, error in niʔwatsꞟkatꞟʔ
speech, quiet by niʔtsuʔnarꞟ
speech, tremble in nihkwibihbikitꞟ
speedily, act wꞟʔrabiarꞟ F
spend money suʔmakꞟtꞟ
spherical tohtoponitꞟ, topohtꞟ
spider pꞟhꞟ reʔtsi
spill kꞟʔkwꞟriarꞟ, piʔwꞟʔwenitꞟ, wꞟhtiarꞟ
spill accidentally, knock over and tsakwꞟriarꞟ
spill of own accord nꞟꞟtiʔakatꞟ
spill out on something tokwꞟriarꞟ
spill something nꞟꞟtiʔarꞟ, piʔwꞟriarꞟ, tahkwꞟriarꞟ
spill something on purpose tokwꞟriaitꞟ
spilled narohkwꞟriʔetꞟ
spilled accidentally makwꞟriʔaikatꞟ
spilled by someone taʔokitꞟ
spin around kwinuʔyarꞟ, natsahkwinuʔitꞟ
spinal column kwahiporopꞟ
spinal cord kwahi kupisi
spine kwahinupꞟ
spine, align tahparaʔitꞟ

spinner ku?e kwʉsi?
spirit nanisuwʉkaitʉ
spirit, calm tsʉmʉkikatʉ
spirit, evil pʉe tʉyaai?, tʉtʉsuana
spirit, have an evil poosubʉhkaitʉ
spirit, peaceful tsʉmʉkikatʉ
spirit, quiet tsʉmʉkikatʉ
spirit, unclean tʉtʉsuana
Spirit-talker Mukwoorʉ
spirited nanisuwʉkaitʉ
spit tusitʉ
spit out liquid pai tusi?itʉ K
spit out kʉhkihtserʉ W
spittoon tusi aawo
splash into water pakwa?nuarʉ
splash water on pakwihtsikʉrʉ
splash with water pawʉhpa?itʉ
splatter kuhpuru?airʉ, puruarʉ
splattered kuhpuru?aitʉ
spleen hekwi?
splice nanakatso?arʉ
splinter tsatsia?
split tabakoitʉ, topʉkaarʉ,
    tsahpako?arʉ, tsapʉkarʉ
split into two parts tʉapako?itʉ
split of own accord nʉʉhtsi?aitʉ
split open peko?arʉ
split something tohpakurʉ
spoke of wheel na?omo nasʉwʉhki?
spokes waikina nakwʉʉki
spokesman tekwawapi, tʉnikepisa?
sponged maba?isokitʉ
spongy yokake
spoon tʉe aawo, wʉhibi?
spoon, table- pia rʉ?ewo
spotless tutʉtsaai wahtʉ
spotted naboo-
spouse notsa?ka?
spouse, leave a pʉah kwarʉ
sprain a joint of the body
    wʉkwʉsarʉ
sprain ankle naraminaitʉ K

sprain or break hand or lower arm
    namaminaitʉ
sprained makwʉsetʉ
spray, fly animui wasʉ
sprayed with water pawʉ?we?niitʉ
spread a tablecloth tʉkʉ soonarʉ
spread legs out po?arʉ
spread out something tsahpararʉ,
    wʉhpararʉ
spring parʉtsohpe?
Spring, become tahma ro?itʉ
spring water parʉtsohpe?
sprinkle pasibunarʉ, pa?isokerʉ,
    pi?wʉ?wenitʉ
sprinkled tohpa?isokitʉ W
sprinkling, baptize by ku?e naba
    wʉhtia
sprout pa?mukʉsʉ?arʉ
spun natsahkwinu?itʉ
spur natsiwekwa?
spy on ho?aniitʉ
spy on someone kuhiyarʉ, watsi
    punitʉ
spy on someone secretly watsi iyarʉ
squash makitsarʉ
squash, or crush tsakitsetʉ
squashed makitsetʉ
squat kwanu?itʉ K, wʉnʉhkarʉrʉ
    W, wʉtahkarʉrʉ K
squaw corn nʉmʉ hani
squeak kahúu pipikuniitʉ,
    kʉtsu?tsu?kitʉ
Squeaky Pipiku?
Squeaky-like-a-mouse Kahúu nihku
    pipikure
squeeze kwabarʉ
squeeze hand matsáhtsurʉ
squeeze to a head ma?okwerʉ
squeezed tight tsinʉkʉ
squint tasʉkʉpunitʉ
squirm pisukwitaitʉ,
    pʉhkwinu?itʉ W

squirrel, ground ekwakʉʉpi?, ewa kʉʉpi?

squirrel, tree wokoohwi

stab tonarʉ

stable puku kahni

staff natsihtóo? K

stagger when walking tsimʉami?arʉ

stairs huunaro?i?, naro?i?

stake tʉrawʉna? K

stake down tawʉnarʉ

stake down tightly ʉhtaarʉ

stake something tʉrawʉnarʉ K

staked-down object ʉhta?etʉ

stalk or plant, sunflower hi?oopi

stalked mahooikatʉ

stall nanamʉ?aitʉ K

stallion, wild pʉa watsi

stamen of flower totsiyaa papihtsipʉ

stand tobo?ikatʉ

stand angrily pihiso?aiwʉnʉrʉ

stand hair on end sʉroonitʉ

stand in the sun tabe wʉnʉ?itʉ

stand just above the horizon tabe wʉnʉ?itʉ

stand on someone's back to ease pain tahpara?itʉ

stand still yuu wʉnʉrʉ

stand tall kanaba?aitʉ

stand waiting tahkamʉrʉ

standing wʉnʉrʉ

standing, crowded while tahtsʉkitʉ

standing alone, one hill nookarʉrʉ

standing on hind feet manawʉnʉkatʉ

standing position, help up from sitting to matsákwʉnʉkurʉ

standing up, slide tahkitemi?arʉ

standing up, slip tahkitemi?arʉ

Standing-sun Tabe wʉnʉrʉ

staples, fence tʉʉhtʉmapʉha tʉrawʉna?

star tatsinuupi

star, north kemi?arʉtatsino

start nabihtawʉna, to?aikʉrʉ

start something, roll to to?aikʉrʉ

startle wʉʉyoritʉ, yʉrʉhkitʉ

starve to death tsiharʉyaitʉ

starving ketsihanabenitʉ

statement, misunderstand nanawatsikarʉ

stationary karʉʉrʉ

stay karʉkatʉ 1, yʉkwimi?arʉ

-stay-downstream, Those-who Tinawa

stay late tsʉ?nitʉ

steak tʉhkapa nakoopʉ

steal sikusarʉ, tʉrʉhkarʉ

steam no?yaikʉtʉ

steam bath nakuhkwaraki? K

steam bath, take a kuhkwarʉkitʉ

steam bathe nakuhkwarakitʉ, nasukoo?itʉ

steel tool tʉʉhko?ne?

steeple puha kahni muutsi

stem (of plant) totsiyaa?a sʉʉki

stem, pipe omotoi

step backward pimimi?arʉ

step over something tasarʉ

stepmother paraiboo?

-steps, Yellow Ohawʉnʉ

sternly, order ninabitsiarʉ

stew kohtsáarʉ

stew food tʉkarʉkurʉ

stewed food kohtsáa?, tʉkarʉkʉpʉ

stick hu-

stick, bracing wana tsihparaa?

stick, carry a huuyaarʉ

stick, carry something on a tsihimarʉ

stick, roast on a kuhtsiyarʉ

-stick-and -hit-someone, Take-a
Huuwɨhtɨkwaʔ

stick, walking tɨʔehkooiʔ W

stick for hand game tuhhuuʔ

stick to sanarɨ

sticks, pillow- tsohpe tawɨnaʔ

sticks, possess huuhimarɨ

sticks into ground, pound pillow-
tsohpe takwɨnarɨ

sticks, roast on kuʔtsiyaarɨ

stiff, be tsihturuarɨ K

stiff neck, have a woʔrohtsarɨ

still ɨkɨ, ɨkɨsɨ, yunahkatɨ

still, lie yuu habíitɨ

still, sit yukarɨrɨ

still, stand yuu wɨnɨrɨ

sting, insect tonarɨ

stinger of an insect tonaʔ

stingy otɨ suakatɨ

stingy person nahkɨepɨ K

stir wɨnoʔyarɨ

stir around yoʔmitsaitɨ

stir up dust huukɨhɨnɨrɨ

stir up excitement toyɨsekaitɨ

stir up fire kumaʔomerɨ, maʔomerɨ

stirred wɨnoʔyaitɨ

stirrup narahtɨkiiʔ, taʔnikaʔ W

stock, laughing- nanɨsuʔuyaatɨ,
suʔuyaʔiʔ

stockings wana napɨ

stomach sapɨ, sapɨ

stomach ache kohikamɨkatɨ, sapɨ
nɨɨtsikwarɨ

stomach, extreme pain in sapɨ
wɨnɨkatɨ

stomach, full wɨtsɨʔmi

stomach of cow, second sekwi biiʔ

stomach or abdomen, side of
sahpáanaʔ

stomp tanɨʔyɨkitɨ

stone tɨmakɨmaʔaaiʔ, tɨpi, tɨɨpi

stone, grinding tɨsoyuni

stone, whet- tɨmakɨmaʔaaiʔ, tɨpi
tɨmatsuneʔ

stone or brick house tɨpi kɨni

stone someone tɨpi táhparɨ

Stonehouse Tɨpi kɨniʔ

stool tahtɨkiʔiʔ

stool, foot- tahtɨkiʔiʔ

stoop nuhtsairɨ, tumuurɨ

stooped tumuukatɨ

stop toboʔihupiitɨ, tɨtsanɨnɨʔitɨ

stop, cause to tsanɨnɨrɨ

stop crying pɨhkai

stop flow tohtɨmarɨ

stop following someone nɨnɨʔitɨ

**stop hitting with fist or palm of
hand** tohpɨarɨ

stop movement toward something
wɨnɨ hupiitɨ

stop quarreling kekɨnabeniitɨ

stop raining pɨhkitɨ

stop someone by force tahkoonitɨ

stop suddenly tsuhni kwɨnɨrɨ K

stop talking nihpɨʔaitɨ

stopped up tohtɨmapɨ

store narɨmɨɨʔ

store, drug- natɨsuʔɨ narɨmɨɨʔ,
natɨsuʔɨ kahni

store, Indian nɨmɨ narɨmɨɨʔ

store, red ekanarɨmɨɨʔ

store away nabinaʔetɨ

store-bought food tɨkɨ tɨmɨɨpɨ

stories, tell off-color tɨtsɨ
narɨmiʔitɨ

stork paʔa toyokatɨ huutsuuʔ K

storm kɨhtáanɨetɨ

storm, dust huhkukwɨnɨrɨ,
huukɨhɨnɨrɨ

storm, wind nɨepi

storm cellar ohta kahni W,
sekwikɨni, sokokɨni

story narɨmuʔipɨ

story, fairy narɨkuyunapɨ

storybook nanáarᵾmuʔi tᵾboopᵾ, narᵾmuʔi tᵾboopᵾ

stove nakohtóoʔ

straight kewesi̱katᵾ, tuna

straight, be kewesi̱ketᵾ

straight, set up tsayᵾkwikᵾ

straight, sit tsayᵾkwitᵾ

straight pin piitsᵾnᵾaʔ

straighten tsahtunaabarᵾ

straighten something kᵾhpararᵾ

straighten something wrinkled tahtunaabarᵾ

straighter-than-straight tuʔrunaasᵾ

Straighter-than-straight Tuʔrunaasᵾ

strain out something tsasoʔarᵾ

strained natsamarᵾnitᵾ

strange nanakuyaʔarᵾ, natsuwᵾkai

stranger. kᵾᵾkᵾmeʔ

strangle tsaʔokᵾrᵾ

strangle on water paabitsanitᵾ

strangle someone kuitsi̱marᵾkᵾtᵾ

strangled kuitsi̱marᵾkitᵾ, makuhpᵾkatᵾ, tsaʔoibehkatᵾ

strap, jock tsaʔnikaʔ

strap, saddle nakwᵾsi tsaʔnikaʔ, narᵾnooʔ namᵾkᵾ

straw hat soni tsoʔnikaʔ

strawberry ekapokopi

stream hunuʔbi̱, okwèetᵾ

stream, bank of ekatotsa̱

stream, clear pahtsi okweʔ

stream, fork of a atahunubi

street kawonokatᵾ

streetcar ohawaiki̱na̱, waikina

strength natsu̱wi

strength, pull with full tsahturerᵾ

strengthen kebisaʔmakarᵾ, natsu̱witᵾmakaʔeetᵾ

stretch tsahturerᵾ, turetᵾ

stretch arms or body narurerᵾ

stretch out haahpi̱tᵾ

stretch out arm maruruʔarᵾ

stretch out something wᵾhpararᵾ

stretch something out tsahturᵾ

stretched pohitᵾ, tsahtunehtᵾ

strike out wᵾhpohtoʔitᵾ

string tᵾᵾhtamaʔ, wᵾhtamaʔ

string, G- kohinehkiʔ, tsaʔnikaʔ

string, shoe- napᵾ tsakwᵾsaʔ

strip, cut a wᵾsiʔkwarᵾ

strip off makwi̱teerᵾ

striped naboo-, nawoʔorᵾ, wanatsihtaraaʔ

stroke nisutaitᵾ, tohtarakiitᵾ

stroke, pet or tohtarakiʔarᵾ

strong kᵾhtáatᵾ, kᵾtáatᵾ

strong physically natsu̱witᵾ

strung napᵾ saarᵾ

strut nᵾᵾhtonitᵾ

stubborn person sutenapᵾ

stuck between two things tsᵾki̱katᵾ

stuck down in tsᵾhkarᵾ

stuck fast pimᵾni̱katᵾ

stuck in the mud sekwi sᵾhkai, yubutsᵾhkatᵾ

stumble tahtsanitᵾ

stump huupita tᵾrahna̱

stump, tree huupita kwiita

stupid suapᵾwahtᵾ

stutter nigwatsᵾkatᵾ

suck mubi̱ tsooʔnitᵾ

suck on body (to draw out pain) musoopitᵾ

suck (on something) mukwihterᵾ

suck through nose simuhtarᵾ

sucker (candy) mubi̱ tsooʔniʔ, mukwiteʔ

suddenly, stop tsuhni kwᵾnᵾrᵾ K

suffer abdominal pain kohikamᵾtᵾ

suffer an illness tᵾʔoibᵾkᵾrᵾ

suffer chest pain amawᵾnᵾtᵾ

suffer from a toothache tamanᵾᵾtsi̱kwatᵾ

suffer gall-bladder pain
puʔiʔwɨnɨrɨ
suffer on deathbed pisukwitarɨ
suffer temptation masuyakerɨ
sufficient food, satisfied with
wɨtsɨʔmitɨ
sugar pihnáaʔ W
sugar, brown otɨ pihnàaʔ W
sugar ant tɨe anikuuraʔ
sugar cane huupihnàa, soni
bihnáaʔ
Sugar Eaters Pena tɨhka, Penanɨɨ
suggest something, meet to
nanikaʔwitɨ
suicide, commit nabakɨtɨ
suitcase wosa
sulky pikwɨsiiʔ
sulky, horse-drawn sɨmasɨ
nooi K
sumac huutsúʔa tɨahkapɨ, pahmo
namahya, tatsipɨ
sumac, smooth tɨmaya huupi
summer plum, late- parawa sɨkɨ
summer season taatsa
summer wind yuʔanee
summer-dried meat tahmai napɨ
summertime tatsatɨ
summit kuʔe
sun tabe-
sun goes down tabeʔikamiʔarɨ
sun-dry, partially wɨhtakɨmiitɨ
sun to dry, sit in mabasahtɨkitɨ K
sun to dry, sit in the
pasahtahtɨkitɨ W
sun, stand in the tabe wɨnɨʔitɨ
-sun, Standing Tabe wɨnɨrɨ
-sun-does-not-tell-a-lie, This-
midday Sihka tabe ke isopɨ
Sun-eagle Tabe kwiʔne
Sunday Puha rabeni, Puha rakatɨ
sunflower ohayaaʔ
sunflower head hiʔoopitaohayaa

sunflower salve hiʔookwanaʔ
sunflower stalk or plant hiʔoopi
sunflowers hiʔoo-
-sunrise, Voice-of-the Tabe nanika
supernatural power puha
supernatural power, having
puhakatɨ
supper yɨihtɨhkaʔ
supper, eat yɨihtɨhkatɨ
supply, deplete a tsahtsuʔmarɨ
supply, exhaust kehewaʔitɨ
supply, exhaust food tɨkɨ
tsuhmarɨ
support something tsihtɨroorɨ
supported marɨrooniitɨ K,
tohtɨrooniitɨ W
sure noo
surely kewáhabahku, tɨbitsi
surface, file a tɨmatsunarɨ
surface, rasp a tɨmatsunarɨ
surface, skim from the yunarɨ
surfaced road tɨpi puʔe
surgery nɨɨpɨtsapɨ
surgery, perform wɨpɨtsarɨ
surgical operation nɨɨpɨtsapɨ
surprise, hit by wɨnɨʔyɨʔitɨ
surprised tɨɨmoo
surrender manɨsutarɨ, nasutarɨ
surrender someone
manɨsutaʔaitɨ
suspended, hang tsanikatɨ
suspenders hapianaʔ
swab out wɨhkwinarɨ
swallow, to kuʔnuitɨ
swallow something tɨyuwarɨ,
yɨwitɨ W
swamp pamɨpɨtsoʔni
swamp rabbit ekaeʔree W,
taʔwokinaeʔree eka K
swamp weed pakɨɨka
swat down wɨʔanirɨ
sway yɨʔbanaʔitɨ

swear mahiyaru, tabéʔaitu
sweat takusitoʔitu, takwusipu
sweat bath nakuhkwarakiʔ K,
    nasukooʔiʔ
sweater yuʔa kwusuʔu
sweathouse nasukooʔi kahni
sweep wunuaru
sweep something tuunuaru
sweet, taste pihnákamaru
sweet bread pihná nohkopu
sweet cider amawóoʔa pàa
sweet potato kamúutaʔ
sweetbreads toyo tahkaʔmiitsa
sweetheart notsaʔkaʔ,
    tuuʔurapu W, K
sweets pihnáaʔ W
sweets, crave pihná ruhkaru
swell atabaroʔitu, paroʔikitu,
    pekwitu
swell up pohtokitu
Swift-moving Wuʔrabiahpu
swim pahabitu
swim, make tapuhabi
swim dog paddle masuʔwaʔnekitu,
    paruhparu
swindle tutsikwusaru
swine poʔroʔ
swing natsawenitu, wepukaitu
swing, playground piʔwesurúuʔiʔ
swing back and forth
    natsakwenitu
swing sitting down
    piʔweesuʔruʔitu
swinging hips, walk piʔweke
    miʔaru
switch kwibukitu, suuki,
    tukwibukiitu, wukutsaru
switches parukwihtsipu
swollen pekwipu
sword tutsiwaiiʔ K, uwíhi
sympathize suakutuaitu
syrup huupihnàa

T t

table, set the awotsawuniʔitu
table fork tuhkaʔ
tablecloth tuku soona
tablecloth, spread a tuku soonaru
tablespoon pia ruʔewo
taboo mamusuakatu K,
    nabiʔatsikatu
tadpole paʔwuhtakóoʔ
tail, animal kwasi-, kwasi
tail, cat- pisibuniʔ
tail, cat's pisibuniʔ
tail, pony kuwikusii
tail, scissor- kukuburaakwaʔsiʔ
tailbone piwoʔsa
-tailed deer, white piʔtohtsíaʔ W
take a steam bath kuhkwarukitu
take an oath narabeeʔaitu
take apart tsahpukusuʔaru W
take away something live
    tahtukitu
take down tsayumiʔi
take down a teepee tsahtuwaru
take down off of something
    tsahpuheru
take oath mahiyaru
take off maboʔayaru, tohkweʔyaru
take off a shoe tahkweʔyaru
take off layer tsahkwuruʔaru
take one or several things yaaru
take out tsahkuaru, tsahtoʔiru
take, over- tahtsaitu, wuhpitu
take several objects himaʔaru
take someone by force sutena
    betu
take someone home as guest
    panimiʔaru
take something in the mouth
    kuhyaaru
take to eat W tuku yaaru
take women along notsaʔkaaru

Take-a-stick-and-hit-someone
Huuwʉhtʉkwa?
taken, object (or item) yaapʉ
talcum powder homoroso?yoki?
tale narʉkuyunapʉ, narʉmu?ipʉ
Talk Loud Pibia niwʉnʉ?nʉʉ
talk, pester by nimʉsasuarʉ
talk rough tuhu rekwarʉ
talk someone into something
nitsʉbahikʉ?itʉ
talk to someone niwʉnʉrʉ, tekwarʉ
talk tough nimakwihtsetʉ
-talker, Spirit Mukwoorʉ
talking, stop nihpʉ?aitʉ
tall panihputʉ mabà?atʉ, tsihtararʉ
tall, stand kanaba?aitʉ
tall and slender kanaba?aitʉ,
kʉbʉráata
tame kesósoorʉ
tame a wild thing manʉsu?narʉ W
tame an animal masuyu?ikarʉ K
tamed, un- pʉewatsi
tamp down tanʉkʉtʉ K, tonʉkʉrʉ
tan koropitʉ
tan a hide kwiipʉsiarʉ, tʉso?arʉ
tangle kwisikatʉ K, sakwʉsikʉtʉ,
takwʉsiskʉrʉ, tsakwʉsikʉkatʉ K
tangle, cause to kwisihkarʉ
tangle something tokwʉsikʉtʉ,
tsakwʉ?ikʉrʉ W
tangled kwisihka, kwʉsipʉ W
tangled by hand makwʉsikʉkatʉ
tangled hair papi tsʉnʉ?itʉ
tangled up tomʉsiketʉ K
tanned deer hide pikapʉ
tanned hide narʉso?ipʉ, tʉso?ipʉ?
tanning a hide, process of narʉso?ipʉ
tap on something wʉhtarakiitʉ
tape, bias tʉkʉma?ai
tape measure tʉmanahke?
tar tusanahpi
tarantula pia pʉhʉ re?tsi

tardy keyu K
taste kamatʉ, kʉhpunitʉ, kʉsukarʉ,
kʉ?kwiyarʉ
taste good tsaa kamarʉ
taste oily or greasy wihi kamatʉ
taste sour mohakamarʉ
taste sweet pihnákamarʉ
taunt ni?he?bunitʉ
tax collector tʉniwaitʉ?
taxi nʉmi noo?etʉ
tea, dry puhi huuba
tea, liquid puhi tuhpaa W
tea, mormon sanaweha
teach suabetaikʉrʉ
teach someone something
nisuabetarʉ
teach something to someone
tʉnisuabetarʉ
teacher tʉboo bia?, tʉnisuabetai
wapi W
teacher, female tʉboorʉʉ pia?
teacher, male tʉboo wapi
tear masi?warʉ 1, ohpepʉ
tear apart tsahpako?arʉ
tear at something tsahkwanitʉ
tear down tsahperʉ
tear off sʉmʉ sihwarʉ
tear skin nʉʉsihwa?itʉ
tear something puhkarʉ, sihwarʉ,
tosi?kwarʉ, tsai?warʉ K
tear with the foot tasi?kwairʉ
tear with the teeth kʉsi?kwarʉ
tears, shed many pa?okwetʉ
tears flow ohpeto?ikarʉ
teaspoon tʉe aawo
teatowel awomatsuma?
teepee kah-, kahni, nʉmʉkʉni
teepee, peyote puha kahni, wokwe
kahni
teepee, take down a tsahtʉwarʉ
teepee, ventilator at top of
natsihpara?

teepee pole huutsiyaa?, waahuupi̱, waata̱

teepee poles, travel carrier made of tu̱?noo?

teepees, set up yu̱kwiku̱

teepees, skins or other covering for nu̱mu̱ku̱ni

teeter-totter na?atsiyaa?, na?tsiyaa?

teeth, break up with the ku̱nutsaru̱

teeth, chatter the ku̱u̱htarakiitu̱

teeth, chattering saatitamakatu̱

teeth, clack the ku̱hkwitsitu̱

teeth, crack with the ku̱tu̱baru̱

teeth, false tamatsa?nika?

teeth, grind the ku̱hporokitu̱

teeth, grit the ku̱hkwitsitu̱, ku̱hporokitu̱

teeth, gums of tamaruhku̱

teeth, roots of the tamakwita̱

teeth, sever (or break) with the ku̱hkobaru̱

teeth, tear with the ku̱si?kwaru̱

Tejas), Proud People (Wichita name for Comanches of Natai

telegram namu̱si buhihwi tekwapu̱

telephone puhihwi tekwapu̱

telephone pole puhihwi tekwapu̱hana huupi

tell naru̱mu?ikatu̱, tu̱?a̱wetu̱, watsih tekwaru̱

tell a fortune nipu̱karu̱

tell-a-lie, This-midday-sun-does-not- Sihka tabe ke isopu̱

tell fortunes nu̱nipu̱karu̱

tell off-color stories tu̱tsu̱ naru̱mi?itu̱

tell to feed makahtu̱nikatu̱

teller, fortune- mapaana?, nipu̱kaa?eetu̱, nu̱mi nipu̱ka? K, tu̱nipu̱kawapi̱ W

telling, finish nimaru̱kaitu̱

temple pui?

tempt (by describing something) nisuyakeetu̱

tempt one to sin tu̱rape suwaitu̱

tempt (or test someone) mabunihkaru̱

tempt to turn aside tsapu̱hesuwaru̱

temptation, suffer masuyakeru̱

tempted, be masuyakeru̱

ten su̱u̱maru̱

Ten-elks Paruwa su̱mu̱no

tenant na?raiboo?

tent, canvas nu̱u̱soo?

tent pin tu̱rawu̱na? K

termite wobi muwo?ne? K

termites muwo?ne?

terrain, rough wohtsa?wu̱tu̱

terrible nasu?ana

test tohpunitu̱

test something natsahpunitu̱

test (or tempt someone) mabunihkaru̱

test someone, tempt or mabunihkaru̱

tested marahpunihkatu̱

tested item maru̱mabunipu̱

than, smaller inaaru̱

thank you ahó, u̱ra

thanks, prayer of ahotabenihtu̱

thanksgiving ahotabenihtu̱

that one suhkapu̱

that way suni

That's all sube?tu̱

That's It Tasúra

That's life! namami?aku̱

their maru̱u̱, pu̱u̱

them marii, urii

them, two of mahri

them, of two of mahru̱

then wihnu

then, since sube?su̱

these two itu̱kwu̱, situ̱kwu̱

they uru̱

they say that tʉa
thick pohotatʉ
thief tʉrʉhka?
thieves, den of tʉrʉkʉ kahni
thieves, house of tʉrʉkʉ kahni
thigh tohoobe̱
thigh meat pabo tuhku
thin hʉnʉketʉ, tahi, tapi̱tʉhtsi
thin person kanabʉʉtsi?, wehuru?i
thing hihini
thing, discarded namaro?ihkatʉ
thing, play- nohi?
thing, tame a wild manʉsu?narʉ W
things, say mean nimakwihtsetʉ
things, stuck between two tsʉki̱katʉ
things, take one or several yaarʉ
think suatʉtʉ
think, lie down and nasutamʉ habitʉ
think about sukwʉ̱kitʉ
think about something nasutamʉ̱katʉ tamai, su?atsitʉ, tʉsu?atsi̱katʉ
think good thoughts suakʉtʉ
thinness hʉnʉ-
thirst takʉsuaitʉ
thirst, die of takuhtʉyaaihumi?arʉ
thirst to death takuhtʉyaaihumi?arʉ
this ihka, isʉ, itʉ
this direction ibu, inakwʉ̱
this evening yʉihka̱
This-midday-sun-does-not-tell-a-lie Sihka tabe ke isopʉ
thistle po?aya?eetʉ, wokwe
thistle, Texas ebitotsiya?
thorn wokwe
thorn apple tu?amowoo, wokwekatʉ huupi
thorn tree wokʉ̱ huupi̱
thornapple tubokóo

thorny weed wokwesonipʉ̱
thorough sʉmʉ makʉkatʉ
thoroughly sʉmʉ
thoroughly, soaked papoosinʉ
those ehka, etʉʉ, setʉʉ, surʉʉ
Those-who-are-always-against Komanche
Those-who-stay-downstream Tinawa
thought sua, suapʉ̱
thoughts suana
thoughts, kind tʉsu?ʉrʉ?
thoughts, think good suakʉtʉ
thread wana ramʉ
thread, crochet wana ramʉ
threadbare pupʉkatʉ
threatening movements, make tahkuya?arʉ
three pahihtʉ
three groups of people pahibahtʉnʉnʉ
three separate families pahibahtʉnʉnʉ
three separated groups pahibahtʉ
thresh tusurʉ
throat kuitsi̱
throat, clear nanihkanuitʉ
throat, have a sore kuitsi̱sʉatʉ
through nana-
through, peer wihtekatʉ
through, soak parʉbʉʉ?itʉ
through nose, suck simuhtarʉ
throughout nana-
throughout a location oyo?rʉtu
throw takwʉ̱kitʉ, tokwʉ̱ki?arʉ, wihirʉ
throw a light on something kupi̱tarʉ
throw at something tahtʉkwarʉ
throw away petihtarʉ, wihtaitʉ
throw body on the ground kwanu?itʉ K

throw down tsayumarʉ
throw down a person
tsahkwaʔnuʔitʉ
throw into the fire kuhtsahwirʉ
throw out of something
wʉʔkwʉriarʉ
throw overhand kwihitʉ
throw with nose or mouth
muhwitʉ K, mukwʉbʉarʉ W
throwing arrows naroʔtoneetsiʔ,
tiroʔwoko
thrown (forcibly from a horse)
wʉpʉherʉ
thumb mahtokooʔ
thunder tomoyaketʉ
thus sunihku
tick kaʔraʔáaʔ
tickle someone pinakʉtsʉrʉ
tidings, upset people by bad
niʔyʉsʉkaitʉ
tie wʉhtsʉkʉnarʉ
tie, un- wʉhtoʔyarʉ
tie a child to back wʉpitoorʉ
tie a knot wʉtsʉkʉnarʉ
tie in round bundle or round knot
wʉhtopʉʔnoorʉ
tie something wʉhtamarʉ
tie up a horse tʉʉtsʉkʉnarʉ
-tied person, tongue ekotʉyaipʉ
tied up nʉʉtsʉkʉnarʉ
tied up, wrapped and nʉʉhtamiʔitʉ
ties tʉʉhtamaʔ
tight kʉhtáatʉ, kʉtáatʉ, matsʉkikatʉ
tight, squeezed tsinʉkʉ
tighten wʉnʉkʉtʉ
tightly kʉhtáaku
tightly, packed in manʉkʉtʉ
tightly, stake down ʉhtaarʉ
till tsatʉsukitʉ
Timber Creek Huuhunuʔbi
Timber People Huuhʔinʉʉ
time, day- taahkatʉ

time, next kwasikʉ
time, one sʉmʉsʉ
time, one at a sʉsʉmʉʔ,
sʉʔsʉmʉʔnʉku
time, past the ʉi
time, summer- tatsatʉ
time, winter kwihneʔ
times, few hʉʉsʉ
tin cup sʉʉ awo
tin or other shiny metal pisayuʔneʔ
tip off ninakʉakʉrʉ W
tire makwʉʔnikʉ W, narahpanaʔ
tire, automobile naʔbukuwàaʔa
narahpaana̱ W
tire, (blow out a) tʉrapʉtsarʉ W
tire, puncture a tʉrapʉtsarʉ W
tire of something manʉʉʔmaitʉ
tire oneself nananʉʉʔmaitʉ
tire out kweʔyʉkatʉ, nʉʉʔmaitʉ
tired of something nakʉnʉʉʔmaitʉ,
wʉʔtsikwarʉ
tired person namakʉnʉmapʉ
title (or deed to land) nabinai
tʉboopʉ
title deed soko bookʉtʉ
to, speak niikwiitʉ
to deceive emʉahkatʉ
to die kooitʉ
to dry, sit in sun mabasahtʉkitʉ K
to dry, sit in the sun
pasahtahtʉkitʉ W
to disconnect tsahtukarʉ
to fish hʉarʉ
to haul away noorʉ
to swallow kuʔnuitʉ
to the right tʉbitsi petutʉ
to trap hʉarʉ
to turn aside, tempt tsapʉhesuwarʉ
to you ʉnʉ
toad, horned kuhtsu tʉbiniʔ
toast bread wesikʉrʉ
toast corn hanikwasʉkʉrʉ

toasted wesikatʉ

toasted maize kukʉmepʉ

tobacco pahmu, yokabahmu

tobacco, chewing yokabahmu

tobacco, Indian tabahko

today tabéni

toe tookaatso

toe, big tahtokooʔ

toe, little tahtúaʔ, tʉeh tahtuaʔ

toe, middle tahtʉpinaaʔ

toenail tasiito

toes tasakwʉʉhkiʔ

together naha-, nahmaʔai, sʉʉ

together, come naʔakʉtʉ

together, crowded narahtsʉkikatʉ

together, drive taʔookitʉ

together, gather kaʔwitʉ,
   narahkaʔwitʉ, sʉʉmaʔaitʉ

together, pin tsihtʉpʉkarʉ,
   wʉhtʉpʉkarʉ

together, rake manuarʉ W,
   marʉʔokitʉ K, tanuarʉ

together, rub hands namʉsuʔnetʉ

tomato kwasinabooʔa tʉahkapʉ

tomb (burial mound) nabʉkapʉ W

tomorrow, day after piʔnakwʉ
   bʉetsʉ

tongue eko-

tongue, lap with the kaʔamoorʉ

tongue hanging down, pant with
   hehekʉbʉniitʉ

tongue-tied person ekotʉyaipʉ

tonic, hair papi wihtʉʔekaʔ

**tool (any sharp-pointed
   implement for punching holes
   through which** sinews pass)
   wiiyʉ

tool, peeling huusibeʔ

tool, steel tʉʉhkoʔneʔ

too late ʉi

tooth taama, tama-

tooth, decayed woʔataama

tooth, loose saatitamakatʉ

tooth, wisdom kʉʉtsi

toothache, suffer from a
   tamanʉʉtsikwatʉ

toothache tree kunanatsu

toothbrush tamamatsumaʔ

toothpaste tamakotseʔ

top kuʔe

top, house- kahni kuʔe

top of, on kuʔe

top, quilt sona boʔa

top of teepee, ventilator at
   natsihparaʔ

Tope Tope

torment aibuniitʉ

torn puhkapʉ

torn by a foot tasiʔkwaitʉ

torn object sihwapi

torn up completely tsasikwaitʉ

tornado nʉepi

tortilla tohtíaʔ

-totter, teeter naʔatsiyaaʔ,
   naʔtsiyaaʔ

touch marʉkitʉ, masukaarʉ, tasukarʉ

touch, cure partially through
   marebunitʉ

touch (lightly with the hand)
   makwʉʔnetʉ

touch, reach out and maʔwʉminarʉ

tough, talk nimakwihtsetʉ

toward someone or something
   mawakatu

**toward something, stop
   movement** wʉnʉ hupiitʉ

towel awomatsumaʔ, kobe
   matsumaʔ

towel, face kobe matsumaʔ, nakobe
   matsumaʔ

town narʉmʉʉʔ, sookʉni

town crier tekwʉniwapi

towsack soni narʉsoʔ

toy nohiʔ

toy wagon nohiwaikinu
tracks, horse tuhuyena puni W
tracks, railroad kunawaikina puʔe
trade narumuuru, tumuuru
trade goods wanapu K
trading post ekanarumuu?, numu
narumuu?
tradition nanihpuʔeʔaikupu K,
puʔeʔaikupu W
trail napu, napuhu, napuhu miʔaru,
puʔe
trail a human or an animal
nayaaru
trail something tunahyaru
trailer pitsaka?, tubiyaaku? W
trailer house kahni tubitsika? K
train kunawaikinu, kunawobipuuku,
waikina
train, freight tunoo kuna waikina K
train someone suabetaikuru
traitor natsaka?uhtu?etu?
trampling on it, soften something
by tahpararu
transparent pabo-, pabokopitu
transplant tsihtaboʔikutu,
wunukutu
trap huaru?
trap, to huaru
trap, bear wasápe pumata
kwuhuru?
trap, fish pekwi pumata huaru
trap, mouse kahúu pumata huaru?
trap, rat- kahúu pumata huaru?
trapper huawapi
trash tutsakwuriapu K
travel carrier made of teepee
poles tuʔnoo?
tread heavily tanuʔyukitu
treasure puhihwi ta ahweetu,
tsaanahapu
treat muuru
treat with respect pahnaʔaitu

treaty mahyaru,
nanihpuʔeʔaikupu K
tree hu-, huu-
tree, ash tosa seyuʔyuki?
tree, bois d'arc ohahuupi
tree, cottonwood soho obi,
tahpooku?, weʔyuku sohoobi K
tree, dead putsi waipu
tree, domestic humasuapu
-tree, Peeping-from-behind
Kuhiyai
tree, plum parua sukui?
tree, silver maple kweʔyuku
sohóobi
tree. single- pihtsaku huupi
tree, thorn woku huupi
tree, toothache kunanatsu
tree bark huupi poʔa?, huupita poʔa
tree limb huupita mooka
tree root huupita turahna
tree squirrel wokoohwi
tree stump huupita kwiita
tree trunk owóora
tree trunk, burned out kuwoʔnepu
trees, clump of huukabatu
tremble kwibihpikitu W, suhkwibitu
tremble in speech nihkwibihbikitu
tremble with cold suutsunitu
tremor of earth soko
yuʔyumuhkuru
tribe, Eating- Maruhke
tribe, enemy tawohho
tributary atahunubi, nabatai K
trick kaabehkaru
tried item marumabunipu
tried on marahpunihkatu
trim kuhpomaru, kumakooru,
wuhuwuʔniitu, wuʔyukwitu K
trip and fall nuuhkupatu,
nuuhpisiʔmaitu
trip someone tanuuhkupaitu
triplets paʔabeʔnuu

troll nʉnʉ pʉhiʔ
trolley ohawaikina
trot aimiʔarʉ, pohyamiʔarʉ
trot, made to poyohkarʉ
Trotter Waakakwa
troublesome tʉmabisoʔaitʉ
trough, water puku hibikʉʔ
trousers pitʉsohkoʔ
trousers, put on pitsohkorʉ
truck tʉnoona bukuwaʔ, tʉnoo
waikina, waikina
true tʉbitsiyu
trunk wobi aawo
trunk, tree owóora
trunk, tree (burned out)
kuwoʔnepʉ
trunk of a white putsi waipʉ
trust tʉmayokʉrʉ
trust someone tokʉsuakʉtʉ
truth, doubt the (of a statement)
tsuwíhnu
try naniʔookitʉ
try on headwear tsohponiitʉ
try on shoes tahpunitʉ
try or want to hit with fist
tosoʔwaitʉ
try out kʉhpunitʉ, tohpunitʉ
tub, wash- wana kotse aawo
tuber ahwepʉ
tuber, edible taʔwahkóoʔ W,
totohtʉ
tuber, wild payaape, tutupitʉ
tuberculosis monʉ ohni
tug-of-war natsaaturuʔitʉʔ
tunnel kahnitaikʉ
turkey kuyuʔnii, puhitóoʔ K
turkey grass puhitóoʔ
turn wʉhbuikatʉ W, wʉnʉkʉtʉ
turn around koonitʉ, kooniʔetʉ,
kwinuʔyarʉ
turn around (and come back),
cause to tsahkooʔitʉ

turn around, caused to
tsakwʉhwitʉ
turn around quickly pikwebuitʉ
turn aside, tempt to tsapʉhesuwarʉ
turn away from wʉhbuikatʉ W
turn cold kwihnerʉ
turn loose pʉarʉ, wʉhtoʔyarʉ
turn over natsamʉritʉ
turn red hot ekawehaarʉ
turn something around, cause to
tsakwʉhburʉ
turn something over tsamʉrikarʉ,
wʉmʉʉrʉ
turned nakʉmʉʉʔetʉ W
turned over wʉmʉʉrihkatʉ
turtle pitsohka kwaba W,
wakaréeʔ K
Turtle Wakaréʔe
turtle, snapping kwasi nʉrʉʉʔwʉʔ,
paʔkwakʉme
twig sʉʉki
twigs, willow sʉhʉ tsitsinaʔ
twine soni wiyaaʔ
twins waʔwaʔ
twist kwipunarʉ, makwipunarʉ K
twist oneself nʉʉkwitsʉnarʉ
twist oneself around something
nʉʉʔkwipunarʉ
twist something tsakwipunarʉ
twist the body kwitsunairʉ
twitch yʉʔyʉturʉ
twitch, hand mayʉʔyʉrʉ
two waha-, wahati
two apiece waʔwaʔ
two of them mahri
two of them, of mahrʉ
two, of us taa
two, of you mʉhʉ
two, these itʉkwʉ, sitʉkwʉ
two, you mʉkwʉ
two years old tomohtootʉ W
two-by-two waʔwaʔ

two-man handsaw huutsihkaa?
two parts, split into tʉapako?itʉ
two-seated buggy natsa?ani?
two things, stuck between tsʉki̱katʉ
two-year-old wahatomopʉ̱ K
two-year-old item tomohtoopʉ̱ W
-type handkerchief, work pʉesúube? K
typewriter mo?o rʉboo?
typhoid fever narʉ?ʉyʉ̱ kuhtsʉni?

U u

ugly tʉtsʉ-
umbrella hʉkiai, hʉʉki?ai?
unable mʉnitʉ
unable to breathe sua?su?maitʉ
unable to do something kemahpʉ?arʉ, tsuhitʉ
unbolt wʉhkwe?yarʉ
unbridle a horse tʉpe tsahkwe?yarʉ
uncle ara?
uncle and niece, marriage of arakwʉ?ʉtʉ
uncle, paternal great kʉnu?
unclean spirit tʉtʉ̱suana
uncoil pʉrʉ̱su?arʉ
uncoil something wʉhpʉkʉ̱suarʉ
unconcerned, live yukahnibarʉ
unconscious sua watsikʉ
uncontrollably, continue kenaninabenitʉ
undecided wahabi̱suatʉ
undependable person senihtʉhtsi?
under water, hit and push wʉhpaaku?nerʉ
under water, pushed tohpaaku?netʉ W
underarm ahna, ana-
underarm hair anapʉhʉ

underarm to waist ama-
undershirt tuhkanaai kwasu?ʉ̱
understand someone nahkʉsuaberʉ
understood kenanawatsitʉ
undertaker K tʉyaipʉ̱ha noo?ee?tʉ̱
underwear tsa?nika?
underwear on, have tsa?nikʉkatʉ
undress natsahkwe?yarʉ, tsahkwe?yarʉ
uneven ho?yopi̱pʉ̱, pihpokaarʉ
uneven land wohtsa?wʉtʉ̱
unfold marʉpi̱su?arʉ W, tsahpʉkʉ̱su?arʉ W
unfriendliness nakahanupʉ̱ W
unfriendly kwetʉ̱sapʉ̱
unhitch too?itʉ
unhitch a horse noro?yarʉ
unhitch an animal to?yarʉ W
unhorse tsiperʉ
unlace tsahkwʉmarʉ
unlighted tukanikatʉ
unload tsahpʉ̱herʉ, tsapʉ̱yetʉ, tsayumi?i
unlock tsihtʉ̱warʉ
unmarried man, young wohka?ni?
unplug to extinguish tsahtukarʉ
unravel pʉrʉ̱su?arʉ
unravel of own accord nʉʉpʉrʉ̱suarʉ
unravel something nʉʉpʉrʉ̱suanʉpurʉ
unroll tsahkwʉmarʉ, tsahpʉkʉ̱su?arʉ W
unsaddle a horse narʉnoo?ro?yarʉ
unscrew wʉhkwe?yarʉ
unseal something tsahto?arʉ K
unseat tsiperʉ
untamed pʉewatsi
untie wʉhto?yarʉ
unwind pʉrʉ̱su?arʉ, tsahkwʉmarʉ, tsahkwʉnunúukitʉ, wʉhpʉkʉ̱suarʉ
unworthy tʉtaatʉ

unwrap mahkwᵾmarᵾ,
   tsahkwᵾmarᵾ
unwrap an object tsahpekoʔarᵾ
unwrap something tahkwᵾmarᵾ
**unwrap something with the
   mouth** kᵾhtoʔyarᵾ K
up, dry kuwaaitᵾ, waaitᵾ
up, fill muʔibuikᵾrᵾ
up, filled wᵾtsᵾʔmitᵾ
up, fix maʔyᵾkwiitᵾ
up, fly yorimiʔarᵾ, yᵾtsᵾrᵾ
up, give narahkupaitᵾ, nasutarᵾ
up exhausted, give anitᵾ
up, go yᵾtsᵾrᵾ
up, heap pia wᵾʔutsitᵾ
up, help matsáyᵾtsᵾrᵾ
**up, help (from sitting to standing
   position)** matsákwᵾnᵾkᵾrᵾ
up, high tsihtararᵾ
up, hill maʔohtaʔaitᵾ, wᵾnoʔkarᵾrᵾ
up, hitch mahkarᵾ W
up, hitch (horses and buggy)
   nomohkarᵾ
up, hung narohtsanarᵾ,
   natsahkweniitᵾ
up, hurry namᵾsohitᵾ
up, lace tsakwᵾsarᵾ W
up a horse, lead tsakᵾhunitᵾ
up, lift toyarᵾ, tsahhᵾkwᵾʔniitᵾ W
up, load tᵾnookᵾrᵾ
up someone, lock taʔikᵾrᵾ
up, locked taʔikᵾkatᵾ
up something, mash mapitserᵾ
up animal, pen taʔikᵾrᵾ
up, penned tawekwit
up several objects, pick himaʔarᵾ
up, pile wᵾʔutsitᵾ
up the ears, prick toʔyabaitᵾ
up, pry tsahtoʔarᵾ K
up, puff pohtokitᵾ
up, pull tsahkᵾarᵾ, tsahtoʔirᵾ
up, pull oneself natsahtoʔitᵾ

up, pulled tsahtoʔitᵾ
up, rake tsaʔoorᵾ
up, reared manawᵾnᵾkatᵾ
up, rise yorimiʔarᵾ, yᵾtsᵾrᵾ
up, roll namakwatubiitᵾ,
   tᵾmakwatᵾbiʔetarᵾ
up to itself, roll wᵾhkwitubikatᵾ
up with something, roll
   tohtopoʔnarᵾ
up, rolled makwatubiitᵾ
up, round tahkoonikarᵾ, taʔookitᵾ
up, saddle narᵾnooʔrᵾkitᵾ
up, scoop mahorarᵾ
up earth, scratch taʔsiʔwoorᵾ
up, set karᵾkᵾrᵾ, maʔyᵾkwiitᵾ
up straight, set tsayᵾkwikᵾ
up teepees, set yᵾkwikᵾ
up from heat, shrivel
   kuhtakwitsooʔnitᵾ W
up, slide standing tahkitemiʔarᵾ
up, slip standing tahkitemiʔarᵾ
up dust, stir huukᵾhᵾnᵾrᵾ
up excitement, stir toyᵾsekaitᵾ
up fire, stir kumaʔomerᵾ,
   maʔomerᵾ
up, stopped tohtᵾmapᵾ
up, swell pohtokitᵾ
up, tangled tomᵾsiketᵾ K
up a horse, tie tᵾᵾtsᵾkᵾnarᵾ
up, tied nᵾᵾtsᵾkᵾnarᵾ
up completely, torn tsasikwaitᵾ
up, use tsuʔma
up, wake tᵾbunitᵾ
up someone, wake tsayoritᵾ
up, warm yuʔaʔitᵾ
up, wrap tᵾmakwatᵾbiʔetarᵾ,
   wᵾhkwitunarᵾ
up, wrapped and tied nᵾᵾhtamiʔitᵾ
**up to or onto someone or
   something** maatu
upright, set tsahkarᵾkᵾrᵾ
upriver obutᵾmaʔ

uproot tsahtobarʉ

upset people by bad tidings niʔyʉsʉkaitʉ

upside down paʔarai

upward tukuhputʉ

urge on nihtunetsʉʔitʉ

urinate siitʉ

urine siipʉʔ

us nʉmi, tai

us two, of taa

us, procreated by nʉmʉ rʉborarʉ

use, rawhide ready to pahkipʉ

use up tsuʔma

used to noha

using an instrument, scratch tsahkiʔaitʉ

uterine grandchild, man's tokoʔ

uterine grandchild, woman's kakuʔ

V v

vagabond noyʉkaʔ

valley, level haapane

various directions ebu

various ways seni

vase paboko aawo, totsiyaa aawo

vase, flower totsiyaa tsakwʉnaʔ

vegetable garden narʉhkaʔ sokoobi̱, tʉmʉsʉa sokobi K

vegetable garden plot tʉkʉ masʉa sokoobi W

vegetables, fry meat or kwasʉkʉrʉ

vegetation, hairy pʉhʉʔ

vehicle, haul in a manoorʉ

vein paai

velvet cloth pʉesúubeʔ K

ventilate tsihpʉrarʉ

ventilator at top of teepee natsihparaʔ

verbally, rejoice naninaʔukitʉ

vertebra kwahitsuhni̱

very mohatsi̱, nohi

vessel aawo, awo-

vessel, wooden huu aawo

vexed pihisoʔai

victory, songs of wohho tʉikwʉpitʉ K

vigorously, shake tsobokitʉ

village sookʉni

vine totsiyaaʔa sʉʉki̱

vine, grape- natsamukweʔa sʉʉki̱

visit kahni miʔa, puni kwarʉ

visiting, go kahni miʔa

voice tʉʔaape̱

Voice-of-the-sunrise Tabe nanika

vomit ooʔitʉ

W w

waddle or move clumsily masuʔwaʔnekitʉ

wag wʉhkwitsunarʉ

wagon tʉnoo waikina̱, waikina

wagon, covered nakʉnikatʉ waikina̱

wagon, toy nohiwaikinʉ

wagon crossing naʔweeʔ, puʔe nagwe

wagon wheel waikina naʔoomo̱

wahoo waaʔakitʉ

wail hubiyaa piayakeetʉ

wail, death hubiya piayakeetʉ

waist area kohi̱

waist, underarm to ama-

waist, wear something around the kohinehkitʉ

wait wʉhtuitʉ

wait for someone makamaitʉ

wait on mananaaʔwaihkarʉ

waiting for someone, give up wʉsuwarʉkiitʉ

waiting, stand tahkamʉrʉ
wake someone tsahtʉbunitʉ
wake someone by pounding
 wʉhtʉbunitʉ
wake up tʉbunitʉ
wake up someone tsayoritʉ
waken tahtʉbunitʉ
waken by speaking to someone
 nihtʉbuniorʉ
walk yʉkarʉ
walk, able to nʉmirʉ
walk around nahnʉmiitʉ
walk away natsihtóo mi?arʉ
walk backward pimimi?arʉ
walk dragging one foot
 tasi?womi?arʉ
walk fast pohyami?arʉ
walk, help someone tsami?akʉrʉ
walk lamely wihnai mi?arʉ
walk swinging hips pi?weke mi?arʉ
walk with cane natsihtóo noorʉ
walking around, crying
 yakeyʉkarʉ
walking, come soko kimarʉ
walking, go sokomi?arʉ
walking, raise dust by
 tahuhkuwʉnʉrʉ
walking, rocking way of
 yʉ?bana?itʉ
walking, stagger when
 tsimʉami?arʉ
walking cane tʉ?ehkooi? W
walking stick tʉ?ehkooi? W
wall kahni tʉbanaa, tʉbanaa?
wallet puhihwi narʉsọ W
wallow na?anitʉ
wallpaper kahnị tʉboopʉ, tʉbanaa
 rʉbopʉ
walnut mubitai
walnut, black tuhmubitai
wander (from place to place)
 noyʉkarʉ

Wanderer Nookoni
Wanderers Noyʉhkanʉʉ
want suwaitʉ
want to flirt K na?ịsa suakʉtʉ
want to hit with fist, try or
 toso?waitʉ
want to lay an egg nohabị
 suwaitʉ
war nabitʉkʉrʉ
-war, tug-of natsaaturu?itʉ?
war bonnet pia tso?nika?
war club wʉpitapu?ni
war paint, apply wohho napʉsarʉ
war songs wohho tʉikwʉpitʉ K
war-bonnet bag tuna wosa
wardrobe case, rawhide
 natʉsakʉna
warm kusuatʉ, yu?a
warm, luke- pakuyu?atʉ
warm clothing, wear yu?a
 namʉsoorʉ
warm up yu?a?itʉ
warn ninakaba?ikʉtʉ
warpath wohho namaka?muki?arʉ
warpath, go on mahimi?arʉ
warpath, return from mahiko?itʉ
wart ku?miitsạ, ta?ka?miitsa?
wash dishes awomakotserʉ,
 tʉmakotsetʉ
wash feet narakotserʉ, takotserʉ
wash hand namo?o kotsẹtʉ
wash out earth patowo?nerʉ
washcloth tʉehna matsuma?
washing machine tʉkotse? K
Washita River Tusoho?ọkwe?
washout patowo?nepʉ
washtub wana kotse aawo
wasp otʉ peena
waste aibuniitʉ
wasted tu?rʉmetʉ
watch tʉpunirʉ
watch, wrist- tabe-

watch chain tabe narᵻmuhkᵾ, tabe wenuakᵾ?

watch for iyaa?itᵾ

watch oneself na?iyaitᵾ

watch someone watsi punitᵾ

watchdog tᵾ?iya?i wapi̱

watchman tᵾ?iya?i wapi̱

water pa- W, paa, pai, tuu-, tuupᵾ

water an animal hibikᵾtᵾ

water, be in deep kenawᵾnᵾrᵾ

water boy tuu?etᵾ

water, channel patsanuarᵾ

water dog pa?boosi?

water, draw tuurᵾ

water, drip paa kᵾa?etᵾ

water, duck head under paku?nerᵾ

water, eyes ohpeto?ikarᵾ

water, fetch tuuhuniitᵾ W

water, fetch (for someone) tuukᵾmi?arᵾ

water, fill with paa ma?ibu?ikᵾtᵾ K, pawᵾsa?naitᵾ W

water, filled with (by drinking) pakwᵾ?sᵾ?mitᵾ

water heavily, eyes pa?okwetᵾ

water, hit and push under wᵾhpaaku?nerᵾ

water, immerse oneself in nabawᵾhtiarᵾ

water, paddle masu?wa?nekitᵾ

water, paddle feet in pawᵾpa?itᵾ

water, paddle hands in the paruhparᵾ

water lily, plant similar to pa?mutsi

water on, pour payunitᵾ

water, press down with hands to expel mabitsoorᵾ

water, pushed under tohpaaku?netᵾ W

water, rain ᵾmahpaa?

-water-is, *See-***how-deep-the** Paa roponi

water, sink to the bottom in pa?ikarᵾ

water, soak in parᵾkitᵾ

water, soak oneself in naparᵾkitᵾ

water, splash into pakwa?nuarᵾ

water on, splash pakwihtsikᵾrᵾ

water, splash with pawᵾhpa?itᵾ

water, sprayed with pawᵾ?we?niitᵾ

water, spring parᵾtsohpe?

water, strangle on paabitsanitᵾ

Water Horse Band Tasúra

water jug pihpóo?

water lizard pa?boosi?

water moccasin tuhparokoo?

water pump patsahto?i?, patsa?aikᵾ

water something payunitᵾ

water trough puku hibikᵾ?

water well pahorapᵾ

water-filled pa?ibuikatᵾ

watered mabáa?aitᵾ

watermelon ohapi̱, puhi bihnáa?

wave po?hibahpakitᵾ, wᵾhpetsᵾrᵾ

wave hair wesibapi?arᵾ

wax, ear naki̱ oona̱

wax, weed hi?oosanahkòo

way, doing another atapu

way, lose watsitᵾ

way of walking, rocking yᵾ?bana?itᵾ

way, rub the wrong masu?naitᵾ K, masᵾroonitᵾ W

way, that suni

way? how?, what hakaniiku

ways, different seni

ways, various seni

we nᵾnᵾ

weak kenatsᵾwitᵾ, tsihkwinumai

weak person or animal tᵾ?ọnaapᵾ

weakness tᵾ?ọnaa?

wean a baby pitsi makatᵾ

weaned pitsimai

weapon, attempt to hit with a
wᵾsukwarᵾ W

weapon, force to lie down
wielding a wᵾhhabiʔarᵾ

weapon, kill with a wᵾhkuparᵾ,
wᵾhtokweetᵾ

wear a hat tsoʔnikarᵾ

wear out clothes wᵾkwiʔarᵾ

wear out shoes tawiarᵾ W

wear something natsaʔnikarᵾ

wear something around the neck
korohko̱rᵾ

wear something around the waist
kohinehkitᵾ

wear something out wihtoʔarᵾ

wear warm clothing yuʔa
namᵾsoorᵾ

weary wᵾʔtsikwarᵾ

weather, hot ᵾrᵾʔitᵾ

weave tᵾkwᵾsiitᵾ

wedge tᵾroh pakuʔi?

weed, croton kupi̱sinamaya

weed, horse- tosa wahtsuki

weed, loco esinᵾᵾhparabi

weed, mesquite namabitsooni
sonihpᵾ

weed, quinine pohóobi

weed, smart- ekawoni

weed, sneeze- natsaakᵾsi,
tᵾrᵾkwobamᵾ

weed, soap mumutsi?

weed, swamp pakᵾᵾka̱

weed, thorny wokwesonipᵾ

weed wax hiʔoosanahkòo

weeds paʔsonipᵾ

weeds, cut (or grass) soni
wᵾhpomarᵾ

weeping willow yusᵾhᵾbi

weigh something narayaakᵾrᵾ

weight, gain yuhu bᵾhkaitᵾ

well kenamaʔᵾbᵾʔitᵾ, pahorapᵾ,
tsaa

well, live yunᵾmitᵾ, yᵾyᵾkarᵾ

well, oil nabaai tokwaaitᵾ, tukaʔa
nabaa

well, water pahorapᵾ

well behaved yᵾyᵾkarᵾ

well-behaved, be yunᵾmitᵾ

west kahpinakwᵾ, tabeʔikᵾnakwa̱?

west, north- kwihne kahpinakwᵾ

west, south- yuʔa nᵾe kahpi̱nakwᵾ

western ragweed woʔanatsu?

wet patsoʔitᵾ, paʔi̱soketᵾ

wet seat pihpárᵾbᵾʔai

what way? how? hakaniiku

what? hina, hini

what? On hipaʔa

what? on what?, with himakᵾ

(what one is doing), slow down
nᵾnᵾʔitᵾ

what place?, where? hakᵾ̱

wheat tohtía masᵾa?

wheat flour pᵾmata nookoina

wheat plant tohtía sonipᵾ

wheel makwᵾʔnikᵾ̱ W, naʔomo̱

wheel, spoke of naʔomo̱
nasᵾwᵾhki?

wheel, wagon waikina naʔoomo̱

wheel game aratsi?

when? hipe?

where? hakᵾse?

where? what place? hakᵾ̱

whetstone tᵾmakᵾmaʔaai?, tᵾpi
tᵾmatsune?

which?, who? hakarᵾ

which way? where to? hakaapu

while, once in a sᵾsᵾʔana̱

while moving, rope someone or
something kuʔnikakᵾrᵾ

whip kwibukitᵾ, tᵾkwibukiitᵾ

whir kasabipi̱kurᵾ

whisky poʔsa baa

whisper watsih nikwᵾnᵾrᵾ

whisper gossip watsih tekwarᵾ

whistle huukumuyake?,
kusitekwaru, tsuhni muyake?

white tosa-

white, appear to be tosa nabunitu

white, trunk of a putsi waipu

white elm pimoroo?a korohko?

white farmer tutsakwoo raiboo?

white horse tosa?

white man huuyukkwi?, pabo
taiboo?

white man, bearded motso taiboo?

white oak tosa tukanai huupi

white person taiboo?

White-eagle Kwihne tosabitu

white-tailed deer pi?tohtsía? W

who? which? hakaru

-who-are-always-against, Those
Komanche

who betrays, one
kaanatsaka?uhtupu

who gossips, one isanaramu?itu?

who-rides-buffalo, One- Kuhtsunu
kwahipu

-who-stay-downstream, Those
Tinawa

whole keho?yopitu

whom hahka

whoop tsu?tsukitu

whoop, woman's katakakitu W

whooping cough tsuu?tsuki?

why? hakani?yu

Wichita language, speak
tuhka?naai rekwaru

Wichita language, Speakers of
tuhka?naai? niwunu

Wichita people Tuhka?naai?

wick, lamp tuka?a nawanapi

wicked aitu

wide pia wekitu

wide open pia tsatuakatu

wide, open mouth pia kusaru

wide, open something pia tsatuaru

widely piapu

wife kwuhu?, nupetsu?

wife, chief (among multiple
wives) paraiboo?

wife, grandson's (granddaughter
-in-law) tso?apia?

wife, lead away a nupetsu?itu

wig papi tsa?nika?

wigwam mutsikuni

wild puewatsi

wild currant huwabo?kóo?

wild grape mutsi atsamukwe?,
natsamukwe?

wild hyacinth siiko

wild onion kuukanaruhka?, kuuka,
pakuuka, puewatsi kuuka,
tuetutaatu kuuka

wild onion, poisonous
kuhtsutsuu?ni?

wild potato paapasi

wild stallion pua watsi

wild thing, tame a manusu?naru W

wild tuber payaape, tutupitu

wildcat matusohpe?

will suana, tusu?atsipu

willow suhu

willow, black ohasuhuubi

willow, weeping yusuhubi

willow twigs suhu tsitsina?

wilt takwitsoo?nimi?aru

win a prize turahwikatu

win in a contest against someone
tahni?aru

win in a contest by cheating
kaakwakuru

win over someone kwakuru K

wind nuena, nuetu, wuhkwatubi,
wunukutu

Wind Nuena

wind, be carried/blown away by
mabo?ayaru

wind, south yu?anee

wind, summer yu?anee

wind, un- pᵾrᵾsu?arᵾ, tsahkwᵾmarᵾ, tsahkwᵾnunúukitᵾ, wᵾhpᵾkᵾsuarᵾ

wind into a ball wᵾhtopo?nitᵾ

wind instrument, any woinu

wind instrument, play a muuyaketᵾ

wind storm nᵾepi

Wind-running-here Nᵾenuhkiki

windbreak wᵾhturu?aipᵾ

windbreak, make a wᵾhturu?arᵾ

windbreak, natural huukono?itᵾ

windmill patsahto?i?

window nanabuni?

window blind nanabuni tsahpara?

window screen nanabuni saawᵾ?, nasaa?wᵾ? W

windpipe worᵾrokᵾ, wo?rorooki W

wine ekapaa, natsamukwe?a paa

wine, Communion pᵾᵾpi

wing kasa

winged kasakatᵾ

wings, flap kasabipikurᵾ

wink puih tsahtsurᵾ, wᵾhtsobokitᵾ

winnow po?himarᵾ

winter tomoorᵾ, tomopᵾ 2

winter, rain shelter for yu?a ᵾmakᵾni

wintertime kwihne?

wipe matsumarᵾ, tahkwinerᵾ W

wipe away tahtsukitᵾ

wipe, dab to (or erase) tohpᵾsakᵾrᵾ K, tohtsomarᵾ W

wipe feet tasu?netᵾ

wipe off completely wᵾhtsu?marᵾ

wipe off with the hand makwineetᵾ

wipe something off tahtsumarᵾ K

wipe something with the head tsotsomarᵾ

wiping, cloth for tᵾmatsuma? W

wire soni wᵾhtᵾma?

wire, barbed puhihwi tᵾᵾhtᵾma?

wire fence, put up a barbed puhihwi tᵾᵾhtᵾmarᵾ

wire, chicken kokorá?a arᵾhtᵾma?

wire brush puhihwi natsihtu?ye?

wire cutter tᵾkᵾh poma?

wire pincers tᵾkᵾh ka?a?

wisdom tᵾsu?ᵾrᵾ?

wisdom tooth kᵾᵾtsi

wish for nasuyaketᵾ

witch doctor tᵾtsᵾ puha?

(Wichita name for the Comanches of Tejas), Proud People Natai

witchy wᵾtsᵾpai

with a saw, saw something huutsika?arᵾ

with brains, rub kupisi?arᵾ

with each other naha-

with fingers, rip tsahtᵾrᵾ?arᵾ

with fingers, snuff fire W tsahtukarᵾ

with fist or palm of hand, stop hitting tohpᵾarᵾ

with fist, try or want to hit toso?waitᵾ

with foot, rub nara?worᵾ K

with full strength, pull tsahturerᵾ

with something, prick someone piso?arᵾ

with something, puncture oneself nabiso?arᵾ

with something, roll up tohtopo?narᵾ

with sufficient food, satisfied wᵾtsᵾ?mitᵾ

with fringes, shawl na?sᵾkia?

with palm of hand, slap tohpa?itᵾ

with water, splash pawᵾhpa?itᵾ

with water, sprayed pawᵾ?we?niitᵾ

with the foot, tear tasi?kwairᵾ

with the teeth, tear kᵾsi?kwarᵾ

with the hand, touch lightly makwᵾ?netᵾ

with respect, treat pahnaʔaitʉ

with cold, tremble sʉʉtsʉnitʉ

with the mouth, unwrap something kʉhtoʔyarʉ K

with cane, walk natsihtóo noorʉ

with the hand. wipe off makwineetʉ

with the head, wipe something tsotsomarʉ

with hands, wring out tsahpitsoorʉ

with or on someone or something maa

with what? on what? himakʉ

wither kʉhtakwitsooʔnitʉ W, takwitsooʔnimiʔarʉ

wolf kʉʔtseena, pia tseenaʔ, tuhtseenaʔ

Wolf-drinking Esahibi

wolf-howl, Echo-of-the- Isananakaʔ

woman, elderly hʉbi tsiitsiʔ, pʉetʉpʉ

woman, menopausal tsihhabʉhkamapʉ

woman, middle-aged hʉbi

woman, working tʉrʉʔai waipʉ

woman, young naiʔbi

woman's agnatic grandchild huutsi̱

woman's breast pitsiiʔ

woman's brother's child pahaʔ

woman's female kinsman waʔihpʉʔ

woman's purse puhihwi wosa K

woman's uterine grandchild kakuʔ

woman's whoop katakakitʉ W

women nanawaʔihpʉʔanii

women along, take notsaʔkaarʉ

womenfolk nanawaʔihpʉʔanʉ W

wonder at suyoroʔarʉ

wonderful nanaarʉʉmoa, nani̱suwʉ̱kaitʉ, suyoroʔakapʉ

wood hu-, huu-, wobi, woobi̱

wood, bois d'arc etʉhuupi

wood, chisel tohtsiʔarʉ K

wood, cotton- soho obi̱, tahpookʉʔ, weʔyʉkʉ sohoobi K

wood for archery bows (bois d'arc) eetʉ

wood ant tuʔanikuuraʔ

wood plane huusibeʔ

wood shaving wʉsibepʉ

wood shavings kunapi̱soʔni̱

woodchuck huunaʔ, paʔarai moʔo

wooden bench huunakarʉʔ, wobi nakarʉʔ

wooden chair wobi nakarʉʔ

wooden comb huunatsihtuʔye?

wooden drum wobi wʉhpai K

wooden mallet huutʉrohpakoʔiʔi

wooden pestle tʉrayuʔne?

wooden vessel huu aawo

woodpecker pitʉ̱sʉ nuʔye? W, wobi tohtaraki̱ K, wʉpʉ̱koiʔ

woods huukabatʉ̱, soo huuhpi̱

word tekwapʉ

word on, pass nimʉʉmiʔarʉ W

word to someone to return, send nʉníhkoonirʉ

work tʉrʉʔaipʉʔ

work, do tʉrʉʔaitʉ

work someone to death namakupakʉrʉ

work-type handkerchief pʉesúubeʔ K

worked to death namakupʉ̱katʉ̱

working woman tʉrʉʔai waipʉ

workman tʉrʉʔai wapi̱

worm woʔaabi̱

wormwood (silvery) pasiwona pʉhʉbi

wormwood, silvery pasiwona pʉhʉbi

wormy woʔa-

worn out wihtoʔaitʉ

wornout napatawi?aitɨ
-worn-out, Salt- Onawai
worried tsamʉsasuakatɨ
worry musasuarɨ, pisukwitarɨ
worry, caused to tsamʉsasuakatɨ
worse nahaya?ni
worse!, It is namanoke
worse, much nasu?ana
worthy, un- tɨtaatɨ
wound ɨ?a?
wound, cut someone to tsahki?aitɨ
wound, foot narahki?apɨ
wound oneself natsahki?arɨ
wounded person kwɨhti?
wrap namakwatubiitɨ, wɨhkwatubi
wrap, un- mahkwɨmarɨ, tsahkwɨmarɨ
wrap an object, un- tsahpeko?arɨ
wrap something, un- tahkwɨmarɨ
wrap something with the mouth, un- kɨhto?yarɨ K
wrap around wɨhkwitunarɨ
wrap around and around nɨɨhkwitubitɨ
wrap up tɨmakwatubi?etarɨ, wɨhkwitunarɨ
wrapped and tied up nɨɨhtami?itɨ
wrapper plant, cigarette- tɨmakwatui?
wrappers for cigarettes, leaf puhi tɨmakwatubi?
wren pasahòo
wrestle narohparɨ
wriggle pɨhkwinu?itɨ W
wring out with hands tsahpitsoorɨ
wrinkle kuhtakwitsoo?nitɨ W
wrinkle something takwikakwo?arɨ
-wrinkled, Skinny-and Tekwitsi M
wrinkled, straighten something tahtunaabarɨ
wrinkled all over takwikakwo?apɨ
wrist ma?wiitsa̱

wrist, lose something from hand or ma?kwe?yarɨ
wristwatch tabe-
write tɨboorɨ
wrong nɨnɨmɨni̱ tɨhtsɨ
wrong one atɨrɨ
wrong way, rub the masu?naitɨ K, masɨroonitɨ W
wry face, make a sɨkɨbuninitɨ

Y y

Yap-eaters Yapai tɨhka
yard, lumber- huunarɨmɨɨ?, wobi narɨmɨ̱?
yarn aawɨ́ɨtama?, tɨɨhtama?
yaupon holly ekapokopi
yawn ɨhtamakɨ?atɨ
year toh-, tomopɨ, tomopɨ̱
-year-old, two wahatomopɨ̱ K
-year-old item, two tomohtoopɨ̱ W
years ago, many soo be?sɨ
years old, two tomohtootɨ W
yell waa?akitɨ
yell noisily hubiyaarɨ
yelling, make noise hubiyairɨ
yellow ohapi̱
yellow color oha-
yellow fever ohakuhtsɨni
yellow jacket otɨ̱ peena
yellow lotus kɨrɨ?atsi̱
yellow pond lily kɨriata
Yellow-back Ohapi̱tɨ kwahi
Yellow-bear Ohawasápe
Yellow-steps Ohawɨnɨ
yes haa, tsuh
yesterday kɨtu
yet ɨkɨsɨ
yolk, egg noyo?na ohapi̱yuna
you mɨi, mɨmi, mɨnɨ̱, si?ana
you, thank ahó, ɨra

you, to ʉnʉ
you two mʉkwʉ̱
you two, of mʉhʉ
young pʉesúube? W, ʉkʉ-, ʉkʉbitsi̱,
ʉkʉnanakatʉ̱
young catfish tuume?so̱
young man tuibihtsi?
young unmarried man wohka?ni?
young woman nai?bi
younger brother tami?
younger generation ʉkʉ nʉmʉnʉʉ
younger sister nami?
younger than inaarʉ

youngest generation ʉkʉ nʉmʉ
roopʉnʉ̱ K
your mʉmʉ, mʉʉ, mʉʉ
youth, songs of wʉyakeetʉ̱ W
youthful ʉkʉnanakatʉ̱
yucca mumutsi?

Z z

zebra naboohmura?
zigzag wakʉ?wʉtʉ̱
zipper natsakwʉ̱sa?

Part III

Comanche Grammar

Comanche Grammar

The format for the following description of the Comanche language conforms in broad outline to that used by Langacker in his *Overview of Uto-Aztecan Grammar* (1977). Comanche did not play a role in the workshop leading to the series *Studies in Uto-Aztecan Grammar,* of which Langacker's work was the first volume, nor is the present grammar sketch a part of that series. Nevertheless, it was felt that the sketch could have the most value, particularly to those already familiar with the structure of another Uto-Aztecan language and the series referred to above, if Langacker's descriptive framework were adopted in large part. Our debt to him will be obvious to all those who know his work.

Choice of orthography has been influenced by the fact that the majority of Comanches are readers and speakers of English as a first language. This is due, of course, to government policy and not to personal choice, as the Comanche language was not taught in the schools and, in fact, children were not allowed to speak Comanche in school. Thus, the majority of Comanches today are not fluent in the Comanche language.

Many of the changes in the Comanche language in the past thirty years are due to the influence of English, since Comanche children have studied English exclusively in public schools or Indian schools. One way the English influence shows up is in loanwords. Aside from English, there are various loanwords from Spanish, Kiowa, and Siouan.

Some examples of loanwords are listed in (1).

(1)　　*waraatsi*　　from Spanish *huarache* 'sandal', with wider meaning 'shoe'
　　　　papaasi　　from Spanish *papa* 'potato'
　　　　hooki　　　from English 'hog'

waikina	from English 'wagon'
kabitsị	from English 'cabbage'
haa	from Kiowa and Chiwere 'yes'
ahó	from Kiowa and Chiwere 'hello; thanks'

Comanche had contact with Spanish both in the United States and from early raids into Mexico, bringing back Mexican captives who became integrated into tribal life. This contact brought loanwords chiefly in reference to material culture, fauna, and flora. In Oklahoma, aside from English, closest contact seems to have been with the Kiowa and the Siouan (Chiwere), from which more words have been borrowed than from other languages.

1

Phonology

Given the various audiences for whom this work is intended, some compromise on notation had to be reached. The orthography used in both the dictionary and the grammar reflects actual pronunciation fairly closely, but the grammar reflects the abstract phonological analysis given in (2). Where the underlying phonological form of a particular grammatical morpheme differs from the surface form cited in example sentences, the underlying form is often presented in the text set off by diagonals.

(2)		bilabial	dental	palatal	velar	rounded velar	glottal
	stop	p	t, c		k	kw	?
	fricative		s				
	nasal	m	n				
	glide			y		w	H, h
	vowel			i	ʉ	u	
				e	a	o	

This is not the place for an exhaustive treatment of Comanche phonology. We briefly describe some major aspects of pronunciation having to do with consonants, vowels, and stress.

1.1. Consonants. Given the English-language background of most Comanche readers, and in conformity with Canonge's *Comanche Texts*, source of most of our illustrative examples, we treat /c/ and /kʷ/ as clusters /ts/ and /kw/, respectively. Our orthography does not reflect the fact that /y/ is often pronounced as **[dž]** (*ma yaa* **[ma džaa]** 'takes it') nor that /kw/ is often voiced *nʉ kwʉhʉ* (**[nʉ gwʉhʉ]** 'my wife'). We do not write the predictable glottal stop ʔ at the begining of vowel-initial words such as *okwe* **[ʔokwe]** 'to flow', but we do write it within a word, as in *sʉmʉʔokwe* 'to flow completely'.

Comanche exhibits a pattern of consonant gradations brought about by important processes affecting stops whenever they are within a breathgroup (i.e., not preceded by a pause), and a pattern of metathesis.

Spirantization. When preceded by a vowel, /p/ is a voiced bilabial fricative *b* **[ƀ]** : *pabiʔ* **[paƀiʔ]** 'brother', but *nʉ babiʔ* **[nʉ ƀabiʔ]** 'my brother'. Similarly, /t/ is a voiced tap *r* **[r]** , but only when preceded by one of the nonfront vowels /ʉ u a o/: *toyabi* 'mountain', *nʉ royabi* 'my mountain', but *esitoyabi* 'grey mountain'. An intervening /h/ or /ʔ/ does not block spirantization of either /p/ or /t/: *puibaʔa* 'on the eye' (/**puih**/ 'eye'), *tuaʔbaʔa'on* the son', *tuaʔruhka* 'under the son' (but *puituhka* 'under the eye').

Preaspiration. If /H/ precedes a stop, spirantization does not occur and /H/ surfaces as **[h]** , i.e. preaspiration of the stop. Consider the instrumental prefix /wʉH/ 'with body, sideways': *wʉhpitʉ* 'to reach a destination', *wʉhtokwe'to* kill with a weapon', *wʉhtsitoʔa* 'to peel', *wʉhkoba* 'to break'. If /H/ occurs in any other context, it has no surface manifestation or effect: *wʉsiboʔa* 'to shave off', *wʉnʉʔyʉʔi* 'to make a heavy noise, thud', *wʉhabi* 'to march in formation', *wʉʔani* 'to chop down'. /H/ also fails to surface if the following syllable has an organic voiceless vowel (§1.2): *nanaHkwʉhʉ* → *nanakwʉhʉ* 'married couple'.

Nasalization. Historically, Comanche exhibited a process similar to preaspiration, but involving nasals rather than surface *h*. As currently spoken, the language does not retain syllable-final surface nasals, but /n/ is still systematically present, in that it blocks spirantization before being deleted: *ʉn panpi* → *ʉ papi* 'your head'.

Metathesis. A fairly regular process permutes the sequence cV1hV2 to hCV1V2, where c is voiced. The process applies only sporadically if c is voiceless. If the two vowels are identical, they merge as a single short vowel. Metathesis is most common in pronominal forms such as *otʉnhʉh* → *oruhʉ* → *ohrʉ* 'they (dual)', but is also seen elsewhere: *naniha* → *nahnia* 'name', *tsaHwihi* → *tsahwi* 'to open, turn over'.

Historically, all stops were voiceless and unaspirated, aside from preaspiration as indicated by *h*. As early as the forties, and probably before, some speakers had aspirated stops arising through loss of voiceless vowels (§1.2). Thus, older *nʉnʉpʉhi* 'midget', elicited by Canonge in the Yapai area, is some thirty years later given as *nʉnʉpʰi* in the Kwahare-speaking area around

Cache. Similarly, *pitsipᵾha* 'milk (A)' is replaced by *pitsipʰa*. Historical change has also affected preconsonantal *ʔ* and *h*, which many speakers omit. In place of preaspiration, a long vowel is found (*aakaaʔ* for *ahkaaʔ* 'devil's horn'), or preaspiration is used in free variation with the long vowel.

1.2. Vowels. The distinction between vowels such as /a/ vs. /ᵾ/ and /o/: vs. /u/ is often reduced or lost phonetically. The details vary between dialects, but careful pronunciation of the deictic roots with distance ranking *(i, o, ᵾ)*, for example, preserves the systematic distinction in many pronouns, demonstratives, and adverbials.[1]

Many occurrences of the vowel *e* derive historically from the cluster ai as seen by comparison with Shoshone cognates: SH *ekon* 'tongue', C *eko*, SH *enka* 'red, C *eka;* but SH *aisen* 'gray', C *esi*.[2] Morphophonemic changes in certain forms also give rise to *e,* as in the postpositions *waka* 'toward' and *wahketᵾ* 'away from'. The two forms *ai* and *e* cannot be used interchangeably in Comanche since they stand in contrast in certain forms: *aiʔmiʔa'to* lope, trot (SG SUBJ)', *eʔmᵾa* 'be without self-dignity, crazy'; *aitᵾ* 'bad, wicked', *etᵾ'bow,* gun', *etᵾᵾ* 'those scattered'.

Aside from such matters, the major processes affecting vowels are devoicing and lengthening. There are two forms of devoicing, so-called organic and inorganic.

Organic devoicing. Phonemic /s/ and /h/ always devoice a preceding unstressed short vowel that is not part of a cluster: *sitᵾsuʔa* 'this one also', *wanaʔᵾhᵾ* 'cloth blanket', but *sitᵾᵾsuʔa* 'these ones also', *tᵾasᵾ* 'and, again, also'. Vowel quality other than voicing is generally preserved, except that voiceless a shifts to ᵾ unless a glottal stop *ʔ* precedes it: *miʔahtsi → miʔatsi* 'having gone', but *kimahtsi → kimᵾtsi* 'having come'. As these examples also show, consonant deletion (§1.1) removes /h/ except before a vowel, so that the conditioning factor for organic devoicing is often not apparent. Two adjacent syllables cannot both have organic voiceless vowels. In such a situation the second vowel does not devoice: *nakihkah → nakika* 'at the ear'. Note that preaspiration /H/ does not induce devoicing: *nanaHtena → nanahtena* 'male kinsmen'.

---

[1]See Wistrand Robinson (1989) for the corresponding Cashibo set and discussion relating Pano-Tacanan to Uto-Aztecan. An example of the phonetic overlap of /u/ and /o/ can be seen in the prefixes *koh-* and *kuh-,* both meaning 'of fire, by means of fire'. The unstressed form preceding a stressed, stem-initial syllable is *koh-,* while the stressed form is *kuh. koh-to* 'to build a fire', *koh-tsáaʔ* 'cooked or stewed food', *kuh-te* 'chop firewood', *kuh-kwarᵾki* 'take a steam bath'. Unstressed *koh* 'by fire' must be distinguished from *koh* 'break, broken', of different origin.

[2]Shoshone forms are retranscribed from Miller 1972:105.

Inorganic devoicing. A short vowel that is not part of a cluster is optionally devoiced at the end of a breath group. Vowel quality other than voicing is generally preserved and a preceding preconsonantal /H/ is not deleted: *kasa̱* 'wing', *tunehtsu̱* 'to run', *uhtu̱* 'to give'. Inorganic devoicing may apply even if the preceding vowel has undergone organic devoicing *pitsipu̱ha̱* 'milk (A)', *pu̱etsu̱ku̱* 'in the morning'. An inorganic voiceless vowel conditions optional lengthening of a voiced penultimate vowel if there is no intervening /H/: *kaasa̱* 'wing', *oomo̱* 'leg'.

1.3. Stress rules. Comanche has alternating stress according to the number of syllables in a word or compound. Monosyllabic words are without stress or pitch; others have stress on the first or second syllable. Normal initial stress is on the first syllable of a two-syllable word. Acute accent will be used here for primary stress; grave accent for secondary stress. A preconsonant aspirate (h) or glottal (?) usually groups in the syllable with its respective consonant, but it may at times phonologically group with the vowel preceding it.

(3)   *kú.ʔè*   'top'   *pí.ʔtò*   'bob-tailed'
       tó.sà   'white'   *ká.hpè*   'bed'
       tó.sàʔ   'white horse'   *tá.ʔòoʔ*   'dried meat'
       wí.hnù   'then'   *sú.nì*   'that way'

The compound-forming, proclitic form of a noun is basic, having a short vowel. The first vowel of an isolation or citation form of a noun is often lengthened under primary stress and the vowel of the second syllable is voiceless, which is to say, it often undergoes inorganic devoicing.

(4)   *wapi-*   *wáapi̱*   'cedar'
       awo-   *áawo̱*   'cup'
       tama-   *táama̱*   'tooth'

Possessive pronouns, which serve as phonological proclitics to the noun, do not change root or stem-initial stress. These are seen especially with nouns which require possessive pronouns such as body parts and kinship terms.

(5)   *u̱ + náki̱*   'your ear'   *nu̱ + námi*   'my sister'
       u̱ + púi   'your eye'

Diphthongs *ai, oi,* and *ui* act as one vowel with one mora of time.

(6)   *nái.ʔbì*   'young woman'   *wói.nù*   'bugle, music'
       ái.tu̱ì   'bad'   *púi.ku̱.sò*   'chigger'

Initial stress falls on the first syllable of three-syllable words; normal secondary stress falls on the third syllable.

(7)   *tá.pi̯.kò?*   'heel' (of foot)   *ná.kwʉ.sì?*   'pumpkin'
      tú.hʉ.bʉ̀ì   'hide, raw skin'   *má.kwʉ.sà?*   'sleeve'

In three-syllable words which are two-syllable words with an added prefix or suffix, the second syllable does not become voiceless, or may be voiceless if the main stress moves to the second noun of a compound noun.

(8)   *tá.si + ?à*   'smallpox, freckles'   *pù + sí + ?à*   'head louse'
      pò + sáa.ki   'bridge'   *à.ma + wóo*   'apple'
      àa.ta + kîi   'grasshopper'   *tù.nʉ + háa*   'cymopterus plant'

Words of four, five, and six syllables have normal alternating stress when nouns of a compound are coequal, or the root or stem has a one-syllable suffix. Examples with four syllables are:

(9)   *á.ni.mùi*   'housefly'   *á.ta + bì.tsi̱*   'foreigner'
      yú.pu.sì.a   'louse'   *ná.na + bù.ni*   'window'
      wʉh + tú.pʉ.kà?   'buckle, button'   *tʉ̀ì .rʉ + è + tʉ*   'child'

Words or compounds of five syllables also have primary stress on the first syllable and secondary stress on the third syllable.

(10)   *ká.wo + nò.ka.tʉ*   'street'   *nó.hi + tʉ̀ì .e tʉ*   'doll'
      ná.tsa + mù.kwe?   'grapes'   *só.ni + nà.rʉ.so?*   'towsack'

Words or compounds of six syllables have primary stress on the first and secondary stress on the fourth syllable.

(11)   *kú. ?i.na.kʉ̀ì .?e.tʉ*   'roasts for'
      ná.ro.htsa.nì. ?i.ku   'as hanging'
      tʉ̀ì .kwʉ.sʉ kʉ̀ì .e.yu   'cooks on coals for'
      ná.mʉ.so.hì.htsi   'hurrying up'

Again, a prefix or enclitic which is not stem-changing does not receive initial stress, so that the alternating stress begins on the second syllable as in the following words of six syllables, following the pattern of five-syllable words:

(12)   *wʉ.hká. ?a.mì. ?a.nu̱*   'went to cut down'
      wʉ.sú.wa.rʉ̀ì .ki.nu̱   'began to miss'

When a form may seem to have stress on the third syllable, as marked in Canonge's Comanche Texts, what is marked as primary stress (apparently) is secondary stress, except in cases when both a proclitic and prefix are used.

(13) *kú.tsi̠.tò.na.nu̠*   'set on fire'
      há.b̠i̠ + *hu.pí̠i.tu̠*   'stopped and lay down'
      ká.ru̠ + *hu.pí̠i.tu̠*   'stopped and sat'
      wà.ka + *ré?ee?*   'turtle'

A three-syllable word with an added one-syllable suffix or enclitic retains the stress form of the main word, in spite of the added fourth syllable.

(14) *tsú.hnì.pu̠* + ha   'bone (A)'
      káa.be.hkà + nu̠   'cheated'
      tú.ne.htsù + nu̠   'ran'

In narratives, verbs often exhibit stylistic stress shift when occurring at the end of a breath group. Stress moves one syllable to the right if that syllable is voiced; otherwise, it skips over the voiceless vowel to the next syllable.

(15) *pohpínu̠*   'jumped'   *noru̠náku̠nu̠*   'made a bed'
      tu̠hká?eeyu̠   'would eat'   *tsatu̠wánu̠*   'opened'

2

The Simple Sentence

Here and in following sections, the syntax of the various forms of simple
sentences is discussed, with chief divisions according to mood—declarative
mood, interrogative mood, imperative mood, and their corresponding subdi-
visions. Other types of modality and nondistinct argument phenomena follow.
First, however, a few comments concerning interjections and other discourse
phenomena need to be made.

An interjection may stand alone or occur preceding a sentence. A number
of common interjections are listed in (16) and an interjection with following
sentence is illustrated in (17).

(16)   *aahe*   'I claim it!'   *yaa*   'oh' (used by women)
        ahó   'thank you'   *yee*   'oh no!' (disapproval by
        ai   'I'm disgusted'   men)
        anáa   'ouch! (physical pain)'   *ʉbiaʻ*   oh; oh, my!' (surprise by
        haa   'yes'   women)
        haʔii   'oh, my!'   *ʉra*   'thank you'
        kee   'no'   *ʉrʉʉ*   'ouch!' (It burns!)

(17)   haa   tsaatɨ   uʔ
       yes   good^NOM   D4NS[3]
       Yes, it is good.   (78:13)[4]

An extended treatment of Comanche discourse phenomena is beyond the
scope of this sketch, but a few morphemes which function at the highest levels
of narrative form are introduced in this section.

The quotative morpheme *tɨa* occurs in the initial sentence of all but three
of the narratives in *Comanche Texts*. It can be translated 'they say, it is said',
or more colloquially 'the story goes'. The following sentences illustrate its use.

(18)   soobeʔsɨ   -kɨtsaʔ   rɨa   kuyunɨiʔ-nɨɨ   bisikwanúuʔi-bɨnɨ
       much^MEAS   EVID-DECL QUOT   turkey-Np   slide-AUG
       Long ago, they say, (some) turkeys were doing a lot of sliding.   (5:1)

(19)   soobeʔsɨ   nɨnɨ   tɨa   tɨ-híma-ʔee-yu
       much^MEAS   1xNp   QUOT   food-take-REP-DUR
       Long ago, they say, we would get rations.   (129:1)

Another quotative morpheme, *me(h),* marks embedded direct discourse introduced by a verb of saying or thinking (which may be covert). It appears in
final position as meh; elsewhere as me.

(20)   surɨ -kɨ-seʔ   wihnu   tanɨ   hakanih-ku ma   hanɨ me   yɨkwii-yu
       D4   EVID-CTR then   1piN   how-A   D2A do   QUOT say-DUR
       Then that one said, "What shall we do with him?"   (6:19)

(21)   surɨ   -kɨ-seʔ   anáa   meh
       D4   EVID-CTR   ouch!   QUOT
       That one said, "Ouch!"   (6:13)

---

[3]The rich deictic system of Comanche which underlies pronouns and demonstrative
adjectives is presented in detail in §12.1. Note here, however, that four degrees of
distance from the place of the speech act are abbreviated in illustrations by D1, D2,
D3, and D4, respectively, and that plural referents may be designated as D5 to denote
that they are in some respect scattered. Pronouns and adjectives may be further
marked for case as nominative (N), genitive (G), accusative (A), locative (L), or manner
(M), and for number as singular (S) or plural (P).

[4]In examples, references are to page and sentence number in *Canonge's Comanche
Texts* unless otherwise noted. Examples given without references are from Comanche-
speaking consultants.

Enclitic *kɨ-kɨ* is an evidential, which indicates remote past or speaker un-involvement. Given these conditions, its occurrence is obligatory in second position for the initial sentence of each successive paragraph of a discourse. Another narrative enclitic, *-seʔ*, marks successive paragraphs of a discourse, again occurring in second position and following *-kɨ* if that is also present. See *Comanche Texts* for extensive use of these morphemes in context. They occur in sentences (20) and (21) and in many other sentences throughout this sketch.

The temporal conjunctions *wihnu* 'then' and *subeʔ* 'then' reinforce the temporal relationship between a prior event and a subsequent one, as in (22) and (23).

(22)   *setɨ -seʔ   nɨɨmɨ   suhka tabeni ukɨhu   sɨmɨ-no-kima-ʔe-tɨ*
           D5   CTR   Comanche D4As   day   D4ˆatˆto all-haul-come-REP-PROG

              no-bitɨ-ʔee-yɨ   *wihnu*   *tɨeh-buha-rabeni*   *pɨetsɨku-sɨ*
              haul-arrive-REP-DUR   then   small-power-day   agoˆA-INTENS

              tɨ-hima-ʔee-yɨ
              foodˆtake-REP-DUR
              That day various Comanches, having moved there would camp and then early Saturday morning (they) would get rations.   (129:5, 6)

(23)   *mia-ruʔ   nɨʔ me   yɨkwii-yɨ surɨ   -kɨ-seʔ   wihnu*
           goˆUNR   1xNs QUOT   say-DUR   D4   EVID-CTR   then

              hunuʔbɨ-hoi-ki̠   nuhkí-nɨ̠
              creek-around-at   run-PST
              "I will go," (he) said. Then he ran off around the creek.   (6:22, 23)

The adverb *siʔanetɨ* 'at this place' functions equally as a locative and a temporal adverb. In narrative it might be translated as 'at this point' or 'meanwhile at another location', indicating a change in location or scenery, depending upon whether reference to time or location is intended. In (24), this adverb marks a change back to an earlier scene.

(24)   *sitɨ -kɨ-seʔ   u   kumahpɨʔ siʔane-tɨ uhri   kuhíya-miʔa-nɨ̠*
           D1   EVID-CTR   D4G husband   D1L-from   D4Ad   spy-go-PST
           At this point, her husband went to spy on them.   (105:22)

Note that the usual position for these elements is after the first major constituent of a clause following the modal enclitic, although they occasionally occur between a demonstrative and the rest of a subject.

(25)   *suru*   *-ku̯-se?*   *si?ane-tu̯*   *oha?ahnakatu̯*   *nuhkí-nu̯*
        D4   EVID-CTR   D1L-from   coyote   run-PST
        At this point, coyote ran away.   (23:31)

2.1. The declarative mood. The second-position enclitic -tsa? marks declarative sentences in conversational speech and sets the dramatis personae on stage in narrative structure. In this manner, the mood is made explicit to begin narrative. In subsequent narrative clauses, mood is not explicitly marked until a change of mood is made.

(26)   *nai?-bi*   *-tsa?*   *ubitu̯ku̯u̯-tu̯*
        girl-ABS   DECL   flirt-PROG
        The girl is flirting with him.

If the evidential *-ku̯* (remote past) occurs with *-tsa?* (declarative), the evidential precedes the declarative morpheme, as in (27).

(27)   *su̯mu̯-?* *-ku̯-tsa?*   *raiboo?*   *waahpi-hta*   *wu̯hká?a-mi?a-nu̯*
        one-NS   EVID-DECL   white^man   cedar-A   chop-go-PST
        A white man went to chop down a cedar tree.   (27:1)

2.2. Nonverbal sentences. The basic, or neutral, word order for sentences which predicate prototypically nonverbal notions by means of a predicate nominal or predicate adjective is S (MODAL) P,[5] with the modal being enclitic to the subject noun phrase.

(28)   *i*   *-tsa?*   *nu̯*   *kahni*
        D1   DECL   1xG   house
        This is my home.   (38:22)

(29)   *u̯*   *tua?-nu̯u̯*   *-tsa?*   *tahu̯*   *haitsi̱-nu̯u̯*
        2sG   son-NP   DECL   1diG   friend-Np
        Your sons are our friends.   (Canonge 1949)

(30)   *nu̯*   *kwu̯hu̯* *-tsa?*   *ke-sua-tu̯*
        1xG   wife   DECL   NEG-want-NOM
        My wife is mean.   (38:23)

---

[5]Where P stands for PREDICATE.

(31)   *i*   *-tsa?*   *pɨeh-tɨ-pɨ*
         D1   DECL   ago-NOM-ABS
         She is elderly.

There are a number of BE-verbs in Comanche, but these occur in contexts other than simple nonverbal sentences, primarily with intransitive verbs such as *naahka* 'live, become', *karɨ'sit,* live', *wɨnɨ* 'stand', and *habi* 'lie'.

2.3. Intransitive sentences. The basic, or neutral, word order for intransitive sentences is S (MODAL) V. Verbs of this intransitive type take full tense/aspect suffixation.

(32)   *itɨ*   *-tsa?*   *tahɨ*   *napɨhu*   *ɨkɨsɨ*   *kima-rɨ-tuku*
         D1   DECL   1diG   trail   still   come-PROG-same
         This one is still coming on our trail.   (42:21)

(33)   *surɨɨ*   *tɨkɨ-tsi*   *yuu-?ɨh-kooi-nɨ*
         D4Np   eat-SS   quiet-eye-die-PST
         Having eaten, they slept unconcerned.   (8:46)

(34)   *ibu*   *nɨ?*   *mia-ru?i̠*
         D1DIR   1xNs   go-UNR
         I will go this way.   (43:24)

(35)   *wahah-tɨ-kwɨ̠*   *wasáasi?-tena-nɨ-kwɨ̠*   *nɨ-waka*   *bitɨ-?i̠*
         two-NOM-d   Osage-man-NOM-d   1xA-toward   arrive-REAL
         Two Osage men arrived by me.   (105:21)

2.4. Transitive sentences. The basic, or neutral, word order for transitive sentences in full form, where new information is being introduced, is S (MODAL) O V. Full forms of tense/aspect are used with the verb.

(36)   *surɨɨ*   *-se?*   *hani-bi-hta*   *tɨ-rɨni?i-nɨ̠*
         D4Np   CTR   corn-ABS-A   INDEF-putˆaway-PST
         They planted corn.

Various temporal, locative, or other adverbial elements may also occur, normally falling after the S, although only a limited number of grammatical elements may fall between the subject and the verb.

(37) | *situkwu* | *wihnu* | *puhu* | *ina-na* | *maruka-nu* |
|---|---|---|---|---|
| D1Nd | then | COGd | jerk-NOM | finish-PST |

Then these two finished their jerking. (112:24)

(38) | *situkwu* | *si-hkutu* | *puhu* | *kahni-ku-hu* | *nuraa-nu* |
|---|---|---|---|---|
| D1Nd | D1-toˆfrom | COGD | house-at-to | run-PST |

These two ran from here to their house. (116:13)

(39) | *situ* | *-ku-se?* | *pu* | *paka-maku* | *tsah-tunehtsu-nu* |
|---|---|---|---|---|
| D1 | EVID-CTR | COGS | arrow-onˆA | INSTR-run-PST |

He stretched (it) with his arrow. (100:15)

Accusative pronouns precede verbs as proclitics. An indirect object follows a direct object, in the order S O IO V.

(40) | *situu* | *kwasinaboo?-nuu* | *ma* | *ma-nuki-ku-nu* |
|---|---|---|---|
| D1Np | snake-Np | D2A | INDEF-run-CAUS-PST |

These snakes chased her. (52:21)

(41) | *maruu* | *nanah-tena-nuu* | *-ku-se?* | *tai* | *makaa-ka* | *me* | *urii* |
|---|---|---|---|---|---|---|
| D2Gp | RECIP-man-Np | EVID-CTR | 1iAp | feed-!p | QUOT | D4Ap |

niikwii-yu
say-DUR

Their menfolk said to them, "Feed us." (128:16)

Simple, nonemphatic subject pronouns, without added enclitics, are themselves enclitic. They regularly move out of first position and into the sentence to the right of the second constituent, with which they are pronounced as one word. This second constituent may be as small as a word or as large as an entire phrase.

(42) | *noha* | *u?* | *nu* | *kwuhuru?i* |
|---|---|---|---|
| nearly | D4Ns | 1xA | catchˆUNR |

He nearly caught me. (105:28)

(43) | *soobe?su* | *nunu* | *tua* | *tu-híma-?ee-yu* |
|---|---|---|---|
| longˆago | 1xNp | QUOT f | ood-take-REP-DUR |

Long ago, they say, we would get rations. (129:1)

(44) | *waikinu-ba?a* | *-ku* | *urukwu* | *mi?a-?i* |
|---|---|---|---|
| wagon-on | EVID | D4Nd | go-REAL |

They went by wagon. (115:2)

(45)   *wasápe?-a*   *kobe*   *nʉ?*   *puni-tu?i*
       bear-G   face   1xNs   see-UNR
       I'll see the bear's face.

Note that if the verb is in second postion with no other grammatical element intervening, the subject when moved is in sentence-final position.

(46)   *mia-ru?i*   *nʉ?*
       go-UNR   1xNs
       I'll go.   (96:20)

Because a pronoun object is a proclitic on the verb, these two elements cannot be separated by moving a subject pronoun into second position. Hence, the verb ends up out of final position, with the order O V S.

(47)   *ma*   *buni-tu?i*   *nʉ?*
       D2A   see-UNR   1xNs
       I will see it.

(48)   *tai*   *wʉh-tokwʉ-ki-tʉ*   *ma?*
       1iAp   INSTR-club-come-PROG   D2Ns
       He is coming clubbing us.   (4:15)

Movement of subject pronouns rightward into the sentence imparts no special significance semantically. However, movement of some constituent leftward into initial position is a syntactic means of emphasizing that constituent. The sentence topic can be shifted to make it more prominent. Indirect object is brought into focus in (49).

(49)   *pʉʉ*   *kah-tʉi i?-nii*   *surʉ*   *u*   *kwʉhʉ*   *ke*   *u*   *pitʉ-na*
       COGp   house-friend-Ap   D4Np   D4G   wife   NEG   D4G   arrive-NOM

       narʉmu?i-kʉ–nʉ
       tell-CAUS-PST
       His wife told their neighbors of his not having arrived.   (28:13)

In (50), the manner constituent is brought into focus.

(50)   *sunih-ku*   *surʉʉ*   *usúni*   *hani-mia-?ee-yʉ*
       D4M-A   D4N   always   do-go-REP-DUR
       They always go on doing like that.   (130:14)

There is also a type of postposing, involving either an object or an adverbial element as complement of a verb of motion. This takes place either because the two positions preceding the verb are occupied by other grammatical material, to make a verb more prominent, or to lend definiteness to an object.

(51) *situkwu*   *-ku-se?*   *si?ane-tu*   *mi?a-nu*   *puu*   *kahni-ku-hu*
      D1Nd   EVID-CTR   D1L-from   go-PST   COGp   house-at-to
      These two, at this point, went to their house.   (125:12)

2.5. HAVE **sentences.** Although there is no independent verb meaning 'have', there are two verbalizing suffixes that express this meaning (§8.2).

(52) *suhka*   *na-hnía-ba-?i*   *toya-ma*   *karuu-ri*
      D4As   REFL-name-have-REAL   mountain-on   sit-PROG^A
      (He) had that name, Sits-on-mountain.   (72:35)

2.6. DO sentences. DO sentences are of four types. The most neutral of the verbs in this semantic range is *muu* 'do, treat (someone), work (something)'. It is used in a generic and referential sense, referring to actions named more specifically in prior discourse, or understood in context.

(53) *suru*   *-ku-se?*   *wihnu*   *suni*   *uhka*   *bui*   *-hka*   *mia-ru?i*
      D4   EVID-CTR   then   D4M   D4As   COAp   do-DS   go-UNR

         nu?   *me*   *yukwii-yu*
         1xNs   QUOT   say-DUR
      When they had done thus to him, that one said, "I'll go."   (6:22)

The suffix *-?ai* 'do, make, create' forms numerous verbs from noun stems.

(54) *nah*   *ranu*   *ke*   *kahni-?ai-wa?i-tu-u*
      just   1iNp   NEG   house-make-UNR-PROG-P
      Let's just not make a house.   (111:3)

Other examples of this form are *isa?ai* 'tell a lie', *pu?e?ai* 'make an agreement', *huba?ai* 'make coffee', and *puha?ai* 'prepare medicine'.

Two additional verbs expressing 'do' are *naha* 'happen, continue' and *naahka* 'continue, become'.

(55) hakani   ʉnʉ   nahá-nʉ
      how?   2Ns   happen-PST
      What happened to you?   (6:14)

(56) suni -kʉ-seʔ   urii   naha-miʔa-ku   ata-bitsi-nʉʉ   urʉʉ-ma   pahí-nʉ
      D4M EVID-CTR   D4Ap   happen-go-DS   other-ABS-Np   D4Np-on   fall-PST
      As they continued on that way, non-Comanches attacked them. (41:3)

The verbalizing suffix -tu/-ru expresses the meaning 'do so as to have', as in
kuhmaru 'marry (of a woman)'.

3

Interrogative Mood

3.1. Yes/No questions. Questions anticipating a 'yes' or 'no' response are formed by the interrogative enclitic -ha in the second, modal position of a sentence.

(57) *nʉ*   *kahni*   *-ha*   *tsaa-yu̱*
      1xG   house   QUES   good-VB
      Is my house good?   (Canonge 1949)

(58) *nʉ*   *-ha*
      1x   QUES
      Me?   (5:9)

(59) *ʉ*   *-takʉ*   *-ha*   *nʉmii-yu̱*
      2Gs   alone   QUES   move-DUR
      Is it only you moving around?   (95:7)

3.2. Alternative questions. An alternative question is a special type of yes/no question which employs the interrogative enclitic *-ha* in second position, but which also provides alternatives to choose between.

(60) **ʉnʉ**   *-ha*   *pihi-ʔa-nii*   *tʉanoo*   *tʉrʉe-waʔihpʉ-ʔa-nii*   *puni*
      2Ns   QUES   boy-?-Ap   or   little-woman-?-Ap   see
      Did you see boys or girls?

(61) **nʉnʉ**   *-ha*   *pimoróoʔ-a*   *pehka-ʔi̱*   *tʉanoo*   *arʉkaʔ-a̱*
      1xNp   QUES   cow-A   kill-REAL   or   deer-A
      Did we kill a cow or a deer?

325

3.3. Information questions. An information question requests information and is introduced by a question word in initial position, which for Comanche begins with the syllables *hi-* or *ha-*. Other constituents can precede the question word for emphasis. A number of forms distinguish subject from object and singular from plural.

(a) hini 'what? (subject)'. The underlying form of this nominative form of the question word is /hinin/, final *n* blocking the spirantization of a following stop before being deleted (§1.1).

(62) *u-sʉ*   *hini*   *pahí-nʉ*
      D4-INTENS   what?ˆN   fall-PST
      What is that that fell?   (17:30)

(63) *i-sʉ*   *ʉ*   *hiní*
      D1-INTENS   2Gs   what?ˆN
      What is this of yours?   (Canonge 1949)

(64) *hini-paʔi*   *ʉnʉ*
      what?ˆN-have   2Ns
      What do you have?   (Canonge 1949)

(b) hina 'what? (object)'. This is the accusative form of the question word.

(65) *hina*   *ʉnʉ*
      what?ˆA   2Ns
      What do you want?   (31:7)

(66) *hina*   *ʉnʉ*   *ʉ-pi-nakwʉ-ku*   *yaa-hkạ*
      what?ˆA   2Ns   2As-INSTR-DIR-A   take-ST
      What are you taking behind you?   (82:17)

(67) *hina*   *ranʉ*   *taa*   *tʉrʉeʔ-tii*   *tʉhká-kʉ-hu-tuʔi*
      what?ˆA   1iNp   1iGi   child-Ap   eat-CAUS-INDEF-UNR
      What are we going to feed our children?   (119:3)

When the word for 'what?' occurs as object of a locational postposition, it takes the shortened form *hi*.

(68) *hi-paʔa*   *tanʉ*   *yʉkwi-hka*
      what?-on   1iNi   sit-ST
      What are we sitting on?   (60:19)

(69) *hi-tuhka-ti*   *u?*   *wuhka?a-buni*
      what?-under-at   D4Ns   chop-AUG
      What is he chopping a lot under?

(c) hipe 'when?'

(70) *hipe*   *suuru*   *mi?a-hu-tu?i*
      when?   D4Ns   go-INDEF-UNR
      When will he go?   (Canonge 1949)

(71) *hipe*   *unu*   *kima-nu*
      when?   2Ns   come-PST
      When did you come?   (Canonge 1949)

(d) hipeka?i 'how big?' is a compound verb *hipeka* 'what size have?' Compare *Nu batsi? tsa? u pabi? betu* 'My sister is the size of your brother' (Osborn and Smalley 1949). Its presumed underlying structure is /hin-pe-?-kan-?ih/ 'what-MEAS-Ns-have-REAL'.

(72) *hipeka?i*   *u*   *tua?*
      whatˆsize   2Gs   son
      How big is your son?   (Canonge 1949)

(e) hakaru 'who?/which? (Ns)', *hakaruu* 'who?/which? (Np)'. These forms consist of the root *haka* followed by suffixes *-tun* (nominal) and *-u* (plural).

(73) *u-su*   *hakaru*   *hibi-hka*
      D4-INTENS   who?ˆNs   drink-ST
      Who is that (who is) drinking?   (59:7)

(74) *hakaru*   *maruhu-mati*   *u*   *hii-pu*
      who?ˆNs   D2d-PARTˆA   2Gs   thing-ABS
      Which of the two is yours?   (Canonge 1949)

(75) *i-su*   *hakaruu*
      D1-INTENS   who?ˆNp
      Who are these?   (Canonge 1949)

(f) hahka 'whom?' The underlying form of this nonnominative question word is /ha-Hka/ 'QUES-As'.

(76)   *hahka*   *ʉnʉ*   *tʉrʉʔai*
        whom?   2Ns   work
        For whom do you work?'   (Canonge 1949)

(77)   *hahka̱*
        whom?
        To whom?   (Canonge 1949)

(78)   *i-sʉ*   *hahka*   *petʉ*
        D1-INTENS   whom?   daughter
        Whose daughter is this?   (Canonge 1949)

(g) hakai 'how? (state of being)'. This form consists of the root *haka* and the verbal suffix *-i* (be).

(79)   *hakai*   *ʉnʉ*   *nʉʉ-suka?*
        how?   2Ns   REFL-feel
        How do you feel?   (Canonge 1949)

(h) hakani 'how?'. This manner interrogative consists of the root *haka* and the suffix /-niH/ (manner).

(80)   *mʉnʉ*   *esi-ʔahtamúuʔ-nʉʉ*   *hakanih-ku*   *nananịsuyake-ku*   *naboo-hka̱*
        2Np   gray-grasshopper-Np   how?-A   beautifully-A   design-ST
        How are all you gray grasshoppers designed so beautifully?   (33:20)

(81)   *hakani*   *-kia*   *ʉnʉ*   *nahá-nʉ*
        how?   INFER   2Ns   happen-PST
        (I) wonder what happened to you?   (105:20)

(i) hakaniʔyutʉ 'why?' The interrogative of purpose is made up of the root *haka* and suffixes /-niH/ (manner), /-yun/ (verbalizer), /-tʉn/ (nominal).

(82)   *hakaniʔyutʉ*   *ʉnʉ*   *yake-nʉ*
        why?   2Ns   cry-PST
        Why did you cry?   (Canonge 1949)

(83)   *hakaniʔyutʉ*   *ʉnʉ*   *sinih-ku*   *tai*   *hanị-tʉì nị*
        why?   2Ns   D1M-A   1iAp   do-tell
        Why are you telling us to do (it) this way?   (75:25)

(j) *haku* 'where?'. This locative interrogative has the underlying form /ha-kah/ 'QUES-at'.

(84)   *haku*   *suru*   *poko-pi*   *u*   *tu?awe-na*
       where?   D4N   fruit-ABS   2Gs   tell-NOM
       Where is that fruit you told of?   (16:12)

(85)   *haku*   *-se?*   *u*   *kuma-hpu?*
       where?   CTR   2Gs   husband-ABS
       Where is your husband?   (104:14)

(86)   *haku-ku*   *u*   *sarii?*   *tuhkaa-yu*
       where?-A   2Gs   dog   eat-DUR
       Where is your dog eating?   (Canonge 1949)

(k) *hakahpu* 'to/from where?'. This directional interrogative has the form /hakaH-pun/ 'QUES-DIR'.

(87)   *hakahpu*   *u*   *pia?*   *mi?aa-yu*
       where?   2Gs   mother   go-DUR
       Where is your mother going?   (Canonge 1949)

(88)   *hakahpu*   *noo*   *nu?*
       where?   NEC   1xNs
       Where must I [go]?

(l) *huu* 'how many?'.

(89)   *huu*   *u*   *a-hpu?-a*   *tomo-pu*
       how^many? 2   Gs   father-ABS-G   year-ABS
       How old is your father?   (Canonge 1949)

4

Imperative Mood

4.1. Positive imperative. The singular positive imperative form is the simple verb stem.

(90)   *kima*   *habi-k̲i*
           come   lie-come
           Come lie down!   (48:20)

(91)   *ihka*   *buni*   *tɨi-h*
           D1As   see   friend-VOC
           Look at this, friend!   (41:7)

Dual and plural imperatives are indicated by the simple verb stem with a second-position coreferential pronoun showing number agreement. Dual imperative is indicated by *pɨhɨ* or *pɨkwɨ*.

(92)   *ɨhkooi*   *bɨhɨ*
           sleep   COd
           You two, sleep!   (Canonge 1949)

(93)   *nɨ*   *rami?a*   *bɨkwɨ*   *buuni?*
           1xG   brother   COd   see
           You two, look at my brother!   (Osborn and Smalley 1949)

Plural imperative is indicated by *-ka* (!p) suffixed to the simple stem when only the verb is used, or in second position following any other sentence-initial element.

(94)   *mʉʉ   taʔwoʔiʔ-a -ka   makaʔmuki*
        2Gp   gun-A   !p   get^ready
        All of you, get your guns ready!   (122:9)

(95)   *ohka   -ka   kwasinabooʔ-a   wʉhkuupa*
        D3As   !p   snake^A   kill
        All of you, kill that snake!   (51:8)

(96)   *namʉsohi-htsi   -ka   namʉsi   tuhkandaiʔ-niwʉnʉ*
        hurry-NOM   !p   quickly   Wichita-speak
        Hurrying, all of you, quickly speak Wichita!   (78:15)

The pronoun *nʉʉʔ* (second-person nominative) may occur in second position as the pronoun of address and subject of an imperative when needed for reference or emphasis in the singular. Dual and plural suffixes follow *nʉʉʔ* in their respective uses.

(97)   *tai   tʉkʉhmani-bʉni   nʉʉʔ*
        1iAp   cook^food-AUG   2N
        You (sg), cook a lot for us!   (81:3)

(98)   *nʉkʉ-tsi   nʉʉʔ   -ka   nahma   moʔo-tsaai-htsi*
        dance-SS   2N   !p   together   hand-hold-NOM

        sʉmʉ--ʔʉhtsumi- hki-na
        one-close^eyes-come-CONT
        All of you, dancing, holding hands with each other, keep coming with your eyes tightly closed.   (3:11)

Other pronouns sometimes, though rarely, serve as overt subjects of imperatives.

(99)   *ʉnʉ   ma kumahpʉʔ-a weki-kwa*
        2sN   D2G husband-A seek-go
        You, go look for her husband!   (104:17)

4.2. Hortatory. Comanche expresses the hortatory by combining an obligatory first-person dual or an overt plural subject and a simple verb stem

optionally inflected for unrealized (= future) aspect. Since these forms overlap entirely with simple declaratives, context is crucial for understanding
them as exhortations.

(100) *meeku   rakwu̠   ma-baʔatu   nararuu̠na̠*
     now   1diN   D2-over   gamble
     Now let's (us two) gamble over it.   (9:8)

(101) *kima   oruu̠-ku̠hu   tanu̠   raibooʔ-nuu̠-ku̠hu   nuraa*
     come   D3-PART   1piN   white^man-P-to   run
     Come. Let's (pl) run to those white people.   (60:11, 12)

(102) *mia   ranu̠*
     go   1piN
     Let's (pl) go!   (29:30)

5

Polarity

5.1. Affirmation. As seen previously, the word for 'yes' is *haa*, frequently pronounced with nasalization on the lengthened vowel, although this is not indicated in our transcription. This form is also used as a greeting.

There are two known forms of emphasis in addition to the preposing considered earlier. Some of the personal pronouns have special forms used in contrastive or emphatic environments.

(103) *sitʉ*   *tsuhni-pʉ*   *-kʉ-seʔ*   *ke*   *marʉ*   *nʉe*   *tʉʔʉya-tʉ-ʉ*
     D1N   bone-ABS   EVID-CTR   NEG   D2Np   1xAs   fear-PROG-p

       ʉmi   *marʉʉ*   *ʉkwi-hka-tʉ*   *tahi*   *tʉʔʉya-tʉ-ʉ*   *me*   *yʉkwii-yʉ*
       2As   D2Gp   smell-ST-PROG   1iAd   fear-PROG-p   QUOT   say-DUR
       This skull said, "They are not afraid of me, but smelling you, they are afraid of us."   (43:31, 32)

Besides the special emphatic pronouns, the postposition *-masʉ*, from /-man/ 'on' and /-sʉn/ (intensifier), can be added to an element for emphasis.

(104) *poʔsa*   *pimoróoʔ*   *nʉ-ma-sʉ*   *ʉ*   *kaa-bekʉ-tsi*   *ʉ*   *tʉ-behka-nu*
     crazy   cow   1x-on-INTENS   2As   deceit-kill-SS   2As   food-kill-PST
     Crazy cow, cheating you, I have killed you.   (20:27)

5.2. Negation. As seen in §2.1, the word for 'no' is *kee* in its free form. The shortened form *ke* (/ken/) marks negation within sentences, and usually occurs directly before the predicate. In sentences with *ke*, the verb takes the aspective suffix -*wa?i̱* (unrealized) rather than -*tu?i̱* (unrealized).

(105)   *tena-hpu̱?*   -*tsa?*   *ke*   *tu̱-ru̱-?ai-tu̱*
        man-ABS   DECL   NEG   RDP-INDEF-do-PROG
        The man doesn't work.   (Canonge 1949)

(106)   *sarii?*   -*tsa?*   *ke*   *u*   *suwai-tu̱*
        dog   DECL   NEG   D4A   want-PROG
        The dog doesn't like him.   (Canonge 1949)

The negative imperative marker keta? (/ken-ta?/) always occurs in initial position. Negative imperatives do not occur with a simple verb stem, but with one of the variants, according to number, of /-tu̱n/ (progressive).

(107)   *keta?*   *nu̱*   *kuya?a-ku̱-tu̱*
        NEG!   1xAs   fear-CAUS-PROG
        Don't be afraid of me.   (96:18)

(108)   *keta?-ka*   *mu-bi̱si-tu̱-u̱*
        NEG-!p   INSTR-blow-PROG-p
        Don't blow your noses.   (127:7)

The verbalizing suffix -*wai* means 'be without, lack', indicating negative possession.

(109)   *situ̱*   *kwasinaboo?*   *kwasi-waai-tu̱*
        D1   snake   tail-lack-PROG
        This snake lacks a tail.   (36:14)

In the verb *kehewa* 'be all gone, no longer have', -*wa* combines with the negative *ke* (cf. *kehena* 'nothing').
The verb *mu̱ni* 'fail to do, be unable to do' indicates negative ability.

(110)   *pu̱u̱*   *muhyi*   *urii*   *mu̱ni-hka-ku̱-su̱*   *suru̱*   *oha?ahnakatu̱*
        COGp   door^A   D4Ap   unable-ST-DS-INTENS   D4   coyote

        sooti   *wu̱h-tókwe-nu̱*
        much^A   INSTR-kill-PST
        They still being unable to do their door, Coyote clubbed many.   (4:17)

6

Other modality

Three forms which mark modal notions are presented in this section. The form witsa (obligation) occurs in the second position, usually reserved for a mood marker, with otherwise normal declarative sentence syntax.

(111)   *tanʉ*   *-witsa*   *nah*   *paa-kʉ-hu*   *ma*   *wihi-nʉ*
          1iNi   NEC   just   water-in-to   D2As   throw-PST
          We ought to just throw him in the water.   (6:20)

(112)   *ʉnʉ*   *-witsa*   *nʉ*   *nakɨ-ma*   *tsaai-miʔa-rʉ*
          2Ns   NEC   1xGs   ear-on   hold-go-PROG
          You ought to go holding onto my ear.   (20:17)

Normal declarative syntax is again used with the inferential mood enclitic *-kia* 'I wonder if, I guess'.

(113)   *sitʉ*   *-kʉ-seʔ*   *pia-rʉrahyapʉ*   *ʉnʉ*   *-kia*   *siʔana*   *habii-yʉ*
          D1   EVID-CTR   big-meatball   2Ns   INFER   D1L   lie-DUR

               me   *u*   *niikwii-yʉ*
               QUOT   D4A   say-DUR
          This big meatball said to him, "(I) guess you're lying here?"   (21:12)

(114) *surɨ* *-kɨ-seʔ* *suhka* *bɨ*   *tɨeʔti*   *sɨmɨ-ʔ* *-kia* *ɨ-paʔa-tu*
       D4   EVID-CTR D4As COG childˆA   one-NS   NFER   2As-on-along

       tusí-nɨ   *me-kɨ*
       spit-PST   QUOT-EVID

That one said to her child, "I wonder if one spit on you?"   (13:8)

The form *noo* (evidential necessity), meaning 'must', occurs in second position following either a word or a phrase. The following example shows that *noo* and *-kia* (inferential) may occur together as a unit in modal position.

(115) *surɨ*   *noo* *-kia* *hini*   *huhtsúuʔ* *ma* *ra-pɨhe-htsi*   *tai*
       D4   NEC   INFER what?   bird   D2A   INSTR-drop-SS 1iAp

       tsaah-tɨhka-kɨ-nɨ
       good-eat-CAUS-PST

I guess some kind of bird, dropping it, must have caused us to eat well.   (18:35)

7

Nondistinct Argument Phenomena

A predication normally entails reference to persons or objects which stand in particular grammatical relations to a predicate as its ARGUMENTS. There are cases, however, in which one or more such referents is either unknown and, therefore, unspecifiable or is for some reason left indefinite. There are also cases in which a single referent stands in more than one grammatical relation to the same predicate. Such phenomena are treated together as NONDISTINCT ARGUMENTS under the headings UNSPECIFIED SUBJECTS, UNSPECIFIED OBJECTS, REFLEXIVES/PASSIVES, and RECIPROCALS.

7.1. Unspecified subject. A semantically unspecified subject is indicated by *ta*. This form distinguishes neither person nor number.

(116) *so-ko̱*   *ra*   *sooh-kahni-bai-hku*   *uru̱-u̱-ku̱*   *no-bitu̱-nu̱*
       D3-at   UNSP^A much-house-have-DS   D4-p-at   haul-arrive-PST
       There where they had many teepees, (those ones) camped among them.   (106:34)

Ta is frequently used to form neologisms, such as *ta u̱kwiʔena* 'ether' (lit. what one smells), *pu̱ku̱ ra nohkoʔena* 'oven' (lit. place in which one bakes [biscuits]), and *pu̱paʔaku ra tu̱rahkwiʔneʔena* 'ironing board' (lit. place on which one irons).

7.2. Unspecified object. An unspecified object is indicated by one of two verbal prefixes, either *ma-*, having to do with some object related to activity by the hand, or *tu̱-*, having to do with some object's lower end or foot.

(117)   *ma-kwinuma*   'make one dizzy/drunk'
        ma-kwitso?ai   'save someone'
        ma-tsu̲baki   'glue/stick something to'
        tu̲h-tu̲ki   'plant something (pointed end down)'
        tu̲-boo   'write something'
        tu̲-?eka   'paint something'

7.3. Reflexive/Passive. The verbal prefix *na-* marks a reflexive or passive sense.

(118)   *na-maka?muki*   'get one's self ready'
        na-maru̲ni   'hurt oneself'
        na-buni   'look at oneself'
        na-suwatsi   'lose one's mind'
        na-ropu̲sa   'be beaded'
        na-rohtsana   'be hung up/hanging'
        na-ru̲hka?   'groceries (that which is bought to be eaten)'

Special semantic constraints distinguish which occurrences of *na-* are reflexive and which reference an inanimate object. This lies partially in the final syllable of the stem *-ki/-ni/-tsi/-i* 'being' or *-sa/-na/-ka/-a* 'doing', respectively.

(119)   *suru̲*   *-ku̲-se?*   *na-maru̲ni-?*   *nu̲?*   *me*   *yu̲kwi-htsi*   *nahu̲binii-yu̲*
        D4   EVID-CTR   REFL-hurt-REAL   1xNs   QUOT   say-SS   groan-DUR
        That one saying "I hurt myself," was groaning.   (6:14)

(120)   *tsaa*   *nu̲?*   *na-boo-ri*   *kwasu?-i*   *suwaai-tu̲*
        good   1xNs   REFL-draw-NOMˆA   coat-A   want-PROG
        I want a nice designed coat. (32:8)

7.4. Reciprocal. The verbal prefix /nanah-/ (reciprocal) may be a reduplicated form of *na-* (reflexive).

(121)   *nana-kwu̲hu̲*   'marry (each other)'
        nana-buni?   'window (thing for seeing each other)'
        nana-watsi   'misunderstand (lose each other)'

8

Derivational Morphology

While the distinction between derivational processes and inflection is not always sharp, this section presents those more clearly derivational principles by which nouns, verbs, and adjectives are formed by the addition of affixes to various stems. Inflectional noun suffixes are discussed in §9.

8.1. Noun morphology. While some nouns are not made up of smaller units, others can be analyzed as stems plus derivational affixes. These stems and affixes are of several types. They are discussed below in terms of whether they are derived from underlying nouns or verbs.

One class of affixes derives nouns from stems that are themselves nominal. The suffixes *-htsiʔ* and *-weeʔ* are affective in that they carry the notions DIMINUTIVE and ENDEARMENT,which generally, although not always, overlap in each of the two suffixes.

(122)   *tuibi-htsiʔ*   'young man, brave'
        sitɨ-htsiʔ   'this little one'
        tɨeʔtɨ-htsiʔ   'dear child'
        nɨmi wɨʔyɨrɨhki-htsiʔ   'scares people' (name of a quail)

(123)   *tɨtaa-tɨ*   *nɨ*   *ruaʔ*   *tɨʔɨya-tɨ-weeʔ*
      little-NOM   1xGs son   fear-NOM-DIM
      My poor little son is afraid.   (83:29)

The suffix *-htsiʔ* may also have a pejorative sense, as in the noun *senihtɨ-htsiʔ* 'one of an inferior kind'.

The prefix *na-* derives nouns from nominal stems, designating a part-whole relationship, as in *na-ʔomo* 'wagon wheel', *na-rohtɨmaʔ* 'lid' (lit. its stopper), na-rɨnooʔa saddle' (lit. its loader).

341

The prefix *na?-* derives nonspecific kinship relationships from general terms referring to humans.

(124)   *na?-wa?ihpu?*   'female kinsman'
        na?-renahpu?   'male kinsman'
        na?-numu   'kinsman'

Other suffixes derive nouns from verbal stems. The suffix *-tu* (/-tun/) forms an imperfective participle indicating the person or thing which performs an action or possesses a quality.

(125)   *oha?ahnaka-tu*   'coyote' (lit. one who has yellow underneath)
        kokorá?a?arahima?e-tu   'chicken hawk' (lit. one who steals chickens)
        tosapi-tu   'white (color)'
        poyohka-ru   'trotter'
        namamohka-ru   'hitched animal or object'
        nawo?o-ru   'striped object'
        takwusa-ru   'item loosened (by foot)'

The suffix *-pu* (perfective participle), with underlying form /-Hpuh/, marks nouns derived from verbs through completed process or change. The nouns name those things that result from the activity of the verb, or less frequently those things that are simply acted upon through the verbal activity. The noun resulting from an adjective stem with the suffix *-pu* indicates 'one who has the quality of being'.

(126)   *tekwa-pu*   'word' (lit. that which is spoken)
        ahwe-pu   'tuber' (lit. that which has been dug up)
        naboo-pu   'picture' (lit. that which is drawn/sketched)
        kwuhu-pu   'a captive' (lit. one who has been captured)
        pia-pu   'giant person' (AJ stem)

The suffix *-na* (continued action) derives a range of nouns in relation to the continued action named by the intransitive or transitive verb with nonspecific or cognate object. Some of the nouns refer to physical objects related to the verbal activity as instrument or object, and some refer to more abstract notions.

(127)   *poma-na*   'picking'
        nuhka-na   'dancing, dance'
        pitu-na   'arriving, arrival'
        tuhka?e-na   'food'
        yuhkwihka-na   'seat'
        yahne-na   'laughing, laughter'

The suffix *-wapi* (agentive), from /-wapih/, may more rightfully be termed a compound-forming noun with agentive meaning. It marks the person or animal that carries out the action of a verb.

(128) *tɨnoo-wapi*   'pack animal'
       hɨa-wapi   'fisherman'
       tɨnisuabetai-wapi   'teacher'
       tɨe-tekwɨni-wapi   'Indian brave'

A person named by such a noun does not just occasionally carry out the named activity, but is, rather, a professional, a specialist, or one paid to carry it out. Thus, a term with the suffix *-wapi* has honorific overtones.

The suffix *-ʔ* (nominal) derives nouns and pronouns from verbs and demonstrative elements.

(129) *tuka-ʔ*   'light, lamp'
       kwasinaboo-ʔ   'snake' (that whose tail is striped)
       narɨmɨɨ-ʔ   'town, store'
       kwɨhti-ʔ   'victim' (one who is shot)
       taʔwoʔi-ʔ   'gun'
       nɨ-ʔ   'I'
       u-ʔ   'he, she, it' (remote distal)

8.2. Verb morphology. While many verbs are not reducible to smaller parts, others consist of a stem and a verbalizing suffix. The suffix *-ʔi* (temporary state), for example, has the meaning 'being in the state or condition of' or may reference quality.

(130) *esi-tɨyaʔi-*   'faint' (*esi-tɨyaitɨ* 'unconscious')
       esi-tsɨnɨʔi-   'gray in appearance'
       haʔwoʔi-   'hollow, loose'
       papi-tsɨnɨʔi-   'having tangled hair'
       pɨhɨ-noʔi-   'pluck hair/eyebrows' (cause to be taken away)

The examples of (130) name temporary conditions and require either *-tuʔi* (unrealized) or *-tɨ* (progressive) as aspect marker; otherwise the forms might be confused with those having the suffix *-i* (realized). The presence of the suffix *-ʔi* (temporary state) can be determined by adding *-tuʔi*, as in *pɨhka-ʔi-tuʔi* 'will (temporarily) stop crying'. These forms do not have *-i* (realized); they only state that a condition will be present (*-ʔi-tuʔi*) or is temporarily present (*-ʔi-tɨ*).

Postpositions have forms with an added *-i* meaning 'be' in some locative constructions. Such postpositions include *-paʔai* 'be over', *-kuhpai* 'be inside', *-kabai* 'be in or among', and *-nai* 'side' or 'direction'.

(131) situkwu   -ku-seʔ   pu-hu   ina-puh-a   pu-hu   ina-wata-paʔa-i-ki
       D1d   EVID-CTR   CO-Gd   jerk-NOM-A   CO-Gd   jerk-pole-on-VB-at

       roh-tsániʔi-nu
       INSTR-hangˆup-PST
       These two hung their jerked meat over their meat poles.   (112:25)

The verbalizing suffix *-nai* 'become' derives compound verbs from nouns.

(132) situ -ku-seʔ si?ahru   maruu-ku-hu   toʔi-nu   pu   kwasuʔ-i
       D1   EVID-CTR D1Lˆalong D2p-at-to   goˆup-PST COGs   dress-A

       sumu-sihwapu-nai-hku
       one-torn-became-DS
       This one along here went up to them, her dress having become completely torn.   (53:24)

The verbalizing suffix *-pai* 'have' with an inanimate noun shows possession of the item named by the noun. The noun is not grammatically marked as accusative.

(133) *puhihwi-pai*   'have money'
       pianohkoʔawo-bai   'have a large biscuit oven'
       kahni-bai   'have a teepee/house'

Possession of a noun referring to the personal characteristics of an animate being is marked by the suffix *-ka* 'have' (as personal characteristic).

(134) *puʔe-ka*   'be a Christian' (lit. have a road/path)
       ohaʔahna-ka   'Coyote' (lit. have yellow underarms)
       turueʔtu-ka   'have children'

The verb suffix *-ʔa* indicates 'do, make' forming a verb from a basic noun.

(135) *piso-ʔa-*   'stick someone, puncture'
       nariso-ʔa-   'give an enema'
       puʔe-ʔa-   'make/construct a road'

The suffix (/-yun/) -*yu* (verbalizer), possibly related to -*yu* (durative aspect [§13.7]), forms a verb stem from an adjective root or quantifier.

(136)   *soo-yo*   'be many'   (cf. *soo* 'much')
         tɨmarɨɨmoa-yu   'be a lot'   (cf. *tɨmarɨɨmoa* 'much')

8.3. Adjective morphology. As with nouns and verbs, adjectives are simple or derived by a derivational suffix. In many instances this suffix is identical to those found in nouns, particularly the imperfective participial suffix -*tɨ/-rɨ* and the perfective participial suffix -*pɨ*. Certain adjectives cannot occur as free forms without the addition of one of these suffixes, although they may be combined with other elements to form compounds without them.

A few stems which take the imperfective participial suffix -*tɨ/-rɨ* are listed in (137).

(137)   *tɨeʔ-tɨ*   'small'
         sɨmɨ-rɨ   'one' (and other numerals)
         tɨtaa-tɨ   'small'
         nɨɨtsɨkɨna-rɨ   'tied up'
         sɨɨhpe-tɨ   'level, flat'
         paʔitsiʔwɨnɨ-rɨ   'short' (stand short)
         taʔoki-tɨ   'spilled'
         pihpokaa-rɨ   'uneven' (as a hem)

The perfective participial suffix -*pɨ* forms adjectives which reference completed action, as in (138).

(138)   *pia-pɨ*   'big, large'   *papɨsi-pɨ*   'rotten'
         yuu-pɨ   'fat'   *pasa-pɨ*   'dry'
         nuhtsa-pɨ 'bent, stooped'   *namɨsokoa-pɨ*   'buried'

Reduplicated adjectives indicate duality or plurality, whether in immediate succession or habitually.

(139)   *soobeʔsɨ*   -*kɨ-tsaʔ*   *rɨa*   *suʔana*   *u*   *toya-kɨmaʔ-kɨ*
         long^ago   EVID-DECL   QUOT   D4L   D4G   mountain-edge-at

         pɨ-bɨeh-tɨ-u   *kahní-bai*
         RDP-ago-NOM-p   house-have
         Long ago, they say, somewhere there beside that mountain, people of
         long ago had a camp.   (69:1)

(140)   nʉ-   bia?   -se?   pi-bia-pʉh-i   waa-wata-yʉkwi-?ee-yʉ
        1xGs   mother   CTR   RDP-big-ABS-A   cedar-pole-set^up-REP-DUR
        My mother would set up long cedar poles.   (109:2)

Numerals are never reduplicated, except for *sʉmʉ?* 'one', which has a reduplicated form *sʉsʉmʉ?* 'some' (§4.6).

(141)   su?ana -kʉ-tsa?   -rʉa   sʉ-sʉmʉ?-nʉʉ   nʉmʉ-nʉʉ   nobitʉ-nʉ
        D4L   EVID-DECL QUOT   RDP-one-Np   Comanche-Np   camp-PST
        Somewhere there, they say, some Comanches camped.   (73:1)

Similarly, the nonnumeric quantifiers *soo* 'much, many' and *tʉmarʉʉmoa*
'much, many' are never reduplicated.

Adjectives dealing with certain qualities and properties are modified in
terms of extent or degree. This may be through the use of separate lexical
items, such as *nohi?* 'very' or *tʉbitsi* 'really', or through the use of the intensifying suffix /-hʉn/.

(142)   nohi?   tʉh-tʉtaa-tʉʉ   tʉ-rʉehpʉ?-rʉʉ   tai   tsaah-tʉhka-kʉ-nʉ
        very   RDP-little-NP   RDP-child-Np   1iAp   good-eat-CAUS-PST
        Very little children fed us well.   (75:28)

(143)   surʉ   -se?   tʉbitsi   tsaa   sanahkóo-?   kama-nʉ
        D4N   CTR   really   good   gum-Ns   taste-PST
        That tasted like really good gum.   (110:20)

(144)   su?ana   pia-pʉ-hʉ   pimoróo-?   paa-kʉma?-ru   kimaa-yʉ
        D4L   big-ABS-INTENS cow-Ns   water-edge-along come-DUR
        Somewhere there, a big cow was coming along the edge of the
        water.   (19:1)

9

Noun Inflection

Nouns have different forms depending on their function in sentences or as isolated words.

9.1. Absolutive. Quoting Langacker, "Absolutive suffixes are one of the more distinctive and characteristic features of [Uto-Aztecan] grammar. An absolutive suffix, in UA terms, is an ending with no apparent semantic value that appears in citation forms but may drop when a noun is subjected to various morphological processes, such as affixation, compounding, or reduplication" (1977:77). This general statement for UA is true for Comanche.

Although no constant semantic value can categorically be given to any particular absolutive suffix in Comanche, there are small classes of nouns which have a certain semantic cohesiveness. The absolutive ending *-pi*, for example, seems to mark a class of mass or collective nouns.

(145) *toya-bi*   'mountain'   *hani-bi*   'corn'
       ona-bi   'salt'   *hunuʔ-bi* 'creek, river'
       waah-pi 'cedar tree'   *huuh-pi*   'tree, stick'
       tʉah-pi 'chickasaw plum'   *poko-pi*   'berries, nuts'

The suffix *-pi̱* marks a class of color nouns.

(146) *oha-pi̱*   'yellow'   *tuhu-pi̱*   'black'
       otʉ-pi̱   'brown'   *tosa-pi̱*   'white'

A set of kinship terms has the suffix *-hpʉʔ*.

(147) *a-hpʉʔ*   'father'   *waʔi-hpʉʔ*   'woman'
       samo-hpʉʔ   'sibling'   *tuinʉ-hpʉʔ*   'boy'
       tʉe-hpʉʔ   'child'   *tena-hpʉʔ*   'man'
       kuma-hpʉʔ   'husband'

Absolutive suffixes are often absent when a noun is followed by a postposition or is part of a compound.

(148) *huu-ma* 'with the stick'   *waa-watayʉkwi* 'set up cedar poles'

A form homophonous with the perfective participial suffix *-pʉ* (§8.3) functions as an absolutive suffix.

(149) *soni-pʉ* 'grass'   *puhi-pʉ*   'weeds, leaves'
       soni-tu 'through the grass'   *puhi-kabaiki* 'through the weeds'

9.2. Dual and plural number. Nouns other than proper, mass, color, and collective nouns may be inflected for number by the suffixes (*-nʉ-hʉh* →) *-nʉhʉ* (dual), (*nʉ-wʉh* →) *-nʉkwʉ* (dual), or *-nʉʉ* (plural). These distinctions of number are usually not marked for nonhuman nouns, except in contexts where number is emphasized or in narratives where it is used rhetorically to personify an otherwise inanimate object. Where context makes number clear, forms unmarked for number predominate. The two forms for dual number are used interchangeably. A simple noun, a derived noun with *-pʉ* (perfective participle), and a derived noun with final glottal are presented in (150) to illustrate formation of dual and plural forms.

(150) **Singular**   **Dual**   **Plural**
       kahni   *kahni-nʉhʉ*   *kahni-nʉʉ*   'house'
       hibi-pʉ   *hibipʉ-nʉkwʉ*   *hibipʉ-nʉʉ*   'drunk'
       hʉarʉʔ   *hʉarʉʔ-nʉhʉ*   *hʉarʉʔ-nʉʉ*   'trap'

Derived nouns with *-tʉ/-rʉ* (imperfective participle) omit the *-nʉ* portion of dual and plural suffixes, resulting in the shortened forms *-hʉ/-kwʉ* (dual) and *-ʉ* (plural).

(151) **Singular**   **Dual**   **Plural**
       ohaʔahnakatʉ   *ohaʔahnakatʉ-hʉ*   *ohaʔahnakatʉ-ʉ* 'coyote'
       ooʔrʉ   *ooʔrʉ-kwʉ*   *ooʔrʉ-ʉ*   'clothing'

Nouns derived from adjectives show reduplication of their first syllables in dual and plural forms.

(152)	**Singular**	**Dual**	**Plural**	
	tʉtaatʉ	tʉh-tʉtaatʉkwʉ	tʉh-tʉtaatʉ-ʉ	'child'
	mutsipʉ	mu-mutsipʉ-nʉhʉ	mu-mutsipʉ-nʉʉ	'sharp one'

Some kinship nouns add -*a* before dual and plural suffixes.

(153)	**Singular**	**Dual**	**Plural**	
	tuibihtsiʔ	*tuibihtsiʔ-a-nʉhʉ*	*tuibihtsiʔ-a-nʉʉ*	'brave'
	waʔihpʉʔ	*waʔihpʉʔ-a-nʉkwʉ*	*waʔihpʉʔ-a-nʉʉ*	'woman'

9.3. Accusative. Comanche nouns are overtly marked for only three cases—genitive, accusative, or vocative. In subject position, for example, a noun may be inflected for number or may have an absolutive ending; but it has no nominative ending associated directly with its syntactic function as subject. Accusative, on the other hand, is overtly marked on nouns functioning as direct or indirect objects, as well as on those functioning as subjects of certain subordinate clauses (§15.2). Singular nouns are marked for accusative case by -*i* or -*a*. For singular nouns ending in voiced, high *u* or *ʉ*, -*i* replaces that final vowel. In the examples which follow, forms listed as nominative are, as indicated above, actually unmarked by a case ending.

(154)	**Nominative**	**Accusative**	
	puku	*puki*	'horse'
	ʉhʉ	*ʉhi*	'blanket'
	tʉehpʉʔrʉ	*tʉehpʉʔri*	'child'
	ohaʔahnakatʉ	*ohaʔahnakati*	'coyote'

For nonderived singular nouns ending in low vowels *a* or *o*, -*i* replaces that vowel and lowers to -*e* (actually coalescence of *ai* or *oi* to *e*).

(155)	**Nominative**	**Accusative**	
	moʔo	*moʔe*	'hand'
	paka	*pake*	'arrow'

Singular nouns ending in phonemic *h* add -*a* (accusative).

(156)	**Nominative**	**Accusative**	
	animui	*animuih-a*	'fly'
	haitsi̱	*haitsi̱h-a*	'friend'
	pitsipʉ̱	*pitsipʉ̱h-a*	'milk'
	tʉnoowapi̱	*tʉnoowapi̱h-a*	'pack animal'

Singular nouns ending in glottal also add -*a* (accusative).

(157) **Nominative**   **Accusative**
       taiboo?   *taiboo?-a*   'stranger'
       kwasinaboo?   *kwasinaboo?-a*   'snake'

Singular nouns ending in -*pi*, -*bi*, or -*wi* require -*hta* (accusative).

(158) **Nominative**   **Accusative**
       huuhpi   *huuhpi-hta*   'stick'
       wobi   *wobi-hta*   'board'
       puhihwi   *puhihwi-hta*   'money'

Many singular nouns do not follow the above rules for formation of the accusative case. Known exceptions have been indicated in the dictionary, but there are undoubtedly many exceptions of which we are unaware.

(159) **Nominative**   **Accusative**
       kahni   *kahni*   'teepee'
       po?a   *po?a-i*   'bark, skin'
       woinu   *woinu-i*   'horn'
       motso   *motso-i*   'beard'

Note, in particular, that derived nouns ending in -*na* have no special accusative form.

(160) **Nominative**   **Accusative**
       pomana   *pomana*   'picking'
       pitɨna   *pitɨna*   'arriving'

Dual nouns are inflected for accusative case by adding the suffix -*i*. Stem-final *h* is deleted and, by vowel harmony, preceding vowels ɨ also become *i*. (Dual suffixes -*nɨkwɨ* and -*kwɨ* do not occur in accusative forms.)

(161) **Nominative**   **Accusative**
       ahpɨ?nɨhɨ   *ahpɨ?nihi*   'fathers'
       tɨhtɨtaatɨhɨ   *tɨhtɨtaatihi*   'children'

Similarly, plural nouns are inflected for accusative case by adding the suffix -*i*. By vowel harmony, preceding vowels ɨ also become *i*, and the cluster is reduced to *ii*.

(162) **Nominative**   **Accusative**
     nɨmɨnɨɨ   *nɨmɨnii*   'Comanches'
     tɨrɨeʔtɨɨ   *tɨrɨeʔtii*   'children'

9.4. Genitive. A noun or pronoun functioning as possessor precedes its head noun, some being distinctively marked as genitives but others not. Singular derived nouns ending in (underlying) /-tɨn/, for example, occur with -a (genitive) when functioning as possessors, as do other nouns having a final *n*.

(163) *tɨehpɨʔrɨn-a nohiʔ*   'child's toy'
     ohaʔahnakatɨn-a kwasi   'Coyote's tail'
     atɨhɨn-a ahpɨʔ   'stranger's father'
     uʔahrɨn-a moʔo   'anyone's hand'

Other singular nouns functioning as possessors are marked by -*a* or -*hta* (accusative) (§9.3).

(164) *animuih-a kobe*   'fly's face'
     wasápeʔ-a kwɨhɨ   'bear's wife'
     huuhpi-hta moka   'tree's branch'

Dual nouns add -*ɨ* (genitive). Plural nouns have no special genitive form but like other possessors they precede the possessed noun.

(165) *wasápeʔnɨh-ɨ kahni*   '(two) bears' house'
     tɨhtɨtaatɨɨ nohiʔ   'children's toy'

9.5. Vocative. Kinship terms used as forms of address or in calling have special vocative forms. Most of the known examples involve an *h* substituting for stem-final glottal.

(166) **Nominative**   **Vocative**
     piaʔ   *piah*   'mother'
     tɨiʔ   *tɨih*   'friend'

Derived-noun kinship terms ending in -*pɨʔ* undergo regular phonological changes when the vocative -*h* substitutes for the final glottal.

(167) **Nominative**   **Vocative**
     ahpɨʔ   *apɨ*   'father'

Other dual and plural nouns have no special vocative form.

10

Postpositions

Postpositions are a rich and varied class, expressing locative, directional, instrumental, and other notions. While most postpositions are enclitic and can occur only in association with a head noun or pronoun, a few are free forms that can also occur alone. Many postpositions combine with each other and some have different forms depending on phonological considerations or on the type of verb with which they occur. Most postpositions reference semantic ranges of location or direction.

10.1. Locative. Several postpositions, such as *-ka/-kʉ* 'in, at, on', locate a referent spatially.[6]

(168) *pʉ*   *tʉʔikúuʔ-kwasʉ-kʉ-pʉ-ka*   *pitʉ-nʉ*
       COG   prairie^dog-cook-CAUS-NOM-at   arrive-PST
       (He) arrived at his cooked prairie dog.   (10:20)

The vowel of the postposition often assimilates to a preceding deictic root, as (169) shows.

(169) *so-ko̠*   *ma*   *kuʔe-kʉ*   *marii*   *bitʉ-hka*
       D3-at   D2G   top-at   D2Ap   arrive-DS
       ... as they arrived there at the top of it.   (28:25)

Other locative postpositions include those of (170).

---

[6]The first form occurs following a voiceless vowel; the second after a voiced vowel.

(170)   *-hi/-ti*   'in, at'   *-miihtsiʔ*   'near'
        -hoi   'around'   *-munakwụ*   'in front of'
        -kaba   'among'   *-paʔa*   'over, above, on'
        -kuhpa   'inside, within'   *-pinakwụ*   'behind'
        -kuʔeku   'on top of'   *-tuhka*   'under'
        -kụmaʔ   'beside'   *-tụbịnaaʔ(weki)*   'in the middle of'
        -ma   'on'   *-yahne*   'at/on the other side of'

The postposition *-hi/-ti* may, in fact, be considered an agreement marker in that its distribution is severely restricted by a verb of movement.

(171)   *ụ*   *manaaʔ-nakwụ-hi*   *ma-sukaa*
        2Gs   further-side-at   UNSPEC-feel
        Feel on your further side!   (61:30)

(172)   *sụmụ-ʔ*   *-kụ-seʔ*   *tena-hpụʔ*   *hunuʔ-betu-ti*   *buni-nụ*
        one-Ns   EVID-CTR   man-ABS   creek-toward-at   see-PST
        One man looked toward the creek.   (122:14)

10.2. Allative. The general allative postposition is *-ku* 'to, into'. It occurs in clauses with verbs of motion.

(173)   *paa-ku*   *-kụ-seʔ*   *surụ*   *kima-nụ*
        water-to   EVID-CTR   D4Ns   come-PST
        That one came to the water.   (93:5)

Other directional postpositions include those of (174). Of these, *-metụ* 'at' deserves special mention in that it is apparently limited to occurrence with verbs of laughing.

(174)   *-hu*   'to, into'   *-petu*   'toward'
        -kahtu   'into'   *-tu*   'through, along'
        -metụ   'at'   *-tụ*   'from'
        -nai   'from'   *-waka*   'toward'
        -nakwụ   'side, direction'

10.3. Instrumental. The postposition *-ma* 'with, by' marks an instrument involved in an action.

(175)   *sitụu*   *kuyuníiʔ-a*   *pụụ*   *wasụ-ʔị-ma*   *tsihá-kwitsoʔai-nụ*
        D1Np   turkey-A   COGp   kill-REAL-INSTR   hunger-save-PST
        They were saved from starvation by turkeys they killed.   (120:21)

10.4. Partitive. There are two postpositions signalling that part of an object or group of items is being referred to, rather than the whole object or group of items. These partitive postpositions are /-kʉhu/ and /-mantʉn/.

(176) *sʉmʉ-ʔ urʉʉ-matʉ ma-waka nahá-biitʉ*
one-Ns D4Np-PART D2A-toward happen-arrive
One of them happened onto him. (86:18)

(177) *urʉʉ-kʉhu u yuhu-wehki-pʉ wihnu surʉ pi-sikwanúuʔi-nu*
D4N-PART D4 fat-search-NOM then D4Ns INSTR-slide-PST
Then that one, the fattest of them to be found, slid down. (5:11)

These two postpositions occur with *-i* (accusative) when the noun or pronoun they mark is functioning as an object.

(178) *situ- kʉ-seʔ ma piaʔ u-kʉhi yaa-ʔe-tʉ ma-rii*
D1 EVID-CTR D2G mother D4-PARTˆA take-REP-PROG D2-Ap

himi-miʔa̲
give-go
Taking some of it, her mother went to give it to them. (73:8,9)

(179) *u-mati nʉʉʔ noo-htsi miʔa-nu*
D4-PARTˆA 2N haul-SS go-PST
Carrying some of it, you go. (97:27)

10.5. Miscellaneous. Several other postpositions express diverse concepts. Simple coordination of two nominal elements is marked by /-maʔaiн/ 'with' following the second element. More generally, this postposition expresses the notion of accompaniment.

(180) *...sʉmʉ--ʔ rena-hpʉʔ pʉ kwʉhʉ-maʔai pʉ-hʉ tʉeʔtʉ-maʔai*
...one-Ns man-ABS COGs wife-with CO-GD child-with

no-miʔa-nʉ
haul-go-PST
...a man, his wife, and their children moved away. (99:1)

Coordination of two elements from one clause to another is indicated by *-suʔa* 'and' in a second clause.

(181)   *sitʉ*   *-suʔa*   *-kʉ-seʔ*   *ma*   *haitsi*   *suʔah-ru*   *ku-roʔi-nʉ*
     D1   and   EVID-CTR   D2G   friend   D4L-along   INSTR-go^up-PST
     His friend also bobbed up along there.   (58:17)

There is a qualifier -taka 'just, only' and two intensifiers -sʉ and -tuku, the latter often translatable as 'same'.

(182)   *nah*   *nʉkwʉ*   *u*   *tohobe-mati*   *-taka*   *tʉ-tsih-kaʔa-ruʔi*
     just   1xNd   D4G   hindquarter-PART^A   only   food-INSTR-cut-UNR
     We will cut off only part of its hindquarter.   (97:29)

(183)   *yee*   *surʉ-sʉ-tuku*   *ʉnʉ*   *nʉ*   *kaa-behka-noo-rʉ*
     oh   D4-INTENS-INTENS   2Ns   1xAs   deceit-kill-haul-PROG
     Oh, you are the same one who is moving along cheating me.   (23:30)

Finally, similarity of conditions is marked by the postposition -*waʔi* 'like, similar to'.

(184)   *ihka*   *buni*   *pʉ-waʔi*   *tahʉ*   *naah-kwabi-ka-tuʔih-a*
     D1As   see   COs-like   1iGd   continue-lie-ST-UNR-A
     Look at this which we will continue to lie like.   (41:8)

10.6. Ordering. Postpositions may combine to form complex forms. It is useful to distinguish first-order postpositions, second-order postpositions, and so forth, in the structure of these complex forms. A second-order element can follow a first-order element, a third-order can follow a second-order, and so on. Not all possible combinations actually occur, and the exact limits are unknown. Most of the simple forms are first-order elements, and therefore are not listed here. Other orders are as listed in (185).

(185)   Second order: *-tu/-ru*   'through, along'   /-tun/
                            -ka/-kʉ   'at'   /-kah/
         Third order: *-hu*   'into'   /-hun/
                             -ku   'to'
         Fourth order: *-tʉ*   'from'   /-tʉh/
         Fifth order: *-hi/-ti*   'in, at'
         Sixth order: *-taka*   'just'
                             -tuku   (intensifier)

(186)   *...paa-kʉmaʔ-ru*   *kimaa-yʉ*
       water-edge-along   come-DUR
       ...was coming along the edge of the water.   (19:1)

(187) ...*hunu?-ma-tu*   *pohpí-nu*
         creek-on-along   jump-PST
       ...jumped into the creek.   (52:15)

(188) ...*paa-ku-hu*   *ma*   *wihi-nu*
         water-in-to   D2   throw-PST
       ...throw him into the water.   (6:20)

Postpositions, whether simple or complex, directly follow a noun or pronoun to form postpositional phrases. With a few minor exceptions, the noun in such a phrase is otherwise unmarked for case. As two exceptions, the two postpositions -*kuma?* 'beside' and -*tubinaa?(weki)* 'in the middle of' follow a noun optionally marked as genitive. A pronoun in a postpositional phrase is usually a normal nominative form less any -*?* nominalizer, but again there are a few exceptional forms, as indicated in (189).

(189) *tamu*   1i (with postposition)
       mumu   2p (with postposition)
       pu   sˆREFL (with postposition)

Demonstrative adjectives or other elements that modify a noun marked by a postposition are themselves also marked by a copy of that same postposition.

(190) ...*sii-ma*   *pia-huu-ma*   *ma*   *wuh-kúpa-nu*
         D1-INSTR   big-wood-INSTR   D2A   INSTR-kill-PST
       ...killed him with this big club.   (17:23)

(191) ...*si-ku-hi*   *taitu-ku-hi*   *ma*   *puni-hka*
         D1-at-toˆA   cave-at-toˆA   D2A   see-DS
       ...as he looked into this cave.   (91:9)

11

Noun Modifiers

11.1. Demonstrative adjectives. Demonstrative elements reflect a spatial ranking from the point of view of the speaker. There is a three-way distinction between PROXIMAL, DISTAL, and SCATTERED—the last of these encompassing both spatial scattering and type scattering in the sense of the word 'various'—and within the first two categories a further distinction between IMMEDIATE and REMOVED. The demonstrative stems are listed in (192).

(192)		PROXIMAL	DISTAL	SCATTERED
	IMMEDIATE	*i-*	*o-*	
				e-
	REMOVED	*ma-*	*u-*	

Demonstrative adjectives may be simple, as in (192), or may be derived by the suffix *-tʉ/-rʉ* (imperfective participle), and can be further marked for dual or plural number. Since number distinctions are generally optional, derived demonstrative adjectives may appear unmarked for number, as *itʉ* (immediate proximal) and *orʉ* (immediate distal), or marked for plural number, as *itʉʉ* (immediate proximal plural) and *orʉʉ* (immediate distal plural), and similarly for *-e* (scattered). The forms *etʉhʉand *etʉkwʉ which would encode SCATTERED DUAL are semantically anomalous and do not occur.

All vowel-initial demonstrative adjectives may also occur with initial *s* (*si-, so-,* etc.) to indicate that the speaker presupposes the hearer to have prior knowledge of the thing or person referred to.

(193)   *setɨɨ*   *waʔihpɨʔa-nɨɨ*   *kohtoo-htsi*   *tɨkɨh-manii-yɨ*
        D5NP   woman-Np   makeˆfire-ss   food-prepare-DUR
        The various women, making fire(s), were preparing food.   (56:16)

(194)   *surɨ* *-kɨ-seʔ*   *tena-hpɨʔ* *hina*   *mɨkwɨ* *me*   *uhri* *niikwii-yɨ*
        D4   EVID-CTR   man-ABS   what?ˆA   2Nd   QUOT   D4Ad   say-DUR
        That man asked those two, "What do you two want?"   (57:3)

A demonstrative adjective may be inflected for accusative or genitive case. In the accusative case, dual and plural derived forms have the vowel *i* common to other nouns and adjectives with the derivational suffix *-tɨ/-rɨ* (imperfective participle). Singular derived forms, however, are marked with the special accusative ending /-Hka/ that occurs elsewhere only in *hahka* 'whom?'. Genitive dual and plural forms are identical to the corresponding nominative forms, while genitive singular forms are identical to accusative singular forms, as indicated in (195) and (196).

(195)

		As	Ad	Ap
IMMEDˆPROX	(D1)	*(s)ihka*	*(s)itɨhi*	*(s)itii*
REMˆPROX	(D2)	*mahka*	*mahri*	*marii*
IMMEDˆDIST	(D3)	*(s)ohka*	*(s)ohri*	*(s)orii*
REMˆDIST	(D4)	*(s)uhka*	*(s)uhri*	*(s)urii*
SCATTERED	(D5)	*(s)ehka*	——	*(s)etii*

(196)

		Gs	Gd	Gp
IMMEDˆPROX	(D1)	*(s)ihka*	*(s)itɨhɨ*	*(s)itɨɨ*
REMˆPROX	(D2)	*mahka*	*mahrɨ*	*marɨɨ*
IMMEDˆDIST	(D3)	*(s)ohka*	*(s)ohrɨ*	*(s)orɨɨ*
REMˆDIST	(D4)	*(s)uhka*	*(s)uhrɨ*	*(s)urɨɨ*
SCATTERED	(D5)	*(s)ehka*	——	*(s)etɨɨ*

A demonstrative adjective precedes the noun it modifies. An adjective or possessive pronoun occurs between the demonstrative and the noun. Any element that may move to the second, modal position of the sentence may interrupt these constituents. A demonstrative adjective may occur alone, with an overt head noun following it.

(197)   *sitɨ*   *-kɨ-seʔ*   *ma*   *piaʔ*   *pɨ-hi*   *muhne-htsi*   *miʔa-nɨ*
        D1   EVID-CTR   D2G   mother   CO-Ad   precede-ss   go-PST
        His mother went, leading them.   (81:9)

(198) *urɨ-tuku*   *maʔ*   *na-rɨʔɨya-tɨ*   *kwasinabooʔ*
       D4-INTENS   D2Ns   REFL-fear-NOM   snake
       It's that same dangerous snake.   (28:21)

11.2. Nonnumeric quantifiers. There is no particular form characteristic of nonnumeric quantifiers. Some are free forms, others bound; some are derived from more basic forms, others are not. A few such quantifiers are listed in (199). Most are unmarked for case, but three have special accusative forms and one a genitive form as well.

(199) *sɨɨhpeʔsɨ*   'all together'
       oyetɨ   'everyone'
       -etɨ   'each one'
       oʔyɨsɨ   'every time'
       tɨmarɨɨmoa, tɨmarɨɨmoaku (A)   'much'
       soo(-tɨ), sooti/sooko (A), *sootɨna* (G)   'many, much'
       soobeʔsɨ   'long ago'
       sɨsɨmɨʔ, sɨsɨmɨʔ-nɨɨ (Np), *sɨsɨmɨʔ-nii* (A)   'some'

(200) *suʔana*   *sɨ-sɨmɨʔ-nɨɨ*   *kahní-baʔi*
       D4L   RDp-one-Np   house-have
       Some people had a camp there.   (85:1)

A quantifier normally precedes the noun it modifies, but some may also occur alone, without a noun.

(201) *soo*   *maʔ*   *hibi-hka-tɨ*
       much   D2Ns   drink-ST-PROG
       She has drunk a lot.   (56:21)

(202) *sɨɨhpeʔsɨ*   *u*   *kwɨtɨkú-nɨ*
       together   D4A   shoot-PST
       They all shot it at the same time.   (28:21)

(203) *sitɨ*   *-kɨ-seʔ*   *tɨmarɨɨmoa-ku*   *tomoa-nɨ*
       D1   EVID-CTR   much-A   cloud-do-PST
       It clouded up a lot.   (51:2)

A few quantifiers may be verbalized by /-yun/, the vowel of which harmonizes to *o* following *soo*.

(204)   *situu*   *-ku-seʔ*   *u*   *puetsu-ku*   *soo-yo-tu*
        D1Np   EVID-CTR   D4G   early-A   much-VB-PROG
        There were many of them that morning.   (29:24)

(205)   *suru*   *-ku-seʔ*   *paa*   *tumaruumoaa-yu*
        D4   EVID-CTR   water   much-VB
        That was a lot of water.   (93:3)

A type of partitive construction exists with certain quantifiers. In this construction, the quantifier may precede both a demonstrative adjective and the noun, occur between them, or follow them both.

(206)   Q   D   H
        tumaruumoa-ku   *sihka*   *kuruʔatsih-a*   *ahwé-nu*
        much-A   D1As   lily-A   dig-PST
        (They) dug up lots of these water lily roots.   (127:6)

(207)   D   Q   H
        suruu   *-seʔ*   *su-sumuʔ-nuu*   *waʔihpuʔa-nuu*   *suhka*   *wanakotseʔ-a*
        D4Np   CTR   RDP-one-Np   woman-Np   D4As   soap-A

        petihtai-ʔee-yu
        drop-REP-DUR
        Some of those women would throw away that soap.   (129:7)

(208)   D   H
        wihnu   *maruu*   *nanawaʔihpuʔa-nuu*   *sehka*   *kuyuníiʔ-a*
        then   D2Gp   womenˆfolk-Np   D5As   turkey-A

        Q
        soo-ko   *kwasuì -ku-nu*
        many-A   cook-CAUS-PST
        Then their womenfolk would cook many of those various turkeys.
                                                                     (120:20)

There are no special existential quantifiers for indefinite quantification, but the question words *hini* 'what? (NOM)' and *hina* 'what? (ACC)' function in this role (cf. §3.3). There is, in addition, a derived nominal form *uʔahru* 'anyone' (NOM), with accusative and genitive forms *uʔahri* and *uʔahruna*, respectively, which appear to be restricted to negative clauses; but this is not certain.

(209) *o-bo-ti-ka*   *hunu?-ru-ti*   *noo*   *hina*   *tu-hani̱-ki-ti*
     D3-DIR-at-!p   creek-along-at   NEC   what?ˆA   black-do-come-PROGˆA

       okwe-hki-ti   *puhwai-hbʉʉni̱*
       flow-come-PROGˆA   look-AUG
       Look along the creek for some blackish thing coming floating down
       toward us over there! (6:24)

(210) *keta?* *kwasi-kʉ* *si-nih-ku* *u?ahrʉn-a* *atʉhʉn-a* *nohi?-a* *yaa-rʉ*
     NEG!   tail-at   D1-M-A   anyone-G   stranger-G   toy-A   take-PROG
     Next time, do not take any stranger's toy like this! (83:32)

11.3. Numerals. Little information is available concerning the numerical system. The stem *sʉmʉ-* 'one' also expresses notions of completeness and totality (§13.3). The form *hayarokwe* 'four' is analyzable as *haya* 'two times' (?) plus *tokwe* 'exact' and *mo?obe?* 'five' is clearly *mo?o* 'hand' plus *-be?* (measure).

The suffix *-?* marks *sʉmʉ?* 'one' as a derived noun or adjective. Similarly, the stem *waha-* 'two' may appear in derived form with *-tʉ/-rʉ* (imperfective participle), where it is in addition marked overtly with the dual suffix, as *wahahtʉhʉ* or *wahahtʉkwʉ*. Other numerals can be marked as plural forms, all making use of this same *-tʉ/-rʉ* plus *-ʉ* for plural. All derived numerals are marked as genitive or accusative in appropriate contexts.

The suffix *-bah* can be added to at least some numeral stems to express separateness (i.e., the items are not a natural set) or distribution over two or more items.

(211) *surʉ* *-kʉ-se?* *suhri* *bihi?a-nih* *waha-bah-tih* *na-ropʉsi?i-tih*
     D4   EVID-CTR   D4Ad   boy-Ad   two-SEP-Ad   REFL-bead-Ad

      uhri   *napʉ-máka-nʉ*
      D4Ad   shoe-give-PST
      She gave each of the two boys a pair of beaded moccasins. (74:19)

Other processes are hinted at, but how productive these are is not known. Reduplication of *sʉmʉ?* 'one' yields *sʉsʉmʉ?* 'some', and *sʉsʉ?ana* 'sometimes'. Addition of the intensifier *-sʉ* to the same basic form yields *sʉmʉsʉ* 'once, one time'.

Finally, there are two ways to express 'half'. The form *sʉkwee-bi* originally has to do with working down a row but not returning. The postposition *tʉbi̱naa?(weki̱)* means both 'half' and 'in the middle'.

A numeral normally precedes the noun it modifies. Genitive pronouns are proclitic to nouns and, therefore, follow numerals. The postposition *tʉbịnaaʔ(wekị)* 'half' naturally follows its noun.

(212) Q   H
       wahah-tʉkwʉ   *taʔwoʔiʔ-nʉkwʉ*   *na-mahtowʉnʉ-kạ*
       two-Nd   gun-Nd   REFL-lean-ST
       Two guns stood leaning (against the wall).   (92:12)

(213) Q   PO   H
       sʉmʉ-ʔ   *u*   *tʉiʔ*   *toya-ma-tu*   *poma-miʔa-nʉ*
       one-Ns   D4G   friend   mountain-on-along   pick-go-PST
       Her friend went up into the mountain to pick.   (111:10)

12

Pronouns

In general, the pronoun system distinguishes three persons (speaker, spoken to, spoken about) and three numbers (singular, dual, plural). The system further distinguishes inclusive and exclusive forms for nonsingular first person—inclusive pronouns including person(s) addressed, exclusive pronouns excluding them. Third-person pronouns exhibit another embellishment of the system in distinguishing the same spatial ranking of third persons as is found in demonstrative adjectives (§12.1). Nominative forms of pronouns are introduced first, followed by accusative, genitive, and reflexive forms, in that order.

12.1. Nominative pronouns. Nominative forms of pronouns occur primarily as main clause subjects. First-person nominative pronouns are listed in (214). There are two singular forms, the second of which is emphatic and occurs only rarely. There are three dual forms, one exclusive (x) of a second person and two inclusive (i) of a second person, the two inclusive forms being used interchangeably. There are two plural forms, one exclusive and one inclusive.

(214)   *nʉʔ, nʉʉ*   (1xNs)
       nʉkwʉ   (1xNd)
       nʉnʉ   (1xNp)
       tahʉ, takwʉ (1iNd)
       tanʉ   (1iNp)

The second-person nominative pronouns are listed in (215). The two dual forms are interchangeable. The second-person form *nʉʉʔ* (2Ns/p) occurs exclusively in imperatives (§4.1) when addressing a single or plural number of persons, but not two persons.

(215)   *ʉnʉ*   (2Ns)
        mʉhʉ, mʉkwʉ   (2Nd)
        mʉnʉ   (2Np)

Third-person pronouns are based on demonstrative adjective roots (§11.1) and distinguish four of the five spatial categories of the demonstrative system—IMMEDIATE PROXIMAL, REMOTE PROXIMAL, IMMEDIATE DISTAL, and REMOTE DISTAL. Third-person-singular nominal pronouns add the suffix -*ʔ* to a demonstrative root, while dual and plural forms add the suffix -*tʉ/-rʉ*, as indicated in (216). There are two interchangeable endings for each of the dual forms.

(216)	3Ns	3Nd	3Np
IMMED^PROX (D1)	*iʔ*	*itʉhʉ, itʉkwʉ*	*itʉʉ*
REM^PROX (D2)	*maʔ*	*mahrʉ, marʉkwʉ*	*marʉʉ*
IMMED^DIST (D3)	*oʔ*	*ohrʉ, orʉkwʉ*	*orʉʉ*
REM^DIST (D4)	*uʔ*	*uhrʉ, urʉkwʉ*	*urʉʉ*

12.2. Accusative pronouns. Accusative forms of pronouns occur in main clauses as direct or indirect objects, and in subordinate clauses marked by -*ka*, -*ku*, or -*tsi* as either subjects or objects (§15.2).

First-person accusative pronouns are listed in (217). As with nominative forms, there is a second, emphatic form of the first-singular accusative pronoun.

(217)   *nʉ, nʉe(tʉ)*   (1xAs)
        nʉhi   (1xAd)
        nʉmi   (1xAp)
        tahi   (1iAd)
        tai   (1IiAp)

Second-person-singular accusative pronouns are listed in (218). The second singular form is emphatic, but the two plural forms are interchangeable.

(218)   *ʉ, ʉmi*   (2As)
        mʉhi   (2Ad)
        mʉi, mʉmi   (2Ap)

Third-person accusative pronouns are listed in (219). The singular pronouns are identical to corresponding nominative forms, except that they lack the derivational suffix -*ʔ* of nominatives. Dual and plural accusative pronouns have the ending -*i* common to many other accusative forms (§9.3).

(219)			3AS	3AD	3AP
	IMMED^PROX	(D1)	*i*	*itʉhi*	*itii*
	REM^PROX	(D2)	*ma*	*mahri*	*marii*
	IMMED^DIST	(D3)	*o*	*ohri*	*orii*
	REM^DIST	(D4)	*u*	*uhri*	*urii*

12.3. Genitive pronouns. A genitive pronoun occurs primarily as the possessor constituent of a noun phrase, with the genitive form preceding the head noun. There are five first-person genitive pronouns, as listed in (220). All but the singular form end in an underlying *n* which prevents spirantization of a following stop (§1.1).

(220)	*nʉ*	(1xGs)
	nʉhʉ	(1xGd)
	nʉmʉ	(1xGp)
	tahʉ	(1iGd)
	taa	(1iGp)

There are four second-person genitive pronouns, distinguishing the three number categories, but with two competing plural forms, as indicated in (221). All four have an underlying final *n*.

(221)	*ʉ*	(2Gs)
	mʉhʉ	(2Gd)
	mʉʉ, mʉmʉ	(2Gp)

Third-person genitive pronouns are listed in (222). These also have an underlying final *n*.

(222)			3Gs	3Gd	3Gp
	IMMED^PROX	(D1)	*i*	*itʉhʉ*	*itʉʉ*
	REM^PROX	(D2)	*ma*	*mahrʉ*	*marʉʉ*
	IMMED^DIST	(D3)	*o*	*ohrʉ*	*orʉʉ*
	REM^DIST	(D4)	*u*	*uhrʉ*	*urʉʉ*

(223)	*nah*	*nʉʔ*	*mʉʉ*	*kahni-kʉ-hu*	*ʉ*	*tsa-wee-hkwa-tuʔį*
	just	1xNs	2Gp	house-at-to	2As	INSTR-descend-go-UNR

I'll just haul you off to your camp.   (39:35)

(224)   nʉ   kwʉhi nʉʔ   nʉ   rʉrʉeʔ-tii   puni-tuʔi̠   ʉkʉnaa
        1xGs   wifeˆA 1xNs   1xGs   child-Ap   see-UNR   first
        I'll see my wife and my children first.   (39:25)

An IMPERSONAL GENITIVE form (*tan* →) *ta* 'one's, our, people's' does not distinguish either person or number.

12.4. Coreferential pronouns. Nondistinct argument phenomena were
discussed in §7, where forms designating unspecified subjects, unspecified objects, reflexives, passives, and reciprocals were discussed. There is also a set of
coreferential pronouns that serve an intensifying function in apposition with
other pronouns or full nominal forms. These forms make no distinction as to
person, but do distinguish singular, dual, and plural number, as well as case,
as indicated in (225). Competing forms are separated by comma (,). Genitive
forms have underlying final *n* and are used within an object noun phrase
when the possessor of the object noun is also the subject of the sentence or is
included in the subject.

(225)

	COS	COD	COP
N	*pʉnʉ*	*pʉhʉ, pʉkwʉ̠*	*pʉmʉ*
A	*pʉmi*	*pʉhi*	*pʉi, pʉmi*
G	*pʉ*	*pʉhʉ*	*pʉʉ*

(226) (*sitʉ-kwʉ̠*) su-kʉ-hu bʉʉ kahni-kʉ-hu urii bʉa-htsi pʉkwʉ miʔa-nʉ
        D1Nd   D4-at-to   COGp house-in-to D4Ap leave-SS CONd go-PST
        Leaving them there in their teepee, (these two) themselves went.
                                                                        (103:4)

(227) sʉ-sʉmʉʔ -kʉ-seʔ   pʉmʉ   u   yuhu-kʉ̠   u   kwasʉì -kʉ-nʉ
        RDP-one   EVID-CTR   CONp   D4   fat-in   D4   cook-CAUS-PST
        Some of them fried it in the fat.   (127:12)

13

Verbs

13.1. Verb stems. Each verb stem occurs in two forms, an unmodified form and a combining form. In general, the combining form of a verb stem is identical to the unmodified form except that it has either a final voiceless vowel or triggers an added *-h*. There are regular phonological patterns reflected in these forms, but these will not be considered here.

The unmodified form of a verb occurs in isolation as a citation or elicitation form. It can also take various suffixes. The combining form never occurs alone. It must have one of a special set of suffixes or be part of certain types of compounds. Since the special suffixes are scattered through several sections of this grammar summary, they are listed together in (228) for the sake of convenience.

(228) *-ka*   'stative'
       -ka   'dependent clause (different subject)'
       -ki   'motion toward (come)'
       -kwa   'motion away (go)'
       -kwai   'motion around, back and forth'
       -pɨni   'much'
       -tsi   'dependent clause (same subject)'
       -tɨki   'begin'
       -tɨni/-rɨni 'tell'

Many verbs are irregular in the sense that the stem used in the singular is different from that used in the dual and the plural. There is never a distinction between dual and plural in verb stems. In all cases, suppletion is determined by the number of the subject for intransitive verbs and by the

369

number of the object for transitive verbs. Each form is alphabetized separately in the dictionary, but with the other form supplied as well. Thus, one can find *tʉyaai* as the singular stem for 'die', with the nonsingular form *kooi* also given; or one can find *kooi* as the nonsingular stem, with the singular stem *tʉyaai* also given.

Suppletion is widespread, with several phonological patterns distinguishing the singular and nonsingular stems, but space does not permit discussion of these here. However, it was noted in section §9.2 that it is common for nominal elements not to be overtly marked for number, particularly if context makes clear the number involved. Suppletion in verbs can now be seen as one device available to the speaker for an indirect indication of number, whether of subject or object. In example (229), the object is not overtly marked as plural, yet *tʉkʉwasʉ* 'kill (PL OBJ) for food' rather than *tʉkʉhpehka* 'kill (SG OBJ) for food' provides sufficient indication of number for the object.

(229) soobe?sʉ   nʉnʉ   su-nih-ku   puhitóo?-a   rʉkʉ-wasʉ-?e-tʉ-ʉ
       long^ago   1xNp   D4-M-A   turkey-A   food-kill-REP-PROG-P
       Long ago we killed turkeys for food in that way.   (119:9)

(230) sitʉ   -kʉ-se?   ma   wʉh-kúpa-nʉ
       D1   EVID-CTR   D2A   INSTR-kill-PST
       He clubbed it to death.   (125:8)

(231) tai   wʉh-tokwʉ-ki-tʉ   ma?
       1iAp   INST-kill-come-PROG   D2Ns
       He's coming clubbing us to death.   (4:15)

Note that in (232) and (233), the verb is chosen on the basis of the subject even though there is an object in the sentence. *Yʉkwi/niwʉnʉ* 'say' is intransitive in the sense that it cannot take an indirect object; suppletion is controlled by the number of the subject.

(232) surʉ   -kʉ-se?   oha?ahnakatʉ   taa   haitsi   na-marʉni-nʉ   me
       D4   EVID-CTR   coyote   1iGp   friend   REFL-hurt-PST   QUOT

       yʉkwii-yu
       say-DUR
       Coyote said, "Our friend hurt himself."   (6:18)

(233) surʉʉ   -kʉ-se?   na-kwʉsʉ-?i-tuku   marʉkwʉ   me   niwʉnʉʉ-yu
       D4Np   EVID-CTR   REFL-kill-REAL-same   D2Nd   QUOT   say-DUR
       Those ones said, "They killed each other."   (94:18)

While not common, reduplication in certain verb stems can be used to signal a number of actions performed by subjects acting individually rather than as a group. The known examples are almost all verbs of motion or have an adjective as their first element.

(234) *surʉʉ*   *-kʉ-seʔ*   *pʉʉ*   *kahni-kʉ-hu*   *tu-runehtsʉ-nʉ*
      D4Np   EVID-CTR   COGp house-at-to   RDP-run-PST
      They ran to their houses.   (4:16)

(235) *marʉʉ*   *ooʔrʉ*   *tʉa-sʉ*   *marʉʉ*   *kahni*   *o-ʔokwenu-nạ*
      D2Gp   clothes QUOT-INTENS D2Gp   house   RDP-flow-CONT
      Their clothing and teepees are floating.   (122:19)

13.2. Instrumental prefixes. A prominent feature of many verbs is the incorporation of an initial, usually instrumental, element. Most instrumental prefixes relate to body parts, but a few relate to other notions such as 'mind', 'speech', and 'fire'. Several of the prefixes have two or three different forms depending on phonological considerations, but each has been alphabetized in such a way that related forms fall together in the dictionary. Examples of prefixes follow, with illustrative sentences below.

(236) *hu-*   'with back'   *to(h)-*   'with violent motion of hand'
      ki-   'with elbow'   *tsa(h)-*   'with inward, upward motion
                                              of hand'
      ku-   'with head'   *tsi(h)-*   'with sharp pointed instrument'
      kʉ(h)-   'with teeth'   *tso(h)-*   'with head'
      ma-   'with hand'   *wʉ(h)-*   'with body/sideways'
      mu-   'with nose'   *ku(h)-*   'with heat'
      pi(h)-   'with buttocks'   *ni-*   'with speech'
      sʉʉ(h)- 'with feet'   *su-*   'with mind'
      ta(h)-   'with foot/leg'

(237) *nʉ-mati-tʉ*   *sʉmʉ-sʉ*   *pia-kʉh-kaʔa*
      1sAs-PART-Ns   one-INTENS   big-INSTR-cut
      Take one big bite of me!   (22:14)

(238) *sitʉ*   *-kʉ-seʔ*   *waʔihpʉʔ*   *pʉ*   *tʉeti*   *soko-ko*   *ma-hbé-nʉ*
      D1   EVID-CTR   woman   COG child^A earth-on   INSTR-drop-PST
      This woman dropped her child to the ground.   (61:32, 33)

(239)   *sitʉ*   *-kʉ-seʔ*   *u*   *sʉʉh-poʔtse-nʉ*
        D1   EVID-CTR   D4A   INSTR-jerk-PST
        She kicked it.   (41:7, 8)

(240)   *sitʉ*   *-kʉ-seʔ*   *ma*   *kwʉhʉ*   *ma*   *ku-ʔina-nʉ*
        D1   EVID-CTR   D2G   wife   D2A   INSTR-jerk^meat-PST
        His wife roasted it.   (126:14)

13.3. Temporal prefixes. Other, noninstrumental, prefixes are generally temporal in nature. These include *ʉkʉ-* 'still, just', *namʉsi-* 'quickly',
and *sʉmʉ* 'completely, thoroughly'. There is also an augmentative *pia-*
'big, loud'.

(241)   *me*   *u*   *ʉkʉ-yʉkwi-ka*   *pia-woinu*   *pi-pikúu-yu*
        QUOT   D4A   just^now-say-DS   big-horn   RDP-sound-DUR
        Just as he had spoken, a big bugle sounded.   (85:13)

(242)   *namʉsohi-htsi-ka*   *namʉsi-tuhkanáaiʔ-niwʉnʉ*
        hurry-SS-!p   quickly-Wichita-talk
        Hurry and quickly speak Wichita!   (78:15)

(243)   *sitʉ*   *-kʉ-seʔ*   *siʔah-ru*   *marʉʉ-kʉ-hu*   *toʔi-nʉ*   *pʉ*
        D1   EVID-CTR   D1L-along   D2p-at-to   go^up-PST   COG

        kwasuʔi   *sʉmʉ-sihwapʉ-nai-hkʉ*
        dress^A   one-torn/become-BE-DS
        This one came up to them along here, her dress having become all
        torn.   (53:24)

(244)   *surʉ*   *-kʉ-seʔ*   *wihnu*   *ohaʔahnakatʉ*   *pia-yake-nʉ*
        D4   EVID-CTR   then   Coyote   big-cry-PST
        Then Coyote cried loudly.   (6:18)

13.4. Number agreement. Syntactic marking in verbs is limited to number
agreement and various subordinating suffixes. Verbs optionally take suffixes
to mark them as agreeing with their subjects. This marking option is most often realized with dual subjects, less often with plural. In both circumstances,
number agreement is a type of emphasis.

With *-tʉ/-rʉ* (progressive aspect), agreement is by addition of the dual suffix
-hʉ or *-kwʉ*, used interchangeably, or the plural suffix *-ʉ*. These verbs therefore look like derived nouns (§8.1) or adjectives (§8.3).

Verbs   373

(245)   **Singular**   **Dual**   **Plural**
         tɨhka-rɨ   tɨhka-rɨ-hɨ   tɨhka-rɨ-ɨ   'eat'
         wihi-tɨ   wihi-tɨ-kwɨ   wihi-tɨ-ɨ   'throw'

In verbs not marked with progressive aspect, optional agreement is by the
dual suffix -nɨhɨ or -nɨkwɨ, used interchangeably, and the plural suffix -nɨɨ.
These verbs therefore look like nonderived nouns (§9.2).

(246)   **Singular**   **Dual**   **Plural**
         nɨhkaʔi   nɨhkaʔi-nɨhɨ   nɨhkaʔi-nɨɨ   'danced'
         nɨkɨbɨni   nɨkɨbɨni-nɨkwɨ   nɨkɨbɨni-nɨɨ   'dance much'

Whether or not a speaker chooses to mark number overtly by adding an
agreement suffix, number is sometimes indicated through verb-stem suppletion or reduplication (§13.1). Thus ɨhpɨi 'sleep (SG SUBJ)' is distinct from
ɨhkooi 'sleep (PL SUBJ)', and okwe 'flow' (with no subject indication) is distinct
from oʔokwe 'flow' (with reduplication showing that several subjects are acting as individuals and not collectively).

13.5. Causative/Benefactive. Many verbs are inherently causative or
benefactive, such as *tsaka* 'lead by the hand/reins' or *maka* 'feed'. Other
noncausative or benefactive verbs can be made such by the addition of the
suffix -kɨ (causative). In terms of sentence structure, this suffix normally
makes an intransitive verb transitive, and a transitive verb ditransitive.
As (247) and (248) show, the subject of the originally intransitive verb
may become the object of the causative verb marked with -kɨ. In (248),
the benefactive *kohtookɨ* 'build a fire for' accepts an object where originally no object would have been permitted (because *kohtoo* 'build a fire'
is intransitive).

(247) surɨ   -kɨ-seʔ   u   kwasɨ-hka   pɨ   tɨ-rɨeʔ-tii   nimai-nɨ
       D4   EVID-CTR   D4A cook-DS   COG   RDP-child-Ap call-PST
       When it had cooked, he called his children.   (7:30)

(248) sitɨ   -kɨ-seʔ   wakaréʔeeʔ   moʔobe-tii   tɨʔrikúuʔ-nii   kwasɨi-kɨ-bɨni̠
       D1   EVID-CTR   turtle   five-Ap   prairie^dog-Ap cook-CAUS-AUG
       This turtle cooked (transitive) five prairie dogs.   (9:1)

(249) sɨmɨ-ʔ   ruibihtsi-ʔ   pɨi   kohtóo-kɨ-nɨ
       one-Ns   young^man-Ns   COAp   make^fire-CAUS-PST
       One young man built a fire for them.   (70:16)

At times the syntactic structure in which verbs with and without -*kʉ* occur is more complex. For example, *tuhubʉhka* 'get angry' takes a human subject and no object, but *tuhubʉhkakʉ* 'get angry about' takes the same human subject plus a direct object noun phrase which expresses the source of anger.

(250) *sitʉ*   -*kʉ-seʔ*   *ohaʔahnakatʉ*   *tuhú-bʉhka-nʉ*   *pʉ-metʉ*
       D1   EVID-CTR   Coyote   black-hush?-PST   CO-at

      u   *yahne-na*   *ruhú-bʉhka-kʉ-nʉ*
      D4G   laugh-NOM   black-hush?-CAUS-PST
Coyote got angry, got angry at her laughing at him.   (16:15)

13.6. Motion. Some of the adverbial suffixes expressing motion are shown below, along with related independent verbs. The suffixes without an asterisk (*) never attach to the combining form of a verb (§13.1). Those marked with an asterisk can occur with the combining form or with the unmodified verb stem. With these suffixes, a difference in meaning is expressed by choosing the combining form over the unmodified form. The combining form expresses the notion of action either followed by the indicated motion or occurring simultaneously with the indicated motion, while the unmodified form of the stem expresses the notion of indicated motion resulting in or for the purpose of the named action.

(251) -*miʔa*   'unspecified motion' (*miʔa* 'go')
       -*nii*   'motion around, from place to place (SG)'
       -*yʉhka*   'motion around, from place to place (PL)', (*yʉka*
                        'move about, walk (PL)')
       *-*ki*   'motion toward' (*kima* 'come')
       *-*kwa*   'motion away'
       *-*kwai*   'motion around, back and forth'

(252) *sitʉ*   -*kʉ-seʔ*   *yʉtsʉ-miʔa-rʉ*
       D1   EVID-CTR   fly-go-PROG
       This one goes flying.   (31:6)

(253) *hini*   *u-waka-tu*   *kasá-bi-pɨku-hki-na*
       what?ˆN   D4-toward-along   wing-RDP-beat-come-CONT
       Something kept coming toward him making wing noises.   (27:3)

(254) *sitʉʉ*   -*sihka*   *raibooʔ-a*   *noo-nʉ-kwa*
       D1Np   D1As   white^man-A   haul-PST-go
       These ones carried off this white man.   (28:23)

(255) *setɨ   ma   noo-pɨh-a   hima-hkwai-tɨ*
      D5   D2G   haul-NOM-A   take-back^and^forth-PROG
      These various ones come and go taking his load.   (97:34)

As the above examples show, the adverbial suffixes expressing motion can occur with aspect markers (§13.7). These suffixes are sometimes used redundantly, so that the indicated motion is doubly indicated.

(256) *kima   habi-ki̱*
      come   lie^down-come
      Come! Come and lie down!   (48:20)

Three other adverbial affixes will be mentioned here. The suffix -*etɨ* 'each one' indicates identical or similar action distributed over several subjects. The suffix -*pɨni/-bɨni* 'much' is augmentative, indicating that a good deal of the action named by the verb is going on. It takes the combining form of the verb (§13.1). Of these two suffixes, only the second can occur with a singular subject. Finally, the proclitic numeral **sɨmɨ-** 'one' indicates that the action named by the verb is done completely or thoroughly.

(257) *sitɨɨ   pɨɨ   kahni-kɨ-ku   kohtoo-ʔetɨ-tsi   sihka   pɨɨ*
      D1p   OGp   house-at-A   make^fire-each^one-SS   D1As   COGp

      ahwe-pɨh-a   tɨkɨh-mani-nɨ
      dig-NOM-A   food-prepare-PST
      Each making a fire in her home, they cooked their diggings. (127:10)

(258) *sitɨ   -kɨ-seʔ   siʔana   wɨnɨ-rɨ   na-buih-wɨnɨ-bɨni̱*
      D1   EVID-CTR   D1L   stand-PROG   REFL-eye-stand-AUG
      This one stands here and examines himself a lot.   (32:11)

(259) *nɨkɨ-tsi   nɨɨʔ-ka   sɨmɨ-ʔɨʔ-tsumi-hki-na̱*
      dance-SS   2N-!p   one-eye?-disappear-come-CONT
      Dancing, keep coming with your eyes completely closed.   (3:11)

13.7. Aspect. There are apparently no tense markers as such, but a rich array of aspect markers. Tense refers to specification of when, in the flow of time, an event takes place. Aspect does not place an event in time, but rather focuses on other features of the event—its beginning or ending, whether it is ongoing or not, whether it is to be considered as an action or as a state, and so on.

A common possibility is for the verb stem to occur in uninflected form. This is clearly the semantically neutral or unmarked state, where context is sufficient to make intended meanings clear, and the addition of specific aspect suffixes is dependent on the judgment of the speaker as to the ability of the hearer to keep up with the flow of information. Considerations of emphasis may of course dictate the addition of one or another aspect marker even when one is not otherwise required.

(260) *suruu*   *-ku̱-se?*   *na-rah-ka?wi̱-tsi*   *nuku̱-bui̱ ni̱*
       D4Np   EVID-CTR   REFL-INSTR-gather-SS   dance-AUG
       Those ones, having gathered together, were dancing a lot.   (3:2)

(261) *surukwu̱* *-ku̱-se?*   *tena-nukwu̱ tsaa-tu̱*   *ma?*   *me*   *niwu̱nu̱*
       D4d   EVID-CTR   man-Nd   good-NOM   D2Ns   QUOT   say
       Those two men said, "It's good."   (111:5)

Inceptive. There are two verb markers that focus on the beginning of a named event, /-tu̱ki/ and /-pitu̱/. The first marker may be related to the independent verb *tu̱ki* 'place, put'; the second is clearly related to the independent verb *pitu̱* 'arrive'.

(262) *suruu*   *-ku̱-se?*   *wihnu*   *uruu*   *wobi-wihtua*   *piku̱-rui̱ u̱ki*
       D4p   EVID-CTR   then   D4Gp   wood-bucket   beat-begin
       Those ones then began beating their drum.   (70:19)

(263) *su̱mu̱?*   *uruu-matu̱*   *ma-waka*   *nahá-biitu̱*
       one^Ns   D4p-PART   D2-toward   happen-arrive
       One of them happened onto him.   (86:18)

(264) *situ̱*   *-ku̱-se?*   *u̱mu̱-hú-piitu̱*
       D2   EVID-CTR   rain-INDEF-arrive
       It began to rain. (51:4)

As (264) shows, *-piitu̱* may be preceded by /-hun/ (indefinite), the two elements appearing as *-hupiitu̱*. Both forms are sometimes translated 'suddenly', suggesting that there may be an element of spontaneity or unexpectedness present. Notice also that *-tu̱ki takes* the combining form of the verb, *-piitu̱* takes the unmodified form of the stem.

Completive. The suffix *-ma* (completive) focuses on the coming to completion of an event that is presupposed to have been ongoing. It attaches to the unmodified form of a verb stem. The suffix *-?i̱* (realized) is similar to *-ma* in dealing with the completion of an event, but -ʔi states that the event is over and done while -ma specifies more closely the coming to be over and done. It also attaches to the unmodified form of the stem.

(265)   *sitɨɨ*   *-kɨ-seʔ*   *suhka*   *tɨhka-rɨ*   *wihnu*   *tɨhká-ma-nɨ*
       D1   EVID-CTR   D4As   eat-PROG   then   eat-COMPL-PST
       This one was eating that, and then finished eating.   (39:30)

(266)   *wahah-tɨkwɨ*   *wasáasiʔ-tena-nɨkwɨ*   *nɨ-waka*   *bitɨ-ʔi*
       two-Nd   Osage-man-Nd   1xA-toward   arrive-REAL
       Two Osage men arrived where I was.   (105:21)

(267)   *sitɨɨ*   *-kɨ-seʔ*   *ma*   *pitɨ-ʔi-ma-tu*   *na-ʔoki-tɨ*
       D1p   EVID-CTR   D2G   arrive-REAL-on-along   REFL-rejoice-PROG
       These ones are rejoicing over her return.   (40:43)

As (267) shows, a verb marked with -ʔi may serve as the stem to which postpositional elements can be attached. As such, it may be possible to analyze -ʔi as a nominalizer. The ramifications of this analysis will not be pursued here.

Stative. The suffix /-kan/ (stative) focuses on events as states rather than actions, expressing the notion that such-and-such a state exists. The suffix attaches to the combining form of the verb. The stative forms are often translatable as 'be X-ing' or 'be X-ed'.

(268)   *surɨ*   *-kɨ-seʔ*   *sɨmɨ-bekwi-ka*
       D4   EVID-CTR   one-swell-ST
       That one was all swelled up.   (28:17)

(269)   *sitɨɨ*   *-kɨ-seʔ*   *sehka*   *taʔsiwóoʔ-a*   *soni-too-hka-ku*   *marɨɨ-kɨ-hu*
       D1p   EVID-CTR   D5As   buffalo-A   grass-graze-ST-Ds   D2p-at-to

       kɨa-hu-piitɨ
       comeˆup-INDEF-arrive
       As the buffalo were grazing, they came up to them.   (69:6, 7)

Repetitive. The suffix -ʔe marks repeated action. It occurs with the unmodified verb stem. Since -ʔe contains no indication of how frequently an event is repeated, it can be used for a variety of contexts. In (270), repeated action over a short time span is expressed. In (271), the sense is more along the lines of habitual activity, presumably over an indefinitely long time period.

(270) situ   -ku̱-se?   u   tsuhni-pu̱h-a   u̱mah-paa-ku̱-hu   wihí-?ee-yu̱
       D1   EVID-CTR   D4G   bone-ABS-A   rain-water-in-to   throw-REP-DUR
       This one threw its bones in the lake.   (10:22)

(271) suru̱u̱   -ku̱-se?   ma-nakwu̱-hi   tuu-?ee-yu
       D4p   EVID-CTR   beyond?-side-at   fetch^water-REP-DUR
       They would get water far away.   (81:2)

Continuative. The suffix -*na* (continuative) focuses on the continuation
of an event and attaches to the unmodified form of the verb stem. The suffix
-*mi?a* 'go' (§13.6) has apparently been extended to have much the same sense.
It sometimes occurs with a preceding -*hu* (indefinite). Both markers might be
translated 'keep on X-ing'.

(272) si?ana   -ku̱-se?   pi-bia-kwasinaboo-?   ma-waka-tu
       D1L   EVID-CTR   RDP-big-snake-Ns   D2-toward-along

       pa-kwabi-hkwai-na̱
       water-lie-back^and^forth-CONT
       Here big snakes were swimming around toward her.   (52:18)

(273) tukani̱-hu-mi?a-ru̱   ma?
       night-INDEF-go-PROG   D2Ns
       It is about to get dark.   (82:13)

(274) nu̱nu̱   -se?   paa-ku̱   wihnu   u   kotsé-mia-?ee-yu̱
       1xNp   CTR   water-in   then   D4A   wash-go-REP-DUR
       We would then go wash it in water.   (110:17, 18)

Progressive. The suffix /-*tu̱n*/ (progressive) focuses on an event as being in progress. The distinction between progressive and continuative is
often subtle. Continuative expresses the idea that the event keeps on going, while the progressive says nothing about continuation but merely
reports that the event is occurring. This suffix attaches to the unmodified
form of the verb stem.

(275) nu̱   na?-nu̱mu̱-nii   nu̱?   nu̱e   no-bu̱a-hrai-kwu̱-ka
       1xGs   kin-Comanche-Ap   1xNs   1xAs   haul-leave-final-go-Ds

       uru̱u̱   napu̱-hu   mi?a-ru̱
       D4Gp   foot-to   go-PROG
       My relatives having abandoned me, I am following their trail. (38:14)

(276)   *surɨ*   *-seʔ*   *pia-nohko-ʔawo-baai-tɨ*
       D4   CTR   big-bake-vessel-have-PROG
       She had a big oven.   (109:8)

Unrealized. The suffixes /-tuʔih/ and /-waʔih/ (unrealized) mark an event as not having taken place although potentially capable of taking place. They attach to the unmodified form of a verb stem, with *-tuʔi* occurring in an affirmative clause and *-waʔi* occurring if *ke* (negative) is in the same clause. The suffix *-hu* (indefinite) often occurs preceding *-tuʔi* (never before *-waʔi*). Both suffixes can take a following *-tu* (progressive) to express ongoing potentiality, and both are often translatable as the English future.

(277)   *...ke*   *tamɨ-ma-tu*   *musa-sua-waʔi-tɨ*
       NEG   1INd-on-along   ?-think-UNR-PROG
       ...will not be concerned about us.   (78:14)

(278)   *sitɨ*   *-kɨ-seʔ*   *ma*   *petɨʔ*   *rɨʔɨya-na*   *pɨ*   *ahpɨʔ-a*   *pɨ*
       D1   EVID-CTR   D2G   daughter   fear-CONT   COGs   father-A   COGs

           tɨrɨhka-ruʔih-a   *ke*   *su-waai-kɨ*
           steal-UNR-A   NEG   INSTR-lack-Ds
       Her daughter is afraid, because her father does not want her to steal.
                                                 (66:20, 21)

(279)   *noha*   *uʔ*   *nɨ*   *kwɨhɨ-ruʔi*
       nearly   D4Ns   1sAs   catch-UNR
       He almost caught me.   (105:28)

Other. In this section the suffixes /-nuh/ and *-yu* will be mentioned, although their exact status remains unclear. Each of these attaches to the unmodified verb stem. /-nuh/ most often occurs in contexts where English uses the past tense. It appears to express the notion of a relatively short-lived event. On the other hand, *-yu* expresses the idea of a longer-lived event (here glossed DURATIVE). These suffixes thus contrast with each other, although they are compatible with the *-ma* (completive). /-nuh/ is incompatible with *-ʔe* (repetitive).

(280)   *uhka*   *orii*   *wɨh-paʔi-ku*   *-seʔ*   *u*   *piaʔ*   *yake-nɨ*
       D4As   D3Ap   INSTR-beat-Ds   CTR   D4G   mother   cry-PST
       When they beat him, his mother cried.

(281)   *uhka*   *orii*   *wɨh-paʔi-ku*   *-seʔ*   *u*   *piaʔ*   *yakee-yu*
       D4As   D3Ap   INSTR-beat-Ds   CTR   D4G   mother   cry-DUR
       When they beat him, his mother was crying.

(282)   *sitɨ*   *-kɨ-seʔ*   *pitɨ-sɨ*   *pitɨ-nu*
       D1   EVID-CTR   back-INTENS   arrive-PST
       This one arrived back.   (105:24)

(283)   *nohiʔ*   *tsaa*   *na-buni-yu*   *nɨɨ*
       very   good   REFL-see-DUR   1xNs
       I look very nice.   (32:12)

Note that of the two suffixes under discussion, verbs of saying *(niikwi, yɨkwi, niwɨnɨ)* regularly take *-yu* and apparently never /-nuh/.

Summary. Since the preceding examples of aspect markers do not adequately illustrate their sequential possibilities, these are summarized as follows.

As noted it is common for a verb to be marked with no overt aspect suffix. For verbs taking *-ma* (completive), *-tɨki* (inceptive), *-pitɨ* (inceptive), *-miʔa* 'go', and *-ka* (stative), there is usually no further indication of aspect. The combination *-ka* + *-tɨ* (temporary state) occurs frequently enough, however, that it deserves special mention. Also note that *-nɨ* (short-lived) falls before the motion suffixes *-ki* and *-kwa* (§13.6), even though it would seem that it should follow them.

(284)   **Aspect sequences**

Repeated	**Motion**	**Realized**	**Other**
-ʔe	*-ki*	*-ʔi*	*-tɨ*
-nɨ	*-kwa*	*-tuʔi/-waʔi*	*-na*
			-yu

14

Adverbs

Apart from their linking function between successive clauses in discourse, adverbial elements are of various types and play varying roles within the sentence. Temporal, locative, manner, directional, and other adverbials may be individual lexical items, nominals, postpositional phrases, or entire subordinate clauses. Whenever a clause contains two or more adverbials of the same type (temporal, locative, etc.), the normal order is from more general to more specific. Adverbs of degree precede the elements they modify.

(285) nohiʔ   tᵻh-tᵻtaa-tᵻᵻ   tᵻ-rᵻe-hpᵻʔ-rᵻᵻ   tai   tsaah-tᵻhka-kᵻ-nᵽ
       very   RDP-little-Np   RDP-small-ABS-Np   1iAp   good-eat-CAUS-PST
       Very small children caused us to eat well.   (75:28)

14.1. Temporal adverbs. Temporal adverbs include *kwasikᵻ* 'next time', *ᵻkᵻnaa* 'first', *meeku* 'now', *ᵻkihtsiʔ* 'now', *kᵻtu* 'yesterday', *pᵻetsᵽku* 'in the morning', *pᵻetsᵽkusᵻ* 'early in the morning', and others. When noun phrases are used as temporal adverbs, they are in the accusative case.

(286) setᵽ   -seʔ   suhka   tabe-ni   u-kᵽ-hu   no-bitᵻ-ʔee-yᵽ
       D5   CTR   D4As   sun-?   D4-at-to   haul-arrive-REP-DUR
       That day, they would camp there.   (129:5)

14.2. Locative adverbs. Locative adverbs include *kᵻmaʔkᵻ* 'beside', *kᵻmaʔru* 'alongside', *uhtu* 'along there', *unaʔru* 'along the other side', *hunaikᵻ* 'outside', and many others.

(287) *situ̱*   *-ku̱-seʔ*   *ma*   *kwu̱hu̱*   *hunai-ki̱*   *pu̱nu̱*   *nu̱mii-yu̱*
       D1   EVID-CTR   D2G   wife   outside-at   CONs   move-DUR
       His wife herself was moving about outside.   (48:19)

14.3. Directional adverbs. Directional adverbs include *ku̱maʔku* 'to the edge of' and *pitu̱su̱* 'back'. With verbs of motion, directional adverbs distinguish between motion toward and motion away from, as in *hunaku̱hu* '(toward) outside' and *hunakwu̱hi* '(from) outside'.

(288) *siʔane-tu̱*   *situ̱hu̱*   *pitu̱-su̱*   *mia-hu-tu̱ʔi̱*
       D1L-from   D1Nd   back-INTENS   go-INDEF-UNR
       At this point, these two are about to go back.

(289) *situ̱* *-ku̱-seʔ*   *uh-tu*   *toʔi-kwa̱* *e-ku̱-hu* *huna-ku̱-hu*   *toʔi-nu̱*
       D1   EVID-CTR   D4-along   go^up-go   D5-at-to   outside-at-to   go^up-PST
       He went up through there and climbed outside there.   (92:17)

(290) *su̱mu̱-ʔ* *-ku̱-seʔ*   *waʔi-hpu̱ʔ*   *hu-nakwu̱-hi*   *ke*   *bu̱-ku̱-hu*
       one-Ns   EVID-CTR   woman-ABS   out-side-at   NEG   CO-at-to

       toʔi-waʔi̱   *na-naka-ku*   *-ku̱-seʔ*   *su̱ru̱*   *nu̱*   *-tsaʔ*
       go^up-UNR   REFL-hear-Ds   EVID-CTR   D4   1xNs   DECL

       toʔi-tu̱ʔi̱   *me*   *yu̱kwii-yu̱*
       go^up-UNR   QUOT   say-DUR
       Sounding from outside like a place not to go out to, one woman said,
       "I'll go out."   (52:11)

14.4. Demonstrative adverbs. Demonstrative adverbs are based on the same roots and conceptual scheme as demonstrative adjectives (§11.1), consisting of a demonstrative root plus an additional element. As might be expected, the patterns for locative and directional demonstrative adverbs are the most elaborate.

Locative and allative demonstrative adverbs. Three locative adverbs consist of a demonstrative root plus the general locative postposition /-kah/ 'in, at, on'. In these simple forms the vowel of /-kah/ is always devoiced and assimilates to that of the preceding root vowel.

(291) *i-ki̱*   'here (D1)'
       o-ko̱   'there (D3)'
       u-ku̱   'there (D4)'

Further semantic material in the form of other postpositions may be added. One set, formally allative and not strictly locative, overlaps with the above in distribution. This set uses the same three roots and the postposition /-kah/ (locative), but in addition has the postposition -hu 'into'. With the stem o (immediate distal), the postposition -hu appears as -ho. These forms can be used as locatives or allatives.

(292)   *i-kʉ-hu*   '(to) here (D1)'
        o-kʉ-ho   '(to) there (D3)'
        u-kʉ-hu   '(to) there (D4)'

Another set of allative demonstratives consists of a demonstrative root plus -bu 'way, direction'. After the stem o-, the vowel of -bu harmonizes to o.

(293)   *i-bu*   'this (D1) way'
        o-bo   'that (D3) way'
        u-bu   'that (D4) way'
        e-bu   'various (D5) ways'

All these forms may occur with initial consonant s, indicating presupposed prior knowledge of the location or direction on the part of the hearer. These and other possible forms are illustrated in (294)–(296).

(294)   *surʉ*   -kʉ-se?   *o-kʉ-ho*   *hunu?-ba?a-tu*   *to?i-nʉ*
       D4   EVID-CTR   D3-at-to   creek-on-along   go^up-PST
       She came out over there along the creek.   (37:7)

(295)   *su-kʉ-hu*   *sitʉ*   *tʉmarʉʉmoa-ku*   *urii*   *kʉhtá-nʉe-nʉ*
       D4-at-to   D1Ns   much-A   D4Ap   hard-blow-PST
       The wind blew hard on them there.   (53:26)

(296)   *pʉʉ*   *omo-mʉ-sʉ*   *surʉʉ*   *u-kʉ*   *bitʉ-nʉ*
       COGp   leg-on-INTENS   D4Np   D4-at   arrive-PST
       They arrived there on foot.   (119:10)

There are also three indefinite locative adverbs based on demonstrative roots and the suffix -?a which mean 'somewhere', having the same spatial ranking scheme as that underlying demonstrative adjectives. As with adjectives, initial s indicates that a location, even though indefinite, is presupposed to be a part of the hearer's knowledge.

(297)   *(s)i-ʔa*   'somewhere (D1)'
        (s)o-ʔa   'somewhere (D3)'
        (s)u-ʔa   'somewhere (D4)'

Three suffixes can occur with these stems: *-na* 'at somewhere' marks a narrowly focused location. (/ʔah-tun/) *-ʔahru* along/through somewhere', a variant of the postposition *-tu*, marks a location characterized as having span. *-netu*, a fusion of *-na* and *i* (verbalizer), with the postposition *-tu* 'from', signals change from one location to another or (in discourse) from one scene to another, either in location or time.

(298)   *suru*   *-ku-seʔ*   *so-ʔa-na*   *bu*   *tu-rue?-tuu-ku*   *bitu-nu*
        D4   EVID-CTR   D3-L-at   COGS   RDP-small-Np-at   arrive-PST
        That one arrived somewhere there among his children.   (6:23)

(299)   *situ*   *-ku-seʔ*   *ohaʔahnakatu*   *si-ʔah-ru*   *toʔi-ki*
        D1   EVID-CTR   Coyote   D1-L-along   go^up-come
        Coyote comes up along here somewhere.   (10:23)

(300)   *situ*   *-ku-seʔ*   *si-ʔa-ne-tu*   *toʔi-nu*
        D1   EVID-CTR   D1-L-at-from   go^up-PST
        At this point, he came out.   (20:26)

Temporal demonstrative adverbs. Temporal demonstratives consist of a demonstrative root with presuppositional *s*, *-be* (measure), the suffix *-ʔ* (nominalizer), and usually with /-sun/ (intensifier). The variety of forms characteristic of locatives and allatives is not found. The two known forms are listed in (301).

(301)   *si-beʔ-su*   'at this time, now (D1)'
        su-beʔ-su   'at that time, then (D4)'

As (302) and (303) show, these forms can be used to express temporal notions extending beyond the purely punctual.

(302)   *su-beʔ-su*   *-ku-seʔ*   *su-sumu?*   *kwasinabooʔ* *piʔtoʔ-naʔi*
        D4-MEAS-INTENS   EVID-CTR   RDP-one   snake   bobtailed-become
        Since then, some snakes are bobtailed.   (36:16)

(303) *puhihwi-kahni-kų*   *ra-kwų*   *ta-hų*   *puhiwi-hta*   *si-beʔ-ni-kị-yu-tų*
     money-house-in   1i-ND   1i-GD   money-A   D1-MEAS-M-in-VB-from

     tahniʔi-ʔe-tuʔi
     put-REP-UNR
     From now on, let's put our money in the bank.   (49:33)

There are two indefinite temporal adverbs, *hipeʔsų* 'at some time' and *susųʔana* 'sometimes'. The former is related to the question word *hipeʔ* 'when?'

Manner demonstrative adverbs. Manner demonstratives consist of a demonstrative root and -*ni* (manner), the root always occurring with either initial *s* indicating the referent is presupposed to be known to the hearer or with a definite referent. Little elaboration is observed, forms apparently being limited to the those listed in (304).

(304) *si-ni*   'in this (D1) way, thus'
      so-ni 'in that (D3) way, thus'
      su-ni 'in that (D4) way, thus'
      se-ni 'in various (D5) ways'

(305) *ketaʔ* *kwasi-kų* *ų* *puhiwi-hta* *suni* *mųų-rų*
     NEG! tail-in 2Gs money-a D4M do-PROG
     Next time, do not treat your money like that.   (49:33)

In constructions where these manner adverbials relate to objects, they are optionally marked with the accusative adverbial ending -*ku*.

(306) *surųų* *wihnu* *su-hku-tų* *miʔa-nų* *sunih-ku* *uhri* *buni-htsị*
     D4Np then D4-at-from go-PST D4M-A D4Ad see-SS
     They then went from there, having seen them like that. (94:19)

One additional manner demonstrative adverb is mentioned here, although it does not contain any of the demonstrative stems that figure in the forms considered above. This adverb is *su-me* 'thus', used in contexts of saying or thinking. The first element of this form may be a demonstrative stem that no longer occurs elsewhere in the language. The second element is the quotative particle *me(h)* which was discussed in §2.

(307) *su-me* -*kų-seʔ* *u* *yųkwi-hka* *siʔana* *ohaʔahnakatų* *kimaa-yų*
     ?-QUOT EVID-CTR D4A say-Ds D1L Coyote come-DUR
     As she thus spoke, somewhere here Coyote was coming. (19:4)

15

Complex Sentences

The following sections treat complex sentences—those involving coordination, clausal complements, and relative clauses.

15.1. Coordination. We here distinguish between 'and', 'but', and 'or'. The most common expression of 'and' in coordinate sentences is simply by a succession of constituents, that is, by no overt conjunction. These constituents may be of any size up to an entire phrase or clause.

(308)   *nʉ*   *kwʉhi*   *nʉ?*   *nʉ*   *rʉrʉe?-tii*   *puni-tu?i̢*   *ʉkʉnaa*
          1xGs   wifeˆA   1xNs   1xGs   child-Ap   see-UNR   first
          I'll see my wife and my children first.   (39:25)

(309)   *mahrʉ*   *natsa?ani?*   *muh-pa?araih-tu*   *wʉh-tʉìkwa-nʉ*   *mahri*
          D2Gd   buggy   INSTR-inverted-along   INSTR-hit-PST   D2Ad

          ma-na?koroomi-nu̢
          UNSP-coverˆup-PST
          Their buggy fell upside down and covered them up.   (57:14)

The word (*tʉa-sʉn* 'QUOT-INTENS' →) *tʉasʉ* 'and, also' can be used to emphasize the notion of conjunction. It occurs between the elements being conjoined.

(310)   *nʉ*   *rʉʉhkaʔaʔ-a*   *tʉasʉ*   *nʉ*   *kukʉmeʔawe-tuku*   *nʉʔ*
        1xGs   axe-A   and   1xGs   skilletˆA-same   1xNs

        na-su-watsiʔ
        REFL-INSTR-lose
        I forgot my axe and my skillet.   (123:20)

(311)   *su-kʉ-hu*   *sitʉ*   *tʉmarʉʉmoa-ku*   *urii*   *kʉhtá-nʉe-nʉ*   *pahoopi-ma*
        D4-at-to   D1   much-A   D4Ap   hard-blow-PST   hail-with

        tʉasʉ   *urii*   *ʉma-nʉ*
        and   D4Ap   rain-PST
        It blew hard on them there, and also hailed on them.   (53:26)

In contrastive environments where English would use 'but', the realization of conjunction is zero.

(312)   *sitʉ*   *-kʉ-seʔ*   *tena-hpʉʔ*   *sihka*   *mahrʉ*   *tʉ-noo-pʉh-a*
        D1   EVID-CTR   man-ABS   D1As   D2Gd   UNSP-haul-NOM-A

        tsa-pʉhe-su-waai-tʉ   *u*   *mʉni-nʉ*
        INSTR-drop-INSTR-lack-PROG   D4   fail-PST
        This man tried to throw off their packs, but couldn't.   (96:22)

(313)   *situ*   *-kʉ-seʔ*   *tukani-nʉ*   *tsaa*   *mʉah-tabe-baʔi̱*
        D1   EVID-CTR   night-PST   good   moon-sun-have
        Night fell, but there was good moonlight.   (59:4)

The word for 'or' is *tʉanoo*, from *tʉa* (quotative) and *noo* (necessitative). It separates two equal constituents.

(314)   *orʉ*   *-tsaʔ*   *rena-hpʉʔ*   *hube*   *tʉa-noo*   *pitsi-pʉh-a*   *hibi-tuʔi̱*
        D3   DECL   man-ABs   coffeeˆA   QUOT-NEC   milk-ABs-A   drink-UNR
        That man will drink coffee or milk.

(315)   *pihiʔa-nii*   *tʉa-noo*   *tʉrʉeʔ-waʔihpʉʔa-nii*   *nʉnʉ*   *puniʔi̱*
        boy-Ap   QUOT-NEC   small-woman-Ap   1xNp   see-REAL
        We saw boys or girls.

15.2. Complement clauses. Complement clauses are marked with one of three subordinating suffixes and take subjects marked as accusative. The major distinctions are whether an event occurs simultaneously with the event of the next higher clause (or is overlapped temporarily by it), or whether subordinate and main clause subjects are different or identical.

No simultaneity or overlap. The subordinate suffix is *-ka* if the subject of the subordinate clause is different from that of the next higher clause. If the subjects are identical, the subordinate clause suffix is *-tsi* and its subject does not occur overtly. Both *-ka* and *-tsi* can attach to the combining form of the verb, and *-ka* can also be preceded by the inceptive marker *-hupitu̱* and either *-tu̱ʔi* or *-waʔi* (unrealized).

(316) u   yu̱i-hka   -ku̱-seʔ   maru̱u̱   nanah-tena-nu̱u̱
     D4A   evening-Ds EVID-CTR D2Gp RECIP-man-Np

      soo-ku̱ni-ku̱-hu   hibi-miʔa-nu̱
      much-house-at-to drink-go-PST
      When it had gotten evening, their menfolk went into town to drink.
                (59:3)

(317) hunakwu̱ mahri toboʔi-hu-pitu̱-ka   -ku̱-seʔ u kwu̱hu̱
     outside D2Ad stand-INDEF-arrive-Ds EVID-CTR D4G wife

      mahru̱-waka-tu   toʔi-nu̱
      D2Nd-toward-along goˆup-PST
      When the two had come to a stop outside, his wife came out towardthem.
             (39:26)

(318) suru̱u̱   tu̱ku̱-tsi   yuu-ʔu̱h-kooi-nu̱
     D4Np   eat-SS   quiet-eye?-die-PST
     Having eaten, they slept undisturbed.   (8:46)

(319) suhka u tu̱iʔ-a   bu̱a-htsi uhri miʔa-ku -ku̱-seʔ
     D4As D4G friend-A leave-SS D4Ad go-DS EVID-CR

      taʔsiwóoʔ   nu-nura-wu̱-na̱
      buffalo   RDP-run-?-CONT
      As they went, having left her friend, buffalo ran off. (43:30)

There is a restriction having to do with *-tsi* (same subject) and *-tu̱ʔi/-waʔi* (unrealized). Since UNREALIZED cannot occur syntactically with *-tsi*, there is a problem in sentences having identical main and subordinate clause subjects with unrealized aspect in the subordinate clause. The solution is to choose *-ka* as the subordinate clause in a special way to indicate that it is identical to the next higher subject. The special subject marking involves coreferential pronouns *pʉ* (singular), *pʉhi* (dual), and *pʉi* (plural).

(320) *soo-beʔ-sʉ*   *nʉmʉ-nʉʉ*   *pʉi*   *puhihwʉ-hima-ruʔi-ka*
       much-MEAS-INTENS   Comanche-Np   COAp   money-take-UNR-DS

      nʉmʉ-na-rʉmʉʉʔ-nʉʉ-kʉmaʔ-kʉ   *no-bitʉ-nu*
      Comanche-REFL-trade-Np-edge-at   haul-arrive-PST
       Long ago when Comanches were about to receive money, they camped near Comanche trade stores.   (59:1)

Simultaneity or overlap. The subordinate clause suffix is *-ku*, which attaches to the unmodified verb or is preceded by *-ka* (stative) or *-ʔe* (repetitive). If the next higher subject is different from the subordinate subject, the structure is straightforward.

(321) *urii*   *kima-noo-ko*   *suʔana*   *urʉʉ-mu-nakwʉ* *pia-ʔʉmah-paa-baʔi*
       D4Ap   come-haul-DS   D4L   D4p-INSTR-side   big-rain-water-have
       As they came traveling, there ahead of them was a big lake.   (93:2)

If the subjects of the two clauses are identical, the coreferential pronouns mentioned above are used in the lower clause. The subjects of the clauses can be identical since *-tsi* does not allow a preceding *-ka* (stative). Instead, *-ku* is found along with a coreferential pronoun in the complement.

(322) *sitʉ*   *-kʉ-seʔ*   *tʉtaati wihtue*   *pʉ*   *tsa-yaa-hka-ku*   *u*   *boma-nʉ*
       D1   EVID-CTR   little^A bucket-A   COGs   INSTR-take-ST-DS   D4A   pick-PST
       As she is carrying a little bucket, she picked it.   (73:4, 5)

Finally, note the following construction involving the word *kesʉ* 'before' (*ke* 'not' + *-sʉ* 'still').

(323) *sitʉ*   *-kʉ-seʔ*   *kesʉ*   *pʉ*   *waikina*   *u*   *wʉh-pitʉʉ-ku*   *u*
       D1   EVID-CTR   before   COGs   wagon^A   D4A   INSTR-arrive-DS   D4A

      kʉh-tsía-nʉ
      INSTR-bite-PST
       Before he could reach his wagon, this one bit him.   (27:9)

Subject and object. Both subjects and objects of complement clauses are marked syntactically as accusative. For accusative case-marking nouns, see §9.3. The accusative form of pronouns is presented in §12.2. Since only a single accusative pronoun can be proclitic to the verb, in a complement clause with both pronominal subject and object in OSV order, the first pronoun is stranded in nonproclitic position.

(324) *suni*   *urii*   *tai*   *mʉʉ-hka*   *-seʔ*   *taa*   *nanah-tena-nʉʉ*   *oh-to*
       D4M   D4Ap   1iA   do-DS   CTR   1iGp   RECIP-man-Np   D3-along

      toboʔi̱-hu-tuʔi̱
      stand-INDEF-UNR

When we have done thus to them, our menfolk will stand along there.   (119:18)

(325) *urii*   *urii*   *maka-hka*   *-kʉ-seʔ*   *urʉʉ*   *piaʔ*   *nohiʔ*   *tsaa-ku*
       D4Ap   D4Ap   feed-DS   EVID-CTR   D4Gp   mother   very   good-A

      mʉnʉ   *nʉ*   *rʉrʉeʔ-tii*   *maka-nʉ*
      2Np   1Gs   child-Ap   feed-PST

When they had fed them their mother said, "You fed my children very good."   (74:15)

Whenever a third-person-singular pronoun object would be stranded before another pronoun in a complement clause, a demonstrative (in the accusative case) substitutes for it. Third-person-singular accusative pronoun forms can occur only directly before the verb.

(326) *meeku-ka*   *na-makaʔmuuki̱*   *uhka*   *rai*   *buni-kwa-tuʔi̱-ka̱*
       now-!p   REFL-getˆready   D4As   1iAp   see-go-UNR-DS

Get ready now, so we can go see him!   (7:36)

(327) *uhka*   *u*   *wʉh-kaʔa̱-buni-ku*   *-kʉ-seʔ*   *hini*
       D4As   D4A   INSTR-chop-AUG-DS   EVID-CTR   what?ˆN

      kasá-bi-pi̱ku-hki-na̱
      wing-RDP-beat-come-CONT

As he was chopping it, something was coming making wing noises.   (27:3)

Coreferential forms. If the subject of a higher clause is also the object of a complement clause, a coreferential pronoun (§12.4) is used in the complement clause.

(328) *sɨtɨ*   *-kɨ-seʔ*   *wakaréʔeeʔ*   *suni*   *pɨmi*   *u*   *mɨɨ-miʔa-ku*
       D1   EVID-CTR   turtle   D4M   COA   D4A   do-go-DS

       ma-hoi-ki   *nɨɨʔ-kwipu-nɨ-kwa*
       D2-around-at   REFL-wrap-PST-go

This turtle, when he (the snake) treated him (the turtle) in that way,
he (the turtle) went off wrapping himself around [some weeds].
                                                              (36:12)

Similarly, if the main clause subject is included in the subject or the object
of a complement clause, then the latter will be a coreferential form.

(329) *surɨ*   *-kɨ-seʔ*   *suni*   *uhka*   *bɨi*   *mɨɨ-hka*   *mia-ruʔi*   *nɨʔ*   *me*
       D4   EVID-CTR   D4M   D4As   COAp   do-DS   go-UNR   1xNs   QUOT

       yɨkwii-yɨ
       say-DUR

When they treated him that way, he said, "I'll go."   (6:22)

(330) *sɨtɨ*   *-kɨ-seʔ*   *ma*   *piaʔ*   *pɨhi*   *muhne-htsi*   *miʔa-nɨ*
       D1   EVID-CTR   D2G   mother   COAd   lead-SS   go-PST

His mother, leading them, went.   (81:9)

15.3. Relative clauses. The most common type of relative clause has a
verb marked with the suffix *-a*. The verb takes either the suffix *-ʔi* (realized) or
one of the suffixes *-tuʔi/-waʔi* (unrealized). Both subjects and objects of relative clauses are marked as genitives (§§9.4 & 12.3). Relative clauses normally
directly follow the nouns they modify, but may sometimes precede them.

(331) *nɨ*   *buhiwi-hta*   *nɨʔ*   [*narohtɨma-kɨ*   *nɨ*   *rɨki-ʔih-a*]   *watsi-kɨ-ʔi*
       1Gs   money-A   1xNs   can-in   1Gs   put-REAL-A   lose-CAUS-REAL

I lost my money that I had put in a can.   (49:27)

(332) *sɨmɨ-ʔ* *-kɨ-tsaʔ*   *raibooʔ*   [*pɨ-ma-ku*   *bɨɨ*   *waahima-ruʔih-a*]
       oneˆNs   EVID-CTR   man   CO-on-a   COGp   Christmas-UNR-A

       waah-pi-hta   *wɨh-káʔa-miʔa-nɨ*
       cedar-ABS-A   INSTR-chop-go-PST

A white man went to cut down a cedar tree with which they would
celebrate Christmas.   (27:1)

It is common for a noun modified by a relative clause to be present only semantically and not syntactically. Even if a noun is not overt, however, a demonstrative adjective may be present.

(333) *u-mati*   *takwʉ*   *[taa*   *tʉhka-ruʔih-a]*   *pomaa-kwạ*
      D4-PARTˆA   1iNd   1iGp   eat-UNR-A   pick-go
      Let's go pick from it what we will eat.   (16:10)

(334) *sitʉ*   *-kʉ-seʔ*   *[surʉʉ*   *pihiʔa-nʉʉ*   *pʉmʉ*   *aiʔ-ku*   *hani-ʔih-a]*
      D1   EVID-CTR   D4Gp   boy-Gp   COGp   bad-A   do-REAL-A

      nasúwatsi-nụ
      forget-PST
      He forgot what bad things those boys had done.   (80:30)

(335) *sitʉʉ*   *-kʉ-seʔ*   *taibooʔ-nʉʉ*   *sehka*   *[bʉʉ*   *toh-kʉa-ʔih-a]*
      D1p   EVID-CTR   man-Np   D5As   COGp   INSTR-goˆup-REAL-A

      sʉʉ-ma-tu   *tsoʔmẹ-tsi*   *u*   *ku-tsitóna-nụ*
      one-on-along   gather-SS   D4A   INSTR-setˆfire-PST
      These white men, gathering together that which they had blown out, set it on fire.   (29:29)

(336) *sitʉ*   *-kʉ-seʔ*   *tuibihtsiʔ*   *suhka*   *[pʉnaʔ-waʔi-hpʉʔ-a*
      D1   EVID-CTR   youngˆman   D4As   COG   kin-woman-ABS-G

      tʉhka-ruʔih-a]   *hima-nụ*
      eat-UNR-A   take-PST
      This young man got that which his woman would eat.   (71:27)

As in complement clauses, if a relative clause has pronominal subject and object, the order is OSV. A proclitic third-person-singular pronoun cannot stand as an object in this structure, so a demonstrative in genitive case substitutes for it. Note also that the use of coreferential pronouns in relative clauses is identical to that used in complement clauses.

(337) *...[mahka*   *pʉ*   *tʉkʉ-hima-kʉ-ʔih-a]*   *ma*   *maka-nụ*
      D2GS   COG   food-take-CAUS-UNR-A   D2A   feed-PST
      ...fed her what he had taken for her to eat.   (71:28)

Selected Bibliography

Armagost, James L. 1982. The temporal relationship between telling and happening in Comanche narrative. *Anthropological Linguistics* 24:193–200.

Armagost, James L. 1984. The Grammar of Personal Pronouns in Comanche. In David S. Rood (ed.), *1983 Mid-America Linguistics Conference Papers*, 25–35. Boulder, CO: University of Colorado.

Baker, Theodor. 1882. Über die musik der nordamerikanischen wilden. In Songs of the Comanche, 10–13, 37–41, 50–51, 59–79.

Beals, Ralph L. 1943. *The aboriginal culture of the Cahita Indians*. Volume 19. Berkeley and Los Angeles.

Becker, W. J. 1936. The Comanche Indian and his language. *Chronicles of Oklahoma* 14:328–342.

Becker, W. J. 1951. The compounding of words in the Comanche Indian anguage: A Thesis. M.A. thesis, University of Oklahoma, Norman, Oklahoma.

Canonge, Elliott D. 1949. Comanche Frames. Unpublished manuscript.

Canonge, Elliott D. 1957. Voiceless vowels in Comanche. *International Journal of American Linguistics* 23:63–67. Rev.: D. Hymes in *Language* 35:370–371 (1959); Tovar in *Word* 16:407–409 (1960).

Canonge, Elliott D. 1958. *Comanche texts*. (Repub. 1962, 1974.) Norman, Oklahoma: Summer Institute of Linguistics of the University of Oklahoma. (Coyote tales, fables, histories, food preparation. Includes vocabulary of about 1,300 entries.)

Carlson, Gustav A. and Volney H. Jones. 1939. Some notes on the uses of Plants by the Comanche Indians. *Papers of the Michigan Academy of Science, Arts and Letters* 25:517–542.

Casagrande, Joseph B. 1948. Comanche baby language. *International Journal of American Linguistics* 14:11–14.

Casagrande, Joseph B. 1954. Comanche linguistic acculturation I. International *Journal of American Linguistics* 20:140–151.

Casagrande, Joseph B. 1954. Comanche linguistic acculturation II. *International Journal of American Linguistics* 20:217–237.

Casagrande, Joseph B. 1955. Comanche linguistic acculturation III. *International Journal of American Linguistics* 21:8–25.

Chomsky, Noam and Morris Halle. 1968. *The sound pattern of English.* New York: Harper & Row.

Espinosa, Aurelio Macedonio, ed. 1907. Los Comanches. *University of New Mexico Bulletin, (Language Series I)* 1:1–46.

Fehrenbach, Theodore R. 1974. *Comanches: The destruction of a people.* New York: Knopf.

García Rejón, M. 1866. *Vocabulario del idioma Comanche.* Mexico.

Gilles, Albert S., Sr. 1974. *Comanche Days.* Dallas: Southern Methodist University Press.

Gladwin, Thomas Favill. 1948. Comanche kin behavior. *American Anthropologist* 50:73–94.

Hale, Kenneth. 1958. Internal diversity in Uto-Aztecan: I. *International Journal of American Linguistics* 24:101–107.

Hale, Kenneth. 1959. Internal diversity in Uto-Aztecan: II. *International Journal of American Linguistics* 25:114–121. (Comanche on p. 116).

Hoebel, E. Adamson. 1939 Comanche and Hekandika Shoshone relationship systems. *American Anthropologist* 41:440–457.

Hale, Kenneth. 1940. Political organization and law-ways of the Comanche Indians. *American Anthropologist Memoir 54 (supplement).*

Hoffman, W. J. 1886. Remarks on Indian tribal names. *Papers of the American Philosophical Society* 23:299–301.

Lanacker, Ronald W., ed. 1977. *An overview of Uto-Aztecan grammar. Studies in Uto-Aztecan grammar.* Summer Institute of Linguistic and the University of Texas at Arlington Publications in Linguistics 56. Dallas: Summer Institute of Linguistics and the University of Texas at Arlington.

Marcy, Randolph B. [with remarks by W. W. Turner]. 1853. Vocabularies of words in the languages of the Comanches and Wichitas. U.S. Senate Doc. Ex. No. 666 (Exploration of the Red River of Louisiana.), Appendix H, pp. 307–311. Washington.

McLaughlin, John E. 1982. From aspect to tense, or what's *-nuh* in Comanche. *1982 Mid-America Linguistics Conference Proceedings,* 412–427. Lawrence, Kansas: University of Kansas.

Miller, Wick. 1972. Newe natekwinappeh: Stories and dictionary. *University of Utah Anthropological Papers 94.* Salt Lake City: University of Utah.

Neighbors, Robert S. 1852. Comanche (Nauni) vocabulary. In Henry Rowe Schoolcraft (ed.), *Information respecting the history, conditions and prospects of the Indian tribes of the United States* 2:494–505. Philadelphia.

Osborn, Henry and William A Smalley. 1949. Formulae for Comanche stem and word formation. *International Journal of American Linguistics* 15:93–99.

Richardson, Rupert N. 1929. The culture of the Comanche Indians. *Texas Archeological and Paleontological Society Bulletin* 1:58–73.

Osborn, Henry and William A Smalley. 1933. *The Comanche barrier to South Plains Settlement.* Glendale, California.

Riggs, Venda. 1949. Alternate phonemic analyses of Comanche. *International Journal of American Linguistics* 15:229–31.

Shimkin, Demitri Boris. 1940. Shoshone-Comanche origins and migrations. *Proceedings of the 6th Pacific Science Congress* 4:17–125.

Shimkin, Demitri Boris. 1941. The Uto-Aztecan System of Kinship Terminology. *American Anthropologist* 43:223–245.

Smalley, William A. 1953. Phonemic rhythm in Comanche. *International Journal of American Linguistics* 19:297–301.

Tilghman, Zoe A. 1938. Quanah: *The eagle of the Comanches.* Oklahoma City: Harlow.

Voegelin, Florence M. and Kenneth L. Hale. 1962. Typological and Comparative Grammar of Uto-Aztecan: I (Phonology). *Indiana University Publications in Anthropology and Linguistics,* Memoir No. 17.

Wallace, Ernest and E. Adamson Hoebel. 1952. *The Comanches: Lords of the Southern Plains.* Norman: University of Oklahoma.

Wistrand-Robinson, Lila. 1976. Sample cognate list and preliminary sound correspondences toward a North and South American Indian language relationship. Paper read at Southeastern Conference on Linguistics XXVIII Meetings, University of Maryland at College Park, April 8, 1983.

Wistrand-Robinson, Lila. 1985. Bi-directional movement in historical change Shoshone: Comanche. Paper read at the 1985 Annual Meetings, American Anthropological Association, Washington, D.C.

Wistrand-Robinson, Lila. 1991. Uto-Aztecan affinities with Panoan of Peru I: Correspondences, in Mary Ritchie Key, (ed.), Language change in South American Indian languages. Philadelphia: University of Pennsylvania Press.

SIL International Publications
Additional Releases in the **Publications in Linguistics** Series

SIL International Publications
7500 W. Camp Wisdom Road
Dallas, TX 75236-5629

Voice: 972-708-7404
Fax: 972-708-7363
publications_intl@sil.org
www.ethnologue.com/bookstore.asp